MW00388210

Exploring Theatre

Exploring Theatre

Nancy Prince

Jeanie Jackson

 National Textbook Company

a division of NTC/CONTEMPORARY PUBLISHING GROUP
Lincolnwood, Illinois USA

Acknowledgments begin on page 445, which is to be considered an extension
of this copyright page.

Student Edition: ISBN 0-314-07016-8
Teacher's Annotated Edition: ISBN 0-314-07017-6

Published by National Textbook Company, a division of NTC/Contemporary Publishing Group, Inc.
4255 West Touhy Avenue, Lincolnwood, (Chicago), Illinois 60712-1975 U.S.A.

03 04 05 06 KR 15 14 13 12 11

About the Authors

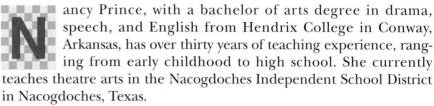

Nancy Prince

Nancy Prince, with a bachelor of arts degree in drama, speech, and English from Hendrix College in Conway, Arkansas, has over thirty years of teaching experience, ranging from early childhood to high school. She currently teaches theatre arts in the Nacogdoches Independent School District in Nacogdoches, Texas.

She serves as a discipline-based theatre education facilitator at the Southeast Institute for Education in Theatre, Chattanooga, Tennessee. Her program "Puppets Add Pizazz" has been featured as part of the teacher training programs at the John F. Kennedy Center for the Performing Arts in Washington, D.C.

Presently she serves as a mentor teacher for the Stephen F. Austin University Center for Professional Development and Technology in Nacogdoches, Texas, training interns and student teachers in her classroom. As a professional public speaker, puppeteer, and motivator, Mrs. Prince has traveled and given presentations throughout the nation.

In 1988, for her role in the education of youth and adults, Mrs. Prince received the Texas Educational Theatre Association Secondary School Educator of the Year Award.

Jeanie Jackson

Jeanie Jackson, with a bachelor of science degree from East Texas State University and a master of education degree from Stephen F. Austin University, is certified to teach secondary education in theatre, speech, English, and Spanish, as well as kindergarten through eighth grade. Jeanie has taught for twenty-eight years, ten of which were spent as Fine Arts Department Middle School Chair in the Lake Travis I.S.D., Austin, Texas. She is presently the Creative Drama Specialist in the Harleton Independent School District, Harleton, Texas.

Mrs. Jackson is a member of numerous associations, including the Association of Texas Professional Educators, Texas Educational Theatre Association (TETA), and the Creative Drama Network. She has taught numerous drama and speech workshops throughout Texas, including TETA summer workshops, TETA conventions, and The Texas Elementary Principals and Supervisors Association State Convention. She has also given presentations at numerous national conferences such as the Educational Theatre Association National Convention in Chicago. She has served as the summer drama clinician for the Tennessee Arts Academy, Nashville, Tennessee.

In 1989 Mrs. Jackson was honored as the Educator of the Year and was selected as one of the top three finalists for the Texas Secondary Teacher of the Year. In 1992, she received a Texas Educational Theatre Association Educator of the Year Award.

Dedication

To George, my friend, husband, and number one encourager;
To Mother and Dad, who guided me with unconditional love;
To "Sister," my computer specialist, and Steve, who taught me to
follow my dreams; and
To my colleagues and friends who provided ideas and support.

Jeanie Jackson

To my mother and late father, Vera and Frank Olive, who first instilled in me the joy of hard work and the satisfaction of a job
well done;
To my family—my husband Phil, my daughters Kelly and Marty,
and my sister Debbye—who lovingly supported this work in
countless ways;
To my friend and mentor, Kim Wheetley, who has provided unlimit-
ed opportunities for me; and
To my friend and colleague, Lou-Ida Marsh, who taught me much
about theatre and life.

Nancy Prince

■ ■ ■

Preface

T heatre arts teachers have been pleading for a new introductory theatre arts textbook for many years. They have needed a single teaching tool that could combine in one book reliable theatre information and suggestions for appropriate and effective theatre activities. Theatre teachers have wanted each student to have his or her own textbook so that they could more easily involve all their students in personally rewarding theatre experiences, and evoke in their students an excitement and appreciation for both creating and attending theatre. They wanted all this in a cost-effective, time-saving form that would help validate their courses.

Exploring Theatre is the authors' response to these pleas. The two authors represent a combination of almost sixty years of theatre teaching experience. The book is the result of the authors' desire to share their theatre adventures with all the theatre teachers who have been forced to teach their courses without a text for too many years.

The focus of *Exploring Theatre* is on the development of the total student, which includes the development of the students' personal resources, self-confidence, and ability to work well with others. In *Exploring Theatre*, students learn how to bolster their self-concepts, build an ensemble, observe people and places more closely, move expressively, and become more aware of their senses. They learn basic acting skills such as improvisation, characterization, preparing a role, and stage movement. The students are also guided through the various aspects of the production process, from rehearsal to backstage crews, and they explore a range of career opportunities in theatre and theatre education. An array of special topics such as storytelling, clowning, oral interpretation, readers theatre, and puppetry make the text broad enough and versatile enough for up to two full years of theatre instruction.

Exploring Theatre's handling of theatre history requires a special note. Many teachers said that they did not spend much time on theatre history with their beginning students, while other teachers preferred to include a fairly strong history component in their courses. Almost all teachers agreed, however, that beginning students enjoyed and retained information about theatre history more when the content was provided in short, discrete segments rather than in broad, lengthy overviews. Therefore, you will find one- and two-page *Our Theatre Heritage* features on selected topics in theatre history sprinkled chronologically throughout *Exploring Theatre*. You will also find, between Chapters 1 and 2, a colorful theatre time line to which the students can refer repeatedly throughout the course. It is hoped that this type of theatre history presentation will stimulate, rather than stifle, your students' appetites for theatre history.

Additional special features of *Exploring Theatre* that will help motivate your students and provide them with effective study tools are:

Lesson Organization—Each chapter is divided into short lessons to present information in manageable segments for students and to provide you flexibility in your course planning. *Lesson Objectives* are stated at the beginning of each lesson.

Warm Ups—Also at the beginning of each lesson is a Warm Up activity to introduce students to the key concept or skill of that particular lesson. You will want to use many of these activities repeatedly throughout the text.

Quotes—Interspersed throughout the text are quotes from theatre people and other literary sources to help stimulate class discussion and promote student thinking with regard to theatre concepts and practices.

Action—At the conclusion of every lesson, an Action section provides numerous activity suggestions to reinforce and extend the content of that lesson. Approximately one-third of the textbook is made up of these Action segments.

"Reader-Friendly" Writing Style—*Exploring Theatre* is written in a light, conversational style that will capture and hold the students' interest.

Theatre Vocabulary—Because theatre confronts students with an extensive, highly specialized vocabulary, *Exploring Theatre* provides several study aids to help students learn theatre terminology. So that students can preview the important new terms in each chapter before reading the chapter, the terms are listed in *Spotlight on Terms* at the beginning of the chapter. These terms are then highlighted in yellow within the text, and are both defined in text and called out in margin definitions. Students will also be able to find definitions in the Glossary whenever they need them.

Illustrations—Approximately 300 full-color photographs and drawings make *Exploring Theatre* a visually appealing textbook that will hold students' attention, as well as illustrate concepts for greater understanding.

Curtain Call—At the end of each chapter, on the Curtain Call page, is a range of exercises, including objective questions (*Focus on Facts*), critical thinking questions (*Reflections*), exercises for showing students how their theatre experiences will benefit them in other areas of their lives (*Theatre in Your Life*), and more activities (*Encore*).

Playbook—This special section at the end of the text contains over thirty excerpts from plays that students can use to practice their skills. There are passages for male and female monologues; and scenes for two females, two males, one female and one male, and for various groups. In the *Playbook*, you will also find selections for readers theatre.

Exploring Theatre provides a solid beginning for students studying theatre arts—a beginning that will encourage students to take more theatre courses and to participate in and appreciate theatre throughout their lives. But even if they were to never enter a theatre again, the authors believe that students who have used *Exploring Theatre* will be more assertive and more confident in their daily lives, more aware of their surroundings, more expressive in their communications, and more cooperative in their dealings with others.

■ ■ ■

Acknowledgments

The authors would like to thank Lynn Murray, Kim Wheetley, and Krin Brooks Perry, without whom they might not have had the opportunity to write *Exploring Theatre;* the many members of the Texas Educational Theatre Association (TETA) who have provided innumerable ideas and suggestions over the years; Judy Matetzschk for the time, effort, and knowledge that she invested in *Our Theatre Heritage;* Lynda Belt, Rebecca Stockley, and Charles Pascoe for their theatre games ideas; Bob Cassel, Lynda Kessler, Carole Balach, Chrisztina Kowalski, Lee Anne Storey, John Orr, and all the people at West Educational Publishing Company who produced such a beautiful book; and the people at Federal Express who helped us meet the strictest deadlines.

Nancy Prince would also like to thank the 1995 and 1996 TAPS classes, Sandi Elsik, Jean Ferraro, Jennifer Franklin, Gigi Bollinger, and Melissa Bahs.

Jeanie Jackson would also like to thank George Edna Hooten Wallace, Marilyn Swinton, Becky Chenevert, and Becky Kasling.

The authors would also like to thank the following theatre arts teachers for their valuable comments and suggestions during the development of the *Exploring Theatre* manuscript.

Reviewers

Cynthia Allen
Alief I.S.D.
Houston, Texas

Mary Bill
Richardson I.S.D.
Richardson, Texas

Mary Bowles
Fort Worth I.S.D.
Fort Worth, Texas

Diane M. Brewer
Eanes I.S.D.
Austin, Texas

Beverly Burnside
North East I.S.D.
San Antonio, Texas

Ann Crofton
Carrollton/Farmers I.S.D.
Carrollton, Texas

Marla Crowe
Klein I.S.D.
Spring, Texas

Jean Danna
Cypress Fairbanks I.S.D.
Houston, Texas

Vicki Dickerson
Aldine I.S.D.
Houston, Texas

Sandra S. Fitzhugh
Ysleta I.S.D.
El Paso, Texas

Darla Howard
Northside I.S.D.
San Antonio, Texas

Professor Judith Kase-Polisini
University of South Florida
Tampa, Florida

Peter D. Kinser
Alvin I.S.D.
Alvin, Texas

Donna Lampman
Northside I.S.D.
San Antonio, Texas

Judy Matetzschk
Zachary Scott Theatre Center
Project InterAct
Austin, Texas

Carol Mize
Austin I.S.D.
Austin, Texas

Sheila Rinear
North East I.S.D.
San Antonio, Texas

Mike Storey
Corpus Christi I.S.D.
Corpus Christi, Texas

Paulette Van Atta
Plano I.S.D.
Plano, Texas

Cynthia Winters
Austin I.S.D.
Austin, Texas

Contents in Brief

Contents

Building Your Acting Skills 80

UNIT 3

Producing and Appreciating Plays 168

Special Topics in Theatre 266

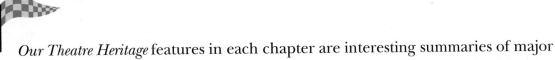

OUR THEATRE HERITAGE
Historical and Cultural Perspectives

Our Theatre Heritage features in each chapter are interesting summaries of major theatrical developments throughout history. You can find them on the following pages:

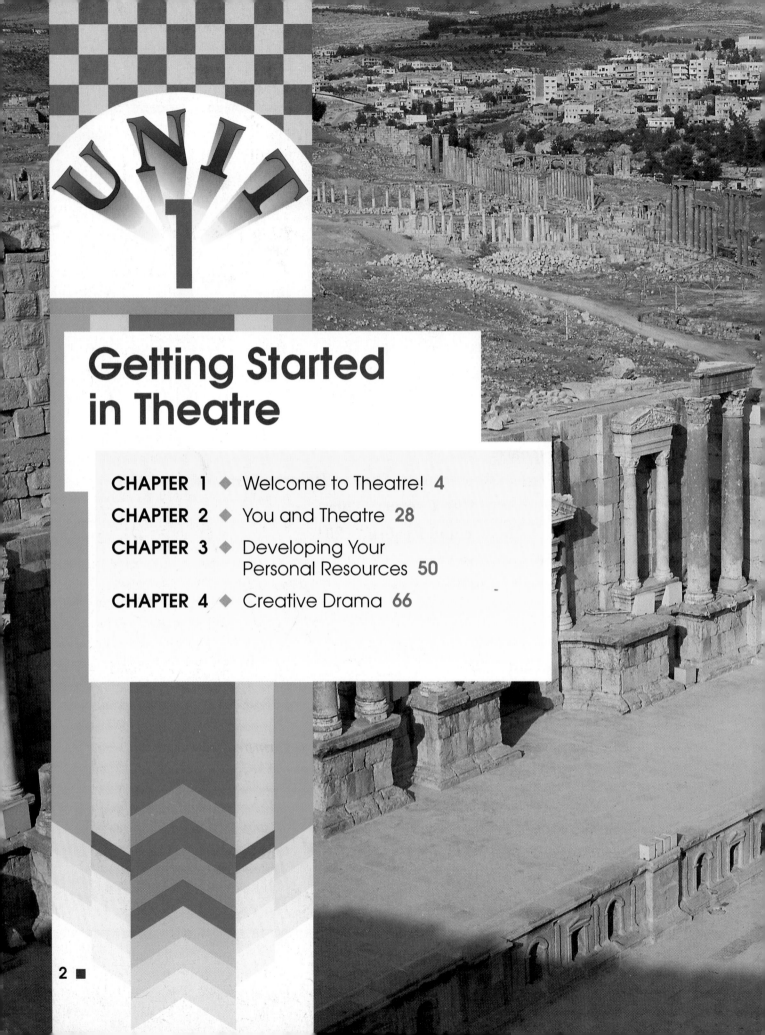

UNIT 1

Getting Started in Theatre

CHAPTER 1

Welcome to Theatre!

Chapter Outline

Spotlight on Terms

- ◆ acting
- ◆ actor
- ◆ characters
- ◆ dialogue
- ◆ drama
- ◆ dramatic structure
- ◆ filmed
- ◆ play

- ◆ player-audience relationship
- ◆ playwright
- ◆ ritual
- ◆ script
- ◆ stage directions
- ◆ theatre
- ◆ theatre arts

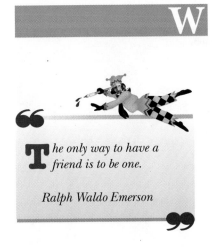

elcome to theatre—one of the most exciting classes you will ever take. Why is theatre so exciting? Because it's entertaining, obviously, but also because it is based on human experience. In a sense, theatre is a class about life. As Roy Scheider, the actor, once said, "Theatre doesn't exist because it's entertainment. It exists because it's a part of the energy of living, of humankind."

In some ways you might think of this class as preparation for living your life to the fullest. This class will provide opportunities for you to get to know yourself, to involve yourself with others, to take safe risks, and to actively participate in activities and projects—all of which will help you respond to the world around you with increased energy and sensitivity. You should begin this class with the eager anticipation of an explorer about to embark on a new adventure.

> *The only way to have a friend is to be one.*
>
> *Ralph Waldo Emerson*

Getting to Know You

LESSON OBJECTIVES

- ◆ Meet the other members of the class.
- ◆ Develop a feeling of acceptance.
- ◆ Communicate with people your own age.

Warm Up

At your teacher's signal, introduce yourself to the students seated around you. Even if you already know each other, go through the introduction process to encourage participation. Speak your name clearly, and listen carefully when others tell you their names.

Seeing old friends and making new friends are important parts of the education process. Today you probably arrived at school hoping that some of your friends would be here waiting for you. That's a feeling that everyone knows; everyone likes to connect with someone familiar. For that very reason, one of the first things you will do in this class is become better acquainted with your classmates.

Getting to know the people you will be working with can help you feel *included*. Psychologists tell us that feeling included is one of our most important social needs. We need this sense of belonging in order to work, play, and contribute effectively to society.

In theatre, special "getting-to-know-you" activities help students and teachers learn each other's names and get to know each other in an enjoyable way. These activities will help your class learn to work as a group and will also help you respond to your teacher as the leader. These activities also help you learn to listen and pay attention. These two skills are important both in theatre and everyday life.

In our society, our names are an important part of our identities. One of the nicest sounds in the world is to hear someone call us by name in a pleasant way. It is meaningful to each of us that we be called by name rather than referred to as "her," "him," "the red-haired girl," or "that tall boy." Think of how good it makes you feel when someone you hardly know calls you by your given name. This courtesy is especially important in theatre class, since you and your classmates will be working together throughout the course.

ACTION

In this lesson, you will learn the names of your classmates through fun, non-threatening games. Complete one or more of the following activities.

1. **Circle of Friends.** This is a game about meeting people. Make two circles, an outer circle and an inner circle, with participants facing each other. When your teacher gives you the signal or begins to play music, the inner circle will move with small steps to the right, and the outer circle will move to the left.

    When the music stops or when the teacher calls "Make a friend," stop moving and introduce yourself to the person you are facing. Use the name you wish to be called. For example, if your name is Mary Ann Jones and you wish to be called Ann, introduce yourself as Ann.

    Continue for several rounds. Try to connect each person's name with his or her face. After the game, decide how many new names you have learned.

2. **A-to-Z Name Game.** This game helps you recognize the names of others by putting them in alphabetical order. At your teacher's signal, arrange yourselves in a circle or line from A to Z, using first names or the names you want to be called. Students having the same first names can use second names or birth dates to determine their rank order. When your teacher asks for a roll call, step forward and call out your name in a clear voice. Listen carefully to the names of all the other students.

3. **Right/Left.** The purpose of this game is to think quickly and correctly call out the name of the person to your right or left. Begin this game by standing in a circle. The game is easier if you are still in first-name alphabetical order.

The leader stands in the center of the circle and points to someone, calling "right 1 2 3 4 5" or "left 1 2 3 4 5." Before the count is completed, the person to whom the leader is pointing must correctly call out the name of the person specified. The first person who hesitates to call out a name, forgets a name, or calls out the wrong name automatically becomes the next leader.

If, after several calls, the leader hasn't been replaced, the teacher can call "Switch places," and everyone, including the leader, must find a different place in the circle. The person who is left out of the circle becomes the new leader.

An Introduction to Theatre

LESSON OBJECTIVES

♦ Recognize a scene written in script format.
♦ Understand the player-audience relationship.
♦ Recognize the contribution of theatre to your life.

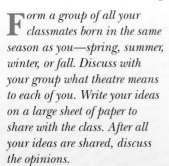

Warm Up

Form a group of all your classmates born in the same season as you—spring, summer, winter, or fall. Discuss with your group what theatre means to each of you. Write your ideas on a large sheet of paper to share with the class. After all your ideas are shared, discuss the opinions.

drama

a story written to be played out on the stage.

theatre arts

the term used to cover all parts of training or instruction in the field of theatre.

script

a written copy of the dialogue that the actors will speak.

Drama, the dramatic tradition which began with primitive people nearly three thousand years ago, comes from a Greek word meaning "to act" or "to do." We usually think of drama as a story written to be played out on the stage. **Theatre arts** is the term used to cover all parts of training or instruction in the field. This lesson is designed to help you understand what drama is, how it has changed through the ages, and how the study of theatre arts relates to your life.

The format of this lesson is unique because it is written as a **script**, a written copy of the conversation between **characters**. Characters are the personalities actors portray in a scene or a play, which are different from their own personalities. Like all scripts, this play is meant to be presented by **actors**, performers who play the roles or take the parts of specific characters, and who project the characters to the audience. Such presentation is called **acting**.

The way **plays** are written is a special style of writing called **dramatic structure**. This style is different from the way a short story, novel, or poem is written. In a play, the talk, or conversation between two or more characters is called **dialogue**. Dialogue is not set in quotation marks. Instead, the character's name appears before the spoken part. Plays are made up entirely of dialogue and **stage directions**, additional information provided by the **playwright** or author. Stage directions help the actors know how to feel or what to do when certain lines are spoken. Such directions are usually printed in italics and set apart from the dialogue by parentheses. You'll learn more about the structure of plays in Chapter 8.

character

the personality an actor portrays in a scene or play that is different from his or her own personality.

actors

males or females playing character roles.

acting

an actor's assumed behavior for the purpose of projecting a character to an audience.

play

story in dialogue form to be acted out by actors before a live audience.

dramatic structure

the special literary style in which plays are written.

dialogue

the conversation between actors on the stage.

playwright

one who writes plays.

The Wonderful World of Theatre

Mrs. Logan's Theatre Class

Characters

Mrs. Logan . . the teacher
Matt . . . . a football player taking the class because of his girlfriend, Sydney.
Sydney . . . . . . a good student; wants her boyfriend, Matt, to enjoy theatre.
Vanessa . . . . . a new student who hopes to find friends in theatre class.
José . . . . an extremely intelligent student who enjoys studying history.
Thomas . . . . . someone who thinks about food and fun all the time.
Holly . . . . a good-natured person, but not a good student.
Rosa . . . . someone who enjoys attending plays with her family.
Kristen . . . . . . an insecure classmate with serious family problems.
Katie . . . . a student who loves to perform and wants to be a ballerina.
Lo . . . . Matt's best friend, a good-natured tease.

Scene: *A theatre arts classroom in any school. As the play begins, class has just begun. The students are seated and are talking quietly to each other as the teacher finishes checking roll.*

Mrs. Logan: (*After putting away the roll, moves to the front of the classroom.*) Welcome to the wonderful world of theatre! (*She smiles, and there is excitement in her voice.*) This class is going to be fun as we explore theatre together. Theatre requires active participation. Each one of you will have many opportunities to perform, observe, organize, create, and evaluate. You may not be aware of this, but your background in theatre began long before today. Think back on some of your past experiences. When you were little children, did any of you ever like to pretend? (*Students respond by nodding their heads and smiling.*) What were some of the things you pretended? (*Class responds simultaneously with different answers*—superhero, cop, doctor, fireman, nurse, *etc.*)

■ ■ ■ ■ ■ ■ ■ ■ ■ ■ ■ ■ ■ ■ ■

Participate. You will probably be nervous at first—almost everyone is—but you will soon be as eager as these students to perform for your classmates.

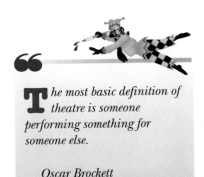

Everyone likes to pretend. When we're young, it's called *dramatic play*. When we're older, it's called *acting!*

> The most basic definition of theatre is someone performing something for someone else.
>
> Oscar Brockett

Sydney: *(Laughing as she speaks.)* I was always a popular movie star.

Lo: Every Monday, I always pretended I was sick, so I wouldn't have to go to school. *(Class laughs.)*

Mrs. Logan: Most children just naturally pretend as they play. Pretending, or acting out, is an important part of growing up. Through these play experiences, young children learn to use dialogue, act out different characters, and create and solve problems. Acting out, or pretending, is considered dramatic play. *(Students nod and respond.)* Have any of you ever been in a play?

Rosa: I love being in plays. My first starring role was as Cinderella when I was in the fourth grade. That was the year I tripped over a pumpkin.

Thomas: *(Reacting with humor.)* Oh, I remember that! Because I was the pumpkin!

Lo: *(Boasting.)* When I was about seven, I played a dairy product in a play about food groups.

Matt: Wow! Big deal! Did you "butter up" the teacher to get the part? *(Class makes faces at the pun.)* I bet you really "milked" that part for all it was worth. *(Group responds with such comments as* Ugh! Great! Way to go, Matt! Real funny!*)*

Holly: Ugh, Matt! That was bad!

Thomas: *(Rubbing his stomach.)* Speaking of milk, I'm hungry! *(Class groans.)*

Mrs. Logan: Has anyone else been in a play?

Katie: Last year, I was a dancer in *Oklahoma!* at the community theatre. We had a full house at every performance. It was great!

Kristen: In kindergarten, I was a partridge in our Christmas play. I was so nervous, I ran off the stage to my mom. She was so embarrassed that she never let me be in a play again. *(Class laughs.)*

Over the past 2000 years, the theatres, the costumes, and even the audiences have changed a great deal. What has not changed is the human need to act out life's situations and to enjoy and learn from those performances.

Imagine what it would be like to perform in an ancient outdoor theatre like this one. What special skills would you need?

Mrs. Logan: *(Smiling at the class.)* Well, I can certainly see that many of you have had stage experience. But perhaps some of you have never been in a play before. *(Several students begin to nod their heads.)*

Matt: *(Leaning over to* Sydney.*)* I can't believe you talked me into taking this class! All she's talking about is being in a play. I'd rather be in some other class. I think I better go get my schedule changed before they close out all the other classes.

Sydney: *(Whispering.)* Shhh! Be quiet, that's not all it's about. Just wait, you'll see. Besides, you promised that if I would go to your ballgames, you'd be in this class. (Matt *slumps down in his chair disgusted.)*

Mrs. Logan: *(Looking at* Matt *and smiling.)* I can see that some of you are a little worried about what we're going to be doing. I promise I'll talk about that soon. *(Class settles down to listen.)* But first I'd like you to answer a question! Just what is theatre? Does anyone know?

Vanessa: A place to see plays.

Rosa: *(Excited.)* Live performances like the ones my family and I have seen on Broadway.

Kristen: Entertainment.

Lo: This class! *(Everybody laughs.)*

Mrs. Logan: You're all right! Today, *theatre* has many different meanings. In this class, theatre refers to the writing or performing of plays, to the buildings where those plays are performed, and to your activities and experiences in this class.

Thomas: *(Raises hand proudly.)* Wait! I know something else that theatre is! It's a place to watch movies and eat popcorn!

Mrs. Logan: That's true, Thomas. Both movies and television are forms of entertainment featuring actors in a **filmed** or photographed presentation. We will discuss some of the ways in which

filmed

preserved as a moving photograph.

movies, television, and live performances are alike as well as different. But for now, let's think back to the beginning of theatre. When do you think theatre first began? *(Students shrug their shoulders and give each other puzzled looks.)* Suppose I gave you the assignment to look up the word *theatre* in your dictionary.

Matt: *(Leaning over to* Sydney *and whispering loudly.)* Thanks a lot, Sydney! You didn't say anything about homework! *(Mutters to himself while Sydney ignores him and continues to listen to Mrs. Logan.)* Now I know I'm changing classes! *(Slouches down low in his chair.)*

Mrs. Logan: *(Continuing.)* You would find that the word **theatre** comes from the ancient Greek word *theatron*, meaning "a place for seeing." But we think that theatre actually began long before the Greeks gave it a name. *(Looking directly at* Matt.*)* Matt, when you and your friends get together, how do you tell your friends what happened in a football game?

Matt: *(Sits up and speaks hesitantly.)* Well, most of the time I just say, "Hey, man, guess what happened to me?" and then I tell it.

Mrs. Logan: *(Dramatically.)* Well, what if you saw someone make a great catch in a football game on television and you wanted to share it with the team at practice? What would you do?

Matt: *(Beginning to get interested.)* I'd probably grab a ball and show everyone. *(He demonstrates catching the ball, then acts out passing to* Lo, *who catches it. The class laughs.)*

Mrs. Logan: You know, Matt, you are exactly right. People have always shown, or "acted out," things they thought were important. Historians think that even primitive people may have acted out certain events.

Holly: *(Looking puzzled.)* You mean the caveman did Shakespeare?

Mrs. Logan: No, Holly, the first theatre wasn't exactly the way you and I think of it. Primitive people told about things that happened to them. One of them might have discovered, just as Matt has, that

theatre

the writing or performing of plays, as well as the formal study of the art form. Also, a building in which plays are performed.

We're all actors every day. Think about the ways you use gestures and facial expressions to communicate with your friends.

The Beginning of Theatre

Although every culture on earth celebrates some form of performance, no one really knows for sure where or how theatre began. Most experts believe that today's theatre began with the myths and rituals of ancient people. Artifacts (hand-made objects such as tools and ornaments) from the Ice Ages have shown that humans may have been performing rituals of various types as many as 30,000 years ago. From 10,000 to 30,000 years ago, tribes of humans also left records of what seem to be rituals in the wall paintings found in caves in Africa, France, and Spain. All drawings of people performing ritual ceremonies seem to involve man's need to hunt for food.

Anthropologists believe that early in human history, societies became aware of forces that seemed to influence their climate and food supply. With little or no scientific knowledge, these early people believed that good and bad occurrences were due to magical, unexplainable, supernatural forces. To ensure their well-being, societies tried to find ways to win the favor of these unknown forces. In their ignorance of how nature works, an ancient society might have perceived a connection between some of their activities, such as dancing or chanting, and the desired results in nature. The society would then begin to repeat and refine those actions. Over time, these actions would become formal, fixed rituals or ceremonies enacted for the sole purpose of ensuring the tribe's safety and prosperity.

These early rituals have several elements in common with theatre. For example, certain movements in the rituals were performed by a person, possibly a *shaman* (priest), who wore symbolic clothing and used symbolic items. These priests are in some ways like actors who perform scripted movements while wearing costumes designed specifically for their characters.

Rituals were performed in a space set apart from the other tribal members so that the actions performed by the priest or shaman could be watched by members of the tribe. It is easy to see how this spatial arrangement might reflect the stage area and the audience area found in theatres today.

Still another similarity between ancient rituals and today's theatre is based on the fact that ancient rituals had a set order of events. Participants in ancient rituals probably repeated certain actions many times in a predetermined order to win the favor of the supernatural spirit they were trying to please. This ritual order is roughly equal to the plot of events found in modern plays.

Other theatre historians believe that what we call theatre today grew out of early dances humans may have developed after observing animals in their environments. Still others believe that theatre grew out of storytelling. If hunters returned to their tribes with exciting stories to tell about their day of work, they may have demonstrated some of their adventures to those who were not along to see the excitement for themselves.

We may never know exactly how or why theatre as an art form was invented. However, similarities between ancient myths, rituals, dance, and storytelling, and the structure of theatrical performance today, seem to indicate a close connection. They may have been the beginning of today's theatrical performance. ■

Prehistoric cave paintings, such as this one in Altamira, Spain, provide evidence about the nature of early rituals and dances, which many experts believe were the beginnings of theatre.

ritual

repeated action that becomes a custom or ceremony.

stories really come alive when they are acted out. We also think that primitive people believed that acting out something would make it happen. Their actions were repeated over and over until a pattern, or **ritual**, developed.

Matt: *(Now very interested.)* What did they use for a stage?

Mrs. Logan: That's a good question, Matt. What do some of you think?

José: Didn't they act out and dance around the campfire?

Mrs. Logan: Very good, José. So the campfire would be considered the first stage, and the first audience would have been the other tribe members. What do you suppose were some of the things they acted out?

Vanessa: How about trying to survive a big storm without any shelter or friends? *(Whispers.)* Like me.

Holly: Maybe struggling with a big animal, like a bear.

Rosa: What about things they considered sacred? Did they have some sort of religious customs?

Thomas: Maybe they acted out how hungry they were. I know that's what I'd act out. *(Class groans, some rolling their eyes, as they look at Thomas.)*

Matt: Oh! *(Getting involved.)* Oh, I know! They probably acted out one tribe defeating another tribe.

Lo: *(Smiling.)* That sounds like our football team. *(The class laughs.)*

Mrs. Logan: All of you are right. From the time humans were civilized enough to have some sort of community, their lives and rituals focused on their attempts to survive, to please the gods, to understand life, to learn about other people, and to be successful despite the problems facing them. At first, no records were kept. But from the time recorded history began, we believe that these rituals included some of the very things that we see in performances today. Historians think that people dressed in masks and animal skins and pretended to hunt while others gathered around to watch the action.

These tribesmen in the Sudan are celebrating the completion of the king's hut, a community activity where they recognize their accomplishments.

Theatre, as you and I know it, may have its roots in such primitive events.

Sydney: That was all so long ago. How did theatre change? When did it become more of a performance or production?

José: I know! As civilizations progressed, so did theatre.

Mrs. Logan: *(Smiling approvingly at* José.*)* José's interest in history is really beginning to pay off. As humans progressed, so did their rituals. Much of what we experience in today's theatre we owe to the early Greeks, who participated in dramatic ceremonies and celebrations at great public festivals honoring the god Dionysus. We will follow the progression of theatre through special features in your textbook called *Our Theatre Heritages.* These features will help you see how theatre has evolved since the days when the ancient Greeks began performing for each other.

Katie: But what about entertainment? I thought that's what theatre was. I like to watch a play just to escape my own world for a couple of hours. I don't think of theatre as a ritual.

Vanessa: Yeah! I like to be in plays to escape my boring life. I don't act in plays to put food on the table. My mom takes care of that.

Mrs. Logan: Whether we are performing or watching, Vanessa, most of us do consider theatre to be entertainment and also a pleasant escape from reality. But we can also see from our study of theatre history that the theatre of a period reflects the people of that period as well as their behavior. Over 400 years ago, William Shakespeare, a famous English playwright, felt that theatre was such a true reflection of human behavior that it was "to hold as t'wer a mirror up to nature." In other words, theatre reflects life as if it were a mirror.

Rosa: I guess you're right. And some human behavior is pretty funny. *(She glances toward* Lo *and* Matt, *who are making faces.)*

Mrs. Logan: Theatre also gives us the opportunity to explore humanity. We are able to try on different roles and view life from different perspectives.

Matt: I really don't see what good theatre will do me. I don't plan to be an actor. I plan to be in politics.

Lo: Yeah, right!

Sydney: Well, then, you'll really have to be a good actor!

Mrs. Logan: *(Continuing.)* Matt, whether you are a politician, a teacher, or a football player, your theatre experiences will help you become more self-confident as you talk to others. You'll learn to speak clearly, to think quickly, and to use expression in your presentations. Those skills are important in whatever job or career you choose.

Sydney: See, Matt! *(Class laughs.)*

Mrs. Logan: *(Voice building in enthusiasm.)* Theatre students also learn to make good decisions, form sensible judgments, take safe risks, and develop self-discipline. And those are just a few of the many ways that theatre helps prepare you for life.

Katie: I want to be a ballet dancer, not an actress. What can theatre do for me?

Mrs. Logan: Well, Katie, you will learn to enhance your creativity through self-expression—showing your true thoughts and feelings, just as you do through ballet. Theatre is so diverse that each of you will have many opportunities to discover talents and develop skills that will transfer into your other interests.

Lo: Hey, I'm just an ordinary guy. I don't know what I want to do other than just get out of school. What's this theatre stuff supposed to do for me? It's not like I'm going to open my own theatre or anything! *(Holly giggles.)*

Mrs. Logan: Lo, think of this class as an adventure! You will have the chance to try different experiences, and you may even find a new interest. Theatre has something for everyone. Some students enjoy acting on the stage or performing with puppets. Others enjoy working backstage building sets, running lights, or videotaping the performances. Many just appreciate knowing what it takes to produce a play. Developing such interests in theatre enriches your life.

Sydney: *(Turning and looking at* Matt.) See, Matt, that's what I told you! *(Matt grins.)*

Thomas: *(Thinking aloud.)* How can theatre enrich our lives? Only the stars get rich!

Mrs. Logan: *(Smiling at* Thomas.) Well, that's a good point, Thomas, but that's not the type of "rich" I mean. Enrichment means improving or adding to your life. Theatre not only will give you new interests, but will also give you a different perspective on others. Whether you are playing a role or watching a performance, you will be able to see how others work and live differently from you.

Vanessa: I took theatre at my old school, and the thing I liked best was working with other people.

Mrs. Logan: Yes, Vanessa, and since theatre is a group effort, you do learn to work as a team. *(Looking at* Matt.) Much like a football team.

At this point you are probably not aware of the many tasks involved in producing a play. The good news is that whatever your skills happen to be, there will be a valuable role for you in each and every production.

It takes many talented people working together to make a performance successful.

You will use the teamwork skills you develop in theatre in other classes and organizations. Later, when you have a job, you will realize that teamwork is one of the most important life skills we can learn. Does anyone else have something they would like to add?

Katie: Every time I've been in a play, that special feeling I get performing before the audience is what I remember most. I may forget the songs and the lines from the show, but I always remember that feeling of excitement about performing.

Vanessa: That's why they say "there's no business like show business." *(Starts humming the song.)*

Rosa: I love going to the theatre! There is something really exciting about seeing a live performance. I like it better than going to a movie.

Kristen: Even when I'm just watching, I always feel I'm a part of the play.

Mrs. Logan: What you are talking about is a special "live" connection, or bond, that develops between the audience and the actors. The audience becomes part of the team. In theatre, we call this the **player-audience relationship**. The actors respond to the audience, and the audience responds to the actors. Attending a "live" performance is a once-in-history event. Even though the play may have been performed many times before, it will be different on the night you attend because you are there. Your personality and your interaction with the actors will be part of the energy and excitement. They will respond to you, as you will respond to them.

Matt: I can relate to that! When I'm on the football field, even though the coach says not to pay attention to the crowd, I can feel them. I

player-audience relationship

the special interactive and "live" relationship that exists between the performers and the audience, connecting and bonding them into a team.

can hear them yelling, and it makes me feel like I've got to do my best.

Mrs. Logan: It is a similar feeling, Matt. This interaction with the audience can't occur in movies or television, because the relationship between the performers and the audience is not there. In live theatre, the audience is the essential ingredient. Without the audience, there is no theatre.

Holly: *(Pointing to the wall clock.)* Hey, look! The bell's about to ring. This class really went fast.

Mrs. Logan: That was because you were all so involved in our discussion. That's another good point for theatre. There is opportunity for active involvement. Tomorrow, we will continue to see how the study of theatre can enhance your life. I hope I'll see all of you then. *(Looks at* Matt *and smiles.)*

(The bell rings. Students gather their books, chatting as they exit.)

Complete one or more of the following activities.

1. **What is Theatre?** Ask five people to answer the question, What is theatre? Record their answers. As a class, compile a list of the many different perceptions of theatre.

2. **Your Impressions.** Working in small groups, write your own scene, sharing your impressions of theatre. Read your scene aloud or act it out in front of the class.

3. **Videotape Your Play.** Develop and videotape a scene similar to the one you read in Lesson 2.

Curtain Call!

■ ■ SPOTLIGHT ON TERMS ■ ■

An important part of theatre is understanding the terminology, or vocabulary, used. Add the new terms and definitions to the vocabulary section of your theatre notebook or folder.

■ ■ FOCUS ON FACTS ■ ■

1. Name one of our most important social needs.
2. Why is it important that we call each other by our given names in theatre?
3. Why is pretending an important part of growing up?
4. Give a theory for the beginning of theatre.
5. What were some of the basic needs that primitive people might have enacted?
6. Where did the name *theatre* come from, and what was the early meaning?
7. How will the term *theatre* be used in this class?
8. What are some of the life skills that are used in theatre?
9. What did William Shakespeare mean when he said theatre was a true reflection of human behavior?
10. What is meant by the player-audience relationship?
11. What is an essential ingredient in live theatre?

■ ■ REFLECTIONS ■ ■

Discuss the following questions with your class or answer them on paper as instructed by your teacher.

1. Discuss the ways in which you have seen an audience become part of a team in a live performance. Think about plays, musical concerts, and other live events that require a player-audience relationship.
2. Discuss how theatre can enrich your life.
3. How did the second lesson in this chapter, written as a play, prepare you for theatre class?
4. How did you identify with the characters in the play?

■ ■ THEATRE IN YOUR LIFE ■ ■

Make a list of your personal goals for this class.

■ ■ ENCORE ■ ■

Complete one or more of the following activities.

1. Conduct a survey, interviewing twenty people of various ages, to discover how often each attends the theatre. Report your results to the class. Construct a class graph showing attendance by age-group. Which age-group attends most often?
2. As a class, prepare a questionnaire to determine the most frequently attended entertainment event in your community.
3. Work with a new friend to establish what you believe to be the advantages of live theatre over the movies or television.
4. Create a collage of advertisements for live theatre events in your community or surrounding communities. Mount your collection on a poster to share with the class.
5. Interview an adult who has taken a theatre course to find out how this person has been able to use what he or she learned in his or her job or life experiences. Share your information with the class in an oral report.

Exploring Theatre

TIME LINE

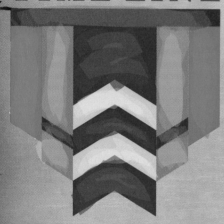

T oday's theatre is the product of many changes. Thousands of years ago, before books, T.V., movies, or computers, human beings felt a need in their lives for art and culture. One of the many ways in which people participated in the arts was to present theatrical productions and dramatic contests. As civilizations progressed, special places were built for these performances. As customs, beliefs, and technology changed, so did theatre. All the playwrights, directors, actors, and technicians who have participated in theatre for thousands of years contributed to the development of theatre into the art form we know today.

This time line is a road map for your journey through theatre history. As you read through the text, you will want to refer back to the time line frequently. Seeing where a particular playwright or new theatre design occurred in relation to other people and events will help you understand and remember the new information.

600 B.C.
Arion, a Greek poet and musician, replaces improvised dithyramb (choral hymn) by writing formal lyrics.

534 B.C.
Thespis, who is credited with introducing the first actor, wins first contest for tragic drama in Athens, Greece.

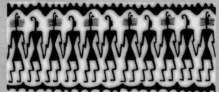

8500–7000 B.C. (approx.)
Primitive tribal dance and religious rituals.

8500

600

B.C.

4000 B.C. (approx.)
Plays written called the *Pyramid Texts* (fifty-five texts found later in Egyptian pyramids and tombs).

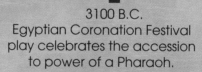

3100 B.C.
Egyptian Coronation Festival play celebrates the accession to power of a Pharaoh.

2750 B.C.
Egyptians participate in ritual dramas.

1887–1849 B.C.
I-Kher-nefert, the first stage director and actor mentioned in recorded history, produces the *Abydos Passion Play*.

Outstanding Playwrights

500 B.C.–500 A.D.

Greece:	Rome (Italy):
Aristophanes	Plautus
Aeschylus	Seneca
Euripides	Terence
Menander	
Sophocles	**India:**
Thespis	Kalidasa

500 B.C.–486 B.C.
Comedy competition begins in Greece.

475 B.C.
Aeschylus adds a second actor.

472 B.C.
Aeschylus writes *The Persians,* earliest surviving Greek play.

471 B.C.
Sophocles introduces a third actor in tragedy and makes less use of the chorus.

465 B.C.
A skene (wooden hut or tent) is added to the theatre for use as a dressing room for actors and chorus.

365 B.C.
First Roman theatrical performance.

365 B.C.
Many Greek theatres are built throughout the Mediterranean area.

240 B.C.
Comedies of Livius Andronicus performed in Rome.

80 B.C.
First Roman amphitheatre built at Pompeii.

55 B.C.
First permanent Roman theatre built of stone.

CLASSICAL PERIOD (500 B.C.–500 A.D.)

500 **400** **300** **200** **100** **0 A.D.**

458 B.C.
Painted stage scenery and stage machinery are used.

449 B.C.
First acting competition for tragic actors at City Dionysia.

435 B.C.
Pericles builds theatre honoring Dionysus.

442–441 B.C.
Sophocles writes *Antigone.*

431 B.C.
Euripides writes plays with parts for up to 11 actors.

423 B.C.
Production of Aristophanes' *The Clouds.*

360 B.C.
Theatre of Dionysus completed.

335–323 B.C.
Aristotle's *Poetics* sets standards for tragedy.

200–160 B.C.
Roman playwrights, Plautus and Terence, write comedies.

179 B.C.
Wooden theatre built in Rome.

22 B.C.
Introduction of pantomime.

4 B.C.
Seneca, major Roman tragic dramatist, is born.

■ 21

80 A.D.
The Colosseum in Rome
is built. Roman gladiatorial
contests become more
popular than theatre.

600 A.D.
Wandering troupes of performers,
usually the troupe owner's slaves,
entertain in Britain and on
the European continent.

80 A.D.
Actors, called mimes,
dress in ordinary clothes
without wigs and masks.

300 A.D.
Christians against
theatre gain force.

80 A.D.
Most actors are slaves,
or low-ranking
members of society..

304 A.D.
Genesius, an actor,
dies a martyr's death
during a performance
in Rome.

700 A.D.
Acrobats, minstrels, puppeteers,
and jugglers entertain at weddings,
banquets, and festivals helping
to keep performing alive.

197–202 A.D.
Christians forbidden to
attend theatre.

CLASSICAL PERIOD (To 500 A.D.)

| 0 | 100 | 200 | 300 | 400 | 500 | 600 | 700 |

A.D.

80 A.D.
Theatres, built with the
stage and audience as a
connected unit, have a
sloping roof over the stage.

304 A.D.
Christians against
theatre becomes
widespread.

712 A.D.
Dance-dramas
are performed in
Chinese court.

175 A.D.
Roman theatre consists of
mimicry, mime, pantomime,
and spectacle.

400 A.D.
Indian classic, *Shakuntala*,
by Kalidasa is written
in Sanskrit.

426 A.D. (approx.)
Saint Augustine opposes
theatre in *The City of God*.

197–201 A.D.
The Roman Catholic Church
excommunicates actors.

568 A.D.
Roman spectacles are stopped.

300 A.D.
Earliest recorded religious plays.

T   I   M   E

Exploring

1204
Religious drama performed outside the church.

1430
Professional actors reappear.

925 A.D.
Earliest known Easter tropes, *Quem Quaeritis*—dialogue of *The Three Marys and the Angels.*

1250
Beginning of German drama

1110
Earliest record of a miracle play, Dunstable, England.

1375
English plays begin to be written in everyday language.

1402
First European acting company is given permission by Charles VI to occupy a permanent playhouse in the Hôpital de la Trinité in Paris

MEDIEVAL PERIOD (500–1550)

800 **900** **1000** **1100** **1200** **1300** **1400** **1500**

1320
Ordinary people participate in performances as the medieval trade unions or guilds take over presentations of religious pageants. Rolling stages or pageant wagons used.

1425
Outdoor staging directions given in *The Castle of Perseverance.*

800 A.D.
Traveling circuses provide live entertainment.

1325
Noh plays developed in Japan.

1469
Mummings and masquerades become popular.

1200
Bards, professional storytellers, popular in Ireland.

1490
Development of Spanish drama.

L I N E

Theatre

Outstanding Playwrights

1450–1700

England:
Jonson
Kyd
Marlowe
Shakespeare
Webster

France:
Corneille
Molière
Racine

Spain:
Calderón
Cervantes
Lope de Rueda
Lope de Vega

Italy:
Ariosto
Goldoni
Machiavelli
Tasso

1599
Globe Theatre built.

1599
Shakespeare's *Julius Caesar*.

1613
The Globe Theatre is destroyed by fire.

1616
Shakespeare's death.

1674
Drury Lane Theatre opens in England.

1680–1780
Bibiena family dominates scene designs using lavish, ornate, baroque-style scenery.

1500
Anonymous morality play, *Everyman*, personifies virtues and vices struggling for the soul of man.

1558
Elizabeth I forbids writing of religious drama.

1633
First performance of Oberammergau Passion Play in Germany

MEDIEVAL PERIOD (to 1550)	RENAISSANCE, ELIZABETHAN, RESTORATION, GOLDEN AGE, NEOCLASSIC (1550–1700)		
1500	**1550**	**1600**	**1650**

1512
The word "masque" first used to denote poetic drama.

1548
Hôtel de Bourgogne, first roofed theatre and first public theatre in Europe since classical times, opens in Paris.

1540
Ralph Roister Doister, English "school play."

1540
Classical drama begins in schools and universities in England.

1548
Religious drama banned in Paris.

1558–1584
Mature plays performed for the English court by companies of young boy actors.

1564
Shakespeare's birth.

1576
The Theatre, first permanent London theatre opens.

1595
Shakespeare's *Romeo and Juliet*.

1618
Teatro Farnese, first Renaissance proscenium arch theatre, is built in Italy.

1634
Théâtre du Marais opens in Paris.

1642
Theatres are closed in England.

1671
Paris Opera opens.

1675–1750
Kabuki Theatre and puppet theatre begin in Japan

1660
London theatres are reopened.

1660
Actresses play female roles.

T I M E

Exploring

1852
First production of
Uncle Tom's Cabin, the
most popular American
play of the century.

1774
Plays banned in America
by Continental Congress.

1716
A theatre opens in
Williamsburg, Virginia.

1864
Edwin Booth (1833–1893)
plays Hamlet for 100 nights
in New York. Long runs of
plays become common.

1790s
More realism in
scenery and costumes.

1732
First record of a play
in New York: Farquhar's
The Recruiting Officer.

1866
Duke of Saxe-Meiningen (1826–1914)
begins reform in staging. Role of
modern director begins in Germany.

1790s
Actors' salaries range
from $4 to $50 a week.

1737
Licensing Act, London,
submits all plays to censorship.

1820s
More historical accuracy
in costumes and sets.

1878
H.M.S. Pinafore, operetta by
Gilbert and Sullivan, is presented.

1741–1742
David Garrick begins his career.

ROMANTIC, VICTORIAN, DAWN OF REALISM,
(1700–1900)

1700   1750   1800   1850   1900

1750
First playhouse
opens in New York.

1822
Gas lighting
introduced at
the Paris Opera.

1880
Madison Square Theatre
opens in New York City.

Outstanding Playwrights

1700–1900

Great Britain:
Congreve
Garrick
Gay
Goldsmith
Gregory
O'Casey
Robinson
Sheridan
Synge
Wilde
Yeats

France:
Labiche
Rostand

Germany:
Goethe
Gottsched
Lessing

Russia:
Chekhov
Gorky
Pushkin
Tolstoy

Norway:
Ibsen

USA:
Bowker
Fitch
Herne
Howard
MacKaye
Moody
Mowatt
Payne

Spain:
Benavente
Echegaray
Quintero
Sierra

Sweden:
Strindberg

1840
Arrival of the
"well-made"
play.

1881
The Savoy in London
is first theatre to be
lighted throughout
with electricity.

1846
Electric arc lighting
used at the Paris Opera.

1883
Metropolitan Opera
founded.

1883
Sarah Bernhardt (1844–1923) becomes
most famous star of the century.

1889
Edison develops the motion picture camera

1895
Oscar Wilde writes *The Importance of Being Earnest*.

L   I   N   E

Theatre

Outstanding Playwrights

1900–1945

Great Britain:
Barrie
Coward
Pinter
Shaw
Synge
Thomas
Williams

Germany:
Brecht

Russia:
Chekhov

France:
Anouilh
Cocteau
Feydeau
Giraudoux
Sartre

USA:
Hellman
O'Neill
Rice
Van Druten
Wilder

Italy:
D'Annunzio
Pirandello

Belgium:
Cromme-linck

1924
Stanislavski's
My Life in Art begins
revolution in actor
training.

1927
Audiences are lured from
theatre to the "talking pictures."

1927
Jerome Kern and Oscar
Hammerstein II write *Showboat*.

1929
First Academy Awards
(Oscars) presented for
the 1927–1928 year by
the Academy of Motion
Picture Arts and Sciences.

1934
Lillian Hellman writes
The Children's Hour.

1943
Rogers and Hammerstein's
Oklahoma! integrates music,
story, dance, and setting.

1946
Electronic computer
invented.

1947
Antoinette Perry
(Tony) Awards
first presented
for excellence in
Broadway theatre.

1949
First Emmy Awards
presented for
excellence
in television.

1905
Gordon Craig writes
The Art of the Theatre.

EARLY MODERN (1900–1945)

1900	**1910**	**1920**	**1930**	**1940**

1903
Pioneering film,
The *Great Train Robbery*,
is produced.

1903
George Pierce Baker
(1866–1935) begins to
teach playwriting at
Radcliffe College.

1904
Thomas Edison
produces the first
sound motion picture.

1912
Non-professional acting
companies—"little theatres"—
appear in the U.S.

1914
U.S.'s first degree program
is established in theatre
at Carnegie Institute
of Technology.

1920
Television is invented.

1930
Marc Connelly writes *The Green Pastures*.
Plays are written for and presented by
black actors.

1931
Group Theatre, modeled
after Moscow Art Theatre,
is founded by Lee Strasberg,
Harold Clurman, and
Cheryl Crawford.

1935
Depression motivates founding
of Federal Theatre Project.
10,000 employed in 40 states.

1938
Thorton Wilder
writes *Our Town*.

1945
Tennessee Williams writes
The Glass Menagerie.

1947
Actors' Studio, founded
in New York City, emphasizing
Stanislavski "Method".

1948
Theatre threatened by
rapid development of TV.

T   I   M   E

Exploring

1954
Joseph Papp establishes the New York Shakespeare Festival. Moves to Central Park in 1957 as free theatre.

1955
Jim Henson's Muppets star in the television show *Sam and Friends*.

1959
First play on Broadway written by an African American woman—*A Raisin in the Sun*—by Lorraine Hansberry.

1966
Movie studios contract movies made for television.

1965
National Endowment for the Arts established.

1968
Negro Ensemble Company founded.

1971
John F. Kennedy Center for the Performing Arts opens in Washington, D.C.

1980s
Musicals by Stephen Sondheim, Andrew Lloyd Webber, and Leonard Bernstein win popular acclaim.

1980s
Broadway productions use spectacular high-tech special effects.

1982
Annie closes after 2,377 performances.

1990s
Over 200 non-profit theatres exist in U.S., mounting over 3,000 productions.

1990s
Escalating production costs force price increases of Broadway tickets.

1993
A spoken drama on Broadway costs over $1.2 million to produce. A musical costs $12 to $13 million.

LATE MODERN (1945–PRESENT)

1950   1960   1970   1980   1990   2000

1962
Theatres introduce subscription tickets to finance productions.

1975
Michael Bennett's *A Chorus Line* opens.

1975
Videocassette recorders marketed.

1977
Charles Strouse's *Annie* opens.

1979
Theatrical companies film plays on video cassette for new VCR market.

1980
Ronald Reagan, an actor, is elected U.S. president

1993
Broadway meets MTV in the telecasted rock opera *The Who's Tommy*.

1995
14 fall "openings" occur on Broadway.

Outstanding Playwrights

1945–Present

Great Britain:		Canada:
Broadhurst	Henley	Beissel
Osborne	Hwang	Campbell
Pinter	Mamet	Deverell
Rattigan	Medoff	Foon
Shaffer	Miller	Ryga
	Rabe	
France:	Saroyan	**Australia:**
Beckett	Shepard	Buzo
Fauquez	Simon	Davis
Ionesco	Williams	De Groen
	A. Wilson	Holman
	L. Wilson	Williamson
USA:	Zeder	
Albee		**China:**
Conley	**Africa:**	Yu
Hansberry	Clarke	
	Fugard	

L   I   N   E

Theatre

CHAPTER 2

You and Theatre

Spotlight on Terms

- artistic discipline
- authentic evaluation
- cooperation
- criteria
- critique
- ensemble
- evaluation
- group process
- interpersonal relationships
- performance evaluation
- respect
- risks
- self-confidence
- self-image
- self-talk
- trust

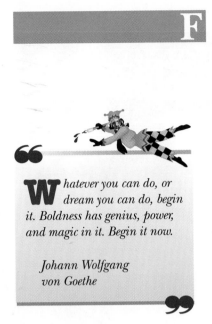

or many of you, Chapter 1 was your first experience with any aspect of drama. As a cast member you discussed many parts of the wonderful world of theatre. You might not have realized the impact of our history on theatrical performances or acknowledged your own personal experiences as an excellent source for theatre arts activities.

In Chapter 2 the focus is on you—your development as a positive person, and your responsibilities in this class. The first two lessons will generate experiences that will enable you and your classmates to grow emotionally, academically, physically, and socially. You will develop team spirit and ensemble skills through cooperation and respect for yourself and each other.

Your participation is crucial to the success of your theatre arts experiences. This is why your teacher will provide a theatre curriculum and safe environment in which you can actively get up in front of others without the fear of rejection and failure. The theatre skills you learn in this chapter will help minimize these fears, which are common for all people. These skills can be applied to other experiences and situations in your everyday life.

> *Whatever you can do, or dream you can do, begin it. Boldness has genius, power, and magic in it. Begin it now.*
>
> Johann Wolfgang von Goethe

LESSON 1

Believing in Yourself

LESSON OBJECTIVES

- ◆ Demonstrate an understanding of self-confidence and the importance of positive self-talk.
- ◆ Participate in activities that will improve your self-confidence.
- ◆ Acknowledge similarities and differences in others.

Warm Up

In your theatre journal, write two positive statements about yourself. Look around the room and choose three of your classmates. List their names in your journal, and write two positive statements about each of them.

self-confidence
belief in your worth and abilities as a person.

self-image
the way we see ourselves.

Self-confidence, belief in your worth and abilities as a person, is the key to success. Throughout this course, you will participate in activities that will help improve your self-confidence. The course will provide you with opportunities to explore and imitate life in a positive and safe environment, which will help build your self-confidence. If you have confidence in yourself and feel accepted by others, you will be able to face each day with a positive outlook.

Having a Positive Self-Image

We all have a self-image. Your **self-image** is the way you see yourself. Usually, your self-image depends on your everyday relationships. If you get negative feedback from your friends, family, and teachers, you will most likely have a negative self-image. When the people you see every day give you supportive feedback, you develop a positive self-image—that is, you like who you are. We all have a need to belong, to be connected to someone or something positive.

Positive feedback from your
"team" gives you a good
self-image.

Self-image is directly linked to respect. A positive self-image is possible only if you have respect for yourself as well as for others. Having **respect** means being considerate and accepting of yourself and others, including other people's property, backgrounds, and opinions. Self-confidence also improves as you learn to appreciate and understand other people's personalities. No two people are exactly alike. In choosing your friends, you probably select people whose likes and dislikes are similar to your own. But to maintain those friendships, you must recognize and respect the many ways in which your friends are different from you.

If we all practiced the principles of respect, the world would be a safer, happier place to live. In fact, many experts believe that there is a direct link between negative self-image and certain crimes. Therefore, in helping to improve people's self-image, theatre can be valuable to society.

The Power of Positive Self-Talk

For most of us, our families, friends, and teachers have made a positive difference in our lives and how we feel about ourselves. Wouldn't it be wonderful if the people who tell us good things about ourselves could be with us to give us pep talks and protect us at all times? Unfortunately, this is not realistic. Each of us must be responsible for his or her own self-talk.

Self-talk is the mental comments and opinions we repeat to ourselves constantly. It is up to you to put forth positive thoughts about yourself. If you give yourself negative thoughts each day, then all you will have are negative thoughts—about yourself and others. When you constantly put yourself down, everything probably seems to go wrong—from schoolwork to friendships to your life at home.

Positive talk must begin with one person, and that person is you. Believe in yourself! To have a good self-image, you have to believe in your

respect
consideration for and acceptance of ourselves and others, including other people's property, backgrounds, and opinions.

self-talk
mental comments and opinions we repeat to ourselves constantly.

You *can* make a difference, whether onstage or off.

> **Y**our attitude and not your aptitude determines your altitude.
>
> *Jesse Jackson*

abilities. In theatre, you will find concepts and activities that will help you feel good about yourself. With a stronger self-image, you may have a greater desire to learn and accept responsibility. You will also have more fun while participating in all the subjects you are required to take.

The power of positive self-talk is truly remarkable. Extraordinary accomplishments and lasting friendships are the result of a strong self-image. Great inventions could never have been completed without determination and an inventor with an "I can do it" attitude.

When you were small, you learned to walk, talk, and even ride a bicycle for the first time. You couldn't have mastered these tasks without a positive attitude and encouraging words. The good grades you make are not the result of negative thoughts, but rather positive thoughts and words. The football team that wins a championship always has a positive coach and teammates as well as fans who believe in the team. The successful theatre activities and performances in which you'll participate will be the result of positive talk and action.

We all have many talents, but often we don't recognize them. Theatre class will give you the chance to use your special abilities. You may not be the best singer in the class or play an instrument, but you may be really good at operating the sound and light equipment. Or you may be just the person to organize the efforts of others. You may be the most responsible person in the class and be assigned to take care of all the props for a production. Perhaps you can follow a script well and mark cues. Or you may have the gift of being the best listener and observer in class. Everyone has special skills and talents, and theatre class can help you develop yours.

We all need to feel that what we say and think has value and matters to others. This is vital to your theatre experience because theatre is cooperation. You will belong to a team, a theatre troupe that will feel like a family. You will have opportunities to develop your special talents as your teammates develop theirs. For everyone to grow, it will be important to hear everyone's ideas equally. In theatre activities, you will be given a chance to express yourself in a safe environment (without being judged). You will have fun and success participating in theatre activities. And with your efforts and the support of your classmates and teacher, you will believe in yourself!

It has often been said that the first step to making friends is liking yourself. After you accept yourself, it becomes much easier to accept others.

Try these activities to reflect on and improve your self-image.

1. **Positive Self-Reminders.** Every day, read the positive journal entries that you write about yourself to remind yourself of what a special person you are. Keep adding positive statements to your journal. Try to become aware of those times in your daily life when you use negative self-talk so that you can guard against it in the future.

2. **Self-Collage.** Make a list of some of your likes, dislikes, and traits that make you the unique individual that you are. Next, choose materials for a collage (a collection of pictures and words from magazines or other printed material). The pictures and words that you choose should reflect your personality. Bring your collage materials to school. Then cut and glue them to a poster board (you may use part of the board or the whole piece). Be creative with the shapes you cut, overlapping the pictures in different directions. Use captions to reflect your personality. Keep the activity positive! You can laminate your collage as a classroom decoration or for your own room at home.

3. **Class Comic Book.** Make a class comic book of personal events. Fold a sheet of typing or drawing paper into six sections. Draw in the most important events in your life. Use only positive events from your life. Examples might be your first day of school; losing your first tooth; a special birthday, holiday, or vacation; learning to ride a bike; getting a favorite pet; being elected to the student council; winning an academic contest; an athletic victory; or making the honor roll. How good you are at drawing is not as important as the events you choose. Share your page with your classmates. Your teacher will collect all the pages and form a class comic book.

4. **Positive Back Talk.** Each person in class should tape a piece of paper on his or her back. Everyone should walk around the room and with a pencil write a positive comment on the paper of each classmate. It is not necessary to sign your name. Keep the comments positive! After the activity, take your "back talk" sheet off your back and read it to build your self-confidence. Follow up on this activity by making a journal entry on what surprised you most on your sheet.

5. **Classmate Similarities and Differences.** Write down the names of your classmates on a sheet of paper. Make two columns, one labeled "Similar," the other "Different." Write down one similarity and one differ-

Confidence in yourself helps you appreciate what you have in common with your classmates. It also helps you respect what is different.

ence between you and each classmate. Then have a class discussion about the similarities and differences in the class. The discussion will help you appreciate what you have in common with your classmates and at the same time help you respect the differences that people have. This activity will help bond your class. Follow up on this activity by writing a contract that all of your classmates will sign, promising to focus on common bonds and respect for differences.

6. **Self-Identity Sack.** Bring three items from home that represent your personality. (These items must be able to fit in a lunch sack.) Place the items into a decorated lunch sack. Don't let your classmates see the items. All paper sacks need to be placed on a table when you enter class. The contents of each sack will be revealed by the teacher or assigned students, and the class will try to guess whose sack it is. After the activity, use the sacks for a class bulletin board.

7. **Personality Clue Game.** Write something unusual about yourself in sentence form on a sheet of paper. For example: "I have nine people in my family." "My family went to Europe this summer." "I take karate lessons." "I always sing in the shower." "I like liver." Do not put your name on the paper. Fold your clue and put it in a box. Your teacher will pass out the clues to the class, each person receiving only one clue. Now everyone will become a detective and try to find the person that matches his or her clue. After all the clues have been matched, talk about them in a class discussion.

8. **Self-Identity T-Shirt.** Bring a T-shirt to class to make a shirt that fits your personality. At the top of the shirt, write a word that best describes you. On the left sleeve, draw or write something that you do well. On the right sleeve, write or draw something that you like about being your age. Write your name in large letters in the center of the shirt. On the bottom left, draw or write something you wish you could do. On the bottom right, draw or write something you do for a hobby. After the shirts are completed, have a fashion show. Discuss modeling postures and poses for the

fashion show. Your teacher or you could select some music to accompany the fashion show. Add other designs and be creative to make the shirt your special possession.

LESSON 2

Working with a Group

LESSON OBJECTIVES

◆ Define group process.
◆ Participate in the group process by using cooperative activities.
◆ Develop drama skills and techniques through the use of warm-ups and theatre games.
◆ Build ensemble and team spirit.
◆ Take risks in a safe environment.
◆ Develop trust among your classmates.

Warm Up

Energy Circle

Make a large circle holding hands. The leader, chosen by your teacher, begins a squeeze of the hand of the person to the left that continues around the circle until it comes back to the leader. Alternate directions of the squeeze, then send squeezes around in opposite directions, letting them cross. The purpose is to work together and keep the flow of the squeeze in rhythm. Watch the energy fly!

"*Go, team, go!*"
"*Go! Fight! Win!*"
"*We're number 1!*"
"*United we stand. Divided we fall.*"
"*We've got spirit! Yes we do! We've got spirit! How about you?*"

So what are all the yells, excitement, and energy about? Building team spirit helps you to connect to a group. You may already know about team spirit from other groups that you belong to, such as a basketball or volleyball team, a dance troupe, or even a debating team. Or possibly you are a member of 4-H, a rodeo club, Scouts, or a church group.

In this lesson, you will become part of another dynamic group—your theatre class. In this class, you will experience learning that is accepting, supportive, and fun! What's more, you will build lasting friendships and memories that you will always cherish.

The Group Process

The group process can be especially effective in helping you relate to your classmates in theatre class. Your social skills will gradually improve, making it easier to get along with and work with others. Your level of participation in the group process is key to improving your individual skills and your group's productivity.

Exactly what do we mean by group process? The **group process** involves two or more students taking a step-by-step course of action and making decisions together that are aimed at achieving certain goals. This process generates experiences that will enable you to change and grow emotionally, socially, physically, and academically. You will learn to take **risks** —actions that are different from everyone else's. And you will participate in activities that require you to trust your classmates.

group process

two or more people taking a step-by-step course of action that takes place over a period of time and is aimed at achieving goals.

risks

actions that are different from the norm.

Greek Theatre

You can go to a play almost anytime you choose. Hundreds of plays are performed almost every night of the week all across the United States. Your opportunities to see a play would have been very limited, however, had you lived in Greece around 400 to 500 B.C.

In ancient Greece, plays were performed only a few times a year at religious festivals honoring Dionysius, the Greek god of wine and fertility. The festivals were held to honor Dionysius in the hope that he would bless the Greeks with many children, rich land, and abundant crops.

An important part of the festival was the dramatic contest. At first there were contests for drama only, but later contests for comedy were added. The first such contest is thought to have taken place in 534 B.C. The winner was Thespis, from whom we derive the term *thespian* (which is still used today to refer to an actor). Other famous winners of the contests were Sophocles, Aeschylus, and Euripides for drama, and Aristophanes for comedy. Of the hundreds of plays written by these famous Greek playwrights, only forty-some remain today. Among those plays, *Oedipus the King* by Sophocles is considered one of the finest dramas, and *Lysistrata* by Aristophanes is perhaps the best-known Greek comedy.

Athens was the center of the Greek theatre. The most important festival of the year was the Great, or City, Dionysia which was held in late March to the beginning of April in the Theatre of Dionysius. This open-air theatre was built much like today's large football or baseball stadiums. Since each play was performed only once, the theatres had to be large enough to hold thousands of people. Historians believe that as many as 14,000 to 17,000 people might have attended each production.

So that all the audience could see, the theatre was built into a hillside. The performance took place on the ground level, a circular floor called the *orchestra*, and the audience extended all the way to the top of the hill. Some historians believe that the audiences were made up exclusively of boys and men. Other experts believe that women and even slaves might have attended.

Since there was no electricity for lighting, sound, or special effects, the plays began early in the morning and lasted until the sun began to set. Imagine the excitement in the air as people prepared to spend an entire day at the theatre.

Many of the Greek actors wore lightweight masks. These masks made it easier for the actors to change characters quickly. Since the first Greek actors were all men, the masks also made their portrayal of female roles more believable.

Much of the action of the Greek play was song and dance by a group of young men and boys. This group was called the *chorus*. Thespis is credited by most historians as being the first playwright, and perhaps the first person, to have stepped out from the chorus to recite the first solo lines, and thereby become the first actor.

The type and style of theatre performed in the United States today can be traced all the way back to these ancient Greek plays given in honor of Dionysius. What better indication of the importance of Greek influence than the fact that such key words as *theatre, drama, tragedy,* and *comedy* all originated with the Greeks? ∎

Can you imagine yourself as a Greek actor or chorus member appearing 2500 years ago in an all-day performance before thousands of people? Would you rather have been a member of the chorus or one of the first actors to speak your lines alone, all by yourself on centerstage?

trust

the ability to risk expressing yourself in front of your classmates without fear of being ridiculed.

■ ■ ■ ■ ■ ■ ■ ■ ■ ■ ■ ■ ■ ■ ■

The group process makes everyone a winner.

interpersonal relationships

the contacts a person has with many different people.

ensemble

a group of people working together cooperatively.

cooperation

the act of working together, getting along, and sharing responsibility.

Trust is the ability to risk expressing yourself in front of your classmates without fear of being ridiculed. You need to be able to trust that your classmates will be supportive, and you must be supportive in turn. Only then can your classroom become a safe environment in which to experiment while you are actively learning.

Benefits of the Group Process. The group process offers many benefits to a theatre arts class. You will feel challenged and motivated, eagerly waiting to explore the next theatre adventure. You will find a positive, enriched, and caring environment that will give you a sense of belonging. You will feel involved, included, and of value to others. You will share responsibility and understand the importance of accepting responsibility. You will develop respect for yourself and others and develop attitudes that value individual differences.

There is power in learning with a group. Together you will learn problem solving, organizational skills, and decision-making skills. The group will work together to accomplish goals and tasks.

The group process is an invitation to express your opinions, and you will have many opportunities to share your talents and resources with team members. Moreover, you will learn how to adapt the group process to other school subjects and everyday life situations.

The group process will also allow you to develop **interpersonal relationships**—the contacts you will have with the many different people in your group activities. The satisfaction of working well together is the key benefit of the group process in your theatre class.

The emphasis on group process will make your theatre arts experience different from most of your other educational experiences. In fact, the group process may turn out to be your favorite aspect of theatre arts.

Building an Ensemble

Building an ensemble is essential in theatre arts. An **ensemble** is a group of people working together with mutual respect for one another. An ensemble not only performs together but creates together. The members of an ensemble practice **cooperation**, working together, getting along, and sharing responsibility. Each member is willing to help the other and strive to do his or her best for the good of the group.

Getting a group of people together doesn't mean that you have an ensemble. A true ensemble doesn't happen in one class period. As you work together throughout the course, the stronger your ensemble-building skills will become.

The positive self-talk and positive self-image that you learned about in Lesson 1 are essential to ensemble building. If you have a positive self-image and use positive self-talk, your theatre group will benefit from your input as you make decisions, choices, and suggestions in the group activities. A positive attitude is critical to building ensemble in theatre and completing activities successfully.

Don't be afraid of embarrassing yourself. According to Dale Carnegie, author of *How to Win Friends and Influence People*, speaking in front of others is the number one fear of students, and most people experience this fear many times in their lives. The activities that your

A good ensemble is creative,
responsible, and cooperative.

group will share will allow you to "let yourself go" and give it your all, without the fear of looking foolish.

Remember to think as a group and be a team player. The participants need to support each member of the group and work together to achieve the group's goals. The key to building an ensemble is to create a group in which each member knows and cares about all the other members. In that way, all the members feel comfortable expressing themselves in various roles—acting, directing, managing, designing, and playwriting. The process of ensemble building must also include evaluation, which you will learn about in Lesson 4. Giving opinions about the strengths and weaknesses of individual and group work, and doing so in a tactful way, is a necessary part of the process.

Guidelines for Building an Ensemble. For the ensemble to work and the team spirit to grow, you and your classmates and teacher must set guidelines. Here are suggested guidelines for your ensemble:

1. Always have respect for the feelings, backgrounds, and property of others.
2. Practice attentive listening.
3. Use nonverbal as well as verbal encouragement for your teammates. Keep the positive energy flowing, and praise others often.
4. Avoid put-downs. No one deserves verbal abuse.
5. Keep the activities G-rated. The classroom is no place for inappropriate remarks or ideas you might use to get laughs. This means following the general school rules about language and behavior.
6. Actively participate in the team effort whenever possible. But also know that you can choose not to participate at times. Be a silent

*A*ll for one. One for all.

from The Three
Musketeers *Alexandre
Dumas*

As an effective member of an ensemble you should speak up and offer suggestions when you have an idea that you think would improve the group's performance. You must also be good at listening when other members of the ensemble are voicing their ideas.

If you treat an individual as he is, he will stay as he is, but if you treat him as if he were what he ought to be, he will become what he ought to be and could be.

Johann Wolfgang von Goethe, German poet and playwright

observer if you choose. Your silent observations can be as valuable as your active participation.

7. Remember to share responsibilities and accept responsibility.
8. Be a thinker as well as a listener and talker.
9. Use the four **F** formula for success: Be **F**air (don't show favor in making judgments), **F**riendly (be on good terms with others), **F**irm (don't yield easily to pressure), and **F**lexible (be able to adapt to new situations and ideas easily).
10. Don't let your teammates down. Always do your best!

Assuming Your Role in the Ensemble. The activity or assignment given to your group will determine the type of role you will have. Your teacher may have a variety of duties for you to perform to complete the activity. The acronym *COPER* can help you identify possible roles in your group. (An acronym is a word formed from the first letters of another word.)

C for Checker: The checker makes sure that all teammates understand the activity.
O for Observer: The observer records what the group is doing, making notes and observing all details. (Two teammates may be needed for this role.)
P for Praiser: The praiser praises good ideas and teammates to keep up the team spirit and to promote self-confidence.
E for Encourager: The encourager encourages all the participants and makes sure that everyone is participating.
R for Reader: The reader reads aloud the activity or assignment.

Did you realize that, by coincidence, COPER is short for *cooperation*?

Preparing for the Activities

Use your creativity to get motivated as you participate in the group activities. These activities will include warm-ups, theatre games, and cooperative activities.

Warm-ups will be provided throughout the book. They are designed to get you ready mentally and physically for theatre activities and performances. The warm-ups should help relax you and reduce any fears that you may have about getting involved in your group or performing in front of others.

Theatre games are activities that give you opportunities to express yourself creatively and to develop your acting skills on stage. The games and cooperative activities provide a participant avenues in which to connect, communicate, respond, experience, and explore with other students in theatre situations. They will help pave the way to successful preparation for your future performances.

Theatre games can help you explore what it means to live in a cooperative society. In games when you make choices, you are practicing making choices in real life. You can take the cooperative spirit you learn in theatre arts class and use it in your everyday experiences. The games are designed to encourage cooperation rather than competition. They create an environment in which you feel valued by others because your input is needed for the game to continue. Teammates learn to trust and support each other. One person's success in a theatre game is everyone's success.

Theatre games can help you tap into your talents, producing unbelievable changes in you. In her book *Theatre Games for Rehearsal*, theatre expert Viola Spolin explains that games provide an important rehearsal technique for groups throughout the world. In theatre class, warm-ups, games, and cooperative activities are all methods of resolving production problems.

In theatre arts, as in life, people have to learn to work together. The purpose of the activities is to begin building the team spirit—the ensemble we have been discussing. Have fun!

Warm-Ups

1. **Balloon Blow-Up.** Pretend that you're a deflated balloon. On a signal from your teacher, "blow yourself up" to fullest expansion. Don't be afraid to make sounds in the process. At the end, when your teacher "pops" each balloon, spin crazily and loudly all over the room. Remember not to invade someone else's space while you are doing this activity.

2. **Ready? Ok!** Your teacher will call out an activity for you to act out—for example, "Let's all shake hands." First a leader shouts "Ready?"; then everyone shouts "OK!" and begins acting out the activity. After several suggestions from the teacher, you and your classmates begin suggesting activities to perform. Possible examples: playing tennis, brushing your teeth, jogging in place, and flying a kite. This is fun because you get to shout and fill the classroom with energy.

Try letting your group "guide" you while you're blindfolded. Do you trust them?

3. **Lift Off!** Divide into groups of three. One student stands in the middle with hands on waist, palms facing down. The other two students stand on each side of the student in the middle, holding that student's wrists and arms gently but firmly. On a count of 3, 2, 1, lift off! the students on the sides lift the student in the middle. As the students on the sides lift the middle student, it is the responsibility of the middle student to jump up. Be careful! The middle student can be lifted extremely high off the floor. The feeling of being lifted is like being on the moon, where gravity is weaker than on earth. Now take turns being the student in the middle.

4. **Trust Tour.** Divide into pairs. One partner should then volunteer to be led with his or her eyes closed or wearing a blindfold or mask. The other member of the pair leads the person for 5 minutes, taking very good care of the partner. After 5 minutes, switch roles. Reflect with your partner about how this activity felt. What was scary? What made you feel secure? Develop trust with your partner by doing and talking.

5. **Acting Companies.** After dividing into groups of four or five, create a name for your company, group, or family. The names could relate to Broadway shows (for example, Cats, Sharks), movie titles (E.T., Jurassic Park), popular songs, popular musicians, or cartoons. Your teacher will change your group often to give you the opportunity to work with everyone in the class. That classmate to whom you never really spoke may become your best friend.

6. **Body Tangle.** In groups of seven to fifteen students, join hands, making sure that you have two different people connected to you, causing a body tangle. Working as a group, don't let go of hands, but untangle yourselves into a circle.

Theatre Games

1. **Two on a Draw.** After being divided into groups of two, you and your partner should take one marker, pen, pencil, or crayon and one sheet of paper. You may not talk to each other before or during the activity. While

These students are working together as an ensemble. What do you think is going to happen next?

your teacher plays a 3- or 4-minute song in the background, you and your partner should hold the drawing tool simultaneously and (without speaking) draw any picture together. When finished, have a class discussion, answering the following questions:

a. What did you draw? Does it represent anything?

b. What did you learn about sharing and cooperation?

c. Who was the leader in your partnership? How difficult was it to share the leadership?

d. How did you feel when you realized that your picture was going to be something? Or did it turn out to be an abstract?

e. Why did you like or dislike this activity?

2. **Who Started That Action?** Your teacher will pick one student to go outside the room. The class then forms a circle, standing or sitting. While the student is out of the room, decide which student in the circle will be the leader. The rest of the circle will follow this student's actions. When the student outside the room comes back in, he or she stands in the center of the circle and tries to identify the leader. Remember not to look directly at the leader or you will give the leader's identity away. The leader tries to change the action when the student in the center looks away, looking for the leader. The class must work together smoothly to keep the student in the center guessing which person is the leader. After two guesses, the leader reveals his or her identity. The class then starts the game again.

3. **Moving an Imaginary Object.** Working in groups, choose a large, imaginary object to move from one place to another. Each member must be actively involved in moving the object, using gestures (no words). When the presentation is over, the other students must guess what the object is.

4. **We Are Where?** After dividing into groups, think of a place anywhere in the world and discuss some of the activities that could happen there.

Your teacher may have a list of locations to choose from in case you can't decide on your own. One member of your group (in a designated acting area) begins doing an activity specific to the place. Your teammates then think of different activities and act them out, so that the entire group is participating. When the scene is completed, your classmates try to guess where the place is and identify the activities being performed there.

Artistic Discipline

LESSON OBJECTIVES

◆ Define artistic discipline and understand its importance in theatre class.
◆ Demonstrate social discipline in dramatic activities.
◆ Practice and develop organizational skills.
◆ Accept the responsibility that comes with freedom.

Warm Up

Answer these questions in your theatre journal:
What is discipline?
Why is discipline necessary in the home? at school? in your personal life?

artistic discipline
maintaining a balance between group cooperation and individual integrity.

Maybe you enrolled in theatre class because you heard that it was fun. To most of us, the word *fun* means little or no work. Theatre is fun, but it is also hard work.

It is possible that you will decide that theatre is the hardest class you have ever been in because it requires self-discipline and self-control. Self-discipline requires order and management in your daily activities. Motivation for this type of discipline comes from within a person. For example, you may not have to be told to clean up your room; or, perhaps you know you must study to pass a test; and any athlete who wants to excel knows that he or she must practice and "go the extra mile."

In the arts, self-discipline leads to artistic discipline. Artistic discipline is more demanding than self-discipline. **Artistic discipline** involves maintaining a balance between group cooperation and individual integrity. Actors, musicians, dancers, and visual artists must train to perfect their crafts, and hard work, commitment, and dedication are essential ingredients. A passion (inner drive and determination) for theatre, dance, music, or visual arts is an integral part of artistic discipline. For example, it isn't unusual for people in the arts to spend hours each day perfecting their skills. Many choose to study their art during the summer in camps, workshops, and seminars, often beginning their study at 7 A.M. and continuing until 9 P.M. Clearly, these individuals have a high degree of artistic discipline.

The theatre activities in which you will participate will give you a certain amount of freedom that you might not experience in some of your other classes. With freedom comes responsibility. It will be your job to accept this responsibility with a mature attitude. Responsibility has its rewards (for example, being allowed to work on costumes alone or being in charge of the tickets for a performance). But you must take such responsibilities seriously.

Artistic discipline develops from self-discipline. Sometimes in theatre class, you will have to accomplish tasks by yourself using the skills you have learned.

> Freedom is not what you like, it is what you want; but you cannot have freedom to express yourself until you have discipline.
>
> Dame Ninette de Valois

While in this class, you will be assigned a variety of theatre projects. Many activities will require you to work with small groups, large groups, and even your entire class. Other projects will allow you to work at your own pace. Often, your teacher will need to work with one group while several other groups continue to work on their own. This means that you and your group will need to stay on task to complete your project. Theatre cannot be accomplished unless you remain focused on your task, even when your teacher is not standing over you.

Your teacher will introduce you to many techniques that can help develop artistic discipline. One such technique is a written contract. As in the business world, people in theatre have to contract, or make a promise, to fulfill certain desired behaviors or tasks. Your teacher might contract with you to learn a specific number of lines by a specific date, or to keep to a certain rehearsal schedule, or to follow certain backstage rules and procedures. To be a responsible member of your group, you must fulfill the requirements of your contract, whether it is written or verbal.

Developing artistic discipline requires organization and commitment. You can begin by keeping up with all the assignments, scripts, and classroom notes that your teacher gives you. A simple folder or notebook will help you get organized. Homework assignments, rehearsal information, and performance times can all be scheduled on a school calendar that you keep in this notebook. Here are just some of the items your theatre notebook can contain:

journal entries
assignments
theatre terms
handouts
class notes
critique sheets from all performances, including self-evaluations

all written or artistic projects
picture and article collections
returned tests
play reports and play reviews
all scripts used

Keeping an organized notebook and knowing where you put it every day will help you acquire organization skills that are needed on every job. But once you get organized, you must remember to stay organized. Being organized will help you feel much better about yourself, even when you're under pressure. Remember, creativity is not born out of chaos. Creativity involves thinking, planning, imagining the unknown, and then getting into action.

Train yourself to always check your classroom "call-board" or designated assignment board for upcoming homework or other responsibilities. As soon as you see that your teacher or director has made an assignment, schedule it on your personal calendar or in your assignment book and plan a time to complete the work. It is important to develop a systematic approach to remembering and completing whatever is required of you. Turning in homework on time and remembering to bring props or costumes from home shows your teacher or director that you are trying hard to discipline yourself.

Finally, if your teacher or director gives you information to take home to your parents or guardians, take it home and return it as soon as possible. Following instructions—and doing it quickly—is an important part of artistic discipline.

Roman Theatre

By 146 B.C., Rome had conquered Greece, and in the years that followed, Rome would gradually absorb the entire Greek world. Because their empire was so vast and their wealth so great, many Roman citizens had a great deal of free time. They didn't have to spend many hours each day growing, gathering, or earning money to pay for their food. As a result, they were a society that loved many forms of entertainment.

Greek-style theatre was only one of many forms of entertainment that the Romans regularly produced. The Romans enjoyed performances of short comedies (similar to our "sitcoms"), athletic events, music and dance, trained animal shows, chariot races, and circus performers such as jugglers and tumblers. Of the different full-length plays produced by the Romans, the comedies were much more popular than the tragedies.

The titles of many Roman plays were recorded in government and festival records, but few of that large number survive. Of the known tragedies, all but one is by a playwright named Seneca (5 B.C.–65 A.D.). Nine of his plays survive. Of these, the best known are *The Trojan Women, Medea, Oedipus,* and *Agamemnon,* all of which are based on Greek plays. The comedy scripts that have survived are by either Titus Plautus (254 B.C.–184 B.C.) or Publius Terentius Afer, who is known to us today as Terence (190 B.C.–159 B.C.).

Most of the surviving Roman plays are based upon plots of Greek plays. This practice of borrowing the main ideas and characters from plays written in earlier periods is a practice which we see repeated by many famous playwrights throughout history. For example, the Roman *Menaechmi* was Shakespeare's source for *The Comedy of Errors,* one of his most popular scripts today.

But the Roman writers did more than copy the Greeks' ideas. They made some important changes in dramatic form. They eliminated the chorus and added music to underscore the dialogue, rather like a movie soundtrack does today. Unlike the Greeks, who restricted the number of actors in each play, the Romans did not limit their writers to any set number of performers.

The stage setting for Roman comedy was always the same city street, regardless of the play being produced. The backdrop (a permanent stone structure known as the *Scaenae frons*) always represented the front of several houses, in which there were doorways. These doorways represented the households of the main characters of the play and served as entrances and exits. For a tragedy, this same structure would represent a palace or temple.

The Romans will always be remembered as great engineers and architects. Their strong sense of design is reflected in their theatre buildings, which were unified, free-standing structures several stories in height. These buildings were unlike the Greek theatre buildings, which were built on hillsides to utilize the natural slope of the ground for better audience visibility. ■

The Romans built enormous theatres, such as this one in Jordan, to accommodate not only plays, but also circuses and sporting events, which the Romans also favored as forms of entertainment.

ACTION

1. **Theatre Notebook or Folder.** Prepare a theatre notebook or folder according to your teacher's guidelines, or use the items suggested in this lesson. If you are using the lesson's suggestions, create (with theatre designs) a cover sheet for each section in your notebook.

2. **Cover Design.** Design a cover for the notebook or folder reflecting your interests or hobbies. This activity could be combined with the self-collage activity in Lesson 1.

3. **Theatre Calendar.** Create a calendar or assignment sheet on which to record theatre assignments.

4. **Interviewing a Professional.** Interview someone involved in theatre or another of the performing arts. Ask how that person developed and maintained artistic discipline in his or her profession. Here are some sample questions:
   a. What training did you have that helped you become successful in your art?
   b. Why are you dedicated to your art?
   c. Where do you go to research your art?
   d. What motivates you to excel in your art?
   e. Who was your inspiration in the arts?
   f. Is there a special time or place that makes you feel most creative?

Evaluation

LESSON OBJECTIVES

◆ Define evaluation and critique.
◆ Identify three types of evaluation methods.
◆ Evaluate and critique theatre activities in class.
◆ Reflect on and form opinions of drama/theatre experiences.

Warm Up

Select one of your classmates, and write in your journal why he or she is a successful theatre student.

performance evaluation

an evaluation of a performance given before an audience.

All through your education, you have been evaluated. At each grade level, someone has evaluated your participation, your work, and your progress. An **evaluation** is a judgment about your strengths and weaknesses. Evaluations have helped determine your progress in developing certain skills and have determined what still needs to be improved.

Evaluation can take many forms. You are no doubt familiar with written and oral tests. Another evaluation method is **performance evaluation**: You perform before an audience and are given a **critique**—opinions and comments based on specific criteria. **Criteria** are evaluation guidelines that your teacher will provide or your classmates will determine before the performance.

As a theatre student, you will learn to rate both yourself and others according to the guidelines on pages 47 and 48. Remember, the purpose of evaluation is not to criticize, but to help everyone, including yourself, improve.

> *If you want to do a thing badly, you have to work as hard at it as though you wanted to do it well.*
>
> Peter Ustinov

evaluation

assessment of strengths and weaknesses.

critique

opinions and comments based on predetermined criteria; used in an evaluation of a person or performance.

criteria

evaluation guidelines to use in judging or grading an activity.

authentic evaluation

an evaluation involving real-life situations and role-playing to test skills and abilities for the real world.

The evaluator is usually your teacher, but your classmates will also be asked to give their opinions of both group and individual work. And the most important evaluator you should learn from is yourself! Self-evaluation is difficult to do because we are usually so hard on ourselves. We seldom see the strengths in our work and performances—only the negatives. Reread Lesson 1 if necessary to remind yourself of the power of positive self-talk.

Evaluation of self is a valuable tool in theatre. It is important to understand that there is not a "right" or "wrong" in theatre. The experiences that you will have in evaluating yourself and others will help prepare you for making sound judgments in later life.

When you have completed an assignment, activity, or performance, the evaluation process comes next. It is one of the most valuable parts of this class. You will often want to hurry this part of the class and go on to the next assignment or activity, but do not rush the evaluations. Class evaluations can be stimulating and encouraging. These discussions can also be an effective learning tool. Use the evaluation process to be positive, but also use it to grow from your mistakes and identify what can be improved.

Another type of evaluation is called authentic evaluation. In **authentic evaluation**, you are involved in real-life situations and role-playing to test your skills and abilities for the real world—your future.

Most people think that the word *criticism* means only negative responses. But a critique in theatre class means forming opinions about strengths as well as weaknesses. The evaluation process will give you many opportunities to explore the world of theatre. Forming opinions and learning to make sound judgments are necessary skills for success in life.

Throughout this course, you will evaluate yourself and your classmates in assignments and activities. Before you perform for evaluation, your teacher will share the guidelines that will be used. By studying

these guidelines, you will have a better understanding of what is expected of you. In giving a critique, remember that comments such as "It's good" or "I didn't like it" are not really helpful to the classmate you are evaluating. Use specific words that reflect the strengths and weaknesses of the assignment, activity, or performance.

Following are three sample evaluation forms.

I. Form for Performance Evaluation (Sample 1)

Be able to discuss the following criteria for the person you are evaluating. Use opinions and comments that reflect the strengths and weaknesses of the performance.

A. Group work
1. Cooperated with the group.
2. Took an active part in the group.
3. Had a good attitude.
4. Shared in responsibilities in getting the task completed.

B. Voice
1. Used correct pronunciation of words.
2. Spoke clearly.
3. Used adequate volume.

C. Body
1. Used expressive facial expressions.
2. Used appropriate posture and body language.

D. Characterization
1. Stayed in character while performing.
2. Was believable while performing.
3. Was motivated in all actions.
4. Listened to other performers.
5. Responded to other performers.

E. Overall performance
1. Was totally involved in activity.
2. Related to other characters.

II. Form for Performance Evaluation (Sample 2)

Answer the following questions in evaluating yourself and your classmates.

1. Did the actor stay focused on his or her assignments and purpose of the presentation? Discuss what he or she did to accomplish this.
2. How well did the actor project his or her voice?
3. Was the actor's use of dialogue effective and clearly pronounced? Explain.
4. Did the actor use appropriate posture and body language? Give examples.
5. In what ways was the actor believable? Be specific.
6. Did the actor skillfully handle the props (if used)?
7. How poised and relaxed was the actor? Give examples.
8. Did the actor achieve his or her purpose? Be specific.

III. Form for Authentic Evaluation (Sample 3)

The following criteria are intended to help evaluate your interview with a person involved in the theatre or other performing arts.

1. What procedure did you use in persuading the professional to be interviewed?
2. How did you determine which questions to use?
3. What was the professional's attitude toward his or her career?
4. What was the professional's attitude toward you?
5. What were the most interesting comments that the professional made during the interview?
6. What surprised you about the person you interviewed?
7. What comments did the professional make that will be the most useful to your life?
8. Was the interview a success? Why or why not?
9. Would you like to interview this person again? Why or why not?

Your teacher will discuss evaluation or critique procedures as you are assigned an activity. The critiques will vary and should have appropriate criteria for the assignments. Brainstorming with your classmates is another excellent method to develop criteria for your future evaluations.

1. **Class Comic Book Scene.** After the class comic book is completed, your teacher will divide the class into groups of three or four for this evaluation project. Your teacher will give each group one of your classmate's comic sheets about his or her life. Your group's assignment is to create a scene depicting one of the pictures that was illustrated on the comic sheet. Everyone in the group must be involved in the scene, and an introduction or title would be appropriate before the group begins. The scene should be no more than 3 minutes in length. The class may also guess, after the scene, who illustrated the picture. Then use appropriate criteria for evaluating the activity. Use one of the sample evaluation forms, or design your own criteria before the performance.

Curtain Call!

CHAPTER 2 REVIEW

■ ■ SPOTLIGHT ON TERMS ■ ■

An important part of theatre is understanding the terminology, or vocabulary, used. Add the new terms and definitions to the vocabulary section of your theatre notebook or folder.

■ ■ FOCUS ON FACTS ■ ■

1. What is respect, and why is it an integral part of theatre class?
2. What is the value of positive self-talk?
3. Explain the importance of having artistic discipline in theatre class.
4. Why should students learn how to evaluate their own work as well as the work of others?

■ ■ REFLECTIONS ■ ■

Discuss the following questions with your class or answer them on paper as instructed by your teacher.

1. Why is it important to continually talk positively to yourself? How can such positive statements affect your everyday life?
2. How does it feel to be encouraged each day in class? What does this do to your self-confidence?
3. What are some positive statements that you can tell yourself each day?

■ ■ THEATRE IN YOUR LIFE ■ ■

1. What people do you respect? Why do you respect them? How does this affect your relationship with them?
2. What situations can you name that could use artistic discipline?

3. How have evaluations helped you?
4. Why did you choose theatre as a class?
5. In what ways do you see yourself applying theatre in your future?

■ ■ ENCORE ■ ■

To help build self-confidence and bond with your classmates, do the following activities.

1. On a sheet of paper, list every person's name in the class, including the teacher's. Beside each name write a positive statement about that person. The statements could be about the person's hair, clothes, personality, and so on. Think about this assignment, and spend time developing a statement about each person that would build his or her self-confidence. After the comments are written, your teacher will collate them and write all the comments for each person individually. When the teacher returns the statements, keep this sheet in a favorite place to remind yourself how great you really are. This can be your personal "ray of sunshine" each day. Read the sheet often!
2. Create a theatre spirit chain by cutting a construction paper or typing paper link (12 inches long and 2 inches wide). On the link, write your name on one side and write or illustrate one or two of your best attributes (things you like about yourself) on the other side. When the class is finished, your teacher will have you staple the links together, forming a long spirit chain. Your classmates can get to know each other better with this activity if everyone shares what is on each link. The spirit chain can then be used as a room decoration to remind everyone that the theatre class has "spirit" and is "connected and bonded."

CHAPTER 3

Developing Your Personal Resources

Chapter Outline

Spotlight on Terms

- aesthetic perception
- choreography
- concentration
- dramatic play
- emotions
- expressive movement
- imagination
- motivation
- movement
- observation
- personal resources
- point of view
- rhythmic movement
- sensory awareness
- visualizing

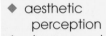

W hat do you remember most about elementary school? Did you look forward to recess, just as most children do today? Schoolchildren cannot wait to go outside and play. Remember? Close your eyes and picture those days. Recess was fun, and it was an important time in your life.

You probably did not realize it, but you were enhancing your personal resources during this playtime. You were preparing yourself for theatre as well as for intellectual and social living in the real world.

While you played, you used *imagination, concentration, observation, sensory awareness,* and body *movements.* These five skills were—and still are—extremely valuable in your personal development. They are your **personal resources** —the techniques and skills that you use to express yourself emotionally, intellectually, socially, and physically.

Your personal resources are essential to you as an actor. They will help you develop a better understanding of yourself and enhance your **aesthetic perception** , your insight into our world of images, sound, color, patterns, forms, and movements. You cannot reach your potential in the theatre without exploring your personal resources and using them daily.

Remember when you played "pretend" and created scenes as a child? You were participating in a type of drama called **dramatic play** . You and your friends were firemen, soldiers, nurses, princesses, athletes, warriors, and movie stars. You could do anything and be anyone because you used your imagination. **Imagination** is the power to create ideas and pictures in your mind. You made up ideas and stories in your mind and then you acted them out. Many dreams are fulfilled and inventions created through the use of imagination. In fact, all of the world's great visionaries have possessed well-developed imaginations.

While you permitted your imagination to run wild, you concentrated on making the characters and scenes feel real. In other words, you thought carefully about what was happening. It took this concentration to make your games work. **Concentration** is the ability to focus and pay close attention.

You knew how to make the people and scenes look real because you used your observation skills. You watched people and animals closely and carefully to learn how to imitate life. **Observation** is the power of seeing and taking notice of the environment.

Your sensory awareness added believability to your play. If you had not remembered what an object looked, smelled, sounded, felt or tasted like, your play and games would have been without meaning. **Sensory awareness** is the ability to use sight, sound, touch, smell, and taste to become conscious of your environment.

Concentration, observation, and sensory awareness are personal resources that are closely related. All three are valuable onstage because they help you make a character believable after you have observed and then re-created the details of how someone walks, talks, and makes gestures.

Finally, recall the importance of movement in your childhood play activities. Movement is also basic to drama. **Movement** is the transformation of ideas into action. This action was your release. It was a natural way to express yourself. It didn't matter if you were inside or outside—you knew you had to move. Movement allows the theatre stu-

personal resources
techniques and skills that we use to express ourselves emotionally, intellectually, socially, and physically.

aesthetic perception
insight into our world of images, sound, color, patterns, forms, and movements.

dramatic play
children's creation of scenes when they play "pretend."

imagination
the power to create ideas and pictures in our minds.

concentration
the ability to focus and pay close attention.

observation
the power of seeing and taking notice.

sensory awareness
the ability to use sight, sound, touch, smell, and taste to become conscious of the environment.

movement
the ability to transform ideas into action.

Our five senses—smell, sight, touch, taste, and hearing—make up the sensory awareness we can use to bring believability to our roles.

dent to explore his or her environment. Acting converts the movement of a character into the expression of ideas and feelings onstage.

When you put all these personal resources together in your childhood play, you had fun and created lifelong memories. In this chapter, we will analyze each of these personal resources to see how they can enhance your life and theatre experiences. Activities will be provided to develop your own personal resources. As you explore these resources, you will understand why they provide a foundation for your acting experiences and performances.

Personal resources are like a door. They must be opened before you can walk through and realize their full potential. Everyone possesses personal resources. They are inside us, even if we seldom use them. You may not think of yourself as imaginative or creative if you have not had the opportunity to exercise and develop your personal resources. Theatre class offers the opportunity you have been needing to become aware of your personal resources and to expand them.

Why do people forget their childhood days and the joy and pleasures that their personal resources gave them? Why do people abandon the skills that worked so well when they were young? If you, too, have forgotten how to apply these resources, welcome back! If you are a person who has realized the value of these techniques and uses them often, congratulations!

Imagination

LESSON 1

LESSON OBJECTIVES

◆ Identify imagination.
◆ Understand the importance of imagination in theatre.
◆ Participate in imagination activities.
◆ Perform with feeling, thought, imagination, and creativity.

Warm Up

While sitting at your desk, imagine you are with your friends at your favorite place to hang out. Who are you with? What are you doing?

visualizing
the act of imagining and seeing pictures in the mind.

Putting imagination and action together is an excellent way to learn, solve problems, and create. Imagination permits us to remember and to dream. Our imaginations allow us to go anywhere and do anything—the sky's the limit!

As an actor, you must use your imagination to make what happens onstage look real. Your imagination is essential in acting. The process of **visualizing**, or imagining, is important if your theatre experience is to have the greatest possible impact on an audience.

Your world of imagination is enhanced by your everyday life experiences. The more you become aware of the world around you, the easier it will be to act believably on stage. It is believability before an audience that makes actors successful.

The activities that follow are not meant to be performed before an audience. Their purpose is to exercise and stretch your imagination. They are pre-acting exercises designed to warm up your mind.

ACTION

Artist Joan Miró is known throughout the world for his imaginative works of art that appeal to many of our senses. This fanciful fountain is in Paris.

1. **Imaginary Snake.** Imagine that a snake crawls into the classroom from the science lab. All the other students are reading an assignment and you notice the snake. What color is it? How long is it? What kind of snake is it? What do you do when the other students see it? What happens in the classroom?

2. **Let's Play Ball!** Imagine that all your classmates are standing in a circle in the classroom. Your teacher tosses an imaginary beach ball to you. How big is it? What color is it? Take your hands and move them about the ball. Now toss the ball to one of your classmates. The ball is tossed back to you, and it becomes a football. How do you catch it differently? What is its shape? Again the ball comes back after being tossed around, and it becomes a tennis ball. Look at your hands. How differently are you holding the ball now? How does it feel? Try the same activity with an imaginary basketball, soccer ball, golf ball, and baseball.

3. **What Is It?** As the class stands in a circle, your teacher tosses a scarf into the middle of the circle. Your teacher then suggests an environment for you to imagine. For example, she might say, "beach." In that case, the first student must pick up the scarf and use it as an object you would

find at the beach. The other students must guess what it is. The students take turns using the scarf as a different beach object until the teacher suggests a new environment.

4. **Musical Scenes.** Listen to some music with your eyes closed. What imaginary action is inspired by this music? Imagine a scene that might take place, or focus on a character and imagine what is happening in his or her life. Discuss these possibilities with the class.

5. **Mental Visual Art.** Your teacher will show the class some visual artwork—perhaps examples of the baroque, Christian, Gothic, naturalistic, realistic, rococo, romantic, and surrealistic styles. Imagine what might have been happening in the picture when the artist painted it. Discuss the painting with the class.

6. **Imaginary Objects.** Your teacher will call out the names of objects that he or she will pretend to give each student while the class is sitting or standing in a circle. For example, the first object may be a coin, the next one a rose, then a cup of hot chocolate, a small puppy, a bag of popcorn, a plate of liver, and so on. How do you react to each imaginary object? How do your classmates react to the objects? Think about why different people react in different ways.

7. **Why Are You Frightened?** Can you remember a situation when you were frightened? Discuss what was happening. Is a feeling easier to imagine than people or objects? Why? If different members of your class react differently, discuss why this range of reactions is normal.

Concentration

LESSON OBJECTIVES

- Identify concentration.
- Understand the importance of concentration in theatre.
- Participate in concentration activities.
- Concentrate on physical detail.
- Demonstrate self-confidence using your concentration.
- Work on problem-solving activities, individually and cooperatively.

Warm Up

Why is it difficult to concentrate in class? In your journal, list reasons you have difficulty concentrating in class.

You have been told to concentrate most of your life. This is a skill that was probably difficult for you as a child because your attention span was so short. You may still have trouble concentrating today because there is so much happening around you, and you do not want to miss any of the action.

Concentration is an important skill for you to develop. With concentration you become a disciplined actor. To concentrate, you must pay close attention to people and objects in your environment and you must remember what you observe. You must also learn to focus in on your thoughts and feelings.

You have played concentration games throughout your schooling. You had to rely on your memory so that you could match math cards, vocabulary cards, or picture cards. You succeeded in those concentration games when you did not let anything else interfere with your goal of concentrating. You remembered what was happening, and you did not let anyone break your concentration. You must maintain the same kind of focus when you are rehearsing or performing onstage. Do not let anything or anyone block your concentration on the character or actions you are portraying.

ACTION

Focus on your goal, whether it's the bulls-eye or learning a certain number of lines each day.

1. **Table of Concentration.** Your teacher will place fifteen to twenty different items on a table. Look at the items carefully, and concentrate on what they are. After a few minutes, your teacher will cover the items with a cloth. List the items on a sheet of paper. Check to see how well you concentrated. Try to draw a map of the tabletop, recalling in detail where all of the objects are in relation to each other.

2. **Staying in Character.** Bring a magazine, book, or comic book to theatre class. Your teacher will assign a character for you to become while you are reading the material you brought to class. Concentrate on how this character would read the material. How would that reading affect your body? Don't let anyone distract you. Possible characters for you to become are a cowboy, nurse, hippie, five-year-old girl, Girl Scout, eighty-year-old man, politician, lawyer, or preacher.

3. **Who's Conversing with Whom?** Try to carry on a conversation with two people at the same time. For example, talk about a language arts assignment with one person and a football game with another, or talk about what happened during lunch and your plans for the weekend. Focus on your purpose, and concentrate to keep the conversations moving and making sense.

4. **Concentration Relay.** Your teacher will divide the class into teams of three. Each team will have to concentrate to win. The first team member carries beans in a spoon and drops them in a bucket. The object is to concentrate and not drop any beans on your way. The second team tosses beanbags into a trash can. The object is to hit inside the can as many times as possible and to concentrate on how many times the beanbag goes in. The third group hits a birdie into a bucket with a badminton racket and must concentrate on how many times the team makes the bucket. This concentration game is a relay race, but the object is to keep count of all that is going on and to concentrate on doing the best job as a team.

5. **Concentration Paper Fold.** Pick a partner to work with for this exercise. Challenge yourself to work with someone you have not worked with before. Sit or stand back to back with your partner. Each student needs two sheets of paper. The first student folds the paper in a particular way and then instructs the second student on how to fold his or her paper

the same way. The goal is for the second student to fold his or her paper correctly by following the verbal directions, without looking. After the concentration activity, the partners turn around to see how well they followed directions. Now switch roles and repeat the activity.

6. **Director, You Said What?** Choose a partner. One student becomes the director and the other student the actor. It is the director's job to give the actor directions for an action onstage. The directions should include several stage movements that would take place in the front, middle, or back of the stage (for example, crossing to another actor, sitting on a couch, and picking up a magazine). The actor then follows the director's directions. Then the partners reverse roles and do the activity again. The actor needs to concentrate in order to do everything the director asks. After you and your partner have each had a turn, discuss how it felt to have to give clear directions.

7. **I Can Make You Smile!** Your teacher will divide the class into two teams—team A and team B. Each team faces the other team, forming two lines. The first member of team A steps to the front of the class and faces the first member of team B. Team member A tries to make team member B laugh or smile. You may not touch the other person while trying to make the person laugh. You may make faces, sounds, or be creative to make team member B laugh. If team member B smiles or laughs, then team member B must join team member A and both go to the end of the line of team A. The first member of team B goes next and the process continues until all team members have had a chance to concentrate in front of the others and not break concentration. Remember if any team member breaks concentration, that member joins the other team.

Observation

LESSON OBJECTIVES

◆ Identify observation and point of view.
◆ Understand the importance of observation in theatre.
◆ Participate in observation activities.
◆ Observe physical detail.

Warm Up

How observant were you this morning? What did your parents and siblings say to you before you came to school? What were they wearing?

Observation skills are valuable in appearing believable onstage. If you do not pay careful attention to people's movements, mannerisms, and dress, your portrayal onstage will be without substance.

The skill of observation requires much attention and study. When you observe people or things, you must look carefully at the details. For example, what was the teacher in your last class wearing? You have to pay close attention to every detail to observe successfully.

The way we think, feel, or act about a person, place, or situation is called our **point of view**. A point of view can be literal, such as the way

point of view

a position from which we perceive (understand) an object, person, or place.

you see actual objects fitting together in a given space. It can also be figurative, involving interpretation, which results from your attitude toward what you see. Your point of view will have an impact on your observation, so try to get into the habit of looking at things and people from several different points of view to get as much detail as possible.

As an actor, you have to observe people every day and remember what they look like and how they behave. You have to pay close attention to the way your body moves—such as how you hold a cup, brush your teeth, or walk through a door.

This sounds like work, and it is. It isn't easy being an actor and creating a believable world onstage. Developing your observation skills will give you ideas to use in your performances and will make you more aware of the world around you.

1. **Daily Actions.** Study these daily activities while at home, school, or places you visit. Observe each detail and be able to perform a simple reenactment of the activity.

making a sandwich
brushing your teeth
channel surfing, using the TV's remote control
working on your computer
dialing a phone number
drinking a cup of hot chocolate
zipping a jacket
turning on a light

opening the door of the car
standing in line at the cafeteria
carrying your books to class
buttoning a coat
shooting a basketball
throwing a football
serving a tennis ball
combing your hair

Ask yourself a detailed set of questions about each activity. For example: How do my hands react to the weight of this object? What is my face doing right now?

2. **A Person Came In?** Your teacher will make arrangements for a visitor to come to your theatre class. The person will come in, stay for a moment, and then exit. After the person leaves, have a class discussion focusing on the following questions:
   a. Who was the person?
   b. What was the person wearing?
   c. How long did the person stay in the room?
   d. What did the person do in the room?
   e. What did the person leave in the room?
   f. What time was it when the person came in?
   g. What time was it when the person left?
   h. What was the person's general attitude, and how could you tell?

3. **Classroom Observation.** Look around the classroom. Observe to your left, to your right, up, down, in front of you, and behind you. After 2 minutes, close your eyes and be prepared to answer questions about your surroundings. For example, your teacher may ask: What is Emily wearing? Who is sitting in the front of the room? Who is directly to your left? What color shoes is that person wearing?

Theatre of the Middle Ages

The theatre created in the Middle Ages (also known as the *Medieval Period*) stretched from approximately 500–1500 A.D. The theatrical performances staged during this period were quite different from the theatrical performances staged in Rome. In the absence of a powerful monarch or government to stabilize trade and daily life, the church took over many of the functions of leadership. Because the church was so powerful, and because so few people could read the scriptures for themselves, theatre became a way to communicate religious messages to the general public in a clear and powerful way.

Most plays performed in the Middle Ages told stories from the Bible. Often several stories were performed, one right after the other in what became known as a *cycle* of plays. An example of such a cycle is the Wakefield cycle staged in Wakefield, England, which consisted of thirty-two plays. The thirteenth play in this cycle, *The Second Shepherds Play,* is considered one of the best English cycle plays.

The cycle plays were often referred to as *mystery plays,* because they focused on the mysterious nature of God's power. These plays dramatized biblical events spanning the period from the creation in the book of Genesis to the last judgment in the book of Revelation. For example, *The Mystery of Adam* tells the stories of Adam and Eve, Cain and Abel, and the prophets who foreshadow the coming of Christ.

Although the plays of this period focused on man's proper response to God, as the period passed, the church began to modify the content of the plays.

Here you see a scene from a Medieval mystery play being presented on a wagon, which will move on to another part of this English town once the scene has been completed. Another wagon will follow with the next scene.

These newer plays, known as *morality plays,* attempted to teach a moral lesson to the audience through the use of allegorical (symbolic) characters. For example, a character in a morality play may have represented all of mankind, or a particular vice or virtue such as greed, anger, or mercy. The main character, often called *Everyman* or *Mankind,* was typically tempted by evil but returned to the side of good in the end.

The plays were presented very differently from the way the Romans had staged their plays. Staged in the church itself or in the churchyard around the church building, or in the street, the setting customarily was comprised of a series of several small, temporary, hutlike houses, each one decorated differently to represent a different location. These were called *mansions.* All of these mansions were visible to the audience at once. Each of the mansions faced a common, shared playing space in front of the row of mansions called the *platea.* This space served as the central acting area for all of the locations. The audience would accept that the space was changing based upon from what mansion the actors entered.

Although they were of minor importance compared to the religious and morality plays, two other forms of theatre—*farce* and *interlude*—were popular in the Middle Ages. Farce was a form of coincidence that originated in the 1200s, emphasizing some of society's more ridiculous behaviors. The interludes were comic plays that served as short breaks between different parts of a celebration ■

Sensory Awareness

LESSON OBJECTIVES

◆ Identify sensory awareness.
◆ Understand the importance of sensory awareness in theatre.
◆ Participate in activities to develop the five senses and utilize them.

Warm Up

Choose one of your senses and in your journal write why you believe it is the most valuable sense.

"
All of us collect fortunes when we are children—a fortune of colors, of lights and darkness, of movements, of tensions. Some of us have the fantastic chance to go back to see his fortune when grown up.

Ingmar Bergman
"

As mentioned early in the chapter, concentration, observation, and sensory recall are all closely related. Together, these three personal resources can help you as you portray characters different from yourself.

When your sensory awareness is sharp, you can easily recall how something tastes, smells, looks, sounds, or feels. Sensory awareness is more than just seeing, hearing, or touching something. When you are truly aware of your senses, you absorb every detail of an item or experience and attempt to make associations with other items and experiences. Colors, textures, and patterns are important in these experiences. Your senses must be so keen that you can recall every detail.

Do not take anything for granted as you participate in the following sensory activities. It is important for the actor to fully expand each of the senses. In fact, it is only when we lose one of these senses that we fully realize its significance in helping us understand the world around us. The actor that makes his or her words and actions work onstage has not missed a single detail, showing great sensitivity to the objects, people, and places surrounding him or her. As you carry out the activities to develop your sensory awareness, think of each sense as a key to your future performances.

1. **Seeing an Object.** Recall in your mind how each of the following objects looks.
   a. a mushroom
   b. a dirty sock
   c. a tulip
   d. a fish in an aquarium
   e. a fish you have just caught
   f. paint that is blue, black, red, yellow, green, or orange
   g. your favorite toy when you were a toddler
   h. a kitten
   i. a $20 bill
   j. a strand of hair

   What other senses besides your sight help you to remember these items? Where were you when you last saw each of these items? What activity were you engaged in? What emotion were you feeling?

2. **Smelling an Object.** Recall how the following items smell.
   a. toast that has burned
   b. roses blooming

c. fudge cooking
d. cough syrup
e. a slice of lemon
f. pine trees or cedar trees
g. car exhaust

h. coffee
i. cabbage cooking
j. someone eating oranges
k. rubbing alcohol

What other senses help you remember these smells? Where were you when you last smelled each of these odors? What activity were you engaged in? What emotion were you feeling?

3. **Hearing an Object.** Recall how the following objects sound.
   a. your favorite music
   b. church bells
   c. a foghorn
   d. a siren
   e. a dog barking

   f. a baby crying
   g. a refrigerator running
   h. students laughing
   i. bacon frying

   What other senses help you remember these sounds? Where were you when you last heard each one of these sounds? What activity were you engaged in? What emotion were you feeling?

4. **Tasting an Object.** Recall how the following objects taste.
   a. freshly baked chocolate chip cookies
   b. a lemon slice
   c. a Snickers candy bar
   d. ice
   e. a hot dog

   f. popcorn
   g. spinach
   h. licorice
   i. strawberries
   j. cough syrup

   What other senses help you remember these tastes? Where were you when you last tasted these items? What activity were you engaged in? What emotion were you feeling?

5. **Touching an Object.** Imagine touching the following items.
   a. sandpaper
   b. velvet
   c. plastic
   d. paper
   e. a hot cup of tea

   f. a glass of iced tea
   g. your skin
   h. the bark of a tree
   i. polyester
   j. seashells

   What other senses help you remember these items? Where were you when you last touched these items? What activity were you engaged in? What emotion were you feeling?

Movement

LESSON OBJECTIVES

◆ Identify movement.
◆ Define rhythmic movement.
◆ Define expressive movement.
◆ Understand the importance of movement in theatre.
◆ Participate in both rhythmic and expressive activities.

rhythmic movement
the ability to move to a beat or pattern of beats.

choreography
the art of planning and composing a dance.

expressive movement
the ability to express feelings through physical action.

■ ■ ■ ■ ■ ■ ■ ■ ■ ■ ■ ■
Perhaps no form of dance is more expressive than ballet.

Movement, the last of the five personal resources discussed in this chapter, is an essential element in theatre. It is the way we communicate with our bodies. The activities for movement will develop your understanding of your own body in motion but will also develop cooperation and ensemble. Two types of movement will be discussed in this lesson: rhythmic and expressive.

Rhythmic Movement

Rhythmic movement is movement to a beat or pattern of beats. A beat is a mark of time or accent given to time. Rhythm is movement with a regular repetition of a beat or accent. Rhythmic movement is especially challenging because it requires discipline and practice. You must try to be in complete control of your body. It requires not only physical attention but mental attention. You may be directed to perform movements at different speeds to produce special effects onstage. You may also be directed to move to music onstage. The rhythmic movements and arrangement of steps are referred to in the theatre as **choreography** .

Expressive Movement

Studies on body language tell us that people often express how they feel through physical movement. This type of movement is called **expressive movement** . You will have a chance to explore nonverbal communication through the expressive movement activities. Emotions and thoughts can be expressed through the use of your entire body, from head to toe.

Movement can reveal what a person is feeling at a particular moment. But when you express yourself physically, you must also think

■ CHAPTER 3: Developing Your Personal Resources ■ **61**

motivation

an inner drive that causes a person to act a certain way.

emotions

strong feelings, such as joy, fear, hate, and happiness.

about what is going on inside you. How you are feeling inside greatly affects how you react on the outside. Emotions are more successfully expressed if you think before you act. In other words, your action must result from an inner drive, or **motivation**—the reason you are acting the way you are. If you do not think first, your expressive movement will be meaningless and incomplete. You will not communicate your feelings effectively, and you will not be believable onstage. Remember, you must respond mentally, as well as physically, to feelings of expression.

We have been talking about emotions. But what *are* emotions? **Emotions** are strong feelings, often reactions, such as happiness, sadness, anger, jealousy, fear, loneliness, grief, joy, excitement, love, hate, and embarrassment, to name only a few. In the following exercises, you will be given the opportunity to try rhythmic movement exercises and expressive movement activities by using facial expressions and other body movements. Some assignments will also include verbal communication to enhance the expression of your feelings.

ACTION

Rhythmic movement can help you warm up and relax before a rehearsal or performance.

Rhythmic Movement Activities

1. **Rhythm of the Beat.** Form a circle with your classmates. Your teacher will have you pass a ball around the circle. Match the rate of passing the ball with the rate of a drumbeat. Each student must focus on the rhythm of the beat.

2. **Rhythm of the Music.** While music is playing, move to the rhythm of the sounds. Stay on the beat and listen to the patterns and rhythm.

3. **Rhythmic Movements.** Create a rhythmic movement that matches the loudness and intensity of these sounds.
   a. a scratching sound
   b. a soft whisper
   c. snoring
   d. a high, shrill whistle

These actors are engaged in some very expressive movements on stage.

e. a popping sound
f. a bang
g. a snap

h. a tap
i. a boom
j. a swishing sound

4. **Animal Motion.** Move to the teacher's or leader's drum beat as each of these animals would if they were searching for food. Next, move to a different rhythm or beat given to you as if the animals were tired from a day's hunt. Do not use any sounds the first time through the list. Use sounds the second time you do the motions.

a. a cat
b. a dog
c. an elephant
d. a snake
e. a rabbit

f. a giraffe
g. a fish
h. a bear
i. a fly

Expressive Movement Activities

1. **Emotional Recall.** Express the following emotions. First, think about the body tension that you have when you feel these emotions. Your teacher will help you express these emotions using your hands, arms, neck, face, and so on.

a. anger
b. sadness
c. happiness
d. jealousy

e. grief
f. fear
g. surprise
h. embarrassment

Now discuss situations in which classmates experienced the different emotions in the past. Replay the expression of the emotions. Which activity was the most successful? Why?

2. **Emotional Relay.** Divide into groups and stand in single file. You will participate in a relay game using movement to express an emotion. Each member must complete four emotions (anger, fear, sadness, and happiness) before tagging the next team member in line. Two chairs are placed on opposite sides of the room. You must remember the order of the emotions and express each one as you run from one chair to the other.

3. **Relay versus Emotional Thoughts.** Use the same emotions as in the previous activity. In a class discussion, think about these emotions and share situations when you have experienced the emotions. Where were you when you felt these emotions? What activity were you engaged in when you felt these emotions? Your teacher will ask you to recall and express each of the four emotions. Compare the outcome of this activity with the outcome of the emotional relay. Name specific differences.

4. **Emotional Fitness.** Form a circle with your classmates. Each student will be given an emotion to express. Each student must think of a facial expression, body movement, and sound that fits the emotion. The activity begins with the first student expressing his or her emotion. The activity continues one student at a time, until everyone in class has had a turn. All of your personal resources are used in this activity.

5. **The Music Moves Me.** Divide into groups of four or five. Your teacher will play some music. After listening to the music for a few minutes, each member of the group—individually, not in unison—must use body movements to express the music.

6. **Expressive Movement and Sound Scenes.** Using the following situations, you will perform individually or with a partner a short scene using expressive movement and sound.
   a. A teenager is excited about going to a sports event.
   b. A student is called to the principal's office.
   c. Your best friend has talked about you behind your back.
   d. You have just lost a pet.
   e. You have been hit with a basketball.
   f. You are coming down with the flu.
   g. You believe that you are being given too much homework.
   h. You walk into the cafeteria, and discover that they are serving your favorite meal.
   i. Your friends start laughing and applauding when you walk into class.
   j. You get your progress report, and there are all A's on the report.

7. **Let's Go on a Picnic.** Imagine that you are at a picnic. Instead of being one of the people at the picnic, become one of the ants or some other animal that sees and smells the food. Move the way the animal would.

8. **Is That Bacon I Smell Frying?** Pretend that you are a strip of bacon in a frying pan. Someone has just started cooking you when the phone rings. The cook answers the phone and forgets about you. How would you move in the frying pan while the cook was on the phone?

9. **Imaginary Walk.** Imagine that you are walking with the following:
   a. a melting ice cream cone
   b. a hot pan you took out of the oven
   c. your toothbrush in your mouth (full of toothpaste)
   d. a newborn baby
   e. bees that are stinging you
   f. a stack of books in your arms
   g. a large musical instrument, such as a tuba
   h. beach equipment (ball, umbrella, lunch basket, towels, suntan lotion)
   i. a pet that is sick

■ ■ SPOTLIGHT ON TERMS ■ ■

An important part of theatre is understanding the terminology, or vocabulary, used. Add the new terms and definitions to the vocabulary section of your theatre notebook or folder.

■ ■ FOCUS ON FACTS ■ ■

1. What are the five personal resources discussed in this chapter?
2. List ways that your personal resources will help you in your everyday activities.
3. What is the importance of imagination in theatre?
4. Why is concentration a significant skill to develop?
5. Which personal resource makes you look believable onstage?
6. Explain the difference between rhythmic movement and expressive movement.

■ ■ REFLECTIONS ■ ■

Discuss the following questions with your class or answer them on paper as instructed by your teacher.

1. Why is it important to believe in what you are doing onstage?
2. How could you better prepare for a role by using observation?
3. Why is it essential to keep an active imagination throughout life?
4. Which personal resource have you developed the most? Why? Which personal resource needs the most work?

■ ■ THEATRE IN YOUR LIFE ■ ■

1. Which personal resource is the most important in your classes?
2. How do you relax, mentally and physically, before a performance?

3. Which activities helped strengthen your self-confidence?
4. How powerful is your imagination?
5. Why is it difficult to focus and concentrate during theatre activities?
6. What does it take for you to be totally involved in an assignment, activity, or performance?
7. Why do actors need to observe people, places, and things?

■ ■ ENCORE ■ ■

1. Write a letter to a famous movie director, such as Steven Spielberg, Spike Lee, or Barbra Streisand. Ask the director questions about the use of his or her personal resources. How did the director prepare in his or her early career to achieve success?
2. Divide into groups of three, four, or five. Everyone should have a Frito corn chip. As you look at the Frito, answer the following questions: What does the Frito look like? What does the Frito smell like? What does the Frito sound like? What does the Frito feel like? What does the Frito taste like? What does the Frito remind you of? After the class discusses these questions in detail, each group will be assigned to plan and present a short commercial about Fritos. The commercial may be a song based on a tune you already know (such as "Twinkle, Twinkle, Little Star"), a short scene, a cheer, or any creative idea that your group may have. After the presentations, the class will judge the presentations for strengths and weaknesses.
3. Form two lines facing each other. Line A will begin with the emotion happiness. The first person in line A will greet the first person in line B by expressing the emotion happiness using only the numbers "1, 2, 3, 4." The first person in line B will respond to the greeting using the same emotion only saying the numbers "5, 6, 7, 8." The two people then walk toward each other, say the numbers, and return to their lines. The greetings will continue to be made, using different emotions as the teacher calls them out.

CHAPTER 4

Creative Drama

Spotlight on Terms

- creative drama
- external characteristics
- formal drama
- improvisational
- internal characteristics
- interpret
- in unison
- leader (or teacher) playing in role
- literary merit
- narrative pantomime
- narrator
- paraphrase
- props
- protagonist
- replaying
- set
- side-coaching
- story dramatization
- transition

I n this chapter, the emphasis is on creative drama, a process of informal acting. Imagination, concentration, sensory and emotional awareness, movement, and being able to communicate through actions and dialogue are all elements of theatre essential in creative drama. This means that in this chapter you will make use of all the personal resources that you explored in Chapter 3. In addition, you will learn about and participate in two specialized areas of creative drama: narrative pantomime and story dramatization.

What Is Creative Drama?

LESSON OBJECTIVES

◆ Define creative drama.
◆ Demonstrate an understanding of creative drama through participation in classroom activities.
◆ Distinguish between creative (informal) drama and formal drama.

Read silently Jack Prelutsky's poem "A Remarkable Adventure" from the book Something Big Has Been Here *found on page 68. Imagine how you could use your facial expressions and your body to act out this poem.*

creative drama

an improvisational, process-centered form of theatre in which participants are guided by a leader to imagine, enact, and reflect on human experiences.

formal drama

theatre that focuses on a performance in front of an audience as the important final product.

improvisational

nonscripted and spontaneous.

Many of your early theatre experiences involved using your imagination and creativity to act out stories, poems, or original ideas. This informal process of acting is called **creative drama** . Creative drama is an improvisational form of theatre in which participants are guided by a leader to imagine, enact, and reflect on human experiences. Creative drama differs from formal drama in that the process of acting out is more important than the end result. That is, how the participants develop the activity is more important than the final product of the activity. **Formal drama** focuses on a performance in front of an audience as the important final product.

Another important difference between formal drama and creative drama is that even though a literary selection might be used as the basis for a creative drama activity, there is no *script* (manuscript written in dialogue form for acting). The acting would be **improvisational** — imaginative and spontaneous. Improvisation is key to creative drama. And since the process is not a performance, creative drama does not require an audience.

Do you remember when you were in elementary school and your teacher read to the class, perhaps from the wonderful book *Where The Wild Things Are*? After the reading, if your teacher had the class act out the story, then you and your classmates were sharing a creative drama experience. Even today, when the students in your science class actively become the parts of a tree, solar system, or immune system, those are creative drama experiences.

In creative drama, you hear a story or get an idea and then plan how to act out the dramatic action. Following careful planning, the scene is then played, either in parts or from beginning to end.

A Remarkable Adventure

I was at my bedroom table
with a notebook open wide,
when a giant anaconda
started winding up my side,
I was filled with apprehension
and retreated down the stairs,
to be greeted at the bottom
by a dozen grizzly bears.

We tumultuously tussled
till I managed to get free,
then I saw, with trepidation
there were tigers after me,
I could feel them growing closer,

I was quivering with fear,
then I blundered into quicksand
and began to disappear.

I was rescued by an eagle
that descended from the skies
to embrace me with its talons,
to my terror and surprise,
but that rapture lost its purchase
when a blizzard made me
    sneeze,
and it dropped me in a thicket
where I battered both my knees.

I was suddenly surrounded
by a troop of savage trolls,
who maliciously informed me
they would toast me over coals,
I was lucky to elude them
when they briefly looked away–
that's the reason why my home-
    work
isn't here with me today.

By Jack Prelutsky,
Something Big Has Been Here

replaying

acting out again.

side-coaching

a method by which the leader talks you through an activity by making suggestions or giving you ideas.

■ ■ ■ ■ ■ ■ ■ ■ ■ ■ ■ ■ ■ ■

During many of your creative drama experiences, your director or coach will help you by giving you ideas for what you might do or say next.

An important part of creative drama is the evaluation that comes after playing out a story or idea. When the acting out is over, all participants evaluate the activity. The leader guides the discussion to focus on what worked well during the playing process. Next, the discussion covers the changes that could make the activity more successful or the story more believable if it were replayed. **Replaying** is acting out the story or activity again using the changes discussed. It enables participants to expand on their ideas. Replaying can occur immediately or it can be saved for another time.

Leaders in creative drama activities often use a technique called side-coaching. In **side-coaching**, the leader (often your teacher) talks you through an activity by making suggestions or giving you ideas. Side-coaching may also provide an internal monologue—the thoughts

of a character. Often, this informal prompting helps participants incorporate important actions or meaningful concepts that might otherwise be missed.

When the leader or teacher in a creative drama actively takes part in the drama by playing one of the characters, we have a **leader (or teacher) playing in role**.

Experiences in creative drama provide you with the opportunity to explore theatre in a comfortable, nonthreatening way. There are no lines to memorize, no stage to stand on, no makeup, costumes, or hot lights to worry about—and, of course, no audience.

Through experiences in creative drama, you will come to understand and appreciate the art of drama—a story told through action and dialogue. Thus, creative drama helps pave the way for future theatre experiences.

leader (or teacher) playing in role

a leader (or teacher) who actively participates in the creative drama process by playing one of the characters.

1. **Reflections.** The class is divided into pairs, with partners facing each other. One partner reflects (mirrors) what the other is doing. Use slow motions and concentrate on following each other by using your peripheral vision. The objective is not to try to trick your partner but to move in unison. Keep the motion smooth and fluid.

2. **Dr. Smart.** The class is divided into teams of four or five. One team stands in a line at the front of the classroom. Your teacher introduces the team as Dr. Smart. The teacher will let the class know that Dr. Smart can answer *any* question. Someone in the class might ask, "What is the definition of a backdrop?" Dr. Smart must answer this question one word at a time per student. For example, the first student in line says, "A," and the second student follows with "backdrop," then the third student says, "is," and the fourth student says "a," and so on, until the team finishes the sentence. The whole answer might be, "A backdrop is a large painted cloth used as a background." Every answer that the Dr. Smart team constructs must make sense and be in logical order.

3. **It's a What?** Stand in a circle with your classmates. Students then pass an object (balloon, book, towel) from one student to the next. Each student pantomimes using the object in an environment named by the teacher. For example, you might be asked to use the object as if it were something at the beach. Students must use their imaginations to turn the object into something different when it's their turn. Students pantomime using the object as if it were a real object at the beach. The rest of the class guesses what each student is using. Your teacher might assign a different place to begin each round for the object.

4. **What Are You Doing?** Stand in a circle with your classmates. One student begins pantomiming an activity, such as brushing his or her teeth. The next student asks, "What are you doing?" While still performing the brushing of teeth, the first student tells the second student to do a different activity—say, driving a car. The second student then begins pantomiming the new activity, while suggesting yet another activity to the next student along the circle. Continue this process around the circle. The goal of each student is to change the activity with speed and rhythm. A single activity must not be repeated.

5. **Story Bag.** Your teacher will prepare a bag filled with various items. Sit with your group in a circle. One student will draw an item out of the bag and begin a story that involves the item. This student will keep that item and pass the bag on to the next person. The next student will draw another object out of the bag and continue the story by incorporating the second item into the plot. The last student must close the story with the last object that is pulled from the bag.

6. **Dictionary Mania.** Divide into groups of four or five. Each group is given a dictionary. One member of the team opens the book to any page. The group then chooses five words on the same page to create an improvised scene. You are not to write a script, but your team will have 5 to 10 minutes to plan your scene. Do not stress the key words in the dialogue of your scene. After you perform your scene, the rest of the class tries to guess the five selected words.

7. **Situation, Problem, Solution.** Divide into two or three teams. Each team is then subdivided into three small teams, named Sit, Prob, and Sol. The first team, Sit, creates a situation or challenge. (We must move a rock from the front of the house to the back.) Sit goes to the acting area and presents the scene. Then Prob decides on a problem and enters the scene. (The rock is too heavy to move.) After the problem is established, then Sol enters with a solution. (Sol may get members out of the audience to help move the rock.) The three small teams may plan among themselves, but should not share their ideas with the other large teams. They must concentrate and see what is happening as the scenes unfold. If the team acting is believable, then the other members of the audience will also believe and can get totally involved when called on.

8. **Opinion Session.** Evaluate the above activities, giving strengths and weaknesses. Discuss how well the groups worked together. What would you do differently next time you participate in the creative drama activities?

Narrative Pantomime

LESSON OBJECTIVES

◆ Define narrative pantomime.
◆ Incorporate the physical, emotional, and social dimensions of characters and scenes.
◆ Pantomime literary selections.

Narrative pantomime provides a fun way to act out literary selections, especially poems and stories. You have probably participated in narrative pantomime most of your life. Many of you will remember when your parents read stories to you at bedtime. You might have used

Before they can successfully perform a narrative pantomime, these students must communicate and cooperate with each other to plan their pantomime.

Warm Up

Recall a poem or story you have read that has a lot of action words. Imagine how you could pantomime the action effectively.

narrative pantomime

a creative drama activity in which a leader reads a piece of literature while the entire class plays the action in unison without words.

in unison

at the same time.

interpret

act out a meaning of a selection and understand it in a unique way.

pantomime (actions without words) as you listened to the story. One reason that narrative pantomime is so satisfying is that it is so easy to perform.

In **narrative pantomime** , a leader reads a piece of literature while the entire class plays the action **in unison** . There is a difference between playing the action "together" and playing it "in unison." Playing in unison doesn't mean acting or improvising with each other. It means performing the same action simultaneously (at the same time), whether in pairs, groups, or by yourself. When playing in unison, it is important to find your own space, so that you do not bump into another student or invade another student's acting area.

Through narrative pantomime, you can become many different characters and be in many places. The sky's the limit when you use your imagination and concentration during the reading of a literary piece. During this process, you will have the freedom to **interpret** the selection, acting out the meaning of the selection and understanding the piece in a unique way. You can interpret a literary selection any way that you choose. For example, if you are acting out a scene from "Little Red Riding Hood," you might play the wolf as a "rapper," grandmother may live on a ranch instead of in the woods, and Little Red Riding Hood may drive a three-wheeler on the way to granny's house instead of skipping along in the forest. There is no right or wrong in how you choose to interpret a selection.

A story can really come alive through narrative pantomime. It's a time to really let loose and not be shy. Just let your imagination soar. Your theatre class will become a safe environment—a place to feel free to express yourself without being ridiculed. For example, if the class decides to act out "The Three Little Pigs," don't hesitate to develop one of the little pigs in a special way. Let your imagination and body create the character. You might use unusual facial expressions and move your body with a little wiggle to develop his character. Do whatever it takes to make a character believable when you play a scene.

Eastern Theatre Traditions

In the early 1400s the Japanese were performing a very stylized and graceful form of theatre called Noh Theatre. Noh has elements of opera, pantomime, and stylized dance.

The first Noh performances were shared with the general public by Zeami, a fifty-year-old actor/playwright who was one of the most outstanding Noh performers to have ever lived and who wrote over 100 Noh plays. In the dramas the main character is always played by a man who wears a beautiful, carved, hand-painted mask. He performs to the constant accompaniment of several on-stage musicians. Most Noh plays are spiritual in nature, having a ghost, demon, or obsessed human whose soul cannot find rest as the main character.

Actors in Noh troupes train for their profession for many years. From the time they are very young children they train to become one of the three main roles in Noh. These are the *slite*, or main character; the *waki*, or narrator; and the *tsure*, or accompanying role. These actors perform on a raised platform stage with a floor of polished wood. This stage is connected to the actor's dressing rooms by a long wooden walkway with the audience viewing from three sides.

Kabuki, another Japanese theatre form, developed in the early and mid–seventeenth century and is still being performed today. The Kabuki plays were based upon the plays written earlier in that country for their very popular puppet theatres, called Bunraku, and from the Noh plays. Most of these were based upon history or folklore, especially ghost stories.

Like the Noh actors, the Kabuki actors train from childhood in singing, dancing, acting, and acrobatics. Many of these actors inherited a character type from their fathers who were famous actors before them. The Onagata were male actors who specialized in playing the female roles. These actors were famous for their ability to imitate the essence of feminine personality through the use of stylized poses and gestures. A major difference between Noh actors and Kabuki actors is that Noh actors always wear masks, while Kabuki actors create their characters' facial features with highly stylized stage makeup.

The Kabuki stage is rather like our common American proscenium stage of today. The audience faces the playing space from only one side, watching the action through a proscenium (picture frame) opening. The Kabuki stage, however, is rather long and has a much lower proscenium opening than most of our theatres today. A unique Kabuki staging feature is the presence of a *hanamichi*, which means "flower way." A hanamichi is a walkway that connects the stage with the back of the auditorium. This walkway is used for many characters' entrances and exits as well as for the performance of short scenes. The configuration of the acting space remains the same, but the plays, unlike Noh, are usually staged with elaborate sets and props.

Kabuki, like Noh, is usually accompanied by an orchestra that plays music to enhance the dialogue. Unlike Noh, however, the Kabuki musicians are sometimes hidden from the audience's view.

The Indian people have a much older theatrical tradition in their Sanskrit drama, which dates from approximately 100 A.D. About twenty-five of these plays remain. These are all based upon stories found in the *Mahabharata* or the *Ramayana*, two great epic writings, which are compounds of myth, history, and legend.

These dramas, which all end happily, are different from Western plays in that instead of being based upon the action and reactions of characters or the examination of thematic issues, the central goal of Sanskrit drama is the creation of an appropriate *rasa*, or mood. This places the focus in Sanskrit drama squarely on the actor, who uses movement and a set style of hand gestures to communicate meaning, rather like sign language functions today. In keeping with this style of communication, there is very little scenery in Sanskrit presentations.

One of the most famous Sanskrit plays, *The Little Clay Cart*, is a social play that features a set of young lovers who struggle to be together. This is common in Sanskrit dramas, as good and evil in these plays are clearly defined and good always eventually wins.

In China, there are very few records of theatrical activity until about 1500 B.C. with no great dramatic literature created until the thirteenth century A.D. Because of the nation's vast size, many regional forms of theatre developed around the country. Early plays were drawn from all sorts of subject matter, ranging from current events to histories and legends, containing characters from all walks of life. Thematically, the plays usually upheld the idea of loyalty to family, friends, and country, and showed that justice eventually was served.

In 1790, on the Emperor Ch'ien-lung's eighteenth birthday, performers from all over the country were brought to Beijing to perform in a huge celebration. Many of these performers remained in the city and established a new form of theatre, which focused upon the performer and acting style rather than text. This new, highly stylized performance mode was called the Beijing Opera and remains the dominant style of theatre in China.

These performers believed that a text or play is merely an outline for a performance. Acting is dancelike in Beijing Opera, with each movement set to a steady rhythm established by the leader of the on-stage orchestra who plays a drum. Each line of dialogue is accompanied by a movement or gesture intended to enhance or explain its exact meaning to the audience. Costumes are ornate and utilize color symbolically to indicate many facts about the character's class, status, occupation, and temperament.

The traditional Chinese stage is modeled on the shape of the covered porches of the temples where the earliest of the dramas were performed. They are simple platforms with an ornate roof supported by four lacquered columns. Many of these early stages were located in teahouses and the audience watched the performances while seated at small tables located in front of the stage. On the stage is little more than a carpet, sometimes a table and a few chairs. Openings in the curtain that hangs at the rear of the stage provide the only entrances and exits. ■

These Japanese actors probably began training for parts in Kabuki Theatre when they were children.

literary merit
that quality of a story that gives readers and actors a deeper understanding about the human condition and human spirit just through experiencing the story. Usually, the story's protagonist must face and triumph over internal and external obstacles.

protagonist
the major character in a story.

internal characteristics
inner, personal qualities, invisible to the human eye.

external characteristics
qualities relating to a character's outwardly visible traits.

What's more, encourage your classmates not to hold back. You and your classmates will discover the fun of doing pantomime if you follow this advice.

Besides being easy and fun, narrative pantomime offers many other benefits. Because you must listen to the leader read a story, your listening skills will improve. Moreover, the story that is chosen for narrative pantomime (or any other creative drama activity) must have **literary merit**. That is, we, as readers and actors, should gain a deeper understanding about the human condition and human spirit through experiencing the story. Usually, such a story has a major character, or **protagonist**, who must face and triumph over internal and external obstacles. A story with literary merit can teach you the elements of good literature, such as introduction, plot, conflict, characterization, and conclusion. These elements will also teach you skills in organization. Listen carefully to how the story is written. You will have the opportunity to write an original story for narrative pantomime at the end of this chapter.

Your major concern in developing your own story will be with action. Action is the key to narrative pantomime. It is important that the material have enough action to allow for continuous movement from beginning to end. Also, write your story in the order in which you want the action to happen. Otherwise, when the story is read to the class, your classmates may get confused about what to act out first. It also helps to use good description words to make the listener's imagination soar with creative movements.

Your story should always have a beginning, middle, and ending. Conflict (the problem or obstacle) creates interest and suspense in your story. Use humans or animals for your characters, and give them clear **internal characteristics** (mental and emotional traits) and **external characteristics** (qualities relating to their physical appearance).

Your best source of stories is your own personal experience. You will be amazed at how many everyday events in your life can be used for narrative pantomime activities. Choose from all the interesting events that happen at home and at school. For example, think of all the stories you can tell involving the family pet. And lunchtime chatter is often a good source for what's happening around school. Athletic events, too, can be exciting topics for writing a story. These experiences are filled with plots that would be excellent for creative drama.

ACTION

1. **Narrative Pantomime Using a Poem.** Bring to class a favorite poem, or select one from your teacher's collection. Work with a small group of your classmates to plan and act out the story using narrative pantomime. Your teacher or a designated leader from your group should read the poem.

2. **Narrative Pantomime Using a Fable.** Bring to class a favorite fable (a story with a lesson), or select one from your teacher's collection. Work with a small group of your classmates to plan and act out the story using narrative pantomime.

Working in unison, students act out a story using narrative pantomime.

> *Tell me and I forget. Show me and I remember. Involve me and I understand.*
>
> *Old Chinese proverb*

3. **Narrative Pantomime Using the Book** *Alexander and the Terrible, Horrible, No Good, Very Bad Day* **by Judith Viorst.** Check this book out from the library, or bring it from home. After your teacher or a leader reads the story, discuss the plot and the protagonist's emotions expressed in the story. When your teacher or a leader reads the story for the second time, the entire class should do a pantomime (in unison) of the scenes of action from the story.

4. **Narrative Pantomime Using the Book** *The Man Who Didn't Wash His Dishes* **by Phyllis Krasilovsky.** Use this book as a basis for a narrative pantomime.

5. **Replaying a Children's Story.** Retell a children's story of your choice while classmates act out the scenes in the story. Discuss what changes could be made and replay the scenes.

6. **Opinion Session.** Evaluate yourself and your classmates using criteria your teacher gives you for the above activities, or use the criteria questions provided at the end of Lesson 3.

LESSON 3

Story Dramatization

LESSON OBJECTIVES

◆ Define story dramatization.
◆ Incorporate the physical, emotional, and social dimensions of characters in scenes.
◆ Convert material from the narrative mode to the dramatic mode.

story dramatization

a playing/acting process to interpret and share a story by using improvisation rather than scripts.

paraphrase

put a story into your own words.

props

handheld items that are used in a performance to make a scene or play more believable.

Before dramatizing a story, discuss the actions and characters you will use.

Most people enjoy reading or listening to a good story. One way a theatre student can interpret and share a story is by acting it out— using improvisation rather than scripts, a process known as **story dramatization** . Participants in story dramatization follow the same creative drama process discussed in Lesson 1 of this chapter. The dialogue in story dramatization gives this activity a much higher level of involvement and expression than narrative pantomime.

The most important part of story dramatization is choosing the right story. Always select a story you like. Also, always choose a story that has literary merit. Select a story that will be interesting and challenging, but not so difficult that you will lose interest.

Another consideration in choosing your story is the dialogue. It needs to be simple, yet interesting to read and act out. Also, choose characters who would appeal to you and your classmates. Choose a story with several strong characters who speak interesting lines, and pick a story whose characters have easy-to-play, yet challenging, actions and reactions. Well-developed plots, as in *Caps for Sale, Stone Soup,* or *The Three Bears,* are a must for story dramatization. The better the story is organized, the easier and more fun it will be to dramatize.

Some stories are great to read but hard to act out. Remember reading Dr. Seuss books, with their rhyming lines? If you tried to act out one of those stories, the rhyming lines might be hard to remember— and even harder to put into your own words. It would be better to choose a story that had easy dialogue to remember or that you could easily **paraphrase** —that is, put into your own words. Be careful about choosing stories that are too descriptive; it is difficult to act out a description. When you are reading a story, a vivid description of a place or person can enhance the images in your mind. But you can't act out a place, nor can you easily act out a person's physical appearance.

Avoid stories that require complicated props, costumes, or sets. **Props** are handheld items that are used in a performance to make a

set

usually large items used to stage a scene or play.

narrator

a storyteller.

transition

description of what is happening while the actors pantomime the action of a story.

A plot is: *The king died and then the queen died. A story is: The king died, and then the queen died of a broken heart.*

E. M. Forster

scene or play more believable. **Sets** are usually larger items used to stage a scene or play. Remember to choose stories that are simple enough to be dramatized in the classroom.

An important role that can be created in story dramatization is that of the **narrator** or storyteller. One or more narrators can open the story, provide **transition** from scene to scene (describe what is happening while the actors pantomime the action), and then close the story. The narrator needs to be very familiar with the story and should be capable of improvising dialogue.

Story dramatization often leads to experimentation with character and plot. After reading a story, the class discusses the story's various elements. Then the teacher or leader becomes the narrator while the story is played out in many different ways. Every member of the class can eventually have a part when the story is played again and again. Or perhaps the class will choose to replay only certain scenes from the story. The class can also be divided into groups, with each group given a scene from the story. The story should then be replayed in chronological order (arranged in the order the events happened). Clearly, methods for story dramatization replay are many and varied.

To succeed with story dramatization, it is important to evaluate the action that has been replayed. The action is the focus of creative drama and must be clear and believable. When you are evaluating your classmates, comment on the characters being portrayed, not the individuals who are playing the parts. Evaluation gives the process of story dramatization closure. After a while, through such evaluation, you will come to a clearer understanding of good pieces of literature.

The following questions may be helpful in evaluating creative drama activities:

1. What was the story about? What was the beginning, middle, and ending of the story?
2. What were the characters like? Compare them to people you know.
3. What did you like best about the creative drama activity?
4. What did you find most difficult about playing out the scenes?
5. What changes could be made the next time you replay the scenes?
6. How well did the class participate? How would you suggest increasing participation in the replay of the scenes?
7. When did you have to concentrate most on the acting during the scenes? Why?
8. How could this type of activity be useful in another class (such as science, language arts, or social studies)?

ACTION

1. Planning Story Dramatization
   a. Research and select a suitable story to dramatize in class.
   b. Working in small groups or acting companies, read one of the selections aloud.

    c. As a group, pick one of the stories to dramatize. Take turns rereading the story until the story line and dialogue are familiar to everyone in the group.

    d. Plan the characters, scenes, and events. Use these questions in your planning:

        1. What does the setting look like, and how will we organize our space for the playing? What will we do for the beginning scene?

        2. What does each character want to do?

        3. In what order will the characters enter?

        4. How will each character sound when he or she talks, and how will each character move? Describe external and internal characteristics.

        5. What events will be played out? In what order will they occur?

        6. How will we conclude the story?

    e. Play the story.

    f. Evaluate the playing using the guidelines given in this lesson.

2. Replaying a Story

    a. Replay your group's story. Make the discussed changes in characters and actions.

    b. Trade stories with another group or acting company and replay the story.

    c. Create a new ending for a familiar children's story. Play out the scene with your group. Discuss the process and replay the new ending again.

3. Sequencing

    a. Break into groups of three or four.

    b. Select a familiar children's story.

    c. Select a scene from the story to act out as a group.

    d. Watch all the performances and decide how to sequence them chronologically.

    e. Perform the scenes again in order.

Curtain Call!

CHAPTER 4 REVIEW

■ ■ SPOTLIGHT ON TERMS ■ ■

An important part of theatre is understanding the terminology, or vocabulary, used. Add the new terms and definitions to the vocabulary section of your theatre notebook or folder.

■ ■ FOCUS ON FACTS ■ ■

1. How does creative drama differ from formal drama?
2. Explain the difference between spontaneous action and scripted action.
3. What is the difference between narrative pantomime and story dramatization?
4. What types of selections work best for narrative pantomime?
5. How would you select a story for story dramatization?

■ ■ REFLECTIONS ■ ■

Discuss the following questions with your class or answer them on paper as instructed by your teacher.

1. Make a list of your favorite stories when you were a child. Why do you still remember them?
2. Why is the process more important than the product in creative drama?
3. After participating in the activities in this chapter, which specialized area do you prefer: narrative pantomime or story dramatization? Why?
4. Which aspect of creative drama was the most interesting for your group: choosing the selection, listening to the selection, discussing the selection, playing it out, replaying it, or evaluating the actions?

■ ■ THEATRE IN YOUR LIFE ■ ■

1. Choose a fairy tale with your group. With your teacher's assistance, use creative drama to present the fairy tale to an elementary school class.
2. Using creative drama, get the elementary school students to replay scenes from your group's fairy tale.
3. Present scenes from fairy tales or folk stories as part of a Saturday children's day at your public library.
4. After the preceding presentations, evaluate the activities.

■ ■ ENCORE ■ ■

1. Rewrite a fairy tale from a different point of view. For example, write the story "Little Red Riding Hood" from the wolf's viewpoint. Write his side of the story. Share the tale with the class, and present scenes from the story using creative drama.
2. Rewrite a nursery rhyme from a different point of view. Share the rhyme with the class, and present scenes from the rhyme using creative drama. Discuss changes that could be made, and replay the scenes.
3. Rewrite a fairy tale with a new twist of character development. For example, rewrite the tale "The Three Bears," making Goldilocks French, African American, or Chinese. After sharing this rewritten tale, present scenes to the class using creative drama.
4. Present the activity in exercise 3, using formal drama.
5. After completing each activity, evaluate the process and activity.
6. Write an original story using the criteria in Lesson 2. Choose a classmate, yourself, or your teacher to read the story while the rest of the class acts out the story using narrative pantomime.

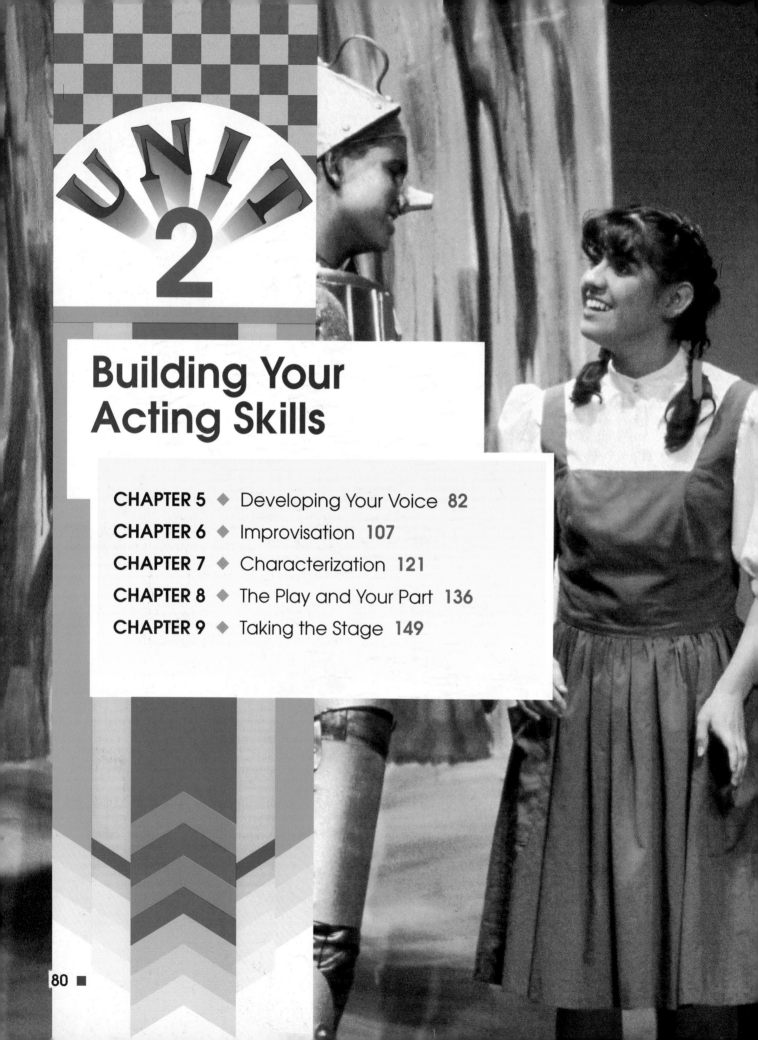

UNIT 2

Building Your Acting Skills

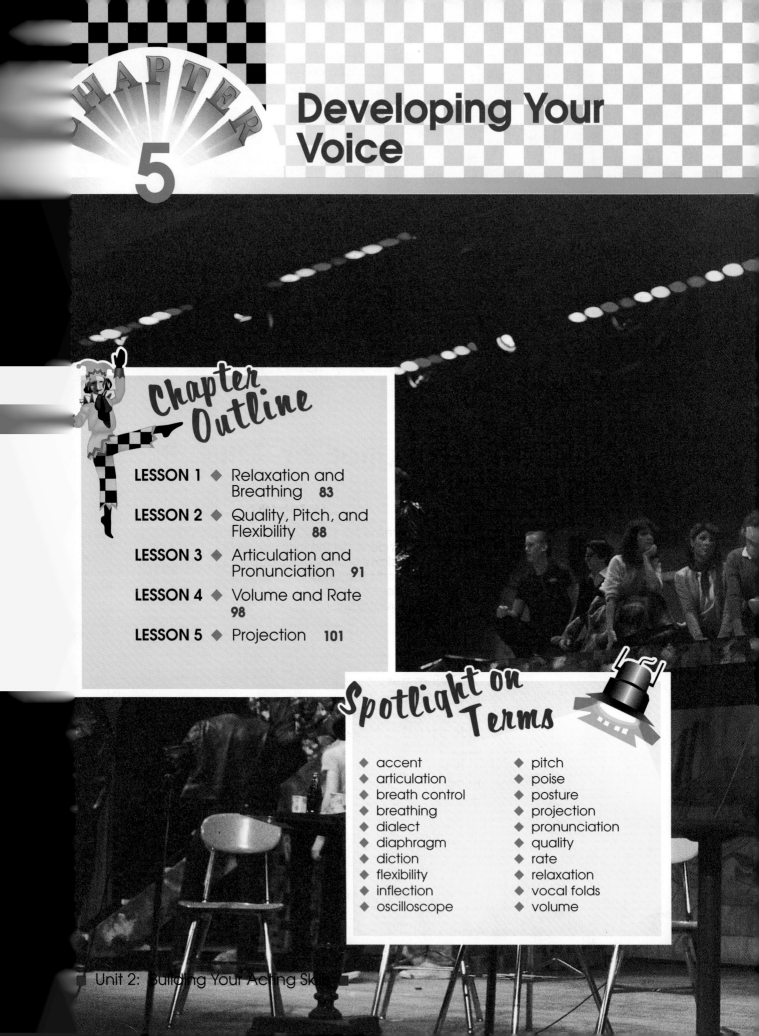

CHAPTER 5

Developing Your Voice

Chapter Outline

Spotlight on Terms

- accent
- articulation
- breath control
- breathing
- dialect
- diaphragm
- diction
- flexibility
- inflection
- oscilloscope
- pitch
- poise
- posture
- projection
- pronunciation
- quality
- rate
- relaxation
- vocal folds
- volume

> **K**now you how much the people may be moved by that which he will utter?
>
> William Shakespeare

The lines that an actor speaks must be heard clearly. Every word must be understood by cast members and audience alike. Thus, the voice is the foundation of an actor's art. Effective vocal communication is important not only onstage, but also at home, in the classroom—wherever you want people to understand what you are saying.

A voice that is used effectively conveys a wide range of emotions and reflects a person's personality, moods, and attitudes. A well-trained actor with an effective voice knows the importance of the following ten elements: relaxation, breathing, quality, pitch, flexibility, articulation, pronunciation, volume, rate, and projection.

If you were fortunate when you were younger, someone encouraged you to develop good speech habits. If this happened, you will probably have more success in theatre class than those who need to change bad vocal habits. Unfortunately, most people fall into the category of those who need vocal improvement. Take a moment now to list in your journal what you like about your voice and what you think needs improving. In this chapter, you will learn about the elements that make up an effective voice. You will also put a plan into action with drills, exercises, and activities to develop and improve your voice.

Relaxation and Breathing

LESSON OBJECTIVES

◆ Define relaxation and breathing.
◆ Understand the function and importance of relaxation and breathing.
◆ Participate in drills, exercises, and activities for developing and improving relaxation and breathing techniques.

Warm Up

Which method helps you relax?
a. music
b. silence in a room
c. daydreaming
d. exercises
e. all of the above
In your journal, explain your answer.

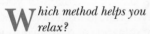

relaxation
freedom from all bodily tensions.

posture
how we sit and stand.

Relaxation

Before using your voice onstage, you must prepare your body by becoming relaxed. Most people do not know how to completely relax. **Relaxation** means freedom from all bodily tensions. It gives the actor a deeper level of awareness and provides the energy needed for the stage.

Being relaxed does not mean having a body like a wet noodle. The body and mind must be keenly alert and ready, yet calm and free from distractions and tension. Relaxation requires that you shut out any wandering thoughts about yourself or others. It also means ignoring unusual sounds, interruptions, and any other distractions. You can train both your mind and body to reach this level of relaxation with the exercises provided in this lesson.

Relaxation will give you physical and mental control and focus onstage, which in turn will help you achieve your theatrical goals. Relaxation techniques will also improve your **posture** (how you sit and stand), which is essential in controlled breathing. Finally, relaxation

For the best possible performance, you need to be relaxed. Actors use a variety of relaxation exercises to prepare for their performances.

will improve the sound of your voice and make your movement smoother onstage.

1. **Musical Relaxation.** While listening to music, lie on your back on the classroom floor. Relax each portion of your body by picturing the muscles with your mind's eye. See them relaxing as you breath slowly and deeply. Start with the top of your head and move down to your toes.

2. **Away With Tension!** Listen to music provided by your teacher and experience the difference between tension and relaxation. Start with the top of your head and move down to your toes. Tighten up the muscles and then completely relax. Concentrate on each section of your body by seeing the muscles in your mind's eye change from bright red to soft pink as they relax. End up completely relaxed, and remain that way for 5 minutes.

3. **Space Walk.** While standing in the classroom (find your own space to perform without bumping or disrupting other students), pretend that you are in space. Move completely relaxed, as if you were floating. Explore the feeling of complete freedom but with the control of slow motion.

4. **Silence is Golden!** During complete silence, sit at your desk for 3 minutes. Relax your entire body. Sit upright, but roll your head down and let your hands dangle by your body. In your mind's eye, see your body completely relaxed during these 3 minutes without interruptions.

5. **Body Parts in Motion.** While listening to music, do the following relaxation exercises three times each: shoulder shrugs; shoulder rolls

forward and backward; head rolls forward and backward; arm swings forward and backward; waist stretches to the left and right; massage your neck and shoulders; leg swings one at a time to the sides, forward, and backward; foot stretches up and down; massage your feet and hands.

6. **Smile!** Smile in an exaggerated manner several times to stretch and relax your face muscles. Repeat this activity, using a frown instead of a smile.

7. **Facial Massage!** Massage your face, and completely relax your facial muscles.

8. **Sleepy Time!** Yawn several times to relax the jaw.

9. **Going Up, Going Down!** Sit on the floor of the classroom and get comfortable. Pretend that you are in an elevator. Start at the twentieth floor and slowly go down. There will be pauses at each floor, but you will not get off. Finally, at the first floor, pretend to get off in a completely relaxed state of mind and body. As the leader calls out the different floors, feel your body get more relaxed at each floor as you go down.

10. **Country Time!** Stand in the classroom (find your own space). Raise your arms up and reach high into the air. Stretch higher and higher. Bend over and relax your body as if it were a limp doll. Remain in this position, and let your arms dangle for 1 minute. Slowly come up, relaxing each part of your body as you rebuild your backbone while gradually straightening up. As you completely stand erect, pretend that you are alone in the country, standing under the most beautiful tree you have ever seen. Smell the country air. Hear the birds. Feel the country grass soft beneath your feet. Stretch your body to the left and to the right. Stand up on the balls of your feet and look to the left and to the right. Look forward and behind you. See the gorgeous countryside with its hills and valleys, flowers, and cool streams. All of a sudden, a beautiful horse comes up to you. Jump up on the horse and ride bareback. Gallop in the wind. Relax and enjoy the ride through the country. Guide the horse back to the tree and get off. Lie down and pretend that a cloud comes down to take you back to the classroom.

Warm Up

Read the introduction of this chapter aloud. How far can you read without taking a breath?

breathing
the necessary process of inhaling and exhaling air to live.

diaphragm
the muscle located between the abdomen and the rib cage.

Breathing

As you know, **breathing** is the necessary process of inhaling and exhaling air to live. As a young actor, you must learn to control your breathing. Controlled breathing gives the performer enough power to carry the voice and be clearly heard.

Onstage, you need to inhale more deeply than you do in regular breathing, which translates into using more muscles. This type of inhalation allows you to build volume and vary your vocal sounds without running out of breath or straining your voice. Exhaling should also be stronger and with more control than in your everyday breathing. Your muscles, especially the **diaphragm** (the muscle located between the abdomen and the rib cage), must be used to supply the air

Developing breath control is always essential onstage. It is especially important in productions that require singing or dancing, such as in this production of *The King and I*.

breath control

the amount of force you use in inhaling and exhaling.

you need to create sound. **Breath control** is how much force you use in inhalation and exhalation.

Controlled breathing will help you develop an effective voice onstage and provide the support you will need to sustain you through performances. But another reason controlled breathing is so important is that it influences the body and its movements. When actors first begin performing onstage, their movements are often awkward and unnatural. They always seem to be out of breath after speaking several lines. But after developing breath control and practicing their breathing exercises every day, most actors notice that they have more energy onstage. Their body movements are then more effective as they rehearse and perform.

1. **Book Rest.** Lie down on the floor in the classroom. Rest a book on your diaphragm (the muscle between the abdomen and the rib cage). Watch the book rise when you inhale and fall when you exhale. Continue this exercise for about a minute.

2. **Observation Time.** Observe closely the difference between everyday breathing and breathing while speaking. Observe inhaling and exhaling for both types of breathing by placing your hands on your stomach, just below the rib cage. Also notice changes in upper body and lower body tension as you breathe.

3. **Air Release.** Breathe deeply and inhale slowly. Hold your breath and release the air slowly, counting 1 to 6. Repeat this process to see how well you can control your breathing as you say the numbers.

4. **Ha, Ha, Ha!** Slowly inhale and hold your breath for 10 counts. Exhale on the sound of "ha."

5. **Ah!!!!!!** Slowly inhale and hold for 10 counts. Exhale on the sound of "ah."

6. **Snake.** Inhale as if you were about to speak. Now exhale and make the sound of a snake—"s-s-s-s-s-s."

7. **Pucker Up!** Pucker your lips, and hold the tip of your finger in front of your lips. Quickly inhale and blow out a stream of air. Concentrate on producing a steady, smooth stream of air each time you repeat this exercise. Feel the difference in the air on your finger when there is a change in the stream of air.

8. **Phrases.** Slowly inhale. Next practice saying phrases, working on your breath control. Suggested phrases are: good morning, good luck, break a leg, nice day, good show, and thank you.

9. **Using Poetry for Breath Control.** Read Jack Prelutsky's poem "Life's Not Been the Same in My Family" to practice breath control. See how far you can read without taking a breath.

Life's Not Been the Same in My Family

Life's not been the same in my family
since the day that the new baby came,
my parents completely ignore me,
they scarcely remember my name.

The baby gets all their attention,
"Oh, isn't she precious!" they croon,
they think she looks like an angel,
I think she resembles a prune.

They're thrilled when she giggles and gurgles,
"She burped!" they exclaimed with delight,
they don't even mind when she wakes us
with deafening screams in the night.

They seem to believe she's a treasure,
there's simply no way I agree,
I wish she'd stop being a baby
and start being older than me.

10. **Poetry Scavenger Hunt.** Find three other poems that would help develop your breath control.

The Italian Renaissance

In the years stretching from the late 1300s through the early 1600s, the cultural center of Europe was Italy. This period of cultural advancement and activity is known as the *Renaissance.* The Renaissance was a time for great advancement not only in the theatre but in all of the arts.

It is during this period that theatre was transformed from its Medieval form to a type of theatre much closer to our modern style. Much of the new theatre activity resulted from the merchants sponsoring artists to create works of art, such as plays, for the enjoyment of their family and friends. This system of providing financial support was known as *patronage.* The subject matter of the arts changed from the religious topics, which had been dominant in the Middle Ages, to more earthly matters, and is focused upon human rather than divine activity. This new way of looking at the world was known as *humanism.*

Neoclassical Ideas

The new Renaissance rules of writing drama, known as the *Neoclassical Ideals,* were very important because they dominated opinions about the best ways to write plays for over two hundred years. The Neoclassical theories were based upon the then recently rediscovered writings of the Greek and Roman playwrights and the writings of the Greek philosopher Aristotle. The Renaissance writers thought they had found the rules about the proper way to write and create theater, so they created plays that copied the stories and themes of the Greek and Roman plays.

The Neoclassical Ideals were concerned with what is called *verisimilitude,* which means "being true to life." Verisimilitude is what the Renaissance playwrights mistakenly believed that Aristotle was dictating. Therefore, the Renaissance philosophy demanded that all characters and situations be recognizable and verifiable from real life. To make sure that this rule of verisimilitude was followed, all plays had to have a unity of time (requiring that the action of the play not cover more than twenty-four hours), unity of place (requiring that the action all take place in one locale), and unity of action (re-

quiring that the plot have only one story line, with no subplots). In some Renaissance theatre, such as that of Elizabethan England and Spain's Golden Age of drama, the Neoclassical ideals were ignored, but most European countries followed the rules of verisimilitude.

Changes in Space and Style

During the Renaissance, changes and discoveries in visual art had a major effect upon the arrangement of space and visual imagery inside the theatre. Italian artists discovered how to use angles and variation in the size of objects represented in the same painting to create the illusion of depth, or a sense of realistic, three-dimensional space. This was called *perspective painting.* The use of perspective in paintings replaced the medieval practices of painting, which made images seem flat.

Some of the most important people in theatre history in this period were architects, who changed forever the way theatre buildings would be built. In the early 1600s, architects first began to design proscenium arches, or picture-frame openings around the stage space. The oldest surviving theatre from this period is located in Vicenza, Italy, and named the *Teatro Olimpico.* It was completed in the year 1585 and could hold up to 3,000 people. Although it had no proscenium arch, the stage had a permanent facade (fake building front built on stage to represent a large building), which reflected the new concern with visual perspective. Like the Roman scene houses in the earlier period, the Olimpico's facade had a series of doorways built into a massive, ornate wall that could be used to represent the households of various families in the plays. These doorways were different from their Roman counterparts in that they had long hallways or alleyways built into them. These alleyways ran at sharp angles away from the audience, giving the illusion of deep interior spaces within the homes of the play's characters.

The concern with perspective was to soon change the use of the facade. The facade gave way to the use of painted scenery, which could be shifted to reveal new settings behind it. Soon, painted flats (painted

The **Teatro Olimpico** in Vicenza, Italy is the oldest surviving theatre from the Italian Renaissance Period. Notice the long hallways leading from the stage that contributed to the illusion of depth.

canvases representing three-dimensional walls) were replacing fixed, architectural stage houses as the basic unit of scenery. This change is what made building proscenium arches popular. The arch gave audience members the sense that they were looking at a walking, talking, moving, transforming, singing painting when they went to the theatre.

In the Middle Ages, the style had been to use mansions to represent heaven, hell, Earth, and other specific settings—all visible to the audience at the same time. In the Renaissance it was much more popular to reveal only one setting at a time. This made it necessary to hide from view all the flats except the one being used at a given time. The proscenium arch was the solution. While serving as a huge picture frame, it also hid the extra flats and the system of ropes, pulleys, and tracking needed to move the flats. As the period progressed, the audience began to want more and more changes of setting, which lead to the building of permanent proscenium arches.

The first theatre to have a proscenium stage was the Teatro Farnese, in Parma, Italy, completed in 1618. For the Farnese scenery, painters used perspective techniques to create a painted series of wings or flats, which were placed one behind the other on both sides of the stage, so that they could be slid away to reveal the next set. These flats usually ap-

peared to be houses along a city street. The setting was closed off at the back of the stage with a painted drop or a large set of wings called *shutters*, which met in the middle of the stage and could be slid away to reveal another backdrop. The use of these multiple settings required that newer theatre buildings have more backstage space to store scenery and equipment. This meant that Renaissance stages became larger and larger, and deeper and deeper, to house all the scenery and to provide the visual depth that had become so popular in visual arts.

Although the Italians were very concerned with perspective, they did not find it necessary to create new scenery for each play. Instead they reused three standard styles of settings, one for tragedies (showing the street of a wealthy neighborhood), another for a comedy (showing a common street lined with lower-class homes), and a third setting for pastoral plays (showing trees, hillsides, and simple country cottages). The practice was to reuse these basic settings over and over, depending upon the style and genre of the play being produced.

The first comedy written in Italian was *La Cassaria* by Ludovico Ariosto. *La Cassaria* is a comedy that combines classical form with a more contemporary sense of earthy humor. The first important tragedy was *Sofonisba* by Giangiorgio Trissino. ■

Quality, Pitch, and Flexibility

LESSON OBJECTIVES

◆ Define quality, pitch, and flexibility.
◆ Understand the function and importance of quality, pitch, and flexibility.
◆ Recognize and break bad speaking habits.
◆ Participate in drills, exercises, and activities for developing and improving an actor's voice quality, pitch, and flexibility.
◆ Begin developing good speaking habits for a lifetime.

Warm Up

List three people whose voices you admire. Why?

quality

the voice element that makes one person sound different from everyone else.

Quality

Quality is the voice element that makes you sound different from everyone else. People recognize you from the unique sound of your voice. You don't have much choice regarding the quality of your voice. But you can eliminate (or at least lessen) annoying habits that produce poor voice quality. Examples of poor voice quality are huskiness, nasality (sounds produced by allowing your breath to pass through your nose when you talk), and a thin, weak quality.

Voice quality and emotional state are closely connected. Your emotions are reflected through the quality of your voice. For example, people can tell if you are happy or angry, depending on whether your voice is pleasant or unpleasant. Even when you aren't aware of it, your voice quality reflects your personality and moods.

As an actor, you will need to use a variety of voice qualities to interpret and portray different characters. When you speak onstage, your voice quality will reflect your character's emotional frame of mind. It is necessary to have effective voice qualities to develop the character that you portray.

ACTION

1. **Quality Warm-Ups.** Roll your head forward, backward, and sideways. Massage your face and lips to loosen the muscles. Relax your tongue, jaw, and throat by yawning slowly. After physically exercising these areas, mentally prepare these body parts before you participate in the exercises to improve your voice quality. To be mentally prepared, focus on keeping the face, lips, tongue, jaw, and throat relaxed for adequate control.

2. **Emotional Survey.** Using different emotions, say these words: yes, no, it's okay, finally, sure, great. Suggested emotions to use are: happy, sad, fearful, angry, and jealous.

3. **Louder, I Can't Hear You.** Say the following words quietly at first.

Then repeat them louder and louder, then finally stronger using more breath support. Practice using your best voice quality.

may	won	play	wink	tune
say	sun	clay	sink	loon
day	done	way	rink	moon

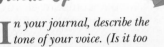

Warm Up

In your journal, describe the tone of your voice. (Is it too high, low, shrill, or nasal?)

pitch
the musical tone of a voice.

vocal folds
muscular membranes in the larynx that produce sound.

inflection
the rising and falling of pitch. Inflection adds meaning, color, and rhythm to spoken words.

Pitch

Pitch is the musical tone of your voice—how high or how low you speak on a musical scale. It is one of the voice elements that gives meaning and color to speech. Pitch is determined by the vibration of your **vocal folds**, muscular membranes located in the larynx, or what is often called the "voice box." The faster the folds vibrate, the higher the pitch. The slower the folds vibrate, the lower the pitch. The shape and size of the vocal folds also make a difference in the tone of a person's voice. The loss of your voice after two hours of yelling at a football or basketball game is the result of strained muscles—your vocal folds. They are swollen and vibrate very slowly when you try to speak, causing a low pitch, often hoarseness.

You can find your pitch by matching your voice against the scales of a piano. Once you find your pitch, remember that this is the level that is best for you personally for the richest tone and greatest ease in speaking. You are born with this pitch, and not much can be done to change your natural pitch. But you can learn to manipulate your pitch for the stage.

Two common flaws onstage are a thin, high tone and a monotone. A high, thin pitch can be corrected with concentration and a conscious effort to lower your speaking tone. A person who speaks in a monotone (speaking without a change in pitch) needs **inflection**, the rising and falling of pitch. Vocal inflection is essential for the actor. Besides giving the voice variety in its pitch, inflection adds meaning, color, and rhythm to words. Inflection makes a voice interesting. When you listen to a teacher who never changes pitch—talks in a flat monotone—it's hard to pay attention; your mind wanders. But a teacher who uses inflection effectively can stimulate your mind for hours.

ACTION

1. **Which Pitch Did You Use?** Say the following three times, changing your pitch each time.
   a. Yes.
   b. No.
   c. I don't know.
   d. I knew that.

   Repeat the activity. Be prepared to explain what you meant each time you said the word or words. For example, "yes," can mean "I will do it," "I'm not sure," or "Sure" uttered sarcastically.

2. **Rising and Falling Inflection.** Say the numbers 2, 4, 6, 8, with a rising inflection. Say the numbers 2, 4, 6, 8 with a falling inflection. Repeat this drill several times.

An oscilloscope displays an electronic graph of your voice.

oscilloscope

an instrument that can be used to record voice vibrations and show voice patterns.

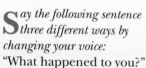

Warm Up

Say the following sentence three different ways by changing your voice: "What happened to you?"

flexibility

the process of varying inflections of the voice.

poise

the effective control of all voice elements and body movements.

3. **What Did You Say?** Using gibberish (senseless chatter) and varying the inflection in your voice, explain the following.
   a. how to get somewhere
   b. what's in an imaginary box
   c. what someone looked like
   d. how to solve a math problem
   e. how to cook an egg
   f. how to operate a small appliance
   g. how to play a sport
   h. where you are from
   i. who's in your family
   j. an idea of your own

4. **Patterns.** If your science lab has an **oscilloscope** (an instrument that records vibrations produced by charges of electricity), take turns reading this sentence: "It wasn't so much what he said as how he said it." Watch the pattern of your voice on the oscilloscope. Compare all voice patterns in the class.

5. **Would You Please Repeat That?** Practice repeating this question—"What did you do?"—five different ways. Place emphasis on the different words in the question to make each way effective.

Flexibility

You will be able to keep the members of an audience on the edge of their seats if you vary your pitch and exhibit flexibility. **Flexibility** is the result of using the muscles in your face, tongue, jaw, lips, and throat in a lively manner. It is also a process of varying inflections as you speak. Vocal flexibility is created in a number of ways: using variety in the sounds of words; placing emphasis, or stress, on certain syllables, words, or groups of words in an unexpected way; phrasing words and sentences in a particular way; and using pauses, which provide the element of timing—not only for the actor, but also for the audience, helping them grasp what is being said.

As an actor, you may be hesitant to use pauses, but they are extremely effective in communicating onstage. A pause can be as meaningful as a spoken line. It can give an audience the interpretation of the script intended by the playwright.

Another skill that you need to develop is poise. **Poise** is the effective control of all your vocal elements and body movements. Poise can give you a calm, confident manner. But it can only come as a result of the self-confidence that you gain from your training in vocal elements and body movements.

Actors find as they develop flexibility that they are able to express the meaning of lines more clearly.

ACT*ion*

1. **It's a Date!** Divide into pairs, a girl and a boy. Carry on a conversation asking for a date and accepting the date, using only first names as the dialogue. Vary your inflection for emphasis and interest.

2. Express Yourself with a Song. Sing the following songs as warm-ups, drills, exercises, activities, and fun.

a. Happy Birthday
b. Row, Row, Row Your Boat
c. London Bridge
d. This Old Man
e. I'm a Little Teapot
f. Old MacDonald Had a Farm

g. Oh! Susanna!
h. Yankee Doodle Went to Town
i. She'll Be Coming Around the Mountain
j. another song—your choice

3. Poetry Inflection. Read the following poem, "A Word" by the famous American poet, Emily Dickinson, three different ways:

> A word is dead
> When it is said,
>   Some say.
>
> I say it just
> Begins to live
>   That day.

4. Short Statements. Practice saying the following short sentences. Concentrate on changing meaning when you repeat them, adding color and emphasis to different words.

a. The world's a stage.
b. You are my sunshine.
c. You haven't seen anything yet.
d. I never met a man I didn't like.
e. Oh, what a beautiful morning.
f. You can't do that.

g. Come on down.
h. United we stand.
i. Divided we fall.
j. Do whatever it takes.
k. Take a risk.
l. Make a difference.

5. Say It Again Sam! Repeat the sentences in exercise 4, assuming a different character each time. Make up your own characters—for example, a cowboy, a doctor, an old woman, a young child, a newscaster, an astronaut, a rock star, a sports hero, a movie star, a preacher.

LESSON 3

Articulation and Pronunciation

LESSON OBJECTIVES

◆ Define articulation and pronunciation.
◆ Understand the function and importance of articulation and pronunciation.
◆ Participate in drills, exercises, and activities that develop and improve an actor's articulation and pronunciation.

Radio announcers or deejays must have excellent articulation. Hearing is the only sense their audience can use in understanding them.

Warm Up

Before reading aloud one of the passages assigned by your teacher, stretch your facial muscles by smiling and frowning three times.

articulation

the shaping and molding of sounds into syllables.

ACTION

Articulation

Articulation is the shaping and molding of sounds into syllables. We use all of our articulators (lips, tongue, teeth, hard and soft palates, jaw, muscles, and nasal passageways) in articulation. The process of learning vowels and consonants begins early in childhood. It is then that many bad speaking habits are formed. Some common bad habits are slurring sounds and words, not completing the endings of sounds and words, and generally not speaking distinctly (clearly).

To develop good vocal habits for the stage, you need to practice your articulation daily. One of the best ways to do this is to recite tongue twisters. Articulation drills will not only improve your articulation for the stage but will also train your ear to hear the way you speak in everyday life.

1. **Tongue Twisters.** Practice your articulation with the following tongue twisters. Practice each one three times. If you have difficulty with any tongue twister, spend more time practicing it until you have mastered all twenty-six tongue twisters.
   a. Ruby red rubber baby buggy bumpers.
   b. Eight great gray geese grazing gaily into Greece.
   c. Tie twine to three tree twigs.
   d. The old cold scold sold the school coal scuttle.
   e. What noise annoys a noisy oyster most? A noisy noise annoys a noisy oyster most.
   f. Did you see Peter Piper's puppy peeping playfully?
   g. She sells seashells at the seashore's seashell store.
   h. Let Letty linger longer at the luncheon.

i. He is a nice man, not an ice man.

j. Sinful Caesar sipped his snifter, seized his knee and sneezed.

k. She says such shabbily sewed seams show seriously.

l. Strange strategic statistics.

m. Round and round the rugged rocks the ragged rascal ran.

n. Thissian Thistle, the successful thistle sifter, sifts sieves full of three thousand thistles through the thick of this thumb.

o. Double bubble gum bubbles double.

p. Six slick slim slippery slimy sleek slender sickly saplings.

q. Can a stammerer flatter a flatterer?

r. The sun shines on shop signs.

s. Truly rural rustic trees.

t. Shy Sarah saw Swiss wristwatches.

u. The sixth sheik's sixth sheep's sick.

v. Are you copper-bottoming them, my man? No, I'm aluminuming 'em, mum.

w. From "A Fly and a Flea in a Flue" by an anonymous poet.

> A fly and a flea in a flue
> Were imprisoned, so what could they do?
> Said the fly, "Let us flee!"
> "Let us fly!" said the flea,
> And they flew through a flaw in the flue.

x. From "Grace at Kirkudbright" by Robert Burns.

> Some have meat and cannot eat,
> Some cannot eat that want it:
> But we have meat and we can eat,
> Sae let the Lord be thankit.

y. From "Weather" by an anonymous poet.

> Whether the weather be fine
> Or whether the weather be not,
> Whether the weather be cold,
> Or whether the weather be hot,
> We'll weather the weather
> Whatever the weather,
> Whether we like it or not.

z. From "A Publisher Who Published Papers" by an anonymous poet.

> A publisher who published papers
> Plenty of pens and pictures wished,
> To pile up his pages with capers
> Of prestigious professors who fished.

2. Clear Articulation Check. Ask your teacher or a classmate to listen to you read the following sentences. Ask a partner to circle the sounds of the words (on a separate sheet of paper) that are not spoken clearly.

a. The healthier, the better.
b. Feel free to leave.
c. It sounds correct to me.
d. I like fried french fries.
e. This will soon pass.
f. The women climbed the mountain.
g. The men ran the race.
h. The hot chocolate burned my tongue.
i. Please go away.
j. Stay another hour.

3. **Rhyme Time.** Practice your articulation with these nursery rhymes.

a. Mary had a little lamb. Its fleece was white as snow.
   And everywhere that Mary went the lamb was sure to go.
b. Jack be nimble. Jack be quick. Jack jump over the candle
   stick.
c. There was an old lady who lived in a shoe.
   She had so many children she didn't know what to do.
d. Jack and Jill went up the hill
   To fetch a pail of water.
   Jack fell down and broke his crown
   And Jill came tumbling after.
e. Row, row, row your boat
   Gently down the stream,
   Merrily, merrily, merrily, merrily,
   Life is but a dream.
f. Three blind mice,
   Three blind mice,
   See how they run!
   See how they run!
   They all ran after the farmer's wife,
   Who cut off their tails with the carving knife,
   Did you ever hear such a thing in your life,
   As three blind mice?
g. Oh where, oh where has my little dog gone?
   Oh where, oh where can he be?
   With his ears cut short and his tail cut long,
   Oh where, oh where can he be?
h. Jack Sprat could eat no fat.
   His wife could eat no lean.
   Betwixt the two of them they licked the platter clean.

4. **Father to Son.** Read the following lines from Lewis Carroll's *Alice's Adventures in Wonderland*. Use all your articulators with energy and vitality.

   "You are old," said the youth, "and your jaws are too weak
      For anything tougher than suet;
   Yet you finished the goose, with the bones and the beak—
      Pray, how did you manage to do it?"
   "In my youth," said his father, "I took to the law,
      And argued each case with my wife;
   And the muscular strength which it gave to my jaw,
      Has lasted the rest of my life."

pronunciation

the way sounds or syllables that represent a word are said and stressed according to the proper notation found in the dictionary.

Pronunciation

Pronunciation refers to the way words are said. Proper pronunciation means that words are spoken according to dictionary notations.

Warm Up

Pronounce the following words:

mischievous   advertisement

indict   get

theatre   acquittal

If you are unsure of the correct pronunciation, which of the following would be the best source?

    a. your smartest friend
    b. the glossary of a language arts book
    c. a dictionary

diction

a person's pronunciation of words, choice of words, and manner in which the person expresses himself or herself.

dialect

a pronunciation of words from different languages blended together to form a distinct language for a group of people.

accent

the manner in which people speak and the way words are pronounced in different parts of the world.

Pronunciation helps us distinguish the correct sounding out of a word, dictating which letters of a word are to be articulated. Proper pronunciation, like articulation, results from people being aware of how our language differentiates the sound of one word from another. You may remember being corrected when you mispronounced a word as a child. If so, you can count yourself as one of the lucky ones. Someone cared enough to correct your pronunciation. Proper pronunciation is seen as the mark of an educated person. It often will result in that person getting a good job.

Who decides the correct pronunciation of a word? Your dictionary is probably your most dependable source. A dictionary is not the only authority for a pronunciation, but people who write dictionaries are experts who have done a great deal of research to determine the accepted pronunciation of a word.

Before rehearsing the lines of a play, use a dictionary (or other accepted source) for difficult pronunciations and unfamiliar meanings. Certain words may not be in the dictionary you are using. You may have to research those words, perhaps getting help from more educated people or people from other cultures. Other sources that may help you with pronunciations are your language arts teacher, your parents, the librarian, and foreign language teachers.

During your theatre experiences, you will probably encounter three other terms related to pronunciation: diction, dialect, and accent. **Diction** is a person's pronunciation of words, choice of words, and manner in which the person expresses himself or herself. Developing good diction is a valuable tool for life and essential for the stage. **Dialect** is a pronunciation of words from different languages blended together to form a distinct language for a group of people. Diction and dialects enhance characterization. A character onstage takes on a whole new dimension when you use, for example, a Jamaican dialect. This type of character development requires time, research, and practice. **Accent** is the manner in which people speak; it is the way words are pronounced in different parts of the world. The use of stress and emphasis contribute to a word's accent.

ACTION

1. **Pronunciation Check.** Check your pronunciation of the following words, which are often mispronounced.

pin	cent	picture	entire	infamous
pen	thin	pitcher	horizon	medicinal
any	can't	town	idea	mischievous
get	catch	debate	ideal	preference
just	measure	disclose	incomparable	

2. **It's All in the Endings.** Pronounce the following words, whose endings are often left off when spoken.

madder	battle	city	tests	toward
ladder	water	rests	tasks	
paddle	wetter	wasps	desks	
saddle	butter	discs	mists	

3. Dictionary Scavenger Hunt. Look up in the dictionary any of the following words for which you are unsure of the pronunciation or meaning. Be prepared to read the list aloud and explain any definition.

abdomen	data	hospitable	oscilloscope	travail
address	detour	illustrate	pianist	vaudeville
automobile	dictionary	interesting	preferable	vice versa
aviation	exquisite	laboratory	presentation	
bouquet	forehead	magazine	route	
clique	grimace	medicinal	status	
coupe	harass	military	suet	
coupon	harassment	ordeal	suite	

Volume and Rate

LESSON OBJECTIVES

◆ Define volume and rate.
◆ Understand the function and importance of volume and rate.
◆ Participate in drills, exercises, and activities for developing and improving an actor's volume and rate.

Volume

volume
how softly or loudly a person speaks.

■ ■ ■ ■ ■ ■ ■ ■ ■ ■ ■ ■ ■

Even with the advantages of modern technology, actors still need exceptional volume, rate, and placement skills when performing outdoors.

Volume is how loudly or softly you speak. The basis for a person's volume is breath control. Actors must develop breath control to regulate the amount of air being used when speaking. They also need to

Warm Up

After class today, keep a mental record of how many times someone asks you to repeat what you said. Also count how many times you ask someone else to repeat what he or she said.

use proper voice placement (directing the voice where the audience is located). Otherwise, the result will be uneven volume or unclear sounds and words.

The distance between the actor and the audience will be a problem if volume is not used properly. As you can imagine, your audience will be disappointed if they can't hear what you are saying. Shouting is never an answer. You can place your voice where it is needed by focusing your vocal energy to your listeners. It is your responsibility, as an actor, to train your voice for adequate volume. You must constantly have the desire to be heard, and you must understand what it takes to reach that goal. A good performance demands it.

Remember that good posture and breath control are essential in the drills and exercises for improving your volume. The diaphragm plays the key role in producing volume for the stage.

ACTION

1. **Counting the 5s.** Count slowly by 5s—5, 10, 15, 20, and so on—increasing your volume with each number.

2. **Counting the 5s with Stress.** Repeat exercise 1, this time emphasizing every other number. On each number that is emphasized, mentally and verbally project the sound farther and farther away.

3. **Hello!** While carefully inhaling, say the word "hello" and repeat it several times. Begin softly and increase the loudness. Repeat the drill in reverse, going from loud to soft.

4. **ABCs.** Recite the letters of the alphabet, increasing the volume with each letter. Repeat the drill starting with the last letter of the alphabet. This time begin loudly and get softer.

5. **The Comics Are Everywhere.** Bring your favorite comic strip or comic book to class. Read the passage in a variety of places. For example, begin by reading to a small group; next, read in front of the entire class; then move to a cafeteria or an auditorium; and finally, read outside to a group. You must physically and mentally adjust your breathing and volume for each location.

6. **Favorite Children's Story.** Repeat exercise 5 using a favorite childhood story.

Rate

Rate is the speed at which you speak. Rate and volume affect each other. Again, breath control is important in having an effective rate both for everyday speaking and onstage. Many actors mispronounce and slur their words when they speak too fast. When this happens, the audience becomes lost and confused.

Never cause your audience to misunderstand what's going on because of rapid speaking. Rate is one of the elements of voice that can be

rate
the speed at which someone speaks.

effectively used for characterization. You must give your audience time to listen and think about what they hear. Onstage, some characters do need to speak rapidly, but it is possible to control articulation inside a rapid rate. Always remember that this is the first time, and probably the only time, the audience will see and hear the performance.

1. **Watching Time Go By.** Using the second hand on a watch, time yourself counting. Count from 1 to 5 in 5 seconds. Count from 1 to 10 in 10 seconds. Count from 1 to 20 in 20 seconds. Learn to control your rate when you speak. Repeat the drill and ask a classmate to listen to your rate. Experiment with speaking at various rates. Have the volunteer suggest your best rate of speaking to be easily understood.

2. **Story Time.** Bring a folktale, fairy tale, or children's story to class. Divide into pairs and read the stories to each other. Practice reading at a rate that is understandable. Vary your rate to make the story interesting and lively.

3. **Rhyme Time.** Read the following poems aloud, varying your rate for the best vocal reading.

> **Silver**
> Slowly, silently, now the moon
> Walks the night in her silver shoon;
> This way, and that, she peers, and sees
> Silver fruit upon silver trees;
> One by one the casements catch
> Her beams beneath the silvery thatch;
> Couched in his kennel, like a log,
> With paws of silver sleeps the dog;
> From their shadowy cote the white breasts peep
> Of doves in a silver-feathered sleep;
> A harvest mouse goes scampering by,
> With silver claws, and silver eye;
> And moveless fish in the water gleam,
> By silver reeds in a silver stream.
>
> *Walter de la Mare*
>
> **City, City**
> **I**
> City, city,
> Wrong and bad,
> Looms above me
> When I'm sad,
> Throws its shadow
> On my care,
> Sheds its poison
> In my air,
> Pounds me with its
> Noisy fist,

Sprays me with its
Sooty mist.
Till, with sadness
On my face,
I long to live
Another place.

II
City, city,
Golden-clad,
Shines around me
When I'm glad,
Lifts me with its
Strength and height,
Fills me with its
Sound and sight,
Takes me to its
Crowded heart,
Holds me so I
Won't depart.
Till, with gladness
On my face,
I wouldn't live
Another place.

Marci Ridlon

4. **Judging Rate from the Stage.** Bring to class an acceptable article from a favorite magazine or book. Choose a paragraph to read aloud. Focus on your rate of speaking. Go to the stage or cafeteria to read the passage. Repeat the activity, but tell from memory what you have read to the class. Notice the changes in your rate.

Projection

LESSON OBJECTIVES

◆ Define projection.
◆ Understand the function and importance of projection in performance.
◆ Participate in drills, exercises, and activities to develop and improve an actor's projection.

projection

the placement and delivery of voice elements used effectively in communicating to an audience.

Projection is the placement and delivery of all the characteristics of an effective voice to communicate with your audience. It makes no difference where you are performing—classroom, cafeteria, small courtyard, or auditorium—your audience must be able to understand you. Projection involves aiming your voice at a directed target. It combines all the voice elements discussed earlier. As an actor, it is your responsibility to use all the techniques available to you.

Projection involves delivering your lines to the audience, and energy is vital in the delivery of those lines. You constantly must be aware of where the audience is. Not only must you remember all the aspects of acting and speaking onstage; you must also remain aware of the audience's need to hear you.

Having the right attitude is critical. Proper and effective projection requires that you *want* to speak and perform well. Voice projection takes desire, study, and hours of work. The result, however, is that your audience will hear and understand the performance. They will enjoy and possibly even learn from the performance.

ACTION

1. **Outdoor Theatre.** Select or write a short monologue (script for one person) using themes involving teenage students (for example, peer pressure, boy/girl relationships, friendships, or problems youth face). Either read or memorize the monologue and present it outside, with the class as the audience. Focus on the placement and delivery (where your listeners are) of your lines.

2. **Alphabet Olympics.** Everyone in class participates at the same time, reciting the letters of the alphabet. Use projection, not volume, to be heard. Choose the classmate with the best projection and write in your journal why this person has effective projection. Be specific with your explanation of the effective vocal elements.

3. **How Far Can You Project?** Locate a large room, such as the cafeteria or auditorium. Work in pairs. Memorize the following sentence: "I have told you a hundred times, and the answer is still the same." Stand 15 feet apart from each other and take turns reciting the line. Continue by moving farther and farther apart. Focus on projecting, not shouting.

4. **Stories for Projection.** Select one of the following stories to tell in front of the class or onstage.
   a. The Three Bears
   b. The Three Pigs
   c. Little Red Riding Hood
   d. Three Billy Goats Gruff
   e. Speaker's choice
   When projecting onstage, remember these points:
   • Warm up the voice and body before performing.
   • Be prepared mentally and physically.
   • Relax the throat, and don't strain your throat muscles or the vocal folds.
   • Use breath control, and breathe from the diaphragm.
   • Use energy to apply effective voice elements clearly, distinctly, and without dropping the last words you speak.
   • Use a clear, distinct tone when you speak—not a yell.
   • Speak to other characters onstage as well as to the audience.
   • Focus your lines as far back as the last seat in the auditorium.

5. Lines for Projection. Read the following lines from various plays in front of the class, onstage, outside, and at home, for practice with projection.

from **Butterflies are Free**

by Leonard Gershe

MRS. BAKER. Of course not. And I know you're not Snow White.

JILL. *(Takes the apple, rises, crosses below Mrs. Baker, through kitchen to D. L. post.)* I may have to wait hours before I read. I'll probably starve to death before their eyes.

MRS. BAKER. *(Crosses to kitchen, takes lettuce, picks off a few pieces, washes them, puts them on plate.)* You're going to get that part, you know.

JILL. What makes you so sure?

MRS. BAKER. Well, you're a very pretty girl and that's what they want in the theatre, isn't it?

JILL. *(Crosses below to D. R. post, away from Mrs. Baker.)* Today you have to have more than a pretty face. Anyway, I'm not really pretty. I think I'm interesting-looking and in certain lights I can look sort of . . . lovely . . . but I'm not pretty.

MRS. BAKER. *(Crosses with lettuce, sits C. sofa.)* Nonsense! You're extremely pretty.

JILL. (Laugh.) No, I'm not.

MRS. BAKER. Yes, you are.

JILL. *(Turns, leans post.)* No, I'm not. I've got beady little eyes like a bird and a figure like a pogo stick. *(Waits for a reaction from Mrs. Baker. There isn't one.)* Well? Aren't you going to deny you said that?

MRS. BAKER. *(Unperturbed.)* How can I, dear? Obviously, you heard it.

JILL. (*Crosses above director's chair.*) There are plenty of true things you can put me down with. You don't have to put me down with lies.

MRS. BAKER. You know what I like about you?

JILL. Uh-huh. Nothing.

MRS. BAKER. Oh yes. I like your honesty . . . your candor. You're really quite a worldly young woman, aren't you, Mrs. Benson?

JILL. I suppose I am. (*Crosses above "picnic," away from Mrs. Baker.*) I wish you wouldn't call me Mrs. Benson.

MRS. BAKER. Isn't that your name . . . Mrs. Benson?

JILL. But you don't say it as though you mean it.

MRS. BAKER. I'm sorry. Why don't I call you Jill? That's more friendly . . . and I'll try to say it as though I mean it. Now, Jill, (Jill—R. *turn, back to audience.*) you were telling me about your childhood.

JILL. I was?

You're A Good Man Charlie Brown

Based on the comic strip *Peanuts*
by Charles M. Schulz

CHARLIE BROWN. I think lunchtime is about the worst time of the day for me. Always having to sit here alone. Of course, sometimes mornings aren't so pleasant, either—waking up and wondering if anyone would really miss me if I never got out of bed. Then there's the night, too—lying there and thinking about all the stupid things I've done during the day. And all those hours in between—when I do all those stupid things. Well, lunchtime is *among* the worst times of the day for me.

Well, I guess I'd better see what I've got. (*He opens the bag, unwraps a sandwich, and looks inside*) Peanut butter. (*He bites and chews*) Some psychiatrists say that people who eat peanut butter sandwiches are lonely. I guess they're right. And if you're really lonely, the peanut butter sticks to the roof of your mouth. (*He munches quietly, idly fingering the bench*) Boy, the PTA sure did a good job of painting these benches. (*He looks off to one side*) There's that cute little redheaded girl eating her lunch over there. I wonder what she'd do if I went over and asked her if I could sit and have lunch with her. She'd probably laugh right in my face. It's hard on a face when it gets laughed in. There's an empty place next to her on the bench. There's no reason why I couldn't just go over and sit there. I could do that right now. All I have to do is stand up. (*He stands*) I'm standing up. (*He sits*) I'm sitting down. I'm a coward. I'm so much of a coward she wouldn't even think of looking at me. She hardly ever does look at me. In fact, I can't remember her ever looking at me. Why shouldn't she look at me? Is there any reason in the world why she shouldn't look at me? Is she so great and am I so small that she couldn't spare one little moment just to . . . (*He freezes*) She's looking at me. (*In terror he looks one way, then another*) She's looking at me. (*In terror he looks one way, then another*) She's *looking* at me.

(His head looks all around, frantically trying to find something also to notice. His teeth clench. Tension builds. Then, with one motion, he pops the paper bag over his head. LUCY and PATTY enter)

LUCY. No, Patty, you're thinking of that other dress, the one I wore to Lucinda's party. The one I'm talking about was this very light blue one and had a design embroidered around the waist.

PATTY. I don't remember that dress.

LUCY. *(Takes a pencil and draws matter-of-factly on the bottom of the paper bag)* Something like this. The skirt went out like this and it had these puffy sleeves and a sash like this.

PATTY. Oh yes, I remember.

LUCY. Yes, well *that* was the dress I was wearing last week when I met Frieda and she told me she'd seen one just like it over at . . . *(The girls have exited. CHARLIE BROWN sits immobile as their voices fade)*

CHARLIE BROWN. *(The paper bag still pulled over his head)* Lunchtime *is* among the worst times of the day for me . . . . . .

Selected Lines by William Shakespeare

Let me have men about me that are fat,
Sleek-headed men, and such as sleep a-nights.
Yond Cassius has a lean and hungry look.
He thinks too much. Such men are dangerous.
  Julius Caesar, Act. 1, Scene 2, 192–195

All the world's a stage,
And all the men and women merely players.
They have their exits and their entrances;
And one man in his time plays many parts.
  As You Like It, Act. 2, Scene 7, 139–142

To-morrow, and to-morrow, and to-morrow,
Creeps in this petty pace from day to day,
To the last syllable of recorded time;
And all our yesterdays have lighted fools
The way to dusty death. Out, out, brief candle!
Life's but a walking shadow, a poor player
That struts and frets his hour upon the stage
And then is heard no more: it is a tale
Told by an idiot, full of sound and fury,
Signifying nothing.
  Macbeth, Act 5, Scene 5, 19–28

Good name in man and woman, dear my lord,
Is the immediate jewel of their souls;
Who steals my purse steals trash; 'tis something, nothing;
'Twas mine, 'tis his, and has been slave to thousands
But he that filches from me my good name
Robs me of that which not enriches him
And makes me poor indeed.
  Othello, Act 2, Scene 3, 155–161

■ ■ SPOTLIGHT ON TERMS ■ ■

An important part of theatre is understanding the terminology, or vocabulary, used. Add the new terms and definitions to the vocabulary section of your theatre notebook or folder.

■ ■ FOCUS ON FACTS ■ ■

1. Why is it important to be relaxed before speaking and moving onstage?
2. How is everyday breathing different from breathing onstage?
3. Which voice element makes the sound of your voice different from all other voices?
4. List three articulators that help you shape and mold sounds.
5. Who or what is the authority on the pronunciation of a word?
6. Explain the difference between diction, dialect, and accent.
7. What is inflection? Why do you need to use it onstage?
8. Discuss the importance of control in using vocal elements effectively onstage.

■ ■ REFLECTIONS ■ ■

Discuss the following questions with your class or answer them on paper as instructed by your teacher.

1. What areas of your voice need improving?
2. In your opinion, what voice element is the most important? Why?
3. Which drill, exercise, or activity has helped you improve your voice?
4. What good speaking habits have you developed?

■ ■ THEATRE IN YOUR LIFE ■ ■

1. Write five goals you would like to accomplish in improving your voice this year.

2. List three drills, exercises, or activities you will use at home to reach the goals you have set.

■ ■ ENCORE ■ ■

1. After memorizing the following lines from the poem "The Lord Chancellor's Nightmare," by W. S. Gilbert, try using this poem as a 5- to 10-minute warm-up.

The Nightmare

You're a regular wreck with a crick in your neck.
No wonder you snore your head's on the floor.

You've needles and pins from your soles to your shins.
Your flesh is a creep, for your left leg's asleep.

You've a cramp in your toes, a fly on your nose, some fluff
In your lungs, a feverish tongue, a thirst that's intense and a
General sense that you haven't been sleeping in clover.

But the darkness is passed—it's daylight at last. The night
Has been long and ditto-ditto my song. Thank goodness
They are both of them over.

2. Make a list of tunes from Broadway shows or movies that the class can use for warm-ups and exercises for developing and improving the voice for the stage.

CHAPTER

6

Improvisation

Spotlight on Terms

- breaking character
- commedia dell'arte
- conflict
- "curtain"
- "freeze"
- improvisation
- improvise
- role-playing
- scenes

When you and your friends get together, how does the conversation begin? Does one of your friends hand out a written script for you to follow? Probably not. Most conversation occurs spontaneously— without a written sheet of instructions telling you what to say and without rehearsal. When young people gather together, the conversation might begin with "Guess what!" or "Hey, man, what's up?" or "You won't believe what I just saw!"

At home, a conversation might begin when someone in your family asks, "What happened at school today?" At this point, anyone might chime in with a comment. You might tell about forgetting your lunch money; your little sister might tell about getting a perfect score on her spelling test; your older brother might tell about the substitute teacher in his math class.

In theatre, conversation between characters is called dialogue. Usually, the actors use a script—a written copy of the dialogue. But actors can also **improvise** —that is, work without a script. This chapter will introduce you to a style of unrehearsed, unscripted theatre called **improvisation** . In improvisation, the actors bring imaginary circumstances to life through action and dialogue. Thus, improvisation is a form of acting.

improvise
to ad-lib, or invent dialogue and actions without a script or rehearsal.

improvisation
a spontaneous style of theatre using unrehearsed and unscripted acting scenes.

Improvisation

LESSON OBJECTIVES

◆ Understand the process of improvisation.
◆ Improvise action and dialogue in character.
◆ Create theatre through group effort.

Like a dinner-table discussion with your family, an improvisation is a spontaneous, unrehearsed, unscripted dialogue.

scene
(1) a short situation to be acted out, as in improvisation, with a beginning, middle, and end.
(2) a subdivision of an act in a play.

Your first try at improvisation might be like your first ride on a giant roller coaster—a little frightening, but thrilling.

In improvisation, you will be working without a script. You will say whatever comes to mind in response to the dialogue of others. Making up the lines as you go along will be a fun way to learn to "think on your feet." You will discover that the more you listen, the more you can participate, and the easier improvisation will become. Improvisation gives actors the opportunity to work together in an informal way developing and creating characters—personalities different from one's own—before beginning scene work. It is also an excellent way to develop concentration, exercise imagination, and become more self-confident while at the same time learning some acting fundamentals.

Listening and responding, two good acting fundamentals, can be learned through improvisation. Actors must learn to listen to each other and to respond to what is being said. These fundamentals are keys to clear, understandable improvisations.

Besides being a good training tool for the actor, improvisation is really fun. In the beginning, the scenes, or short situations, may seem a little silly. Feeling silly can come from being nervous about a first-time experience. Whenever we try something new, we get jittery or afraid. This happens because we want to present a good image in front of our friends and we don't want to "goof up."

Think back to when you were learning to swim or trying to ride a bicycle or stand up on roller skates. If you are like most people, those first attempts weren't easy, but they were fun and exciting. Taking a risk and trying new experiences helps you develop confidence and pride.

Remember the thrill of riding an exciting amusement park ride for the first time? Improvisation is something like that. Relax and try to remember that this is a learning experience, not a performance. Eventually, you and your classmates will enjoy listening to the strange dialogues that just "pop out" spontaneously.

Now think of what you would say if your teacher said any of the following lines:

"I can't believe you are late to my class again."

"I'm afraid you didn't pass the test."

"Why is your homework late?"

Good job! You have just thought of dialogue to use in an improvisation. Try saying your lines aloud. Now that you see how easy it is to think up dialogue, you're ready to learn some additional information about creating improvisations.

Parts of an Improvisation

The basic story line of a well-constructed improvisation includes a beginning, a middle, and an end. These are the same basic parts you will find in every story, movie, or play (see Figure 6–1).

The beginning should introduce the audience to the cast of characters, establish the setting for the scene, or situation, and set up the conflict. The **conflict**, or problem, is the obstacle that the characters must overcome. Opening dialogue should prepare the audience for the scene by letting them know what happened before the scene began.

In the second part of the improvisation, the conflict becomes more complicated as each character establishes what he or she wants or needs. Here it is important for the characters to establish their wants and needs through clearly defined actions and revealing dialogue. The audience must believe the characters and understand their relationships to each other.

The end is the third part of the improvisation. Here the characters solve the problem and conclude the scene.

conflict

the problem or obstacles a literary character must overcome. Often a struggle between opposing forces.

Figure 6–1

■ ■ ■ ■ ■ ■ ■ ■ ■ ■ ■ ■ ■ ■

Three Basic Parts of an Improvisation.

BEGINNING
- ◆ Tells the audience what has happened before the scene
- ◆ Introduces the characters
- ◆ Establishes the setting
- ◆ Sets up the conflict or problem

MIDDLE
- ◆ Problem becomes more complicated
- ◆ Characters reveal wants and needs

END
- ◆ Problem is solved
- ◆ The scene comes to an end

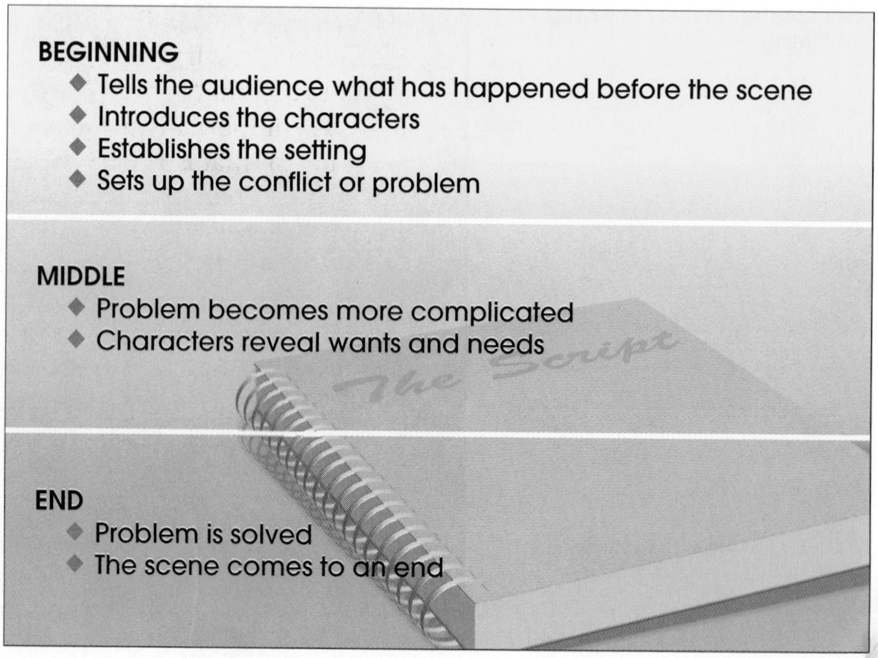

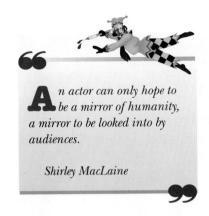

breaking character
losing concentration or
getting out of character. Using
dialogue or behavior
inconsistent with the part you
are creating.

Guidelines for Improvisation

When an improvisation involves working with another person or a group, all the participants need to follow the same guidelines. When the numbered guidelines are used, the improvisation will seem as if it were planned and rehearsed.

1. Before you begin the scene, decide who you are, what you want, and what your relationship is to the other characters. In your early improvisations, you will have very little time to plan or to create an original character. Therefore, you should draw on your memory of real-life characters and imitate them.

2. Once you have established a character in your mind, you need to communicate that character to your audience through your dialogue and actions. Before you begin, make the necessary changes in your own voice and body. Ask yourself several questions before you begin: If you were really the person in this situation, what would you want or need? How would you go about obtaining it? How would you sound? How would you stand or walk? What habits would you have?

3. Try hard to remain the same person during the improvisation. Stay in character. **"Breaking character"** occurs when you say or do something that is inconsistent with the role you are creating. Laughing at yourself or others during a scene is a common form of breaking character. While playing a character with an English accent, if you accidentally use your own voice, you are breaking character. A character's physical traits also need to remain constant. If you create a character with a limp, momentarily forgetting and walking normally is breaking character. If you accidentally break character, get back on track and continue the scene.

4. Begin your dialogue with enthusiasm and confidence.

5. It doesn't really matter who talks first. In scenes with just two characters, you will find it easy to take turns speaking. In larger groups, there will not be a set pattern for the conversation. All of the actors should try hard to participate in the dialogue.

6. It is very important in improvisation to pay attention, listening carefully to what is being said and following what is happening in the scene. Then you can respond appropriately. A rhythm, or pace, will develop once the dialogue and action have begun. This will be much like the tempo of a piece of music. To keep the conversation flowing, concentrate on what is being said, not on yourself. When you really listen to what is being said, you will be surprised how easy it is to think of something to say in response.

7. Remember to keep the dialogue moving. In other words, keep talking. Long periods of silence, unless filled with actions, are boring to the audience. Be especially careful not to dominate the scene by doing all the talking.

8. Avoid "dead-end" words or phrases. Responses such as "No," "Okay," "So?", and "Well?" stop the dialogue. These phrases make it difficult for the other players in the scene to continue the conversation or action. And disagreeing with what your partner

has said with negative responses such as "That's not right," or "No, she's not" makes it difficult to do much more than argue. Another roadblock is to not respond when your partner makes a statement or asks a question. When a member of the improvisation replies with a response such as "Oh?" "Really?" or "What?" build on it and continue the dialogue.

9. Avoid questions that can be answered by "yes" or "no." If you must ask questions, it is much better to ask open-ended questions. A question such as "Why did you come home so late?" would give the other players an easy opening into the conversation.

10. Always look for a way to end the scene. When the natural ending occurs, conclude the scene. Remember, your group is working as an ensemble, so the ending might not be your idea. Part of the fun is finding out what happens to end the scene.

Using Improvisation in Real Life

Many young people participate in behavior that is dangerous or likely to lead to serious consequences: distrust from your parents, a police record, or mention of the incident in your school records. Improvisation can help prepare you for dealing with difficult, even life-threatening situations. Perhaps some of your peers are engaging in self-destructive behavior. When you find yourself caught in an uncomfortable situation, it helps if you have previously acted out courses of action. Some of the situations in this section may lead to classroom discussion. Use your classroom discussion to think of other ways the situation could have been handled. Your class may want to compile a list of other situations for possible improvisations.

ACTION

Follow the guidelines for improvisation in the situations assigned by your teacher. Each scene can be played as a duet or as an ensemble with the entire acting company. Add additional characters to the scene if they are needed.

1. **Sticky Situations**
   a. You and a friend return home from a ball game to find your house locked.
   b. Early on a cold winter morning, the car won't start.
   c. Your mother discovers that she has misplaced the only set of car keys.
   d. You discover that one of your favorite shoes is missing.
   e. You and your friends find yourselves locked in the school building on Friday afternoon.
   f. You and two friends are caught outside the movies in a severe rainstorm.
   g. A newly engaged teacher loses her diamond ring on the school campus. You offer to help her look for the ring.
   h. By accident, your best friend dyes her hair red.
   i. A student you know forgets his lunch money on the first day of school. He asks to borrow money from you.
   j. You are a tough guy who lost your last quarter in the soft drink machine.
   k. Your best friend gives you a tacky gift in front of some peers you would like to impress.
   l. The principal catches you and two other outstanding students skipping class.
   m. You bring the wrong book to the class of the toughest teacher in school.
   n. Your father tells you that you must baby-sit your little sister on the night of the biggest football game of the season.
   o. One of your friends wants to play a trick on the substitute teacher, who happens to be your mom's best friend.
   p. Your friend is wearing a new shirt. While eating in the school cafeteria, you spill red fruit punch on it.

2. **School Situations.** Many situations that occur at school can be the basis for wonderful improvisations. Working with a partner, one of you will play the role of the student; the other will play another character in the scene.
   a. Your locker is stuck.
   b. Your best friend gets the part you wanted in the school play.
   c. You forgot to study for a test.
   d. You lost your lunch money.
   e. You're caught passing notes in class.
   f. You forgot to finish your homework.
   g. The new outfit you are wearing violates the school dress code.
   h. You are a new student who can't find the right classroom.
   i. You didn't make the football team.
   j. You are late to class.
   k. You lose your new jacket the first day you wear it to school.

l. You discover during class that your best friend has invited your boyfriend (or girlfriend) to the movies.

m. You notice that your friend's socks don't match.

n. You dislike math, but the school computer has misprinted your class schedule, and you end up in an advanced math class.

o. You have to make a speech in class, and you are unprepared.

p. You forget part of your costume on the day of the play, and you have to tell the director.

3. Serious Improvisations: What Do I Do Now?

a. While on a school-sponsored trip, your friend decides to walk out of a restaurant without paying the check. You are confronted by the trip sponsor.

b. Your friend, who has been caught smoking in school several times, asks you to hold her cigarettes so that she won't get caught again.

c. A new friend hangs around with a group of teenagers who are known to get in trouble. Your friend invites you to join the group after school.

d. Your friend's mother appears to have been drinking when she picks you and your friend up after a party. She insists on driving you home.

e. While on a school trip, someone hides alcohol in your luggage. You get caught.

f. Two seemingly nice guys you've just met offer to buy you and your friend pizza after the movies.

g. A new car in the parking lot at school belongs to a teacher you dislike. Your friend suggests that you scratch the car with a key to get back at the teacher.

h. You are alone at your house. Two of your friends stop by to visit. Your parents do not allow you to entertain guests unless they are home.

i. You share a locker in the gym with a very popular athlete. You open the locker one morning and discover a small plastic bag with something in it that looks suspicious.

j. Your friend wants you to slip out of your bedroom window after your parents are asleep.

k. You and your friend notice an expensive camera lying on the backseat of an unlocked car. Your friend would really like to have the camera.

l. While spending the night at a friend's house, one of your friends produces a can of spray paint and a paper bag to get high.

m. You and your date arrive at a party and discover that the host is serving alcohol. Everyone at the party is a minor.

n. Your group suggests writing hate letters to a foreign exchange student, threatening what you will do if he doesn't go back home.

o. When the boy next to you in class opens his backpack, you see what you think is a switchblade.

p. A classmate offers you some prescription medicine for your headache.

q. Several times your friend comes to school with unexplained bruises. You suspect abuse.

r. An extremely thin friend who sits with you in the school cafeteria never eats lunch, yet constantly complains of how fat she is. You suspect that she has an eating disorder.

s. Your cousin has been slipping out of the house in the middle of the night and driving the family car around town. He doesn't have a driver's license.

t. One of your friends has the teacher's answers to your math textbook. He offers you the answers.

u. You and a friend are hanging out at the mall, and your friend decides to shoplift a CD from one of the shops. He asks you to watch for the manager.

v. Your friend has just been dumped by his girlfriend. He doesn't think life is worth living.

w. When you walk down the hall at school, a certain group of students leer at you, shouting "catcalls." You are uncomfortable.

x. Your friend has no rules at his house, and your parents won't allow you to spend the night. Your friend is having a big party, and you want to attend.

y. A group of your friends is going to meet at a local park to gang up on a group from another school. You best friend wants you to be there.

z. When you are absent from school, your best friend "shares your secret" with the teacher.

4. **Opening Lines.** A common problem in improvisation is thinking of an opening line. Your teacher will assign partners for this activity. One of you will begin with the opening line; the other will continue the dialogue.
   a. "I can't believe you said that."
   b. "Where did you get that?"
   c. "I have a date with John Saturday night!"
   d. "That's mine!"
   e. "How could you doubt me?"
   f. "Stay here! I'm going to call the wrecker."
   g. "What is that supposed to mean?"
   h. "Wait for me!"
   i. "How can you be so insensitive?"
   j. "I told you to pick that up!"
   k. "So, does that mean we have to do this assignment?"
   l. "I need to talk to you."
   m. "Did you really believe him?"
   n. "Tell me one more time."
   o. "Lower your voice."
   p. "What do you mean, I have to leave?"

5. **Creating Endings.** Thinking of appropriate endings for improvisations takes lots of experience. Try working with a partner to create a situation that could end with one of these final statements.
   a. "You're grounded!"
   b. "Aw, Mom!"
   c. "I love you, too."
   d. "For the life of me, I cannot imagine."
   e. "Good night!"
   f. "Stay here! I'm going to call the fire truck."
   g. "Don't be like that!"
   h. "You're not getting a puppy, and that's final."
   i. "I'll meet you at McDonald's."
   j. "Thank you so much. You're a lifesaver."
   k. "What about your mom?"
   l. "Very nice!"
   m. "Look what you did!"
   n. "Well, if you need anything, just ask."
   o. "I'm really sorry."

Commedia dell'arte

Commedia dell'arte was a form of improvisational theatre that began during the Renaissance, in the early sixteenth century. Troupes of actors toured the Italian countryside performing anywhere they could find an audience.

Each troupe had a set of stock characters, familiar characters, who appeared in most plays. Characters such as *Pantalone*, an old man, *Arlecchino* or *Harlequin*, the clever prankster, and *Pulchinello*, the malicious servant, are examples of exaggerated stock characters. These comic characters were easy for the viewers to identify dressed in their leather masks or half masks and special costumes. Other characters such as the young hero, the heroine, and the *fontesca*, a serving maid, were unmasked.

Hero

The plot for the story was usually based around the lives of the young hero and heroine, who were very much in love. Problems occurred when the heroine's grumpy old father tried to hamper their romance. The *zanni*, male servants, and the Fontessa, created comedy by helping or hindering the couple's courtship.

Performers in the commedia dell'arte memorized a basic outline for the action; however, dialogue was improvised, created on the spot without a script. Audiences in the 1500s enjoyed this style of theatre and were always eager to watch a performance. ■

Pierrot

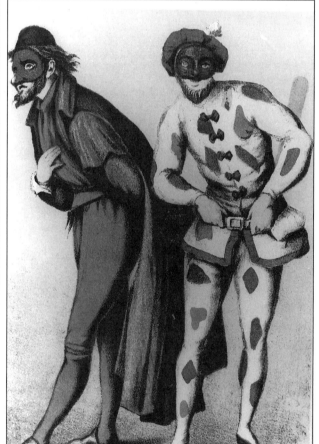

Pantalone and *Harlequin*

Role-Playing

LESSON OBJECTIVES

◆ Develop skill in improvising action and dialogue.
◆ Identify experiences from other classes to role-play.

Warm Up

Discuss with your class specific historical events that have been altered or influenced by the role of one person.

role-playing

trying on the role of others, or assuming the part of another person in society.

Try on the roles of these immigrants coming to America. What is each one of them thinking as they view the Statue of Liberty? Are they excited? Fearful? How would you react in their place?

Have you ever wondered what you would have done if you had been at the scene of a famous historical event?

◆ What if you had been a runaway slave trying to find your way to freedom?
◆ What if you had been an early colonist during the winter of 1612?
◆ What if you had been a twelve-year-old seamstress working under terrible conditions in a garment factory during the early 1900s?
◆ What if you had been in Dallas, Texas, watching the parade, the day President Kennedy was assassinated?

You were not there, but you can experience the event through a form of improvisational theatre called role-playing.

Role-playing is taking on the role of a person other than yourself in an improvisation based on a given dramatic situation. Role-playing can help you grow socially. When you "try on" the roles of others, you have the opportunity to discover how they feel and what they want or need. Thinking as someone else helps you to expand your way of looking at things and strengthens your own decision-making skills. Often, the views and opinions you act out will be different from your own. Role-playing allows you to take safe risks with thoughts and ideas in order to establish your own set of values and beliefs.

ACTION

1. **Bringing History to Life.** Think about some of the historical events you have learned about in social studies or history, or look through your history book. Make a list of characters and circumstances that could be acted out. How could these scenes be re-created through role-playing? Select a character to portray in one of the situations. Remember to create the attitudes, voices, and actions that the real people would have experienced.

2. **Historical Scenes.** Invite social studies or history classes to suggest or outline different historical scenes based on their units of study.

3. **Presenting History to History Class.** Prepare the scenes as you would an improvisation. Invite the social studies or history classes to watch the scenes and judge them for authenticity.

LESSON 3

Point of View

LESSON OBJECTIVES

◆ Develop skill in improvising action and dialogue.
◆ Confront various personal behaviors through role-playing and role reversal.
◆ Demonstrate attitude changes and various viewpoints through role-playing.

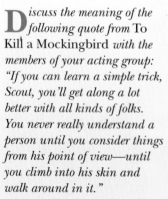

Warm Up

Discuss the meaning of the following quote from To Kill a Mockingbird *with the members of your acting group:* "If you can learn a simple trick, Scout, you'll get along a lot better with all kinds of folks. You never really understand a person until you consider things from his point of view—until you climb into his skin and walk around in it."

The way we think, feel, or act is called a point of view. Our personal point of view toward a person or situation is determined by who we are and also by where we are in our lives. Our needs and desires also influence the way we view a situation. A three-year-old who wants a dog would view the animal simply as a plaything and would not see the responsibilities that go along with having a pet. You, too, might want a dog, but because you are older, you would understand the expenses and responsibilities that are involved.

When we have the opportunity to think and act like someone else, we should consider, or evaluate, the situation from another point of view. A father being transferred to a job in a different city would have different needs, desires, and responsibilities than the other members of the family. If you were playing the role of the father, you would have to think about the situation from his point of view. In acting out the role, you would use appropriate dialogue and actions that would reflect his viewpoint to the audience. Acting out situations from different points of view helps you to become more sensitive and understanding as problems are confronted and worked out.

ACTION

1. Exploring Different Points of View. To explore different points of view, try acting out some situations. By playing more than one role in each scene, you will be challenged to extend your own point of view.

Work with your class to establish characters with four very different viewpoints for each situation given. Work with your acting company to select one of the scenes to play, or try one your teacher suggests. Next, decide who will play each role.

Prepare a sign for each viewpoint by writing the character's name on a 12-by-4-inch piece of poster board with colored markers. Punch one hole at each end of the sign. Run approximately 10 inches of yarn through the holes to create a hanging sign. Wearing these signs will help the players maintain their particular point of view.

Begin the scene when your teacher or a member of your group calls **"curtain."** The scene should begin with each player acting "in character." Each participant in the scene should try to stand, sit, walk, talk, and respond as suggested by the character's point of view. When your teacher calls **"freeze,"** all dialogue and action should stop. Then each sign will be passed one character to the right. After the signs are exchanged, the dialogue must continue with the viewpoints established by the four beginning characters. After all participants have explored the four roles, the scene should draw to an appropriate conclusion. If an ending cannot be reached, your teacher will verbally terminate the scene by calling out "curtain."

Here are some suggested scenes to play. Four different viewpoints are given for the first scene. For each of the remaining scenes, work with your group to develop viewpoints for each character.

a. A student has not been turning in her homework. The teacher calls a conference with the parent and the principal.
  - The student thinks that the teacher doesn't like her because the teacher keeps "nagging" her about the homework.
  - The single parent, working two jobs, wants her daughter to pass.
  - The teacher, who really cares, wants to give the student another chance.
  - The tough, authoritarian principal thinks the student needs more discipline at home.

b. A teenager has abused her phone privileges. A family discussion includes the parent, a nosy neighbor, the teenager, and a younger sibling.

c. A student who has just moved from a small town to a large city is having a hard time adjusting to the new school environment. The principal and a concerned teacher call the new student in for a conference and invite a popular, well-adjusted student to make suggestions.

d. A teenager has stayed out past curfew. He arrives home to find his mother, grandmother, and kid sister worried and "waiting up."

e. A star athlete's grades are extremely low in science class. To stay on the track team, he must raise his grades. He is thinking of cheating on a major test. He discusses the situation with an older brother who dropped out of school, a classmate who cheats often, and his best friend, who is in the National Honor Society and would never cheat on a test, no matter what the circumstances.

"curtain"

a verbal command starting or ending a scene.

"freeze"

a verbal command given by the director to stop the dialogue and movement in a scene.

Curtain Call!

CHAPTER 6 REVIEW

■ ■ SPOTLIGHT ON TERMS ■ ■

An important part of theatre is understanding the terminology, or vocabulary, used. Add the new terms and definitions to the vocabulary section of your theatre notebook or folder.

■ ■ FOCUS ON FACTS ■ ■

1. In theatre, what is conversation between actors called?
2. What is improvisation?
3. What are the three parts of an improvisation? What should happen in each part?
4. What is meant by "breaking character"?
5. In improvisation, what are "dead-end" phrases? How can you avoid them?
6. When do you end an improvisation?
7. What is role-playing?
8. What is a point of view?

■ ■ REFLECTIONS ■ ■

Discuss the following questions with your class or answer them on paper as instructed by your teacher.

1. What did you learn about the needs and feelings of each of the characters you portrayed?
2. Which roles were the most difficult to portray? Why?
3. Which roles were the easiest to portray? Why?
4. What were some strong points of the improvisations?
5. How did your viewpoints change as you changed characters?
6. If you could play one of your scenes again, which scene would you choose? What would you do differently?

■ ■ THEATRE IN YOUR LIFE ■ ■

Discuss aloud or as a journal entry in your theatre notebook the ways improvisation and role-playing help you in real-life situations.

■ ■ ENCORE ■ ■

1. Work with your acting company to create an improvisational scene based on a popular television sitcom. Use classroom furniture to create a set for the show. Act out the situation, trying to portray the characters as realistically as they appear on television. When each acting company has completed its scene, discuss the similarities and differences between the classroom show and the television show.

   If your class has access to a video camera, it would be worthwhile to film the scenes and later view the tape as if you were watching a televised program. As a class, watch and analyze the videotaped class sitcoms. Discuss with your class the changes that are needed in each scene to create a program as believable as "real" television. As a result of videotaping your improvisation, what have you learned about acting for television?

2. Create a new language for improvisation using only the letters of the alphabet. The dialogue "Are you going with me?" might become "A bcd kyz oe mni?" Avoid spelling out real words. This technique, sometimes called "gibberish," uses silly sounds to help you focus on *the way* you speak rather than on what you say. Concentrate on staying in character as you replay the Action activities in this chapter using gibberish.

3. Here are some additional scenes for practicing the development of different viewpoints as you did in the activity on the preceding page.
   a. A doctor discusses a father's need for a kidney transplant with the father, the son, and the grandmother. The grandmother and the son are possible donors.
   b. Three friends are walking to school when they are approached by a drug dealer who has an easy way for them to make some quick cash.
   c. An eighth-grade girl who lives with her grandparents wants to attend the high school homecoming dance with a tenth-grade boy. Her brother knows that the boy has been in trouble with the law.

7 Characterization

Chapter Outline

Spotlight on Terms

- analyze
- characterization
- first person
- mannerisms
- monologue
- soliloquy
- stereotypical character
- stock character

characterization

developing and portraying a personality through thought, action, dialogue, costuming, and makeup.

The pretending that you did when you were younger was the first step you took toward learning characterization.

Pretending to be someone else is a game that most of us have played. Perhaps you have seen your younger brothers or sisters act out characters as they play with their action figures or dolls. Most of us have participated in this form of characterization we call pretending. In the theatre, however, **characterization** involves more than just pretending to be a character in a scene or play. It also involves making others believe that you are someone else. Whether you have created your own original character or are portraying a role written by a playwright, your job as an actor is to make the character real for the audience.

One of the most exciting parts of theatre is to have the opportunity to "try on" and experiment with different characters. Professional actors know that there are techniques they can use to make the characters they play seem real. These trained actors know that their inner thoughts and outward actions work together to develop a character that the audience believes is real. Actors find it is enjoyable, yet challenging, to use the mind, face, body, and voice to think, talk, act, and react like someone else.

Improvisation activities have given you a foundation for portraying different characters. Now you will participate in activities that will help you understand how to develop a believable character. The characters that you create in this chapter will be based not only on your imagination but on all the characters you have ever met—in books, in movies, on television, and in real life.

Stock Characters and Stereotypical Characters

LESSON OBJECTIVES

◆ Understand the process of characterization.
◆ Begin to create stock and stereotypical characters.

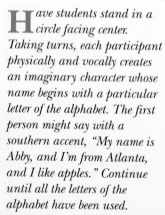

Warm Up

Have students stand in a circle facing center. Taking turns, each participant physically and vocally creates an imaginary character whose name begins with a particular letter of the alphabet. The first person might say with a southern accent, "My name is Abby, and I'm from Atlanta, and I like apples." Continue until all the letters of the alphabet have been used.

Sometimes when you watch a play, movie, or television program, you recognize a character type and automatically know how that character will act. Many of the popular 30-minute situation comedies on television have character types that are easy to recognize. These character types are known as stock characters and stereotypical characters.

Stock Characters

A **stock character** is a familiar character who is the same type of character in every play. Stock characters were an important part of the commedia dell'arte style of theatre. The audiences of the 1500s quickly identified each character based on what they had seen the character do or say in previous plays. Characters such as the villain, the hero, the

clever servant, the fool, and the heroine were expected to appear in play after play, always looking and acting the same way.

Stereotypical Characters

stereotypical character
a familiar character identified by an oversimplified pattern of behavior that typically labels the character as being part of a group of people.

Another type of character we often see played by beginning actors is the stereotypical character. A **stereotypical character** is a familiar type of character whose tag, or label, identifies a particular group or segment of society. If the labels "politician," "cheerleader," "television evangelist," and "jock" automatically bring to mind visual images, then those particular character types have probably become stereotyped for you. The stereotypical picture that many of us have of a grandmother is a gray-haired old lady wearing sturdy shoes and a knitted shawl. But how many grandmothers do you know who fit this picture?

When creating characters, it is important to avoid negative ideas concerning occupation, race, gender, age, ethnic heritage, or religion. Negative stereotypes result when groups of people or individuals are misrepresented in a discriminatory or prejudicial way.

Beginning actors find stock and stereotypical characters an easy starting point, choosing to portray characters from books, plays, and movies. If you re-create the role of the class clown, the helpful policeman, the spoiled brat, or the teenage bully, you have an idea of what to do and how to act, because you have seen these characters played many times before.

Think of the way you would use your body and face to physically create a frozen statue of these modern stock and stereotypical characters:

psychiatrist	secret agent
handsome movie star	clumsy waiter
cowboy/hero	photographer
rich socialite	district attorney
miserly businessman	traffic cop

secretary	bellhop
nanny	cab driver
baby-sitter	butler
newspaper reporter	flight attendant
writer/poet	mad scientist
gangster	stern teacher
dentist	surgeon
short-order cook	rock star
gorgeous fashion model	snoopy neighbor
strict school principal	nurse
private detective	clown
military officer	librarian

ACTION

1. Trying on Characters

a. Take turns moving around a chair or walking around the room as your teacher calls out the various character types from the preceding list. Notice how you and your classmates change physically and mentally each time a new character is assigned.

b. Select one of the characters from the list. Write down the way you would walk, talk, and act as that character. Give yourself a name, occupation, hometown, and reason for visiting the classroom. Become the character as you walk to the front of the classroom or to the center of the acting area. In character, introduce yourself to the class.

c. Working with a partner, improvise the meeting of two of the characters from the list. Talk and act as if the characters were meeting in one of the following places:

at the grocery store	at a laundromat
in a shopping mall	on another planet
in the school cafeteria	in a haunted house
on an airplane	on a television talk show
on a desert island	at a trial
at an amusement park	at the beauty/barber shop
in the principal's office	

Creating Original Characters

LESSON OBJECTIVES

◆ Use observation, emotional memory, and imagination in creating original characters.
◆ Develop skill portraying the physical attributes of characters.

As you continue your study of characterization, you will move beyond stock and stereotypical characters to ones you create on your own. In this lesson, we will concentrate on creating original characters.

Observation—*Your teacher will divide your class into pairs. After observing each other for at least 1 minute, each student will write a detailed description of his or her partner on a 3-by-5-inch index card. Your teacher will then collect the cards and pass them out at random. Each student will read aloud the card received and attempt to identify the student described.*

> **A**n actor's art is like a beggar's bag . . . he should pick up everything he comes across.
>
> Sakata Tojuro

If you are like most people, you frequently find yourself in large crowds, such as you see here. Next time, pick out different individuals in the crowd and observe them carefully.

Observation

One of the most important skills you can develop is the ability to observe real people. Observing real people in real situations will help you develop original characters. Your purpose in observing is to "collect" as many different qualities as you can. As you begin to "people watch," your memory bank will become a virtual storehouse for all the wonderful ideas you will collect. By borrowing bits and pieces from many different characters, you can actually create a whole new being. You will then use your own mind, voice, face, body, and imagination to give your own interpretation of the character, making the character come alive for your audience.

It is a good idea to record in a notebook the different ideas that you collect from your observations and relationships with real people. Then when you need to create an original character for class, you can refer to your notebook. You might choose to speak with the British accent you heard on television but walk and move like the man you see every week in the grocery store. Your character's unconscious habits of pushing up her glasses and shifting from foot to foot could be the same unconscious gestures you observed your history teacher use.

External Characteristics

When you observe people, you will first notice their outwardly visible qualities, or external characteristics. Suppose that a new student comes to your class. What is the first thing that you notice? Appearance, of course! Now look at your classmates. What are the different components of their appearance? Your answer probably includes age, gender, height, weight, hair color, skin tone, manner of dress, and degree of attractiveness.

The Elizabethan Age

In England, the Renaissance is known as *The Elizabethan Age.* This period was named after the powerful English ruler Queen Elizabeth I, who ruled Great Britain for forty-five years, from 1558 to 1603. Elizabeth's reign began a period of English history during which language and literature flourished. At the heart of the English Renaissance was the love of language and the art of theatre.

Several developments during Elizabeth's reign helped the theatre to thrive. As one example, acting changed from an amateur to a professional status. The citizens who had performed the medieval religious plays and the plays in the homes of nobility were replaced by companies of professional actors who played regularly around London and throughout the country. This development gave playwrights a more stable and experienced group of performers for whom to write more detailed and complicated plays.

Along with this rise in the profession of acting came the building of permanent theatres, public buildings where all classes of people could attend performances. These permanent buildings began to replace the temporary stages that had been set up in the town squares or in cathedral yards. The new theatre buildings created spaces dedicated specifically to the presentation of theatrical events.

Because of the church's earlier policy, which looked at all theatre that was not religious in nature as an evil activity, the city of London did not permit theatre buildings to be erected inside the city limits. Therefore, the permanent theatres so popular during the Elizabethan period were located outside the city, across the Thames River, and audience members had to leave the city to see a play. The audience knew that a play was going to be presented at one of the theatres across the river by seeing a flag fly from high atop the theatre, which was the signal that there would be a performance that day. Of these theatre spaces, the most famous was the Globe Theatre, which was the location for the presentation of Shakespeare's plays.

Most Elizabethan theatres were circular or octagonal structures of about three stories, with an open roof. We know that the Globe was such a building.

The raised platform stage was surrounded by the audience on three sides, and was closer to a contemporary thrust stage than to a proscenium arch stage, which was so popular at this same period in time in Italy. Behind the platform stage was a stage house, known as a *tiring house,* which served as a backdrop

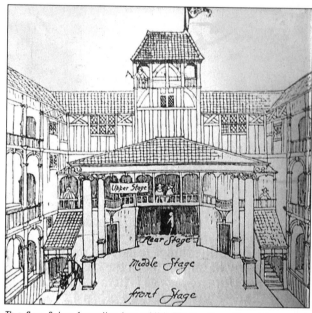

The flag flying from the top of this Elizabethan theatre meant that a play was to be presented that day.

for the action. This structure served as backstage space for changing and storing costumes and props and the few scenic pieces used in the productions. At the back of the platform was an area called the *inner stage,* a roofed area that could be separated from the front of the platform to suggest an interior setting. Above this, on the roof of the inner stage, was a second playing space, a sort of balcony where some of the scenes might be played. This was, no doubt, where Shakespeare's famous balcony scene in *Romeo and Juliet* would have been played. There was a third level of platforming above this balcony stage space, which was called the *musicians' gallery,* where a small group of musicians might be stationed to provide music during the play. There was usually a roof coming out from the top of the stage house to

Historical and Cultural Perspectives

The Elizabethans loved to go to the theatre. In this artist's rendering of an Elizabethan production of Shakespeare's *A Midsummer Night's Dream* you can see that the least expensive seats actually meant no seats at all. How would you feel about standing up through an entire play?

times, a character might signal the next location by announcing it in the early lines of the scene. This type of signal to the audience is called *spoken decor.* Language was important in Elizabethan plays in all respects, even scenery!

Another noted feature of Elizabethan drama was the use of poetry. Christopher Marlowe (1564–1593) was one of the first playwrights to utilize a special type of dramatic poetry called *iambic pentameter,* which is written to contain five beats or stress points per line. Words in iambic pentameter have two syllables to each beat and when spoken, stress is placed upon the second beat. This makes the language almost musical in nature.

By far the most important playwright during this period was William Shakespeare, whom you will read about later in this book. ■

protect the various layers of playing space from direct sunlight or rain.

The form of the English plays written in this period was different from the plays being written in Italy and on the European continent. The English did not follow the new neoclassical ideal (which required their plays to observe strict unities of time, place, and action). Instead, the English dramas of the period were structured in a series of brief scenes, which frequently changed location from place to place. These quick shifts in action required that the Elizabethans adopt a much freer use of stage space. They didn't use the perspective painting and wings used by the Italians. Instead, the Elizabethan stage was an open platform with little or no scenery placed on it. This platform was a neutral playing area, which could become many different locations in the same play. When one group of characters left the stage and another group entered, the audience knew that the scene was changing. An actor might carry on a single piece of furniture to suggest the location of the next scene. A throne, for example, might indicate a palace setting; a table and a few props might indicate a dining hall. At other

Notice the sparse set in this modern-day recreation of an Elizabethan drama. Elizabethan theatre-goers were accustomed to using their imaginations to visualize the play's settings.

> *An actor should be observant not only on the stage but also in real life.*
>
> *Konstantin Stanislavski*

mannerisms

unconscious habits or peculiarities.

Next, notice the posture and stance of the students in your class. Do they stand tall and straight or slouched and slumped? What about the way they sit? Do you notice any particularly interesting forms of posture?

Watch as your classmates move around the room. Everyone moves with a unique rhythm. One student might move at a frantic pace, while another might bounce or glide from place to place. These movements can be imitated as you develop your original characters.

Take special note of interesting habits. When simple behaviors such as nail biting, raising an eyebrow, or twisting a lock of hair are unconsciously repeated, they are called **mannerisms** . Certain mannerisms may become associated with a particular character. Whenever we see that character, we expect to see the familiar mannerisms as well.

Vocalization

Once you have developed your original character, you will want to be sure that the character can come alive vocally. A character's voice is easier to discover after you have established the external and internal characteristics. Actors need to be able to adapt their own voices to reflect a character's external and internal characteristics.

As a student actor, you will want to listen to as many different voices as possible. For each voice, notice the quality and tone, the patterns of speech, and the accent or dialect. The illusion of a character can be totally lost if the character's voice is not suitable. For example, if you have created an authoritarian, masterful character who dominates everyone around her, you will want your character to have an appropriately powerful voice to go along with her personality. A deep, brusque voice might be more believable to the audience than a soft, sweet voice.

Listen to teachers, friends, television personalities, and public figures to hear the special qualities in each voice. As you listen to differ-

Have you seen the famous Christmas movie *It's a Wonderful Life* with Jimmy Stewart? Watch this movie, then discuss with your classmates the ways that this famous actor makes his character's internal characteristics apparent. Does his voice contribute to his characterization?

ent voices, take notes about the way they sound. Professional actors often work with recordings of dialects and accents to achieve vocal variety, master a particular vocal quality or tone, and build a collection of voices. Many actors study for years with vocal coaches or voice teachers to enhance their voices.

Internal Characteristics

Learning about a character is like opening a present. Regardless of the size of the package or the way it is wrapped, you never really know what is inside until you open it and take a good look. As we get to know a person or a character, we discover that there is more involved than just the outside packaging, or external characteristics. Your goal as an actor is to look beyond one-dimensional stock or stereotypical characters and create a character who is complex and three-dimensional.

The dimension, or depth, of a character is based on what's inside the character. In addition to thinking about how your character looks, you also need to think about your character's inner qualities—the internal characteristics. These internal qualities include every aspect of the character's identity: background and life experiences, personality, intelligence, educational opportunities, personal interests, job or occupation, and physical, mental, and emotional health. Also included would be the character's place or role in society, as well as beliefs, attitudes and values, and wants and needs.

Desires, thoughts, feelings, reactions—these are all internal characteristics that are revealed as you get to know the character. Getting to know a character is much like becoming friends with a new acquaintance: It takes time and careful study.

In 335 B.C., Aristotle, an important Greek philosopher, defined character as the sum total of an individual's actions. In theatre, it is the actor's responsibility to use words and actions to explain to the audience what the character is doing and why. When the actor is able to think the inner thoughts of a character and react as the character would in a given situation, then the audience is able to see and believe.

ACTION

1. People Watching
   a. Carefully observe your friends, classmates, parents, teachers, and even total strangers for a length of time specified by your teacher. Look for interesting external characteristics to use when creating original characters.
   b. Notice the different ways that people walk, sit, stand, and carry their bodies.
   c. Pay special attention to unusual mannerisms and habits.
   d. Listen, and try to reproduce the different ways that people talk.
   e. Record all of your observations in your theatre notebook.

2. Building a Character
   a. Physically and vocally build an original character, putting together the bits and pieces obtained from your observations of people. Try

walking, sitting, standing, and talking like your original character. Check your original character in front of a mirror to see if you are physically projecting the image you want to convey.

b. On the assigned day, come to class as your original character. At the appropriate time, your teacher will invite you to model your character in front of the class.

c. Discuss with your classmates the value of observation and "people watching" when developing a character's external characteristics.

3. **Character Improvisations.** Working with a partner, use your observations of real people to develop and perform believable characters in one or more of the following improvisational situations.

   a. A daughter tells her elderly mother that she has to move to a nursing home because the daughter can no longer care for her mother at home.

   b. There are two survivors at the scene of an airline crash.

   c. The principal tells a first-year teacher that her discipline in the classroom is ineffective.

   d. A surgeon must tell his patient that he has an incurable disease.

   e. Two waitresses discuss the manager, who is misusing the restaurant's money.

   f. Two elderly people are bird-watching in a city park.

   g. A woman's fiancé has just given her a diamond ring that she suspects is fake.

   h. A very shy girl is asked to the dance by the school's most popular boy.

   i. A wife encourages her overweight husband to go on a diet before his high school reunion.

   j. A bellhop delivers numerous pieces of luggage to a hotel room, and the businessman gives him a $1 tip.

   k. The president of the United States and his head of security must decide how to respond to a threat on the president's life.

   l. A young bride serves a less-than-desirable meal to her husband.

   m. A couple are dividing up the property during a divorce settlement, and they can't decide who gets the vacuum cleaner.

   n. After an unsuccessful weekend of fishing, an inexperienced fisherman attempts to purchase fish from an old man who has a plentiful catch.

   o. A teenager backs into a new car in the parking lot. The driver of the other car is hard of hearing.

   p. While in the veterinarian's office, two pet owners brag about the talents of their cats.

   q. A judge sentences a pickpocket to 3,000 hours of community service.

   r. An airline reservation clerk is unable to find a reservation for an impatient businesswoman trying to get to Chicago.

   s. On the afternoon of the prom, a hairdresser cuts a teenager's hair too short. The teenager becomes hysterical.

   t. An elderly man and an elderly woman meet on an airplane and compare grandchildren.

   u. A receptionist refuses to allow an impatient customer to see her boss.

   v. A husband tells his ill wife that he has lost his job.

Writing Original Monologues

LESSON OBJECTIVES

◆ Use analysis in developing a character.
◆ Write a monologue revealing the innermost thoughts of an original character.
◆ Perform a monologue using vocal and physical characterization.
◆ Perform a monologue using appropriate staging techniques.

Warm Up

Do you ever express your thoughts aloud, even when no one is around to listen? Think about some of the advantages and disadvantages of talking to yourself.

monologue

a long speech spoken by one person, revealing personal thoughts and feelings.

soliloquy

a monologue usually delivered while the character is alone onstage, thinking aloud.

analyze

to study carefully or examine critically.

Playwrights sometimes use monologues to help the audience understand the thoughts and emotions of a character. A **monologue** in dramatic literature is a long speech spoken by one character, usually revealing the character's personal thoughts and feelings. The use of the monologue in drama dates back to the ancient Greeks. A monologue can be delivered with or without other characters on the stage.

A **soliloquy** is a monologue in which a character is thinking aloud, usually alone onstage. The soliloquy is used throughout the plays of William Shakespeare. Hamlet's famous "to be or not to be" speech is a good example.

Performing an original monologue gives the theatre student an excellent opportunity to **analyze** a particular character, studying it carefully and critically, and then to share the character at a particular moment in time with the audience. Writing an original monologue is a good first step in the playwriting process.

There are many reasons for writing an original monologue. Some students really enjoy the writing process and look forward to using that skill in theatre class. Writing for theatre allows us to share our personal thoughts and feelings, to make statements about our beliefs or needs, and to explore another dimension of theatre—the craft of the playwright.

In her workshop Playmaking and Playwriting, Lou-Ida Marsh suggests six ideas leading to a monologue, a scene, or a play:

1. things we have done or not done in our own lives
2. people we have met, known, loved, hated, feared, or respected
3. ageless stories or myths, perhaps told from a new viewpoint
4. group interaction and artistic collaboration
5. ideas for resolving various conflicts
6. a puzzlement (something we don't understand)

Any of these six ideas could be developed into a dynamic monologue. Which one would you choose?

There are no set rules in playwriting, but some established principles work best. It is important for the audience to know the five Ws (who, what, when, where, and why) as early as possible in the scene or play. The same holds true for your original monologue. Your audience

You may find that you enjoy writing original monologues. Start with a photograph or a single characteristic and let your imagination take over.

should be able to answer the following questions as soon as possible:

◆ Who is speaking to whom?
◆ What is happening?
◆ When is this occurring?

◆ Where is this occurring?
◆ Why is this happening?

Monologue writing is a wonderful way to develop a "life story" for an original character. A good way to start is with a photograph. Your teacher may have a collection of interesting photographs for you to choose from, or you may prefer to bring a few pictures from home. Also, the librarian in your school library may allow you to look

---

The following monologue, from the unpublished work *A Full House*, by Vera Olive, is based on something that the author herself once did. See if you can answer the five Ws from the information provided in the monologue.

THE CIRCUS

I'm so excited! Mama just said if we kids would get our baths and go to bed early, tomorrow all of us would load up the wagon and go to the circus with our cousins from El Dorado. I'd really like to go to a circus. Come to think of it, I've never been to a circus in all of my seven years. I say, Vera McDonald, you're going to bed early tonight because tomorrow you're going to a real live circus!

There are seven of us kids, plus mama and papa, it will be hot and crowded in that wagon, but I don't mind. Mama said we'd take lots of food. It's almost twenty miles to El Dorado. That's the longest trip I've ever made.

And, we'll get to spend the night away from home. I'm glad mama and papa will be with us. Once, my sister Pearle and I spent the night away from home. We stayed at our piano teacher's house, when it was raining so hard we couldn't get home from our piano lessons. Our clothes were so wet, we had to put on Mrs. Muse's big old night gowns and she tied ribbons around the waists to hold them up. After supper she made us a big plate of fudge. It was fun until we were all in bed and I began to get homesick. That was my first night away from home. Pearle said I was just being silly, but I thought that daylight would never come. The next day we had to wear our same clothes to school and our studies seemed like they would never end. By the time we got home, I felt I'd been gone a week. I was really glad to see my mama and papa.

I'm coming mama, I'm going to bed. I don't want to miss that circus.

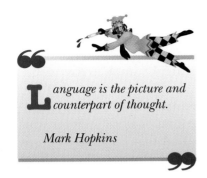

through the discarded magazines and newspapers. Take special note of the interesting photographs of people in articles and advertisements. Select a variety of characters for whom you could create an imaginary story.

Carefully study your collection of photographs. Select one picture to bring to life through characterization. You are now ready to begin your character analysis.

Character Analysis

Use your awareness and imagination to answer the following questions as you develop a background and personality for your chosen character. Answer the questions as if you yourself were really the character.

1. Who are you? What is your name?
2. What is your ethnic background?
3. How would you describe yourself physically? Include your height, weight, facial features, hair color, and skin tone. Also, be sure to note any outstanding physical trait or condition that makes you unique.
4. How would you describe your stance, posture, walk, and movement?
5. What rhythm or tempo do you associate with yourself? Think of a piece of music that would describe yourself. Would the tempo be a waltz, a cha-cha, a march, country swing, or contemporary jazz?
6. What gestures, mannerisms, or habits do you use unconsciously?
7. How do you dress?
8. How do you sound? Describe your voice quality. Is it high or low, nasal or guttural? Do you speak with a drawl, twang, accent, or dialect? Do you make any unusual sounds, such as wheezing or grunting?
9. Think about your background. Where did you grow up? What type of environment shaped your early life? What kind of relationship do you have with your family?
10. Where do you live now? What is your present family status?
11. Think about your intellect. How would you describe your mental capabilities?
12. What is your position in society? Are you rich, poor, important, or powerful?
13. What is your job or occupation?
14. What are your attitudes, values, and beliefs?
15. What is your emotional state?
16. How do you treat other people? How do others treat you?
17. Do you have a secret that you try to hide?
18. What is your greatest want or need?
19. What is the problem or obstacle standing in the way of fulfilling the want or need?
20. To what extent are you willing to go to eliminate the obstacles?
21. What do you enjoy or do for fun?
22. What are you thinking at this moment?
23. What do other people say about you?
24. What phrase or expression do you use frequently?

Lily Tomlin became famous for her comedy monologues as Edith Ann and Ernestine when she appeared on the TV comedy revue *Laugh In*. She still performs monologues before sold-out audiences today.

ACTION

Writing the Monologue

Now that you have completed your character analysis, you can begin to write the thoughts that your character might want to say aloud. Write these thoughts (the monologue) in the **first person**—as if you are the person to whom this story is happening.

Your teacher may want to give you a time limit or word limit for your first monologue. Most beginning students find that they are comfortable memorizing and performing 2 to 3 minutes of speech, or about 200 to 400 words.

Rehearsing and Presenting the Monologue

Prepare for your presentation by memorizing the material you have written. Tape-record your rehearsals and listen carefully to the playback. Are you presenting the character in the way you intended? Hearing a friend read your monologue aloud can sometimes help you with phrasing and emphasis.

When it is your turn to share your monologue, walk to the performance area or to the stage as yourself. If you have planned introductory remarks, they should be delivered as yourself. Pause after the introduction, allowing yourself enough time to physically and mentally take on your characterization. The first words of the monologue should immediately create a picture of your character for your audience. Imagine your character in the setting that you pictured as you wrote the monologue.

If your character is speaking to someone else onstage, also picture that person in your mind. Situate this "listener" downstage, or in front of you, so that you are facing the audience. Once the imaginary listener is placed on the stage, your glances at this character tell the audience a lot about the scene. If the imaginary listener is an adult and the character you are portraying is a child, you would look upward. If the imaginary listener is seated in a chair, you would direct your attention to the level of the listener's eyes.

Remain in character throughout the monologue. Stay onstage, clearly visible to the audience, until after you have completed the final sentence. Pause slightly, allowing the audience time to realize that the scene has ended. Then leave the stage as yourself.

1. **Performance Time.** Practice what you've learned in this lesson as you do each of the following activities:
   a. Perform your original monologue for your class or for an invited audience.
   b. Rehearse a prepared monologue selected from the Playbook in this text or from a book of monologues. Perform the monologue for the class or for an audience.
   c. Adapt a cutting from a novel or short story into a monologue. Prepare and present the monologue before the class.

Curtain Call!

■ ■ SPOTLIGHT ON TERMS ■ ■

An important part of theatre is understanding the terminology, or vocabulary, used. Add the new terms and definitions to your vocabulary list in your theatre notebook or folder.

■ ■ FOCUS ON FACTS ■ ■

1. Explain characterization.
2. Why do beginning actors sometimes choose to portray stock characters?
3. What are negative stereotypes?
4. Why should actors become "people watchers"?
5. Explain the difference between external and internal characteristics.
6. Name five interesting mannerisms you could use in a characterization.
7. How can character analysis help the actor develop a character?
8. What five things should the playwright tell the audience as soon as possible?
9. Explain the difference between monologue and dialogue.
10. Explain the difference between monologue and soliloquy.
11. How should the actor prepare for a monologue performance?
12. Describe the steps an actor uses to effectively perform a monologue.

■ ■ REFLECTIONS ■ ■

Discuss the following questions with your class or answer them on paper as instructed by your teacher.

1. Describe something new that you learned about characterization in this chapter.
2. What part of characterization presented the most challenge for you? Why?
3. What did you learn about the needs and feelings of each of the characters you portrayed?

4. If you had the opportunity to present your original monologue again, what changes would you make? Why?
5. How can you use the processes of character analysis and writing original monologues in other school subjects?
6. Describe the activity that helped you best understand characterization. Why did you select this particular activity?
7. What did the study of characterization teach you about yourself? Was it a pleasant or unpleasant discovery? Why?
8. Is there anything you would like to change about yourself or your acting after studying this chapter on characterization?

■ ■ THEATRE IN YOUR LIFE ■ ■

Discuss aloud or explain in a short journal entry in your theatre notebook how this chapter has helped you have a clearer understanding of yourself and others.

■ ■ ENCORE ■ ■

The following activities are additional opportunities to portray the original character you developed for your monologue.

1. Your teacher will play the on-the-spot news reporter for television station KWHO, broadcasting live from your classroom. Respond in character to the questions addressed to you during the television interview.
2. Create a French restaurant scene in the acting area using a small table and two chairs. Add a tablecloth and flowers to enhance the mood. Because this Paris restaurant is so crowded, the waiter insists that two strangers dine at the same table. By asking questions, the strangers get to know each other. The focus of the questions should reveal character development to the audience.

The Play and Your Part

Chapter Outline

Spotlight on Terms

- act
- antagonist
- business
- climax
- comedy
- cues
- exposition

- melodrama
- plot
- spectacle
- subtext
- theme
- tragedy

I n the previous chapters, you explored activities preparing you to interpret and develop a role from a playwright's script. You used imagination, concentration, observation, sensory recall, and movement to become aware of your personal resources. You used vocal exercises to prepare your voice for creative vocal expression. Improvisation and characterization activities provided opportunities for you to explore simple character portrayal and plot development. All of these activities were preparatory techniques for acting. Now you are ready to bring a character from the written page to the stage.

The Structure of Plays

LESSON OBJECTIVES

◆ Understand the dramatic structure of a play.
◆ Recognize several types of plays.
◆ Understand how a play is organized.

Warm Up

A s a class, play a short game of charades. Use the titles of plays and musicals or the names of famous actors.

Much of an actor's time is spent working from materials written by playwrights. You have probably read plays in your language arts classes. Thus, you probably already know that a play is a story written in dialogue form to be acted out by actors before a live audience as if it were real life.

Other forms of literature, such as short stories and novels, are written in prose form and are not intended to be acted out. Poetry also differs from plays in that poetry is arranged in lines and verses and is not written to be performed.

These students are bringing literature to life in much the same way that Aristotle first described drama over 2,000 years ago.

Plays have distinguishing characteristics that make the style easy to recognize. These characteristics—the way a play is put together—make up what is often called the play's dramatic structure.

The Elements of a Play

The dramatic structure of a play dates back to 335 B.C., when Aristotle described the six basic parts, or elements, of a play. Playwriting has changed through the years, but Aristotle's basic components of *plot, character, thought, diction, song,* and *spectacle* still exist to some extent in all plays. Still, different plays may place more importance on one component than on another. In some plays, plot is the key ingredient. Others might feature spectacle. In still others, song might be the most important feature. Today, many teachers refer to the six basic parts of dramatic structure as *plot, character, theme, language, music,* and *spectacle.*

Plot. Aristotle tells us that the **plot** is the arrangement of the incidents that take place in a play. A plot has three basic parts: the beginning, middle, and end. The beginning introduces the audience to who, what, where, when, and why through revealing information called **exposition**. The middle is composed of a series of complications or conflicts, which result in a **climax**, or turning point. In the final part of the plot, the conflict is resolved and the story ends.

Character. The plot of the play is carried out through the action and dialogue of personalities or figures called *characters*. It is through these characters that the playwright reveals his or her message. The principal character, who represents the main thought of the play, is called the protagonist. Standing in the protagonist's way and opposing the protagonist is a character known as the **antagonist**. All other important characters in the play will side with one of these two characters.

Thought/Theme. Playwrights have an overall meaning, or basic idea, that they wish to get across through the play. This idea, known as the thought or **theme**, ties the characters and events together and gives the play purpose. The theme of a play is usually suggested, or implied, rather than directly stated.

Diction/Language. The playwright tells the story of the play through words, or language. Careful selection of language gives the audience a better understanding of the type of play, the characters, and the plot. The lines of the play and even the stage directions are all considered the language of a play.

Song/Music. During Aristotle's time, Greek plays were chanted or sung, often accompanied by musical instruments. In today's theatre, song, or music, includes the sound and characteristics of the actors' voices, as well as songs, instruments, recorded background music, and even sound effects. These musical elements are used to establish mood and enhance believability in a play.

plot

the arrangement of the incidents that take place in a play.

exposition

detailed information revealing the facts of the plot.

climax

turning point in the action of a play.

antagonist

the character opposing the protagonist.

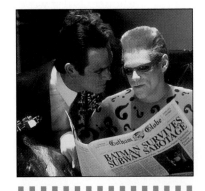

Are these two characters from *Batman Forever* protagonists or antagonists? Even if you didn't see the movie, what clues help you answer the question correctly?

theme

the basic idea or purpose of the play. It ties together all the characters and events.

Spectacle. The last of Aristotle's six elements is spectacle. **Spectacle** includes all visual elements of production. Today, scenery, properties, lighting, costumes, makeup, stage movement, and dance are all used to create spectacle in theatre. Although scenes and plays can certainly be staged without these elements, the addition of some form of spectacle enhances most productions.

Organization of a Play

The first Greek plays ran continuously from beginning to end without a break. It was Horace (65–8 B.C.), a Roman poet, who was the first writer to divide a play into five acts. An **act** is a major division of a play. Breaking up the action of a play is now a common practice. Today, most plays are divided into two or three acts, and many plays have just one act. Acts can be further divided into sections called scenes. Thus, a *scene* is a subdivision of an act. Scenes are often used to show the change of location or the passing of time. (See Figure 8–1 on the following page.)

Types of Plays

As you work with different scenes and plays, you will begin to notice the different ways that plays are classified. One play may be called a tragedy, while another may be considered a comedy. Let's look at what makes plays different.

The oldest type of dramatic literature is the tragedy. A **tragedy** deals with a serious situation in a serious way. In a tragedy, the protagonist dies or is defeated at the end of the play. Tragedies are often named after the defeated hero or heroine. *Antigone, Romeo and Juliet,* and *The Diary of Anne Frank* are all examples of tragedies.

A drama is also a play dealing with a serious subject in a serious way. It differs from a tragedy in that the protagonist does not die and is not

spectacle
all visual elements of production, such as scenery, properties, lighting, costumes, makeup, stage movement, and dance.

act
major division of a play.

tragedy
a play that deals with a serious situation in a serious way. The protagonist dies or is defeated at the end of the play.

Figure 8-1

Divisions of a Play.

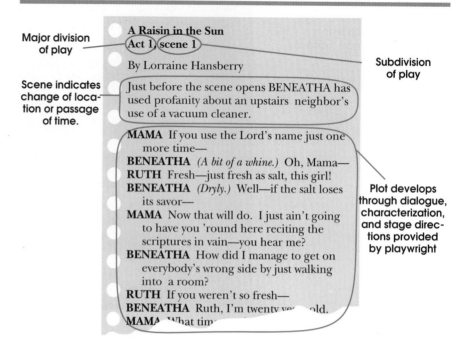

Major division of play

Subdivision of play

Scene indicates change of location or passage of time.

A Raisin in the Sun
Act 1, scene 1

By Lorraine Hansberry

Just before the scene opens BENEATHA has used profanity about an upstairs neighbor's use of a vacuum cleaner.

MAMA If you use the Lord's name just one more time—
BENEATHA *(A bit of a whine.)* Oh, Mama—
RUTH Fresh—just fresh as salt, this girl!
BENEATHA *(Dryly.)* Well—if the salt loses its savor—
MAMA Now that will do. I just ain't going to have you 'round here reciting the scriptures in vain—you hear me?
BENEATHA How did I manage to get on everybody's wrong side by just walking into a room?
RUTH If you weren't so fresh—
BENEATHA Ruth, I'm twenty ve   old.
MAMA   What tim

Plot develops through dialogue, characterization, and stage directions provided by playwright

defeated at the end. In fact, the drama often offers hope for the protagonist's situation. Some dramas that you might enjoy reading are *Little Women, The Chalk Garden, The Miracle Worker,* and *Raisin in the Sun.*

Another type of dramatic literature is the comedy. A **comedy** presents both theme and characters in a humorous way. A popular comedy plot involves two young people who are in love but who almost don't get together. After several complicated situations, the characters

comedy

a play that presents its theme and characters in a humorous way. All characters come together at the end of the play.

The novel, *Little Women* has been successfully staged and filmed as a drama.

finally overcome the opposition and come together at the end of the play. *The Importance of Being Earnest, The Taming of the Shrew, Butterflies Are Free,* and *The Star Spangled Girl* are all comedies.

Often a play is a mixture of both comedy and tragedy. One of the most common mixtures is the melodrama. A **melodrama** is an exaggerated, fast-moving play in which action is more important than characterization. In the melodrama, there is a clear-cut distinction between good and evil. In the end, we see the "good guys" win and the "bad guys" punished. Melodramas that you may have read or viewed on videotape are *Dracula, Deathtrap,* and *Dial "M" for Murder.*

ACTION

1. Reading a Play

a. Select and read a one-act play.

b. Identify each of Aristotle's six elements. Describe how these elements are used in the play you have read.

c. Prepare a short written report on the play you have read. Plan to discuss your work with your acting company or class.

Preparing Your Part

LESSON OBJECTIVES

◆ Learn to analyze a play.
◆ Develop a character from a script.
◆ Learn how to memorize lines.
◆ Perform a role portraying thought, feeling, and character.

Warm Up

Working with your acting company or in small groups, discuss your favorite actors. Compile a list of today's top five male and female actors, and give two reasons for your decision. Compare your group's list with those of the other groups. Discuss the reasons for choosing the actors.

When you participated in improvisation, you focused on creating an imaginary character in a specific situation. Now you are ready to focus on developing a character from a play. Once you are assigned a role in a scene or play, it becomes your responsibility to do everything possible to bring that character to life for the audience. Your job is to learn as much as possible about the character in order to make the character an exciting, well-developed personality. The actions of well-developed characters are much more interesting and harder to predict than those of the stock or stereotypical characters we explored in Chapter 7.

Analyzing the Play

You should begin, as professional actors do, by reading the play for enjoyment and understanding. You should then reread the entire script, looking carefully for all the information the playwright has pro-

William Shakespeare

"All the world's a stage,
And all the men and women merely players:
They have their exits and entrances;
And one man in his time plays many parts,
His acts being seven ages."

You can't study theatre without hearing the name William Shakespeare. He is considered by many to be the greatest dramatist of all time. As hinted at in the lines above from his play, *As You Like It*, his plays portray the many stages of man throughout life. Although he lived almost 400 years ago, his plays are still read and produced throughout the world today, more so than the plays of any other playwright.

Like many, you may at first be fearful of studying Shakespeare's work. The difficult language—poetic and figurative dialogues, and allusions to the time in which he lived, will be difficult to understand. But putting some time and effort into appreciating Shakespeare's plays can pay off. He had a keen awareness of human nature, and it is this awareness that makes his plays relevant and enjoyable today. The best way to experience Shakespeare is not just through the reading of his plays, but through the seeing of them. This is when his characters truly come to life.

Shakespeare, one of eight children, was born in 1564 in Stratford-upon-Avon, a town about 75 miles northwest of London, England. His parents, John and Mary Shakespeare, were prominent citizens in Stratford, and they were able to provide their son with a good education. Shakespeare married Anne Hathaway in 1582 and the marriage produced three children.

It is thought that Shakespeare left Stratford and his family in about 1587 to go to London. He probably got his start in the theatre by becoming a hireling for an acting company, and then working his way up to actor. He was a member of a very successful theatre company, The Lord Chamberland's Men, and became an expert in all areas of theatre. Eventually he even became a shareholder in the company and helped finance the building of the most famous of all Elizabethan theatres, The Globe Theatre. It was in The Globe that most of his best-known plays were first produced.

Scholars have raised questions about whether or not Shakespeare really wrote all the plays attributed to him. Did he put his name on someone else's plays, just revise someone else's work, or is he the actual author? Most Shakespearean experts agree that he borrowed stories from many other sources, but that he reworked them until they became distinctly his own. He adapted and elaborated on stories from English and Roman history and from Italian literature to create his beautiful and original plays.

Shakespeare returned to Stratford from time to time, especially when the theatres were shut down to prevent spreading of the plague. After The Globe Theater burned to the ground in 1613, Shakespeare retired permanently to Stratford-upon-Avon. He died in Stratford in 1616 at the age of 52, having written 38 plays and 154 sonnets. His plays represent a wide range of styles and types, such as tragedy, comedy, history, and fantasy. Some of the more familiar plays are *Romeo and Juliet, Hamlet, and Julius Caesar.* To this day, actors from all over the world consider it a credit to their careers to have performed Shakespeare. ■

Doesn't this look like a perfect setting for reading and analyzing a play? If you don't have access to a theatre, a quiet room at home or in the library will work almost as well.

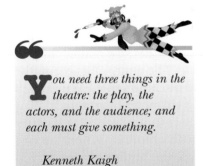

You need three things in the theatre: the play, the actors, and the audience; and each must give something.

Kenneth Kaigh

vided about your character. Become a detective. Make a list of every piece of information you know about the character. Various descriptions of your character might include references to physical traits, such as age, gender, height, weight, hair color, eye color, race, stance, posture, walk, and mannerisms. Also pay special attention to what other characters say and think about your character. Note any references to voice quality, accent, or dialect.

Once you have written down all of the descriptions from the script, try to create a mental picture of your character. Use your imagination to fill in any information not provided by the playwright. Refer to the character analysis questions in Chapter 7 (p. 133) for additional help.

Now ask yourself these questions:

◆ Who are you?
◆ In the play, what do you need or desire?
◆ What obstacle stands in your way of fulfilling this need or desire?
◆ What is your relationship to the other characters in the play?
◆ Where are you in each scene of the play?
◆ What are you specifically doing in each scene of the play?

As you read the play again, picture your character in each scene. Concentrate on understanding the character through his or her actions and thoughts. Personalize the character by making comparisons between your character and yourself.

Researching the Play

Suppose that you were going to play the part of Black Elk in the play *Black Elk Speaks*, based on the eyewitness account of the Sioux Indians. You would no doubt want to research the history behind the play. Research is an important part of preparing for a part in any play. You might begin in your school library or media center, looking up information on the background or period of the play. If possible, you would interview someone who was living during that time or a direct descendant of someone who had lived during that period. To further your understanding of the period, you would try to find the answers to the following questions:

◆ What were the major world events at the time of the play?
◆ What were the social customs of the time?
◆ What type of clothing was worn?
◆ What music was popular?
◆ What famous political or social characters were popular?
◆ In what type of dwelling or shelter would your character have lived?
◆ What type of food was eaten?
◆ What would have been the job opportunities for your character?
◆ What was your character's relationship to society?

At this point in your study, you should have developed a strong impression of the character you are to portray. But before you begin rehearsing the play, discuss your ideas with the director. With the director's help and guidance, you will continue to develop the character.

It is very important that each character in a play—even the ones with very few lines or no lines at all—seem believable to the cast and to the audience. Many directors encourage cast members to create backgrounds, memories, and "life stories" for the characters they portray. These exercises help make a role more than just a name in the script.

The more real and meaningful a character becomes, the more relevant the character is to the plot of the play. When the actor playing the guard creates a background for his character, it doesn't matter that his entire part is to stand silently at the castle gate. The entire cast accepts the role with the same understanding as they do the king's role, even though the king has many lines. See Figure 8–2 for a character biography.

A clear understanding of all the characters in a play makes it easier for everyone in the cast to act and react with emotion. When the cast understands and believes in the characters, the audience also understands and believes. That is the essence of theatre.

Memorizing Lines

As an actor, you have many new responsibilities. One of them is memorizing your lines. Actors must memorize a script exactly as written, "word for word." Missing a line could leave out important information or confuse another actor.

The other members of the cast depend on you, just as you depend on them, to deliver the correct line at the appropriate time. Some of the lines may be cues for the other actors. **Cues** are the lines or signals that alert another actor to be ready to speak, enter, or exit. If you don't say your line correctly, an actor might miss his or her cue. Missed cues often cause actors to leave out lines. Missed cues also slow down a rehearsal or performance, causing the show to drag.

To memorize your lines, you need to understand them. When you first receive your script, take time to read it carefully. The lines will be

cues

the dialogue, sounds, movement, or business signaling an actor or technician to respond as rehearsed.

easier to memorize if you understand them completely. Look up the meanings and pronunciations of all words you are not sure of in a good dictionary.

It is also important to understand the meaning *behind* the words and actions of each line. This is called subtext. You often use subtext in your everyday life, so it shouldn't be a hard technique to master as an actor. **Subtext** is the hidden meaning or interpretation of each line. It is what your character thinks but does not say. For example, when a character says, "What a lovely dress you're wearing," she really might be thinking, "That dress certainly makes you look fat!" or "Girls with red hair shouldn't wear orange dresses!"

It is important for each actor to know what his or her character is thinking, not just when delivering a line, but also while other characters are moving or speaking. When you know your character's hidden thoughts, it is easy to respond with your face and body in a natural way. Because subtext is so important, many directors have the actors write out their character's unspoken thoughts.

Another way to increase your understanding of the play or scene is to listen carefully to your director's interpretation of the play or scene. You will have several rehearsals where you spend time becoming familiar with the script. Ask questions when you don't understand something.

Once you understand the script, begin to memorize your part. Nothing can slow down a rehearsal more than actors who are having trouble reading their lines. Not much progress can be made onstage until you know your lines. Memorize the lines exactly! Do not paraphrase or put the lines into your own words.

Memorizing becomes easier the more you do it. Scripts are actually fun to learn. Most students are really surprised at how quickly they can memorize a script. One of the best ways to memorize is to read the script over and over with a partner.

It's nice to have another member of the cast for your study partner, but sometimes that's not possible. Don't hesitate to ask a friend or a

subtext

the underlying meaning or interpretation of a line, which is not indicated in the script but is supplied by the actor.

■ ■ ■ ■ ■ ■ ■ ■ ■ ■ ■ ■ ■ ■ ■

A good memorization technique is to study lines with a member of your family or a cast member. Your study partner should help you learn your cues and prompt you if you forget.

member of your family to help you with your lines. Soon you will be ready to put down the script, relying on your partner to prompt you—tell you the word or line—only when you forget. A good way to let your partner know that you need a prompt is to say "line" without breaking character.

As you go over the lines, visualize what is happening in the scene. Note your character's movements and personal **business** (mannerisms, actions, or use of props) at that moment in the play. These mental "action" pictures help you remember the scenes as you master the script.

There are other ways to memorize. A good way to memorize when working alone is to cover your lines with an index card, removing the card after you recite the line to check for accuracy. Many actors like to memorize by acting out the lines as they move about. They associate certain movements with certain words.

Actors with many lines often divide their parts into small sections, or scenes, memorizing one scene at a time. Other actors record their cues on a tape recorder, leaving time on the tape after each cue to speak their lines. Some actors find that reading their lines aloud just before going to sleep is helpful.

Whatever method you use, memorization requires time, concentration, and drill. As an actor, it is your responsibility to spend the time needed to learn the lines of the script.

business

small movements and actions that do not require the actor to move from place to place.

*E*very role is a challenge. *You always start from scratch.*

Jessica Tandy

ACTION

1. **Letters of Introduction.** Write a letter in character introducing yourself to the other characters in the play you are rehearsing. Share these letters in one of the early rehearsals.

2. **Character Collage.** Create a collage of magazine or newspaper clippings. Include descriptive words and pictures that might reflect your character's personality. Mount these on posterboard or construction paper and label with your character's name. Create a cast "art gallery" for display during the run of the play.

3. **Memory Box.** Prepare a special "memory box" to fill with memorabilia that your character might consider important enough to save. Look through your closets or attic to see if you might have something that is similar to what you need. Secondhand stores, estate sales, or flea markets may have just the right items at low cost.
   a. Prepare your box and share it in class or at rehearsal.
   b. Select the one item from the box that your character would consider most precious. You might choose a locket, a lock of hair, or even a special rock. Prepare a 1-to 2-minute monologue revealing the item's value and importance to your character. Share your monologue "in role" in class or at rehearsal.

4. **Character Bag.** Create a "character bag." Decorate the outside of a grocery sack to reflect your character's external traits. Use pictures and captions that reflect the outer images that the audience will be able to view immediately. Fill the inside of the sack with several items that repre-

sent the internal characteristics that will be discovered as the audience gets to know the character. Bring the bag to class or rehearsal to share with the other members of the cast.

5. **Composing Subtext.** Write the complete subtext for your assigned part in the play.

6. **Research Your Character.** Combine your knowledge of your character in the play with your research on the historical period in which the play takes place. Put all the information together as a "life story," or biography, for the character you will portray (see Figure 8–2).

7. **Analyzing a Character.** After reading the character biography in Figure 8–2, describe Monica.
   a. What is her habit, or mannerism?
   b. What does she enjoy doing?
   c. What things does she dislike?
   d. What is her greatest desire?

Figure 8–2

■ ■ ■ ■ ■ ■ ■ ■ ■ ■ ■ ■ ■ ■

Character Biography.

The following part of a character biography, written by theatre student Melissa Bahs, describes Monica from the play *Twelve Dancing Princesses*, by I. E. Clark. After reading the excerpt, decide what you know about the character.

Student Example Character Biography

Monica

Monica is a very sarcastic and resentful princess. She resents being forced to sneak out of her father's castle to attend the nightly dances at the castle of the Demon Prince. She also resents that she isn't as beautiful as all of the other princesses. One of the things she wants most is to be as beautiful as her sisters. Being beautiful would make her feel as important as all of the other eleven sisters.

Monica is probably about sixteen years old. It would have taken her at least this much time to form such a resentful attitude toward herself and toward the other characters in the play. We know from history that young princesses were allowed to date and even marry at a very young age.

Monica's posture is not very good because of her lack of confidence. She walks slowly and reluctantly as she journeys to the far away kingdom. She has a habit of twirling a ring on her right hand. Perhaps this ring was given to her by a prince with whom she was once in love.

Although Monica is not as beautiful as the other princesses, she is clean and neat. She has straight brown hair and greenish-blue eyes. She looks a little like I look.

She is physically healthy, but she is mentally unhealthy because of her constant depression over her situation with her sisters and her father. Her depression shows in her movements, in her reactions to other characters, and in her voice. Each time she speaks, her deep mature voice is harsh and cruel and very sarcastic.

Monica's lines indicate that she is intelligent and that she has a good imagination. She is well read and well-versed on the current affairs of the kingdom, although she does not share these facts with her sisters.

Curtain Call!

CHAPTER 8 REVIEW

■ ■ SPOTLIGHT ON TERMS ■ ■

An important part of theatre is understanding the terminology, or vocabulary, used. Add the new terms and definitions to the vocabulary section of your theatre notebook or folder.

■ ■ FOCUS ON FACTS ■ ■

1. Explain the elements that make up the dramatic structure of a play.
2. In what ways are plays different from short stories and novels? In what ways are they similar?
3. What steps should an actor follow when developing a character from a script?
4. How does researching the play benefit the actor?
5. Explain one method of memorizing lines.
6. What is meant by subtext?
7. Describe one way a playwright might tell you about a character.

■ ■ REFLECTIONS ■ ■

Discuss the following questions with your class or answer them on paper as instructed by your teacher.

1. How did working with a script differ from improvisation?
2. What memorization technique worked best for you?
3. Which activity in this chapter did you enjoy the most? Why?
4. In what ways was this a challenging or an easy chapter?
5. Why do you think Aristotle's six elements are still basic to the dramatic structure of a play?
6. Which type of play would you prefer to read? Why?

■ ■ THEATRE IN YOUR LIFE ■ ■

Discuss aloud or explain in a short journal entry in your theatre notebook the personal challenge that this chapter presented for you.

■ ■ ENCORE ■ ■

1. Prepare and perform a monologue.
   a. Analyze the scene, writing subtext for your character's lines.
   b. Develop a character using the character analysis questions given in Chapter 7.
   c. Memorize your lines and prepare the scene for performance.
   d. Perform the scene according to your teacher's instructions.
2. Recall plays (or parts of plays) that you have studied in your language arts classes. Did you enjoy reading these plays? Why or why not?
3. Make a list of all the plays (and parts of plays) included in your literature textbook. Next to each play, write the type of play (tragedy, comedy, etc.) you think best describes that play. Be prepared to explain why you categorized the play as you did.
4. Pick a character from a play to analyze. Write out answers to the six questions toward the top of page 143. Use your imagination to answer the questions. There are no right or wrong answers.

CHAPTER 9

Taking the Stage

Chapter Outline

Spotlight on Terms

- acting areas
- apron
- arena stage
- blocking
- body positions
- flexible staging
- grand drape
- house
- level
- planes
- proscenium stage
- stage
- stage picture
- thrust stage
- wings

ow it is time to think about taking your scene or play to the stage for rehearsal and production. In this chapter, you will be introduced to different types of stages and to the specialized language used in directing and staging a play. You will begin to see why acting requires a great deal of hard work, intense discipline, and years of training.

Types of Stages

LESSON OBJECTIVES

◆ Understand performance space.
◆ Recognize basic types of stages.

Warm Up

With your acting company, discuss how the stages at your school differ from the stages illustrated in this textbook. Where are the stages located in your school? What other events take place in those spaces?

Figure 9–1

The Proscenium Stage.

stage
the area where the players perform; usually a raised platform.

proscenium stage
a four-sided stage built like a box with one side cut away, enabling the audience to view the play as if it were in a picture frame.

A play must have a performance space. This space should provide a **stage**, or area where the players perform, and a separate area where the audience watches. The stage in your school might be in a theatre or auditorium, or it might be part of the classroom. A performance space can be any area designated for acting that is set apart from the audience.

The Proscenium Stage

The most common stage in educational theatre is the proscenium stage. A **proscenium stage** is usually a raised picture-frame stage, or box stage (see Figure 9–1).

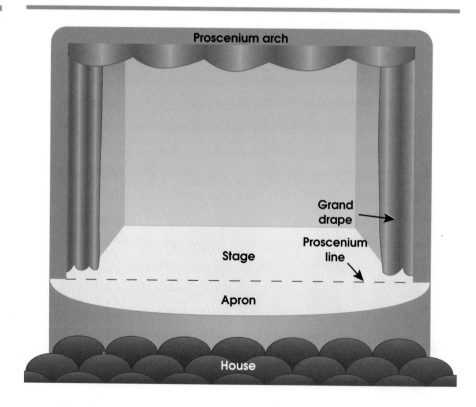

Proscenium arch

Grand drape

Proscenium line

Stage

Apron

House

Figure 9–2

Overhead View of the Proscenium Stage.

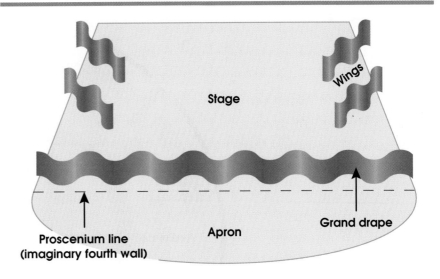

grand drape

the draperies covering the proscenium opening (picture frame), separating the audience from the stage.

wings

offstage spaces to the sides of the acting area.

apron

the part of the stage extending past the proscenium arch toward the audience.

arena stage

a stage constructed so that the audience can sit on all sides; also known as "theatre-in-the-round."

thrust stage

a stage that extends into the seating area. The audience sits on three sides of the stage.

A *proscenium arch*, or frame, surrounds the opening of the stage much like a giant three-sided picture frame. A **grand drape**, or curtain, hangs across the imaginary *proscenium line*, and can be opened to reveal the picture, or scene, to the audience.

Entrances onto the stage are made by the actors from offstage spaces to the right and left of the acting area called **wings** (see Figure 9–2). An actor making an entrance from the wings is hidden from the audience's view by curtains or scenery.

Often in front of the grand drape is a portion of the stage extending past the proscenium arch toward the audience. This part of the stage is called the **apron** (see Figure 9–2). Scenes are sometimes played on the apron with the grand drape closed, often while scenery is being changed behind the curtain.

The Arena Stage

The **arena stage** is a stage constructed so that the audience can sit on all sides of the production. Often this stage is lower than the audience. Notice in Figure 9–3 on the next page that entrances and exits must be made through the audience. Staging of this type is also known as "central staging" or "theatre-in-the-round."

The Thrust Stage

Another type of stage extends, or projects, into the seating area of the audience. This type of stage is called a **thrust stage** (see Figure 9–4). The audience sits on three sides of the stage. The thrust stage has qualities of both the proscenium stage and the arena stage.

Figure ■ 9–3

The Arena Stage.

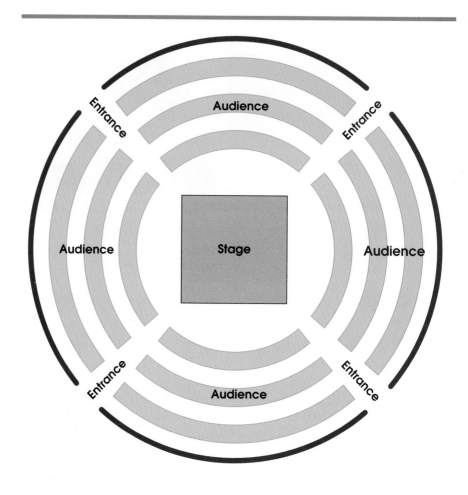

Figure ■ 9–4

The Thrust Stage.

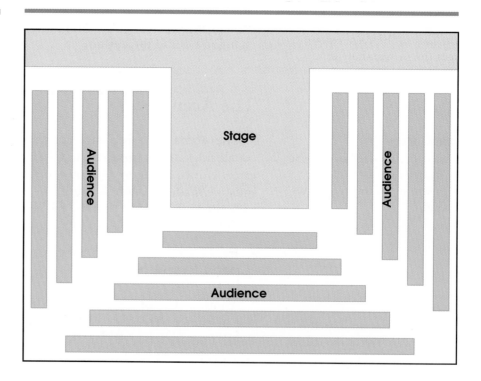

Flexible Staging

When a performance space does not fit into one of the three basic shapes or categories, it is usually called **flexible staging** (see Figure 9–5). A current trend is to stage plays in spaces other than actual theatres. If your school does not have an auditorium or theatre with a stage, flexible staging might be used in a classroom, cafeteria, gymnasium, corridor, or band or choir room. Through the use of flexible staging, performances are often staged inside empty commercial buildings, libraries, shopping centers, and malls, as well as outside in parks and recreation areas. The many ways and places in which plays can be staged remind us of William Shakespeare's words over 400 years ago—"All the world's a stage."

Figure 9–5

An example of flexible staging.

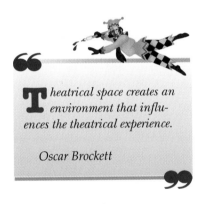

Theatrical space creates an environment that influences the theatrical experience.

Oscar Brockett

1. **Theatre Tour.** If your school has a theatre or auditorium, tour the facility. Based on the information in this lesson, determine the type of stage at your school.

2. **Finding Flexible Staging.** Brainstorm with a partner or your acting company to think of other areas in your school or community that could be used as flexible staging for a play.

3. **Creating Performance Spaces.** As a class, plan as many ways as possible to create a performance space in your classroom.

Stage Terminology

LESSON OBJECTIVES

◆ Identify the different parts of the performance space.
◆ Identify the proscenium stage acting areas.
◆ Follow basic stage directions using the acting areas.

Warm Up

Stage Terms Relay. *As directed by your teacher, match your assigned theatre term with the corresponding part of the proscenium stage or performance space.*

As you take your place onstage, you will discover that the theatre has a language all its own. This language has evolved over many years, reflecting the techniques commonly practiced by actors and directors. Knowledge of this basic theatre language is as important to the actor as knowledge of the alphabet is to the child learning to read. Once you have learned to use this language, you will be able to effectively communicate onstage with your director and the other actors.

The Performance Space

First, you need to become acquainted with the parts of the performance space. As you study the new terms, be sure to look at the diagrams that have all the parts labeled (see Figure 9–6). Anything within the stage setting and visible to the audience is considered *onstage*. Anything beyond the stage setting and not visible to the audience is considered *offstage*.

Figure 9–6
■ ■ ■ ■ ■ ■ ■ ■ ■
The Basic Parts of the Stage.

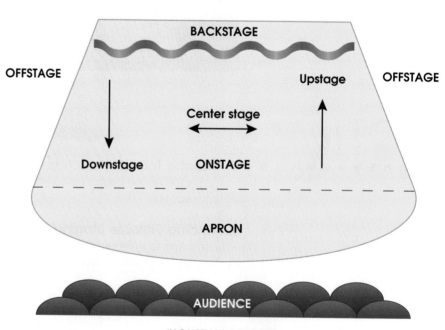

154 ■ Unit 2: Building Your Acting Skills ■

house

the section of the theatre where the audience sits; also called "out front."

The area of the performance space where the audience sits is often called *out front,* or the **house** . The areas behind the stage and not seen by the audience are usually called *backstage.* In your school, backstage could be just a small area behind the back curtain, or it could be large enough to include storage rooms, rehearsal rooms, and dressing rooms.

Stage Positions

Directors use a set of standard terms to guide the actors on the stage. On the proscenium stage, the directions *downstage* and *upstage* date back to the days when stages were built with the rear of the stage slanting upward away from the audience. Downstage (D) was the area closest to the audience, and upstage (U) was away from the audience. Although all stage floors no longer slant, the names for these areas have remained. Other directions, such as *stage right* (R), *center stage* (C), and *stage left* (L), are always given as if the actor were standing on the stage, facing the audience. When you are onstage, stage right and stage left will always be *your* right and left as you face the audience.

acting areas

nine to fifteen divisions of the stage floor, used by directors when moving actors or placing furniture or scenery.

blocking

planning and working out the movements and stage grouping for a play.

Acting Areas

The proscenium stage floor is divided into imaginary blocks called **acting areas** , in which the director can move people or place furniture and scenery. Small proscenium stages are usually divided into nine acting areas (see Figure 9–7) and large stages (see Figure 9–8) into fifteen. Planning the movement for the play is **blocking** the play.

Figure 9–7

Proscenium Stage with Nine Acting Areas.

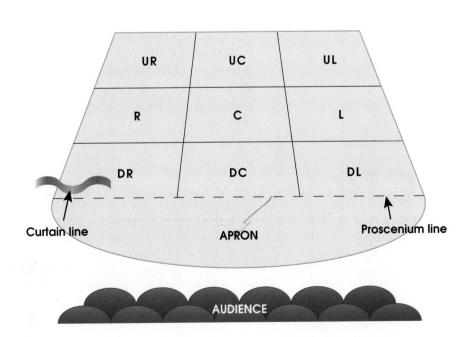

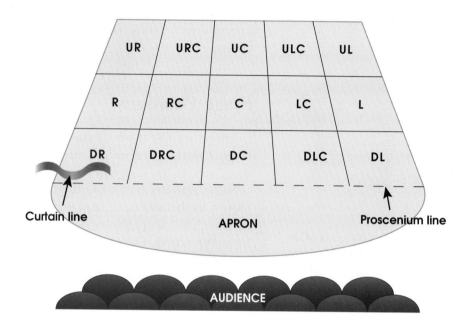

Dividing the stage helps the director to block the play and provides a guide, or road map, for the actors and technicians.

In arena theatre, because the audience is seated on all sides, the terms *upstage* and *downstage* cannot be used. Instead, the arena stage is usually viewed as either a map (north, south, east, west) or a clock (see Figure 9–9). During a performance, some actors will naturally have their backs to the audience, while others will be facing the audience. The director's challenge is to position the actors so that they can be seen by the greatest number of viewers.

The thrust stage can be thought of as a combination of a proscenium stage and an arena stage. The upper part of the stage, away from the audience, is usually treated like a proscenium stage. The part of the stage closest to the audience is treated like an arena stage.

Because of the vast differences in flexible staging, no one set of practices exists. Directions in flexible staging would depend on the shapes of the acting areas and audience areas. Directors often use a combination of techniques from both proscenium staging and arena staging.

■ ■ ■ ■ ■ ■ ■ ■ ■ ■ ■ ■ ■

1. **Labeling a Proscenium Stage.** Do the following activities to make sure you know the areas of a proscenium stage.
   a. Draw an outline of the proscenium stage. Label these areas: on-stage; offstage L and R; wings; backstage; proscenium line; proscenium arch; apron; house.
   b. Draw an outline of the proscenium stage. Label nine acting areas: DR, DC, DL, R, C, L, UR, UC, UL.

Figure 9-9
▪ ▪ ▪ ▪ ▪ ▪ ▪ ▪ ▪ ▪ ▪ ▪ ▪
Dividing the Arena Stage.

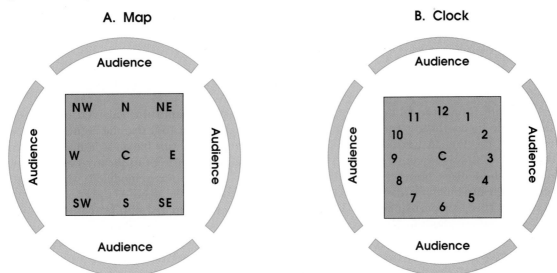

A. Map

B. Clock

2. Arena Floor Plans. Draw two floor plans illustrating how movement might be directed on an arena stage.

Acting Technique

LESSON OBJECTIVES

◆ Understand and use basic body positions.
◆ Use basic stage movement and composition to create meaning.

Every day we receive over 90 percent of our communication without the use of words, through nonverbal messages—facial expressions, gestures, or body language. In a play, much of the meaning comes nonverbally—from the way the actors relate onstage to the audience and to each other, as well as from basic stage movement and composition. It is important to understand the acting techniques involved in such communication.

Body Positions

The actor's position onstage in relation to the audience can be described by five different angles, called **body positions** (see Figure 9–10 on page 160). Each position makes a different emotional contact

OUR THEATRE HERITAGE

Seventeenth-Century French Theatre

France was greatly influenced by the changes taking place in the Italian theatre during the Italian Renaissance, but the French Renaissance did not reach its peak until the seventeenth century. It was the French, not the Italians, however, who built the first permanent theatre buildings after the fall of the Roman Empire. This first permanent theatre was the Hôtel de Bourgogne, built in 1548 for the purpose of doing religious plays. The Hôtel de Bourgogne remained the only permanent indoor theatre building in Paris for almost a hundred years. Originally, the Bourgogne was a long, narrow building with a platform stage at one end. Staging was basically medieval, with several settings appearing on the stage at the same time. The audience knew that the play's location changed as the actors moved from setting to setting. Most of the audience stood and watched the performances from the open floor space in front of the stage. The side and back walls of the theatre were lined with enclosed boxes and gallery seating for wealthy audience members who could pay for a seat. The theatre was owned and strictly controlled by the crown, who had the final say in all matters concerning appropriate stage practices and dramatic content.

It was not until the Palais-Cardinal theatre was built in Paris in 1641 that the French had a proscenium arch stage with Italian-style machinery for shifting set pieces. After this theatre was built, the Hôtel de Bourgogne was remodeled, with a proscenium arch added to the stage. As the French became more and more fascinated with changing the spectacular sets, they began to utilize painted perspective scenery in the same sort of sliding wing and shutter system that had become so popular in Italy. The newer French theatre buildings provided more and more backstage space to store scenery waiting to be shifted into the view of the audience. An example of this increasing depth in stage space is found in the Hall of Machines, a theatre built in 1660. Although the stage was only 52 feet wide, it was 140 feet deep from the front of the stage to the back wall behind the backdrop. This practice of creating such deep stage spaces made it possible for some audience members to sit on stage in the wing spaces on benches to watch the action! By the close of the seventeenth century, members of the French upper class were often seated on stage for performances. One of the theatres built with this practice in mind was the Comedie Française, which was built in 1689 and served as the home of the French national theatre company for over eighty-one years.

It is important to remember that these huge indoor theatres had no electric lighting and were very dim places. Lighting was provided by huge chandeliers equipped with candles that were lighted by lowering the chandelier with a pulley system. These chandeliers provided a dim and smokey light, which kept both the audience space and the stage lighted throughout the performance. Designers in this period also used oil lamps with open flames on stage, mounted near the scenery to light the stage. These open flames offered very little or no means of modifying the intensity of lighting during the performance and made theatre fires a very real danger.

Of the playwrights of this period, easily the most famous is Jean-Baptiste Poquelin (1622–1673), who took the stage name of Molière. His plays, like the plays of Shakespeare, are still being produced around the world today. Molière was the son of the

Given his own theatre and troupe of players by King Louis XIV, Molière wrote, directed, and starred in one hit play after another in the 1660s and early 1670s.

upholsterer to the royal family and was expected to follow in his father's footsteps. Instead, he developed an interest in theatre. But his first attempts at theatre in Paris were failures. He left the city and traveled with an acting company for many years. These years were important in his artistic development as he became a much more experienced actor and began to write plays. When he returned to Paris, he established himself as the country's leading actor-manager and playwright with his own company performing his plays.

Molière specialized in creating comedies with a central comic character who had extreme mannerisms and character flaws. He created exaggerated character types, like those he saw in commedia dell'arte troupes during his years of touring, and put them in plots that made fun of their eccentricities. Molière also utilized a great deal of the slapstick comic gags just like those he saw in commedia. He blended these characters with the French appetite for spectacle and special effects. He frequently employed a plot development called a "deus ex machina" which means "the god of the machine." This was a theatrical practice from ancient Greece of bringing in a god on a spectacular flying machine. The god solved the problems for the characters and ended the play. In most of Molière's plays, deus ex machina meant a god or higher authority (a king or ruler) appeared at the last minute to save the protagonist from disaster. Although there were seldom plot elements supporting these miracle endings, the French audience's love for special effects made these endings very popular.

Molière's *Tartuffe* is frequently produced today, but even though the King liked the play when he first saw it at a festival in 1664, he did not allow it to be shown publicly until 1669 because of protests from the Church.

But being popular with the French audiences did not keep Molière out of trouble. Some of his plays made fun of people in power, suggesting that they were not reasonable, good people. For example, his play *Tartuffe* (1664) was not allowed to play in France when it was first written because its main character, Tartuffe, was very pious and wore a religious outfit. This was a problem because the action of the play showed that Tartuffe was actually a greedy womanizer. The play makes fun of his hypocrisy and the gullibility of those around him, who do not see through his religious act. Although the play is a comedy, many church leaders believed that it was an attempt to make fun of the church. Therefore, they would not allow the play to be performed. Eventually, *Tartuffe* was performed in Paris and was a raging success. It remains a standard comedy performed by many theatre companies today. Some other very popular Molière plays include *The Misanthrope* (1666), *The Miser* (1668), *The Learned Ladies* (1672), and *The Tricks of Scapin* (1671).

Important writers of tragedy in this period include Pierre Corneille, Thomas Corneille, and Jean Racine. The most important of these is by far Jean Racine (1639–1699), whose most famous plays was *Phedre* (1677). Racine is remembered for his ability to create interesting plot developments based upon the internal conflicts of his characters. These characters are usually torn between their sense of duty and responsibility and their strong, uncontrollable desires.

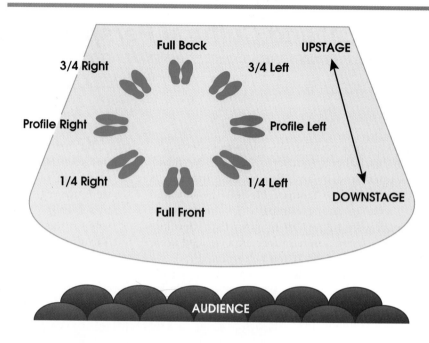

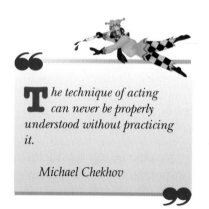

> *The technique of acting can never be properly understood without practicing it.*
>
> Michael Chekhov

with the audience. On the proscenium stage, *full front position* means directly facing the audience. *One-quarter position* (¼ right or ¼ left) means turning slightly, about 45 degrees, away from the audience. *Profile position* (½ right or ½ left) means turning to face the side of the stage, 90 degrees away from the audience. *Three-quarter position* (¾ right or ¾ left) means turning about 135 degrees away from the audience. *Full back position* means turning completely away from the audience and facing the rear of the stage.

In order to be seen by everyone in the audience, the actor is often given special instructions. To *open* or *open up,* means to position or turn the body more toward the audience. When an actor is told to *turn in*, turning should be toward the center of the stage. The direction *turn out* means to turn more to the side of the stage.

Other directions frequently given to actors relate to the actor's position in relation to other actors onstage. To give the audience a better view of the body and face, actors *cheat out* during conversations, turning more toward the audience than they would in normal conversation. This is called cheating because the audience isn't aware of the action. Frequently, actors are told to *share.* This means that they are to assume positions of equal strength by opening up to the audience equally, thus sharing the scene equally. If an actor is told to *give* or *give stage,* then that actor moves to a different part of the stage to allow another actor more emphasis or attention. The actor receiving more emphasis *takes* the scene. (See Figure 9–11.)

Movement and Composition

Movement is an exciting part of the actor's role onstage. Actors enter, exit, cross, sit, and rise based on motivation. Motivation is the

Figure 9-11

Ways for Two Actors to Share a Scene.

A. Four *shared* positions for two actors

B. Three *give and take* positions for two actors

Takes

Gives

Takes   Gives

Takes

Gives

purpose for or reason behind the move. When a character moves across the stage, it could be to answer the phone, open a door, or write a letter—but the move must have a reason and serve a purpose. Directors plan stage movements to emphasize the meaning in the playwright's work. All stage movement is planned and rehearsed, giving the director the opportunity to guide the actors. Actors will find many helpful suggestions in the "Guide for Basic Stage Movement and Business" featured in this chapter (see page 162).

As you know, planning the movement for a scene or play is called blocking. Some directors invite improvisational movement during rehearsals, thus working out the blocking with the actors. All entrances,

Guide for Basic Stage Movement and Business

Entrances

Get into character before the entrance. Begin your entrance in the wings, at least 5 to 6 feet away, in order to take on the physical attributes of the character. Go over in your mind the reason you are entering the scene and what you are going to do onstage. If two characters share an entrance, the speaking character should enter last.

Exits

Remain in character until you are 5 to 6 feet into the offstage area. If the exit requires a long cross, make sure the last few lines are spoken near the exit. When several characters exit at the same time, the character with lines should exit last.

Professionalism Onstage

Remember to avoid turning your back to the audience unless so directed. Avoid standing in front of another actor or upstaging an actor by forcing that actor to turn his or her back to the audience in order to talk to you.

Crosses

Take "strong" crosses downstage (below) other actors, "weak" crosses upstage (above). Most crosses are made downstage (below) of the standing character and upstage (above) of the seated characters. "Strong" and "weak" crosses are determined by the purpose of the movement and the lines spoken. The shortest distance between two points is usually the best guide for a cross. A cross can be softened by moving in a curved pattern. Curved crosses can be used to convey a casual approach, hesitation, or doubt.

Gestures

Avoid covering the face with a gesture. When handling stage props such as a telephone or making large gestures, use the upstage hand.

Walking

Carry your weight in the chest rather than the feet. Head and shoulders should be up. Steps should be even and not too long. When moving, step off with the foot closest to your destination.

Backing Up

This is a weak move and should be avoided unless the move backward makes a dramatic point.

Walking Up and Down Stairs

Practice leading with the toes and coming down on the heel without looking down at the steps. Avoid bouncing up and down the stairs. Before descending a flight of steps, pause slightly, drawing attention to the movement.

Sitting

Approach the piece of furniture without staring at it. Secure your position of the furniture with the back of your upstage leg. Keep the weight of your body on the upstage leg as you lower

Guide for Basic Stage Movement and Business

yourself onto the seat by bending your legs. Avoid plopping or slumping into an easy chair or sofa. Sit near the front edge of the chair to make rising easier. Unless told to do so, avoid crossing your legs onstage. Females usually sit with ankles crossed or one foot slightly in front of the other; males sit with legs slightly apart.

Rising
Keeping the back straight, push up with the upstage leg. Next, shift your weight to the downstage leg, allowing you to move forward with the upstage foot.

Kneeling
The downstage knee should touch the floor, helping to keep an "open" position. When kneeling on both knees, the downstage knee should be lowered first; then the upstage leg can be lowered into position.

Turning
Always turn toward the audience unless your director tells you otherwise.

Stage Slaps
Using a cupped hand, strike the receiver on the chin or jawbone, away from the ear. Be especially careful not to hurt the receiver when administering a stage slap.

Falls
To prevent injury, all stage falls should be planned and rehearsed. Place your body weight on the leg opposite from the direction you will fall. As the fall begins, the knee (on the side that is falling) relaxes and bends. The fall is broken as the knee, hip, and shoulder hit the floor (in that order). The head can be supported by the outstretched arm on the floor.

Eating
Eating while talking always poses problems, especially onstage. Avoid foods that get stuck in the throat or foods such as crackers which dry out the mouth and make talking more difficult. Also avoid carbonated beverages to prevent unwanted burps or belches onstage. Weak tea and fruit juices such as lemon and grape are easy to drink. Use tea and lemon for light-colored drinks and grape juice for dark drinks such as coffee.

Movement
Visible movements, such as entrances, exits, crosses, sitting, and rising, draw focus (the attention of the audience). Always move or gesture on your own lines, so as not to steal the audience's attention during another actor's lines. All movement should be in character. All movement should be motivated. Make every movement count.

Personal Business
This consists of small actions that a character performs without moving from place to place. An actor enhances characterization with appropriate personal business, such as handling a cup, straightening clothing, reading the newspaper, fanning with a fan, or writing a letter.

Figure 9–12
■ ■ ■ ■ ■ ■ ■ ■ ■ ■ ■ ■ ■ ■
Cross and Countercross.

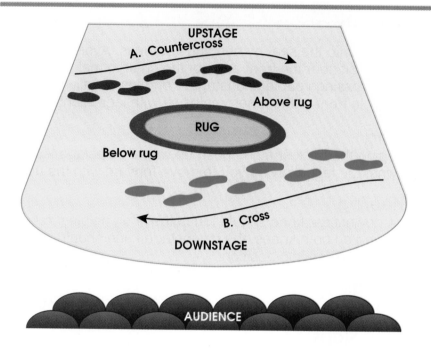

exits, crosses, and stage groupings are planned. After blocking, the actors add the plans to their scripts in pencil, in case changes occur as rehearsals progress.

Moving from one point to another onstage is called a *cross*. Indicate a cross in your script with an X. You should begin crosses with your upstage foot, which helps keep your body open to the audience. To complete a cross, the director may ask an actor to cross above or below a piece of furniture or an actor. *Above* means upstage, or behind the object or person; *below* means downstage, or in front.

After one actor has moved, often another actor will need to move in the opposite direction, or *countercross* (see Figure 9–12). A countercross is sometimes needed so that the audience can see all the actors. A countercross might also be needed to call attention to a new focal point, or center of interest.

Inexperienced actors tend to line up onstage or clump together in a bunch. When this happens, the director may tell the actors to *dress stage*. This means that the actors need to look at the *composition*, the way they are grouped on the stage, and adjust their positions to balance or improve the stage picture. A **stage picture** is an appealing arrangement or grouping formed onstage by the performers. The director creates stage groupings to present a picture for the audience in much the same way that a photographer arranges people for a magazine layout.

Important considerations in planning a stage picture are levels and planes. The term **level** refers to an actor's actual head height. An actor is at his or her highest level when standing or when elevated in some way, as by a platform or set of steps. Different meanings can be created in the stage picture by placing characters at various levels to each other (see Figure 9–13).

stage picture

an appealing and meaningful arrangement of performers on the stage; the picture that the audience sees onstage.

level

the actual head height of the actor as determined by his or her body position (sitting, lying, standing, or elevated by an artificial means such as a step unit or platform). Meaning is created in stage pictures by placing actors at different levels.

Figure 9-13

▪▪▪▪▪▪▪▪▪▪▪▪▪▪▪▪▪▪

Using Levels to Create Meaning.

A. Standing and kneeling

B. Sitting and standing

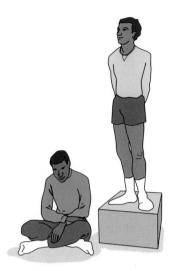

C. Sitting on floor and standing on box

D. Sitting on ladder and standing on floor.

planes

imaginary divisions giving depth to the proscenium stage. An actor moves through the stage planes as he or she moves downstage toward the audience or upstage away from the audience.

Planes are imaginary divisions giving depth to the proscenium stage. An actor moves through the stage planes as he or she moves downstage toward the audience or upstage away from the audience. Each imaginary plane is about 2 feet deep. An actor in plane 1 would seem more important to the audience than an actor in plane 6 (see Figure 9–14). When one actor causes another actor to turn his back to the audience, it is called *upstaging*. This can be avoided by actors playing in the same plane.

Using their knowledge of body positions, levels, and planes, directors can create a composition, or stage picture, to establish the mood of a scene, help create emphasis, and show character relationships.

Figure 9-14

▪▪▪▪▪▪▪▪▪▪▪▪▪▪▪▪▪▪

Imaginary Planes Showing Depth of Proscenium Stage.

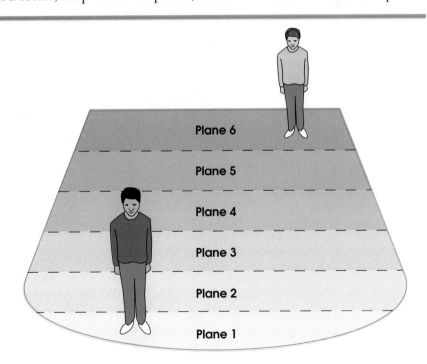

Plane 6

Plane 5

Plane 4

Plane 3

Plane 2

Plane 1

ACTION
■■■■■■■■■■■

1. **Creating an Acting Area.** Working with your acting group, use masking tape to mark off nine or fifteen acting areas on the floor of your classroom.
   a. Make a set of stage directions, including entrances, exits, and crosses, using the areas on the floor (for example: Enter UR; X to DL; X UC; exit UL).
   b. Take turns instructing your group in stage direction and movement.
   c. Create a motivation for each set of movements you design. For example, motivation for the stage directions suggested in part (a) (Enter UR; X to DL; X UC; exit UL) could be: enter UR from the upstairs in response to phone ringing; X to DL to answer phone; X UC to sofa to pick up car keys; exit UL through kitchen door to get to car.
   d. Repeat the stage directions using the motivated movements.
   e. Discuss your observations.

2. **Meaningful Stage Pictures.** Work with a small group, using body positions, levels, and planes, to create a stage picture reflecting one of the following themes:

loss	triumph	separation	revenge
distrust	peace	celebration	hope
power	shame	grandeur	jealousy
grace	relief	gratitude	unhappiness

3. **Dramatize a Photograph.** Using body positions, levels, and planes, bring to life a still photograph (use an art print or magazine photograph). Work with the same number of actors as people shown in the picture. Plan the movements that you imagine occurred prior to the "picture," ending with the frozen image captured by the photographer.

Figure 9–15
■■■■■■■■■■■■■■■■

Stage Picture.

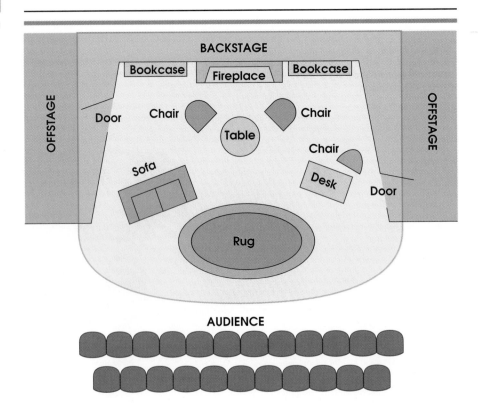

▪ ▪ SPOTLIGHT ON TERMS ▪ ▪

An important part of theatre is understanding the terminology, or vocabulary, used. Add the new terms and definitions to the vocabulary section of your theatre notebook or folder.

▪ ▪ FOCUS ON FACTS ▪ ▪

1. Describe the basic types of staging defined in this chapter.
2. List several places where flexible staging might be used.
3. What is the primary difference between a proscenium stage and an arena stage?
4. Draw and label the nine acting areas of a small proscenium stage.
5. Illustrate the two methods of giving directions on an arena stage.
6. What is the difference between onstage and offstage?
7. Explain what is meant by stage right and stage left.
8. How do body positions change the actor's relationship to the audience?
9. What is the purpose of blocking a play?
10. What does *give* or *give stage* mean?
11. What is meant by the term *dress stage*?
12. How does an actor avoid upstaging another actor?

▪ ▪ REFLECTIONS ▪ ▪

Discuss the following questions with your class or answer them on paper as instructed by your teacher.

1. If you were the director, on which type of stage would you prefer to direct? Why?
2. Assume that you have all the money that you need to build a new theatre space. How would you design your stage?
3. Which activity in this chapter did you really enjoy? Why?

4. What new ensemble work did you experience in this chapter?
5. How will your knowledge of stage terminology help you in acting?

▪ ▪ THEATRE IN YOUR LIFE ▪ ▪

Discuss, through a short journal entry, something new that you learned from this chapter.

▪ ▪ ENCORE ▪ ▪

1. Working with a partner, or group, plan the blocking for one of the duet scenes included in this textbook. Develop the characters and prepare the scene for performance. When your scene is ready, share it with the class.
2. Plan the blocking for a scene from a play you have recently read. Direct a member of your group in the movement for the scene.
3. In the drawing on the opposite page, notice placement of the doors and furniture. Using basic classroom furniture, follow the drawing to arrange the stage, then rehearse the movements. Make additional directions so each member of the class can have one or more turns.
   a. Enter UR door, X DL above desk, sit in chair.
   b. Enter DL, X above sofa, straighten cushions, exit UR.
   c. Enter DL, X UR, stand full back, remove book from bookcase, X UR to exit.
   d. Enter DL, X below desk, sit on rug profile R.
   e. Enter UR, X below table UL, sit in chair R, X DR to exit.
   f. Enter UR, X DR below sofa, sit downstage, ¼ R.
   g. Enter DL, X UC, pause, pick up table, X DR, place table below sofa.
   h. Enter UR, X UC, sit full front.
   i. Enter DL, X UC, stand full front below fireplace.

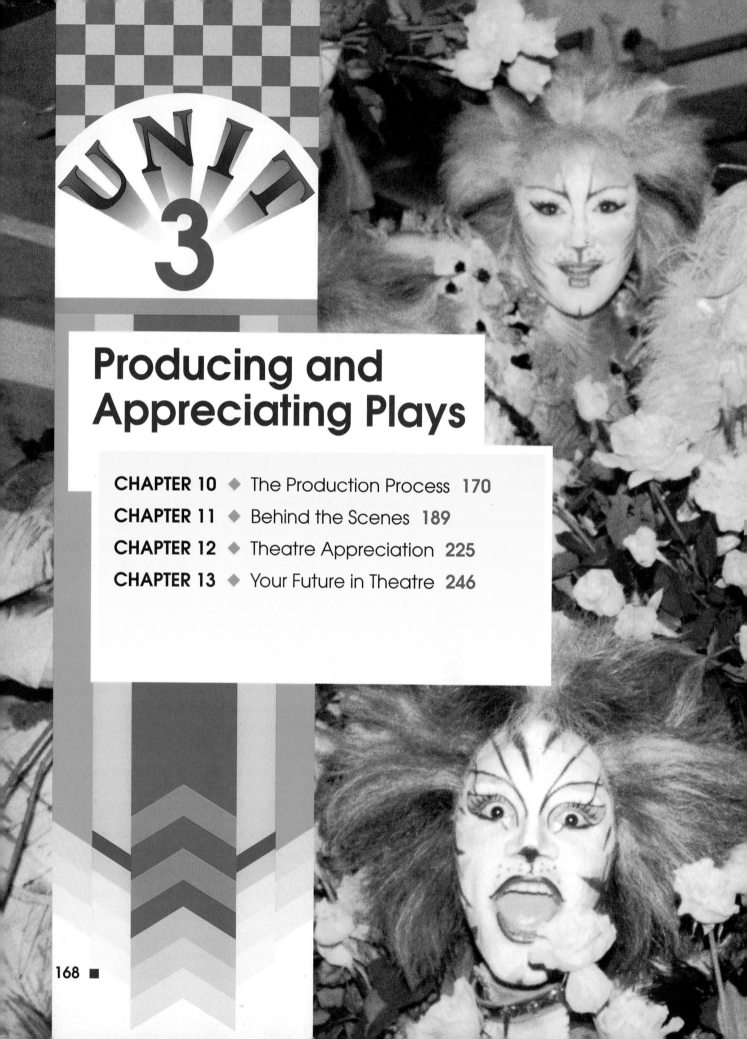

UNIT 3

Producing and Appreciating Plays

CHAPTER 10

The Production Process

Spotlight on Terms

- auditions
- blocking rehearsals
- callbacks
- casting
- copyright
- costume parade
- developing rehearsals
- director
- dress rehearsal
- floor plan
- line check
- polishing rehearsals
- promptbook
- reading rehearsals
- rehearsals
- royalty
- run-throughs
- strike
- technical rehearsals
- understudy

our teacher or director has just announced that your class or drama group is going to produce a show. It is to be a one-act play. The director could have selected a three-act play, a series of scenes from several plays, a readers theatre production, or even a show made up of a variety of "acts." In each production, most of the preparation techniques will be the same.

All productions require careful planning, weeks of preparation, dedication, and hard work on the part of everyone involved. Your teacher or director will be the person in charge of the production. In educational theatre, a teacher is usually the director and is assisted by students who are interested in theatre or enrolled in a theatre class. These students assume the responsibilities for all jobs other than directing.

In this chapter, you will become familiar with the entire production process—from selecting the play to bringing down the final curtain and dismantling the set.

Selecting the Play

LESSON OBJECTIVES

◆ Recognize the role and responsibilities of the director in selecting a play.
◆ Understand the process of selecting a play to produce.

Warm Up

Working with your acting company or class, list as many play titles as you can. See who can think of the most.

director
person in charge of the artistic production of a play.

Before the title of the production was announced, several decisions had already been made. First, the play was selected. This was a major responsibility for your teacher or director.

The **director** is the person in charge of the artistic production of a play. Directors spend many hours reading and studying plays as well as attending theatrical productions to enrich their background in dramatic literature. Directors want to enjoy directing the play, they want the cast and crew to enjoy working on the show, and they especially want the audience to have a rewarding theatrical experience. For those reasons, directors try to select plays that have good literary merit, that will challenge the actors as well as the director, and that will offer more than mere entertainment to those attending.

There are many things to consider in selecting a play. Directors need to know what type of show would be suitable for the school and community. They also need to be aware of the budget, the availability of the play, the talents of the actors, and their own directing capabilities. Finally, directors must be aware of any special needs involved in staging a particular show, such as the sets, costumes, stage facilities, style of acting, and time needed to produce the show. For example, a director might really want to direct the musical *Peter Pan*, but she might also feel that the stage is too small to accommodate the cast, or perhaps she doesn't feel comfortable "flying" the characters across the stage. Each director must carefully consider these many different elements before selecting a particular play.

In some cases, a play might be selected by committee, or students might vote on a favorite play, or the class could work together to write a script. The method of play selection is determined by the director.

Obtaining Permission

After selecting the play, the director must secure permission to produce the play and purchase copies of the script. Any material protected by copyright should not be photocopied and requires permission from the publishing company for production. A **copyright** is the registration of ownership of a piece of literature or music. In most cases, there is a fee charged for each time the show is produced. This fee is called a **royalty**. A portion of this payment goes to the playwright. Writing is the playwright's occupation, and receiving payment each time the play is produced helps the playwright earn a living.

Most likely your drama teacher will be the director of your first play. Look to your teacher for guidance since it's the director's job to combine the roles of all the actors and crew members to create a successful production.

copyright

the registration of ownership of a literary or musical work.

royalty

a fee required to produce a play or musical.

The **copyright notice** tells who owns the rights to a literary or musical selection. You must contact this source for permission to use any portion of the work. (This is an example of an acknolwedment for an extract used in this textbook.)

From ANTIGONE, by Jean Anoulih, trans. Lewis Galantiere. Copyright © 1946 by Random House Inc. and renewed 1974 by Lewis Galantiere. Reprinted by permission of Random House, Inc.

The **royalty notice** warns that fees are payable each time the material is used. Royalty payments are made both to the publisher and to the playwright.

CAUTION: Professionals and amateurs are hereby warned that "THE CHALK GARDEN," being fully protected under the copyright laws of the United States of America, the British Commonwealth countries including Canada, and the other countries of the Copyright Union, is subject to a royalty. All rights, including professional, amateur, motion picture, recitation, public reading, radio, television and cable broadcasting, and the rights of translation into foreign languages, are strictly reserved. Any inquiry regarding the availability of performance rights, or the purchase of individual copies of the authorized acting edition, must be directed to Samuel French Inc., 45 West 25 Street, NY, NY 10010 with other locations in Hollywood and Toronto, Canada.

The Director's Concept

Before the director begins to work with the cast, the director will spend much time studying the play, developing ideas for interpreting the playwright's work. The director's plan, or vision, is known as the *overall*

floor plan

a drawing of the stage setting as seen from above (bird's-eye view).

promptbook

usually a loose-leaf notebook containing the script marked with all stage movement, entrances and exits, technical cues, and special instructions for the production. The stage manager is usually in charge of the promptbook.

concept of the play—the big picture. It is the director's job to decide what the play means. What's more, the director must be able to imagine the play being performed in its finished form. Thus, the final production reflects not only the work of the playwright, but also all of the choices the director has made regarding every aspect of the play—characterization, movement, costumes, lighting, props, scenery, and so on.

There are as many different ways to put on a play as there are directors. The playwright may have included ideas for production in the script, but those aren't the only ideas the director can use. To interpret a play, the director will analyze it in much the same way you learned to analyze characters, reading the play several times to study the style, theme, dramatic structure, characters, and dialogue. The director needs to thoroughly understand the entire play, and research may be needed. The director will study the people and customs of the historical period as well as furnishings and clothing.

After determining the concept for the play, the director will work out a plan for the stage showing all the entrances and exits, levels (different heights), and main furniture pieces that will be needed onstage. This is called a **floor plan**. If the director has a designer or technical director, the two of them might work together to plan a suitable design for the play.

Many directors continue at this point to plan the play's blocking and begin the promptbook. The **promptbook** is usually a loose-leaf notebook containing a script that is marked with all stage movement, entrances and exits, and special instructions for the production. Many directors also include the phone numbers and addresses of cast and crew members and any emergency numbers that might be needed.

ACTION

1. **Analyzing Scripts for Production.** Look through a catalog from a company that publishes plays. Select a play that you think you would enjoy seeing produced onstage.
   a. Make a list of the cast requirements (number of males and females) for the play you selected.
   b. List the number of scenes and acts.
   c. What information about staging is mentioned in the play catalog?
   d. Discuss your selection with your acting company, giving reasons for your choice.

2. **Paying Royalties.** Suppose that your class wants to produce the play you have selected. Determine the amount of royalty you will have to pay if you present the play four times.

3. **Calculating Script Costs.** Determine how much it will cost to purchase scripts of the play for all members of the cast and the director, assistant director, and stage manager. Also include eight additional scripts for the heads of the production crews.

4. **The Director's Concept.** Read a one-act play and imagine it being staged. In one paragraph, describe your overall concept from a director's point of view.

5. **Creating a Floor Plan.** Draw the floor plan for the play you selected.

Selecting the Cast

LESSON OBJECTIVES

♦ Understand the process of auditioning and casting.
♦ Experience the audition process.

While analyzing the play, the director begins to form an impression of the kinds of characters the playwright has created. With these characters in mind, the director's next major responsibility is to choose actors that can bring those characters to life. Matching up characters and actors is called **casting**. In educational theatre, casting is usually accomplished through a selection process called **auditions**, in which actors try out for the parts that they want.

Auditions

During auditions, actors try different parts for the director. Auditions are extremely competitive, so always come prepared. Reading the play before the auditions will give you time to think about the play as a whole as well as to pick individual roles that you think you might like to play.

Directors conduct auditions in different ways, depending on the needs of the particular school or group. If the play is to be produced as a class project, the director might choose to hold auditions during class time; other times, auditions could be held before or after school. The auditions might be limited to only students in theatre classes, or they might be open to the entire school.

During auditions, the director might ask all interested persons to "read cold" (without preparation) for each part. This could be done as a private reading or a group reading. Or the director might ask each actor to prepare (memorize) a speech from the play. Still other directors like to have actors improvise scenes from the play. Directors may choose to use a combination of these techniques to audition actors privately or in groups.

When a production requires specific talents, such as singing or dancing, the director might require songs or a short dance routine to be included in the audition. Such important information is usually specified in the audition publicity. If you are unsure, ask questions on your own. To feel comfortable about the audition process, find out as much as possible before the day of auditions.

Warm Up

Play the game "Actor Wants a Role" (based on the game "Kitty Wants a Corner"). The students (pretending to be directors) sit in a circle, and one student stands in the center of the circle playing the part of the actor seeking a role. The actor goes to one director and says, "Actor wants a role." Each director sends the actor to another director, saying, "No part, see another director." While the actor is walking from director to director, the directors (players) try to exchange places. The objective is for the actor to get a job by getting into one of the empty places in the circle. The person left without a place becomes the actor wanting a role. The director (player) can call out additional playing directions, such as "Audition in character," "Speak with an accent," or "Play in slow motion."

A cting seems to be the easiest of all the arts because everybody walks, talks, gestures, and makes faces. But then he is just being himself and one sees immediately how different that is from acting as soon as one puts him on stage and gives him a part to learn and interpret.

August Strindberg

callbacks
additional opportunities for the actor to audition.

Often the director must weigh many factors and then choose just one person, from the many people who auditioned, for a particular part. If you don't get the part you want, taking another part or working on one of the crews will increase your chances for success at the next audition.

Most directors distribute a proposed rehearsal schedule along with an audition application to be filled out before you try out. It is very important to review this schedule with your family to make sure that you can attend all of the scheduled rehearsals. If you foresee conflicts, write them on your audition application. Directors like to be aware of all conflicts as soon as possible.

If possible, fill out the audition application before you get to auditions. Audition applications will differ, but the sample in Figure 10–1 on the next page will give you an idea of the type of information you might be asked.

Casting

When selecting the cast, the director must consider each actor's ability to interpret the character and project the character vocally and physically. The director needs to consider each actor's physical attributes—gender, appearance, height, and size.

The director also looks for growth potential. In educational theatre, a director wants an actor who will not just be good in auditions but will continue to grow, giving the character depth as the rehearsals progress. Dependability, cooperation, and attitude are other factors that a director considers when selecting a cast.

Along with all these qualities, the director must also pay attention to an actor's attendance record at school as well as the actor's grades. Actors must be able to attend classes and keep up grades in spite of numerous rehearsals and performances.

After the first auditions, directors sometimes need a second or third "look" at an actor. These second and even third audition opportunities are called **callbacks**. These callback auditions help narrow the selections by giving the director another chance to see and hear the actor. They also give the director an opportunity to combine several actors in scenes to see how they look and work together. After making the "final

Figure 10–1

Audition Application Form.

Name ____________________ Phone number ______________

Address ________________ Age _____ Sex _____ Grade _____

Height _____ Weight _____ Hair color ______________

PLEASE COMPLETE THE FOLLOWING INFORMATION:

SPECIFIC TALENTS OR ABILITIES ______________________________

____

____

CONFLICTS WITH PROPOSED REHEARSAL SCHEDULE:

____

____

____

CLASS SCHEDULE

PERIOD	CLASS	TEACHER	ROOM NUMBER
1.			
2.			
3.			
4.			
5.			
6.			
7.			
8.			

ROLES FOR WHICH YOU WILL AUDITION:

______________ ______________ ______________

______________ ______________ ______________

DO YOU WISH TO BE CONSIDERED FOR ANY ROLE IN THE PLAY? _____ yes _____ no

WHICH ROLE WOULD YOU NOT ACCEPT? ______________

WHY? ______________________________________

CHECK THE AREA/S WHERE YOU WOULD BE WILLING TO WORK:

_____ SCENERY _____ PROPS _____ COSTUMES

_____ MAKEUP _____ LIGHTING _____ SOUND/MUSIC

_____ HOUSE/PUBLICITY _____ STUDENT DIRECTOR

_____ STAGE MANAGER _____ TECHNICAL DIRECTOR

underststudy

a person who learns a part in order to substitute in a performance should the original actor not be able to appear in the show.

cuts" (eliminations) and casting the show, the director posts the cast list or announces to the actors their assigned roles.

Many directors assign understudies when the cast list is posted. An **understudy** is a person who attends all rehearsals and is prepared to perform if the original actor is absent from a performance.

1. Getting Ready to Audition.
   a. Copy the audition application on a separate sheet of paper and complete it as though you were auditioning for a play.
   b. Prepare a selection from The Playbook at the back of this text to use in a real or simulated audition.
   c. Participate in a simulated or real audition.

The Rehearsal Process

LESSON OBJECTIVES

◆ Understand the rehearsal process.
◆ Understand the purpose of each type of rehearsal.
◆ Recognize the ways the play benefits from the guidance of the director.
◆ Demonstrate the ability to cooperate with a director.

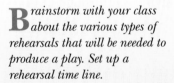

Warm Up

Brainstorm with your class about the various types of rehearsals that will be needed to produce a play. Set up a rehearsal time line.

rehearsals

production sessions in which the actors and technicians prepare by repetition.

Once casting is complete, it is time for rehearsals to begin. **Rehearsals** are preparation sessions for the production. Rehearsals provide an opportunity to discuss and analyze the play, to learn lines and blocking, and to perfect every aspect of the play.

How much rehearsal time is needed will depend on the abilities of the actors, the length of the play, and the difficulty of the play. Your group will probably have four or five weeks to put together a one-act production, six to ten weeks for a three-act play or musical. That really isn't very long, considering all that has to be done. Therefore, rehearsals are extremely important, and your full cooperation is needed.

Before rehearsals begin, everyone involved in the production should take time to review the Actor Etiquette guidelines featured on the next page. These guidelines are helpful reminders of good production etiquette, which is appropriate behavior and common courtesy.

Each rehearsal is planned for a specific purpose. Although your director may call the rehearsals by different names, most rehearsals follow a

NOTICE

ACTOR ETIQUETTE

1. Abide by all school and classroom rules.
2. Be on time for rehearsals and performances.
3. Leave only when dismissed.
4. Attend every rehearsal, unless you have special permission to be absent.
5. Immediately contact the director in case of an emergency.
6. Come to rehearsal willing and prepared to work. Bring a pencil, your script, and any other items the director has required. Learn your lines as soon as possible.
8. Observe common courtesy to other members of the cast before, during, and after rehearsals.
9. Avoid touching anything that doesn't belong to you—including costumes, props, makeup, lights, mikes, or scenery.
10. At the end of a rehearsal or performance, put away your props and costumes. Also check the backstage area or dressing rooms for any of your personal possessions.
11. Once in costume or makeup, the audience should not see you in the theatre or peeking out from behind the curtains.
12. Be quiet backstage during rehearsal and performances.
13. Listen while backstage to avoid missing cues or entrances.
14. Avoid "mouthing" the lines of others.
15. Call "line" if you need a prompt.
16. Keep up your grades. Let your director know if you are having academic difficulty.
17. Continue to study your part during the run of the show.
18. Give 100 percent at all rehearsals, work sessions, and performances.

---

similar pattern: reading rehearsals, blocking rehearsals, line checks, developing rehearsals, run-throughs, polishing rehearsals, technical rehearsals, costume parade, and dress rehearsals. You are now ready to learn what happens from the first rehearsal all the way through until you put away the show.

Reading Rehearsals

reading rehearsals
rehearsals for the purpose of reading and analyzing the script as well as discussing and understanding characterization. They can be referred to as *read throughs*.

Reading rehearsals are rehearsals set aside for reading and understanding the script. These are the first rehearsals after the show is cast. These rehearsals can take place in the classroom, in a rehearsal room, or on the stage. The cast is usually seated informally in a circle, if possible around a large table. Some directors like to have everyone involved in the play attend this first rehearsal. This is a good opportunity to introduce everyone, briefly go over job descriptions, pass out any revised rehearsal schedules, and make any general announcements. At this time, all changes or cuts should be made in the script in pencil.

■ ■ ■ ■ ■ ■ ■ ■ ■ ■ ■ ■ ■ ■ ■

At the reading rehearsal, you will have an opportunity to see how your character interacts with the other characters in the play. You will begin to get a feel for the theme and mood of the play.

The director must not use his actors as instruments to make his own music, but orchestrate theirs until it becomes one song which he can then share in singing.

Robert L. Benedetti

Everyone should bring a pencil, a notebook, and a copy of the script. (Some crew members may not need to have a script.)

The director's purpose in the first reading rehearsal is to briefly explain the theme of the play, to describe how the playwright tells the story, and to share his or her plans for telling the story onstage. The director might also describe the characters, show a drawing of the floor plan, explain any problems in staging, and share other relevant ideas about the production.

Next the cast reads the play aloud, carefully considering pronunciation and interpretation of lines. Reading rehearsals provide the actors time to ask questions and to develop a clearer understanding of the characters and the play.

Reading rehearsals can take several days, depending on the play. During these rehearsals, the director may assign research assignments pertaining to the play's time period, culture, or customs. An individual character analysis may also be assigned. Refer to Chapters 7 and 8 for help with such assignments.

Blocking Rehearsals

Blocking rehearsals are used for planning all stage groupings, basic movement, body positions, crosses, entrances, exits, and stage business. For ease in blocking, the director will divide the play into workable units, or scenes. Next, most directors will ask the actors to disregard all stage directions in the script. Those directions probably will not suit your director's interpretation of the play or the floor plan for your set.

The stage manager will have taped the floor plan on the stage floor with masking tape, marking all entrances and levels. Chairs may be placed onstage to represent other pieces of furniture. The director will guide the cast through each scene. Be sure you understand the motivation behind each move you make.

blocking rehearsals

rehearsals for planning stage movement and groupings.

The English Restoration: Theatre Returns from Exile

In 1649, Oliver Cromwell and his followers, the religiously conservative Puritans, beheaded King Charles I, and for over eleven years England was ruled by Cromwell. In 1658, after Cromwell died, the royal family was asked to return to England from France, where they had been living in exile. In 1660, Charles II became king and the monarchy was "restored" to power, which is why this period of time is called the *Restoration Period.*

When the English royalty and nobility returned to England, they brought with them a taste for the French theatrical practices that they had enjoyed as audience members in France. This pleased the English because the Puritans had closed all theatres in 1642. With the Restoration came a resurgence of theatrical activity. As you may recall, English theatre during the Renaissance had not been like the theatre popular in Italy and France. English playwrights and producers did not use painted perspective scenery, for example, but had continued to use very few furnishings to suggest a location for the action. After the Restoration, the Elizabethan practices and the Italian and French stage arrangements were merged to form a unique, new kind of theatre. This combination of styles affected the form of the plays, the organization of the theatre companies, the theatre buildings themselves, and the use of scenery on stage.

The Restoration was not a period of great tragic plays. Most of the Restoration tragedies were heroic tragedies about extraordinary heroes who did extraordinary deeds. While entertaining, these plays were usually too far removed from reality to have much credibility. The really popular plays of the period, the ones still performed today, are the comedies, which are known as "comedies of humours" or "comedies of manners." Thomas Shadwell (1642–1692), who wrote *The Sullen Lovers*, was a popular playwright during this period and one of the first to write comedies of manners. His plays focused on eccentric characters in modern-day settings. Other important playwrights include John Dryden (1631–1700), Sir George Etherege (1634–1691), and William Wycherley (1640–1715), who wrote *The Country Wife*, a very popular play from the period.

William Congreve (1670–1729), who wrote *The Way of the World*, which is still produced, and Sir Richard Steele (1672–1729), who wrote *The Conscious Lovers*, also wrote the sentimental comedies that were so popular during this period.

These comedies of manners usually made fun of members of the upper class and nobility, and of their preoccupation with appearances, reputation, and piety. These characters were always shown to be greedy, vain, and obsessed with flirting and romance. The audience members, most of whom were from the upper class and nobility, used the plays as a way to laugh at themselves and their neighbors. Going to the theatre during this period usually had as much to do with "being seen" as it did with enjoying the play.

Theatre companies were changing drastically during the Restoration. For example, for the first time in English history, women were performing the roles of the female characters. Another change was taking place in the way actors, both male and female, were being paid. Prior to the Restoration, the Elizabethan companies of actors were paid by collecting a share of the profits of the production. During the Restoration period, outside investors began to own the buildings and finance the productions, keeping the profits, if there were any. The actors were contracted at a set fee for a set period of performances. This change marked the beginning of today's commercial theatre.

The theatre buildings were also changing. The Elizabethan theatre buildings had been circular, open-air structures. The new Restoration theatre buildings were enclosed with a roof. They merged the popular Italian and French staging practices, which included a proscenium stage opening, and an apron. This apron was an extended platform that spread out in front of the proscenium arch, upon which much of the play's action was performed. The apron was a lasting reminder of Elizabethan staging practices that focused on the use of an open platform. Another addition to the stage in this period was a "raked" or slanted floor. This type of floor improved the audience's ability to see the action on the back of the stage.

The audiences at Restoration theatres had a choice of pit seating, box seating, or gallery seating. The pit (the floor space closest to the stage) was unlike the French pit in that it was furnished with benches. The boxes, which offered the most comfort and privacy to the wealthier audience members, provided eye-level viewing. The galleries were rows of seating recessed into the side and back walls of the theater building, rather like balconies.

Restoration scenery was much like the Italian Renaissance scenery. The scenery was painted in perspective on wings, shutters, and sometimes rolled backdrops. Painted boards were added to hide stage-hands who shifted the wings to change the set. Unlike the Italians, who used a complicated system of ropes to move the wings simultaneously, the English depended upon stagehands to slide the flats out of the way, revealing the new setting behind them.

By the end of the Restoration period, in the late 1700s, society was changing and the middle class made up of merchants and traders was emerging, becoming increasingly powerful financially and politically. As a result, theatre changed, reflecting this cultural change by dramatizing the lives of people from the middle class. ■

Look closely at the facial expressions and postures of these four characters from a 1957–58 Broadway production of William Wycherley's *The Country Wife*. What adjectives would you use to describe these stock characters from a Restoration comedy of manners?

In developing rehearsals, your director will continue to work with you and your fellow actors to refine and improve all aspects of your performance.

line check

a test run of the show's dialogue to ensure that all lines have been memorized; also called a line rehearsal.

developing rehearsals

rehearsals in which the actors work under the director's guidance to prepare the show for performance; also called *working rehearsals.*

run-throughs

rehearsals conducted without any stops.

Some directors draw the plans on a chalkboard, others talk and walk the cast through, and still others let the actors experiment through improvisation. However your director directs, you should make careful notes in your script in pencil. Blocking can change as rehearsals progress.

After each scene is blocked, the actors walk through it several times to clearly establish the movement and business in their minds. That is also the actor's signal to memorize lines for that scene in the play, unless told otherwise. Blocking rehearsals continue until the entire play is completed. Meanwhile, all actors are memorizing their parts. When an actor has completely memorized his or her part, that actor is said to be "off book" or "off script."

Line Checks

To make sure that the entire cast is off book, a director may call a line check, or line rehearsal. During a **line check**, the cast sits in a circle performing only the lines, without any movement or action. The purpose of this rehearsal is to be sure that all the actors have memorized their lines. Provided everyone is off book, the director may also use this opportunity to time the run of the show from opening line to closing line.

Developing Rehearsals

Developing rehearsals are also called *working rehearsals* because that is exactly what happens. The director and cast are working as they go over and over the play, making changes and adjustments as needed. As the play develops, sometimes new action or stage business is added to help the audience understand what the characters are doing and how they are doing it. Props are added during these rehearsals so that the actors can become accustomed to their use. During this period, directors often work individually with actors or with small groups of actors to strengthen their scenes without rehearsing the entire company.

Run-Throughs

Run-throughs are rehearsals without any stops. These rehearsals should take place after all actors are off book and the blocking is firmly established. These rehearsals must take place at least two weeks before the production. Run-throughs give the director an opportunity to see the strengths and weaknesses of the show.

During the run-throughs, both the assistant director and the director make notes. Some directors use a small tape recorder to "talk" their comments. The tape is then played at the critique session. Many directors like to videotape these rehearsals and view the tape with the cast at the next rehearsal. At least two run-throughs are beneficial to the performance.

Polishing Rehearsals

Polishing rehearsals are used to smooth out all the rough spots discovered during the run-throughs. The play is now in the final stages of the rehearsal process, and it is important to continue to improve. These rehearsals often stop and start, focusing on problem areas and strengthening the weaker scenes. These rehearsals also give actors time to fine-tune characterization, vocal projection, and "picking up cues"—qualities that contribute to a well-polished production.

Technical Rehearsals

Technical rehearsals focus on all of the technical aspects of the play, including set changes, lighting, sound, music, and special effects. Once the scenery is in place, the first technical rehearsal may be held with just the stage crew so that they can get the feel of moving the set pieces without the cast. Some directors have similar rehearsals for lighting, sound, and special effects, with the assistant director reading the cues.

All technical elements must be completed for a full technical rehearsal. During rehearsal the actors walk through the play delivering only lines that are cues for a technical effect. Doorbells ring, lights go up and down, scenery changes, doors open and close—all at the proper time. Enough of these rehearsals must be scheduled to have the technicians feeling comfortable and all the technical elements running smoothly by dress rehearsal.

Costume Parade

The **costume parade** is an informal modeling of all costumes under the lights. The director and costume crew sit in the audience and view the costumes, making notes about possible changes. Holding the costume parade a week before dress rehearsal gives the costume crew time to make the needed changes before the first dress rehearsal.

If your director plans to have the cast take a curtain call, this is a good time for blocking and rehearsal. If you are performing your show during the school day, you may just have time for one curtain call. When the lights fade or the final curtain closes, the cast should line up along the proscenium line, alternating males and females. Your director may wish to place the principal characters in the center of the line. When the curtain opens, the cast should smile and bow graciously in response to the audience's applause. After the bow, the lights fade as the curtain closes.

There are other ways to take a curtain call, and your director may wish to block it differently. If time permits, several curtain calls can be taken. The first call is the entire cast, the second is usually the secondary parts, and the third is reserved for the principal actors. If there is a fourth call—and in educational theatre there can be—this curtain call can be for all of the crews, the stage manager, the student director,

---

polishing rehearsals

rehearsals used to correct problems that occurred in the run-throughs. The rehearsals give the actors the opportunity to fine-tune character believability, vocal projection, and "picking up cues."

Several technical rehearsals will be held, with and without the actors, to solve problems and perfect the timing for lighting, scenery, sound, and all the other technical parts of the play.

technical rehearsals

rehearsals emphasizing the performance of the production's technical elements—prop changes, scenery shifts, light changes, sound effects, and so on.

costume parade

actors modeling costumes under the appropriate stage lights. This parade gives the director and costume designer the opportunity to evaluate the costumes and make any needed changes before the production opens.

and anyone else who has played an important part in the show. On the night of the performance, the curtain call is a good time for the actors to acknowledge and thank the director.

Dress Rehearsals

A **dress rehearsal** is a rehearsal that is conducted as though it were an actual performance. The crews are in place. The actors are costumed and in complete makeup. The show runs without stopping unless there is a major problem. After the rehearsal, the director will gather the cast and crews and go over any problems that need to be corrected before the next dress rehearsal.

At least two dress rehearsals are required, and three are usually needed. The final dress rehearsal should be completely under the direction of the stage manager.

ACTION

1. **Evaluating Your Rehearsal Time Line.** Working with your acting company, compare the rehearsal time line you developed at the beginning-of-the-lesson warm-up with the suggestions given in the lesson. Discuss your findings with the class.

2. **Organizing Rehearsals.** You are the director for the next production. Prepare a chart for the cast, showing what will be done at each rehearsal.

3. **Reviewing Types of Rehearsals.** Summarize, in one sentence, the purpose of each type of rehearsal.

The Performance

LESSON OBJECTIVES

◆ Demonstrate an actor's responsibilities before, during, and after a performance.
◆ Explore performance as an actor.
◆ Reflect on and form opinions of the performance experience.

The day you have waited and worked for has finally arrived. Excitement is in the air! Everything has been planned, rehearsed, and prepared for the moment when the curtains will open to a real live audience. Even if the play is to be performed in the morning or afternoon, during class or after school, for classmates or paying patrons, you will experience the feeling of "opening night"!

Under the guidance of your teacher or the student director, physically stretch and warm up your body to the music of a Broadway musical. Warm up vocally, repeating the letters of the alphabet with a variety of inflections. Breathe deeply and relax the body as well as the vocal mechanisms. Think about your role. Begin to get into character.

Before the Performance

Everyone should arrive at the school or theatre early—your director will tell you how early. Be sure you have made arrangements for transportation so that you won't be late. Once you arrive, you will need to report to your assigned place for makeup and dressing. Always check your own props to be sure that they are in place and ready to go. Once you are in makeup, you should begin relaxation exercises and vocal warm-ups. These can be done individually or as a group. Some directors ask the assistant director to plan and lead these activities.

Thirty minutes before "curtain," the stage manager will call "half-hour," announcing 30 minutes remaining before the show begins. Five minutes before the curtain opens, the stage manager will call "places," and all cast members should report to the areas designated by the director.

This is a most exciting time in an actor's life. The hours of training and rehearsal will now pay off in the performance. It is time to take a deep breath, swallow, and think about your character. As you go onstage, you must become your character rather than being just an actor playing a part.

Beginning with the stage manager's signal, the performance should go as rehearsed. This is not the time to try something new. If a problem should arise or a line is missed, follow the guidelines that your director has instilled in you to keep the show moving.

After Each Performance

After each performance, you will be exhilarated. But you must remember to put away your personal props, hang up your costume, and take off your makeup. Although you may be tempted, don't ever go out

■■■■■■■■■■■■■■■

You will want to arrive at the theatre in plenty of time to prepare for the performance. You will be part of the team, and every member of the team must be ready if the show is to be a success.

When the curtain comes down, it will be time for celebration and congratulations. You will enjoy the feeling of having been part of a team that has worked hard to entertain and enlighten an audience.

into the audience or crowd dressed in your costume and makeup—unless your director has planned a "meet the cast" time. Your parents and very closest friends will probably come backstage to congratulate you.

Crews will carefully check for any repairs or replacements that need to be made before the next performance. Everyone should help clean up to make sure that everything is ready for the next show.

After the Final Curtain

It is sad, but every show has to end and be "put away." In theatre, putting away everything that was used in the performance is called the **strike** . This part of the production process is also a team effort. Your director will plan the best time for the strike.

To *strike the set* means to disassemble the scenery. The stage crew will be responsible for the majority of the tasks, but the cast must also help. Besides striking the set, there are many things that need to be done. Costumes must be cleaned and returned to the wardrobe closets. Props must be put in their proper places. Letters of appreciation must be written to anyone who was not part of the company but extended their help. All persons or companies who loaned props or furniture for the show should also receive thank-you letters. All of the posters or advertising should be taken down, and the theatre area must be cleaned. Every director has a special plan for what needs to be done and when it needs to be completed, so be prepared to do your share.

Closing Traditions

Theatre groups often have special traditions that take place after all of the performances are over and the show is struck. Casts sometimes gather to discuss the show's success or to enjoy viewing the videotape

strike

take apart the stage setting, remove it from the stage, and store all parts of the production for future use.

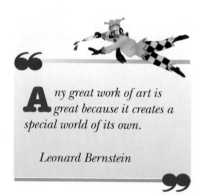

*A*ny great work of art is great because it creates a special world of its own.

Leonard Bernstein

together. Classes usually complete an evaluation or a self-critique. Lasting memories of the show can also be created by autographing programs, scripts, or cast shirts at a cast party. Your director will have a special way of "putting the show away."

1. **Describing Your Theatre Experience.** Using colored markers on 3-by-5-inch index cards, write one word or a short statement summing up your response to being part of a performance. Share your comments aloud or post the card on a bulletin board for all the cast members to read.

2. **Appreciating a Team Member.** Write a note of appreciation to another member of the cast or to a member of one of the production crews, expressing admiration for something in that person's performance.

3. **Thanking the Person in Charge.** Write a short letter to your director, assistant director, or stage manager, expressing appreciation for that person's role in the production.

■ ■ SPOTLIGHT ON TERMS ■ ■

An important part of theatre is understanding the terminology, or vocabulary, used. Add the new terms and definitions to the vocabulary section of your theatre notebook or folder.

■ ■ FOCUS ON FACTS ■ ■

1. What are four responsibilities a director must complete prior to rehearsals?
2. What is a royalty? Why is it paid?
3. What is a copyright?
4. What is the purpose of filling out an audition application?
5. Outline the rehearsal process from reading rehearsals to dress rehearsals. Explain what happens at each type of rehearsal.
6. List the actor's responsibilities before a performance on the night of a show.
7. What are an actor's responsibilities following a performance?
8. What is meant by "off book"?
9. What is meant by "striking the show"? When does this "strike" take place?

■ ■ REFLECTIONS ■ ■

Discuss the following questions with your class or answer them on paper as instructed by your teacher.

1. Why do you consider it important to prepare a promptbook for a play?

2. If you were the director, how would you audition twenty female actors for a play with only three female parts?
3. Your theatre class has $200 to produce a one-act play. How will you spend the money?
4. Which warm-ups would you choose to prepare your own voice and body before a performance?
5. What specific ensemble or team growth did you see in the cast of this play during the production process?

■ ■ THEATRE IN YOUR LIFE ■ ■

1. Discuss aloud or in your journal what you liked best about being part of the production.
2. Pass around your scripts to be autographed by members of the cast and crew.
3. Suggest a tradition you feel would be a meaningful way to close your next production.

■ ■ ENCORE ■ ■

1. Prepare a promptbook for a production.
2. Design an appropriate audition application for first-year theatre students.
3. Design a self-evaluation form to be used by the cast of a one-act play.
4. Write a letter to a publishing company requesting the right to perform a play at your school.
5. Check on plays and scripts available from your school library. Ask your librarian for help in selecting these plays.

CHAPTER

11

Behind the Scenes

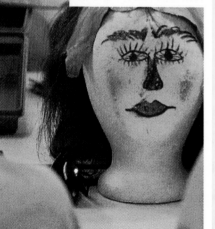

Spotlight on Terms

- ◆ assistant director
- ◆ basic makeup
- ◆ character makeup
- ◆ costume
- ◆ costume crew
- ◆ costume plot
- ◆ crew
- ◆ cue sheet
- ◆ cyclorama
- ◆ house crew

- ◆ light crew
- ◆ lighting plot
- ◆ makeup crew
- ◆ makeup plot
- ◆ masking
- ◆ prop crew
- ◆ publicity crew
- ◆ scenery
- ◆ set pieces
- ◆ sight lines

- ◆ sound
- ◆ sound crew
- ◆ sound plot
- ◆ stage crew
- ◆ stage lighting
- ◆ stage makeup
- ◆ stage manager
- ◆ theatre safety

ake a deep breath. It's time to prepare for the production from another direction. And because theatre is a group effort, there's a job for everyone.

A director could never stage a show alone. Behind the scenes, a support team is hard at work. There is a lot to be done in a short amount of time. Sets must be built, lights hung, sound effects created, music selected, makeup planned, costumes and props found or made, and publicity begun. In this chapter, you will discover the many ways to get involved in theatre by working backstage.

Theatre Safety

LESSON OBJECTIVES

◆ Understand the importance of theatre safety.
◆ Recognize potential dangers in the theatre.
◆ Practice theatre safety.

Working with your acting company, make a list of possible dangers involved in producing a play. Compare your group's list with those of the other acting companies.

theatre safety
keeping the crews, cast, and audience free from harm, danger, risk, or injury.

Before you begin work on a production, your director will discuss theatre safety with everyone involved in the production. **Theatre safety** means keeping the crews, cast, and audience free from harm, danger, injury, or risk. Safeguarding all the people involved in the play requires thinking ahead and eliminating hazardous situations. Theatre safety requires that every member of the company develop a "safety attitude"—always thinking, feeling, and acting in the safest manner for everyone concerned. Most accidents in theatre occur as a result of carelessness, taking unnecessary risks, being in a hurry, not knowing any better, or getting too excited. Most of these accidents could be avoided if everyone practiced the "safety attitude."

To be effective, theatre safety must be rehearsed until it becomes part of the everyday routine. Because no two theatres, scene shops, or backstage areas are exactly alike, each theatre should have its own specific guidelines for safety. After you study the theatre safety guidelines in Figure 11–1, help your company develop similar guidelines for your school theatre.

1. **Safety Tour.** Tour your theatre, making a list of possible hazards or unsafe areas. Compare the lists and compile them into one.

2. **Creating Safety.** Brainstorm with your class about ways to make any unsafe areas in your theatre safer.

3. **Fire Prevention.** Locate all fire extinguishers in the house and backstage areas. Then invite the city fire marshal or a local firefighter to discuss safety practices in the theatre.

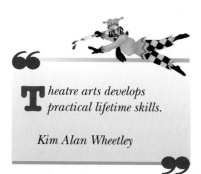

*T*heatre arts develops
practical lifetime skills.

Kim Alan Wheetley

Basic Theatre Safety Guidelines

1. Understand and observe all safety procedures and regulations.
2. Be observant of possible hazards or potential dangers. Report such situations to the stage manager or director.
3. Respect all tools and equipment. Never touch equipment without proper training.
4. Understand basic emergency procedures as established by your director (immediate report of injury; evacuation of building; use and location of fire extinguishers, flashlights, and master electric switches), and practice them when necessary.
5. Help keep exits and access to exits unobstructed at all times.
6. After you are finished, remember to put away all materials, tools, set pieces, props, and costumes in the safest manner possible.
7. Avoid running, throwing props or tools, pulling on curtains or ropes, jumping on or off the stage or from one level to another, playing practical jokes, or any other activity that might endanger either yourself or others.
8. When lifting objects, always bend the knees, keep the body erect, and push upward with the legs.
9. Always ask for assistance when moving set pieces or scenery to avoid possible strain or injury.
10. Help pick up and clean up after each work period or rehearsal.
11. Wear proper clothing, shoes, and safety goggles when working backstage or in the scene shop. Use gloves when working with solvents.
12. According to your local fire code, avoid using any open flame, hay, or untreated paper onstage.
13. Always use a sturdy wooden ladder rather than a box or chair to reach another height. Have another person "spot," or hold the ladder, when you are climbing.
14. Do not use tools or lights with frayed cords or broken connections. Extension cords should be heavy duty (UL listed) and of the proper size and length.
15. Make sure that all extension cords and microphone cords are taped to the floor to avoid tripping over them.
16. Be aware of potentially toxic materials: paint, glue, dyes, fireproofing chemicals, aerosol sprays, paint solvents, powdered pigments.
17. Avoid breathing vapors, and be sure to have proper ventilation when working with any potentially toxic material.
18. Remember that only authorized and trained crew members are to run lights or work rigging.
19. Make sure that crew members always wear shoes for safety.
20. Work on the grid or rigging only after the stage is cleared of actors and crew.
21. Keep all food and beverages out of the scene shop, backstage area, and light control area.
22. Always be sure that scenery is properly secured, braced, or weighted.
23. Practice your "safety attitude" during the "strike." The combination of excitement and exhaustion makes this one of the most dangerous times of the production.

4. Designing Safety Posters. Design and make a safety poster to post as a reminder to cast and crew.

5. Safety Cleanup. Properly dispose of all unsafe materials or substances found in the theatre work areas.

The Production Team

LESSON OBJECTIVES

- ◆ Recognize the responsibilities of the production team.
- ◆ Understand delegation of responsibilities.
- ◆ Recognize the function of management in theatre production.

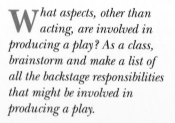

Warm Up

What aspects, other than acting, are involved in producing a play? As a class, brainstorm and make a list of all the backstage responsibilities that might be involved in producing a play.

stage manager

the person in charge of supervising backstage.

assistant director

the person who helps the director with such duties as warming up the cast before rehearsal, checking roll, posting rehearsal schedules, writing directorial notes during rehearsal, running errands, and filling in as an understudy when an actor is absent.

When the cast is announced, the director also announces the production team. One of the most important backstage roles is that of the stage manager. The **stage manager** reports directly to the director and is the person in charge of all backstage work—scenery, props, lighting, music, special effects, costumes, and makeup. During rehearsals, the stage manager acts as the director's assistant, supervising everything backstage. The stage manager is also responsible for handling the promptbook and prompting the actors when they forget their lines.

On the day or night of the performance, while the actors are getting into costumes and makeup, the stage manager will conduct a safety check to be sure that everything is in order for the performance. Once the performance begins, the director's job is over, and control of the show is left entirely to the stage manager. The student assigned this responsibility should be able to direct people in a firm but pleasant manner. Theatre students usually work their way up to the role of stage manager, since it is such a responsible position.

Another important behind-the-scenes position is that of assistant director. As the name implies, the **assistant director** serves as the director's assistant, helping the director with various jobs. These jobs include warming up the cast before rehearsal, checking roll, collecting production contracts, posting rehearsal schedules, photocopying notices to parents or cast members, writing directorial notes during rehearsal, running campus errands, and filling in as an understudy when an actor is absent.

It is important that the assistant director be dependable and self-motivated. The assistant director should be someone who is willing to

crew

committee of technicians who work behind the scenes creating the scenery, costumes, props, and so on.

take responsibility for seeing that the routine tasks are not forgotten during theatre class or rehearsal.

The backstage production team also includes various crews. A **crew** is a group of people, other than actors, who work behind the scenes to prepare the technical aspects of the show. The crews are as important as the actors. Many directors believe that a show cannot be successful without an intelligent, talented, responsible production team. Many great theatrical moments have been ruined by a technician who didn't do a good job. Some jobs, such as pulling the curtain, are not as easy as they look.

A director selects crews according to what is needed for a particular show. In some schools, a technical theatre class might be responsible for backstage work—scenery, lighting, and props. Other classes, too, such as art, wood shop, or sewing class, might be able to help the theatre department. Usually, the teacher of one of those classes becomes an assistant to the director, serving as technical director to oversee the technical work. Sometimes, interested parents organize "booster" groups and volunteer to help with the work backstage.

While the actors are learning their lines and movements, the production crews are also working hard, preparing to meet the deadline set by the director. Everything needs to be completed at least two weeks before the opening of the show. If there is a technical director, he or she is in charge of the production crews. Otherwise, the director or stage manager is in charge.

A leader, called the *crew head*, is usually assigned to each technical area—stage, props, costumes, makeup, sound, lighting, publicity, and house. Crew members are assigned by the director or recruited by crew heads. In the following lessons, you will explore the basic responsibilities of each of these crews.

ACTION

1. **Stage Manager Responsibilities.** You are the stage manager for a play. Make a list of your responsibilities during the production process. As the stage manager for the production, what must you remember to always check before the performance?

2. **Assistant Director Responsibilities.** You are the assistant director for a play. Make a list of all of your responsibilities. As the assistant director for the play, plan a series of physical, vocal, and breathing exercises to use to warm up the cast at the beginning of each rehearsal.

The Stage Crew

LESSON OBJECTIVES

◆ Understand the responsibilities of the stage crew.
◆ Select specific scenic elements to represent a visual environment.

Warm Up

Tour the onstage and backstage areas of your theatre. Look for basic pieces of furniture, folding screens, or set pieces that could be used to transform the empty stage.

stage crew
the group of technicians responsible for building the scenery. During a production, this crew is in charge of any scene changes.

scenery
curtains, backdrops, or any structures constructed to transform an empty stage into a suitable background for the play.

The job of the **stage crew** is to transform the empty stage into a suitable setting for the play. Through the use of **scenery**, anything hanging or constructed to create a background for the play, the setting is established for the audience and the actors. The ease or complexity of the job depends on many elements—the play's requirements, the theatre facilities, the budget, the time allotted, and the crew's capabilities.

Scenery serves several purposes. It helps to create the stage setting, showing the audience where and when the play takes place. It defines the acting area, giving the actors a basic plan for entrances, exits, and movement and providing a physical background for their work. Finally, scenery can create a mood or atmosphere for the play or even make a statement about the theme.

An effective stage setting is an important part of the play. The stage design should enhance the total production by working in harmony with the costumes, props, lighting, and acting. It is the job of the stage crew to work with the director or technical director to interpret the overall concept of the play and to support that interpretation through the set.

After carefully studying the script, the director or technical director designs a floor plan for each scene in the play. The floor plan is a drawing of the stage setting as seen from above (see Figure 11–2). Next, a scenic design is created from this floor plan. A watercolor sketch and often a model of the design might then be presented to the stage crew

Figure 11-2

Floor Plan of Set Design.

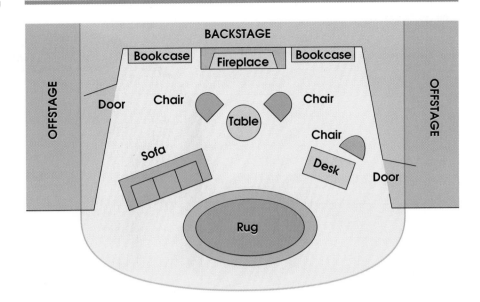

so that they can see how the set is to look (see Figure 11–3). Working plans are then developed, and the construction begins.

It is the stage crew's responsibility to construct and complete the scenery. In some schools that could mean arranging and repainting unit set pieces—platforms, ramps, steps, and pylons, structures that resemble a pillar or column (see Figure 11–4). In some theatres, the set might consist of a large backdrop on which scenery has been painted. In many performances, furniture and freestanding set pieces, such as trees and fences, are placed in front of a cyclorama. A **cyclorama** is a large semicircular curtain covering the back and sides of the stage (see

cyclorama

a large curtain covering the back and sides of the stage.

Figure 11-3

Set Design Sketch.

Figure 11-4
■ ■ ■ ■ ■ ■ ■ ■ ■ ■ ■ ■ ■ ■ ■ ■

Unit Set Pieces.

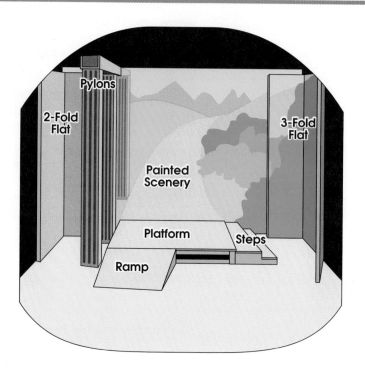

Figure 11-5). Schools with a scene shop and technical supervision might build a complete set from the stage floor up. Your director will explain the types of scenery used at your school and how the sets are to be constructed.

Completing the set also means finding or building set pieces. **Set pieces** are large, portable pieces of the setting. They may consist of furniture, a fountain, movable rocks, a throne, or a tree stump (see

set pieces

large portable pieces of the stage setting.

Figure 11-5
■ ■ ■ ■ ■ ■ ■ ■ ■ ■ ■ ■ ■ ■ ■ ■

Freestanding Set Pieces.

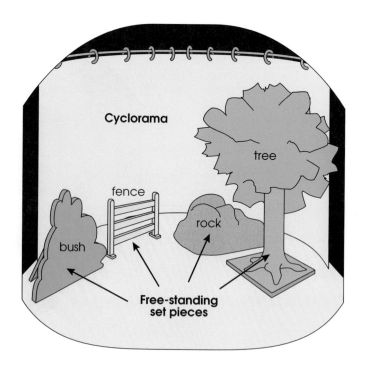

Stage crew members must be sure heavy set pieces like the king's table are safely moved where they belong for every scene in the production.

sight lines

imaginary lines defining the areas of the stage where the actors can clearly be seen by the audience.

Figure 11–5). In most schools, the prop crew handles the hand props and the stage crew is responsible for finding and setting up the set pieces. Your director will probably make these large pieces the responsibility of the stage crew, since they tie in with the overall design of the set. Other decorative items, such as pictures, banners, flower arrangements, tablecloths, and wall mirrors, also help decorate the set, and they, too, could be the responsibility of the stage crew.

Some accessories or furniture items may need to be borrowed. Before you go to a local furniture store or antique shop, look around campus to see what bits and pieces you can find. The guidance counselor might have a great rocking chair, the librarian a brass hat tree, the principal a perfect end table, and the school secretary just the right painting for the wall. What's more, a plywood circle from the scene shop, when attached to a wooden stool and covered with a long velvet (or corduroy) skirt, can become an elegant table.

Another way to collect decorative items and furniture is to send out notes to the parents of the cast and crew. Sometimes, all it takes is a note in the school bulletin or an article in the school newspaper to alert interested students, teachers, and friends of your needs.

If scenery needs to be painted, your director or the technical director will instruct you in special painting techniques used to create textures and designs (see Figure 11–6). Almost any look can be created with paint. Water-based flat paint is the best paint to use for most scenery needs because it doesn't reflect light onstage and the cleanup is easy.

It is the stage crew's responsibility to have the scenery and set pieces ready by the scheduled deadline. This will give the actors ample time to become comfortable working on the completed set.

Establishing sight lines is an important part of the stage crew's job. **Sight lines** are imaginary lines on the stage that indicate those areas where the actors can be seen by the audience (see Figure 11–7). The

Figure 11–6

Ways to Paint Scenery.

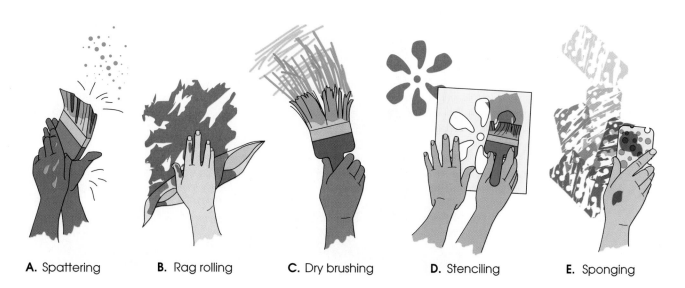

A. Spattering **B.** Rag rolling **C.** Dry brushing **D.** Stenciling **E.** Sponging

■ CHAPTER 11: Behind the Scenes ■ 197

masking

any materials such as curtains
or scenery used to block
an audience's view of the
backstage area.

stage crew must be sure that each member of the audience can see all
of the stage that is being used. People seated in the back rows will have
a different view from those seated near the front of the house. By
checking out the sight lines from different areas of the house, the
stage crew makes sure that the scenery doesn't block the sight of any
member of the audience.

Another job of the stage crew is to be sure that the backstage areas
are hidden from view of the audience. This is called **masking**, and it
can be accomplished with curtains, flats, or screens (see Figure 11–8).

Figure ■ 11–8

Masking.

You need not be an actor to play an important part in your school's next performance. Many different kinds of skills are needed to create a successful production.

*I*n the last analysis the designing of stage scenery is not the problem of an architect or a painter or a sculptor or even a musician, but of a poet.

Robert Edmond Jones

During rehearsals and performances, the stage crew will move any set pieces or scenery that need changing during the scene changes. If the stage is shared with other groups, the set will need to be "struck" (taken down) after each rehearsal or performance. To make setting up easier, the stage crew can spike (mark) the stage floor with colored tape to show the placement of scenery and set pieces. After each rehearsal, the stage crew will carefully move the scenery and set pieces and store them as directed by the stage manager.

At the end of each rehearsal, the stage crew head should note any changes or repairs that need to be made before the next rehearsal. The stage crew will also clean the stage floor before the next rehearsal. Most stage floors need to be cleaned with a vacuum cleaner, dust mop, or damp mop to pick up all the dust that accumulates during a rehearsal. Sweeping with a regular house broom usually just stirs up more dust.

The final job of the stage crew is to strike the set. All usable set pieces and scenery items should be stored under the guidance of the stage manager. Borrowed items should be returned and appreciation letters written and mailed. After everything is stored, the crew thoroughly cleans the stage and backstage area. If there is a scene shop, that, too, should be put into good order and cleaned according to the director's instructions.

ACTION

1. **Stage Crew Responsibilities.** First pretend that you are the head of a stage crew and make a list of your responsibilities. Then pretend that you are a *member* of the stage crew and make a list of your responsibilities.

2. **Where Are the Sight Lines?** Sit in different areas of the theatre to establish sight lines for your particular stage.

The Prop Crew

LESSON OBJECTIVES

◆ Recognize the responsibilities of the prop crew.
◆ Experience the technical aspects of production.

Figure 11–9
▪ ▪ ▪ ▪ ▪ ▪ ▪ ▪ ▪ ▪ ▪ ▪ ▪ ▪

Props.

prop crew
the crew in charge of stage
properties (props).

The **prop crew** is the name of the crew in charge of stage properties. Props (stage properties) are all articles handled by the actors or
used to "dress," or decorate, the set. Props are important additions to a
play. They reveal information about the plot, they help the audience
place the play's action, they aid the actor with stage business, they enhance characterization, and they often add symbolism to the play.

The prop crew is usually responsible for obtaining and maintaining
all props (see Figure 11–9). The prop crew's first job is to carefully read
the script to determine the needed props. A meeting between crew
heads from the prop crew, costume crew, and stage crew will ensure
that several crews are not assuming responsibility for acquiring the

same items. After completing the prop list, the prop crew head attends the blocking rehearsals to find out how the props are used in the play.

Once the types of props and their uses are determined, the prop crew begins the challenge of supplying the props. The crew checks to see what is available from the storage cabinets or prop room. These items are then checked off the list. Finally, the crew makes a list of all the items they need to locate. Different members of the crew might take responsibility for acquiring certain props.

Props can be acquired in several ways: by buying them, renting them, borrowing them, and making them. For many educational theatre groups, buying and renting may be out of the question because of the cost. In these cases, making and borrowing are the only solutions. One rule to remember: Never borrow anything too expensive for your group to replace if it were to become broken, lost, or stolen. Accurate records should be kept of all props that are borrowed, and the props should be returned immediately following the final performance.

Making props is one of the most exciting parts of working backstage. Papier-mâché, Styrofoam, and modern molding products from your local craft store or theatrical supply store will make your job fun. Your crew will probably have lots of creative ideas. But if you should need help constructing a particularly difficult prop, remember to consult a book on prop making from your school library or art teacher.

All props need to be ready by the first rehearsal after blocking. Some of the props will be easy to find; others will be more difficult to come by. While your crew is busy locating and creating the more difficult ones, you will need to supply substitute props for the actors. Plastic fruit can be used for real fruit, cardboard tubes can make temporary swords, and a cutoff broomstick can be used as a scepter. While creating the real items, use your imagination for substituting props.

One of the responsibilities of the prop crew is to have all props in place and ready for each rehearsal. Some props need to be onstage at the beginning of a scene; others need to be in the wings, waiting to be carried onstage by actors later in the scene. It helps to organize hand props by scenes. Small props can be stored together in boxes, milk crates, or baskets, with a list of the contents taped to the box. To save time and frustration during rehearsals and performances, these prop boxes can be organized backstage on two prop tables—placed offstage right and offstage left. These tables should also have room for any props too large to fit into boxes.

It is the prop crew's responsibility to make sure that the correct prop is handed to an actor as the actor prepares for an entrance. One crew member can be assigned to each of the prop tables. These crew members must learn to check that the actors actually have the props in their hands. Sometimes, an actor will absentmindedly put down a prop while straightening a costume and not remember to pick it up.

When props must be removed or replaced during a scene change, careful planning and coordination are needed. Crew members should have specific responsibilities in such situations to ensure that all props are in place by the end of the scene change. Small pieces of tape marking the locations for the props make setting up arrangements on table-tops, bookshelves, or buffets go much faster. It is best if the same people set up the arrangements at each rehearsal. If there are lots of

In the theatre you have to make the unreal believable.

Jean Vilar

Movie prop crews operate much the same as theatre crews. They have to be sure all props, including special effects pieces, are in place and in good working order for every scene.

scene changes, place photographs of the finished arrangements in the promptbook to serve as reminders for the crew head.

After rehearsals or performances, the prop crew will gather up all the props and store them behind a locked door. Check carefully to be sure that you have collected all the props. Actors sometimes put props down in strange places backstage or carelessly take them to the dressing room. It is the prop crew head's responsibility to make sure that all props are found and returned to the proper storage place at the end of each rehearsal or performance. If props need to be repaired, the prop crew head sees that it is done before the next rehearsal or performance. When props become wilted (real flowers) or soiled (paper products), the prop crew head replaces them.

After the final production, it is the prop crew's responsibility to collect all the props. The day after the show, all borrowed props should be returned and a letter of appreciation written and mailed to each lender. Then the crew sees to the cleaning and repairing of any props needing attention. Finally, any reusable props should be stored for later use.

ACTION

1. **Prop Crew Head Responsibilities.** You are the head of the prop crew. Make a list of your responsibilities in preparing for the production.

2. **Prop Crew Member Responsibilities.** You are a member of the prop crew. Make a list of your responsibilities during a performance.

3. **Preparing a Prop List.** Read a play and prepare a prop list based on the script.

4. **Scene-by-Scene Prop Checklist.** Make a checklist or chart of props used in each scene of the play in activity 3.

5. **Prop Rehearsal.** Working with your acting company, plan the props for two scenes from the play you read in activity 3. Rehearse a quick change of props from one scene to the next. Use a stopwatch to see how long it takes to "switch out the props."

6. **Creating Props.** Design and make a stage prop for an upcoming production.

The Costume Crew

LESSON OBJECTIVES

◆ Recognize the responsibilities of the costume crew.
◆ Experience the technical aspects of production.

Warm Up

Working in pairs, create a hat or headdress using newspapers and masking tape. One student models the creation while the other describes with "colorful" language what the costumer would like the audience to see.

costume crew
the committee in charge of costuming the show.

costume
an outfit, including accessories and undergarments, worn by an actor in a production.

The **costume crew** prepares the costumes for the play. A **costume** is any outfit worn by an actor in a production. The costume also includes accessories.

Costumes are a vital part of any production because they carry such strong meaning for the audience and actors. Costumes help the audience "see" the characters—help them to know the age, personality, tastes, social standing, and even occupation of a character. And through their color and style, costumes complete the visual impression of time and place established by the scenery. Finally, costumes help the actors feel and move as characters rather than as themselves.

In professional theatre, a costume designer confers with the director, researches the period of the play, and then designs all of the costumes for the entire play, coordinating them to harmonize with each other and with the scenic design. These costume designs are then taken to the costumer, who transforms the designs into costumes. In educational theatre, the director and the costume crew usually plan the costuming for a play.

In most schools, the director depends on the costume crew, parents, and sometimes a professional to help create the needed costumes. Costumes can be obtained by renting, borrowing, making, or buying. The process followed in your school will most likely depend on the theatre department's budget.

The responsibilities of the costume crew will vary, depending on the type of production and the resources of the school. Many costume crews design and make as many costumes and accessories as they can. A meeting with the director will put the costume crew in the right direction.

A good way to costume a production on a small budget is to first study the play for all references to costume, paying close attention to what the playwright says about the characters' clothing. (Check both dialogue and stage directions.) Some clothing needs may be determined by the period of the play, the time of day, or the season of the year. If a character is to go outside in the snow, the costume crew will need to "bundle him up" appropriately.

costume plot
a chart listing each character, the acts or scenes in which they appear, and all garments, undergarments, and accessories needed.

Next, the costume crew makes a costume plot. A **costume plot** is a costume chart listing every character in the show and each scene in which the character appears (see Figure 11–10). Beside each character's name is the actor's name and every garment, undergarment, and accessory needed for that scene. This gives the crew an idea of the outfits needed, the type of garments required, the number of changes for each character, and any special requirements. At this point, the crew should meet again with the director to create a color scheme and design the costumes, making sure that all parts of the play work well together.

After the costume plot is prepared, the costume crew meets with the actors individually to see if they can supply any of their own personal items. This is especially helpful with accessories such as shoes and tights. These individual meetings could also include a measurement session. Having accurate measurements for each actor is vital for the correct sizing of costumes. Discuss this session with your director, who may want to be included. If the director cannot present, invite a parent to assist in this session.

With the costume plot in hand, the next stop is the costume storage closet, or wardrobe, to evaluate the collection of costumes from previous plays. Basic costumes can be embellished (decorated) or altered to make them suitable for the current production. Often, costumes can be "put together" in different ways. The costume crew will need to think creatively.

Figure 11–10

Costume Plot.

Play Title *Calling Dr. Curemee* Date *11/12, 11/13*

Act *3*
Scene *2*

Character	Actor	Costume	Accessories	Special Notes
Sylvia	*Megan*	*blue silk dress*	*hat, scarf, heels*	*help tie scarf over shoulder*
Walter	*Eric*	*brown suit*	*spectator shoes, pipe, glasses*	
Grandma	*Andrea*	*blue bathrobe*	*slippers, tissue box*	*must look very rumpled*
Bobby	*Justin*	*jeans & T-shirt*	*baseball cap, glove*	
Suzie	*Jackie*	*soccer uniform*	*soccer ball, water bottle*	
Dr. Curemee	*Roberto*	*blazer, navy pants, white shirt, tie*	*stethoscope, notepad, pencil*	

If you are involved in a play set in a time or place different from your own, costumes will become an especially important part of the production. For these plays, students with sewing skills or a knack for clothing design will become valuable members of the production team.

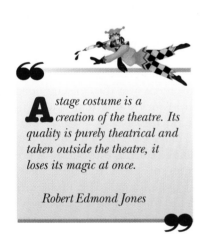

Meet again with the director to decide how to continue with your crew assignment. The next step may be a trip to the local thrift stores, where for very little money, many garments can be found to restyle into great costumes. Begin by looking for clothing similar in style to the period you are costuming. A suggestion of the historical period can go a long way onstage. Also think about how a modern garment might be used for another historical period. By removing the collar, cuffs, and pockets from a man's shirt and adding binding to the neck and elastic to the sleeves, you can create a loose-fitting shirt for a peasant.

Look for fabric and accessories that can be turned into costumes. A king's robe can be made from an old velour blanket or a pair of brocade drapes. A fur collar from an old coat can be cut apart and used to trim the robe.

Vests, white ruffled blouses, long full skirts, and full evening dresses always offer possibilities. Remember to keep in mind the color scheme your director has suggested—but don't overlook the possibility of dying clothes with premixed fabric dye from the grocery store. Many fabrics take dye beautifully. Once the costume crew gets started, you will find that there are endless possibilities for developing attractive and appropriate costumes, even when the budget is slim.

Some costumes will probably need to be sewn. Theatrical costume books give instructions on drafting and cutting patterns for various time periods. Even today's modern pattern books have a selection of basic period designs in the section on costuming.

Once all costumes and accessories are completed, the actors should try them on to be sure they fit properly. Then the crew irons or steams the costumes and hangs them neatly on clothes hangers. All accessories for each ensemble can be grouped together and placed into plastic grocery bags or in the drawstring bags you get from a shoe store. With permanent marker, label the bag with the character's name, and hang the bag on the hanger with the correct costume. The actor's costume is then organized.

After each rehearsal or performance, group the costume and accessories together and hang them up. The costume crew head is in charge of checking out the costumes to the actors. The costume crew head is also in charge of making sure that the actors turn in all pieces after taking the costumes off.

Before any dress rehearsals or performances, the costume crew should assist the actors when they need help. If an actor has a quick change between scenes, a member of the costume crew should be there to help the actor make the change. The costume head should be prepared with a costume first aid kit containing safety pins of various sizes, needles, thread, masking tape (for quick hems), a glue gun, glue sticks, and even a stapler and staples.

After the final performance, the costume crew is responsible for checking to see that each actor has checked in all costumes and accessories. Next, all borrowed costumes should be cleaned and returned. If they were borrowed from someone other than a cast member, a letter of appreciation should be written and mailed immediately. Finally, all costumes and accessories should be stored according to the director's instructions.

OUR THEATRE HERITAGE

Theatre In the Nineteenth Century

For theatre, like most of society, the 1800s were a time of change. Technology was changing throughout society and the new inventions were bound to affect the way theatre was produced. Europe's farming economy shifted to an economy controlled by the big factories of the Industrial Revolution, the period of time when machines replaced hand tools in many trades.

No nineteenth century theatre actor was more well-known around the world than the French star Sarah Bernhardt (1844-1923). In addition to playing the leads in the most popular French plays of her time, she managed and owned several theatres and traveled regularly with her own acting company to places such as London and New York.

You wouldn't think that the invention of the steam engine would have a major impact on the theatre, but it did. The steam engine made it possible to transport theatre to areas that had never had the opportunity to see theatre regularly. European stars and productions even began to tour with their shows in America!

Even more important, the steam engine led to the building of large steam-powered factories, which offered hundreds and hundred of new jobs, so workers started swarming into the cities. This trend, called *urbanization,* had a major effect on the theatre. The crowds of people moving into the cities in Europe wanted entertainment and the members of the growing middle class had more free time on their hands than ever before. Theatre grew and grew in popularity. In fact, theatre became a very fashionable pastime, an actual fad! By the late 1800s, theatre and other live entertainment were in endless demand, as common to the people of that day as movies are to us today. This great popularity of theatre resulted in the construction of more and larger playhouses. After 1817, these new theatres were lit with gas, a vast improvement over the constant need to replace the hundreds of candles that it took to light theatres prior to the use of gas.

The way in which plays were written during the 1800s was also changing. During this period there were three main types of plays: romantic plays, well-made plays, and melodramas. The Romantics (writers who wrote in the romantic style) rejected all the current artistic rules, stating that if the playwright were a real genius, he or she needed no rules, such as those that had dominated the neoclassical period. Romantic plays are noted for the way they created a feeling, an atmosphere, and a mood, often at the expense of believable plots or characters. The romantic playwrights believed that there was no subject matter inappropriate for the stage. They built conflict in their plays between the characters' spiritual and creative wishes and their physical inabilities.

The second type of play that was popular during the 1800s was melodrama. Melodrama emphasized action and spectacular stage effects and was always accompanied by music and song, which helped establish a tense mood for the play. These dramas were designed to pull on the heartstrings of the audience by pitting good characters against bad characters, heroes against villains. The main characters in melodrama were either totally good in nature or totally evil, making it very clear which of the two the audience was to applaud. This form of theatre has remained popular in various forms, often comic, up to our present day. You have probably seen some light comedies in which a villain in a dark cape and mustache is defeated by a hero.

The third category of drama popular in the 1800s was the *well-made play*. This name refers to the structure of the play, which builds to a climax through a development of plot events that take place logically in a cause-and-effect fashion. In a well-made play, the audience has all of the information it needs to understand all of the characters, and the play constantly foreshadows the action to come. There are no surprises changing the expected outcome of the plot. The action moves predictably forward as new information is discovered by the characters through means such as letters or documents. The surprise endings to plays, which had been so popular in earlier periods of history, lost their popularity as the new scientific and mechanized society demanded reasonable, logical endings.

During this period, interest in the theatre was beginning to revolve around the popularity of certain stars rather than around highly popular playwrights or play titles. Stars such as Sarah Bernhardt in *Pelléas and Mélisande*, Edwin Booth as Hamlet, and Eleonora Duse drew great crowds and were very influential. Duse, for example, was an influence on Stanislavski and contributed to his development of a new method of acting, which you'll read about later. This period could be thought of as an age of stars.

While the actors were becoming more powerful and more well respected, the theatre was developing a new artistic position, the director. As you will remember from earlier history sections in this book,

prior to this period actors were largely self-directed. The actors decided where and how to say their lines, most often under the supervision of one head actor who gave a few suggestions about how to deliver dialogue during a very few rehearsals. This practice began to change radically in the late 1800s. Individuals known as "directors" tried to create a "unified stage picture" in which all of the visual elements of the play matched each other and visually suggested the same historical period. The directors also began to take great care that all costumes and set designs reflected the fashion popular at the time of the play's setting. This meant that more rehearsals were needed to coordinate these unified choices. Important early directors include Madame Vestris and Henry Irving in London and Richard Wagner and the Duke of Saxe-Meinigen in Germany. ■

George II, Duke of Saxe-Meiningen (1826-1914) helped establish the importance of the director. He took total control of his productions and was especially effective at producing and directing crowd scenes.

1. **Costume Crew Head Responsibilities.** You are the head of the costume crew for the next play. Make a list of your responsibilities in preparing for the production.

2. **Costume Crew Member Responsibilities.** You are a member of the costume crew. Make a list of your responsibilities the day of the performance.

3. **Designing a Costume.** Draw a costume design for a major character in a play you have recently read.

4. **Thank-You Letter.** Write a sample letter of appreciation to thank community members who donated costumes to the theatre department.

The Makeup Crew

LESSON OBJECTIVES

◆ Recognize the responsibilities of the makeup crew.
◆ Select and use makeup to suggest character.
◆ Apply basic stage makeup.

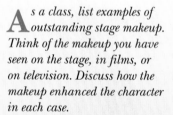

Warm Up

As a class, list examples of outstanding stage makeup. Think of the makeup you have seen on the stage, in films, or on television. Discuss how the makeup enhanced the character in each case.

stage makeup
any cosmetic effect, including hair, that enhances or changes an actor's appearance.

makeup crew
the crew in charge of designing and applying makeup for each character.

Working on the makeup crew is one of the most exciting parts of backstage theatre. It brings out the artist in every crew member. **Stage makeup** is more than just cosmetics added to the face or body. It also includes beards, goatees, mustaches, wigs, hairstyles, hair color, scars, warts, and false noses. Any cosmetic effect that enhances or changes an actor's appearance might be defined as stage makeup. It is the responsibility of the **makeup crew** to plan a makeup design for each character and to apply the makeup for each dress rehearsal and performance.

Stage makeup helps create a visual character. It can help a character's features show up from the stage, or it can actually change an actor's facial or body characteristics. **Basic makeup**, or straight makeup, uses the actor's natural features (see Figure 11–11). **Character makeup** alters the actor's features (see Figure 11–12 on page 210). In movies, television, and live theatre, we can find many examples of character makeup used to age a character or turn the actor into something from the world of fantasy.

The responsibilities of the makeup crew will vary with the director and theatre. The application of stage makeup, even in professional theatre, usually is the job of each individual actor. In educational theatre, a crew might prepare, set up, and assist inexperienced actors in the application of stage makeup.

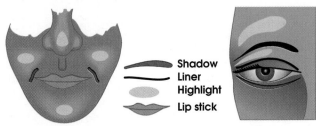

- Shadow
- Liner
- Highlight
- Lip stick

1. Beginning with clean skin, apply the foundation or base makeup with small dots of color to face, neck, ears and other exposed areas. Smooth out and blend the dots of makeup with fingertips or sponge until all the skin has a light covering - makeup should not appear heavy or greasy. Dipping your fingers into water aids the smoothing and blending process.

2. All shading and highlighting is added to contour the face shape. This process helps highlight features, correct features, or change features. Choose a shadow color several shades darker than the foundation, or use dark brown or maroon liner. Shadows are added with a flat sable paint brush - building up and blending the shadows through several applications. Shadows are added where contours are needed - under the chin, around the nose, above the eyebrows, and following the jaw line. For each shadow (lowlight), there must be a highlight. Pale highlights are formed by using white liner or foundation several shades lighter than the face color. Highlights are applied with a brush or sponge above the shadows or on parts of the face that protrude - bones such as cheeks, brow, and jaw. It is often added down the center of the nose and above the lips.

3. Moist rouge is added to shape the face and add warmth to the cheekbones, center of forehead, and chin. Beginning at the highest point of the cheekbone, apply three dots of rouge in a triangle shape. Blend dots together with fingertips or sponge working upward and out. Add moist rouge to lips. Males require less rouge than females.

4. Eye makeup is used to make the eyes stand out. Apply eye shadow to the upper lid blending from darkest (near the eyelid) to lightest (near the brow) keeping the strongest color just above the center of the eye. Use liner to line the upper lid just above the eyelashes; the lower lid from e center to the outer corner - meeting the upper and lower lines together. An eye liner pencil or a fine brush can be used.

5. After checking the makeup under stage lights, powder is used to set the makeup keeping it from smudging. Powdering also softens the lines created by shadowing and removes the shine of the greasepaint. Apply a light coat of powder, pressing it into the face with a puff. Allow the powder to set for a few minutes and then brush off the excess with a soft powder brush.

6. Finishing touches, false eyelashes, mascara, brow color, dry rouge, or additional lip color, are added after powdering. Lips can be lined for more definition.

7. To remove, soften the makeup by covering with makeup remover, cold cream, cleansing cream, baby oil, mineral oil, or white vegetable shortening. After the makeup is softened or liquefied, it is easily removed with tissues. The face should then be cleansed in the normal fashion.

basic makeup

cosmetics applied to the face or body using the actor's natural features.

character makeup

makeup used to change an actor's natural features.

makeup plot

a chart listing the makeup needs for each character in a play.

Although the makeup crew does not really go to work until the first dress rehearsal, it needs to begin preparations earlier in the production process. The first step is to read the play carefully, making notes about individual characters, plot, theme, time, and place.

After reading the play, the crew may need to research the styles of the play's period. A good research technique is to look at art prints and books with illustrations from the period.

Next, the makeup crew should review the techniques of basic makeup application in Figure 11–11 above, and if necessary refer to one of the more complete makeup guides. *Stage Makeup,* by Richard Carson, is an excellent guide to stage makeup. Also, several videotapes are now on the market demonstrating the step-by-step application of all makeup styles. If the crew is inexperienced, the crew head should schedule a demonstration and practice application session.

It is the makeup crew's responsibility to compile a makeup plot for the play. A **makeup plot** is a chart listing the makeup needs for each character. The list should include basic makeup colors as well as any special effects—warts, scars, or hair additions (see Figure 11–13). The makeup plot can also include a makeup sketch showing how the makeup will be applied. Sometimes, it helps to support the sketches with magazine photographs illustrating the finished "looks." The makeup crew will then ask the director to approve all plans. At this point, a con-

Figure 11-12
■ ■

Steps for Old-Age Character Makeup.

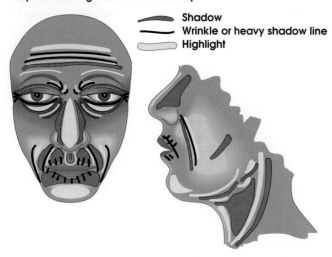

— Shadow
— Wrinkle or heavy shadow line
▭ Highlight

1. Because skin becomes paler with age, choose a foundation color lighter than the natural skin tone or one with a yellow cast. Apply the base color following the steps for basic application.

2. Shadow the soft spots of the face coloring areas that will sag or sink in with age - above and beneath the eyes, around the outside folds of the mouth, under the cheek bones, under the chin, at the temples, and along the neck. Use a purplish mix of brown, red, and blue liners to achieve effective shadows. Contrast these shadows using white highlights.

3. Add age lines under and around the eyes and wrinkles to the forehead. Determine the natural placement of lines and wrinkles by smiling and frowning. Follow the lines with a fine brush and cream liner or a pencil liner. Adding a white line to the upper side of each dark line helps create the illusion of wrinkles. Add "crows feet" to the outer corner of each eye. Add age lines across the bridge of the nose, around the mouth, and on the neck. Blend the lines with a brush or the narrow side of a makeup sponge.

4. Lightly add a reddish brown color to the lips.

5. Age the hands using the same principles of shadows and highlights. Add lines and shadows between the tendons and on either side of the hand. Highlight the tendons. Lines can also be added to the knuckles.

6. Use a toothbrush to apply hair whitener or white shoe polish in fine streaks to age the hair. Hair first begins to turn white around the temples. Eyebrows can be aged in the same way.

7. Check the makeup under stage lights and make necessary changes.

8. Additional age treatment can be created by aging or discoloring the teeth with tooth enamel, adding "liver" spots with yellowish brown liner, and coloring the veins in the hands to stand out prominently.

9. Powder the face using a powder puff to gently press a light coat or powder over all made up areas. After the powder has absorbed the oil, gently brush off the excess with a soft powder brush.

10. To remove makeup, soften it by covering with makeup remover, cold cream, cleansing cream, baby oil, mineral oil, or white vegetable shortening. After the makeup is softened or liquefied, it is easily removed with facial tissues. The face should then be cleansed in normal fashion.

ference with the crew heads from costuming and lighting will be called to make sure that all of the technical aspects are compatible.

Once the makeup needs are determined, the crew needs to check the existing supply of makeup, making a list of all items that need to be replaced (see Figure 11–14). The director will tell the crew head what the policy is for ordering needed makeup or supplies.

It's a good idea to meet individually with each actor to go over the makeup plot. Some actors may need to be reminded not to make any radical changes to their hair, such as haircuts or hair colors, without first consulting the makeup crew. Others may need to be informed of changes needing to be made, such as different hairstyles, haircuts, or hair color.

Although today's theatre makeup causes few problems to the skin, it is still important to conduct a skin sensitivity check on each actor. At the end of one of the early rehearsals, place a "smear" of base makeup on the wrist of each actor. Ask the actors to be alert to any redness or itching that might occur. At the next rehearsal, the makeup crew should question the actors as to sensitivity. If itching or redness occurred, switch brands of makeup or test a new container. Most students do not react, but occasionally a student will have a sensitivity or allergy to one product but not to another.

Figure 11–13

Makeup Plot.

Makeup is an integral part of making your character believable.

> *Just as robes or rags can give the actor the "feel" of a character, so also can makeup.*
>
> Uta Hägen

PRODUCTION _____ DATE _____
CHARACTER _____ ACTOR _____

(Insert sketches or photographs
to show the effect you want to achieve)

Foundation/Base _____ Shadows _____ Highlights _____

Rouge _____ Powder _____

Special Needs: _____ Notes: _____

_____ _____

_____ _____

_____ _____

| Eyes | Cheeks | Mouth | Nose | Forehead |

Shadow
Liner
Brows

Hair   Mustache/beard   Special Effects

The makeup crew will need to prepare the supplies before the first dress rehearsal. Ask each actor to bring a large cover-up to protect clothing and a washcloth and bath towel for cleanup. A man's shirt turned backward works well for the cover-up. Some theatre groups also ask individual actors to supply their own cold cream and facial tissues for removing makeup. All of these supplies need to be organized the best way possible for your facility.

For dress rehearsals and performances, the dressing room or a classroom needs to be set up for the actors. Each actor needs a "spot" set

Figure 11–14

Makeup Supplies.

Foundation: Base makeup comes in a variety of skin colors.

Clown white: Used for highlighting or as a base in fantasy or stylized makeup.

Liners: Greasepaints in a variety of colors. In cream or stick form. Use as liners, eye shadows, or anywhere color is needed.

Rouges: Comes in dry or moist forms. Used to add cheek color.

Powder: Comes in translucent or in skin shades. Used to set makeup.

Makeup pencils: Wooden pencils filled with greasepaint. They come in all colors and are used to darken eye brows, draw lines, and line lips or eyes.

Mascara: Used for darkening eyelashes, mustaches, or beards.

Hair whiteners: Liquid or solid. Used to whiten hair.

Makeup removers: To remove grease-based makeup, use purchased makeup removers, cold cream, cleansing cream, baby oil, even white solid vegetable shortening. Water-based makeup is easily removed with soap and water or soapless facial cleansers.

Crepe hair: Natural hair-colored wool or human hair. Purchased by the yard, it comes woven in tight braids. It can be used to make beards, sideburn, mustaches, even eyebrows.

Spirit gum: An adhesive used to glue on beards. Must be removed with spirit gum remover or rubbing alcohol unless it is water-based spirit gum.

Liquid latex: Used to attach beards, buildup features, create skin texture, and form wrinkles.

Nose putty: Used to build up bony features such as the nose, form scars, or add warts.

Collodion: Can be used to make scars. Comes in a flexible and nonflexible variety.

Tooth enamel: Used to block out or age teeth. Comes in a variety of colors.

Powder puffs: Used to apply powder. Buy puffs that can be cleaned.

Powder brushes: Used to brush off excess powder.

Makeup brushes: Camel's hair paintbrushes in various sizes and widths to use in drawing lines and shading.

Makeup sponges: Used to apply makeup.

Stipple sponges: Used to add texture.

Cotton swabs: Used to blend liners or remove small makeup smudges.

Toothbrushes: Used to add hair whiteners.

Miscellaneous supplies: Tissues, large mirrors, paper towels, combs and brushes, hairpins and hair clips, stretchy headbands.

---

aside with the appropriate supplies. When base makeup is to be shared from a large container, no fingers should ever be placed in the container. A more sanitary way is to use craft sticks to dip out the makeup, placing the "dabs" on small plastic plates. To prevent eye infections, the makeup crew should encourage the actors not to share eye makeup such as mascara or eyeliner.

All stage makeup needs to be checked under the stage lights before rehearsal. Stage lights are different from most dressing room lights and tend to distort, or change, the overall look of the makeup. By examining the makeup under the stage lights before powdering, you can easily make any necessary changes.

After the rehearsal or performance, the makeup crew is responsible for putting all makeup in order and cleaning up the room where the makeup was applied. After the final performance, the crew should clean up and store all makeup equipment and supplies.

1. Makeup Crew Head Responsibilities. You are the head of the makeup crew. Make a list of your responsibilities.

2. **Makeup Crew Member Responsibilities.** You are a member of the makeup crew. What are your responsibilities before rehearsals and performances?

3. **Designing Makeup Plots.** Design the makeup plot for one of the characters in a play.

4. **Applying Makeup.** Apply stage makeup for an upcoming production.

5. **Comparing Stage Makeup.** Collect ten photographs showing different examples of old age.

The Sound Crew

LESSON OBJECTIVES

◆ Recognize the responsibilities of the sound crew.
◆ Recognize the contributions of technical elements in a production.
◆ Select and use sound effects and music to enhance a production.

Warm Up

Sound Improv. *Working in groups, use objects in the classroom to create sounds to enhance a specific mood. Share the sound improvisation with the class.*

sound
artificially produced sound effects or music as well as the amplification of voices so that they can be heard.

sound crew
the group responsible for planning and preparing all sound effects needed for a production.

sound plot
the plan of all the sound effects and music needed for a production.

In theatre, the term **sound** means artificially produced sound effects and music as well as the amplification of voices so that they can be heard. In addition to enabling the audience to hear the play, sound helps set the mood for the play, makes the play more realistic, and helps the audience understand the plot.

The **sound crew** is responsible for planning and preparing all sound effects needed for a production. Depending on the theatre facilities, this crew might also be in charge of setting up and running the sound system. In some schools, this may mean setting up and taking down microphones and setting the sound levels. Clearly, equipment and sound systems vary considerably. In this lesson, we will explain the basic responsibilities of a sound crew. Your director will then adapt the information to fit the situation at your school.

The sound crew's first responsibility is to read the play carefully, making a **sound plot** or plan of all the sounds needed for the show. Many of the sound effects will be mentioned in the script. The sound crew will also look for other places in the script where the addition of sounds or music would enhance the production. Once needed sounds or music is determined, the sound crew decides the best way to create the music or produce each special sound.

Commercially produced sound boards containing basic sounds—a doorbell, telephone, or buzzer—can be purchased from theatre supply companies. Other live sounds—a door knock, alarm clock, or bicycle horn—can easily be produced "live" backstage by the sound crew.

Many sound effects can be obtained from the numerous sound effects tapes sold at sound shops, or the tapes can be ordered from a theatrical supply company. For some shows, such as a fantasy show, the sounds might need to be invented. In that case, a short trip to the music shop, hardware store, and discount toy store often results in unique "sound makers."

Music should be carefully selected to complement the mood and theme of the play. Sound crew heads often consult with choir, band, or orchestra teachers for suggestions. Because of their musical backgrounds, these professionals often save the sound crew hours of listening time.

Sound crews must remember to have backup tapes of all recorded music and sound effects in case a tape breaks. It is even helpful to have a backup tape recorder.

The sound crew (usually a very small crew) should have a clear view of the stage, since every cue must be perfectly timed with the action onstage. Most directors have a special area they like to use for the sound technicians.

cue sheet

a chart or list for lighting or sound showing all of the changes that will occur during a production.

The sound crew needs to have all of the sound effects ready at least by the first technical rehearsal. The technical rehearsals are vital to the sound crew if split-second timing for cues is to be perfected. Sound cues should be marked in a copy of the sound crew's script or on a **cue sheet**. A cue sheet is a chart of all sound changes, when they occur, and how long they last.

At the end of each rehearsal or performance, the sound crew should make sure that all electrical equipment is turned off and unplugged. Most directors prefer that all sound equipment and tapes be locked up until the next rehearsal or performance. The sound crew head is responsible for making sure the director's instructions are followed.

When the show closes, the sound crew will store all school equipment, return any borrowed items, and write letters of appreciation to all those who offered assistance.

ACTION

1. **Sound Crew Head Responsibilities.** You are the head of a sound crew. Make a list of your responsibilities.

2. **Sound Crew Member Responsibilities.** As a member of the sound crew, what are your responsibilities?

3. **Analyzing Sound Effects.** Read the class play or a play of your choice, and make a list of all sound effects that will be needed in the production.

4. **Creating Cue Sheets.** Make a cue sheet for the sound effects and music in the play you read.

5. **Sound Makers.** Invent a "sound maker" to be used in a children's production.

The Light Crew

LESSON OBJECTIVES

◆ Understand the responsibilities of the light crew.
◆ Use available stage lighting instruments to focus attention and establish mood.
◆ Recognize the contributions of the technical elements in a production.

Warm Up

Working in your acting company, think of ways to change the atmosphere in the classroom through lighting. Share your ideas with the class.

stage lighting

illumination of the actors and acting areas; includes any special lighting effects.

light crew

the technicians responsible for planning, preparing, and running the stage lights for a production.

lighting plot

a floor plan of the set showing the placement of basic lighting and any special lighting. This plot should also include a list of what lights are turned on and off and where the switches are located. These cues are marked in the light technician's promptbook for use in production.

Another vital area of a production is **stage lighting** —the illumination of the actors and acting areas. The most important purpose of stage lighting is to create visibility, enabling the audience to see the actors. Stage lighting also helps the audience understand the location, time, and emotional mood of each scene. Specific lighting can be used to highlight important stage areas and scenes or to create special effects, such as moonlight, sunlight, and lightning. The people in charge of lighting are called the **light crew** .

Stage lighting depends on the available equipment, the way it is hung, and the way it is controlled. Although lighting equipment varies in complexity, most school stage lighting is achieved through the use of spotlights, scoop floodlights, and border lights (see Figure 11–15 on page 216).

Just like the lights in your own home, stage lights are controlled by switches and dimmers. A switch merely allows you to turn the light on and off. A dimmer is a device that allows you to control the intensity (level of brightness) of the light. By using a dimmer, you can fade the light gradually from brightness to darkness.

Stage lighting instruments are connected to dimmers, and the dimmers are connected to a lighting control system. The lights are set at different levels of intensity from the control board, or dimmer board. Many control systems are equipped with preset functions and memory devices (see Figure 11–16 on page 217).

Much of today's stage lighting can be planned and controlled by digital dimmers and computerized light boards. Because of the rapid growth of technology in the stage lighting industry, today's equipment will be outdated tomorrow.

The light crew needs to work closely with the director or technical director to learn the lighting capabilities at your school. Electrical lighting equipment for the stage is expensive and extremely dangerous. Technicians should not attempt to hang, set, or run lights without supervision.

In preparing the lighting for a production, the light crew studies the script to determine basic lighting needs as well as any special lighting effects that will be needed. The light crew will need to work closely with the director or technical director as well as with scenery, costume, and makeup crews to make sure that all of these aspects complement each other.

After determining the play's lighting needs, the crew head will plan the lighting plot. A **lighting plot** is a floor plan of the set showing the

Figure 11–15

Illustration of Common Stage Lights.

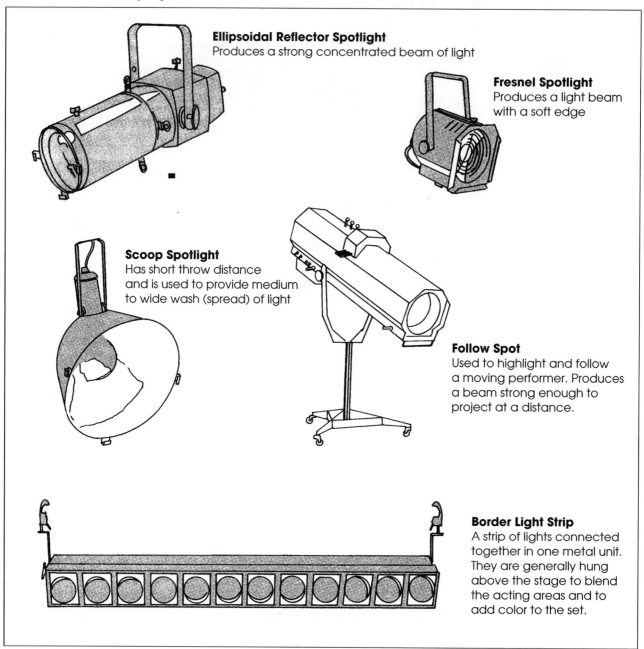

Ellipsoidal Reflector Spotlight
Produces a strong concentrated beam of light

Fresnel Spotlight
Produces a light beam with a soft edge

Scoop Spotlight
Has short throw distance and is used to provide medium to wide wash (spread) of light

Follow Spot
Used to highlight and follow a moving performer. Produces a beam strong enough to project at a distance.

Border Light Strip
A strip of lights connected together in one metal unit. They are generally hung above the stage to blend the acting areas and to add color to the set.

*L*ighting *makes the other elements of theatrical production visible.*

Oscar G. Brockett

placement of basic lighting and any special lighting (see Figure 11–17). The lighting plot also contains a list of the instruments to be used, where they will hang, and the color that will be used on each instrument.

Illumination onstage is usually achieved in five basic ways: front lighting, side lighting, back lighting, down lighting, and background lighting (see Figure 11–18 on page 218).

After the lighting plot is designed, a cue sheet is prepared for each member of the crew working the control board or special lights. The lighting cue sheet is a list of all lighting changes (see Figure 11–19). Many directors also require members of the crew to mark all lighting

216 ■ Unit 3: Producing and Appreciating Plays ■

Figure 11–16

Lighting Control System.

cues in their scripts, using various colors for coding. This makes following the dialogue of the play easier. It is a good idea to indicate an upcoming cue with a "warning signal" several lines before the cue. Think of this as your "caution light" to think and get ready for a light change.

Figure 11–17

Lighting Plot.

LIGHTING PLOT FOR: "A Day at Grandma's"						
FUNCTION	INSTR. #	TYPE	LOCATION	LOAD WATTS	COLOR	NOTES
R. Center Wash	1	8" ellipsoidal	Balcony-L	1000	50	
L. Center Wash	2	8" ellipsoidal	Balcony-R	1000	50	
Area 2 Fill	3	8" ellipsoidal	Beam-R	750	45	
Area 1 Fill	4	8" ellipsoidal	Beam-R	750	45	frame off desk
Area 1 Key	5	8" ellipsoidal	Beam-L	750	30	frame off couch
Area 2 Key	6	8" ellipsoidal	Beam-L	750	30	
UR Fill	7	6" fresnel	1st. stage-R	500	31	
UL Fill	8	6" fresnel	1st. stage-R	500	31	
UR Key	9	6" fresnel	1st. stage-L	500	50	
UL Key	10	6" fresnel	1st. stage-L	500	50	
DL Exit Special	11	6" ellipsoidal	1st. stage-L	500	15	
UR Exit Special	12	6" fresnel	2nd. stage-R	200	20	
R Back Light	13	6" ellipsoidal	2nd. stage-R	500	47	
C Back Special	14	tray	2nd. stage-C	–	–	3rd Act only
L Back Light	15	6" ellipsoidal	2nd. stage-L	500	47	
Fireplace Special	16	Roll log	Fireplace	200	12	

Front Lighting:

Used for visibility. Lights are hung out front to focus on individual acting areas. Follow spots are examples of movable front lighting.

Down Lighting:

Used to tone and blend lights, providing shadowless lighting when used with other types of illumination. These filler lights hang down over the acting areas.

Side Lighting:

Often used in musicals to accent arm and leg movements. Lights are hung on ladders on the sides of the stage.

Back Lighting:

Used to add a halo effect to the actor's head and shoulders and visually helps to separate actors from scenery. Lights are focused from behind the actors.

Background Lighting:

Used to focus on the background or scenery and to silhouette actors.

Figure 11–19

■ ■ ■ ■ ■ ■ ■ ■ ■ ■ ■ ■ ■ ■ ■

Cue Sheet.

Production: *A Day in the Life of a Kid*				Lighting Cue Sheet: Page 1	
Warning	**Cue**	**Page**	**Controls**	**Areas**	**Effect**
House lights down at 5	#1 Music begins	1	1–6	1,2,3	Slowly up to 8
Alarm clock sounds	#2 "Good Morning World!"	1	35/36	4,5,6	Strips up to 10

Under the guidance of the director or technical director, the lighting instruments will need to be cleaned, hung, and focused on the appropriate areas. Before hanging the instruments, the light crew adds the appropriate colors, placing translucent plastic sheets called gels onto the metal frames in front of the lamps. Gels are produced to withstand the heat of the lamps without melting or burning, but they need to be changed once they begin to fade or sag.

Before the technical rehearsals, it is helpful if the light crew can have several "dry tech" rehearsals. These technical rehearsals without any actors give the technicians time to feel comfortable running the equipment.

Before the first performance, your director will tell you when the crew should report for duty and give you instructions for last-minute safety checks. Most directors like the crew to run a safety check early enough to make any adjustments before the theatre begins to fill with people.

When it's "show time," the members of the light crew report to their positions as the stage manager calls the "5 minutes 'till curtain" warning. (Some directors may want the crew in place before that time.) At this time, the house lights flash or blink several times, giving the audience notice that the show is about to begin. The light crew will need to bring up (on) the house lights for any intermissions and again at the end of the show. After the performance, the light crew should follow the director's guidelines for turning off or unplugging equipment.

When it is time to strike the show, the light crew will take down, clean, and store all equipment, according to the director's instructions. The light crew will also make a list of any repairs that are needed. It is the light crew head's responsibility to reset the control board for general stage use.

■ ■ ■ ■ ■ ■ ■ ■ ■ ■ ■ ■

1. **Light Crew Head Responsibilities.** You are the head of a light crew. Make a list of your responsibilities.

2. **Light Crew Member Responsibilities.** As a light crew member, what are your responsibilities?

3. **Developing Lighting Plots and Cue Sheets.** Design a lighting plot for a one-act play using your school's lighting equipment. Prepare a cue sheet to use in production.

4. **Lighting Research.** Research the life of a famous theatre lighting designer.

The Publicity Crew

LESSON OBJECTIVES

◆ Recognize the responsibilities of the publicity crew.
◆ Recognize the function of management in theatre.
◆ Explore a variety of publicity techniques.

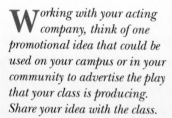

Working with your acting company, think of one promotional idea that could be used on your campus or in your community to advertise the play that your class is producing. Share your idea with the class.

publicity crew

the committee responsible for organizing and implementing all advertising for a production. Often in charge of ticket sales, this crew is sometimes combined with the house crew.

The **publicity crew** is responsible for organizing an advertising campaign and publicizing the show. The advertising campaign should begin as soon as the cast is announced. A short article announcing the play should be the first story released to the school newspaper and the local newspaper. Include the playwright's name and the publishing company, a brief synopsis of the plot, and the names of the director, cast, and crews. Check with your director concerning your school's policy on releasing news to the media.

After rehearsals begin, prepare several publicity photos and stories to release to the school newspaper or local newspaper. Show members of the cast in rehearsal or crew members working on interesting parts of the show. Every picture should look like fun and make all who see it want to be part of the audience. Your director will help you organize a photograph session before one of the early rehearsals. Photograph sessions of the actors in costume are usually scheduled closer to the dress rehearsals. Photographs made at those sessions can be used as part of a lobby display as well as for opening night photographs.

Schoolwide advertising is extremely important. Consider placing posters in the halls, classrooms, and cafeteria. A handmade banner above the auditorium entrance, a decorated bulletin board in the hall, or an attractive lobby display can draw much attention to the upcoming production. Even something as simple as placing bookmarks in the school library can help advertise the production.

Many commercial radio and television stations have public service programs that will announce school events without charge. Some stations have local talk shows that will interview members of the crew "on the air." Call the stations during business hours for this information.

Before you go "on the air live," it is important to have all the necessary information about the show. You should know the name of the

play, the playwright, the publishing company, the theatre where the play is being presented, the dates and times of the performances, and the cost of the tickets.

The week tickets go on sale, try using short announcements or reminders on the school intercom and in the school bulletin. These reminders seem to help increase ticket sales. If your school has the equipment to broadcast into the classrooms via in-house television, consider producing several television spots to advertise the play.

Consider using a variety of advertising techniques to reach as many people in your community as possible. Have several actors or the house and publicity crews dress in costumes and makeup to pass out flyers at a local mall. With permission from mall management, set up a ticket booth, making tickets available on the spot.

After the final performance, it is important for the publicity crew to remove all posters or advertisements for the production. Letters of appreciation should be sent to all persons or businesses who helped promote the production.

ACTION

1. **Publicity Crew Responsibilities.** Make a list of the responsibilities for both the head and the members of the publicity crew.

2. **Creating Play Advertisements.** Design and make a banner or poster advertising a play of your choice.

3. **Play Announcements.** Plan a series of announcements to be broadcast over the school's public-address system.

LESSON 10

Warm Up

Working as an acting company, discuss how you, as house crew, would handle the following situation: An extremely loud group of students arrive several minutes after the play has begun. Their reserved seats are in the front row of the theatre. Share your decisions with the class.

The House Crew

LESSON OBJECTIVES

♦ Recognize the responsibilities of the house crew.
♦ Identify the process of box office operations.
♦ Recognize the function of house management in theatre.

The **house crew** is in charge of printing tickets and programs and managing the box office and house during the performances. This crew can be combined with the publicity crew, or it can function as an independent crew. The person in charge of this crew is known as the house manager.

Working with the director, the house crew decides the most cost-effective way to produce the tickets and programs. Investigate the cost of commercial printing and compare this with the cost of using school facilities. Perhaps there is a parent who can help with the printing.

If the publicity crew and house crew do their jobs effectively, you will have large crowds of people at your performances and everyone who comes will have a seat to match his or her ticket.

house crew
the group responsible for printing tickets and programs and managing the box office, audience, and physical theatre during a production.

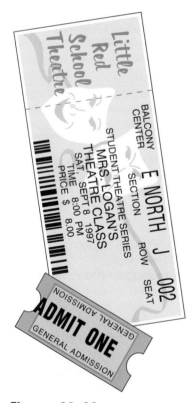

Figure 11–20

Sample Tickets.

Two types of tickets are commonly sold: reserved seating tickets and general admission tickets (see Figure 11–20). Reserved tickets require that all rows have a letter and all seats be numbered. These correspond to the tickets. When a ticket is sold, that seat must be recorded on a master seating chart. The person purchasing the ticket has a guaranteed seat. Selling reserved tickets requires more organization than selling general admission tickets. General admission means that all seats are one price, although the price for student tickets is usually lower. With general admission tickets, there are no reserved seats. This means less work for the house crew. Your director will advise you on the correct type of ticket to print.

Keep your tickets in an affordable price range. Remember your targeted audience. If your performance is to be held during the school day and your audience will be students, don't overprice the tickets.

Tickets sold before the show serve as a written reminder for the patron. Most theatre tickets include the following information:

- title of play
- name of theatre
- day and date of performance
- time of performance
- name of school and or performing group
- price
- ticket number (for accounting purposes)
- section, row, and seat number (when reserved)

Play programs can vary in size, color, even shape. They can be one sheet or several pages. The important thing to remember is that the program is printed to share important information with the audience. A general format for a printed program would include the information as shown in Figure 11–21.

On the night of the performance, the house crew is in full force. The printed programs are passed out to patrons entering the theatre. Ushers (usually members of the crew or other theatre students) might want to dress in similar attire—"dressy clothes" or costumes appropriate for the production.

If tickets are to be sold at the door, a special table should be set up in the lobby, with several ticket sellers on duty. The crew head should be prepared with a cash box and ample change.

When the show opens to a "full house," every member of the company will appreciate the work of the house and publicity crews. It's impossible to fill a theatre without effective promotion of the show and good house management.

After each performance, the house crew should follow the director's instructions for handling extra tickets and money. Cash should be deposited in the bank or locked in the school safe overnight.

Once the production has come to a close, the house crew is usually responsible for putting the house, ticket office, and lobby back in order. It is this crew's responsibility to write letters of appreciation to all people or businesses who helped the house crew in any way.

Figure 11–21
■ ■ ■ ■ ■ ■ ■ ■ ■ ■ ■ ■ ■ ■ ■
Program Format.

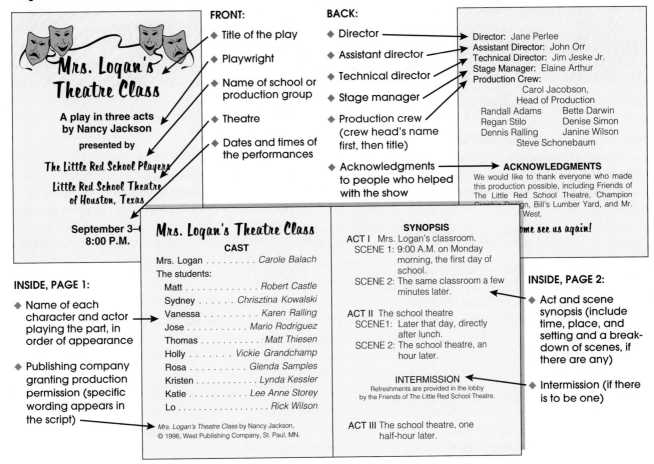

FRONT:
◆ Title of the play
◆ Playwright
◆ Name of school or production group
◆ Theatre
◆ Dates and times of the performances

BACK:
◆ Director
◆ Assistant director
◆ Technical director
◆ Stage manager
◆ Production crew (crew head's name first, then title)
◆ Acknowledgments to people who helped with the show

Director: Jane Perlee
Assistant Director: John Orr
Technical Director: Jim Jeske Jr.
Stage Manager: Elaine Arthur
Production Crew:
　　　Carol Jacobson,
　　　Head of Production
Randall Adams　　Bette Darwin
Regan Stilo　　　Denise Simon
Dennis Ralling　　Janine Wilson
　　　Steve Schonebaum

ACKNOWLEDGMENTS
We would like to thank everyone who made this production possible, including Friends of The Little Red School Theatre, Champion Graphic Design, Bill's Lumber Yard, and Mr. West.

me see us again!

Mrs. Logan's Theatre Class

A play in three acts
by Nancy Jackson
presented by

The Little Red School Players

Little Red School Theatre
of Houston, Texas

September 3
8:00 P.M.

Mrs. Logan's Theatre Class
CAST
Mrs. Logan . . . . *Carole Balach*
The students:
　Matt . . . . *Robert Castle*
　Sydney . . . . . . *Chrisztina Kowalski*
　Vanessa . . . . *Karen Ralling*
　Jose . . . . *Mario Rodriguez*
　Thomas . . . . *Matt Thiesen*
　Holly . . . . *Vickie Grandchamp*
　Rosa . . . . *Glenda Samples*
　Kristen . . . . *Lynda Kessler*
　Katie . . . . *Lee Anne Storey*
　Lo . . . . *Rick Wilson*

Mrs. Logan's Theatre Class by Nancy Jackson,
© 1996, West Publishing Company, St. Paul, MN.

SYNOPSIS
ACT I　Mrs. Logan's classroom.
　SCENE 1: 9:00 A.M. on Monday morning, the first day of school.
　SCENE 2: The same classroom a few minutes later.

ACT II　The school theatre
　SCENE 1: Later that day, directly after lunch.
　SCENE 2: The school theatre, an hour later.

INTERMISSION
Refreshments are provided in the lobby by the Friends of The Little Red School Theatre.

ACT III　The school theatre, one half-hour later.

INSIDE, PAGE 1:
◆ Name of each character and actor playing the part, in order of appearance
◆ Publishing company granting production permission (specific wording appears in the script)

INSIDE, PAGE 2:
◆ Act and scene synopsis (include time, place, and setting and a breakdown of scenes, if there are any)
◆ Intermission (if there is to be one)

ACTION
■ ■ ■ ■ ■ ■ ■ ■ ■ ■ ■ ■ ■ ■

1. **House Manager Responsibilities.** You are the house manager for the upcoming production. Make a list of your responsibilities.

2. **House Crew Member Responsibilities.** As a member of the house crew, what are your responsibilities?

3. **Creating a Lobby Display.** Plan an interesting lobby display for use during an upcoming production at your school.

4. **Developing Seating Charts.** Count the number of rows and seats in your theatre or auditorium. Plan how to label the rows and number the seats for reserved seating.

5. **Designing Tickets and Programs.** Design a printed program and a ticket for an upcoming production.

■ ■ SPOTLIGHT ON TERMS ■ ■

An important part of theatre is understanding the terminology, or vocabulary, used. Add the new terms and definitions to the vocabulary section of your theatre notebook or folder.

■ ■ FOCUS ON FACTS ■ ■

1. Explain the difference between a director, stage manager, assistant director, and crew head.
2. What is the job of a crew member?
3. Define theatre safety, and explain its importance.
4. What is the purpose of scenery?
5. Why are sight lines important?
6. Why might props be used in a production?
7. What are four ways to acquire costumes for a production?
8. What is the purpose of a costume plot?
9. What is the difference between basic makeup and character makeup?
10. What are the various ways to get special sounds needed for a performance?
11. Explain the major differences between a light plot and a light cue sheet.
12. What can the publicity crew do to advertise a play?
13. How does reserved seating differ from general admission seating?
14. What information should be included on a theatre ticket?
15. What duties and responsibilities does the house crew have on the night of a performance?

■ ■ REFLECTIONS ■ ■

Discuss the following questions with your class or answer them on paper as instructed by your teacher.

1. Which crew is the most important in the production of a play?

2. Why do you think the preparation of a prompt-book is important?
3. If you were the director, how would you teach theatre safety so that all of your students would understand its importance?
4. Your theatre class has $200 to produce a one-act play. What are some of the ways you can stretch the money?
5. In what ways can your group show appreciation to individuals in the community who support the theatre program?

■ ■ THEATRE IN YOUR LIFE ■ ■

Discuss aloud or write as a journal entry how working on a theatrical crew teaches you practical life skills. What are some specific skills you developed?

■ ■ ENCORE ■ ■

1. If your class is producing a play, make a checklist of responsibilities for the crew on which you will serve.
2. Design the set for a play or scene. Draw and color the design or build a model.
3. Design a costume for a female to be made from 3 yards of blue velvet, 10 yards of white lace, and twenty pearl buttons.
4. Make a collection of realistic-looking papier-mâché stage foods to be used as props in a play.
5. Attend a production with other members of your crew. Take special note of the way crew responsibilities are handled.

CHAPTER 12

Theatre Appreciation

Chapter Outline

Spotlight on Terms

- ◆ actor viewpoint
- ◆ aesthetic appreciation
- ◆ audience commitment
- ◆ audience etiquette
- ◆ audience viewpoint
- ◆ blackout
- ◆ camera shots
- ◆ constructive criticism
- ◆ curtain call
- ◆ illusion
- ◆ intermission
- ◆ mass media
- ◆ performance space
- ◆ production techniques
- ◆ program
- ◆ spectacle viewing
- ◆ suspend belief
- ◆ theatre conventions
- ◆ vista shots

225

The main focus of this chapter is on appreciation—learning to enjoy, understand, and evaluate performances. In this chapter, you will learn about established theatre practices and theatre etiquette. You will also be given the opportunity to compare live theatre with media such as television, video, film, and computers. As you explore live theatre and various other media, you will learn the importance of making judgments about each of them.

The evaluation process in theatre arts can help you think as an individual rather than accepting what others write or say about a performance. Questions will be provided for you to determine the value of various performance media. It is essential today to learn to make sound judgments about what you choose to see and hear. The world has more choices than ever before, and your theatre arts class can guide you in making wise decisions.

Theatre Conventions

LESSON OBJECTIVES

◆ Recognize and respond to live theatre.
◆ Identify and explain theatre conventions.
◆ Reflect on and form opinions of dramatic experiences.

Warm Up

Do you remember attending your first theatrical production? Divide into pairs and share your experiences.

theatre conventions
established techniques, practices, or devices unique to theatrical productions.

performance space
an area set aside for a performance.

program
printed sheet of paper or booklet that provides information about the production.

When you attend a live performance, you encounter several theatre conventions. **Theatre conventions** are established techniques, practices, or devices unique to theatrical productions. Although not all of the theatre conventions will be used in your classroom, school auditorium, or community theatre, it is important that you know about and recognize them.

Many theatre conventions can become part of your classroom performances. By putting the following conventions into practice in the classroom, you will know what to expect when you attend other events staged in a theatre or auditorium.

Performance Space

There has to be an area set aside for the performance. In theatre, this is called the **performance space**. In many schools, the performance space is an auditorium stage. But theatrical performances can also take place in a gym, cafeteria, or regular classroom. The important thing to remember is that there must be a space set apart so that the actors are physically separated from the audience.

The Program

As you enter a theatre to attend a production, you are often presented with a **program**. This printed sheet of paper or booklet provides

When you attend a live production, get to the theatre or auditorium early. Take your seat promptly so that you don't ruin the performance for other audience members by making noise and walking in front of them after the show has started.

you with interesting information about the production. A program should include the title of the production, the name of the playwright, and credit to the publishing company. Also listed should be the cast of characters and the actors playing the roles. Most programs give credit to the director, the designers, and the technicians. A more detailed program would give a brief explanation of the plot to guide the audience's understanding of the play.

Many shows sell advertising space in the program to help pay the cost of producing the publication. A program not only provides information, but also makes a nice souvenir of the performance.

House Lights

A universally used signal that the show is about to begin is the blinking of the house lights. The house lights are the lights in the ceiling above the audience. In some theatres, when these lights are turned on and off in succession, the lobby lights and rest room lights also blink. This signal is a notice to the audience that they should take their seats because the performance will begin in about 5 minutes.

Approximately 5 minutes after the blinking of the house lights, the same lights will begin to slowly dim, or become softer. As the lights fade out into total darkness, the audience is aware that the show is beginning. The slowly dimming lights give the audience time to become quiet and prepare to enjoy the show.

Curtain Up/Open

Even though most school curtains pull from side to side, many professional curtains are flown (rise above the stage) and actually go up into the fly area, the area above the stage floor. The expression "curtain up" or "curtain open" refers to the rise or opening of those curtains. Not all stages have curtains, however, and in many performances, the

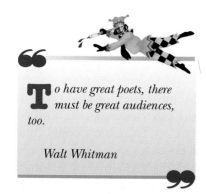

To have great poets, there must be great audiences, too.

Walt Whitman

curtains are already open when the audience enters the theatre. In these cases, the audience knows that the performance will begin by another signal—perhaps the entrance of an actor, a special sound effect, the beginning of the music, or the dimming of the lights.

Intermission

intermission
a short break in the action of the play for the audience.

An **intermission** is a short break in the action of the play for the audience. One-act plays or short performances do not usually have an intermission. A long performance or a play that has more than one act usually does have intermissions. The length of the intermission is usually printed in the program. During intermission, members of the audience can stand up, move around, go to the rest room, get a drink of water, or visit quietly with friends. It is important to be aware of the time and be ready to sit down quietly toward the end of the intermission. To be courteous to others in the audience, you should be in your seat by the time the performance resumes.

Blackout

blackout
turning out all the stage lights at one time.

When all of the stage lights are turned out at one time, it is called a **blackout** . Blackouts are often used to show the passage of time at the end of a scene or act. If an actor is stretched out on a couch, pretending to sleep, a blackout could make the passage of time more believable for the audience.

Blackouts are also used for special effects. Because some actions cannot be portrayed in broad view of the audience, a director might choose to "chop off a head" or "melt down" a character during a split-second blackout. When the lights go up again, the "deed" will have been accomplished, and the show can continue.

Curtain Down/Closed

The term "curtain down" or "curtain closed" refers to the fall (or close) of the curtain at the end of an act or at the end of the play. The closing of the curtain at the end of an act is often followed by an intermission. The closing of the curtain after the last act means that the play is over. This is usually followed by a reopening of the curtain for a curtain call.

Curtain Call

curtain call
following a performance, the appearance of the actors onstage to acknowledge the appreciation of the audience and to take a bow.

To an actor, the curtain call is one of the most exciting and rewarding parts of the performance. The **curtain call** occurs at the end of the performance, when the actors come onstage to acknowledge their appreciation of the audience and to take a bow.

Some directors allow each actor to come forward alone or in small groups to receive the applause. Other directors prefer to open the cur-

tains to the entire cast in a line across the stage. Most often, at some point in the curtain call, the entire cast holds hands and bows in unison.

Applause

Applause is the opportunity for the audience to let the entire company know how much they enjoyed and appreciated the performance. Applause is acknowledgment and reward for all the hard work and team effort that went into putting on the production.

Applause is given at the end of scenes and acts, at the end of the performance, and during the curtain call. During a performance, if there is an especially touching moment or outstanding scene, sometimes an audience will burst into a spontaneous "round of applause." This is appropriate, and the actors will hold their lines until the applause dies down.

Applause in the theatre is not cheering, whooping, catcalling, or stomping feet, as you might see at a pep rally or athletic competition. Rather, it is a sincere, dignified recognition of the performance.

A standing ovation (all members of the audience standing while applauding) is often given at the end of a production. A cast that receives a standing ovation is receiving the ultimate display of appreciation from an audience.

ACTION

1. **Stage Scavenger Hunt.** Explore your school for appropriate places to stage theatrical activities. Compile a class list. Which places would be the easiest to use? Which places would present the most challenges? Why?

2. **Scrapbook for Theatre Programs.** On your own or with your class, compile a collection of old theatre programs. Compare the programs for content and design. Determine the one best suited for a theatrical event at your school. After the assignment, arrange the programs in a class scrapbook.

LESSON 2

Audience Etiquette

LESSON OBJECTIVES

- ◆ Recognize and respond to live theatre.
- ◆ Use appropriate audience etiquette.
- ◆ Reflect on and form opinions of dramatic experiences.

Warm Up

Imagine that you are one of a group of teachers taking your students on a field trip to see a play. As an acting company, create a list of expectations for your students.

Having the opportunity to attend a play is a very special event. You cannot view a play every day, as you might a television program. You cannot even attend plays with the same frequency that you see movies. Even though live productions are extremely popular today, plays are not always readily available. In fact, many of you may view as many television programs in a week as you will attend live theatrical productions in a lifetime.

Audience etiquette is appropriate audience behavior at a theatrical event. Your parents and teachers have stressed the importance of good social etiquette. Most of you have been taught the proper way to greet

Modern Theatre and Realism

Changes in philosophy and religion that began in the mid-1800s had a great impact on theatre in the late 1890s and early 1900s. Influenced by writers such as Darwin and Marx, people began to question their religious, political, and economic beliefs. This questioning led to a wider variety of opinions, and the art of the period began to reflect the conflicting beliefs.

The neoclassical rules for drama (page 88) were being applied in fewer and fewer productions, even though more theatre was being produced than ever before.

The theatre of the late nineteenth and early twentieth century can be roughly divided into two broad types, realism and departures from realism (which you'll read about later). The realists wrote plays in which characters spoke, dressed, and behaved just as people did in everyday life. Scenery began to look like rooms in which many of the audience members lived.

The playwright who is often considered to be the first realistic writer was Henrik Ibsen, a Norwegian playwright. Some of his plays, such as *A Doll's House* and *Ghosts,* were very controversial when they were first staged because of their subject matter and style. Today, these plays are considered classics.

The realists, like Ibsen, believed that plays should be as close to lifelike as possible. These attempts at realism sprang from the playwrights' beliefs that theatre had the power and responsibility to instigate change. These playwrights believed that if the audience members recognized an injustice in society and became emotional about it as a result of seeing the play, the audience would try to bring about changes. Therefore, realists dealt with subject matter that had been taboo on the stage before this period—topics such as social injustice and unhappy marriages. Plots were not clearly resolved at the end of the plays as they had been in previous periods. Instead, the fu-

This is a scene from *An Enemy of the People,* one of Ibsen's most popular and least complicated plays. In a satiric, realistic style, the play dramatizes Ibsen's belief that the majority of people do not think for themselves and are, therefore, easily manipulated.

ture of characters seemed to depend upon the forces of heredity and environment, two forces that the character could not control.

Characters in realistic plays have several notable characteristics. First of all, they are not stereotypes. None of them are clearly evil, nor are they clearly good. Instead, they are a mixture of complicated impulses and motivations, just as people are in real life.

These characters are revealed to the audience in great detail, in such a way that the audience understands what forces, such as heredity and environment, made them the way they are. These characters speak in everyday speech patterns rather than verse. And the setting that the audience sees them moving through is usually a very thoroughly detailed room, filled with all of the items that one might find in one's own home.

Other playwrights who provide wonderful examples of early realism are August Strindberg and Anton Chekhov. ■

someone and even the proper way to answer a telephone. Appropriate audience behavior is just another important social grace you need to learn as you grow up. Because attending a live theatrical event is different from watching a movie or television program, it is important to know what is expected of you at a play, opera, ballet, musical, or concert.

Appropriate behavior begins when you arrive at the theatre or auditorium. If you do not have a ticket for the show, you should allow time to purchase one before the performance begins.

Before the Performance

Always arrive on time. It is annoying to the other members of the audience when they cannot see part of the performance because latecomers are walking in front of them or climbing over them. People arriving late also make noise as they are being seated, which prevents audience members who arrived on time from hearing the dialogue or music.

Gum, food, and drinks have no place in the theatre! Chewing, eating, and drinking are all noisy activities that can distract the actors as well as the audience. To be a good citizen and theatre patron, remember to use the trash receptacles in the lobby of the theatre before you enter the seating area. Save all eating and drinking until after the performance or during the intermission.

Remember also to take care of rest room business and drinks of water prior to being seated. If you have to leave in the middle of the show, you will miss some of the performance as well as distract the people seated near you.

Once you are seated, be considerate of those who are seated around you. Keep your hands, arms, feet, and personal belongings such as umbrellas to yourself. Be especially careful not to put your feet on the chair in front of you. If you want to visit with friends, do so quietly before the performance begins.

As a safety precaution, always take note of the exit nearest your seat. Law requires exit signs to be lighted and clearly visible. If an emergency should arise and the exit needed, you would know where to go.

During the Performance

Be considerate of those seated near you. Do not distract anyone's attention from the performance by talking or making noises. Even if you know all the lines to the show or all the words to the songs, others in the audience did not come to hear or see you perform. Speaking aloud or singing along from the audience is considered in extremely poor taste.

As a member of the audience, you can best show your respect for the actors by giving them your full attention. Shouting out comments or whistling is not considered appropriate theatre behavior. Such responses should be saved for football games and track meets. Responses such as laughter, tears, or even gasps of surprise are expected from the audience. Performers enjoy such reactions and hope that they will

come from the audience at the appropriate times. These types of reactions give the actors feedback, letting them know how their performance is affecting the audience.

Avoid leaving your seat once the performance begins unless you have an emergency. If you must leave, do so as quietly and inconspicuously as possible. If you are attending a performance with your class or with a school group, quietly notify your teacher or director that you have an emergency.

Many productions use special theatrical techniques, such as unusual sound effects, spectacular lighting, or blackouts. If you are viewing a performance with younger brothers and sisters who have not attended the theatre before, prepare them for such occurrences so that they will sit calmly if the lights go out.

Recording music, videotaping performances, and taking photographs are all prohibited during a theatrical event. Recording any music during a performance without written permission of composers and performers is a serious violation of the copyright law. Cameras are distracting to other audience members as well as to the performers. Flashes on cameras can momentarily blind a performer or cause a break in character or dialogue.

After the Performance

When the performance is over, wait until the house lights are turned up so that you can see the aisles and exits clearly. As you wait patiently for your turn to exit, it is appropriate to quietly discuss the performance with your friends. Check under and around your seat for any personal belongings that you might have left.

As you exit the theatre or auditorium, avoid pushing against those in front of you. Remember to be courteous, even though you may have to wait several minutes before you can exit. Climbing under or hopping over seats only demonstrates to others that you lack good judgment. This type of behavior is rude and extremely irritating to those who enjoy the theatre experience.

ACTION

1. **Rules for Audience Etiquette.** Create a short positive rule for appropriate audience etiquette. Illustrate the rule on a poster that would be appropriate for your classroom or for a hall in your school. Follow your teacher's guidelines for poster design.

2. **Dos and Don'ts for Theatre Etiquette.** Demonstrate appropriate and inappropriate audience behavior in a scene prepared for an elementary school class. Lead the elementary school students in a discussion of the importance of appropriate behavior in the theatre.

3. **Theatre Etiquette Video Show.** Create a scene that would appeal to students your age, teaching appropriate etiquette in a fun way. Videotape the performance to share with other classes at your school. Ask the classes to evaluate the tape.

Comparing Theatre with Other Media

LESSON OBJECTIVES

◆ Recognize and respond to live theatre and other media.
◆ Compare live theatre, television, and film.
◆ Participate in class activities to become aware of the differences in live theatre, television, and film.

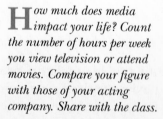

Warm Up

How much does media impact your life? Count the number of hours per week you view television or attend movies. Compare your figure with those of your acting company. Share with the class.

mass media
communication that can reach large audiences.

You are fortunate to be playing a role in today's live theatre and mass media. **Mass media** are various channels of communication that can reach large audiences. During the twentieth century, the world has seen an explosion in the development of technology in live theatre and media such as television, video, film, and computers.

Computers have had a tremendous impact on live theatre. People in theatre now use the computer to design sets, costumes, programs, posters, and tickets. The computer is also valuable in keeping track of inventory and business records for theatre productions. On a larger scale, theatres use computerized lightboards and use the computer to operate the set pieces in productions. Clearly, the computer is an asset to the production of live theatre.

So far, you have been learning about live theatre, which is the form that drama took for centuries. But today we have other means—other

You can make yourself much more comfortable while watching television, as opposed to attending a live performance. Do you think, however, that you are as attentive in front of the television as you are in the theatre audience?

audience viewpoint
the way the audience sees and responds to the cast members.

spectacle viewing
a medium through which film is viewed with wonder and amazement.

suspend belief
pretend that what is happening onstage is real.

audience commitment
audience responsibility.

media—for communicating drama. In this lesson, we will look at some of the similarities and differences that occur when drama takes place in other media.

Live theatre, television, and film are all connected and similar. But they also have unique differences that are fascinating to explore. Even though the subject of this book is theatre, you experience drama more frequently through television and film. Therefore, you need to understand the similarities and differences between live theatre, television, and film. These similarities and differences can be divided into three categories: the audience viewpoint, the actor viewpoint, and the production techniques.

Audience Viewpoint

The **audience viewpoint** is the way the audience sees and responds to the cast members. Actors are viewed live at the theatre, but television and film are prerecorded and edited (except for live television shows) before they are presented to an audience. This means that the audience does not see the actors in television and film firsthand. Television and film audiences do not have the same personal connection with the cast members that is felt in live theatre. In general, television and film have larger casts and have less connection with the audience.

The actual presence of the actors onstage helps establish a unique relationship between the audience and the players. The player-audience relationship is a connection, or bond, between the audience and the players that aids the understanding and appreciation of the play and cast. Television, however, is viewed in small, private settings. And films are shown on large screens suited for extravaganza or **spectacle viewing**, allowing films to be viewed with wonder and amazement by large audiences. For example, many movie theatres provide their patrons today with wall-to-wall screens, stereo sound (DTS Digital Sound and THX Sound System), and listening aids. This type of viewing is impressive, but it doesn't have the player-audience relationship that live theatre can offer.

Another difference in the audience viewpoint has to do with imagination. A live theatre audience must imagine that what is happening onstage is happening in the real world. Live theatre cannot produce the real world as effectively as television and film. For example, the painted backdrop onstage may present an outdoor scene, but you must **suspend belief**—allow yourself to pretend that what is happening onstage is real—to associate the backdrop with the scenery outdoors.

The **audience commitment** (audience responsibility) is quite different for live theatre and other media. Live theatre requires the most audience commitment. People who choose to go to the theatre must pay to enter the theatre. Once they are seated, they become an integral part of the performance. They must use imagination, observation, and concentration while watching the actors. The audience must believe in what is happening on the stage, even though many of the scenes may be pantomimed or performed in front of a set that is obviously not the real thing. The audience becomes involved in the production by listening, applauding, and oftentimes laughing or crying at the scenes that

You need three things in the theatre: the play, the actors, and the audience; and each must give something.

Kenneth Kaigh

are taking place. The audience is important to the actors, too. The two work together to create the wonder of live theatre and establish the player-audience relationship mentioned earlier.

Less commitment is required by the film audience than by those attending live theatre. In general, the movie audience pays about one-third the cost of live theatre. What's more, less imagination is required by this audience because the movies are often brilliantly produced, directed, and edited so as to create a realistic setting. Millions of dollars are spent to create realistic sets or to take the actors to real locations. The audience may eat popcorn and candy and drink beverages while watching the movie. They may talk to the people sitting next to them, even though to do so is inconsiderate of others in the movie theatre. Of course, the actors do not know who might be in the audience, and there is no personal audience-actor relationship as in live theatre.

Television requires the least amount of audience commitment. The small television screen has a remote control that often is used to "surf" from channel to channel in search of the best entertainment. People watch television in their homes, and many obstacles get in the way of what is happening on the screen. Audience members eat, talk, laugh, play games, and walk from room to room during the programs. The actors do not develop a relationship with the home audience, although many television programs have studio audiences to enhance the outcome of the program. The live studio audience helps evoke natural responses from the actors. Directors like to use them to make the show more appealing.

Actor Viewpoint

actor viewpoint

the way the cast members react to the audience and the situation.

■ ■ ■ ■ ■ ■ ■ ■ ■ ■ ■ ■ ■ ■

How do you think this actor's viewpoint would change if she were performing her role in front of a live audience rather than in front of the director and members of the movie crew? Do you think acting in movies would be harder than acting on the stage, or vice versa?

The **actor viewpoint** is the way the cast members react to the audience and the production situation, and the way they contend with working in live theatre and other media. Onstage the actors perform

live. They must have their lines memorized and rehearsed. They spend endless hours during and outside of rehearsals perfecting their roles. They use their voices and bodies in ways that would not be used in television and film. The voice, body movements, and gestures often must be exaggerated for the theatre audience to see and hear. But in television and film, the slightest movement, gesture, or sound is easily recorded by the camera filming the scene.

Film and television actors also must work hard and rehearse endlessly and diligently. They have to perform for specific cameras and work around many obstacles, equipment, and crew members without breaking character. The actors must use total self-control because the camera picks up every movement. The actor's work is affected by the camera's every move. These **camera shots** (camera angles), which include **vista shots** (faraway shots), long shots, medium shots, and close-up shots, may be altered, spliced (placed elsewhere in the film), or omitted without the actor's knowledge. A *vista scene* is shot from far away to give a sense of place. *Long shots* are still shot from far away but you begin to pick out part of the scene on which to focus. *Medium shots* bring you closer to the focus of the scene. You see what is starting to happen. In *close-up shots* the camera closes in on an expression or detail that the director wants the audience to notice. These procedures are used to help the audience understand the film and are not controlled by the actor, but are the decisions of the director and the producer.

Production Techniques

Production techniques are the methods used to stage a play and the methods used to produce television programs and films. Settings in live theatre are limited, and the audience's sight lines (the positions and places onstage that an audience is able to see) must be considered. In television and film, however, mobile cameras allow the filmmakers to create realistic settings in great detail.

Lighting onstage must approximate time and conditions. But television and film scenes can be filmed on location, and the actual lighting, weather, and environmental conditions can be recorded. "Flashbacks" can be shown immediately in television and film; onstage, "flashbacks" are harder to convey.

An **illusion**—something that looks real but is false—and passage of time are easier to convey in film and television because the camera can start and stop. Special effects can appear realistic on the screen, while the special effects onstage have limited power (although computers have revolutionized stage productions).

camera shots
camera angles.

production techniques
the methods used to stage a play and the methods used to produce television programs and films.

illusion
something that looks real but is false.

Movie lighting and special effects can create much more realistic settings and moods than are possible in the theatre. What does this mean for audiences at movies as compared to audiences at theatre performances?

ACTION

1. **Commercial Time.** As a class project, view and discuss several commercials on television. In small groups, create and dramatize an original commercial for a product. Present the commercials and videotape them. Play the commercials back, and discuss the types of appeals (propaganda techniques used in commercials and advertising) used by each group.

2. **Mock Television Program.** Prepare a television program similar to a talk show or a sitcom. After selecting a type of program and having a purpose in mind, write and edit a script (time limit 10 to 15 minutes). Choose a director, cast, advertising crew, and technical crew. After writing, editing, planning, organizing, and rehearsing the script, videotape the program using various camera shots. Play back for study and evaluation.

3. **Reporter's Viewpoint.** Choose a television program to watch; choose a movie to see; and attend a live theatre production. Pretend that you are a newspaper reporter, and write a story comparing the performers and production techniques with your class.

Evaluating Theatre and Media

LESSON OBJECTIVES

◆ Evaluate and critique live theatre, television, and film performances.
◆ Define and develop aesthetic appreciation.
◆ Reflect on and form opinions of dramatic experiences.

In your journal, list one of your favorite live stage productions, television programs, and films. Explain why you chose each one.

aesthetic appreciation

the ability to recognize, understand, and value that which is pleasing, beautiful, cultured, and tasteful in the arts (theatre, music, visual art, and dance).

Evaluation, as you learned in Chapter 2, helps you understand, analyze, and improve your theatre skills and techniques. In this lesson, you will develop an appreciation of theatrical values by learning how to evaluate live performances, television drama, and film productions.

The ability to evaluate dramatic performance is a valuable skill beyond the theatre classroom. When your class attends a live theatre production or views television drama and films, you will be given an opportunity to study and appreciate theatre as an art form. Through this experience, you will also develop your sense of aesthetic appreciation. **Aesthetic appreciation** is the ability to recognize, understand, and value that which is pleasing, beautiful, cultured, and tasteful in the arts (theatre, music, visual art, and dance). For example, as you develop an appreciation for live theatre, you will feel the responsibility to support only performances that have merit and are worthy of your time and energy.

This lesson will offer guidelines on how to evaluate live theatre, television, and film. Evaluating theatre and other media means forming opinions and making sound judgments about the characters and the production, paying close attention to their excellence and shortcomings. When opinions are formed and judgments made, people do not always agree. Disagreement is part of the process of learning how to evaluate. Important steps are listening to others, asking questions, and

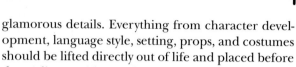

Naturalism

A stylistic movement in theatre occurring about the same time as realism was naturalism. A French playwright, Émile Zola, is considered to be the founder of the naturalistic style of theatre.

Zola had been strongly influenced by the scientific discoveries and practices popular in the early 1900s. He admired the scientists for their apparent ability to observe natural forces at work without influencing the forces that they were observing. So he brought this scientific type of observation to his theatre work.

Zola suggested that artists should present a picture of the real world on stage without making their opinions or presence felt. He and his followers argued that theatre should present a "slice of life" on the stage, that plays and play production should be just like looking into a window on characters' lives and watching them, whatever they were doing. This meant that the playwright was to no longer put only the most important and dramatic moments and conversations on stage, but should also show life's less glamorous details. Everything from character development, language style, setting, props, and costumes should be lifted directly out of life and placed before the audience without adjusting it in any way.

The naturalists, like the realists, believed that theatre should point out society's flaws and try to get audiences to examine social injustice. Therefore, as in many of the realistic plays, the characters in naturalistic plays are from the lower classes and are engaged in situations that had not previously been the subject matter of plays. But unlike realism, naturalistic plays are often made up of a series of brief scenes or episodes rather than the tight dramatic structure of longer scenes found in realistic plays.

The best-known naturalistic dramas from the turn of the century are Gerhart Hauptmann's *The Weavers* (Germany) and *The Lower Depths* by Maxim Gorki of Russia. Gorki's play presents characters in a flophouse who have sunk to the lowest level of Russian society.

Although the naturalistic movement was not popular for long in its original form, it has reappeared in many plays and productions since its beginnings and has also influenced the making of many films. ■

This is a scene from Zola's dramatization of his novel *Thérèse Raquin*. This depressing story involving betrayal, murder, and suicide was not a hit with late nineteenth century French audiences, but is one of the best examples of naturalistic drama.

reading others' comments and reviews before you decide how you judge a performance. It will be worth your time to establish guidelines in choosing what you watch on stage, television, and film.

Evaluating a Live Performance

Johann von Goethe, a German playwright and author of literary masterpieces, gave us an example to follow in evaluating works of art. These can also be used to value theatre events. His writing philosophy involved three questions:

What did the author or playwright do?

Did the author or playwright accomplish the task?

Was it worth doing?

With these thoughts in mind, use the following evaluation criteria after attending a live performance:

1. What was the theme?
2. What was the plot?
3. How were the characters developed?
4. How effective was the dialogue? Was it meaningful language? Explain.
5. How effective were the actors? Were they believable? How effective were the interpretations of their roles, their voices, their movements, their reactions to the other actors, and their projection? Were they disciplined and in control?
6. How effective were the stage designs, set, makeup, costumes, lighting, and special effects?
7. How effective was the director? How effective were the director's selection and casting of the play, interpretation of the characters, and blocking and creation of stage pictures?
8. How smooth was the organization of the crew? How well did they handle the changing of scenes and blackouts?

Once the performance is over, most theatregoers enjoy analyzing and discussing their reactions to the play. Developing your evaluation skills will add to your enjoyment of theatre, television, and movies.

9. Did you agree with the conclusion of the play? Why or why not?
10. Who was your favorite character? Why?
11. What was your favorite scene? Why?
12. What was the reaction of the audience to the play?
13. What was your reaction to the play?
14. In your opinion, was the play a good work of art or a poor one?
15. Did the production make you think?
16. Did the production make you change your view of something?
17. What emotions did you experience during and after the play?
18. How would you change this production?
19. Would you recommend this play to another person? Why or why not?
20. What gives this play merit?

Evaluating Television and Film

There are many fine television dramas and films, but when you make your selection, you must use discrimination, recognizing important differences and distinctions. Television and films can take you anywhere and show you many situations. This is why you must use discrimination. Many dramas on television and on film are not appropriate for all ages, nor do they all have merit. They are also much more accessible than live theatre. There are critics who rate television programs and movies and suggest appropriate viewing. Some critics write for magazines and newspapers; others can be heard on the radio or on television. The Motion Picture Association of America provides movie ratings for parents and young people:

G—all ages admitted
PG—all ages admitted, but use parental discretion
PG-13—parents strongly cautioned
R—restricted; persons under 17 must be accompanied by an adult
NC-17—no children under 17 admitted

Most movie theatres enforce these codes, but it is still in your best interest to learn to be selective in what you see and hear. Use the following criteria to help you select and evaluate television drama and films before you view them.

Before viewing:
1. What comments have you heard about the television program or film?
2. What reviews have you read in newspapers or magazines about the television program or film?
3. Is the television program or film supported or recommended by people you respect or by organizations such as Hallmark and PBS that have a history of producing quality shows?

(You may not agree with the comments and opinions of others, but you may find them helpful in forming your own standards.)

After viewing:
4. Did the story have a well-developed theme and plot? Were the characters well developed?

5. How effective were the actors? Were they believable? How effective were their voices, their movements, and their reactions to other actors?

6. Did the story have human values? Did it have appropriate role models, language, and messages?

7. How effective was the director's work? How effective were the casting directions given to the actors, and message given to the audience?

8. How effective were the set designs, scenery, lighting, and special effects?

9. How effective were the costuming and makeup?

10. How effective were the camera operators?

11. How effective was the television or film editor? Did the television program or film flow together? Did the sequencing make sense? Should part of the program or film have been left out? Was something missing?

12. Did advertising of this television program or film influence you in choosing it?

13. What did you like best and least about the television program or film?

14. What would you change about the television program or film?

15. Would you recommend the television program or film to another person? Why or why not?

In your process of appreciating and evaluating performances, do not be fooled by false advertising or critics who use words to glorify their reviews and create publicity. Select television programs and films that set high standards for living and represent models of ethical conduct. Base your evaluation standards on sound judgment, human values, and literary merit.

Giving Your Evaluations in Class

When you evaluate a live performance, television program, or film production in class, give **constructive criticism**—helpful comments and opinions that are expressed in a positive way. Your judgments and opinions of both strengths and weaknesses are always important and should be voiced. You may be asked to give a critique that is oral or written. Keep in mind how you would like *your* work to be critiqued. Clear and definite comments of how someone or something could be improved are better than vague statements about how bad someone or something was.

As you evaluate live performances and other media, play the role of critic, judge, or reviewer. Your teacher may ask you to play the role of a contest judge to evaluate the activities assigned. Or you and a classmate may role-play the well-known television personalities Siskel and Ebert and conduct your own review of live stage performances, television programs, or movies.

You must have specific evaluation criteria (questions or evaluation comments) before you start judging or forming opinions of performers, live plays, television dramas, or films. These criteria may be provided by your teacher, or you may be asked to develop your own. Use the

This is the reaction we all hope for after every play, TV show, or movie.

constructive criticism

helpful comments and opinions that are expressed in a positive way.

same type of questions that were given in Chapter 2 and in this lesson as a guideline in developing your own evaluation forms. Use appropriate language and a writing style that your class will understand. Above all, do not omit this process from your theatre assignments and adventures.

For each activity, use the following evaluation form (or use one of the forms given earlier in this lesson).

Form for Evaluating Theatre and Other Media

Answer the questions on a scale from 1 to 4. Use these rankings:
1, poor; 2, average; 3, good; 4, excellent.

Evaluation of the Script

Score:

1. Is the theme clear to the audience? _____
2. Does the play offer the audience positive experiences? _____
3. Is the play well written? _____
4. Is the dialogue entertaining? _____
5. Does the dialogue make you think? _____
6. Does the dialogue evoke emotional responses? _____
7. Does the play have a strong plot? _____
8. Are the scenes in the play easy to follow? _____
9. Is there a strong climax in the play? _____
10. Is the ending effective? _____
11. Does the play hold your attention? _____

Evaluation of the Acting

1. Are the characters true to life? _____
2. Are the actors' interpretations effective? _____
3. Are the actors natural and at ease with their techniques? _____
4. Are the actors' movements motivated at all times? _____
5. Are the roles developed into distinct personalities? _____
6. Are the actors' voices effective? _____
7. Do the actors use proper volume, rate, diction, pronunciation, phrasing, inflection, and projection? _____
8. If a dialect is used, is it effective? _____
9. Are the actors always in character? _____
10. Are the actors' facial expressions effective? _____
11. Are the characters relating to each other in sharing scenes, picking up cues, and reacting with each other? _____
12. Is each character believable? _____

Evaluating the Stage Production

1. Is the set appropriate and effective? Does it add to or take away from the play? _____
2. Are the stage designs appropriate to the meaning of the play? _____

---

3. Are the costumes appropriate? Are they true to the time period? Are they clean and tailored properly? _____
4. Is the makeup appropriate in developing the characters? _____
5. Are the special effects an asset to the play? _____
6. Do all the details of the play's production come together for a polished performance? _____

General Comments

1. Are you interested in the play? _____
2. Do you feel a connection with the characters during and after the play? _____
3. Does there seem to be a positive response from the audience during and after the play? _____
4. After the play ends, do you feel an appreciation for the actors, director, and crew? _____
5. Is the performance a positive experience for you? _____

1. **And Now the Envelope Please.** Choose a favorite character on one of the television programs you watch regularly, and evaluate this character's performance. Decide whether or not this character deserves an Emmy. (An Emmy is an award for outstanding television performance.) Repeat the activity with an actor from a movie. Decide whether or not this character deserves an Oscar. (An Oscar is a movie award for an outstanding film performance or association with a film.) Do the activity a third time with an actor from a stage production. Decide whether or not this character deserves a Tony. (A Tony is a stage award for outstanding performance or association with live drama.) Each time, prepare your evaluation using written comments.

2. **Showtime Review.** After attending a movie, select a character who interested you, and prepare an oral critique of his or her performance. Then, with a classmate, role-play a situation in which you are leading movie reviewers sharing your critiques with the other classmates. Ask your teacher to videotape this assignment. Play back the tape and have the class critique you and your classmate orally.

3. **Here Comes the Judge.** Attend a live production with your class. After the class has returned to the classroom, participate in an activity that requires each member to be a critic. Orally give the strengths and weaknesses of the performers and the play.

Curtain Call!

CHAPTER 12 REVIEW

■ ■ SPOTLIGHT ON TERMS ■ ■

An important part of theatre is understanding the terminology, or vocabulary, used. Add the new terms and definitions to the vocabulary section of your theatre notebook or folder.

■ ■ FOCUS ON FACTS ■ ■

1. Explain the following theatre conventions: performance space, program, blinking of the house lights, dimming of the house lights, curtain up, curtain down, blackout, curtain call, and applause.
2. Define audience etiquette.
3. How are computers used in live theatre today?
4. Discuss the similarities and differences of live theatre, television, and film from the audience viewpoint.
5. Discuss the similarities and differences of live theatre, television, and film from the actor viewpoint.
6. Discuss the similarities and differences of live theatre, television, and film from the aspect of production techniques.
7. What do the different movie ratings stand for?

■ ■ REFLECTIONS ■ ■

Discuss the following questions with your class or answer them on paper as instructed by your teacher.

1. Discuss the changes and improvements that you have seen or experienced firsthand in the last few years in live theatre, television, or film.
2. What impact have live theatre, television, and film had on your life?
3. Does advertising play an important role in live theatre and other media? Why?
4. Relate a positive or negative experience in which you have received an evaluation or constructive criticism. Why was it positive or negative? Be specific.
5. Which theatre convention do you think is the most important? Why?

6. How early in school do you think audience etiquette should be taught? Why?

■ ■ THEATRE IN YOUR LIFE ■ ■

1. *Program Design.* On your own, design a program for an imaginary event or an upcoming production.
2. *Theatre Conventions Poster Design.* Create a poster illustrating theatre conventions. Display the posters in your classroom or in the halls of your school.
3. Working in small groups, discuss how your lives are influenced by the media.
4. How often do you use a computer in theatre? Think ahead to the future. How important do you think the computer will be in the theatre? Be specific.
5. Discuss how television and films change, reinforce, or enhance an idea or product in advertising their programs and movies.

■ ■ ENCORE ■ ■

1. *Live Theatre and Media Survey.* Conduct a survey of your peers to find out what live productions they attend, what television programs they watch, and what films they see. Use the computer to create your survey. When finished, conduct another survey of several adults. Compare the two surveys for similarities and differences in written form.
2. *Talk Show.* After attending a play, think of questions you would like to ask the playwright, producer, director, actors, set designers, lighting designer, or costume designer if they were guests on a television talk show where you were part of the audience. Select one student to be the talk show host and persons to assume each of the guest roles. Members of the audience will be called upon to ask their questions. Each guest will form questions by making educated guesses about why certain artistic decisions were made.

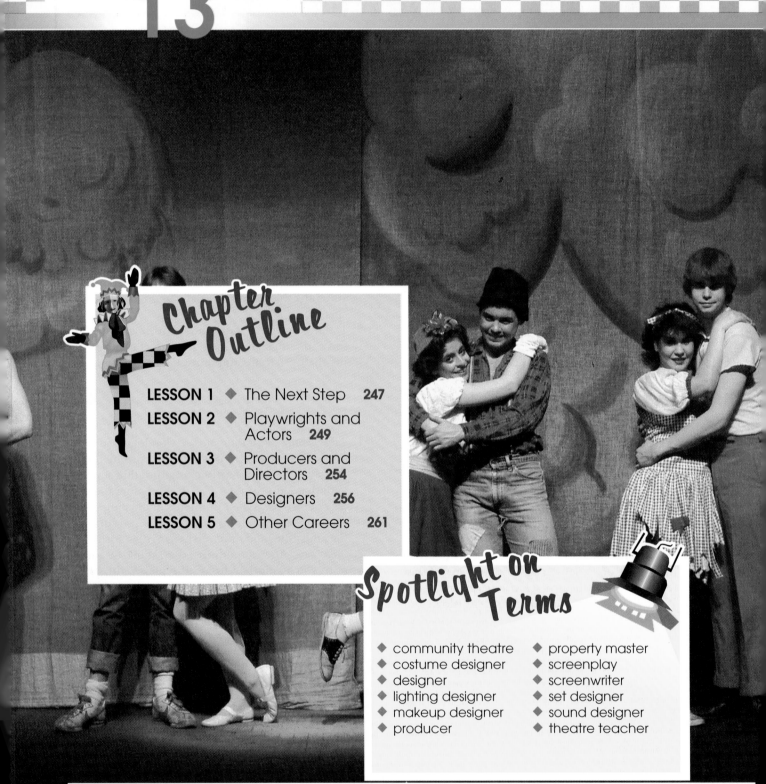

CHAPTER 13

Your Future in Theatre

Spotlight on Terms

- ◆ community theatre
- ◆ costume designer
- ◆ designer
- ◆ lighting designer
- ◆ makeup designer
- ◆ producer
- ◆ property master
- ◆ screenplay
- ◆ screenwriter
- ◆ set designer
- ◆ sound designer
- ◆ theatre teacher

Have you ever wondered what your life would be like if you were an actor, playwright, director, or even a theatre teacher? When you are enjoying an exciting class such as theatre arts, it's only natural for you to imagine a lifetime in the theatre. In fact, it's not too soon to begin thinking of job and career opportunities in the theatre. Perhaps you can picture yourself as an actor or choreographer, director or playwright, stage manager or makeup artist. But there are many other behind-the-scenes job opportunities as well. Many shows hire personnel to publicize the show, to dress the actors, and to work on crews setting up the lights and sound. Every production requires dedicated workers both onstage and backstage to produce the final product that the audience gets to see.

People work in theatre because they love it. It's an uncertain way to earn a living, but very exciting. Theatre jobs do not offer much job security. If a show is unsuccessful, it closes. The closing leaves all those associated with the show jobless. What's more, the pay for work in the theatre is extremely low. To make ends meet, many young people have to work more than one job. Lots of actors work in hotels and restaurants as bellhops and waiters.

In spite of low pay, job insecurity, and job scarcity, theatre jobs and careers offer a wonderful opportunity for creativity, travel, and a taste of life like no other business in the world. In this chapter, you will have a chance to explore some of the career opportunities that await you in the world of theatre.

The Next Step

LESSON OBJECTIVES

◆ Identify community theatre opportunities.
◆ Determine the time requirements for out-of-classroom theatre activities.

Warm Up

Discuss theatre opportunities outside the classroom in which students your age might participate.

community theatre

not-for-profit theatre that uses local talent of all ages to produce plays. The theatre may hire a professional staff but use volunteer actors and backstage workers.

You may want to continue your interest in theatre after school. Many communities have city recreation programs that include dramatic activities. Usually, you can obtain information about local theatre activities and events by contacting your local arts council, city parks and recreation department, or local chamber of commerce.

Volunteers are often needed to help with community theatre productions. **Community theatre** is not-for-profit theatre that uses local talent of all ages to produce plays. Your local newspaper, chamber of commerce, and public library are good sources of information about the kinds of community theatre in your area.

Often, theatre workshops are available for students your age. These might be held after school or on weekends for a short period of time. The workshops usually conclude with a short performance for parents and friends. Ask your theatre teacher if such workshops are available in your area.

Joining a community theatre
production can be a fun and
rewarding experience.

Many colleges sponsor summer theatre programs for a nominal fee. Phone the college theatre department during regular business hours for information. If you live at home, the cost will be much less than if you stay on campus and live in a dorm. Most programs offer both options.

You might want to continue your theatre training by signing up for additional classes in high school. Most high schools offer various classes in theatre, theatre production, and technical theatre. Some also offer musical theatre courses. If your high school does not offer classes in theatre arts, perhaps it has an after-school drama group or club. Some clubs sponsor productions and festivals, providing interested students with a variety of activities in which to participate. Contact the school activities director or guidance counselor to find out what is offered.

Large cities often have special schools for the performing arts. Most of these schools have specific requirements for admittance, such as grade averages, recommendations, or auditions. The counselor on your campus will know what is available in your area.

ACTion

1. Discovering More about Theatre.
    a. Compile a list of theatre opportunities for young people in your community.
    b. Interview a student currently enrolled in another theatre class. Find out the responsibilities and amount of time required for that class.

c. Interview a member of a community theatre group. Find out the responsibilities and amount of time required to be a part of that group.

Playwrights and Actors

LESSON OBJECTIVES

- ◆ Identify a wide range of occupations and careers associated with theatre.
- ◆ Become aware of factors to consider when choosing a career in theatre.

Warm Up

List as many different theatre-related careers and jobs as you can. Remember, acting is not the only job in theatre.

There are many opportunities for jobs in and relating to the theatre. Two jobs you are probably familiar with are playwright and actor.

Playwright

The playwright is the person who creates the script for a play or stage production. The playwright will spend many hours alone writing the dialogue. Some writers work every day, just as if they had a 9-to-5 job, while others work only in their spare time. If you have ever written a play for one of your classes, then you know the amount of time that must be spent thinking, writing, and rewriting.

Playwrights can spend many hours doing research before they begin writing their scripts.

screenwriter
a writer who writes television or movie scripts.

screenplay
the script written for a movie or television show.

Once the script is completed, the playwright must find a producer—someone willing to get the money to produce the play. Sometimes a producer invites, or commissions, a playwright to write a play for a special occasion or based on a special idea. When this happens, the playwright is usually selected based on his or her previous work.

Some playwrights write for television or for film. These writers are known as **screenwriters**. Some **screenplays** (television or movie scripts) originate from the imagination of the screenwriter. Others are based on previously written books or stories. When a book or story is the basis of a movie or television show, a royalty (fee) must be paid to the original author.

Television sitcoms and weekly dramas often have a staff of writers preparing the script each week. Notice the credits that run at the end of your favorite television show and see who the screenwriters are.

Playwrights receive a royalty each time one of their published scripts is performed. Their work is protected by the copyright law. This copyright protects original work, making it illegal for someone to produce a published work without permission from the writer or publishing company. This payment to the playwright is how the playwright earns a living.

If you love the theatre, enjoy writing, and have a good imagination, playwriting or screenwriting might be just the career for you. To prepare for this career, continue getting good grades in school. Reading, attending plays, and writing as much as possible will increase your background knowledge and vocabulary. All areas of education will enhance your theatrical creativity. Besides taking theatre courses in school and working in theatre productions, sharpen your natural writing abilities by taking classes in English, creative writing, and playwriting. Try entering some amateur playwriting contests just to experience the competition. Perhaps your teacher knows of a contest that you can enter. These competitions often offer scholarship opportunities and are ideal ways to open doors to your future.

Actor

Seemingly the most glamorous job in the theatre is that of the actor. Actors, male or female, are people who perform in plays, in films, and on television. Many actors sing and dance as well as act.

Some actors begin their careers in middle school or high school with an active interest in theatre, dance, or singing. Often they work in school and community productions throughout their high school careers.

Some attend a college or university program and earn a degree with a major in theatre arts. A degree is a rank or title that is given by a college or university to indicate that a student has completed a course of study. A major is a particular field of study, such as theatre, that a college student might pursue. One of the advantages in obtaining a college degree is that you will have studied all areas of the theatre. This means that you can rely on other possibilities for employment when acting roles are scarce.

Before an actor "lands a role," an audition usually takes place. Auditions are tryouts for a production. You may have auditioned for one of your classroom shows or after-school productions. In the same way that you auditioned for your teacher or director, the actor auditioning for a professional show reads a part from the script to give the director and producer an opportunity to see and hear the actor perform.

An important part of auditioning for a professional show is providing an 8-by-10-inch photograph and a résumé of your acting experience. The résumé and photograph will help the director and producer remember you later and enable them to check your specific talents and experiences against those they are seeking. (See Figure 13–1.)

Sometimes, callbacks are needed when the director wants to have a second look at the actor. A callback is an additional opportunity for the director and producer to consider the actor for a part in the production. Keep in mind, however, that it is possible to be called back

Figure 13–1

A Résumé and Head Shot.

Kamal Suluki

Height: 6'1"
Weight: 160 lbs.
Hair: Brown
Eyes: Brown

Colours
Model & Talent Agency
(213) 658-7072
8344 1/2 W. 3rd St. L.A. CA. 90048

Film:	Actor:	Directors:
Diggstown:	Boxer in training	Micheal Ritchie
Percy and Thunder:	Boxer workout	Ivon Dixon

Commercials:

Safety for New Years (P.

Training:

Character Development
Monologue
Scene Study
Commercial

Special Skills:
Amateur boxing, skating, Hip-Hop singing, operating computers, bike riding, jogging, also on hand experience with television broadcasting cameras

several times and then turned down for the part. As sad as it may seem, rejection is a big part of an actor's career. Actors need to have a strong sense of self-preservation and be willing to bounce back and try again.

Once a role is offered and accepted, the actor begins to learn the lines, develop the character, and attend the rehearsals, just as you do in your school productions. One of the major differences between school productions and professional productions is that the professional actor is paid for his or her services and can be fired for not doing a good job. Characters are sometimes replaced in educational theatre, but usually a teacher or director tries to convince the student actor to try harder.

The television and film industries have glamorized the role of the actor, making the jobs seem high paying and easy to acquire. In reality, there are many financially successful actors, but many others have to work a second job waiting tables or teaching to support their artistic endeavors.

Actors who have "made it big" often credit not just their talent, but also their willingness to work long and hard. Some actors have said that they were lucky enough to make good connections and to be at the right place at the right time. However, most of the true success stories are the result of ten or more years of hard work getting to the top. It seems that there is no magic formula for what makes an actor a box-office hit. Sometimes it is just chance and good old-fashioned luck.

Where do you find acting jobs? In live theatre, film, and television, of course. Television commercials are another way that actors can practice their craft. The pay for acting in commercials or for performing voice work for commercials is often much more lucrative than acting in the theatre.

1. **Research Project.** Research the life and career of a famous playwright. Write a short report to share with the class.

2. **TV Log.** Keep a list for one week of all your favorite television shows. Indicate those written by individuals and those written by teams.

3. **Writing a Résumé.** Prepare your own résumé. Ask your school guidance counselor for résumé books containing résumé models. In creating your résumé make sure that your final copy is free of errors—employers do not hire job applicants who make mistakes in preparing their own résumés. If you do not have any real acting experience, create make-believe roles for yourself in professional productions. Use a photocopier to enlarge one of your school pictures to attach to the résumé.

Stanislavski and the Moscow Art Theatre

No modern theatre group has been more important to theatre history than the Moscow Art Theatre and the artist, Konstantin Stanislavski, who wrote, directed, and performed for this group in the early years of the 1900s.

The Moscow Art Theatre was founded in 1898 by Konstantin Stanislavski and Vladimire Danchenko. The two men were idealists who spent many hours discussing the nature of life, truth, and beauty and how these forces relate to theatre practice. Stanislavski and Danchenko dedicated their theatre to the presentation of realistic theatre that promoted truth and meaning.

The Moscow artists first gained world attention with Stanislavski's production of *The Seagull* by Anton Chekov in 1898. For this production Stanislavski's group discarded the melodramatic and shallow theatrical style and acting that had characterized the plays of the earlier years of the nineteenth century. Instead of using the old methods, they presented Chekov's characters with the understated, natural voice and movement that his complicated characters demanded. They became famous for their success—so famous that their approach to acting became the model for acting practices for the next century of theatre artists.

The Moscow Art Theatre provided the twentieth century with the first systematic approach to realistic acting. Stanislavski insisted that all actors completely immerse themselves in the roles that they were creating. They were asked to study in great detail the motives and forces of influence at work in the thought process of each character and to let those thoughts, needs, desires, and cultural factors dictate their every move on stage. Stanislavski believed that only through this method could actors depict a totally believable and true-to-life character. He steered actors away from the openly robust overacting that had dominated the popular theatre of the early 1800s. Stanislavski asked his actors to prepare for the roles they would play both mentally and physically, maintaining both muscular relaxation and mental concentration on stage at all times.

Another innovative practice of the Moscow Art Theatre was the teamwork approach to theatre production, which has become known as the *ensemble approach* to theatre. This approach set the Moscow Art Theatre apart from other theatre companies of the period, which were still working under a star system in which the audience's favorite actor was the star of the company and all of the other elements in the production were tailored to support the work of the star. ■

This is the last scene of Stanislavski's 1898 Moscow Art Theatre production of *The Seagull*.

Producers and Directors

LESSON OBJECTIVES

◆ Identify the roles of producers and directors.
◆ Become aware of factors to be considered when choosing producer or director as a career.

Warm Up

How many names of professional producers or directors of live theatre can you name? As a class, compile a list on the board. Can you name one play each person has directed or produced?

producer
the person responsible for the entire production, including obtaining financial backing, paying the bills, and hiring the director and creative staff.

Many important careers in theatre are not onstage. The producer and director play a vital role in every theatrical production long before the audience ever sees the show.

Producer

The producer plays a key role in a theatrical production. The **producer** is the person responsible for the success of the entire show. The producer's major responsibility is to find people or corporations that are willing to invest money in the show. Producing a Broadway play may cost more than $500,000. Musical productions can cost twice as much. Setting the budget and paying the bills are an important part of the producer's job.

A producer may also be required to find a script for the production. Still other important duties include hiring the director and other members of the creative team.

Taking theatre and business courses in school is a good way to prepare for a job as a producer.

Director

The director of a play must be a dreamer, a visionary—someone who can bring the written words of the script to life for the audience. In short, the director is the person in charge of the artistic production of the play.

The director works with the casting director to cast the ideal people to play the various roles in the show. The director also works with the designers to create the set, costumes, makeup, lighting, and special effects. By working closely with all of these artists and technicians, the director coordinates all parts of the production. As a result of the director's efforts, ideas that once were seen only in the playwright's imagination will be shown to a live audience through the magic of live theatre.

A director is sometimes like an athletic coach. The director coaches the actors. As part of the rehearsal process, the director guides the actors in developing the roles they will play. Often, the director helps the actors interpret or understand their lines. The director also studies the script and plans the movement of the different characters onstage. Early in the rehearsal process, the director blocks the characters onstage, showing the actors where to move and how to move. This process is much like a football coach teaching plays to use against the

It is the casting director's job to pick just the right actor for each role.

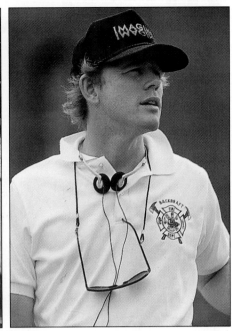

Ron Howard started his career as a child actor, but he is probably best known for playing Richie Cunningham in *Happy Days*. He is now a successful movie director, with such films as *Backdraft* and *Apollo 13* to his credit.

> *he director is the magnifying lens through which the actor's impulse shines; the director is the resonator which lends depth to the actor's music.*
>
> *Robert L. Benedetti*

opposing team. Effective stage blocking strengthens a production, just as effective plays help win a football game.

Once a show is ready to open, the director's job is finished. The director turns the production over to a stage manager and moves on to another production that is just getting started.

Some directors begin as actors and learn as much as possible about the craft. Other directors begin by directing small groups or theatre companies. One of the most important things you can do if you want to be a director is to direct as much as possible in order to make contacts. Contacts—connections with other theatre professionals—may lead to openings in other productions.

Directors need to be quite knowledgeable about all aspects of the theatre. They must also have leadership ability, since people management is such an important part of the job.

We must be realistic and tell you that job opportunities for the professional director are limited. Still, many directors find jobs directing community theatre or nonprofessional companies.

ACTION

1. **Research Project.** Research the life and career of a famous director or producer. Write a short report to share with the class.

2. **What Do You Think?** Read a play and then watch the movie version. Write a comparison/ contrast paper, discussing how they are alike and different. Why do you think the director made certain changes in the movie version?

Designers

LESSON OBJECTIVES

◆ Identify a wide range of occupations associated with design.
◆ Recognize the contributions of designers and technicians in a production.

Warm Up

Discuss with the members of your acting company the importance of set, costumes, makeup, lighting, special effects, and music or sound in a performance. Which of those elements do you think is most important in a production?

designer

a person who creates or plans a specific part of the production, such as the costumes, lighting, set, makeup, or sound.

■ ■ ■ ■ ■ ■ ■ ■ ■ ■ ■ ■ ■ ■ ■

Working with a model of the set enables the designer to solve problems and make improvements without spending a great deal of time and money building an actual set.

set designer

the person who designs the set for a production.

There are many opportunities for designers in the world of theatre. A **designer** is someone who creates or plans a specific part of the production, such as the set, lighting, costumes, sound, or makeup. The job of a designer is to relay to the audience the ideas of the director by enhancing the production using the senses of sight and sound. If you are interested in creating sets, costumes, lighting, sound, makeup, or even props, a career in designing might be just the thing for you.

Set Designer

The scenic designer, also called the **set designer**, is the person who designs the set for the production. This is an important job in the theatre, since the set helps create the mood and provides a background for the play. Part of the set designer's job is to visually set up the stage in a way that gives life to the playwright's words.

Many set designers begin by researching the period of the play, making notes and sketches of colors, styles, and types of furniture that were popular during that time. Then they make sketches of the set for the

director to approve. Later they make floor plans and scale drawings much like blueprints. Today, many set designers create their designs with the help of computer programs.

After the set is designed, the set designer usually builds a scale model of the set. The set designer also oversees the building of the set. Sometimes, a set designer will work on several plays at once.

Many set designers have learned by hands-on training, whereas others have college degrees in art, architecture, or scenic design. This would be the perfect career to combine a love of theatre and architecture.

Many set designers have assistants who help create the sets and find the perfect props for the show. It is important that the set be decorated with furniture and other items that will make it look realistic. Small productions often delegate the job of making or finding props to a **property master** .

property master
the person in charge of the stage properties, or props, for a production.

Props are needed in all theatre, film, and television productions. Modern-day props are easily available and can be purchased. Sometimes, the needed props can be rented from a prop warehouse, museum, or antique shop. To find just the right prop, the prop crew may need to search junk shops, vintage specialty shops, and even flea markets. When the perfect prop just can't be found, the prop crew has to design and construct it.

Lighting Designer

lighting designer
the person who plans and puts into effect the lighting for a play or stage production.

Another important role is that of the lighting designer. The **lighting designer** is the person who plans and puts into effect the lighting. Stage lighting is necessary for the audience to see the actors and the set. But lighting can do more than just illuminate the actors and the stage. Lighting can also establish different moods onstage and

create special effects that enhance the production. The lighting designer must work closely with the director, the set designer, and the costume designer to provide the proper lighting effects on their designs. In small companies, the lighting designer also has the job of making sure that the lighting system is working and running the control board during the performance.

Lighting designers need to be creative and have a thorough understanding of the theatre. Skill as an electrician is also required. And since much of today's lighting is designed and operated by computer, lighting designers should have experience working with computers. Although a college major in theatre arts or design would be helpful to a lighting designer, many designers learn effective lighting techniques just by working on crews and watching others.

Costume Designer

Another exciting career in the theatre is that of the costume designer. The **costume designer** is the person who plans or designs the costumes to be worn in the show. After carefully reading the script, the costume designer decides the type and number of costumes that will be needed for the show.

There are many sources for obtaining costumes. Costumes can be rented or purchased from professional costume manufacturers. Cos-

costume designer
the person who designs or plans the costumes to be worn in a play or stage production.

tumes can also be sewn or constructed by a costumer. In the theatre, this construction is often referred to as "building a costume."

Each play takes place in a particular period in history. The costume designer will spend time researching the styles of the period by looking at pictures, reading books, and visiting museums. Once an impression of the period is established, the costume designer makes colored sketches of costume ideas and meets with the director to finalize the concepts. The costume designer also meets with the lighting designer and set designer to coordinate the production.

After the costume designs are completed and approved by the director, the costume designer oversees or makes the costumes. Selecting appropriate undergarments and accessories is also an important part of the designer's job. In professional theatre, once the ensembles are completed, the costume designer turns them over to the wardrobe department.

Designing costumes is a wonderful career for anyone who enjoys theatre, art, fashion, and design. A knowledge of clothing construction and fabrics is important, and good sewing skills are essential. You might consider taking high school courses in art, design, technical theatre, and clothing construction to explore your interest in this field. Obtaining a college degree in fashion design or costume design would further prepare you for this career.

Makeup Designer

makeup designer

the person who plans and designs the makeup to be worn in a play or stage production. Sometimes this person is also the makeup artist, the person who applies the makeup to the performers.

Makeup designers can transform actors into believable characters such as the scarecrow and tin man in *The Wizard of Oz*.

The **makeup designer**, working closely with the costume designer, plans and designs the makeup to be worn for a production. In many productions, the makeup designer, along with other makeup artists, applies the makeup to the actors.

The purpose of stage makeup is to project the character to the audience as well as to enhance the appearance of the actor. Makeup is sometimes used to change the appearance of an actor. Can you think of a play or movie in which makeup has been used to completely transform an actor into someone else? This transformation might be from youth to old age or from human to monster. The makeup designer works with all the other designers to coordinate the production concept. The designer suits the style of makeup to the particular period or approach of the play.

Sometimes, the makeup designer is also the hairstylist. If so, the research and design for the hairstyles follow the same approach as for the makeup. Once the designer has the basic spirit of the production, sketches are made and a conference is held with the director. The makeup designer and hairstylist always want to work closely with the other designers to provide a "finished look" for the audience.

If you are interested in makeup and hair design, volunteer backstage during high school and community productions. Continue to take high school theatre courses, especially those offered in technical theatre. Many colleges and universities offer classes in theatre makeup. Studying cosmetology and obtaining a state cosmetology license will identify you as a professional cosmetologist. Once you obtain the license, you will want to continue to update your training by enrolling in seminars and classes offered by agencies in the cosmetology field.

Sound Designer

sound designer

the person who plans and puts into effect the sound for a production.

While the other designers in a production are planning the set, lighting, costumes, and makeup—elements that will help the audience "see" the show—the **sound designer** plans and puts into effect the sound so that the audience can "hear" the show. The main job of the sound designer is to project the voices of the actors into the audience. This doesn't just mean making the sound loud.

A knowledge of the architecture of the theatre as well as the physics of sound is important to carry out this job successfully. The sound designer determines what equipment is needed and where it should be placed to obtain the best and most lifelike sound for the audience to hear. Knowing how to mix, blend, and amplify sounds on a sound board is also part of a sound designer's job.

Just as light can create mood, so can sound. Listen to the sound track from a movie, and you can hear the mood that is established by the music. A sound designer's job is not just to project the actors' voices, but also to provide appropriate music and background sounds. If a scene calls for the harsh cry of a crow, it is the sound designer's job to make the crow sound realistic.

The sound designer studies the script to see what sounds are needed in the show. A sound schedule is then planned so that the sound technician—the person controlling the sound—will know when to play music and special sound effects or when to adjust the sound. Just as in lighting, much of the sound today is designed and controlled by computer.

Sound designers often begin as volunteers for school or community productions. If this career is of interest to you, take as many classes as possible in technical theatre, sound, and electronics. Vocational trade schools frequently offer courses in these fields, just as colleges and universities do.

Sound designers have some exciting job opportunities. Many sound designers and technicians travel with road companies, setting up the sound equipment before the show arrives. Jobs for sound designers are available in live theatre, television, and the movie and music industries, as well as at conferences, exhibitions, and other events requiring lighting and sound technicians.

1. **Makeup Morgue.** Collect a file of twenty pictures depicting interesting faces to reproduce with stage makeup. Try to include a variety of ages and races.

2. **Interior Photographs.** Collect a file of twenty pictures of interior settings suitable for stage design. Include a variety of rooms.

3. **Costume Design.** You have just received an invitation to attend a theatre costume party. Use your imagination to design the costume you will wear.

4. **Lighting Projects.** Think of five ways that lighting could change the mood in one of the rooms in your home. Describe and illustrate these changes in a drawing. Be sure to color your design.

5. **Prop Design.** Design and make a prop to be used in a class production.

Other Careers

LESSON OBJECTIVES

◆ Demonstrate familiarity with the job of a stage manager.
◆ Define qualifications and skills required to become a theatre teacher.

Warm Up

Ask your theatre teacher to discuss the most rewarding aspects of his or her job.

Many careers in the theatre require good communication skills and leadership ability. Such jobs are those of stage manager and teacher.

Stage Manager

Do you like organizing people and being responsible for the action that takes place backstage? If so, the job of stage manager might be the ideal career for you. The stage manager sees that everything backstage is ready for the rehearsal and then works closely with the director during the rehearsal.

Before rehearsals begin, the stage manager prepares a promptbook. When completed, this book will contain the script and all the blocking for the show. It will also have all cues marked for curtains, lights, sound, and special effects as well as any special instructions. The director and the stage manager share the book until all the cues are determined and the director has given the cast the blocking. Once that is completed, the promptbook is handled by the stage manager, who marks any changes in the book as they occur. The promptbook is the guide for the show. The stage manager uses the information in the promptbook to keep the show moving smoothly backstage, often prompting actors when they need a line.

Early Theatre in the United States

So far you've read little about the history of theatre in the United States. Let's take a quick look at the beginnings of theatre in our country.

As you know, the land that would later become the United States was ruled by Great Britain for most of the 1600s and 1700s. Therefore, it is only natural that theatre in the colonies would be an extension of the theatre popular in England during that period.

Very few official records of colonial productions exist for theatre activities in the 1500s and 1600s, but we do know that students presented plays at Harvard College and at William and Mary College in the late 1600s. We also know that a theatre was built in 1716 in Williamsburg, Virginia, but we don't really know what was performed there. Small troupes of amateur, strolling players were at work in Philadelphia and Lancaster during the early 1700s, but it was hard for theatre people to make a living performing because strong religious beliefs made theatrical performances unpopular.

In 1745, John Moody, an English strolling player, arrived in North America. He saw the new territory as a great opportunity for performers. Actors in England were having a hard time finding work, so after returning to England, Moody sent a company headed by David Douglass back to Jamaica in 1751. Other English companies also began to tour the Americas. One such company, the Hallam Company, established a theatre in Williamsburg in 1752, making it the first professional theatre in America. From these earliest beginnings, permanent playhouses began to be established in major cities all along the Eastern Seaboard. Acting troupes traveled from one city to another to give their performances since no one area could fully support them.

Theatrical activity diminished during the Revolutionary War, but was quickly re-established in the 1780s. For example, Thomas Wignell (who had acted with Hallam's troupe), built the Chestnut Street Theatre in Philadelphia and traveled to England to gather actors to appear there. Eventually four major theatre areas were established: New York, Philadelphia, Boston, and Charleston. Most of these theatres performed English plays. To these were added plays by American playwrights Royall Tyler, William Dunlap, and John Howard Payne.

After the War of 1812, settlers began to spread west, taking theatre with them. Tour circuits developed that took theatre productions into Pittsburgh, down the Ohio River to Kentucky, and into Ohio, Indiana, Tennessee, and Missouri. This period (1807–1860s) was dominated by steam travel and many companies performed in floating theatres, huge showboats that sailed up and down America's rivers.

While the U.S. was expanding west, the Eastern Seaboard was also booming with new industry. The steam engine had revolutionized the way products were made. Areas such as New York saw huge population growth as more people arrived from Europe and people from rural areas swarmed to the jobs in the new factories. These huge pockets of population needed entertainment, and New York developed into the home of several very large theatres. Investors found it possible to make a profit by financing theatrical productions, which kept citizens in the growing city happy. Soon *Broadway*, the New York City street and neighborhood where several key theatres were eventually built, became synonymous with theatre. ■

Originally called *The New Circus*, and then *The Olympic*, The Walnut Street Theatre in Philadelphia is the oldest theatre in the United States still in use. The Walnut claims among its many "firsts," the first gas footlights (1837) and the first curtain call (Edmund Kean).

The director does not assist once the show is running. At this point, the director's job is finished. In fact, the director will often sit with the audience during the performance. It is the responsibility of the stage manager to see that everything goes as planned. During the production, the stage manager is ready to "call cues" to all of the crews and stagehands.

In most productions, the stage manager sits offstage in the wings during rehearsals and performances. Today's professional shows often have closed-circuit cameras and television monitors to enable the stage manager to see all the important parts of the stage. If there is a problem backstage during the performance or if an emergency occurs, it is the stage manager who handles the situation.

Good stage managers are important to the success of a show. This is an action-filled career that views the theatre from a different perspective. Stage managers need to be well versed in all aspects of the theatre.

Theatre Teacher

One of the most exciting careers in theatre is that of a theatre teacher. A **theatre teacher** is an educator who specializes in theatre arts or drama. Teaching theatre gives you the opportunity to be the director of an elementary, middle school, high school, or college drama group. Theatre teachers enjoy all aspects of theatrical production and also have the privilege of introducing students to the wonderful world of theatre. Educational theatre can be highly competitive and extremely exciting.

theatre teacher

an educator who specializes in theatre arts or drama.

Teaching theatre would be an excellent way for you to combine your love of theatre with an interest in helping to educate others.

Theatre teachers have a broad knowledge about theatre as well as practical experience in theatre. Moreover, their educational training prepares them for using appropriate strategies to motivate and educate their students. Planning and teaching classes, directing plays, supervising crews, and sponsoring drama clubs and fund-raisers are some of the responsibilities of a teacher at the secondary level.

The responsibilities of a college or university teacher might include teaching classes, directing productions, and supervising technical crews. Many colleges and universities require that their teachers write articles for educational journals or even write textbooks—like this one.

If you are considering a career in the theatre, you will want to investigate colleges and universities offering courses of study in theatre or drama. Most four-year schools now offer a degree in theatre. Check with your guidance counselor or school librarian to get the names and addresses of these schools. Your college theatre courses will teach you theatre techniques as well as give you an opportunity for practical theatre experience.

ACTION

1. **Preparing for a Job Interview.** Imagine that you are applying for a job teaching theatre at your school. Make a list of questions you would ask the interviewer about the job.

2. **Finding Out.** Interview a person in your community who holds a job in theatre. Prepare a report to share with your class.

3. **Theatrical Survey.** Interview five of your other teachers to find out if they ever participated in theatrical activities in high school, college, or community theatre. Report your information to your class.

Curtain Call!

CHAPTER 13 REVIEW

■ ■ SPOTLIGHT ON TERMS ■ ■

An important part of theatre is understanding the terminology, or vocabulary, used. Add the new terms and definitions to the vocabulary section of your theatre notebook or folder.

■ ■ FOCUS ON FACTS ■ ■

1. How can a young actor gain acting experience? Where can this happen in your local community?
2. What is one of the major differences between school productions and professional productions?
3. In addition to acting in live theatre, film, and television, what is another area that actors might consider?
4. What are three backstage jobs in theatre?
5. Name and define four important duties of a director.
6. List the different steps that the set designer goes through to create the sets.
7. What happens when the perfect prop can't be found?
8. What are the duties of the sound designer?
9. What career opportunities in theatre require a college degree?
10. Which job opportunities discussed in this chapter do not require a college degree?

■ ■ REFLECTIONS ■ ■

Discuss the following questions with your class or answer them on paper as instructed by your teacher.

1. As you look back on this chapter, which of the theatre jobs or careers appeal to you most? Why? Which ones would you not choose? Why?
2. How can the study of theatre enhance your life, even though you do not choose it as a profession?

■ ■ THEATRE IN YOUR LIFE ■ ■

Picture yourself twenty years from now. You have a career in theatre. Write a short story telling of your career journey. Be sure to include your professional training and some of your experiences along the way.

■ ■ ENCORE ■ ■

1. Invite a theatre professional in your community to visit your class to discuss a specific theatre career.
2. Invite someone from the community theatre to visit your class to talk about how theatre has enhanced his or her life. Ask this person to discuss how he or she manages to stay active in theatre while holding another job.
3. Using this chapter as a guide, compile a list of questions to ask when inquiring about a career in theatre.
4. Prepare a poster depicting career opportunities in theatre.
5. Select one career opportunity in theatre. Research the responsibilities of the job, and prepare a poster depicting this profession.
6. Compile a list of colleges and universities in your state offering degrees related to theatre.
7. Obtain a college or university catalog from a school offering a degree in theatre. Read the description of the courses offered, and make a list of the ones that would benefit you most if you planned to be an actor.
8. Locate the addresses of major motion picture studios, such as Disney, Universal, Warner Brothers, or MGM. Write letters to the studios asking for information about the entry-level positions that each company offers. Bring the information you receive to class and share it with your classmates. Discuss the career opportunities to decide whether or not you might enjoy working for a movie studio.

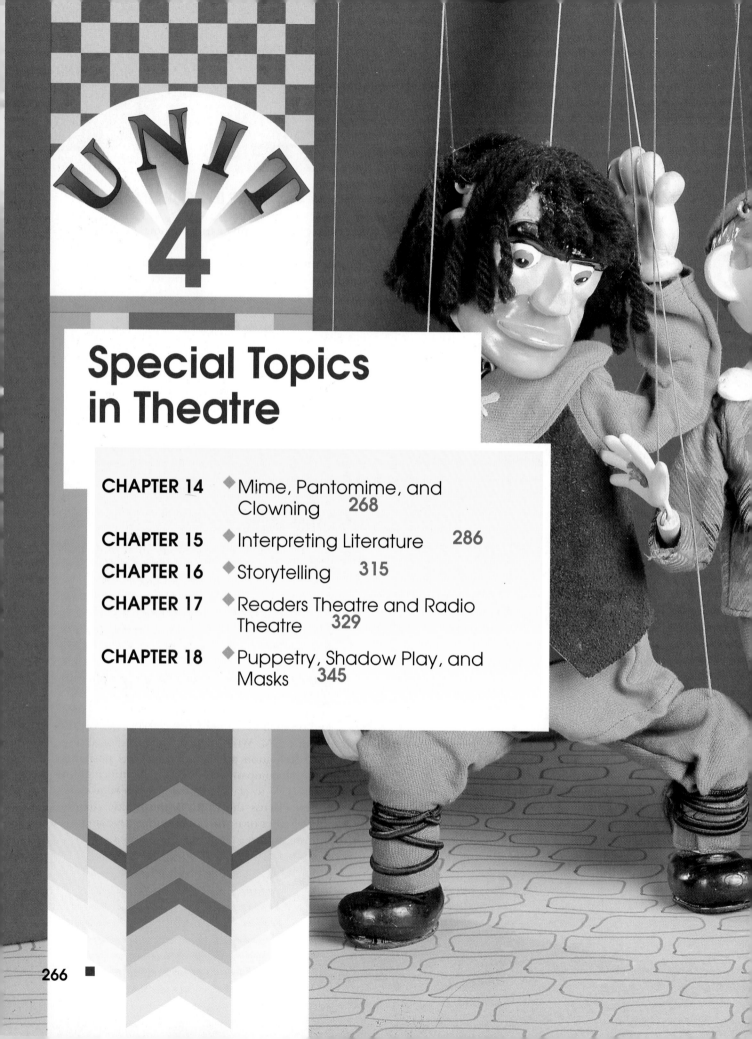

UNIT 4

Special Topics in Theatre

CHAPTER 14

Mime, Pantomime, and Clowning

Chapter Outline

Spotlight on Terms

- auguste clown
- character clown
- clowning
- grotesque whiteface
- mime

- mimesis
- neat whiteface
- pantomime
- pantomimus
- whiteface clown

P antomime, mime, and clowning are closely related. They all express dramatic ideas without words. All three arts require imagination, concentration, observation, sensory awareness, and rhythmic and expressive movement—the personal resources you learned about in Chapter 3. In this chapter, we will explore the similarities and differences among mime, pantomime, and clowning, focusing on the techniques and impact of each art.

LESSON 1

Mime and Pantomime

LESSON OBJECTIVES

- ◆ Define mime and pantomime.
- ◆ Understand and identify similarities and differences between mime and pantomime.
- ◆ Research mimes and their art.
- ◆ Prepare and present pantomime exercises and activities.

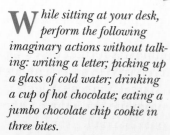

Warm Up

*W*hile sitting at your desk, perform the following imaginary actions without talking: writing a letter; picking up a glass of cold water; drinking a cup of hot chocolate; eating a jumbo chocolate chip cookie in three bites.

Can you communicate effectively with facial expressions and gestures? If so, you might enjoy being a mime.

T he words mime and pantomime are often used interchangeably. They are, however, two different arts. Even experts often disagree on their definitions, resulting in different interpretations of these two skills. Mime comes from the Greek word *mimesis*, meaning "to imitate an activity." Mime's main activity is movement, and its content often deals with the complex meanings and forces of life. Pantomime comes from the Latin word *pantomimus*, meaning "all gestures used in support of a theme." Pantomime revolves around character and plot, using imaginary props and people to tell a story.

Mime and pantomime are similar, however, because they are both ways to communicate by gesturing, a form of acting without words. In both arts, the actors portray characters and scenes through facial expressions and body language that the audience can easily understand.

Many performers believe that the techniques and styles in pantomime are fewer than in mime, with mime involving more body control and dramatic movement. Mime has many different styles, including rituals, commedia dell' arte, silent acting, and French classical mime. Pantomime uses mime techniques to communicate and create characters and plot to its audience.

An important difference between mime and pantomime is the content of the ideas being presented. Pantomime usually has simple and chronological story lines, such as brushing your teeth, playing a tuba, watching a tennis match, or stepping on a piece of gum. Mime is more complex, based on theme, illusion, and plot, requiring a higher level of communication between the performer and the audience. And even though pantomime must be accurate, clear, and performed with precise movements, it does not require the intense study, discipline, and body training required of mime. To explain the contrast in the

The most famous mime in the world is probably Marcel Marceau.

A talented mime can make you believe he is actually doing what he is only pretending to do.

mime
the silent art of using body movements to create an illusion of reality.

two arts, let's use Marcel Marceau, the well-known French mime. He uses pantomime when he performs the famous scene of his character, Bip, at a party, but he uses mime when he produces his intense facial expressions and body movements to communicate a struggle with some force of nature.

We will now look at the two arts in greater detail.

Mime

Mime is the "silent" art of using body movements to create an illusion of reality. The word "mime" can also refer to the performer of this art. Mime is a very old form of theatrical expression. In fact, mime has been the most common dramatic expression in many cultures. The dances at tribal gatherings around campfires, performed by prehistoric people, used elements of mime. Mime shows were presented before performances of Greek tragedies. Phyrrhic dances of the Greek warriors were examples of mime. Romans used mime in their dramatic presentations, which were often based on mythology. Early performers of mime were minstrels, jugglers, dancers, and acrobats. These examples help explain another definition of mime—an art that lies somewhere between drama and dance.

During the sixteenth century, mime was popular in France in the form of the famous commedia dell' arte, which spread to all of Europe in the seventeenth century. In the nineteenth century, Jean-Baptiste Gaspard Deburau from France and Joseph Grimaldi from England developed mime techniques, and both will be remembered for their contributions to this art.

During the twentieth century, the art of mime was further developed by the actor-director Etienne Decroux, often referred to as the father of modern mime. Decroux was the teacher of Marcel Marceau, widely regarded as the master of the arts of both pantomime and mime. Other mimes during this period include Jean-Louis Barrault from France (who became France's greatest stage performer), the famous silent film actor Charlie Chaplin, Paul J. Curtis, Claude Kipnis, Robert Shields, and Lorene Yarnell. Other names associated with mime that you may recognize are Mummenschanz, W. C. Fields, Stan Laurel, Red Skelton, Jerry Lewis, Dick Van Dyke, Jackie Gleason, and Lucille Ball.

Mime techniques are often difficult and demanding to do. They involve a system of exercises and technical strategies of dramatic movements. The mime takes movement and expression beyond simple activities. Trained and skillful mimes create a world of imagery to communicate with their audiences. They create characters, scenes, and even complete plays using only the movements of the body in a world of silence. The mime's physical training and hours of preparing theme, plot, and illusions result in a complete art form—a sophisticated presentation through which the mime and the audience may share a wealth of human experience.

To be a successful mime, you must understand not only *how* to do an action but *why* to do it. Making what you cannot see into something visible through movement is just the beginning of mime. This lesson will not turn you into a Marcel Marceau or any other expert in mime, but

it will help you understand the art form. To become an accomplished mime, you would need to study, perform, and perhaps become part of a mime troupe, a group that is dedicated to the art of mime. It would also help to be guided by a director or teacher willing to give the necessary time and expertise to such an endeavor. This lesson can only give you a taste of mime by introducing this complex theatre form.

Pantomime

pantomime

the use of mime techniques, acting without words, to tell a story.

Mime is the art of creating the illusion of reality and the art of imagining the world together with others.

Claude Kipnis

Pantomime is the extended use of mime techniques in telling a story. Other definitions might include "acting without words," "nonverbal communication telling a story," or "telling a story in chronological order using only gestures." A definition that you will probably add to this list if you have not experienced pantomime is "an art that is fun."

The history of pantomime goes as far back as primitive man. Cavemen told their hunting stories and other adventures using their body movements to express themselves. Pantomime was a popular form of entertainment in ancient Rome. A single actor often played many roles in the form of interpretive dances accompanied by a chorus who told a story from mythology. In medieval times, characters in the miracle plays used pantomime to communicate the good and bad of humankind. Fairy tales and folklore provided material for the pantomimes. The three major characters from these story lines were usually the hero, the dame (an old woman), and the heroine. The elements of pantomime consisted of happy endings, spectacular events, and lavish costumes and scenery. The goal of all the characters was to be at peace with each other and keep harmony among the players. Pan-

Pantomime is closely related to juggling and acrobatics. Throughout history, people have been entertained by artists such as this "jack in the box" at the Drury Lane Theatre in London, who have specialized in pantomime, juggling, and acrobatics.

The art of pantomime is the language of the heart.

Marcel Marceau

tomime is still used in England in farces (comedies performed mostly for laughs) staged around Christmas.

Participating in pantomime will help you develop your confidence, personal resources, and stage techniques. Realistic pantomime requires time, study, and self-discipline, but it is fun. For the theatre student, pantomime is easier than mime. You don't have to be highly trained or skilled to use pantomime. It is basically an art that requires concentration on details in movements and expression. As you master pantomime, you will discover that an expressive body is one of the actor's greatest assets onstage. Physical skills are needed to be able to communicate with your audience. Studying and using pantomime techniques that enhance muscular coordination, poise, and facial expression will help you be more successful.

Pantomime is extremely effective with an audience because people are more inclined to believe what they see than what they hear. This is why an actor's facial expressions and body movements must support the scene. Suppose, for example, that a character onstage approaches a haunted house. An audience will be more likely to believe the house is haunted if the actor's body is shaking and hesitating as he walks up to the front door. Pantomime is an effective and powerful acting skill. This is why your stage movement and pantomime activities in class should be clearly communicated with simplicity, accuracy, consistency, and exaggeration. We will discuss these four elements when you learn how to prepare a pantomime.

In pantomime you should show, not tell, what is happening. You must visualize in your mind the images you want to project to your audience. For example, if you want to pantomime brushing your teeth, in your mind's eye see your toothbrush (size, shape, color), the toothpaste (size, color, weight, shape, amount you squeeze out), and the movements that you normally make in performing this activity each day (brushing up and down, to the sides, or around and around).

272 ■ Unit 4: Special Topics in Theatre ■

Make your actions clear and exact so that your observers are never in doubt about what is happening in your pantomime. You do not want the audience to see any movement or action that is not well planned and prepared.

Begin your preparation by selecting an idea or story line for your pantomime. You might think of a situation you have experienced, such as a stuck locker or a dripping ice-cream cone. The structure of a pantomime story line is prepared with the three basic parts you have already studied—the beginning, middle, and end. These three parts can also be defined another way—an introduction (introduces the character), a conflict (establishes a problem), and the resolution (solves the problem). For example, in the beginning you will want to use your body and face to let the audience see the character you are portraying. Your character would encounter a problem in the middle of the pantomime and resolve it in the end. (See Figure 14–1 for a sample story line.)

To make your pantomime believable, you will want to use some of these key elements in preparing and presenting your pantomime—simplicity, accuracy, consistency, and exaggeration. Simplicity of your

Figure 14–1

▪▪▪▪▪▪▪▪▪▪▪▪▪▪▪

Sample Pantomime Story Line.

Character and Location: Frustrated businessman at bus stop

Conflict: Wristwatch doesn't work

Resolution: Throws down the watch

Imaginary Props: wristwatch, briefcase

Step-by-Step Pantomime:
1. Businessman hurriedly walks to bus stop.
2. Looks up and down the street, frowning.
3. Puts down his briefcase, crosses arms, and looks disgusted.
4. Glances at watch and taps toes impatiently.
5. Looks up and down the street again. This time he shields his eyes to look farther up and down the street.
6. Looks at his watch and begins pacing up and down the sidewalk.
7. Looks at his watch again, stops walking, and stares like it has stopped.
8. Listens to his watch by holding it up to his ear.
9. Frowns at the watch. Then taps at the imaginary watch with his fingers.
10. Shakes his watch arm; listens again.
11. Holds the watch away from him and frowns.
12. Shrugs his shoulders, unhooks the watch band, and throws it down on the sidewalk.
13. Looks up and down the street to see if anyone is watching.
14. Jumps on the watch and stomps on it. Smiles and shakes his head as if satisfied.
15. Picks up briefcase and begins to walk away, shaking his head as if disgusted with the entire experience.
16. Suddenly stops, turns back to the watch, cups his ear, and listens.
17. Returns and picks up the watch.
18. Holds the watch to his ear and acts surprised.
19. Puts down briefcase, fastens on the watch, and holds up wrist as if to listen. Looks very proud as he beams at the watch.
20. Picks up the briefcase and walks down the street shaking head, amazed as he looks at the watch.

Lucille Ball was such a talented pantomime artist and comedienne that her *I Love Lucy* shows are being enjoyed on cable television networks over forty years after they were first produced.

story line will help the audience understand what is happening in your presentation. Don't cloud the story with too many details. Accuracy in pantomime makes the presentation believable and precise. Consistency keeps all the items in a pantomime the same size, shape, weight, and in the same place. Exaggeration makes the actions in pantomime bigger than life, helping the audience see your action with more clarity.

To achieve clarity in your pantomime, try the following techniques: *focus, reach, take, accent,* and *release.* If you focus (visualize) and then reach (approach) for your object (for example, an imaginary glass of water), it is easier for your audience to follow your action. Don't forget to take (establish space) and release (let go of) your object. However, 80 percent of your pantomime is the accent, showing size, shape, weight, level, texture, temperature, and any other detail that will lead to clarity of movement. When all of these techniques are used together with simplicity, accuracy, consistency, and exaggeration, you will succeed in pantomime.

After you have prepared and rehearsed your pantomime activity, your teacher may ask you to use other traditions of pantomime in your presentation. These include wearing clothes that are black, white, and sometimes accented with red; soft, flexible black flat shoes; and white makeup to neutralize the performer's face. The whiteface has only been associated with pantomime during the twentieth century.

Through movement and expression, you can create a whole world of characters, objects, and places in the story, your pantomime. Remember to focus and concentrate, using all of your senses so that the audience can see what you are performing. You, as the pantomime artist, must be totally absorbed in this world to satisfy yourself as well as your audience.

ACTION

Harpo Marx was the brilliant pantomime artist who helped make the Marx Brothers movies among the most popular comedies of the 1930s and '40s.

1. **Famous Mimes.** After researching one of the following mimes, report on his life and work either in written or oral form.
   a. Marcel Marceau
   b. Jean-Baptiste Gaspard Deburau
   c. Etienne Decroux
   d. Charlie Chaplin
   e. Buster Keaton
   f. Harold Lloyd
   g. Laurel and Hardy
   h. Harpo Marx
   i. Claude Kipnis
   j. Jerry Lewis
   k. Jackie Gleason

2. **Mime Films.** Visit the school library, your community library, or the local video store and locate any films about mime or films in which the leading actors use mime throughout the movie.

3. **Warm-Ups for Pantomime Activities.** Use the following exercises to prepare for pantomime activities. Concentrate on learning to control your body.
   a. Loosen up your body by rolling your head to the left and right, shrugging your shoulders up and down, swinging your arms in cir-

cles, swinging your legs forward and backward, rotating your wrists and hands, rotating your ankles and feet, shaking your hands, and moving your fingers and toes one by one in an exercise motion.

b. Stretch your body up and down. Bend your body forward and backward.

c. Put your palms together and apply force when you push them together.

d. Practice sitting and walking with proper posture. As you sit and walk, keep your body straight but easily erect and relaxed.

e. Become aware of body tensions and tightened muscles you may have. Concentrate on reducing these through daily relaxing thoughts and exercises.

4. **Learning to Relax.** Find your space in the classroom and lie down on the floor. As appropriate and calm music is played, relax and relieve any tension in your muscles. Start with the toes and go to the top of your head. Tense up your muscles and then relax them. Compare the difference in the tension and the relaxation of the muscles. Focus on your body parts. Become aware of how your body responds to the music and how the body can move. Your teacher will take you through several exercises to relax the body.

5. **Movement Carousel.** Your teacher will show you various ways to get from one place to the other. For example, your teacher may walk, run, hop, jump, and skip from one side of the room to the other. Notice every detail of your teacher's movement. Now imitate the movements you just observed. You may work in pairs or groups.

6. **Object Focus.** With your classmates, create a list of small objects— for example, a toothbrush, blow-dryer, comb, toilet brush, needle and thread, fingernail file, watch, and contact lens. Mentally focus on an object named by another student. With your mind's eye, see yourself using the object. Note the difference between actually using the object and the mental image of using the object. Name large items now and repeat the process.

7. **Detailing the Object.** Choose one of the objects in exercise 6. Perform in front of the class, pretending that you are using this object. Pay close attention to details. Try to make your performance as believable as possible.

8. **Music Pantomime.** Listen to some music and react to the sound of the music. For this activity, work in groups of three, four, or five. Develop a story to the music, including a beginning, middle, and ending.

9. **Where Are You?** Discuss places that people go. The first volunteer secretly chooses a place that has been discussed and imagines all the senses that would make him or her aware of that place. After preparing mentally, this student approaches the acting area and begins to illustrate where he or she is. Students who think they know what the place is may join in with more and varied movement appropriate to the place. The whole class may join in if they believe they know where the imaginary place is. After the activity, discuss what actions were pantomimed

Musical Theatre

Theatre has always been closely associated with music, movement, and dance. For example, in early Greek theatre, music was used to underscore the meaning of many of the lines delivered by the chorus. It is not until the twentieth century, however, that we find a separate genre of theatre known as *musical theatre*. This is a type of theatre that is actually a product of the United States!

Experts believe that musical theatre developed out of two specialized forms of theatre—vaudeville and burlesque, which provided popular entertainment throughout most of the 1800s. Originally burlesque featured dramatic sketches and songs that made fun of the legitimate theatre. Vaudeville was always filled with music and other variety acts, including acrobatics and comedy scenes, but had more of a tone suitable for family entertainment.

Vaudeville shows, which entertained large audiences with musical numbers and comedy sketches, were among the first steps in the development of the great American musicals.

The popular musical theatre of today actually started by accident! In 1866, the New York producers of a melodrama entitled *The Black Crook* decided at the last moment that their play was not ready to open. At the same time a theatre where a ballet was to open burned to the ground. In a frantic attempt to save both productions the dancers from the ballet were added to the plot of *The Black Crook*, and the show opened. The resulting production was so successful that producers began to create new productions that combined fully staged dance numbers with fully developed plots. Musical theatre was born!

Audiences loved musical theatre. Star performers such as George M. Cohan and composers such as Irving Berlin and George Gershwin specialized in this new form of theatre. These new musicals had a uniquely American perspective of the world and expressed and supported the nation's growing sense of nationalism around the time of World War I in a way that no other medium could. For example, Cohan's "Yankee Doodle Dandy" and "Over There" as well as "Grand Old Flag" played a great role in keeping American spirits up before and during the years of World War I.

At first, the plot lines for musicals were little more than frameworks to hold the musical numbers together. In the late 1920s, however, musical plots became much more structurally sound. These new plots usually consisted of modern, humorous stories. Some of the most popular musicals written during these years were by Rodgers and Hart and Lerner and Lowe. By 1943 when the musical *Oklahoma!* opened in New York, the theatre was in the golden age of the American musical.

During the years after 1940, the musicals dealt with a wide variety of subject matter, from the life of Annie Oakley in *Annie Get Your Gun* to Shakespeare in *Kiss Me Kate*. As time passed, the musical's plot content began to change. In the late 1960s, many musicals became more like musical revues, which feature many songs with little, if any, dialogue. *Hair*, the first major musical of this type, staged in 1967, was built around a theme more than it was built around a unified story. These "non-story" motivated musicals became known as *concept musicals*. ■

and who did what. Correct errors and discuss mistakes. Continue this pantomime activity with several more places.

10. **Moving the Object.** Divide into groups. Your purpose in this assignment is to move a large imaginary object (for example, a large mirror, a computer, a couch, or a large dog) without using words. Each group decides what it will be moving. Note all the details of the imaginary object in your group discussion. You may tell the rest of the class the object you are going to move, or you can let them guess. When it is your team's turn, work as an ensemble and move that object skillfully. After you have moved the object, discuss with the class how you went about moving the object.

11. **Guess Who?** Choose one of the following characters, and then pantomime the actions of that character. After each performance, the class can guess what character was pantomimed.
    a. doctor
    b. painter
    c. football player
    d. nurse
    e. television announcer
    f. cowboy
    g. actor
    h. teacher
    i. parent
    j. principal
    k. chef
    l. waiter/waitress
    m. clown
    n. baby
    o. senior citizen
    p. model
    q. painter
    r. sculptor
    s. photographer
    t. explorer

12. **Zoo Time.** Choose one of the following zoo characters, and then pantomime the actions of that character. Your classmates will then try to guess the character after allowing time to pantomime each animal.
    a. elephant
    b. dog
    c. cat
    d. lion
    e. pigeon
    f. bat
    g. snake
    h. camel
    i. chicken
    j. duck
    k. frog
    l. turtle
    m. fish
    n. bird
    o. tiger
    p. flamingo
    q. monkey
    r. cow
    s. gorilla
    t. pig

13. **Carpet Ride.** Spread a blanket or sheet on the classroom floor, or imagine a carpet on the floor. Divide into groups of four or five. When it is your group's turn, jump quickly on the "carpet" and pantomime the actions needed in one of the following scenes.
    a. in a terrible rainstorm
    b. among beautiful clouds
    c. in the snow
    d. stranded in the middle of the ocean
    e. lost in space
    f. watching doctors perform surgery
    g. playing in a hot tub
    h. in a raft attacked by sharks
    i. being attacked by killer bees
    j. caught in an elevator
    k. having lunch at McDonald's

l. watching a sports event (football, basketball, tennis, soccer, and so on)

m. performing ballet on stage

n. at a 1950s dance

o. at the beach sunbathing and swimming

p. in a covered wagon

q. in a rocket taking off

r. on a roller coaster

s. fishing on a boat

t. snow skiing

u. waterskiing

14. **What Do You Wish For?** Your teacher will place a box in the middle of the classroom floor that will represent a large well. Volunteer to enter the playing area, drop something imaginary into the well (box), make a wish, and then pull out something related to your wish from the well. For example, throw in a coin and take out several dollars, throw in seeds and take out flowers or vegetables, or throw in words from your mouth and take out a book. You must pay close attention to the details of the object you choose to pantomime.

15. **How Are You Feeling?** Pantomime the following physical feelings and emotions. (*Hint:* It is easier and more effective if you think of a situation when you have experienced this emotion or feeling.)

a. bossy

b. angry

c. happy

d. sad

e. frightened

f. sly

g. excited

h. jealous

i. mischievous

j. bored

k. disgusted

l. triumphant

m. tense

n. caring

o. confused

p. lonely

q. shy

r. cheerful

s. suspicious

t. panic-stricken

u. tired

v. sick at your stomach

w. stubbed toe

x. surprised

y. embarrassed

z. rejected

With some makeup and a wealth of facial expressions and body movements, a mime or pantomimist can tell a story or express a profound idea.

16. **Scenes for Pantomime.** Pantomime one of the following scenes as a solo activity. Use only 1 or 2 minutes to plan your activity. Announce the title of the scene, or let the class guess what is happening. Repeat the activity with a partner.

a. walking a dog

b. washing a dog

c. writing a letter, sealing it, and mailing it

d. driving a car

e. changing a flat tire on a car

f. brushing your teeth

g. making a peanut butter sandwich

h. setting a table

i. turning on a computer and using it

j. painting a picture

k. climbing a hill

l. hiking in the woods

m. playing football, baseball, soccer, basketball, tennis, or golf

n. swimming

o. teaching someone how to swim
p. learning a dance step
q. teaching someone how to dance
r. playing an instrument
s. teaching someone how to play an instrument
t. watching a sad, funny, or scary movie
u. building a campfire
v. feeding a pet
w. taking out the trash
x. washing dishes
y. cleaning up your room
z. waterskiing or snow skiing

Clowning

LESSON OBJECTIVES

- Define clowning.
- Relate the history of mime and pantomime to clowning.
- Identify three types of clowns.
- Participate in clowning activities using imagination and creativity.

Warm Up

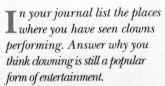

In your journal list the places where you have seen clowns performing. Answer why you think clowning is still a popular form of entertainment.

clowning

the art of entertaining others by provoking laughter, requires the use of personal resources, an understanding of human nature, effective timing, and comedy techniques.

People need to laugh, and laughter is always contagious. In fact, studies have shown that laughter is the best medicine; people actually live longer if they laugh a lot. Thus, the clown's art is one of the best prescriptions for an audience.

Clowning is an art closely related to mime and pantomime. The difference involves the clown's costume, makeup, and goal—to provoke laughter from the audience. Clowning requires the performer to use many skills and talents to provide entertainment. A clown provides an audience with a reason to laugh (the clown's actions and routines) and a way to laugh with others. A clown might be an actor, storyteller, juggler, humorist, acrobat, puppeteer, ventriloquist, magician, or all of these rolled into one. At the heart of the clown's performance is the art of pantomime. Clowning also requires the use of personal resources, an understanding of human nature, effective timing, and good comedy techniques. Clowning demands commitment, physical skills, and acting ability. The clown must mirror life—both comedy and tragedy.

History records clowning being practiced as far back as Greek burlesque (mockery) and the Roman stage. Court jesters, the clowns of the Middle Ages, were talented performers. Many were skilled dancers, acrobats, and musicians. Shakespeare gave the clown respect when he provided lines for him. The clowns were used to relieve the tension in tragedies. In France and Italy, the clowns were great acrobats and colorful figures. (They were named Pierrot and Harlequin in France, Pantaloon in Italy.)

Generations of children have laughed at Bozo the Clown.

Red Skelton began his career as a movie comedian in the 1940s. He regularly performed pantomime sketches on his popular weekly television show in the 1960s.

*I*t's meat and drink for me to see a clown.

William Shakespeare

Today, clowns play a major role in the circus. The first true "circus type" clown, Joseph Grimaldi, was never in a circus. He was a man of the theatre and a mime artist. Many clowns are now named after Mr. Grimaldi; they are referred to as "joeys." Other masters of clowning have been Emmett Kelly (famous for his sad-faced hobo character), Joe E. Brown, Red Skelton, Jackie Gleason, Carol Burnett, Dick Van Dyke, and Jim Carrey, popular in today's films. These experts and others have provided hours of entertainment and laughter for millions.

Clowns must have a good sense of humor and a clear understanding of how to communicate while entertaining an audience. The clown's suspense, wit, ability to surprise, and ability to interact with an audience are all related to the clown's humor.

As clowns perform, they create situations for the audience to think about—to wonder what's going to happen. For example, a circus clown might follow a tiny dog around in circles. He stops, watches the dog, and pulls out a gigantic bone and the audience is probably eagerly wondering what the clown is going to do next.

The goal of the clown is to convince the audience that the entire act is being performed on the spur of the moment. But only through many weeks of rehearsal and planned action can the clown accomplish the task of presenting a "dumb" and funny show that makes the audience think that the act was effortless. The ultimate reward for the clown is an audience response of joy and pleasure.

Characterization is at the core of the clown's preparation and presentation. Clowns must look within themselves to develop a character uniquely their own. Whatever they do for the audience must fit this character. Although each clown usually plays only one character, clowns can assume any number of roles. The makeup, costume, and movements are usually standardized and always depend on the character.

Because much clowning is acrobatic, clowns must be in complete control of their movements. Exercises and rehearsals are essential.

OUR THEATRE HERITAGE
Historical and Cultural Perspectives

Symbolism

Visual artists have personal preferences for the exact materials they want to use to create their art. In the same way, theatre artists have stylistic preferences about the way they will employ theatrical elements in their productions. For example, not all painters create their images using oil paint, although oil paintings are very popular. The same is true of the theatre artist. While realism was the most popular style of theatrical production, other theatre artists felt strongly that a "slice of life" was not the best use of theatrical space or time.

One of these early departures from realism was a movement known as *symbolism.* This movement, which began in France in the late 1800s, had followers from all around the world. These artists disagreed with the realists about what the proper subject matter for a play should be. The symbolists thought the mysteries of life should fill our stages. They believed that questions about the reasons for living, man's place in the universe, and the potential of the human spirit should be the basis for theatre. In the symbolists' theatre, objects used as symbolic images, rather than the concrete actions of realistic life, filled the stage. Poetry and eloquent language, rather than common speech, made up their dialogue. They believed that by using styles far removed from the images and dialects of daily living, their plays would speak a stronger and clearer message.

Because of the symbolic use of props and set pieces, the mood of a symbolist play is often more

Comparing this scene from Maeterlinck's *Pelléas and Mélisande* (1892) to the Ibsen scene on page 231 will help you see some of the differences between realism and symbolism.

dreamlike than it might ever be in reality. In fact, for the symbolist writers, it was more important to evoke a thoughtful mood or atmosphere than it was to tell a story. For example, water in the form of pools, lakes, and fountains is used to create a mysterious mood and to represent forces that both unite and divide people.

Even the characters in symbolist plays are different from characters in realistic plays. Symbolist characters are not written and developed to be individuals, but rather are created to represent a type of character found in society. In this way, the symbolists hoped to expose the way various forces or attitudes function in relation to each other.

For these same reasons, the symbolists did not believe that all of the details of a setting were necessary. All that was needed, in their minds, were the bare essentials—just those items that suggested the environment to the audience in a dramatic way.

Some of the most noted symbolists are playwrights Maurice Maeterlinck, who wrote *Pelléas and Mélisande* and *The Intruder,* and Paul Claudel, who wrote *The Tidings Brought to Mary.* These plays are excellent examples of symbolist plays. Some of the most noted symbolist directors were Paul Fort and Aurelien Marie Lugne-Poe. One of the English language's best-loved poets, William Butler Yeats, was himself a symbolist playwright who created several outstanding plays and productions for Ireland's Abbey Theater, the group that is now the Irish National Theatre Company. ■

whiteface clown
a clown whose makeup is an all-white face with features of black and red added for detail.

neat whiteface
a type of whiteface clown whose makeup is in proportion and looks normal in size.

grotesque whiteface
a type of whiteface clown whose makeup has exaggerated features.

Clowns must be sure of their movements (each scene must be carefully planned) and provide order in their performances, because the world of the clown looks like it is always in chaos. Movements must flow smoothly and skillfully. Timing is a flowing progression from one action to the next, with one action usually the result of the previous action. This cause-and-effect sequence must be established quickly in a clown's routines.

Clowns must have a vivid imagination and keen observation of others. They must be able to recall their senses skillfully and use complete focus and concentration while performing. They make each of their talents and personal resources conform to the art of clowning for a successful performance.

The clown must find an individual personality that makes his or her features unique from the rest of the clowns. Some well-known personalities include the Pierrot or Pierrette clown (whiteface and usually black and white costume), the court jester (colorful costume), the hobo (sloppy, baggy clothes), the rube (overalls, straw hat, plaid shirt, and red nose), and the policeman (Keystone Kop).

Makeup for the clown's face has changed over the years. Early clowns wore masks or nothing on their faces. Later, makeup and costumes replaced the masks. Both must fit the character that the clown chooses to portray.

There are three standard clown types, each with its own distinct makeup and costume. The first type is the **whiteface clown**, with an all-white face and features of black and red added for detail. There are two types of whiteface clown. If the makeup is in proportion and looks normal in size, the clown is called a **neat whiteface**. If the makeup used has exaggerated features, the clown is called a **grotesque whiteface**. The whiteface clown is the leader and the most commonly

From left to right: the neat whiteface clown, the auguste clown, and a character clown.

auguste clown

a rodeo or circus clown; a clown's makeup that is reddish brown instead of white. Makeup and costume usually consist of exaggerated designs and items, such as a huge painted mouth, accented eyes, a huge bow tie, large shirt and pants, and large shoes.

character clown

a type of clown who uses makeup and clothes to represent a specific person or image; for example, a tramp, hobo, Keystone Kop, and so on.

seen of the three types. A polished performer, the whiteface clown looks elegant and usually drives the action of the plot forward.

The second type of clown is the **auguste clown** . If you have ever attended a circus or rodeo, you have seen the auguste clown. The makeup is reddish brown instead of white. Makeup and costume usually consist of exaggerated designs and items, such as a huge mouth painted white, accented white eyes, a huge bow tie, large shirt and pants, and large shoes. The auguste clown makeup and costume look mismatched, and the clown's demeanor reflects this exaggerated appearance. Slapstick humor is the auguste clown's trademark.

The third type of clown is the **character clown** . An example is the typical tramp or hobo clown, whose makeup looks messy, dirty, and unkempt. Although the costume is skillfully prepared, it looks like it was found at the dump. The hobo clown wears sloppy, baggy clothes. Another example of the character clown is the policeman or Keystone Kop. The character clown usually plays the role of the loser or misfit.

Clowning is a wonderful art that requires intensive study and preparation, both mental and physical. Hours are spent perfecting routines, situations, scenes, and stories that take only minutes to present. The clown knows the importance of personal resources. The successful clown has imagination, understands human nature, and has a sense of both comedy and tragedy.

1. **Clowning for a Week.** Your teacher will assign a day to learn how to apply clown makeup. Choose one of the three types of clowns and plan one type of clown makeup. Draw the features, colors, and ideas on paper. Then apply the makeup for the clown face. On a second day, plan and prepare a costume to match the clown makeup. Bring the costume to class. On a third day, work with a partner to play and rehearse a clown routine using pantomime. Use the plot elements needed for the routine. After planning and rehearsing for a clown performance on a fourth day, plan a field trip to an elementary school or nearby class to perform your clown routine. On the fifth day, be organized and use your time wisely when you perform for the children or other classes.

2. **Another Clown Week.** Collect items for another clown week. Suggested items are hats, funny shoes, wigs, false ears and noses, various clothes, fabrics, and props appropriate to use in routines.

3. **The Magician's Smelly Trick.** Plan, rehearse, and present the following clown scene. Two clowns are needed for the scene. One plays a magician and the other, a person from the audience. The magician pantomimes asking for an audience member to assist him with the trick. As this assistant comes forward, the magician communicates to the volunteer that after he sprinkles his "magic dust" on him the volunteer will pass out and not be able to get up alone. The assistant shakes his head in disbelief. The magician promises his assistant a gift (money, candy) if he can do it and proceeds with the magic act. The magician sprinkles "magic dust" but the assistant doesn't cooperate and passes out. After a few minutes the magician signals for a prop (one that represents an

old dirty shoe). The magician holds the prop close to the assistant's nose and the assistant finally drops to the floor. The magician lies next to his assistant who in turn pantomimes asking which one of them has passed out. The magician points to his assistant and pantomimes that now the assistant cannot get up alone. As his assistant gets up, so does the magician. The magician takes the gift and exits.

Working in pairs create another clown scene using this same format. Plan, rehearse, and present the scene for an elementary school class.

4. **Clowning with a Prop.** Choose one of the following props, and create a clown scene using it.

   a. gum
   b. rope
   c. newspaper
   d. bucket

   e. board
   f. pillow
   g. ball of string

5. **Clowning for Fun.** Work in groups of two or three, and create an original routine for clowning. You may use the following characters to develop your story line, or you may make up your own characters. Each person in the group can play a different character.

   a. football players
   b. doctors
   c. models
   d. cowboys
   e. young children

   f. boxers
   g. cave dwellers
   h. robbers
   i. chiefs
   j. jugglers

Curtain Call!

■ ■ SPOTLIGHT ON TERMS ■ ■

An important part of theatre is understanding the terminology, or vocabulary, used. Add the new terms and definitions to the vocabulary section of your theatre notebook or folder.

■ ■ FOCUS ON FACTS ■ ■

1. Define mime, pantomime, and clowning.
2. What are the similarities and the differences between mime and pantomime?
3. Where does the word pantomime come from and what does it mean?
4. What is considered to be the actor's greatest asset on stage in pantomime?
5. Describe a little of the history of clowning.
6. Why are many clowns referred to as "joeys"?
7. Name a famous pantomimist, mime, and clown.

■ ■ REFLECTIONS ■ ■

Discuss the following questions with your class or answer them on paper as instructed by your teacher.

1. How has pantomime played a part of your life? Be specific.
2. How important will pantomime be in your theatrical experiences?
3. What do you remember about clowns when you were a young child?
4. Other than at a circus, at what places and occasions would clowning be appropriate and beneficial?

■ ■ THEATRE IN YOUR LIFE ■ ■

1. Prepare a mime with a partner. Plot all the story elements (beginning, middle, ending, characters, and conflict) before rehearsing. Make the actions clear, exaggerated, and believable. After preparation and rehearsal, present the story onstage. Discuss the performance and evaluate it effectively. Possible story plots to use:
   - A football coach is demonstrating how to block.
   - You and your best friend both want to meet the new student.
   - Your friend tells your secret to someone else, and it gets back to you.
   - The clerk gave you the wrong change when you purchased a sweater.
   - Your girlfriend (or boyfriend) is trying to teach you a new dance.

■ ■ ENCORE ■ ■

1. Attend a performance of a mime troupe. Use your personal resources to learn from the people who perform.
2. Attend a circus, and observe every detail of your favorite clown. If possible, visit with one of the clowns after the show.
3. Working as an entire class, pantomime playing individual instruments while music is being played. Now become an instrument and pantomime being played while music is played by your teacher.
4. Divide into groups and form a particular family—for example, a television family, cartoon family, or famous family. Pantomime getting ready for a family portrait and having your picture taken.
5. Divide into groups and choose a machine. Pantomime what the machine looks like, and pantomime the actions of the machine when it is turned on. Each member of the group must be a part of the machine. Examples are a carousel, tractor, copier, and computer.
6. Divide into groups and pantomime actions for one of the four seasons. Each member must be included and play a part in the planning and acting. Repeat this activity using holidays.

CHAPTER 15

Interpreting Literature

Chapter Outline

Spotlight on Terms

◆ cutting
◆ feedback
◆ introduction

◆ oral interpretation
◆ poetry
◆ prose

oral interpretation

the skill of reading aloud to convey an author's message to an audience.

You hear people reading aloud every day. As you get dressed, you listen to your favorite disc jockey reading the list of top ten songs, or perhaps you listen to the news and weather. When you get to school, the principal reads several announcements, and throughout the day, your teachers read all sorts of instructions. Your friends read class assignments as well as passages from your favorite magazines between classes and at lunch. And at lunch, someone usually reads aloud the menu for the day ("Oh, no! Not barbecued wieners again!"). After school, more radio is heard. And in the evening, you listen to television commentators reading news, commercials, and a variety of messages from teleprompters. Enough already! Can you believe that the spoken word has such an impact on your life? If we spend this much time hearing the spoken word, then we had better enjoy hearing it, reading it, and understanding it. This chapter is designed for all three pleasures.

Oral interpretation is the skill of reading aloud to convey an author's message to an audience. This skill isn't acquired easily. Much time is needed to develop effective techniques for reading aloud, but eventually the written word comes "alive" when presented orally to an audience.

As you read aloud and interpret literature, you are reading someone else's words. Your goal is to get the writer's meaning across to an audience. To do this successfully, you must fully understand what you are reading. Time and research are essential in this process. You also need to answer the following questions:

1. How do you select material to read?
2. How do you prepare the material?
3. How do you present the material?
4. How do you evaluate the material?

■ ■ ■ ■ ■ ■ ■ ■ ■ ■ ■ ■ ■ ■ ■

The oral interpretation skills that you develop in this chapter might someday help you succeed in a broadcasting career in either radio or television.

Literature has much beauty and charm when interpreted by skilled oral readers. This chapter will offer you the fundamentals for enjoying and interpreting different types of literature. The three types of literature you will use for oral interpretations are poetry, prose, and drama.

Poetry is literature written in verse form, often in rhythmic patterns and in rhyme. To create rhythm and rhyme, poets use different kinds of sentences from those you typically read or speak. The word order may be unusual. Poetry is challenging to read and understand, but it is usually an audience pleaser.

Prose is a composition written without patterns of rhyme or rhythm. When you read and study fiction and nonfiction literature in language arts class, you are working with prose. A special feature of prose is point of view—the narrator or voice that tells the story. It is your responsibility to determine if the story is told from the point of view of the protagonist (the major character), a minor character, or an objective observer—a narrator who is not a character but who knows everything that is happening in the story. Good sources of prose are novels, short stories, and histories.

Drama, the third type of literature, is a composition written in the form of dialogue. As a source for oral interpretation, it can be a short play, a long play that has been "cut," or a scene from a play. Two special features you must confront in interpreting drama are characters and their stage directions.

The skills you will need to use in oral reading or oral interpretation will depend on the type of literature you choose. How you make your specific selection is one of the topics of Lesson 1.

poetry
literature written in verse form, often in rhythmic patterns and in rhyme.

prose
a composition written without patterns of rhyme or rhythm.

Selecting and Preparing the Material

LESSON OBJECTIVES

- Understand how to select literature for interpretation.
- Identify resources for locating selections for interpretation.
- Understand and analyze a selection for interpretation.
- Cut a selection for interpretation.
- Mark a selection for interpretation.
- Write an introduction for a selection.

Selecting the Material

Selecting material for oral interpretation may be your most difficult task. Don't make the mistake of letting your teacher or someone else select material for you. Whichever assignment you have—poetry,

prose, or drama—find a selection that you like. You need to choose your own material. This is the only way to reach your true potential in oral interpretation.

There are many places you can find selections for interpretation. Libraries contain thousands of books from which to make a selection. But don't go to the library and expect to find your selection in 30 minutes. It takes time, time, and more time. Don't try to read every line or every sentence when you pull books from the shelves. If the selection appeals to you, then think about it and save it, but continue looking, giving yourself time to consider other selections.

Your teacher may have a file of selections and may suggest a particular piece to you. But don't take just any selection. And don't forget about selections that you find in your own home, in relatives' homes, or at a friend's home. Make sure that the piece satisfies you and suits you—your personality and background. Your own personal experiences should help you understand and enjoy the selection.

Above all, your selection needs to have literary value; it needs to be worth presenting. A selection that has literary merit is well written and expressed in a way that helps the reader gain a deeper understanding of the human condition. Literature that has merit is likely to have universal appeal and teach lasting lessons of life. Examples of selections with literary value are the poem "Macavity, The Mystery Cat," by T. S. Eliot, the prose selections "The Bremen Town Musicians," by the Brothers Grimm, *Alice's Adventures in Wonderland,* by Lewis Carroll, and the drama *The Diary of Anne Frank* by Frances Goodrich and Albert Hackett. These selections have been read by millions of people over the years and contain the elements of literature that make them favorites. If you start out with a selection worth sharing, you will have more success with your interpretation and your audience will enjoy your presentation.

Select material appropriate for the audience as well as the occasion. Is it for a class assignment, for a contest, for an assembly, or for a festi-

Analyzing your selection is not as difficult as it might sound. It does involve time, however, since the best way to analyze a piece is to read it over and over until you begin to feel that you know exactly what the author intended with every sentence and every word.

val? After all this consideration, you are ready to start preparing the material you have selected.

Preparing the Material

After you have made a selection, you need to make a personal copy or several copies of the poem, prose, or drama. Before you start practicing aloud, you need to understand and analyze the selection. To *analyze* means to study something, often by breaking it into parts. You must study every part of your selection to fully understand it. Understanding the meaning will help you appreciate the selection and help you read it more effectively. Read your selection silently many times to get familiar with it. Then answer the following questions:

1. What words do you need to check for meaning and pronunciation?
2. Who (point of view) is speaking in this selection? Who is the audience?
3. How well are the characters developed in the selection?
4. How effective is the language (descriptive words or dialogue, for example) in the selection?
5. What are the plot elements (introduction/setting, body, climax, and conclusion)? How well is this selection organized?
6. What is the author's mood in the selection?
7. What is the selection's theme (life, death, love, war, and so on)?
8. What is the author's message in this selection?
9. How does this selection affect you and relate to your background?
10. In your opinion, does this selection have literary merit? Why?

If you want a satisfying experience interpreting a piece of literature, you must answer these questions before you start practicing aloud.

Another important skill is the cutting of material if you have selected a long poem, prose composition, or drama to interpret. **Cutting**

cutting
reducing or condensing material for oral interpretation.

material means reducing or condensing it so that you can perform your interpretation within a certain time limit. Be careful when you omit words, sentences, and paragraphs. Do not cut major points, characters, or events from the selection.

The process of cutting will take time and many rereadings. It is important that the final selection retain its value and flow (read easily) when read aloud. Use these guidelines to help "cut" your material:

1. Choose a portion or scene from the selection that will have the most impact on an audience, or choose your favorite part. Find the parts you selected and highlight the amount needed to meet the time limit. You will need to allow a minute for an introduction (to be discussed later).
2. Omit names in the material when they are repeated often in lines such as "Carol said" and "Mark asked."
3. In cutting drama selections, eliminate stage directions and any other lines that are too detailed in explanation.
4. Focus on the protagonist and other major characters when selecting lines from the material.
5. Reread the finished product several times before making a copy for your presentation. Continue to cut portions that are not necessary to the meaning of the selection.

After you have cut your selection, put your copy (typed and double spaced or printed from the computer) into a 7- or 10-inch black binder notebook. If you are small in size, use the smaller notebook. You may need to cut the size of the copy to fit the notebook if you are using the smaller notebook. After many practices and presentations, the holes in the typed copy tend to wear out, so it is a good idea to keep reinforcements on hand.

With different-colored pens, mark your selection for key points to remember before you practice the selection. Underline words you want to emphasize, mark pronunciations you have trouble with, mark places to pause (an extremely useful technique for producing a special effect with your voice), and mark places where you want to use special facial expressions or movements of your head and upper body. If there is more than one character in the selection, you might mark each voice with a different-colored highlighter pen. (See Figure 15–1.)

No two people mark a selection in the same way. Only you will know what each mark means. The selection must become your special possession. But the final product becomes a gift for others when prepared properly and read skillfully after the many hours of preparation.

You will also need to prepare an **introduction**, information that you give your audience at the beginning of the presentation to help the audience understand the selection. The information might include the title of the selection, the author's name and background, why you chose the selection, what is happening in the selection (including any helpful information about the setting, characters, or plot), and how the selection may relate to the audience's life. The introduction should set the stage for the audience, mentally warm them up, and help them feel comfortable as you do your interpretation.

introduction

information that an interpreter gives to the audience at the beginning of the presentation to help the audience understand the selection.

Figure 15–1
■■■■■■■■■■■■■ ■■■■ ■■

Marking Your Selection.

Once upon a sunny morning a man who sat in a breakfast nook looked up from his scrambled eggs to see a white unicorn with a gold horn quietly cropping the roses in the garden. The man went up to the bedroom where his wife was still asleep and woke her. "There's a unicorn in the garden," he said. "Eating roses." She opened one unfriendly eye and looked at him. "The unicorn is a mythical beast," she said, and turned her back on him. The man walked slowly downstairs and out into the garden. The unicorn was still there; he was now browsing among the tulips. "Here, unicorn," said the man, and he pulled up a lily and gave it to him. The unicorn ate it gravely. With a high heart, because there was a unicorn in his garden, the man went upstairs and roused his wife again. "The unicorn," he said, "ate a lily." His wife sat up in bed and looked at him, coldly. "You are a booby," she said, "and I am going to have you put in the booby-hatch." The man, who had never liked the words "booby" and "booby hatch," and who liked them even less on a shining morning when there was a unicorn in the garden, thought for a moment. "We'll see about that," he said. He

	Example of a Mark	Explanation
1.	she said	Cross out "she said" or "he said". Use your voice to distinguish a change in characters after they have been introduced in the selection.
2.	booby-hatch	Circle words with which you want to use a special vocal expression.
3.	narrator husband wife	Use a different color highlighter pen for different voices.
4.	unicorn	Underline words once to give emphasis or stress.
	beast	Underline words twice to give *more* emphasis or stress.
5.	| || |||	1 mark for a pause. 2 marks for a longer pause. 3 marks for a very long pause.
6.	↑ ↓ ←→	Up arrow to raise inflection in your voice. Down arrow to lower inflection in your voice. Vertical arrow to stretch out a word.
7.	mith´-ĭ-kəl	Mark pronunciation of words.

The introduction will be more effective if you memorize it and keep it under a minute in length. The introduction is usually included in the time limit of a selection. For extra confidence, you might type the introduction and secure it to the outside or inside of your notebook—to glance at before you begin.

The following is an introduction written by Shelley Moore, a theatre arts student who chose to interpret the poem "The Scorpion," by Roald Dahl:

Roald Dahl, a popular author of children's books and poems, creates wonderful images in his readers' minds. He also uses humor to delight his audiences as they read or listen to his work. Enjoy his poem "The Scorpion" I have chosen to read. (short pause) "The Scorpion," by Roald Dahl.

You are now ready to practice reading aloud and to develop delivery techniques for oral interpretation.

ACTION

■■■■■■■■■■ ■

1. **Scavenger Hunt for Oral Interpretation Selections.** Go to the library and find three poetry, three prose, and three drama selections you would use for oral interpretation. Make a list of the titles and authors in your notebook. Look in your home for poetry, prose, and drama selections. Make a list of any you find that would be worthwhile selections for interpretation.

2. **Why Those Selections?** Explain why you chose the selections in exercise 1.

3. **Analyzing the Selection.** Choose one of the selections you found in exercise 1 and analyze it by answering the ten analysis questions given on page 290.

4. **Cutting Poetry.** Cut a long poem to fit a time limit of 4 minutes. Examples you might use: "The Highwayman," by Alfred Noyes; "Paul Revere's Ride," by Henry Wadsworth Longfellow; "The Cremation of Sam McGee," by Robert W. Service.

5. **Cutting Prose.** Cut a prose selection to fit a time limit of 5 minutes. Titles you might use: "Jack and the Beanstalk"; "Alice's Adventures in Wonderland," by Lewis Carroll; "The Waltz," by Dorothy Parker; "The Secret Life of Walter Mitty," by James Thurber; *The True Story of the Three Pigs*, by Jon Scieszka.

6. **Cutting Drama.** Cut a drama scene to fit a time limit of 6 or 7 minutes. Dramatic literature you might use: *The Diary of Anne Frank*; *You're a Good Man Charlie Brown*, by Clark Gesner; *A Raisin in the Sun*, by Lorraine Hansberry; *The Odd Couple*, by Neil Simon; *J.B.*, by Archibald MacLeish; *I Never Saw Another Butterfly*, by Celeste Raspanti; *Juvie*, by Jerome McDonough; *A Doctor in Spite of Himself*, by Molière.

7. **Selecting and Preparing Your Presentation.** Select a poem, prose, or drama selection to present in an activity for the next lesson. Take the necessary steps to prepare this selection: Select; type or use the computer for a printed copy; analyze the selection; cut if necessary; hole-punch the selection and put it into a binder; mark the selection; and write an introduction.

Developing and Presenting the Selection

LESSON OBJECTIVES

◆ Develop delivery techniques for oral interpretation.
◆ Present literature for interpretation.
◆ Demonstrate verbal versatility and vocal expressiveness in the development of a variety of characterizations.

Developing the Selection

To practice properly and develop effective delivery techniques, you should read your selection over and over in front of a mirror, to

Warm Up

In your journal describe one of your teacher's delivery techniques when he/she reads to the class. Comment on the effectiveness of the teacher's voice and facial expression.

another classmate, to your teacher, or to the whole class. Your delivery techniques should include eye contact, effective use of the voice elements, effective characterization, character placement, and the right attitude.

Your eyes are powerful tools in oral interpretation. Look at your audience when you present your selection. If you have practiced sufficiently, you will be able to look up often during your presentation. But remember that this is not a memorized activity. You must use your script and notebook skillfully as part of your delivery.

Effective voice elements and characterization can be achieved with many of the lessons you have had in this book. Instead of portraying the characters through stage movements, you will present the characters through effective voice elements, facial expressions, and reactions and movements of your head and upper body. For example, to place emphasis on a line, you might lean forward when you read the line. Or you might shrug your shoulders or tilt your head for special effect. Each upper body movement comes from practice and from feeling confident about how the movement fits the material and the author's message.

Character placement means looking at a different location each time you use a different voice for the characters in the selection. This helps you and the audience establish the different characters while you are interpreting. The major characters are placed visually in the center of where you stand while the minor characters are placed to the left and right of the major characters. Keep these positions the same throughout the interpretation or you and the audience will get confused.

The right attitude in oral interpretation refers to the attitude conveyed by your overall performance. Do you have a real passion to interpret your selection, or do you think of it as only another assignment? Your attitude is clear to the audience from the moment you approach and utter the first word to the moment you utter the last word and walk out. The right attitude shows that you are a caring and positive person—one who genuinely enjoys interpreting literature.

When you practice in front of others, always ask for **feedback**—comments and opinions on how well you read. Ask your listeners to tell you the strengths and weaknesses of your interpretation. They can tell you if you used effective techniques while you were reading.

Practice your selection aloud over and over. The amount of time it takes to get ready for a presentation depends on the individual and on the intensity and dedication used in applying effective delivery techniques. The presentation is your reward for all the hard work.

■ ■ ■ ■ ■ ■ ■ ■ ■ ■ ■ ■ ■ ■ ■
This television newscaster uses her oral interpretation skills every night as she reads news stories that range from the natural disasters that evoke great sadness, to human interest stories that are heartwarming and amusing.

feedback
constructive comments or opinions.

Presenting the Selection

Here are the important points to remember as you present your selection to an audience.

1. *Notebook.* Hold your notebook at a comfortable height. It shouldn't be so high that it covers your face, and it shouldn't be so low that it makes you look down too far to read. Hold the notebook with both hands, one supporting the back of the binder and the other sup-

Theater of the Absurd

Wars and other major social and political conflicts have always had a direct impact upon theatrical form and content. The arts reflect how humans feel and think about themselves in relation to other forces in the universe. If we look at the theatrical developments that took place right after World War II, we can find examples of a new theatrical form and content being shaped in reaction to the seemingly senseless waste of life that had just shaken most of the globe. This new form of theatre is known as *theater of the absurd.*

Because each of the absurdist playwrights wrote and produced plays in vastly different ways, theater of the absurd cannot be called a unified movement or style. There are, however, some basic philosophical beliefs. The absurdist playwrights shared the notion that much of what happens in life cannot be explained logically, no matter how hard humans may try to do so. To the absurdists, life is ridiculous and absurd and cannot ever be predicted. They believed that there was no logical connection between causes and effects, and therefore, human life is futile and pointless. This lack of logic and perceived absurdity to the order of the universe was reflected in both the content of the absurdists' plays and the theatrical elements they selected for use on their stages.

To reinforce their basic philosophy, absurdists created plays that use what appears to be illogical dramatic techniques. Plots do not move from cause to effect as they do in realistic plays. None of the traditional rules about the theatre apply! There are few facts about the past included in the first scenes of the play, and by the end of the play the characters will likely have traveled full circle, so that the audience leaves the theatre with the characters in exactly the same mental and physical states that they were in when the play began.

The stage settings created for absurdist productions vary from elaborate scenery to the use of a nearly empty space. Often the set pieces do not indicate any particular place but instead seem to create the feeling that the characters are hanging in limbo, unable to change their situations. The characters who exist in these absurd places engage in dialogue

The setting of *Waiting for Godot* is a country roadside distinguished only by the presence of a tree. How does the setting shown here contribute to the themes commonly presented in absurdist plays?

that sounds like our usual language, but the characters still seem unable to communicate with each other.

One of the most widely produced absurdist playwrights is Samuel Beckett, who wrote *Waiting for Godot* in 1953. This play is believed by scholars to be the classic example of absurdism. The characters, who in many ways seem like clowns, wait at the roadside for Godot, a character about whom the audience knows nothing, to arrive. They wait by the tree, talking about things that seem to add up to nothing, and they do little but wait. At the end of the play Godot has never come and the characters are just as they were at the beginning of the play. The play implies that humans spend their lives waiting, unable to change their existence. It also implies that we seldom know what it is that we are even waiting for! Because of this helpless mood, absurdism is thought by some people to be the most pessimistic form of drama ever created.

Other influential absurdist playwrights are Eugene Ionesco, Jean Genet, and Arthur Adamov. Ionesco's *The Bald Soprano,* Genet's *The Balcony,* and Adamov's *Parody* are examples of absurdist drama. All of these plays were written in the early 1950s. ■

porting the front of the binder. The notebook must feel comfortable in your hands.

2. *Posture.* Stand with proper but relaxed posture. Stand with your feet a few inches apart or with one foot in front of the other for balance. You need to stand properly yet feel comfortable when presenting your selection, able to move your upper body easily and naturally. Your body should communicate that you are eager for the audience to hear you. Holding your notebook properly and standing with correct posture tell the listener that you have confidence and that you are the best reader that they will hear.

3. *Facial Expression.* Your facial expressions are one of the keys to a successful interpretation and presentation. Facial expressions can help get the author's message across to the audience. Use your eyes and change your facial expression to emphasize important words and lines. Opening your eyes wide, raising an eyebrow, winking, and pouting your lips are just a few expressions you might use. Your facial expressions depend on the selection and the author's intended meaning.

4. *Voice.* In Chapter 5, you studied all the elements for an effective voice: breathing, relaxation, quality, pitch, flexibility, articulation, pronunciation, rate, volume, and projection. Use these voice elements to help you portray characters, give emphasis and meaning to words, and create variety, interest, and suspense. Take a risk. Don't be afraid to experiment with different voices to make the selection more interesting for the audience. Do what it takes to get the author's message across to the audience. It is important for the audience to understand the selection.

5. *Pauses.* Pauses greatly affect you and your audience. Use a pause before you give your introduction and again after you have read the last word of your introduction. This will give you and your audience time to adjust and get mentally ready. At the end of the selection, close your notebook and pause. This effect will give the audience

This student has practiced and is exhibiting proper technique for oral interpretation.

time to think and will give you a moment for reflecting or relief.

6. *Appearance and Attire.* Just as makeup and costume are important to the actor, your appearance and clothes play an important part in your presentation in oral interpretation. This does not mean that you need to buy new clothes for a presentation, but it does mean that you need to look groomed and appropriately dressed for the occasion.

The presentation skills covered in this lesson are essential for oral interpretation, but they can also make a difference in your future—for example, when you apply for a job. In fact, these skills will help you express yourself effectively in all situations. Moreover, developing oral reading skills will increase your overall confidence.

Make your selection different. Make it stand out from all the others. If you take this challenge, you will discover what fun oral reading can be and what joy you and your listeners can have.

ACTION

1. **Oral Interpretation Presentation.** Present one of the literary selections you have found, or choose one of the selections given at the end of this chapter. Prepare the selection by using all the necessary steps.

2. **Oral Interpretation Festival or Contest.** Attend a festival or contest that has oral interpretation as an event. Present your selection at the festival or contest.

3. **Reading Orally for Children.** Present your oral interpretation to an elementary school class.

4. **Saturday Morning Oral Interpretation.** Organize a Saturday Morning Oral Interpretation Program in your library for young children and their parents.

Evaluating the Selection

LESSON OBJECTIVES

◆ Evaluate yourself in oral interpretation.
◆ Evaluate oral interpreters.
◆ Identify oral interpretation techniques that need improvement.

Warm Up

In your journal, list the aspects of oral interpretation you hope to improve in today's rehearsal.

To improve your oral interpretation skills, you must constantly evaluate (judge) your own performance as well as the performances of others. You will also want other interpreters or judges to evaluate your performance. The questions listed in the evaluation ballot are often

Evaluation Ballot for Oral Interpretation

Title of selection:. . . . .

Author of selection:. . . . .

Length of presentation:. . . . .

Be specific with your answers to the following questions:

1. What did the speaker include in the introduction? How did it effectively set the stage? Was it memorized? Did the speaker use a conversational tone, or was the speaker's voice monotone?
2. Was the selection appropriate for the reader and audience? Was the selection too easy or too difficult for the speaker?
3. Did the speaker understand the selection? How could you tell? Was the mood set by the speaker? What was the mood? What was the theme?
4. How well did the speaker develop the characters in the selection? Did the speaker use effective character placement?
5. If the selection was a cutting of a poem, prose composition, or drama, did the selection retain the author's message? Did the selection flow from line to line?
6. How effective was the speaker's eye contact? Did the speaker use effective facial expressions to interpret the selection? Were there too many? Too few?
7. How effective was the speaker's voice quality? Pitch? Inflection? Rate? Volume? Articulation? Pronunciation? Projection? What are the strengths of the speaker's voice? What are the weaknesses of the speaker's voice?
8. Did the speaker change and develop voices for different characters? Which character's voice was effective? Which character's voice needs more practice? How successful was the reader's character placement?
9. Did the speaker use an accent? How effective was the accent?
10. Were the speaker's posture and body movements appropriate? How well did the speaker handle the notebook and script?
11. Did the speaker pause at the end of the presentation? Could you tell if the speaker enjoyed what he or she read? What was the speaker's general attitude toward the interpretation?
12. Was the selection appropriate for the time limit? What was the time length?
13. Do you think that the performer communicated the author's meaning to the audience? Why or why not?

used in judging oral interpretation presentations. You will find them useful in evaluating yourself and others.

These evaluation questions are valuable for you and your listeners when you are rehearsing and presenting your oral presentation. Ask your teacher or a classmate to videotape or audiotape your presentation. Ask your teacher, classmates, friends, and relatives to listen to you and comment on your reading to help you improve. These evaluations and the feedback you receive will contribute to your success, wherever you perform.

1. **Videotape Feedback.** Videotape one of your oral interpretation performances, and evaluate yourself using the evaluation ballot in this lesson.

2. **Partner Feedback.** Working with a partner, evaluate each other after presenting a poem, prose, or drama selection in one of your assignments.

3. **Adult Feedback.** Ask a teacher, principal, or other adult to listen to one of your oral interpretations and make comments that would help you improve. Give this person the evaluation ballot and explain that the criteria on the ballot are what an oral interpretation judge would use.

4. **Reading for Language Arts Class.** Ask your language arts teacher if you could present your selection in the language arts class for extra credit. Ask if the class could give you feedback.

Poetry, Prose, and Drama Selections

The next few pages contain selections of poetry, prose, and drama that you can use in your performances. The material selected consists of samples of literature that theatre arts students have read at contests and class activities. The selections were chosen by the students. Remember, an enjoyable and successful experience in oral reading and oral interpretation can only occur if *you* choose the selection that best suits you and your audience.

Poetry Selections

A theatre arts student selected the following poems because they had humor and dialogue. The audiences for whom she read were delighted every time she read for them. She used a British accent for a special interpretive style. The approximate time for reading the first selection with an introduction is 3 minutes.

The Dentist and the Crocodile

The crocodile, with cunning smile, sat in the dentist's chair.
He said, "Right here and everywhere my teeth require repair."
The dentist's face was turning white. He quivered, quaked, and shook.
He muttered, "I suppose I'm going to have to take a look."
"I want you", Crocodile declared, "to do the back ones first.
The molars at the very back are easily the worst."
He opened wide his massive jaws. It was a fearsome sight—

At least three hundred pointed teeth, all sharp and shining white.
The dentist kept himself well clear. He stood two yards away.
He chose the longest probe he had to search out the decay.
"I said to do the *back ones* first!" the Crocodile called out.
"You're much too far away, dear sir, to see what you're about.
To do the back ones properly you've got to put your head
Deep down inside my great big mouth," the grinning Crocky said.
The poor old dentist wrung his hands and, weeping in despair,
He cried, "No no! I see them all extremely well from here!"
Just then, in burst a lady, in her hands a gold chain.
She cried, "Oh Croc, you naughty boy, you're playing tricks again!"
"Watch out!" the dentist shrieked and started climbing up the wall.
"He's after me! He's after you! He's going to eat us all!"
"Don't be a twit," the lady said, and flashed a gorgeous smile.
"He's harmless. He's my little pet, my lovely crocodile."

Roald Dahl, from *Rhyme Stew* (Viking)

Here is another poetry selection for your interpretation.

"GUILTY OR NOT GUILTY?"

She stood at the bar of justice,
A creature wan and wild,
In form too small for a woman,
In feature too old for a child.
For a look so worn and pathetic
Was stamped on her pale young face,
It seemed long years of suffering
Must have left that silent trace.

"Your name," said the judge, as he eyed her,
With kindly look, yet keen,
"Is—" "Mary Maguire, if you please, sir."
"And your age?" "I am turned fifteen."
"Well, Mary,"—and then from a paper
He slowly and gravely read—
"You are charged here—I am sorry to say it—
With stealing three loaves of bread.

"You look not like an old offender,
And I hope that you can show
The charge to be false. Now, tell me,
Are you guilty of this, or no?"
A passionate burst of weeping
Was at first her sole reply;
But she dried her tears in a moment,
And looked in the judge's eye.

"I will tell you just how it was, sir:
My father and mother are dead,

And my little brothers and sisters
Were hungry, and asked me for bread.
At first I earned it for them,
By working hard all day,
But somehow the times were hard, sir,
And the work all fell away.

"I could get no more employment;
The weather was bitter cold;
The young ones cried and shivered
(Little Johnnie's but four years old);
So what was I to do, sir?
I am guilty, but do not condemn;
I took—O! was it stealing?—
The bread to give to them."

Every man in the courtroom—
Graybeard and thoughtless youth—
Knew, as he looked upon her,
That the prisoner spoke the truth.
Out from their pockets came kerchiefs,
Out from their eyes sprung tears,
And out from old, faded wallets
Treasures hoarded for years.

The judge's face was a study,
The strangest you ever saw,
As he cleared his throat and murmured
Something about the law.
For one so learned in such matters,
So wise in dealing with men,
He seemed, on a simple question,
Sorely puzzled just then.

No one blamed him, or wondered
When at last these words they heard.
"The sentence of this young prisoner
Is for the present deferred."
And no one blamed him or wondered
When he went to her and smiled,
And tenderly led from the courtroom,
Himself, the "guilty" child!

UNKNOWN

Prose Selections

The following prose selection was chosen because of its variety of characters and the opportunity to change voices creatively. It will take approximately 8 to 10 minutes to orally present this selection, including an introduction.

PRISCILLA AND THE WIMPS

by Richard Peck

Listen, there was a time when you couldn't even go to the *rest room* around this school without a pass. And I'm not talking about those little pink tickets made out by some teacher. I'm talking about a pass that could cost anywhere up to a buck, sold by Monk Klutter.

Not that Mighty Monk ever touched money, not in public. The gang he ran, which ran the school for him, was his collection agency. They were Klutter's Kobras, a name spelled out in nailheads on six well-known black plastic windbreakers.

Monk's threads were more . . . subtle. A pile-lined suede battle jacket with lizard-skin flaps over tailored Levis and a pair of ostrich-skin boots, brassed-toed and suitable for kicking people around. One of his Kobras did nothing all day but walk a half step behind Monk, carrying a fitted bag with Monk's gym shoes, a roll of rest-room passes, a cashbox, and a switchblade that Monk gave himself manicures with at lunch over at the Kobras' table.

Speaking of lunch, there were a few cases of advanced malnutrition among the newer kids. The ones who were a little slow in handing over a cut of their lunch money and were therefore barred from the cafeteria. Monk ran a tight ship.

I admit it. I'm five foot five, and when the Kobras slithered by, with or without Monk, I shrank. And I admit this, too: I paid up on a regular basis. And I might add: so would you.

This school was old Monk's Garden of Eden. Unfortunately for him, there was a serpent in it. The reason Monk didn't recognize trouble when it was staring him in the face is that the serpent in the Kobras' Eden was a girl.

Practically every guy in school could show you his scars. Fang marks from Kobras, you might say. And they were all highly visible in the shower room: lumps, lacerations, blue bruises, you name it. But girls usually got off with a warning.

Except there was this one girl named Priscilla Roseberry. Picture a girl named Priscilla Roseberry, and you'll be light years off. Priscilla was, hands down, the largest student in our particular institution of learning. I'm not talking fat. I'm talking big. Even beautiful, in a bionic way. Priscilla wasn't inclined toward organized crime. Otherwise, she could have put together a gang that would turn Klutter's Kobras into garter snakes.

Priscilla was basically a loner except she had one friend. A little guy named Melvin Detweiler. You talk about The Odd Couple. Melvin's one of the smallest guys above midget status ever seen. A really nice guy, but, you know—little. They even had lockers next to each other, in the same bank as mine. I don't know what they had going. I'm not saying this was a romance. After all, people deserve their privacy.

Priscilla was sort of above everything, if you'll pardon a pun. And very calm, as only the very big can be. If there was anybody who didn't notice Klutter's Kobras, it was Priscilla.

Until one winter day after school when we were all grabbing our coats out of our lockers. And hurrying, since Klutter's Kobras made sweeps of the halls for after-school shakedowns.

Anyway, up to Melvin's locker swaggers one of the Kobras. Never mind his name. Gang members don't need names. They've got group identity. He reaches down and grabs little Melvin by the neck and slams his head against his locker door. The sound of skull against steel rippled all the way down the locker row, speeding the crowds on their way.

"Okay, let's see your pass," snarls the Kobra.

"A pass for what this time?" Melvin asks, probably still dazed.

"Let's call it a pass for very short people," says the Kobra, "a dwarf tax." He wheezes a little Kobra chuckle at his own wittiness. And already he's reaching for Melvin's wallet with the hand that isn't circling Melvin's windpipe. All this time Melvin and the Kobra are standing in Priscilla's big shadow.

She's taking her time shoving her books into her locker and pulling on a very large-size coat. Then, quicker than the eye, she brings the side of her enormous hand down in a chop that breaks the Kobra's hold on Melvin's throat. You could hear a pin drop in that hallway. Nobody'd ever laid a finger on a Kobra, let alone a hand the size of Priscilla's.

Then Priscilla, who hardly ever says anything to anybody except to Melvin, says, "Who's your leader, wimp?"

This practically blows the Kobra away. First he's chopped by a girl, and now she's acting like she doesn't know Monk Klutter, the Head Honcho of the World. He's so amazed, he tells her. "Monk Klutter."

"Never heard of him," Priscilla mentions. "Send him to see me." The Kobra just backs away from her like the whole situation is too big for him, which it is.

Pretty soon Monk himself slides up. He jerks his head once, and his Kobras slither off down the hall. He's going to handle this interesting case personally. "Who is it around here doesn't know Monk Klutter?"

He's standing inches from Priscilla, but since he'd have to look up at her, he doesn't. "Never heard of him," she says.

Monk's not happy with this answer, but by now he's spotted Melvin, who's grown smaller in spite of himself. Monk breaks his own rule by reaching for Melvin with his own hands. "Kid," he says, "you're going to have to educate your girl friend."

His hands never quite make it to Melvin. In a move of pure poetry Priscilla has Monk in a hammerlock. His neck's popping like gunfire, and his head's bowed under the immense weight of her forearm. His suede jacket's peeling back, showing pile.

Priscilla's behind him in another easy motion. And with a single mighty thrust forward, frog-marches Monk into her own locker. It's incredible. His ostrich-skin boots click once in the air. And suddenly he's gone, neatly wedged into the locker, a perfect fit. Priscilla bangs the door shut, twirls the lock, and strolls out of school. Melvin goes with her, of course, trotting along below her shoulder.

Well, this is where fate, an even bigger force than Priscilla, steps in. It snows all that night, a blizzard. The whole town ices up. And school closes for a week.

Following is another prose selection for oral interpretation.

HUMPTY DUMPTY IN THE FOOD STORE

By University Interscholastic League, 1986

Humpty Dumpty, the big, big, jumbo egg — proud of his marvelous appearance and neat outfit — stepped into the grocery store. Humpty Dumpty thought that he would surprise everyone in the store. He was very sure that all the customers would remember his grandfather, the famous Humpty Dumpty who "HAD A GREAT FALL" from the wall. And now these people would be so pleased to see the *grandson* of Humpty Dumpty, safe and sound in the grocery store.

Humpty Dumpty had carefully dressed up in a matching outfit to impress everyone who looked at him. He wore a clean white shirt with a beautiful black-and-white bow tie, red and white striped pants tied below his knees like knickers, a pair of red knee socks, and shiny black shoes with silver buckles.

It was a Saturday afternoon and the food store was very crowded. As customers were passing back and forth with their shopping carts, they stared at the shelves looking for their favorite foods. As a matter-of-fact, *no one* noticed that Humpty Dumpty was in the store. This disappointed Humpty Dumpty very much and so he frowned sadly. He began walking very carefully under the edges of the shelves, hoping that he would not be run over by the customers and their shopping carts. Humpty Dumpty was beginning to wonder if perhaps WALKING IN A GROCERY STORE could be as dangerous as SITTING ON A WALL had been for his grandfather.

Suddenly, Humpty Dumpty found himself in front of the EGG SHELVES. He saw dozens and dozens of egg cartons with eggs inside them, so quiet and calm and lying beside each other. "They must be waiting for customers to pick them up and buy them," mumbled Humpty Dumpty. "What a pity."

Then, Humpty Dumpty had a bright idea. "Cheer up everybody, here is the 'Humpty Dumpty'," he cried. "Wake up! Move! I don't want to see my generation of eggs so still and quiet. Let's have fun, let's all sing the 'Humpty Dumpty' song! Come on everybody, cheer up! Here I am, the Humpty Dumpty grandson, the hero of your generation!"

Hearing Humpty Dumpty's voice, the eggs got excited and began to open their egg carton lids to see what was going on. As they looked out, their eyes popped open with glee and they began to call out: "What a surprise! Humpty Dumpty is here. The biggest and most charming egg—our egg hero!" All of the eggs clapped their hands and cheered.

The medium grade eggs started singing Humpty Dumpty's song, which their mothers had taught them when they were little eggs. The grade "A" large eggs were so excited to see Humpty Dumpty, the charming egg in his fancy outfit, that they asked Humpty Dumpty if they could have their picture taken with him. Humpty Dumpty was more than happy to accept their request. So he climbed up to their shelf and SAT on the very TOP between all the jumbo eggs. Then, one of the jumbo eggs called the store manager to bring his camera and snap a souvenir picture of Humpty Dumpty in *their* GROCERY STORE. The store manager was so surprised; he could remember when he was a kindergarten student and heard the tale of Humpty Dumpty, the grandfather egg who sat on the wall and had a great fall and all the king's horses and all the king's men couldn't put Humpty together again. "It is our pleasure to have you visit our store because we remember your famous grandfather who took such a big risk sitting on that big wall," said the store manager.

"You know, sir," began Humpty Dumpty. "Big eggs like grandfather Humpty, who are loved by the people, should sit in high places so that they can be seen and admired—people enjoy watching important eggs! But sadly, my grandfather lost his balance, so he fell and broke apart and couldn't be put back together again. It never *should* have happened that way." Humpty Dumpty began to get very sad.

At this moment, a customer came along with her children. They walked up to the egg shelves to pick out some eggs to buy. The children then noticed that Humpty Dumpty was sitting on the top of the jumbo egg shelf. They began to shout: "Look who's here, mommy! Humpty Dumpty! Won't you buy him for us? Please! Please, buy him for us!"

Hearing these shouts, Humpty Dumpty became very upset. "I am *not* for sale," cried Humpty Dumpty angrily. He began to stand up so that he could get off the top shelf. "I am *not* for sale, I am *not* for sale!" In his excitement, the most terrible, most awful thing happened to Humpty Dumpty on that top jumbo egg shelf: He began to lose his balance in the very same way that his grandfather did. Well, this Humpty Dumpty began to fall, all the way down, down, down to the bottom shelf—oh no!

"Oh! No!" Everyone in the store was crying and screaming. The store manager, the customer and her noisy children, and even the little eggs who loved Humpty Dumpty. They all covered their eyes because no one wanted to watch the great fall of the big and charming Humpty Dumpty. No one wanted to see him break into a million pieces.

But guess what! That big and charming Humpty Dumpty was lucky enough to land in one of the *empty* egg cartons which lay open down on the bottom shelf. So he wasn't broken after all; he just fell into one of these egg cartons and quickly he closed the top over him to hide from the customer's view. What a smart Humpty Dumpty!

So now Humpty Dumpty lives in the grocery store in one of the egg cartons on the bottom shelf. He hopes that no one will ever find him and buy him; Humpty Dumpty is too special and too famous to be bought. So when you go shopping with your parents, remember Humpty Dumpty is somewhere on that bottom shelf in an egg carton and is very happy there. You can go by and say hello to him, but please let him stay hidden in his quiet and safe place forever.

Drama Selections

This drama selection takes 5 to 5½ minutes to read and interpret, including an introduction.

The Imaginary Invalid
Act II

Scene: Argan's sitting room, Paris, France; middle of the seventeenth century
Characters: Louison and Argan
(Louison, a girl of twelve or thirteen, enters)

Louison: Did you call me, papa?

Argan: Yes, little one. Come here.

(She advances part way)

Argan: (beckoning slyly) A little closer.

(Louison comes closer)

Argan: Now then. Look at me.

Louison: (with seeming innocence) Yes, papa?

Argan: Don't you have something to tell me?

Louison: (sweetly) Well, I can tell you a story. Would you like to hear the Donkey's Skin or the fable of the Raven and the Fox?

Argan:: (angrily) That's not what I had in mind.

Louison: My apologies, papa.

Argan: Don't you obey your father?

Louison: Of course, papa.

Argan: And didn't I ask you to report all that you see?

Louison: Yes, papa.

Argan: Have you told me everything?

Louison: (with some doubt) Yes, papa.

Argan: Haven't you seen something today?

Louison: No, papa.

Argan: No?

Louison: (quite doubtful) No . . . . .

Argan: Ah ha. Then I shall have to renew your memory. (Picks up his cane and starts toward Louison)

Louison: (frightened) Oh, papa.

Argan: Is it not true that you saw a man with your sister Angelique?

Louison: (crying) Oh, dear.

Argan: (raising his cane to hit her) I shall teach you to lie.

Louison: Oh, forgive me, papa. Angelique made me promise not to tell. But I'll tell you now.

Argan: Very well. You shall tell me, but only after I have punished you for telling a lie.

Louison: Don't whip me, dear papa. Please don't whip me.

Argan: I shall. (Raises his cane and strikes once. Louison backs against the couch, crying loudly, pretending to be hurt.)

Louison: Oh, I'm hurt. Papa, stop. I'm hurt. Oh, I'm dying, I'm dead. (She falls on couch, pretending to be dead, but keeping one eye open to see what her father will do.)

Argan: What's this? Louison, my little one. Louison, what have I done to you? Oh, dear. My poor Louison. Oh, my poor child.

Louison: (no longer able to hide her laughter, sits up suddenly) Come, come, papa. It's all right. I'm not quite dead.

Argan: (surprised, but relieved) Oh, you imp, you. What a rascal I have. Well, I'll overlook it this once, but you must tell me everything.

Louison: Yes, papa. But don't tell Angelique I told.

Argan: Of course not.

Louison: (looks to be sure no one is listening) Well, while I was in Angelique's sitting room, a handsome man came, looking for her.

Argan: (eagerly) Yes?

Louison: When I asked what he wanted, he said he was her new music teacher.

Argan: Aha. So that is their little plan. Continue.

Louison: Then Angelique came and when she saw him she said (overdramatically) "Oh, go away, for my sake, leave."

Argan: (disappointed) Oh.

Louison: But he didn't leave. He stayed and talked to her.

Argan: (eagerly) What did he say?

Louison: He told her . . . (teasing her father) many things.

Argan: Yes?

Louison: That he loved her passionately, and that she was the most glorious creature in the world.

Argan: And then?

Louison: And then he fell on his knees before her—

Argan: (excitedly) Yes, yes.

Louison: (dramatically) And kissed her hand—(giggles)

Argan: (eagerly) *And then?*

Louison: And then—(pause full of suspense, followed by a matter of fact) mama came and he ran away.

Argan: (disappointed) That's all? Nothing more?

Louison: No, papa. There was nothing more. (She giggles and runs out. Argan groans and sinks into a chair.)

From *The Imaginary Invalid*, by Moliere, adapted by Fran Tanner, *BASIC DRAMA PROJECTS*, Clark Publishing Company.

The filmed version of *The Diary of Anne Frank* is but one of hundreds of productions of this inspirational story.

Here is a selection from the popular *The Diary of Anne Frank.*

The Diary of Anne Frank
Act 2, scene 2

By Frances Goodrich and Albert Hackett

In this play, the heroine is a young Jewish girl forced to hide from the Nazis. The year is 1944. Anne and her parents, a sister and four other people are crowded into an Amsterdam attic where they must remain or be killed. Their only hope is that Hitler will be defeated, and they will be able to resume normal lives. Now, however, they think that perhaps the Nazis are becoming aware of their existence. The play is based on an actual diary of a young girl who later was killed.

In this scene Anne, now fifteen, is talking to Peter, nineteen, the first boy she's ever liked and who is one of those who has shared the attic above the warehouse for two years. This scene occurs in the bedroom where Peter sleeps. It is one of three attic rooms into which everyone is crowded. Peter's room is sparsely furnished with a cot and a chair, and there is barely room to stand or move around.

ANNE: Look Peter, the sky. [*She looks up through the skylight.*] What a lovely, lovely day! Aren't the clouds beautiful? You know what I do when it seems as if I couldn't stand being cooped up for one more minute? I *think* myself out. I think myself on a walk in the park where I used to go with Pim. Where the jonquils and the crocus and the violets grow down the slopes. You know the most wonderful part about *thinking* yourself out? You can have it any way you like. You can have roses and violets and chrysanthemums all blooming at the same time. . . . It's funny . . . I used to take it all for granted . . . and now I've gone crazy about everything to do with nature. Haven't you?

PETER: I've just gone crazy. I think if something doesn't happen soon . . . if we don't get out of here . . . I can't stand much more of it!

ANNE: [*softly*] I wish you had a religion, Peter.

PETER: No, thanks! Not me!

ANNE: Oh, I don't mean you have to be Orthodox . . . or believe in heaven and hell and purgatory and things . . . I just mean some religion . . . it doesn't matter what. Just to believe in something! When I think of all that's out there . . . the trees . . . and flowers . . . and seagulls . . . when I think of the dearness of you, Peter, . . . and the goodness of the people we know . . . Mr. Kraler, Miep, Dirk, the vegetable man, all risking their lives for us everyday . . . When I think of these good things, I'm not afraid any more . . . I find myself, and God, and I . . . [PETER *interrupts, getting up and walking away.*]

PETER: That's fine! But when I begin to think, I get mad! Look at us, hiding out for two years. Not able to move! Caught here like . . . waiting for them to come and get us . . . and all for what?

ANNE: We're not the only people that've had to suffer. There've always been people that've had to . . . sometimes one race . . . sometimes another . . . and yet . . .

PETER: That doesn't make me feel any better!

ANNE: [*going to him*] I know it's terrible, trying to have any faith . . . when people are doing such horrible . . . But you know what I sometimes think? I think the world may be going through a phase, the way I was with Mother. It'll pass, maybe not for hundreds of years, but some day . . . I still believe, in spite of everything, that people are really good at heart.

PETER: I want to see something now . . . Not a thousand years from now! [*He goes over, sitting down again on the cot.*]
ANNE: But, Peter, if you'd only look at it as part of a great pattern . . . that we're just a little minute in the life . . . [*She breaks off.*] Listen to us, going at each other like a couple of stupid grownups! Look at the sky now. Isn't it lovely? [*She holds out her hand to him.* PETER *takes it and rises, standing with her at the window looking out, his arms around her.*] Some day, when we're outside again, I'm going to . . . [*She breaks off as she hears the sound of a car, its brakes squealing as it comes to a sudden stop.*]

Following is a third drama selection for oral interpretation.

A Raisin in the Sun
Act 1, scene 1

By Lorraine Hansberry

The playwright wanted to present three types of women in her play. This scene clearly shows the different attitudes toward life of the three women. Mama is pretty much set in her ways and embraces the more traditional values of right and wrong. Ruth tends to agree with Mama but isn't as much at ease with herself as Mama. In fact, she's uncertain about many things. Beneatha is the militant, ready to embrace the new in opposition to the old. At the same time she flits from one set of interests to another. She has taken to heart the idea that a person must discover her identity. She doesn't realize how foolish her unshakable and absolute beliefs are to others. She is absorbed in herself and so defiantly flaunts attitudes that go against what others in her family believe.

Just before the scene opens Beneatha has used profanity about an upstairs neighbor's use of a vacuum cleaner.

MAMA: If you use the Lord's name just one more time—
BENEATHA: [*A bit of a whine.*] Oh, Mama—
RUTH: Fresh—just fresh as salt, this girl!
BENEATHA: [*Drily.*] Well—if the salt loses its savor—
MAMA: Now that will do. I just ain't going to have you 'round here reciting the scriptures in vain—you hear me?
BENEATHA: How did I manage to get on everybody's wrong side by just walking into a room?
RUTH: If you weren't so fresh—
BENEATHA: Ruth, I'm twenty years old.
MAMA: What time you be home from school today?
BENEATHA: Kind of late. [*With enthusiasm.*] Madeline is going to start my guitar lessons today.
[MAMA *and* RUTH *look up with the same expression.*]
MAMA: Your *what* kind of lessons?
BENEATHA: Guitar.
RUTH: Oh, Father!
MAMA: How come you done taken it in your mind to learn to play the guitar?

BENEATHA: I just want to, that's all.

MAMA: [*Smiling.*] Lord, child, don't you know what to do with yourself? How long is it going to be before you get tired of this now—like you got tired of that little play-acting group you joined last year? [*Looking at* RUTH.] And what was it the year before that?

RUTH: The horseback-riding club for which she bought that fifty-five-dollar riding habit that's been hanging in the closet ever since!

MAMA: [*To* BENEATHA] Why you got to flit so from one thing to another, baby?

BENEATHA: [*Sharply.*] I just want to learn to play the guitar. Is there anything wrong with that?

MAMA: Ain't nobody trying to stop you. I just wonders sometimes why you has to flit so from one thing to another all the time. You ain't never done nothing with all that camera equipment you brought home—

BENEATHA: I don't flit! I—I experiment with different forms of expression—

RUTH: Like riding a horse?

BENEATHA: People have to express themselves one way or another.

MAMA: What is it you want to express?

BENEATHA: [*Angrily.*] Me! [MAMA *and* RUTH *look at each other and burst into raucous laughter.*] Don't worry—I don't expect you to understand.

MAMA: [*To change the subject.*] Who are you going out with tomorrow night?

BENEATHA: [*With displeasure.*] George Murchison again.

MAMA: [*Pleased.*] Oh—you getting a little sweet on him?

RUTH: You ask me, this child ain't sweet on nobody but herself—[*Underbreath.*] Express herself! [*They laugh.*]

BENEATHA: Oh—I like George all right, Mama. I mean I like him enough to go out with him and stuff, but—

RUTH: [*For devilment.*] What does *and stuff* mean?

BENEATHA: Mind your own business.

MAMA: Stop picking at her now, Ruth. [*A thoughtful pause, and then a suspicious sudden look at her daughter as she turns in her chair for emphasis.*] What *does* it mean?

BENEATHA: [*Wearily.*] Oh, I just mean I couldn't ever really be serious about George. He's—so shallow.

RUTH: Shallow—what do you mean he's shallow? He's *Rich!*

MAMA: Hush, Ruth.

BENEATHA: I know he's rich. He knows he's rich, too.

RUTH: Well—what other qualities a man got to have to satisfy you, little girl?

BENEATHA: You wouldn't even begin to understand. Anybody who married Walter could not possibly understand.

MAMA: [*Outraged.*] What kind of way is that to talk about your brother?

BENEATHA: Brother is a flip—let's face it.

MAMA: [*To* RUTH, *helplessly.*] What's a flip?

RUTH: [*Glad to add kindling.*] She's saying he's crazy.

BENEATHA: Not crazy. Brother isn't really crazy yet—he—he's an elaborate neurotic.

MAMA: Hush your mouth!

BENEATHA: As for George. Well. George looks good—he's got a beautiful car and he takes me to nice places and, as my sister-in-law says, he is probably the richest boy I will ever get to know and I even like him sometimes—but if the Youngers are sitting around waiting to see if their little Bennie is going to tie up the family with the Murchisons, they are wasting their time.

RUTH: You mean you wouldn't marry George Murchison if he asked you someday? That pretty, rich thing? Honey, I knew you was odd—

BENEATHA: No, I would not marry him if all I felt for him was what I feel for him now. Besides, George's family wouldn't really like it.

MAMA: Why not?

BENEATHA: Oh, Mama—The Murchisons are honest-to-God-real-*live* rich colored people, and the only people in the world who are more snobbish than rich white people are rich colored people. I thought everybody knew that. I've met Mrs. Murchison. She's a scene!

MAMA: You must not dislike people 'cause they well off, honey.

BENEATHA: Why not? It makes just as much sense as disliking people 'cause they are poor, and lots of people do that.

RUTH: [*A wisdom-of-the-ages manner. To* MAMA] Well, she'll get over some of this—

BENEATHA: Get over it? What are you talking about, Ruth? Listen, I'm going to be a doctor. I'm not worried about who I'm going to marry yet—if I ever get married.

MAMA *and* RUTH: *If!*

MAMA: Now, Bennie—

BENEATHA: Oh, I probably will . . . but first I'm going to be a doctor, and George, for one, still thinks that's pretty funny. I couldn't be bothered with that. I am going to be a doctor and everybody around here better understand that!

MAMA: [*Kindly.*] 'Course you going to be a doctor, honey, God willing.

BENEATHA: [*Drily.*] God hasn't got a thing to do with it.

MAMA: Beneatha—that just wasn't necessary.

BENEATHA: Well—neither is God. I get sick of hearing about God.

MAMA: Beneatha!

BENEATHA: I mean it! I'm just tired of hearing about God all the time. What has He got to do with anything? Does he pay tuition?

MAMA: You 'bout to get your fresh little jaw slapped!

RUTH: That's just what she needs, all right!

BENEATHA: Why? Why can't I say what I want to around here, like everybody else?

MAMA: It don't sound nice for a young girl to say things like that—you wasn't brought up that way. Me and your father went to trouble to get you and Brother to church every Sunday.

BENEATHA: Mama, you don't understand. It's all a matter of ideas, and God is just one idea I don't accept. It's not important. I am not going out and be immoral or commit crimes because I don't believe in God. I don't even think about it. It's just that I get tired of Him getting credit for all the things the human race achieves through its own stubborn effort. There simply is no blasted God—there is only man and it is he who makes miracles!

[MAMA *absorbs this speech, studies her daughter and rises slowly and crosses to* BENEATHA *and slaps her powerfully across the face. After, there is only silence and the daughter drops her eyes from her mother's face, and* MAMA *is very tall before her.*]

MAMA: Now—you say after me, in my mother's house there is still God. [*There is a long pause and* BENEATHA *stares at the floor wordlessly.* MAMA *repeats the phrase with precision and cool emotion.*] In my mother's house there is still God.

BENEATHA: In my mother's house there is still God.

[*A long pause.*]

MAMA: [*Walking away from* BENEATHA, *too disturbed for triumphant posture. Stopping and turning her back to her daughter.*] There are some ideas we ain't going to have in this house. Not long as I am at the head of this family.

BENEATHA: Yes, ma'am.

[MAMA *walks out of the room.*]

The Off-Broadway Movement

In the 1930s in New York, producers and theatre groups rebelled against the expense and constraints placed upon them by the profit-driven Broadway system. Therefore, many of these groups moved their productions out of New York's central theatre district and independently financed their own small productions. But none of these groups could afford to stay in production for long due to the terrible economic conditions of the Depression.

By the 1950s, producing plays as part of the Broadway commercial theatre system had become very expensive. Theatre artists started to search for ways to produce plays in New York City in smaller, less expensive theatre spaces, so that they could produce the plays that really interested them—plays that might not appeal to the large, commercial Broadway theatre audience. This movement away from Broadway became known as the *Off-Broadway* movement. By moving Off-Broadway, producers were able to afford to produce classic plays as well as more experimental drama. This movement is still at work today.

While Off-Broadway theatres vary a great deal from one to the other, most seat less than 200 people. Many are housed in buildings that were converted into theatres from their original purposes. Most were storefronts, nightclubs, or warehouses. Since these building were never originally designed to house an audience, it is common in Off-Broadway theatres for there to be no proscenium. It's also common for the actors and audience to be very close to each other. Producing plays in these

The Circle in the Square Production Company was one the first and most influential Off-Broadway companies. Here you see a scene from their production of *Bus Stop*.

buildings, however, keeps production costs much lower than they would be in the large, expensive Broadway theatres, which in turn, keeps ticket prices much lower.

Among the most historically important Off-Broadway groups are *The Circle in the Square* and the *Phoenix Theatre*. Although the Phoenix Theatre had a proscenium stage and seated over 1,000 people, it presented plays that commercial producers would not produce, including many new plays, as well as classical plays, such as Shakespeare's.

By the 1960s, Off-Broadway was costing too much for many younger theatre artists, and so a new movement, *Off-Off Broadway*, was born. Its beginning is usually dated from 1958 when Joe Cino opened the Cafe Cino, a coffeehouse that served also as an art gallery and as a place for poetry readings and dramatic presentations. As time passed, more young playwrights took advantage of the opportunity to have their plays read in Cafe settings and the Off-Off-Broadway movement took shape.

Some of the most important Off-Off-Broadway companies have been *Cafe LaMama*, the *Living Theater*, the *Open Theater*, *Mabou Mines*, and the *Wooster Group*. These companies are known for their experimental and nontraditional dramas, many of which are highly physical and developed by the group through improvisation. It is not unusual for these companies to produce works motivated by their desire to see political and social change. ■

Curtain Call!

■ ■ SPOTLIGHT ON TERMS ■ ■

An important part of theatre is understanding the terminology, or vocabulary, used. Add the new terms and definitions to the vocabulary section of your theatre notebook or folder.

■ ■ FOCUS ON FACTS ■ ■

1. What is oral interpretation?
2. Define poetry, prose, and dramatic literature.
3. What is meant by literary value?
4. Why is it important for you to choose your own material for oral interpretation?
5. Describe how to analyze a selection.
6. What information could be used in writing an introduction?
7. List important steps in presenting a selection.
8. What is the reason for marking your selection?
9. What are the different delivery techniques used for effective oral interpretation?

■ ■ REFLECTIONS ■ ■

Discuss the following questions with your class, or answer them on paper as instructed by your teacher.

1. What impact has reading aloud had on your life?
2. What makes you enjoy or not enjoy listening to people read?
3. How important is it to interpret material the way the author meant it to be read?
4. When you were younger and had stories read to you, which readers had effective reading skills? Why were they good oral readers? Be specific.

■ ■ THEATRE IN YOUR LIFE ■ ■

1. Prepare an Oral Interpreter's Delight Night. Choose poetry, prose, or drama selections to present to your community. After the selection, preparation, and rehearsals, present the program to an audience. Provide dessert, coffee, or soft drinks following the presentation.
2. On Saturday mornings, or once a month, read stories to elementary school children. Arrange the time and place (possibly the library) with the appropriate administrators. Use all the necessary skills in presenting your stories as an oral interpretation activity.

■ ■ ENCORE ■ ■

1. Attend an academic contest that includes interpreting material as one of its events.
2. Attend a festival that includes oral interpretation.
3. Which event, contest or festival, did you enjoy the most? Why? Did you prepare for the two events differently? Why or why not?
4. Sponsor your own contest or festival for several school districts and include poetry, prose, and dramatic oral interpretation as events.

Storytelling

Chapter Outline

Spotlight on Terms

◆ folklore
◆ story
◆ storyteller
◆ storytelling

story

the narration of an event or series of events brought to life for listeners by a storyteller.

storytelling

the art of sharing stories with an audience.

Everyone has a story to tell. And while we could spend a lifetime learning the art and technique of storytelling—perfecting our style and performance—for most of us, it is the simple telling of a tale that's important.

Jimmy Neil Smith

storyteller

a person who tells stories or tales.

■ ■ ■ ■ ■ ■ ■ ■ ■ ■ ■ ■ ■ ■ ■

If you perfect your storytelling skills, perhaps someone will erect a statue in your honor, as was done for the great Danish storyteller, Hans Christian Andersen. His children's stories, such as "The Ugly Duckling," have been translated into more than eighty languages.

Since the beginning of time, people in all parts of the world have woven words into a simple narration, bringing to life an event or series of events to share with others. We call this a **story**. In ancient times, long before the existence of books, television, and movies, **storytelling**, the telling of a story, was an important part of basic human communication. Although we often think of stories merely as entertainment for the young, years ago stories were told primarily for adults. Wherever there were people, there were stories. And it was those stories that connected people and countries. Stories were shared by different tribal chiefs seated around a campfire. Stories traveled with the traders as they moved with caravans across ancient lands. Stories were told by traveling bards and minstrels during the Middle Ages and by the African griots (gree-yos), who traveled from village to village.

Throughout history and in every land, we find evidence of storytelling. Before the written word, the only way people could relate and preserve historical events, cultural traditions, and even daily life was through storytelling. We still know many of these great stories today because someone told the stories to someone else. Only the stories that were passed down from one generation to the next were remembered. And those stories that were forgotten were lost forever.

The teller of the tales was called by many different names—bard, gleoman, minstrel, griot—all meaning **storyteller**. Storytellers told of the past—people's history, customs, and religion. Storytellers told of the future—the dangers as well as the dreams. The tribal storyteller was often the oldest man or woman in the village. Considered wise and important, this person not only could tell a story but could also explain its meaning. Thus, the storyteller was a powerful figure, both in the history of storytelling and in the history of humankind.

Today, we enjoy reading books and watching television and movies. But stories and storytellers are still an important part of our lives and traditions. In this chapter, you will learn to use effective storytelling

techniques as you explore and help keep alive the ancient art of story-telling. But you say you're not a storyteller? Let's see! Do you enjoy talking with your friends after school and telling them about the funny thing that happened in math class or about the great party you went to? If so, you are practicing the art of storytelling. When you repeat a story aloud to an audience, you are a storyteller. That makes every-one—including you—a storyteller!

Storytelling Techniques

LESSON OBJECTIVES

◆ Identify skilled storytellers.
◆ Recognize effective storytelling techniques.

Warm Up

Think about the way you learned the story "The Three Little Pigs." Write down the way you can use that technique when learning to tell a story in this class.

Do you remember when you were young how much you enjoyed hearing your grandmother tell the daring escapades of your mother and her brothers? Or perhaps you had an uncle who told wild, scary, made-up tales at family reunions. Or was your favorite storyteller a teacher who filled in those minutes before the final bell by telling ex-citing adventures from her favorite book? Sure, you remember those storytellers! What made the stories they told interesting? How did these storytellers hold your attention?

We all know that some people are more skilled than others at telling stories. What we notice most often is the difference in quality and style. In this lesson, you will learn techniques to develop and enhance your natural storytelling abilities. Good storytelling techniques learned and practiced in theatre class can help you in your everyday life. Knowing how to tell a story can help you be a better communicator, whether you are on the telephone, at the dinner table, or in front of another class.

Think about the best storyteller you have ever heard. What tech-niques did that storyteller use to capture your attention? What tech-niques were used to hold your attention and make you want more?

A group of students prepared a list of good storytelling techniques used by their favorite storytellers. What other good techniques would you add to the list?

A Good Storyteller Always:
1. Chooses interesting stories that are suitable for the audience.
2. Prepares and rehearses the story.
3. Uses words the audience understands and explains the ones the audience won't understand.
4. Uses ESP—enthusiasm, sensitivity, and personality.
5. Uses facial expression and body language.
6. Uses vocal variety by changing the tone, pitch, inflection, and tempo to suit the appropriate parts of the story.
7. Adds character voices and dialogue where needed.

Brother Blue is a well-known professional storyteller.

8. Makes eye contact with the audience.
9. Adds humor when appropriate.
10. Adds props or costumes if they will explain or enhance the story.
11. Pauses before and after important ideas so the listener has time to think.
12. Builds up to the climax.
13. Creates the "once upon a time" feeling as the story begins.
14. Enjoys sharing the story with the audience.

1. **Storytelling Techniques.** Working with your acting company or with your class, compile a list of good storytelling techniques.

2. **Critiquing Storytellers.** View a videotaped storytelling presentation. Observe and record the good techniques that were used.

3. **Scouting for Storytellers.** Listen to an adult tell stories. This might be a teacher, a minister, a professional comedian, or a professional storyteller. Observe and record all of the good techniques used by the storyteller. Be prepared to share your list with your class.

4. **Storytelling Festival.** Attend a storytelling festival in your community or a storytelling event at your public library. Observe and record the good techniques used by the storyteller. Be prepared to share your observations with your class.

5. **Researching Professional Storytellers.** Research a storyteller for whom storytelling is a profession. Prepare a short report telling how the person became a storyteller. Some storytellers to consider: Jay O'Callahan, Norman Dietz, Diane Wolkstein, Jackie Torrence, Brother Blue, Mary Carter-Smith, Connie Regan-Blake, David Holt, Barbara Freeman, Laura Simms, Rafe Martin.

Finding Stories to Tell

LESSON OBJECTIVES

◆ Recognize that everyone has a story to tell.
◆ Prepare and tell one or more personal stories.
◆ Prepare and tell one or more family stories.
◆ Use effective storytelling techniques.

Warm Up

Tell a short story that begins with the words "once upon a time" and ends with "they lived happily ever after."

Where do you find stories? Certainly, you can find stories in your school or public library in the great works of literature. The stories that you find in the library may be fiction (made up by the writer) or

Hispanic American Theatre: El Teatro Campesino

The movement of theatre activities away from New York and the Broadway production system for commercial theatre steadily continued as the 1960s passed. Many theatre companies were formed by theatre artists who shared similar political ideas. Many other groups consisted of theatre artists who shared similar cultural backgrounds. One such group was the American Hispanic theatre artists who performed in a wide variety of dialects—some only in Spanish, others only in English, and many presenting bilingual productions.

Perhaps the best known and most influential of these Hispanic companies—El Teatro Campesino—was founded in California in 1965 by Luis Valdez. El Teatro Campesino was organized in conjunction with a labor union, the National Farm Workers Association, and was originally formed as an educational group that would use theatrical methods, such as satirical comedy scores, to communicate with farm workers. During one very difficult strike by the grape pickers, the members of El Teatro Campesino used their dramas to explore the complicated issues involved with the strike in an effort to get more and more of the workers to join the union. El Teatro Campesino was so widely popular that in 1969 it developed into a bilingual theatre company based in San Juan Bautista, California, and toured regularly.

One of the major goals of El Teatro Campesino was to create greater pride among the Mexican American population by making the Mexican Americans more aware of their heritage and the accomplishments of their people. Luis Valdez wrote most of the plays that the group performed, using biographical information about successful and legendary Mexican Americans, Mexican folktales and myths, as well as original plots that explored the issues surrounding discrimination.

The Hispanic American theatre movement grew steadily after El Teatro Campesino was founded. By the mid-1980s, there were over 100 Hispanic theatre troupes, including Chicano, Cuban, and Puerto Rican artists, in the United States. Most of these companies are based in New York, Florida, Puerto Rico, California, and other areas throughout the Southwestern states where there are large concentrations of Hispanic audience members. Unfortunately, even with this large number of Hispanic theatre companies working in our country, there have been very few Hispanic playwrights to gain wide recognition.

Other important names in the history of this vibrant theatrical community include the Bilingual Foundation of the Arts, INTAR (International Arts Relations), Repertorio Español, and the Puerto Rican Traveling Theatre. These companies have done a great deal to raise the awareness of the Hispanic community and the general public about the contributions of Hispanic Americans to our country. They've also dramatized the rich heritage of the Hispanic cultures and the racial challenges still facing our nation. ■

Alma Martinez and Mike Moroff played the leads in a Luis Valdez comedy produced by El Teatro Campesino at the Marines Memorial Theatre in San Francisco.

Looking through family albums is
one way to get ideas for
interesting stories.

nonfiction (based on fact). But stories can also be found within us.
Our stories are everywhere.

Personal Stories

Personal stories are based on the events in a person's life. These
events become "story starters." A story starter is the beginning of a
story. The clever storyteller learns how to take these beginnings and
weave them into a longer narration to capture the interest of the listeners and entertain them. Think of the things that have happened to
you. Which of them might be good story starters? Make a list. The following ideas might help you get started.

• You were four years old and you wandered away from your mother
  in a busy shopping mall.
• You fell out of a tree and broke your arm.
• The first night at summer camp, you were afraid of the dark.
• You believed that monsters lived in your closet.
• You filled the bathtub with water and pretended that you were swim-
  ming in the ocean.
• You were disappointed that your birthday present wasn't a puppy.
• You played with the buttons in your grandmother's button box, pre-
  tending that they were rare jewels.

  Those story starters belong to someone else, and only that person
could create personal stories from them. But the starters might remind you of one of your own experiences—and that would be *your*
story. Your personal stories cannot be found in a library book. The
only way someone else can know your story is if you choose to share it
with that person. The fact that the story has never been heard before

makes it one of the best types of stories to tell. What's more, your personal connection to the event will make the story easier to tell and more meaningful to your listeners.

Everyday events and adventures—your story starters—can be developed and improved upon as you choose. You might make a personal story humorous—the time you stuffed your nostrils full of Grape Nuts cereal, only to discover later in the day that the crunchy nuggets had expanded. Other personal stories, like the time your cat was caught in the motor of your neighbor's truck, might be sad. You are the storyteller, so let's get started! Follow the steps to finding a personal story to discover a story within you.

Steps to Finding a Personal Story

1. Begin by listing "story starters."
   a. List the silly things you did as a child.
   b. List all the "jams" in which you have been "stuck."
   c. List all the problems you imagined you had when you were in elementary school.
   d. List any surprises, adventures, or unusual experiences you can remember from your childhood.
2. Choose your favorite starter from one of the lists you compiled.
3. Add details to make it interesting and develop it into a short story.
4. Rehearse your story aloud.

Family Stories

Family stories are also fresh, exciting, personal stories to share aloud. A family story is a story told by a member of your family about something or someone related to you. These family stories, examples of living history, are handed down in the oral tradition and are not written down. These stories, based on facts, have often been exaggerated to make them more interesting for the listener. Can you think of a story about one of your relatives that you have heard your grandfather or grandmother (or some other relative) tell?

To discover family stories, you could begin by interviewing the oldest living member of your family. This relative may be a grandfather, a great-grandmother, or even a great-great-aunt. You may be surprised to discover that this relative has lived through all of the wars of the twentieth century. You might hear a story about life before television, learning to drive a model T, or surviving the Great Depression.

You can also ask your mother, father, and older brothers and sisters to tell you family stories. These stories could be ones they actually experienced or ones that they themselves were told. After hearing each story, ask questions. Find out as much as you can about life during the time of the story. Details help you form a mental picture of the setting, characters, actions, and historical period.

Discover family stories by looking through family photographs. When you see an unusual photograph of a family member stuck in a tree or wearing a funny outfit or with birthday cake in their hair, ask someone to tell you the story behind the photograph.

Have you been lucky enough to hear family stories told by an older relative?

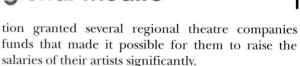

The American Regional Theatre

Prior to the 1950s, New York City, with its powerful theatre investors, was the only major center for theatre production in our country. Many theatre companies based on the East Coast were touring the United States, but few cities had resident companies of actors who regularly produced plays for local audiences. The economic boom of the 1950s, however, made the climate favorable for theatre companies to begin to appear in cities like San Francisco, Minneapolis, Washington, D.C., Chicago, Dallas, and Houston.

A major factor in the growth of these companies, which became known as *regional theatres,* was new financial support. Corporations and foundations began to donate large sums of money for local arts development. The most important of these agencies was the Ford Foundation. In 1959, the Ford Foundation granted several regional theatre companies funds that made it possible for them to raise the salaries of their artists significantly.

This extra money also dramatically increased the producers' flexibility with regard to the plays that they chose to produce. Prior to this time there was a great deal of pressure on local theatre groups to produce the same style of flashy, and costly, musicals and comedies that were popular on Broadway at the time. The new funds from the Ford Foundation made it possible for the regional groups to produce the plays in which they were most interested—those that had become successful in European theatre companies, as well as classic plays such as those by Shakespeare, Ibsen, Chekov, and Molière.

The Ford Foundation later began giving grants to the regional theatres specifically to commission new plays and hire playwrights to create new American dramas. This made the variety of theatre experiences available to American audiences wider than ever before.

By far the most influential of the early regional theatre groups was in Minneapolis. Tyrone Guthrie founded The Minneapolis Theatre Company in 1963. The group built a beautiful 1,400 seat theatre space with a thrust stage and audience seating on three sides so that no audience member was an extreme distance from the stage. This group later changed its name to the Guthrie Theatre, named for its founder. It remains one of the United States' most successful and popular regional theatres.

The Guthrie showed other major metropolitan areas that they, too, could support a resident professional theatre company, if they provided the necessary space and support to make that goal a reality. By the mid-1960s, there were over thirty regional theatre companies in the United States providing jobs for artists and theatre opportunities for audiences who could have never traveled to New York to see professional productions. ■

The success of the plays presented on the thrust stage at the Guthrie Theatre in Minneapolis, and the resulting publicity, helped establish regional theatre in many other U.S. cities.

1. **Story Starters.** Using the steps to finding a personal story as a guide (page 320), prepare your lists of story starters. Then prepare a personal story and share it with the class.

2. **Telling Family Stories.** Prepare a family story and share it with the class.

3. **Family Story Album.** Write a collection of family stories to someday hand down to your children.

Preparing to Tell a Story from a Text

LESSON OBJECTIVES

◆ Recognize folklore as an important part of oral history.
◆ Research and select a story suitable for re-telling.
◆ Prepare and tell a story using effective storytelling techniques.

*W*orking in small groups, compile a list of all the times you heard stories told yesterday. Share your discoveries with the class.

folklore

tales, beliefs, customs, and traditions that were passed down orally from one generation to another.

As you begin to feel more confident telling stories, you will want to learn to tell stories that are not personal. Numerous sources of good stories can be found in your school library or media center. You can choose stories that are as old as civilization or as modern as today.

For the beginning storyteller, the best stories to tell are those designed to be told orally. These stories are classified as folklore. **Folklore** consists of tales, beliefs, customs, and traditions that have been passed down by word of mouth from one generation to another. Legends, fairy tales, folktales, parables, and fables are all considered types of folklore (Figure 16–1 on page 325). Most of these stories were recorded in the way they were told and make good selections for storytelling.

Selecting The Story

How do you choose a story? First, the story should appeal to you. You might like it because it is humorous or because it is sad—but you must like it. You should like the way the story is told. The wording of the sentences should be easy for you to understand, and the plot should be easy to follow. Finally, you should be able to visualize the characters and actions.

You will probably read several stories before you find a selection that you want to learn. If your story is to be told at a special event, choose a story geared to the occasion. Some stories are more suitable for young

To choose a story you really like,
you need to spend time doing
some research.

children, while others are good for any age. If you are going to tell your story outside of your classroom, you will need to know something about the audience before you select the story. Your teacher will prepare you for such an event.

Learning the Story

Storytelling uses many of the acting skills you have already mastered—analyzing a text, developing characters, using vocal expression, and memorizing dialogue. But storytelling isn't acting. In acting, you become the character; in storytelling, you suggest the characters through vocal and physical characterization.

There are many ways to learn the story you plan to tell. All storytellers begin by reading the story several times. During these readings, try to picture in your mind the characters, voices, and actions.

Next, some storytellers make an outline of the plot, or what happens in the story. It is important to tell the story in the correct sequence, or order of events. Telling the events out of order would be like telling a joke and forgetting the punch line. To determine if you know the plot, tape-record yourself telling the story, or tell the story to a friend. Then relearn the parts that were difficult to remember.

Avoid memorizing an entire story word for word. You can easily forget a line and then go totally blank! Memorized stories can also sound too rehearsed and impersonal. More important than memorizing a story word for word is having a clear understanding of the characters and actions. As you rehearse the story, picture the plot of the story just as if it happened to you and your friends. Then memorize only the important lines that need to be phrased exactly as the author wrote them.

For ease in learning, some storytellers divide the story into three parts: the beginning, the middle, and the ending. The beginning sets the stage. We meet the main characters, establish the setting, and are introduced to the problem. The middle takes us on the journey of the

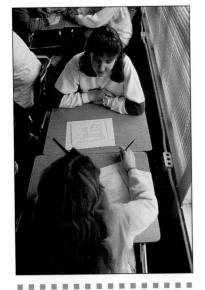

One way to learn the story you
plan to recite is to practice telling
it to a friend.

Figure 16–1
▪ ▪ ▪ ▪ ▪ ▪ ▪ ▪ ▪ ▪ ▪ ▪ ▪ ▪
Types of Folklore.

Folk Tale A story of anonymous origin passed down orally from generation to generation. Such a story usually stresses the virtues of the common people.

Fairy Tale A highly imaginative narrative based on rare powers or magic.

Fable A story using animal characters to point out or teach a lesson.

Myth A traditional story dealing with gods or supernatural beings. Such a story is based on the religious imagination of ancient peoples.

Legend A popular story passed down from generation to generation and originally based on an actual person or historical fact. The story and characters became more exaggerated through the years.

Parable A short story illustrating a truth, moral value, or religious principle.

Ballad A story told through music and song, usually concerned with romance or adventure.

story. During this part of the story, all other characters are introduced, the problem continues, the suspense increases, and the story builds to a climax. The final part of the story is the ending. This part of the story ties up all loose ends and comes to a conclusion when the problem is solved.

Another way to help you remember your story is to sketch out the plot in small pictures, like a comic strip. As you draw the events in sequence, the pictures will help you visually remember the story. Coloring your pictures can help you determine the mood or emotional feelings of each scene.

Don't make a big deal about memorizing or learning your story. If you select a story you really like, it will be fun and easy to learn!

Rehearse your story, telling it to anyone or anything that will listen. Try telling it to your mother, your little sister, your grandfather, even your dog. Listening to yourself tell the story over and over is one of the best ways to learn a story. If you are interrupted while rehearsing, don't start over; pick up right where you left off. It is important that you know the story well enough to do this. Once you have learned the story, work on facial expressions, gestures, and vocal expression.

One of the best ways to become an effective storyteller is to tell a variety of stories. Beginning storytellers should learn several short stories to extend their collections. Select one of the following jokelike stories told by professional storyteller Caroline Feller Bauer in *Read for the Fun of It*. After reading one of the stories aloud several times, try telling it to a friend. Ask your friend to suggest ways you could improve your presentation.

Mario the Beggar
(a story from Italy)

Mario was a great huge man. He had a bushy beard and piercing brown eyes. He made his living by begging. Mario would get close to someone, bend down, and say very softly, "Give me some money, or else . . . ."

This system worked very well. One day a frightened old woman went to her husband and said, "You must do something, I'm frightened of Mario."

The next day Antonio, the old woman's husband, walked close to Mario.

The beggar bent over Antonio and said in his hoarse whisper, "Give me some money, or else . . . ."

Antonio straightened himself up and looked as tough as he could and said in a loud voice, "Or else what?"

"Or else?" said the beggar—"or else? I will go away." And he crept meekly away!

The Lost Donkey
(a Goha story from Saudi Arabia)

Goha's friend came to see him. "I am so sorry, Goha. The donkey you lent me ran away. He is lost."

Goha was sad. The donkey was his only possession. His shoulders slumped and he hung his head.

Suddenly he jumped up and danced for joy.

His friend was astonished. "Why are you laughing? Why are you dancing? Your donkey is gone."

"Well," said the Goha. "I'm happy because if I had been on the donkey I would be lost too."

Three Rolls and a Chocolate Eclair
(a short story from France)

One spring day a young student passed by a bakery in a small town in France. He was poor and hungry. Staring in the window, he counted his money and decided to step into the shop.

He bought a *petit pain*, a small tasty roll, and devoured it as soon as he left the shop. He was still hungry and, so, he reentered the bakery and purchased a second *petit pain*. It tasted good, but since he was still famished, he returned and bought a third roll. He ate it quickly. He still had enough money to buy yet another roll.

"No," thought the student. "This time I shall try one of those divine looking chocolate eclairs." It was delicious.

"The eclair tasted better than the rolls," said the student. "And I am no longer at all hungry. What a fool I was not to buy the eclair first. Now I have wasted my money on three rolls when one eclair would have satisfied my hunger."

Telling the Story

A special event takes place when you share your story with an audience. This is your time to shine. You have found a story you really like, you have spent hours learning it, and you have rehearsed it until you are ready. Have fun! Make your audience enjoy the story as much as you did that first time you read it.

When you begin, pause and take a deep breath. Look out into the audience, make eye contact with several people, and think, "I like this story, and so will they!"

Set the audience up for the story by telling the title, the author, and the story's origin. You may have discovered other interesting facts about the story that would capture the audience's attention. You may include them in the introduction as well.

Once you begin telling your story, don't think about yourself. Focus on telling the story to your listeners, allowing them to enjoy it as much as you do. Watch them. Slow down or speed up, speak louder or more softly, according to their responses to you. As you look into their eyes and faces, you will notice that they are watching and listening—following your every word, your every move.

When you have completed your story, pause and return to your seat. Take pride in knowing that you, as a weaver of words, have joined so many others throughout history in keeping the art of storytelling alive.

66 *N*o, it'll not do just to read the old tales out of a book. You've got to tell 'em to make 'em go right. 99

Richard Chase

ACTION

1. **Folklore Presentation.** Select an appropriate story to share with your class. Then prepare the story for telling. Follow your teacher's special instructions to prepare the story. Finally, share your story with the class.

2. **Stories from Other Cultures.** Select a story from another country or culture and research the storytelling customs of that country. Prepare a short introduction to include this heritage before you tell the story.

3. **Researching Famous Storytellers.** Research a famous storyteller from a period in history. Prepare a short report to share with the class. Some famous storytellers to consider might be: Homer; Hans Christian Anderson; Joe Chandler Harris; The Grimm Brothers; Mark Twain; Rudyard Kipling; Carl Sandburg; or Ruth Sawyer.

Curtain Call!

CHAPTER 16 REVIEW

■ ■ SPOTLIGHT ON TERMS ■ ■

An important part of theatre is understanding the terminology, or vocabulary, used. Add the new terms and definitions to the vocabulary section of your theatre notebook or folder.

■ ■ FOCUS ON FACTS ■ ■

1. What was the importance of the early storyteller in a world without television, radio, or movies?
2. What are five good techniques to use when presenting a story?
3. Why are personal stories good selections for telling?
4. What are some sources for stories written in the oral tradition?
5. What aspects of a story should you consider before choosing a story to learn?
6. Describe the best way for you to learn a story.
7. Before you begin to tell a story, what information should you share with your audience?
8. As you are telling a story, what are some of the things you can do to make yourself more comfortable?

■ ■ REFLECTIONS ■ ■

Discuss the following questions with your class or answer them on paper as instructed by your teacher.

1. Discuss how the audience might react differently to hearing a story told and hearing a story read.
2. What did you like best about hearing the stories in this class?
3. Evaluate the importance of personal and family stories. Why is it important that we hear and retell our living history?

4. How can you use storytelling in classes other than theatre?
5. Discuss professionals, other than storytellers, who might use storytelling in their line of work.
6. What storytelling techniques do you still need to practice to feel more comfortable in front of your classmates?

■ ■ THEATRE IN YOUR LIFE ■ ■

1. As a class, compile a booklet of inspirational stories that have touched your lives.
2. Tell a story that made a difference in your life or record it as a journal entry in your theatre notebook.
3. Using an incident from your life, write an original children's story designed to influence a child to work hard or strive for success.

■ ■ ENCORE ■ ■

1. Interview a senior citizen and listen to a story from his or her life. Share that story with your class.
2. Prepare a story to share in another class—perhaps an event from history, an event from the life of a writer, or a funny story about a scientist or mathematician.
3. As a class, plan a storytelling event for children at a shopping mall, public library, day-care center, or elementary school or for another class at your school.
4. View videotapes of several storytellers. Compare and contrast their styles. Which style would you choose to develop? Why?
5. Bring an interesting small prop to class to put into a "storytelling bag." Take turns drawing a prop from the bag and telling an original story about it.

CHAPTER 17

Readers Theatre and Radio Theatre

Chapter Outline

LESSON 1 ◆ Readers Theatre
331

LESSON 2 ◆ Radio Theatre   338

Spotlight on Terms

- ◆ adapting
- ◆ audience focus
- ◆ characterized
- ◆ double-cast
- ◆ focus
- ◆ narrative bridge
- ◆ offstage focus
- ◆ onstage focus
- ◆ phrasing
- ◆ radio theatre
- ◆ readers theatre

This chapter explores two styles of theatre—readers theatre and radio theatre. Participating in readers theatre and radio theatre combines the skills, techniques, and talents of all those who are willing to spend time and energy to share the beauty of an author's written word orally.

If you are a team player and believe in the power of imagination, the time and energy you invest in these two arts will greatly benefit you academically and personally. First of all, these two styles of theatre are challenging and exciting to present. You and your classmates will have fun learning how to select, prepare, rehearse, and produce readers theatre and radio theatre material to an audience.

Second, your listening, communication, and cooperative learning skills will all improve. As in other forms of theatre, you are an important member of a team. You must be understood, pronounce words correctly, listen to others, use your voice effectively, have a positive attitude, and cooperate with the director and cast members.

Both of these theatre styles focus on an author's written word. The material you select for the scripts may be found in various forms—poems, plays, prose, cuttings from novels, and others. Participation in readers theatre and radio theatre will give you many opportunities to study, analyze, and appreciate literature.

You will have the opportunity to utilize the skills you developed in previous chapters (voice, personal resources, interpreting literature, and so on). The work you have done and the knowledge you have gained will all become intertwined as you actively participate in readers theater and radio theatre.

In both readers theatre and radio theatre, there is a special connection between you, the performer, and the audience. This is where the power of imagination plays a key role. It will be your responsibility as a performer to help your audience visualize settings, characters, and actions. Both the performer and the audience will exercise their imaginations to the fullest.

Readers theatre and radio theatre present special challenges in production. Both styles of theatre will provide the opportunity for your group to explore people, objects, places, and situations together with your classmates cooperatively. The skills you learn from these two arts and your experiences with them transfer to your other classes, at home, and in improving your life skills, giving you more poise, self-confidence, and an understanding of others and their ideas.

Readers Theatre

LESSON OBJECTIVES

◆ Recognize and define readers theatre.
◆ Select suitable materials for a readers theatre script.
◆ Develop a readers theatre script.
◆ Rehearse and stage a readers theatre presentation.

Warm Up

*R*ead the following description of readers theatre scripted in readers theatre style:

"What Is Readers Theatre?"

Reader 1:   Another way of interpreting literature is through readers theatre.
Reader 2:   Readers theatre?
Reader 3:   What's that?
Reader 4:   Readers theatre is . . .
Reader 5:   A form of theatre
Reader 6:   With two—
Readers 1, 4: Or more
Reader 5:   Readers appearing to be reading from the printed page.
Reader 6:   Readers theatre is interpretive theatre.
Readers 2, 3: Interpretive theatre?
Reader 6:   Bringing life to words
Reader 1:   Conveying characters from the printed page to the mind's eye of the listener.
Readers 2, 3: WOW!
Readers 4, 5: Actors using scripts!
Reader 6:   Actors painting with words—
Reader 1:   Settings, movements, and props.
Reader 4:   Readers theatre.
Reader 5:   READERS THEATRE!
Reader 6:   A sharing of literature.
All: Participatory theatre.
Readers 2, 3: READERS THEATRE!!!
All: Readers theatre.

What Is Readers Theatre?

Readers theatre, a style of theatre in which two or more interpreters appear to be reading from a script, is not new although it has gained in popularity in recent times. Throughout the years, similar styles of theatre have been known by such titles as chamber theatre, platform theatre, staged reading, interpreters theatre, and choral reading. Readers theatre seems to be the most suitable title, since the participants interpret the literary selection by reading rather than acting out.

Today's popular style of readers theatre has its origin in primitive ritual chants. These chants may be considered the first oral group performances. Other early examples of group reading, or readers theatre, were the chanting chorus from the Greek theatre and the recitation of Homer's poetry. Homer, the earliest known European poet, had his students read his poems aloud as they memorized them in unison. Throughout the history of religion, we find other examples of group reading. In many religious ceremonies today, we find the "call and response" as part of the worship service.

In the 1930s and 1940s, choral reading was a common activity in speech and drama festivals and contests. This event in public speaking is thought to be the forerunner of readers theatre as we know it today. Because readers theatre teaches students to interpret literary selections and read aloud with fluency, it is as popular in today's classrooms as it is on the stage.

Readers theatre is an exciting way to interpret literature. This theatrical style combines the oral interpretation of literature with the performance of conventional theatre. One difference noticed immediately is that the performers appear to be reading from a script. Another difference is that the actors do not have to dress in costume or act out the character. In readers theatre, the performers merely suggest the characters, settings, props, events, and actions while interpreting the selection for the audience.

Readers theatre becomes participatory theatre for the audience as they actively listen and visualize their interpretation of the selection.

Selecting Material for Readers Theatre

Many commercially prepared scripts are available for readers theatre, but your group might like to prepare your own material. Selec-

These students have developed a unique and pleasing arrangement for their particular readers theatre presentation. Be creative and experiment with your group's presentation.

These students have developed a unique and pleasing arrangement for their particular readers theatre presentation. Be creative and experiment with your group's presentation.

readers theatre

a style of theatre in which two or more interpreters appear to be reading from a script.

tions for readers theatre can come from almost any printed material. Plays, poetry, novels, and short stories are ideal sources. However, readers theatre material can also come from letters, diaries, journals, and even your history book.

Look for selections that will "turn on" the audience's imagination, actively involving the listeners in the presentation. A selection should move the audience to respond in some way. Another aspect to consider is characterization. Choose selections with interesting, easily identifiable characters. Conflict and action are also important. A selection with numerous conflicts offers more action for the actors and is more interesting to the audience.

Consider the language of the selection. You will want to choose a literary selection filled with imagery. Listen to the words of the selection. Do you like the way they sound? Do they paint pictures in your mind? Do you smile or laugh at some of the phrases and become sad when you hear others? Do some of the thoughts linger in your mind after you have finished reading the selection? If you can answer yes to those questions, then your selection will pass the language test.

If you plan to perform published material outside of your classroom, you will need to secure permission from the publishing company. It is against the law to copy or perform material without the permission of the copyright holder, usually the writer or publisher. Copyright is a writer's protection against someone stealing or copying his or her original material. Some companies require a fee to perform their materials. This fee is called a royalty. It is against the law to avoid payment of a royalty. Your teacher will advise you of your school's procedure for paying a royalty.

Adapting the Material

adapting
changing or cutting a literary piece.

narrative bridge
description of characters, actions, and settings provided by one or more narrators.

characterized
divided into characters for readers theatre.

Novels or short stories will have to be shortened to meet the time requirement for your assignment or presentation. Changing or cutting a selection is called **adapting** the material. Read the material several times before you decide on the parts or scenes to cut, or leave out. Descriptions of characters, actions, and settings can be provided by one or more narrators. This narration is often referred to as a **narrative bridge** . Narrative bridges help the audience clarify the scene changes and connect the parts. (You will find additional information on cutting in Chapter 15.)

Your literary selection will need to be divided into parts for each reader. Don't worry about having more characters than participants. Readers can easily play more than one character by changing vocal inflection and shifting posture. A poetry selection should be **characterized**, which means divided into characters. Assign lines to individual characters, and use narrators when needed.

Creating the Script

Using a computer is a good way to create a script, since changes are easy to make.

After adapting your selection, divide the reader parts and prepare the script. (For example, see the Warm Up at the beginning of this lesson.) The left margin of the script should be at least 1½ inches wide to allow room for binding and stage directions. Reader names or numbers are placed on the inside of this margin. The other margins should be about 1 inch wide. Typed scripts are easier to read than handwritten ones. It's also easier to read your manuscript if you have double-spaced the lines.

Here are some other helpful suggestions from students who have participated in readers theatre:

1. Always number your pages.
2. Use at least 12-point (pica) type so you can see it clearly.
3. Avoid dividing a reader's part from one page to the next.
4. Type all stage directions in italics and place in parentheses.
5. Make additional changes to stage directions in pencil. You might have to change them again.
6. Use a stiff manuscript cover or binder for your script. Black is the traditional color for a readers theatre script cover.
7. Underline or highlight your part. Only highlight the words that will be spoken, so that you don't read the stage directions aloud when you are nervous.
8. Each member of your group should use a different color to highlight his or her script in case the scripts get mixed up.

9. To show scene changes in your script, center several symbols (* * * *) where the change occurs.

10. Put your name on the inside of your script.

The final step in preparation is to write an introduction for the presentation. An introduction always includes the title and author or playwright. Background information or special vocabulary could also be included. The introduction is important in setting the stage for the readers theatre presentation.

Rehearsing

Each performer should read the script several times before rehearsals begin. During the first few rehearsals, readers should spend time reading the script aloud, in parts or in round-robin style. Both the text and the characters should be analyzed. These first rehearsals offer readers time to understand the material and prepare the script, making any necessary changes in dialogue or characterization. Once the parts are assigned, each reader should highlight or underline his or her speaking lines.

Early rehearsals are also the time to mark the script for emphasis and phrasing. In each line or group of words, there will be some words you will want to stress. Adverbs and verbs are usually more important than nouns and adjectives. Putting emphasis on these words helps make the meaning clearer for your audience. Your teacher may have a special way to mark scripts, or you may use the same marks you used in oral interpretation. Most readers mark or underline the words they want to stress, using different colors to indicate the amount of stress. Thus, a word marked with two lines in red would be emphasized differently from a word marked with one squiggly green line.

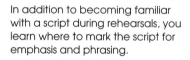

In addition to becoming familiar with a script during rehearsals, you learn where to mark the script for emphasis and phrasing.

phrasing
grouping words to create a specific meaning.

Phrasing is extremely important in readers theatre. **Phrasing** means grouping words to create a specific meaning. Notice two different ways to phrase the following dialogue:

"Oh no! I forgot my lunch." (phrased as if the person is upset at having forgotten his or her lunch)

"Oh! No, I forgot my lunch." (phrased as if the person forgot his or her lunch but isn't too concerned)

Which phrasing is correct? Well, it all depends on the meaning you are trying to get across to your audience. Phrasing should be planned early in rehearsal. Work with your director and group members to determine the best way to phrase all the lines.

Most readers mark their scripts with a "signpost" to signal a pause or break in reading. Use one post (/), or mark, for a short pause; two posts (//) for a longer pause or complete stop. Your acting company or group might create your own signals. Just be sure to remember what they mean.

Once you have a clear understanding of the script, the remaining rehearsals should be used for blocking and staging, developing characters, and polishing the performance.

Staging

Readers theatre is simple to stage. Since the traditional stage, props, costumes, and sets are not required, readers theatre is an ideal style of theatre for classroom presentation.

Performers should be grouped in a visually pleasing manner using chairs, stools, ladders, step units, or cubes. Steps, ramps, and platforms add levels and variety. Using different levels allows all cast members to be visible to the audience. Try experimenting: Use rows, angles, even semicircles to find the ideal grouping for a particular selection. Empty space can be used to show relationships between characters or between the characters and the narrator.

Some time should be spent rehearsing the entrance if the group is to walk onstage or into the performance space. How your group enters depends on the performance space as well as on the blocking. Often in readers theatre, the actors walk in, holding their scripts in their upstage hands. The first or last person to enter, often the narrator, gives a silent signal, such as a slight nod, and all the readers raise their scripts to reading level. Script folders or binders are supported by one hand from underneath, freeing one hand for gesturing. When the free hand is not in use, it rests on top of the script.

focus
in readers theatre, the place or people that the actors look at when they speak their lines.

onstage focus
a type of focus in readers theatre in which the characters focus on each other, as in traditional theatre.

audience focus
a type of focus in readers theatre in which the characters focus on the audience.

offstage focus
a type of focus in readers theatre in which the characters look above the heads of the audience, into an imaginary mirror, focusing on the reflected image of the person to whom they are speaking.

A character enters a scene by stepping forward to speak or by standing. A scene exit is accomplished by stepping back or sitting down. Other exit methods are turning the back, lowering the head, and "freezing" in place. If available, spotlights can also be used to begin and end a scene or to highlight individual entrances and exits.

Focus in readers theatre is one way of achieving action and believability. **Focus** refers to where the actors look or to whom they address their lines when speaking. Three basic types of focus are used in readers theatre. In **onstage focus**, the characters focus on each other, as in traditional theatre. In **audience focus**, the characters focus on the audience. In **offstage focus**, the characters do not look at each other but

Bertolt Brecht (1898–1956)

Bertolt Brecht, a German playwright, director, and writer, had a major impact on contemporary theatre. His innovative plays, his outstanding theatre company, and his writings about theatre have all influenced the way theatre is produced today.

His main goal was to make the audience think about social issues and then act to change the social and political ills dramatized in his plays. To do this, Brecht devised techniques to emotionally distance the audience from the characters in the play. Brecht didn't want the audience to personally identify and become emotionally involved with the characters, as most playwrights did. Instead, Brecht wanted to create a theatrical world that made the audience focus on the social and political forces in the characters' lives, rather than the characters themselves.

To accomplish his goals, Brecht developed what he called *alienation.* He believed in entertaining his audience, but he also wanted to keep the audience members thinking about what they were watching. To do so, he "alienated" the audience from the events they were watching by making events, actions, and characters seem "strange," unlike what is experienced in daily life. This strangeness, he believed, would create sufficient emotional distance between the audience and the play so that the audience could watch objectively and critically.

Brecht's plays constantly reminded the audience (unlike realistic theatre) that they were in a theatre,

not in reality, and that they were watching a reflection of life, not life itself. One of his techniques was to insert songs between each dramatic episode so that the audience would be emotionally pulled away from the action of the previous scene. This gave them time to think about the dramatic event they had just witnessed. Conflict was seldom resolved simply at the end of his plays. Instead, the ending usually suggested that the audience members must find the end, the solution, in their real lives after leaving the theatre. All of these techniques worked toward achieving Brecht's goal of having the audience members realize that they, as citizens, needed to work for social change.

Brecht never tried to hide the mechanics of the stage, such as lighting instruments or scene shifting. Nothing was masked or hidden from the eye of the audience the way it was in productions created by realists. Musicians were not hidden in an orchestra pit, but were placed on stage beside the action. Scenery was fragmentary, using one or two pieces of furniture to represent a whole room. These choices were all made in an effort to keep the audience thinking about the subject matter of his plays.

Some of his best-known plays include *The Three-penny Opera* (1928), *Mother Courage and Her Children* (1938), *The Good Woman of Setzuan* (1940), and *The Caucasian Chalk Circle* (1944–45). ∎

The person you see here is not a television commentator, but a character in the play *Mother Courage and Her Children.* After reading about Brecht, what do you think this character's purpose in the play might be?

Where do you think the reader is focusing in this classroom presentation?

look above the heads of the audience into an imaginary mirror, focusing on the reflected image of the person to whom they are speaking.

In traditional readers theatre, the performers most often use audience or offstage focus. In more informal readers theatre, the characters often use onstage focus, while the narrators use offstage or audience focus. Work with your group, under your director's guidance, to determine the appropriate type of focus for your selection.

When the performance concludes, all readers close their folders at the same time and exit in a prearranged fashion. Remember to rehearse your entrances and exits.

The Presentation

If you have used your rehearsal time wisely, you are ready to share with an audience. You have worked long and hard. You know your material. Now it's time for the fun.

Remember to use all the good presentation techniques you have learned:

- Use appropriate focus.
- Speak out with confidence.
- Follow your marked script.
- Stand or sit tall to avoid slumping.
- Refrain from crossing your legs.
- Enjoy the pleasure that comes from a job well done.

1. Selecting Readers Theatre Material.
   a. Find a short play that can be adapted to readers theatre. Bring it to class to share.

    b. Bring to class three short poems similar in theme to use in a readers theatre performance.

    c. Find two interesting literary characters. These might be found in a novel you are reading or in a short story that you read for language arts class. Share these with your class.

2. **Adapting Material.** Adapt one or more of the following selections for readers theatre:
    a. "Four Vain and Ancient Tortoises," from *Something Big Has Been Here*, by Jack Prelutsky
    b. "Eight Balloons," from *A Light in the Attic*, by Shel Silverstein
    c. "The Camel Dances," from *Fables*, by Arnold Lobel

3. **Developing Material.** Choose one of the following selections to develop for a readers theatre presentation:
    a. "Otherwise Known as Sheila the Great," by Judy Blume
    b. "The Fun They Had," by Isaac Asimov
    c. "A Fable," by Mark Twain

4. **Readers Theatre Performance.** Share your readers theatre performance with your class. Then evaluate your performance using the following criteria:
    a. How well did the members of your group cooperate with each other and the director?
    b. What evidence is there that the group maintained a good attitude and took the assignment seriously?
    c. How effective were the voices in your production?
    d. What blocking was effective during the performance?
    e. Who maintained correct eye focus?
    f. Who handled the script well?
    g. What characters were well developed?
    h. What did you like best about the performance?
    i. What changes would you make in the next performance?

Radio Theatre

LESSON OBJECTIVES

◆ Define radio theatre.
◆ Select material for radio theatre.
◆ Create scripts for radio theatre.
◆ Rehearse and stage radio theatre.

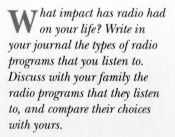

What impact has radio had on your life? Write in your journal the types of radio programs that you listen to. Discuss with your family the radio programs that they listen to, and compare their choices with yours.

During the Great Depression in the 1930s, radio theatre was one of the most inexpensive forms of entertainment in America. The radio, often known as "the furniture that could talk," became a friend to millions of people who did not have the money for any other type of entertainment, including movies. (Remember, there was no televi-

radio theatre

the performance of a play or story on radio by readers using a script that is not memorized. This type of theatre is either broadcast live or taped for later use.

sion!) Radio programming included many titles you will recognize, such as *Superman* and *I Love Lucy*, because many of the successful radio shows were later produced for television.

Many theatre personalities got their start on radio, and many television shows that your grandparents and parents watched—and that you can still see in reruns—originated as radio theatre. Back then, radio had the power to stir one's imagination. It gave people hours of suspense, sorrow, laughter, and adventure. Listeners created vivid images to match the sounds that they heard from the radio. This lost art still has the magic to unleash your creative powers.

What Is Radio Theatre?

Radio theatre is the performance of a play or story on radio by readers using a script that is not memorized. Radio theatre calls for little action. It mainly consists of readers' voices, sound effects, and often music. This type of theatre is either broadcast live or taped for later use.

The radio play requires actors who are skilled in oral interpretation because the imagination of the listener is the key to radio theatre's success. The audience must create images in their minds as they hear the words interpreted by the radio players. To convey the drama of the story, the readers must rely entirely on the energy, emotional range, emphasis, flexibility, clarity, and expressiveness of their voices. Often the readers must develop contrast in their voices to create more than one character as well as sound different from the other readers. This is definitely a challenging role for any young theatre student—as well as for any experienced actor.

Selecting Material for Radio Theatre

You have several choices in selecting a script for a radio play. Your first choice is a published radio play. These plays can be found in your school library, your teacher's personal collection of radio plays, or a public library.

Your second choice is a published play that you want to adapt (change) into a radio play. If you choose to adapt a play, pick one that you think will make thrilling listening for an audience. Also, pick one that you think will be fun to produce with special sound effects and music. (Review the information in Lesson 1 on securing performance rights from a publishing company if you plan to present a published play outside the classroom.)

Your third choice is to write your own radio play. This is perhaps your best choice and the most fun for you and your classmates. You will use all the group skills you learned in Chapter 2 and the techniques of playwriting in Chapter 13 to help you develop and write a play for radio.

Preparing the Material

After choosing or writing the script for your radio play, you must select a cast for the play. The cast size depends on the number of charac-

African American Theatre

The Federal Theatre Project, the government-run theatre of the 1930s, was designed to create jobs for out-of-work theatre artists. Among its most important contributions to theatre was the creation of African American theatre companies.

One of these companies, the Negro People's Theatre, was housed in Harlem in the Lafayette Theatre. It was there, in 1935–36, that John Houseman staged an extremely successful all-black version of *Macbeth* with the help of actor/director Orson Welles.

The 1960s was a time for major changes in American culture. An important cultural change was the appearance of new African American theatre companies, one of the most important of which was the Black Arts Repertoire Theatre, founded in 1964 by LeRoi Jones. This company produced plays with financial support from the federal Office of Economic Opportunity. By the time its funding ended in 1968, there were many other African American companies producing plays all around the nation. Although these were more numerous than before, they represented a small percentage of the total number of theatre companies in the United States at the time.

Other important early groups include Black Arts/West in San Francisco, Concept East in Detroit, and the New Lafayette Theatre in New York. Perhaps the most influential of the African American companies has been the Negro Ensemble Company of New York, which was established in 1968 with financial support from the Ford Foundation. This theatre not only employed a permanent company of actors but also developed a training program for black actors, playwrights, and directors.

By the beginning of the second half of this century, African American playwrights were beginning to be recognized for their powerful and well-written plays, which addressed the needs and issues of black Americans. One of the most important of these early black playwrights was Lorraine Hansberry, who wrote *A Raisin in the Sun* (1959), a warm, moving play that deals with the dreams and setbacks of an African American family in Chicago. This award-winning play was the first play to be presented on Broadway by an African American woman. Other important early black playwrights are Ed Bullins, Douglas Turner Ward, and Ossie Davis.

Lorraine Hansberry's *A Raisin in the Sun* examines a proud African American family and the relationships between its members as they deal with issues such as racism and integration.

In more recent years, African American dramatists have continued to make major contributions to American theatre. One of these playwrights is August Wilson, who was born in 1945. Wilson's first major success, produced in 1984, was *Ma Rainey's Black Bottom*. This play tells the story of vastly talented black musicians who are forced to work for abusive whites during the 1920s in Chicago. Another of Wilson's plays, *Fences*, which was produced in 1985, was awarded the Pulitzer Prize. Wilson's plays tend to explore African American characters who are searching for identity, dignity, and fulfillment—issues still valid today. ■

double-cast

assign an actor to play two roles.

ters called for in the script. If you do not have enough readers, you will need to **double-cast** the actors, requiring each to play more than one character.

You will not need to rehearse this play as often as you would one for the stage, but you must be careful to follow guidelines for the best possible production. You will need enough scripts for the director and every member of the cast. You will also need scripts for the crew members (who will help with sound effects and music), narrators, stage manager, and any announcers.

Mark your scripts as you would in any oral interpretation presentation. Take great care to mark pronunciations, sound effects, words that need special emphasis, places where music is inserted, and places where pauses are needed. Everyone needs to read through the script before rehearsing the play to become familiar with the program and to check the length of the play. Readers should mark their cues to get ready during the last line of the actor who reads before them.

Let's review the vocal techniques discussed in Chapter 5. Volume is important because the voice must be loud enough to be heard over the microphone, but not so loud that it is distorted. Your rate is extremely important in radio theatre. A common mistake that many theatre arts students make is reading too fast. Remember, the performance will probably be the first time that the audience is hearing the production. People read too fast when they are excited or nervous. Mark your script to help pace yourself and try to focus on reading to one listener. This should help with your "mike fright."

As you know, flexibility is the ability to change your pitch and create interest in your voice. You will need flexibility to develop the characters you are portraying in the radio play. Clarity means reading clearly and pronouncing all the words correctly and distinctly. Expression is essential for all interpreters. To hold the interest of your listeners and

Ask your grandparents if they remember listening to the comedy routines of Jerry Colonna on the radio.

create images for them, your voice must be expressive, filled with feeling. By reading with energy, you let the listener know that you are glad to be performing and that you want to do the best job that you can.

Now you are ready to get in front of the microphone. Practice with the microphones two or three times before the live or taped performance. The number of microphones depends on the size of the cast. One microphone is needed for the sound effects and music. You can purchase sound effect records or tapes or be creative and design your own effects with items that you have at school or at home.

Presenting the Material

After two or three rehearsals of the radio play, you will present the play for a live or taped broadcast. As you saw in rehearsal, it takes cooperation from every member of the group to present a radio play. If you are sharing microphones, you need to be ready to move closer to the microphone when it is your turn. You must watch what's going on, listen closely, and be on time for every cue. Avoid unnecessary noise, which the microphone will amplify. Any heavy breathing, sneezing, or coughing will be picked up by the microphone. Have your script in order and in a notebook—or at least not clipped or stapled. Turn the pages without making any noise.

It would be helpful to be familiar with a few radio signals. An index finger pointing to a particular person means "you are on." An index finger that is turning quickly means "speed up." Both hands pulling away from each other means "slow down." A raised hand, palm up, means "talk louder." The opposite move means "talk softer." An index finger pulled across the neck means "cut" or "stop." A thumb and index finger forming an O means "okay."

Evaluating the Material

The radio play is as much a team effort as a play presented for live theatre. Perhaps it is even more challenging than live theatre because the finished product consists only of what the audience hears. Since there is no blocking or movement for the production team to focus on, they should concentrate on selecting the script, casting the play, preparing the play, rehearsing the play, and evaluating the play. Use the following evaluation questions for assessing your radio play.

Radio Play Critique
1. In choosing your play for a radio production, what criteria did you use? What gives the play literary merit?
2. What part did you have in selecting the play?
3. Did you have auditions, or were parts assigned? Which process is better for casting?
4. How cooperative was your group in the process of selecting, casting, preparing, rehearsing, and presenting the radio play?
5. What effective vocal techniques were used to develop your characters? Discuss the volume, rate, flexibility, clarity, expression, and energy in each voice.

6. How effective was the group in its timing and in picking up all cues?
7. How effective were the sound effects?
8. How effective was the music?
9. What directions were given to keep the play running smoothly?
10. How were the scripts used?
11. How effective were the radio signals from the director?
12. What was the length of the production? Was the radio play within the time limit?
13. What did you like about producing the radio play? Why?
14. What was the most difficult aspect of the production? Why?
15. What would you do differently in the next production?

1. **Presenting a Radio Play.** With the help of your teacher, select a radio play, or adapt another work, and present it.

2. **Radio Survey.** After presenting your radio play, prepare a survey sheet for your listeners. Ask your listeners to answer questions that will benefit your radio production staff in the next presentation.

3. **Coping with Life.** As a class, write an original radio play dealing with problems that young people face today. After the preparation and rehearsal of your radio play, present it over the school's public-address system. If the school does not have a public-address system, record the play and share the tape with other classes.

4. **Radio Commercials.** Listen to ten modern radio commercials. Which of the effective radio theatre techniques you learned were used in the commercials?

5. **Listening Skills.** Listen to several radio shows or plays from the 1930s. (Your public library should have a good selection.) Select an outstanding radio actor from each show or play and report on why you found that person outstanding.

Curtain Call!

CHAPTER 17 REVIEW

▪ ▪ SPOTLIGHT ON TERMS ▪ ▪

An important part of theatre is understanding the terminology, or vocabulary, used. Add the new terms and definitions to the vocabulary section of your theatre notebook or folder.

▪ ▪ FOCUS ON FACTS ▪ ▪

1. Why is readers theatre a suitable name for this interpretive skill?
2. List three sources for readers theatre scripts.
3. Give five helpful suggestions in creating a readers theatre script.
4. Discuss the three basic focuses used in readers theatre.
5. Why is the listener's imagination important in radio plays?
6. What is the focus in a radio play?
7. Why are oral interpretation skills necessary for radio theatre?
8. Which type of selection do you think is best for radio plays? Why?
9. Why must cast members be careful around the microphone during the play?
10. Discuss three radio signals your director may give you during a radio theatre production.

▪ ▪ REFLECTIONS ▪ ▪

Discuss the following questions with your class or answer them on paper as instructed by your teacher.

1. Readers theatre and similar styles of theatre have been used for many years. Where have you seen this type of theatre?
2. What is the advantage of using readers theatre instead of conventional theatre?
3. Radio programming and radio theatre were powerful influences during the golden years of radio, 1930–1960. Since people today are fascinated with the past, why is this type of theatre not as popular today?

4. Discuss three changes in today's technology that diminished radio theatre.
5. How has the decline of radio theatre affected people's imagination skills?

▪ ▪ THEATRE IN YOUR LIFE ▪ ▪

1. Compile a class list of favorite poems, short stories, novels, and plays to be considered as readers theatre material.
2. Choose excerpts from literary selections of your choice.
3. Write your own radio play and produce it for another class or to be broadcast over the public-address system at school or by your local radio station.

▪ ▪ ENCORE ▪ ▪

1. Select a novel, short story, play, or poem, and cut and adapt the piece for readers theatre. Working with your group or acting company, prepare the selection for a classroom performance.
2. Attend an academic contest that includes readers theatre as one of its events.
3. Attend a festival that includes readers theatre as an event.
4. As a class, write and rehearse your own radio play. (Cooperate in choosing a subject or theme for the play.) Secure permission from the local radio station to broadcast the radio play at the studio.

CHAPTER 18

Puppetry, Shadow Play, and Masks

Chapter Outline

Spotlight on Terms

- animation
- character mask
- flipping the lid
- full-body puppet
- hand puppet
- lip sync
- manipulation
- marionette
- mask
- mounting the show
- movable-mouth puppet
- neutral mask
- puppet
- rod puppet
- shadow play
- shadow puppet

When you were young, did you enjoy the antics of Big Bird, Cookie Monster, and the Count on the television series *Sesame Street*? Do you remember pretending that you were one of the four Ninja turtles? Did you check out all of the Muppet movies from the video store and watch them at least twice? Did you take a peek at Barney and his friends just to see what all the excitement was about? If you answered yes to any of these questions, then you have observed the pleasure and power of puppetry.

You may have even adopted a puppet when you were younger. Perhaps it was a commercially made Lamb Chop, Bert, or Ernie. Or was it a crocheted lion or felt monkey that your grandmother made especially for you? Possibly you made a puppet in elementary school. Did you use a pattern to create a paper plate puppet or a paper bag puppet? If you were really lucky, you had a creative teacher who provided materials and encouragement for you to design and make your very own creation, a puppet who looked like no other puppet on earth.

After creating the puppet, you were indeed fortunate if you brought your puppet to life, animating it in front of an audience of appreciative friends. Not all students have had that opportunity. Most often, when puppets are created in school, it is merely a craft project, with the puppets soon finding their way into the garbage can. In this chapter, you will learn that puppetry is more than a craft project. You will learn that puppetry is an art form. A skilled puppeteer can bring life to a small puppet, touching the hearts of all who wish to believe.

In this chapter, you will explore the techniques of puppetry, shadow play, and masks. These theatre styles will give you the opportunity to integrate art, dance, music, and literature into your projects.

What you may think of as a modern idea, created for television or the movies, really dates back thousands of years. Early recorded evidence points to the use of masks and puppets in religion, education,

Oscar the Grouch and Zoe are just two of the many popular puppets created by Jim Henson for *Sesame Street*. How many more of the *Sesame Street* puppets can you name?

and entertainment long before people experienced theatre as we know it today. The people behind the puppets, shadows and masks are special kinds of actors who bring to life the characters depicted by their puppets and masks. If historians are correct, these "puppet actors" were in existence long before "human actors" took to the stage themselves.

As you study puppetry, shadow play, and masks you will be exposed to the art, drama, history, and literature of different cultures. These opportunities will give you a new understanding of people throughout the world.

Making a Puppet

LESSON OBJECTIVES

◆ Recognize and identify the five basic puppet types.
◆ Use imagination to design and make an original puppet.
◆ Use other art forms to enhance theatre.

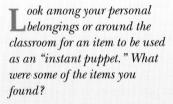

Look among your personal belongings or around the classroom for an item to be used as an "instant puppet." What were some of the items you found?

puppet
almost anything brought to life by a human in front of an audience.

animation
bringing something to life through movement and action.

manipulation
the way a puppeteer moves or works a puppet.

Even though the word *puppet* comes from the Latin *pupa*, meaning "doll," a puppet is not a doll, nor is it limited to being doll-like. A **puppet** can be almost anything brought to life by a human in front of an audience. The puppeteer communicates with the audience through the puppet. Bringing a puppet to life is a form of **animation** .

Years ago, in many different cultures, puppets were used in religious rituals. In our own culture, the popularity of puppets has increased during the twentieth century. It seems that many people still find pleasure relating to colorful puppets with warm, friendly personalities. Today, puppets are being used to teach religion on television and in churches and synagogues. We also see puppets used in advertising, art, celebrations, crime prevention programs, education, entertainment, and therapy.

Types of Puppets

The way a puppeteer works or moves a puppet is called **manipulation** . Puppets are categorized by the way they are manipulated, rather than by the fabric from which they are made. A sock puppet with a hinged mouth, for example, is considered a hand puppet with a movable mouth. A puppet that is made from a cereal box, empty paper towel tubes, and paper cups and is manipulated by strings is considered a marionette.

Five major types of puppets are used in performances today: rod puppets, shadow puppets, hand puppets, marionettes, and full-body puppets. From these five basic puppet types come other variations or combinations, such as hand-and-rod puppets, nonpuppet or object puppets, finger puppets, and even puppets for the feet.

rod puppet

a puppet constructed without shoulders, arms, or legs and manipulated by one or more rods.

shadow puppet

a flat, two-dimensional puppet designed to cast a shadow or form a silhouette on a white screen.

hand puppet

a puppet that fits over the puppeteer's hand, much like a mitten, and is manipulated by the puppeteer's fingers inside the puppet's head and hands.

movable-mouth puppet

a hand puppet with a movable mouth.

marionette

a puppet manipulated by strings connecting a control rod or paddle to the moving body parts.

full-body puppet

a puppet worn over the puppeteer's head and body like a costume.

The rod puppet is one of the oldest and simplest of puppet types. The **rod puppet** is a puppet manipulated by one or more rods. In its most basic form, it is constructed without shoulders, arms, or legs. But a rod puppet can become more complicated by adding joints and body parts such as arms, legs, and shoulders. Traditionally, the puppeteer manipulates the rod puppet from below the stage, although rod puppets can be designed to be controlled from above the stage. The puppeteer indicates that the rod puppet is talking by moving the entire puppet.

A **shadow puppet** is a flat, two-dimensional figure controlled by a wire or rod against a screen. Projecting light from behind the puppet projects the shadow onto a white cloth screen stretched and stapled to a wooden frame. The puppeteer moves the puppet to bring it to life. The earliest shadow puppets were made out of thin animal hides. Today's shadow puppets can be made of cardboard or translucent acetate. (Later in this chapter, we will discuss the shadow technique known as shadow play.)

A traditional **hand puppet**, also called a glove puppet, fits over the puppeteer's hand much like a mitten or glove. The puppeteer manipulates the puppet by placing the second and third fingers into the puppet's head and using the fourth and fifth fingers along with the thumb as the puppet's hands. Since the hand puppet does not have a movable mouth, the puppeteer moves the entire puppet to indicate talking.

A variation of the standard hand puppet is the **movable-mouth puppet**. Although this puppet fits over the puppeteer's hand, it is constructed with a hinged jaw and movable mouth. The puppet's head is manipulated by the puppeteer's four fingers, while the thumb is used to control the puppet's lower jaw. The puppet's mouth opens and closes as the puppeteer's thumb moves up and down.

Puppets controlled and manipulated by strings are called **marionettes**. Built with jointed parts, the marionette moves much like a human or animal. The puppet's moving parts are connected by strings to a control rod or paddle. The puppeteer stands above the puppet stage and manipulates the puppet, moving it along a play board or stage floor.

A **full-body puppet** is a puppet worn over the puppeteer's head and body much like a costume. Most full-body puppets are animated by one puppeteer inside the puppet. Extremely large full-body puppets may be controlled by more than one puppeteer. A few full-body puppets are so large that they are manipulated by remote control.

Puppet Construction

Are you ready to make a puppet? You will need an assortment of materials, but you don't have to spend a lot of money. In fact, making puppets is a fun way to recycle items that would otherwise be thrown away. Make a sweep of your house, collecting some of the materials listed on the materials chart (see Figure 18–1 on page 350). Worthless junk will suddenly become valuable to you as a puppet maker. Items that you do not use can be shared or traded with other puppet makers in your class. Along with puppet materials, you will need to collect basic construction tools and supplies before you begin.

How many of the different types of puppets that you just read about can you identify in these pictures? From top to bottom in the left-hand column: rod, hand, movable mouth, and marionettes; to the right: shadow and full-body puppets.

Figure 18–1

■■■■■■■■■■■■■■■■■■■■

Puppet-Making Tools and Materials.

BASIC CONSTRUCTION TOOLS

scissors
stapler, staples
glue gun, glue sticks
hole punch
colored markers
rulers
tape measure
yardstick
needle
rubber bands
string
several types of tape
   (clear plastic, colored duct, masking)
wire cutters (optional)
sewing machine (optional)
latex paint, tempera paint, acrylic paint
sponge or bristle paintbrushes
coffee cans

Plastic:

colored transparent report covers
margarine tubs
film containers
colored Easter eggs
used ping pong balls
drinking straws
bubble wrap
packing squiggles

Accessory Materials:

sequins
buttons
feathers
fake fur
cotton balls
yarn
rug scraps
costume jewelry
ribbons
lace
fringe
binding
cording
braid
rope
tassels
doll accessories

OTHER MATERIALS

Paper:

construction paper
heavy craft paper
colored tissue paper
decorated wrapping paper
wallpaper samples
foil paper scraps
paper doilies
decorative dots, stars, and gummed reinforcements

Cardboard:

lightweight cardboard and tag board
fillers from shirt and hosiery packages
cereal boxes
various sizes of gift boxes
cardboard tubes
round cartons from speciality ice cream shops

Miscellaneous:

wire hangers
dowel rods
Styrofoam
foam scraps
craft sticks
pipe cleaners
brad-type fasteners
clothespins

Puppets can be as simple or as complicated as the puppet builder wants to make them. Rod puppets, shadow puppets, hand puppets, and movable-mouth puppets are easier to construct than marionettes and full-body puppets. Before making your puppet, consider how the puppet will be manipulated. A good rule to remember is that the closer the puppet is to the puppeteer's body, the easier it is to work and control.

Rather than copying a pattern, let your imagination run free as you design your puppet. Your puppet's greatest asset is the way it looks. Eyes, mouth, nose, ears, and even hair help define and project the

Name: *Lolly Popple*

Voice quality: *Light and sweet*

Personality traits: *Happy, always friendly*

Hometown: *Sweetville, TX*

Job or occupation: *Candymaker*

Talent: *Juggling*

Habits or mannerisms: *Always carries a lollipop*

Clothing taste: *Bright, bold; likes to mix stripes and plaids*

Favorite saying: *"A spoonful of sugar helps everything."*

Favorite food: *Peanut butter*

Figure 18–2

Puppet Profile.

puppet's character. Close your eyes and picture the way you want your puppet to look.

The eyes of the puppet should be large in proportion to the head. Make your puppet's eyes from buttons, rubber balls, jiggly eyes, egg carton cups, pom-pom balls, or wooden beads. Add a little sparkle to the eyes to reflect light by using a small sequin or small white button on top of dark eyes. Placement of the eyes on the face helps to indicate the puppet's focus. Experiment with eye placement before you permanently glue or sew the eyes to the face. Eyebrows and eyelashes help give your puppet facial expression. Try several different combinations to find just the right ones to suit your puppet's personality.

Adding the proper nose can give your puppet character. Even the size and placement of the nose create personality. A puppet with an upturned nose could have a snobbish personality. A puppet with a huge red ball nose might always have the sniffles. A tiny shy mouse could have one small pink bead for a nose.

The mouth of a movable-mouth hand puppet must be glued or sewed as part of the basic construction. When making a puppet without a movable mouth, a permanent mouth can be painted on the puppet's face or cut from felt and glued in place.

Although many puppets do not have ears, the addition of ears can do much to exaggerate a puppet's personality. Ears can be small and understated or large and overdone. A good-listener puppet could be constructed with short perky ears. A hard-of-hearing puppet could be constructed with long floppy ears.

Hair is one of the most important features on any puppet. Instead of trying to create the look of real hair, use unusual materials to exaggerate your puppet's look. Try rug yarn, raffia, pipe cleaners, fake fur, mop heads, feathers, metal scrub pads, gift wrap ribbon, or paper strips for dramatic results.

Hair is one of the easiest ways to emphasize a puppet's character. Style, color, and even hair texture can tell the audience a great deal about the puppet. A female puppet having a "bad hair day" would be believable if her flyaway hair were made of bright orange yarn. Professor Lucas, a mad scientist, would be perfect sporting a tuft of wild wiry hair made from a metal scrub pad.

Every puppet has its own style of dress, just as you do. Dress your puppet to reflect its personal style. Don't forget to add personality with accessories, such as a hat or cap, a gaudy piece of jewelry, weird eyeglasses, a feather boa, or a bow tie. One of these accessories might be just the finishing touch your puppet needs.

Creating an interesting, believable puppet takes time, thought, and lots of work. Take pride in your original creations; each contains a special part of you.

As you just learned, a puppet's character is determined partly by the way it looks. The way it talks and acts also reveals its personality. Once you have made your puppet, give it a name, a voice, and a distinct personality. Completing a puppet profile for each puppet you create will help build your puppet's background and establish its personality (see Figure 18–2). If you need additional help with characterization, refer to Chapter 7. Puppet personalities can be developed the same way character roles are created.

ACTION

1. **Show and Share Puppet Day.** Bring to class one of your personal puppets for a Show and Share Puppet Day. Use your puppet in some of the improvisation activities from Chapter 6.

2. **Object Puppets.** Bring to class a household object you might manipulate as one of the basic puppet types. Give a name, personality, and voice to something as simple as a feather duster, dish mop, folding fan, or kitchen tongs. Create a voice that suits your puppet's personality. Introduce your puppet to the class. Invite the class to ask the puppet questions.

3. **Finger Puppets.** Using a water-based marker, draw faces on your index fingers. By wiggling your fingers, you can create simple puppets. Give each puppet a name, a voice, and a personality. Have the puppets talk to each other. Have them talk with other puppets in your acting company or group.

4. **Design a Puppet.** On unlined white paper, design and color an original puppet from each of the five basic types. Explain to your acting company or to the class how you would transform each design into a puppet.

5. **Search for Supplies.** Collect and bring to class materials to make an original puppet. Use one of the five basic puppet types or a combination of types.

Bringing a Puppet to Life

LESSON OBJECTIVE

◆ Explore puppet manipulations.
◆ Animate a puppet character.
◆ Experiment with puppet voices.

Warm Up

Bring to life your pencil or your pen by moving it and talking as a puppet might.

Puppets are animated (brought to life) when puppeteers give them movements and actions. A simple turn of the body or tilt of the head gives a puppet lifelike qualities. Puppets can use many of the same gestures and movements used by human actors. They can also perform actions that human actors are incapable of doing. Puppets can fly, twist into unusual shapes, or sail into the audience.

Manipulation

Each type of puppet is manipulated in a different way. Here you will learn about basic puppet manipulation for hand puppets. As you

Shari Lewis's well-known puppet Lamb Chop has been entertaining youngsters for many, many years. Recently, a whole new generation of children has been discovering the antics of Lamb Chop on PBS.

lip sync

synchronizing movement of the puppet's mouth with the spoken words.

flipping the lid

improperly manipulating a movable-mouth hand puppet, causing flapping of the upper jaw or head.

A puppet is an inanimate figure that is made to move by human effort before an audience.

Bil Baird

become more interested in puppetry, consult additional books in your school or public library for information on ways to manipulate other types of puppets.

As you know, a hand puppet is worn over the puppeteer's hand, much like a glove. The puppeteer inserts from one to three fingers into the puppet's head and uses the remaining fingers and thumb to serve as the puppet's hands. The puppeteer is able to achieve good hand puppet posture by holding the puppet straight and tall, directly in front of his or her body.

When a hand puppet talks, the entire puppet body should move. You can make your puppet's dialogue even more meaningful by using simple gestures on important words such as verbs and nouns. The movements and gestures of the "talking" puppet help focus the attention of the "listening" puppets and the audience on the talking puppet. To demonstrate that they are "listening," other puppets onstage "freeze," paying attention to the puppet that is speaking.

You can manipulate a movable-mouth puppet by using your fingers to move the top part of the puppet's head and your thumb to move the puppet's lower jaw. Some students have found that they gain upper-hand strength by inserting bent fingers into the upper head. They call this using "knuckle action."

To achieve the best posture for manipulating a movable-mouth puppet, you need to stand or kneel. The arm upon which you place the puppet should be outstretched above your head. Then lock your elbow and slightly drop your wrist, allowing the puppet's eyes to make contact with the audience.

Moving only your thumb, you can make the puppet talk. Try to match the puppet's mouth movements with the words being spoken. This action is called synchronization or **lip sync**. Correct lip sync requires practice and patience. The puppet's mouth should open as it begins talking and close when it is finished. Since a puppet's mouth cannot move rapidly enough to open and close on every word in a sentence, try emphasizing the most important words. Use one thumb movement for one-syllable words, two thumb movements for two-syllable words, and three thumb movements for three-syllable words. Faster speech may necessitate fewer thumb movements.

For ease in manipulation, lightly thrust the puppet forward as the thumb is lowered. By moving only the thumb, you avoid flapping the puppet's upper head. This useless flapping is called **flipping the lid**.

Try not to lean on your elbows or shoulders on the puppet stage or playboard. When a puppeteer leans, the puppet looks tired and lazy. A puppet's physical height should be determined on entrance and maintained throughout the show. Growing or shrinking puppets distract from the performance unless such occurrences are part of the show's action.

Successful entrances and exits are important in a puppet show. A puppet should enter the acting area as if walking up a short flight of stairs. Proper exits include turning the puppet around backward and descending the steps. Special entrances and exits might include a puppet popping up, flying off, or rolling off the stage. These special movements should be included as part of a well-planned script rather than improper puppet manipulation.

Contemporary Theatre:
A World and a Theatre of Change

The world of the 1960s was a world of great change. It is only natural that theatre would reflect this demand for change. Increasingly, theatre was being created and staged as a way to urge political and social reform. Theatre after the middle 1960s was characterized by a number of theatre companies who utilized nontraditional theatre practices.

One of the most well-known of these politically unified groups was the Living Theatre, founded by Judith Malina. Although the original group formed in the 1940s, the group continued to produce plays far into the turbulent '60s. Their work was characterized by the actors not pretending to be characters so much as trying to represent forces in society. They often purposely made their characters stereotypes to dramatize the ways in which the forces of society influenced each·other. Although the Living Theatre

Hair was a radical and influential change from previous Broadway productions. Do you recognize the actor from this original 1968 production who went on to become a famous movie actor? (Diane Keaton, center)

began its production history using scripted plays, their later works were all improvised performances which were loosely practiced and developed around an outline of a story or "scenario." This meant that each performance was truly unique. In most of their later productions, the group performed in everyday clothes. Scenery was sparse, reduced to only a few essential props and set furnishings. Although their popularity declined rapidly as the 1970s passed, they were a very important group in theatre history. They influenced many other groups, such as the Open Theatre group, which utilized improvisation, minimal theatrical elements, and other alternative approaches to theatre.

A common thread running through most of these alternative theatre practices was the understanding that theatre was unique from film and television by virtue of its live, immediate nature. The alternative groups viewed theatre as a communal (shared, group) experience. Many of these artists, such as the Polish director Jerzy Grotowsky, believed that theatre could only survive the electronic, computer age by emphasizing what makes theatre different—direct interaction between actor and audience. Grotowsky and his followers saw theatre as a ritual in which all the people present—actors and audience members alike—are participants. These general beliefs led to the audience participation productions that occurred in post-1960 theatre. This approach has been labeled *environmental* theatre because there is no separation of audience and performer, no fixed seating, little constructed scenery, and a dependence upon improvisation rather than a script.

Today, the theatre is a place of great diversity, involving all of the styles and movements that have come before. Artists today have at their disposal a rich selection of theatrical tools, which they can endlessly recombine to tell their stories.

Some theatre makes us laugh or entertains us with its songs and dances. Other plays move us to feel deep emotions and empathize with characters in situations we understand and identify with. Still other productions motivate us to think hard and ask political and social questions. We can be sure that theatre will continue to embrace and reflect those changes. ■

Additional movements and exercises for hand puppets can be found in *Making Puppets Come Alive*, by Larry Engler and Carol Fijan. This book is an outstanding source for beginning puppeteers.

Regardless of puppet type, the way to discover exactly what your puppet can do is to experiment in front of a mirror. Working in front of a mirror, try several of the puppet movement exercises at the end of this lesson.

Vocalization

One of your puppet's most important features is the way it talks, or its voice. The puppet's voice helps define and communicate the puppet's character and personality. Work at finding the perfect voice for your puppet. Give your puppet a voice of its own—a voice different from yours.

One of the best ways to find a puppet voice is to experiment. Experimenting with voices may seem silly at first, but it is the only way to find just the right tone and quality.

A puppeteer often matches the puppet's voice with its character. For example, a big, gruff goat puppet would need a big, gruff voice. A small, sweet bug puppet would need a small, sweet voice. It is also possible to contrast a puppet's appearance with an unexpected voice. A large lion puppet who is afraid to roar could have a teeny, tiny voice. Contrasting voice and character is another way to reveal the puppet's personality to your audience.

Be sure to choose a puppet voice that you can maintain for the entire show. If you begin puppet dialogue with one voice, you should keep that voice throughout the show. As in formal theatre, switching voices "breaks character" and distracts from the performance.

In your search for the perfect puppet voice, try several vocal exercises. The same vocal exercises used by stage actors are also helpful to the puppet actors.

Movement Exercises

1. **Profile Exercises.** With the puppet in a profile position, have the puppet
   a. look up and down
   b. move as a young, excited child; as a teenager in a hurry; as a sad older person
   c. walk slowly, with head down
   d. skip, hop, run, and jump

2. **Full Front Exercises.** With the puppet facing full front, have the puppet
   a. shift weight from side to side
   b. scratch its head
   c. wipe away a tear
   d. cross its arms
   e. pick up an object
   f. rub its hands together in concern
   g. clap its hands joyfully
   h. rub its head to indicate a headache
   i. pat its chest to indicate a heart attack
   j. pat its chest to indicate "in love"
   k. wave hello or good-bye
   l. nod its head yes
   m. shake its head no
   n. stroke its hair
   o. rub its tummy

3. **Add a Habit.** With the puppet facing full front, try adding a mannerism or habit.
   a. a twitch
   b. a wiggle
   c. a shy head turn
   d. a confident strut

4. **Partner Work.** Working with another puppeteer, have two hand puppets
   a. shake hands
   b. hug
   c. touch shoulders
   d. pat heads
   e. hold hands
   f. stand arm in arm
   g. take turns gesturing "come here"
   h. take turns gesturing "go away"

5. **Stage Movement.** On a puppet stage have your puppet
   a. run
   b. bow
   c. glide
   d. bend
   e. jump
   f. walk
   g. skip
   h. shrug
   i. strut
   j. march
   k. twirl
   l. fly
   m. sit
   n. pace

Vocal Exercises

1. **Vocal Variety.** Exercise your puppet's vocal range by having it count aloud from 1 to 10 in the following ways:

high	whispering
deep	babyish
squeaky	intellectually
creaky	nasal
slow	sweetly
fast	deliberate
angrily	snarling
quavering	with an accent

2. **Sing Along.** In a voice other than your own, have the puppet sing a short familiar song. Puppets always enjoy singing "Happy Birthday," "Jingle Bells," and "The Alphabet Song."

3. **Try This.** Have your puppet try different voices as it recites the alphabet or a nursery rhyme.

4. **Puppet Improv.** Using puppets, try several of your favorite improvisation activities from Chapter 6. Experiment with different puppet voices as you act out different situations.

Writing a Puppet Show

LESSON OBJECTIVE

◆ Write a puppet script using original dialogue.

Warm Up

Working with your acting company or class, make a list of ideas for a puppet show.

Unless you are improvising your puppet show, you will need a script. Writing a puppet script is much like writing a play—you begin by brainstorming plot ideas. Scriptwriters often collaborate on ideas, so try working with your acting company or class to compile a list of ideas.

Great play ideas can come from the simple story lines found in legends, folktales, or fairy tales. Think about personal experiences and school events. What about retelling a historical event, a current event, or a political situation? You can often find a story in practical jokes and funny songs. Or consider writing a play based on a television sitcom, game show, or commercial.

Once your group has compiled a list of possibilities, select one idea from which to develop a script. The most effective shows have simple plots filled with interesting puppet action.

As you learned in Chapter 8, the play's basic structure should have three parts: a beginning, a middle, and an ending. Keep in mind that the beginning of the play captures the audience's attention, sets up the scene, introduces the characters, and establishes the conflict. The middle part of the play, with its rising and falling action, focuses on

how the characters struggle with their problem or conflict. This is the heart of the play, and it determines the length of the show. In the ending, the characters resolve their conflicts, solve their problems, or give up—and the show concludes. Be sure to include all five Ws—who, what, when, where, and why—in your play's three-part outline.

Once the outline is clearly defined, try improvising what you have planned for the puppets. Many puppeteers first act out the situation

It is said that Milton saw a puppet show of Adam and Eve and was inspired to write Paradise Lost. *Haydn composed music for puppet operettas.*

Susan French

A Sample Puppet Show Script

UNDERCOVER BUG
written and performed by
GiGi Bollinger and Jennifer Franklin

Characters:
Daffy—a flower hand puppet
Daisy—a flower hand puppet
Di Dot—a caterpillar rod puppet
Charles III—a caterpillar rod puppet
Charles III—a butterfly rod puppet
The play takes place in a lovely flower garden. Two hand puppet flowers, Daffy and Daisy, stretch and yawn as the scene opens.

Daffy: Good morning Daisy! (*bows*)
Daisy: Good morning Daffy! (*curtsies*)
Daffy: Oh! What a beautiful day! (*nods head*)
Daisy: Yes, Yes, Mr. Sunshine sure makes us grow tall and gorgeous! (*Flowers smile, stretch, and grow taller*)
Daffy: (*The two caterpillars, rod puppets, enter the scene. Di moves quickly but Charles is very slow*) Speaking of gorgeous, here comes Lady Di Dot, OH, MY! and her ugly Prince Charles Caterpillar the Third. (*leans over and whispers to Daisy*)
Daisy: Now, Now, Daffy, you mustn't judge a bug by his cover. (*shakes head to indicate disagreement*)
Daffy: Daisy, Daisy, that sounds just like you—"Miss Goody Two Blooms!" (*shrugs shoulders in disgust*)
Daisy: (*Daisy leans over to listen.*) Listen! The two love bugs are talking.
Charles: Di darling, please walk a little slower. My legs are so tired today. (*dragging along, stops walking*)
Di Dot: Now Charles, you certainly have been acting strange lately. Maybe I should kiss you and make you feel better. (*Di Dot stops moving, leans over and plants a big kiss on Charles*) SMACK!!!
Daffy: Oh my goodness, Daisy. Look at poor Charles, I think he fainted! (*Charles falls rolling off upstage. Charles, butterfly rod puppet, emerges wings first, followed by the entire body*)
Daisy: Look Daffy, look! He's so handsome! Just look at those wings! (*gestures toward Charles*)
Daffy: OH, MY! (*hands on either side of face*)
Daisy: I told you Daffy . . . (*points finger to Daffy*)
Daffy: I know, I know. (*shakes head to indicate "yes"*)
Together: You can't judge a bug by its cover! (*puppets link hands*)
(*Daffy and Daisy turn and walk offstage holding hands. Di Dot and Charles Butterfly freeze in a romantic pose; turn and walk offstage*)

and then write the script. When writing a puppet script, a good rule to remember is that dialogue should be short and filled with lots of puppet action. Successful puppet shows must move along without long, boring speeches. In puppetry, actions speak louder than words.

Audiences enjoy puppet shows filled with humor. The plot and dialogue can both be humorous. Humor can also be achieved through repetition. The audience finds it funny when puppets keep repeating certain words, actions, or reactions.

If you are planning to perform your play, remember that changing scenes usually requires changing sets. It is a good idea for beginning puppeteers to restrict their plays to just one setting. The size of the puppet stage is another important point to consider when planning a puppet script. The number of characters in your puppet play should depend on the size of the stage, the number of puppeteers in the group, and the space behind and below the puppet stage. You can avoid a backstage traffic jam if you remember to limit the number of puppets in the play.

Avoid confusion by including stage directions and puppet actions in the written script. In the example script on page 358, stage directions and puppet actions are printed in italics and included in parentheses.

> *There is no subject that puppetry can't handle but we must always make the strongest use of puppets.*
>
> Bil Baird

ACTION

1. **A One Puppet Show.** Write and memorize a 1-minute monologue for your puppet to share with your classmates. Follow your teacher's directions for sharing the project.

2. **A Comedy Duet.** Working with a partner, write ten lines of comedy dialogue for your puppets. Write the dialogue in script form. Include stage directions in parentheses. Perform the dialogue from the puppet stage.

3. **Write a Script.** Working with the other members of your group or acting company, write a 3- to 5-minute puppet script. Develop the plot from an original idea or from a familiar story line.

Producing a Puppet Show

LESSON OBJECTIVES

◆ Work with a group to produce a puppet show.
◆ Use technical elements to enhance a puppet production.

The script is written and the puppets are made. Now it is time to mount the show. **Mounting the show** means providing accessories and equipment, such as a stage, scenery, lighting, props, sound effects, and music. All of these extras add to a theatrical production. The amount

mounting the show

adding the finishing touches—such as scenery, props, and costumes—to a theatrical production.

of time and work needed to mount the show depends on the complexity of the show. Shows needing several sets and numerous props will take much longer to prepare. Check with your teacher to be sure you have enough class time to produce a complicated show.

The Stage

There are lots of different ways you can share your puppet with an audience. Some puppeteers dress in black and perform onstage in full view of the audience. Other puppeteers wear regular clothes and perform the same way; once the puppets begin to move and talk, the audience doesn't notice the puppeteers. Most puppeteers, however, prefer to work from behind a puppet stage. Unless you have a puppet stage already made, you will need to make a stage for your puppet show.

You can easily make a temporary stage from a variety of materials—a low bookcase, an overturned table, or the back of an upright piano. Cover the furniture with an old bedsheet or a big piece of black felt. Covering the furniture ensures that a makeshift appearance will not detract from the puppets.

A large appliance packing box can also be converted into a stage for a small cast of puppets. Cut an acting window out of the front side of the box and a puppeteer stage door out of the back side. You can then cover the outside of the box with bright craft paper or paint it with water-based paint. Then decorate the outside to suit the theme of the puppet show.

A more permanent puppet stage can be built from hinged plywood panels. One advantage of a plywood stage is that it is sturdy. One disad-

These hand puppets are both performing and being displayed in and around this colorful stage.

vantage, however, is that it is very heavy. A more lightweight stage can be constructed from PVC plumbing pipe and fabric sewn into curtains.

A practical traveling puppet stage can be made by attaching a plywood stage floor to the top of a collapsible ironing board. Once the ironing board is adjusted to the puppeteer's working level, drape a large rectangle of black felt over the entire surface and presto!—instant stage!

Scenery

Color or paint scenery on heavy paper to hang behind the puppets as a background for the action. A longer-lasting backdrop can be designed and painted on fabric and hung on a rod across the backstage area. Fabric backgrounds can be easily folded for storage and reused for numerous shows.

Not all puppet shows require full backgrounds. You can cut simple set pieces from construction paper and pin or tape them to the back curtain of the puppet stage.

Props

Using props during a performance provides stage business and action for the puppets. Props can be used very effectively but should not dominate the show. Puppet action should always be more important than the use of props.

Construct simple props from paper, posterboard, or cardboard. Add a wire rod, wooden ruler, or dowel stick to the props and manipulate them as rod puppets.

Toy stores offer many inexpensive items to use as props. A toy telephone, musical instrument, doctor's stethoscope, or foam football

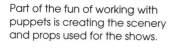

Part of the fun of working with puppets is creating the scenery and props used for the shows.

makes a wonderful puppet prop. Always exaggerate the size of puppet props. Larger-sized props are easier to handle and more easily seen by the audience, and they add a humorous touch to the show. Try combining real props and cardboard props for variety.

If a puppeteer's hand is needed to help the puppet handle props, the hand should be gloved. Brown gardening gloves are a good choice for this situation. They are inexpensive and come in several sizes.

Technical Elements

Technical elements—lights, music or sound, and special effects—all add spectacle to a puppet show. These elements should be planned during the scriptwriting process and should be tried early in the rehearsal process. Often, an idea seems feasible in your imagination, when in reality it is impossible. Never wait until show time to try technical elements for the first time.

Simple show lighting can be obtained using clip-on desk lights, low-cost spotlights, or photographer's floodlights. For all types of puppet shows, other than shadow shows, these are attached to the front of the stage. Shadow shows require lighting from behind the puppet screen. Light from a 35 mm slide projector or a filmstrip projector can also be used to provide a limited amount of stage lighting.

Used at the beginning of a show, music helps set the mood and capture the audience's attention. Musical selections should be simple and appropriate for the show. Show music can be "live" or recorded. Assign one puppeteer to be in charge of the music.

It is fun to manually produce sound effects for a puppet show. As a class, collect a box of noisemakers for the puppet productions. Include inexpensive noisemakers and toy musical instruments, as well as cans and boxes filled with pebbles, dry beans, or pasta.

Sound effects for a puppet show can also be recorded. Use a cassette tape recorder to capture the sound of a squeaky hinge, the closing of a car door, a school bell, crowd noises, or laughter. Professionally recorded sound effect tapes are also available in most music stores or theatrical supply catalogs.

Special effects such as wind, smoke, or thunder should be planned with the safety of the puppeteers in mind. A small electric fan can be used as wind; short puffs from a baby powder box can be used to simulate smoke; and a sheet of tin will rumble like thunder. Be sure to talk over your ideas with your teacher.

Rehearsal

As a puppet show cast member, it is your responsibility to attend all rehearsals. Rehearsals require dedication and concentration, and you will need to work hard during the entire rehearsal. Rehearsals are more than just "playing with puppets."

A puppet show's success or failure depends on the puppeteer's skill in manipulating the puppets. This particular skill can only come from frequent rehearsals. Just because puppets are small actors does not mean that they can rehearse less than human actors.

■ ■ ■ ■ ■ ■ ■ ■ ■ ■ ■ ■ ■ ■
Rehearsals play a critical role in
the overall success of a show. They
require hard work and
commitment by everyone.

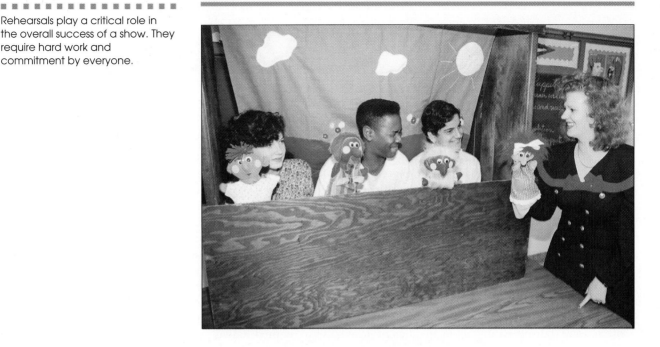

Plan to spend one full class period of rehearsal time for each minute of show time. Once the script for a 5-minute show is memorized, the cast should rehearse at least five full class periods. Extra rehearsal time will be needed to add technical elements, to set up and strike the set, and to store the puppets. Puppeteers kneeling for long rehearsals will want to use foam cushions or wear knee pads for comfort.

Some puppeteers find that rehearsing in front of a large mirror helps them see how to work out basic moves. Videotaping rehearsals after the show is blocked is another helpful rehearsal technique. Viewing the tapes early in the rehearsal process allows you to make necessary changes.

Rather than produce a show "live," it is possible to record the script ahead of time. An audiocassette or reel-to-reel tape recorder may be used in a recording studio or other quiet place to record all puppet dialogue, sound effects, and music. The tape is then played during the performances while the puppeteers lip-sync.

Unfortunately, even in a well-rehearsed show, a cue may be missed or a puppet may fall apart. At this point, the puppeteers must improvise new dialogue or movement and cover the mistake by incorporating it into the show.

The Performance

As you already know, most puppet shows are presented "live," with puppet actors onstage and human actors backstage. A live production is filled with energy and excitement. When it is show time, puppeteers should move backstage as quietly as possible. Always keep a puppet first aid kit backstage for last-minute emergencies. Your first aid kit should include a glue gun, scissors, tape, safety pins, extra puppet eyes, a stapler, and staples.

Masks and Puppetry

Puppetry began thousands of years ago—so long ago, in fact, that historians cannot agree on the exact beginning. We can imagine that centuries ago the religious leader (shaman) created shadow stories using the cave walls as a stage. During dances around the campfire, jaws of animal skulls might have been made to move as part of primitive chants.

We do know that some form of puppetry exists in almost every culture. In most cultures, puppetry is found in the religious rituals or celebrations. Early puppets were used by male adults, not females, and often were buried with people in ancient tombs. The various styles of puppets have mixed together as civilizations, cultures, and religions have merged and migrated. In many lands, the puppeteers were, and many still are, ranked as very important people in society.

The earliest written documentation of puppetry can be traced to India. The *Mahabharata,* an ancient Hindu epic poem, composed about 200 B.C., refers to string-controlled puppets or marionettes. In Indonesia, the rod puppet, or *wayang golek,* was used to tell the story the *Ramayana* as well as to tell the *Mahabharata.*

Authorities tell us that in India, it is possible the puppeteer preceded the actor on stage since religious beliefs of the times did not allow impersonations by humans. Ancient Indians believed that if you pretended to be someone else, or if you acted out the role of another human, you were foreshadowing your own death.

In ancient Greek literature references are made to marionettes by several writers. A Greek writer, Xenophon, tells of the visit of a traveling Greek puppeteer to the home of an outstanding Greek leader named Kallias. Xenophon mentions that one of the guests, who was not interested and would not pay attention, was the Greek philosopher Socrates.

In the fourth century B.C., Aristotle compared man's control of marionettes to the controller of the universe. Other noteworthy Grecian writers, Apuleius, Galen, Plato, and Horace, each compared marionettes to men, and men to marionettes. The "string puller," Potheinos, performing in the Greek theatre of Dionysus, was the first puppeteer referred to by name. Puppetry and other theatrical entertainment were well established in Rome by 400 B.C.

As the Roman Empire began to decay, so did the quality of theatre. Christianity, which at that time opposed the theatre, began to spread rapidly, and by the fifth century the actors were attacked by church councils and forced to wander into the countryside with their shows. Many ventured into other parts of Europe. It was these strolling players who kept theatre, including puppetry, alive during the period called the *Dark Ages.*

African Mask Puppets

Puppetry in Africa is art set in motion. Through the use of music and dance, masked performers become human puppets. The colorful, animated performances are part of life for the entire community. Entertainment, religion, education, and celebrations are all enhanced through this living art form.

In West Africa, in the Segu region of Mali, improvised puppet plays are performed by the young men of the Bamana and Bozo tribes twice a year, during the planting and the harvest seasons. The puppeteers wear large character puppets that cover

These large, colorful wooden puppets are *Bunraku* puppets, which originated in sixteenth century Japan when a puppeteer and a musician combined puppets, narration, and music. It can take up to three puppeteers (seen in black) to manipulate just one Bunraku puppet.

their bodies completely. These large wood and cloth puppets form a moving stage from which smaller rod puppets are manipulated. Young female members of these tribes assume the less important roles, performing as musicians and dancers.

Puppetry in Africa is not performed just for the sake of entertainment. It also offers a way for tribal members to share, without fear of criticism, controversial ideas and opinions that are usually forbidden by individual members of the society.

Masks and Puppetry in America

There were puppeteers in America long before European settlers came. The first puppeteers were the Native Americans. The string puppets used by the Northwest Coast Indians and the Hopi Indians of the American Southwest developed from masks. These puppet styles were used long before puppetry from other countries would migrate to the American shores.

The Spanish explorer, Hernando Cortez, (1485–1547) was accompanied on his voyages by a puppeteer. This puppeteer may well have been the first known puppeteer to arrive on this continent when Cortez conquered Mexico.

In 1738, an English-style marionette show, *The Adventure of Harlequin and Scaramouche,* was performed in New York by a puppeteer named Holt. During the eighteenth and nineteenth centuries, immigrant puppeteers brought their European and Oriental puppetry skills with them to the New World. Soon the exciting Punch and Judy show, so popular in England, was seen on American street corners. Punch, the forerunner of today's circus clown, aimed his humor at the political problems of the day. Speaking as a puppet, Punch was able to voice opinions that most people were afraid to express in public.

An early American puppeteer, Walter Deaves, gained international attention. One of his tours around the world lasted for seven years. Deaves is

Masks are an important part of this Cinco de Mayo celebration in Austin, Texas.

also credited with creating the complicated puppet theatres that fit upon the live theatre stage. His vaudeville puppet shows of the late 1880s were among the favorite entertainments. But interest in puppetry waned, and puppetry was almost a lost art by the early 1900s.

In 1915 Tony Sarg, a talented illustrator of books, moved from London, England, to New York City. He began to create puppets to entertain his friends. It was Tony Sarg's creativity and talent that strongly influenced the art of puppetry in the United States in the early twentieth century. By 1933 Tony Sarg's famous puppets were seen by more than three million people at the Chicago World's Fair.

As early as 1939 the medium of television enabled puppeteers to share the art of puppetry with the entire world. Puppeteers such as Burr Tillstrom and Bil Baird, along with their puppets, were among the first to join the ranks as television personalities. Later Shari Lewis became one of the first female puppeteers to appear on television. And, of course, many of us grew up watching Jim Henson's muppets on *Sesame Street.* ■

Once onstage, puppeteers should perform the show as rehearsed. The performance is not the time to change lines or try to be a star. It is also important to pay attention backstage. See that the puppets enter and exit on cue, clearly projecting all lines. And remember to have fun! Then the audience will, too.

Critiquing the Show

Once the show is performed, you need to spend time reflecting on the project and evaluating the performance. In discussing the show with the rest of the cast, consider these questions:

1. What was the most important thing you learned from this activity?
2. What did you most enjoy about the activity?
3. If you could plan this assignment again, what would you do differently or change?
4. What parts of the puppet performance were successful?
5. What parts of the puppet performance need to be changed or eliminated?

1. **A Puppet Production.** If you have written a short puppet play, now you will need to design and make the set and props and plan the music, sound effects, special effects, and lighting. Work with your group to complete the production project.

2. **Puppet MTV.** Working with a partner or your acting company, choose a short upbeat musical number to lip-sync and choreograph with puppets. Ask your teacher to approve the song's lyrics before you begin rehearsal. Follow your teacher's instructions for performing the musical number. Videotape the performance.

Shadow Play

LESSON OBJECTIVE

◆ Experiment with shadow play.
◆ Create a shadow character.
◆ Use movement to project characterization.

Warm Up

What is a shadow? How can shadows be used to create theatre?

You read earlier in this chapter that a shadow puppet is a flat, two-dimensional puppet designed to cast a shadow or form a silhouette on a white cloth screen stretched and stapled to a wooden frame. Shadow play might be considered a form of shadow puppetry. In **shadow play**,

■ ■ ■ ■ ■ ■ ■ ■ ■ ■ ■ ■ ■ ■ ■ ■
What image has this puppeteer
created? Have you ever created
a shadow puppet like this one?

shadow play
projecting shadow images on a
screen.

the puppeteers use their own hands or bodies to make shadow pictures on a screen.

Shadow play is one of the simplest forms of entertainment, requiring only a shape, a light, and a surface on which to cast the shadows.
You have probably already experimented with shadow play. At night,
alone in your room, have you ever shaped your hands into a dog or
rabbit, moving the animal across the bedroom wall? Have you cast
shadows on the classroom wall when your teacher turned on the movie
projector light? Have you observed how tall your shadow looks on the
sidewalk at certain times of the day? If you've had any of these experiences, you've experimented with shadow play.

Hand Shadows

Your hands can create all kinds of interesting shadow birds and animals. Create a bird in flight by joining your thumbs together and moving your fingers. Try to make a rabbit by holding up your first and
second fingers for ears and forming the head by touching your thumb
to your third and fourth fingers.

What other animals can you create? By moving your fingers in different ways, you can bring the animal to life. See how many parts of
your animal shadow can move. Can it wiggle its nose, flap its wings, or
hop away?

Body Shadows

Hands are just the beginning of shadow play. You can use your entire body to create a shadow character. For human shadows, you will
need a screen large enough for one or more persons to stand behind.
Construct the screen from a white bedsheet stretched and stapled to a
large wooden frame.

You will need a bright light to project the shadows to the audience. Light the screen from behind the actors using an old pole light with three adjustable fixtures (check the local thrift store), or use two clip-on desk lights containing 100- and 150-watt bulbs. When the lights are properly positioned, the actors are sandwiched between the screen and the light. Experiment placing the lights in different positions until the desired silhouette is achieved.

Now you are ready to create a character. Because the audience will only see your silhouette, it is important that you remember to exaggerate everything. Think about what you will wear. Select clothing or a costume that has an exaggerated shape. Shape helps create a better silhouette. Wear loose-legged trousers rather than slim tight-fitting jeans. Wear a large hat or wig, or style your own hair bigger. Further exaggerate the character by selecting large props and by moving with large movements. Playing the character in a profile position allows the audience to view the exaggerated silhouette.

Using the Overhead Projector

Another form of shadow play involves the use of objects as characters. Lighting is provided by an overhead projector with a projector screen. This method allows the participants to see what they are doing.

Place the objects directly on the glass surface of the overhead projector, casting shadows on the projector screen behind you. Placing the overhead projector on the floor allows enlargement of the shadows.

Shadow play on the overhead is not limited to flat, two-dimensional objects. Interesting shadows can be formed from some three-dimensional objects. Think of items in your classroom, purse, or locker that might make good shadows on the overhead. What about a rubber band, a comb, or the wire from your old spiral notebook? Be sure to select items small enough to fit on the glass surface of the overhead.

You can also use an overhead projector for a puppet performance. In your classroom, an overhead projector might be more convenient than a shadow screen. The biggest problem using an overhead projector is making the puppets, props, and scenery small enough to fit on the glass surface of the projector.

Puppets can be designed on white paper, cut out, and transferred to lightweight black cardboard. Using black cardboard makes darker shadows on the overhead screen. Movable parts of the cardboard puppets—heads, arms, legs, and mouths—can be made mobile by connecting joints or body parts using pieces of string or metal brads.

Add color to the puppets by stretching colored plastic food wrap over cut-out sections of the puppets. Simple puppets can become more elaborate by punching out holes or cutting designs in the puppets. Colored report covers can be used in a similar fashion to add color. Clear report covers or overhead transparencies can be colored with colored felt-tip pens and used as decorations or as background designs.

Plastic drinking straws make good rods. They can be cut easily into different lengths. Attach the rods to the puppet's body and movable parts using staples or tape and your puppets will be ready for action.

ACTIO**N**

Using the Overhead Projector

1. Object Shows.
    a. Each member of your acting company should contribute an item to an improvised shadow show. The objects will become the actors on the glass projector stage. One or more members of the group can manipulate the objects while the other group members speak.
    b. Collect five or six interesting objects to use in overhead projector shadow play. Using these objects as the characters, write or improvise a short story or play. Share your story with your class.

2. Shadow Characters.
    a. Make a self-identity character shadow puppet. Use the puppet on the overhead to introduce yourself to the class. Be sure to cover all your interests and hobbies—pets, music, movies, television shows, and school subjects.
    b. Make a shadow puppet character from one of your favorite books or plays. Using the puppet on the overhead projector, conduct a book or play review.
    c. Make puppets of the characters from a favorite folktale or fairy tale. Use the puppets on the overhead projector to share the story with the class. For variation, you might change the ending of the tale.

3. TV Commercials. Working with a partner or your acting company, design an original product that might be advertised on television. Write a television commercial advertising your product. Make shadow puppet characters to use as the product, props, and characters. Rehearse the commercial several times. Then add music, sounds, or special effects to enhance the production. Finally, using the overhead projector as your stage, share your commercial with your classmates.

Using A Shadow Screen

1. Shadow Animals.
    a. Use your hands to create animal shapes on a classroom wall. Experiment, using several different lamps or light sources to find the one that works best in your classroom. Often, the light from a filmstrip projector or movie projector can be used for the proper amount of light.
    b. Develop your shadow animal into a character, giving it a name, voice, and personality. Think of one or two lines of dialogue for your animal to say. Introduce it to the class and let it speak the lines.

2. Human Shadows.
    a. Plan and costume a human shadow character. Create an exaggerated walk and gestures for the character. Prepare to share the character behind the shadow screen.
    b. Parade your character behind the shadow screen. Your teacher will provide appropriate music for this assignment. Be sure your character uses the exaggerated walk and big gestures you planned.

3. Shadow Pantomime. Use each of the characters created by your acting company members in a short pantomimed scene. Stage the scene behind the shadow screen. Encourage feedback from your audience after each scene is presented.

Masks

LESSON OBJECTIVE

◆ Use movement to communicate attitudes, feelings, and moods while wearing a mask.

◆ Explore characterization and improvisation while wearing a mask.

Warm Up

Think about plays or movies in which characters wear masks. What is the purpose of the masks?

mask

a covering worn over all or part of the actor's face to neutralize or create a new character.

neutral mask

a white, featureless facial covering worn to neutralize the actor's own face.

character mask

a mask representing a specific character.

Masks have long been a part of the theatre. The Greeks believed that you put on a mask to become another person. In commedia dell'arte, many of the stock characters were identified by their half masks. In Japan, masks have been part of the traditional Noh theatre since the twelfth century.

In this lesson, you will learn how masks can be effective teaching tools for actors. Masks give the inexperienced actor a sense of security and protection—as though the actor is hiding behind someone else.

A **mask** can be any covering worn over all or part of the actor's face. Making a mask is fun, and learning to work in it presents a new challenge for the actor. When you cannot use your own face for communication, then you must exaggerate your body movements and gestures to project characterization to the audience.

Mask Construction

Masks can be constructed from many different materials. Masks are often a combination of materials. Metal, fabric, paper, and leather can all be used to create a mask. The most common and most easily accessible materials are paper products. Ordinary paper products can be mixed with recyclable materials such as Styrofoam©, plastic, or aluminum to make a unique, one-of-a-kind mask. Unusual masks can also be made from natural materials, such as sticks, leaves, bark, grasses, and weeds.

The puppet materials and supplies listed in Lesson 1 can also be used to create masks. Check with your teacher for a list of additional materials.

The Neutral Mask

A good way to begin working with masks is to wear a **neutral mask**, a plain white mask without any features. The actor's use of exaggerated gestures and body movements appears to make the expression on the mask change. A simple neutral mask can be made from a paper plate or circle of posterboard.

The Character Mask

Unlike the neutral mask, there are masks that represent certain characters. This type of mask is called a **character mask**. A ready-made

Designing your own unique mask can be fun, as well as challenging.

or handmade character mask, such as you might wear to a costume party, has its own personality. The actor can use such a mask as an acting tool, adding appropriate gestures and movements to physically interpret the character.

Begin by spending time studying the character mask. Each ready-made mask, like each puppet, has a mood and personality all its own. Study the ready-made mask; imagine the character that the mask represents. Give the character a name, develop its personality, and create a story about its life. Once you understand the mask, add suitable movements and gestures.

Many actors prefer to make their own character masks. There are two basic approaches. One way is to first develop a character. Following characterization guidelines in Chapter 7, develop an original character on paper. Next, draw a mask to express the character you have developed. Once the mask is designed on paper, select appropriate materials and make the mask.

Another way to create a mask is through experimentation. Using this method, you develop the mask and the character simultaneously. Experiment with different materials until you are pleased with the mask. As you make your mask, think about its character. When the mask is complete, give it a name, personality, and background. Finally, move and gesture as the character dictates.

Working in a Mask

Acting in a mask presents a challenge for the actor. Many actors want to touch or arrange the mask while wearing it. You can avoid this pitfall by thinking of the mask as a character rather than a costume or prop.

Even though your face is covered by the mask and the audience cannot see you, continue to make facial expressions. Exaggerated facial expressions will help you animate and project the mask's personality

Does the idea of creating a character mask and bringing the character to life sound appealing to you?

through your body movements and gestures. Overdoing is important in mask work. Actors sometimes exaggerate movement by slightly bending their knees and lowering their center of gravity.

Modeling the mask in front of a mirror helps you become comfortable with big movements and gestures. Unless your mask covers the entire head, always play open (face the audience). To maintain the illusion of the mask, do not allow the audience to see any part of your face.

When you first enter the acting area wearing a mask, pause briefly to reveal the mask to the audience. This pause gives the audience an opportunity to fully see you in your mask. After performing, exit in character, looking back once at the audience. This last look back is called a tag.

ACTION

1. **Neutral Mask.** Create a simple mask using a paper plate or a circle of poster board. Use scissors to cut out eye holes. Punch a small hole on each side of the plate. Run a 12-inch piece of yarn through each side hole, securing the yarn with a large knot. Using the yarn, tie the plate around your head. For a more secure mask, elastic can be used in place of yarn. Staple the elastic to each side of the paper plate.

2. **Moving in Masks.** Move across the performance area wearing a neutral mask as you physically express the following feelings. Play open using a lower center of gravity.

puzzlement	grief	amusement
resentment	irritation	hatred
misery	rage	depression
love	fear	contentment
agony	curiosity	naughtiness
sympathy	delight	shock

3. **Character Mask.**
   a. Make a character mask using your choice of materials. Pause to reveal the character to the audience as you enter and move across the performance area. Exit in character, remembering the tag.
   b. Working with your acting company, use ready-made masks or hand-made original masks to pantomime a scene with several characters.

4. **Fairy Tale Theatre.** Working with your acting company, plan and create simple masks for a fairy tale. Plan a pantomime to tell the story. (Refer to Chapter 14 for ideas on using pantomime to tell a story.) Perform the story for your class.

5. **Bag It.** Use paper grocery sacks, newspaper, colored craft paper, and other materials to create larger-than-life masks. Plan a style show to model your "bag it" creations.

■ ■ SPOTLIGHT ON TERMS ■ ■

An important part of theatre is understanding the terminology, or vocabulary, used. Add the new terms and definitions to the vocabulary section of your theatre notebook or folder.

■ ■ FOCUS ON FACTS ■ ■

1. Describe the five basic types of puppets.
2. Explain animation.
3. What is manipulation?
4. What is lip synchronization?
5. How can the puppeteer avoid flipping the lid?
6. What should a puppeteer consider before giving a puppet a voice?
7. What technical elements might be used in a puppet show?
8. What are two ways to perform shadow plays?
9. What is the purpose of working in a neutral mask?
10. What is the difference between a neutral mask and a character mask?

■ ■ REFLECTIONS ■ ■

Discuss the following questions with your class or answer them on paper as instructed by your teacher.

1. In what ways could puppetry, masks, and shadow play be used in subjects other than theatre?
2. Why should puppetry be viewed as an art form, rather than just a craft activity for children?
3. How did wearing a mask free your body to move?
4. Where in your culture or community do you see masks used?
5. What part of this chapter appealed to you the most? Why?

■ ■ THEATRE IN YOUR LIFE ■ ■

Think about the many problems facing our society. What puppet could you design to help teach an important lesson to your generation? Discuss your idea with your class, or write a short journal entry in your theatre notebook or folder.

■ ■ ENCORE ■ ■

1. Under the direction of your teacher, write an original play and create shadow puppet characters. Act out the play using the overhead projector as a stage.
2. Write a short puppet play dealing with substance abuse or another social problem that teenagers face today. Create the puppets, rehearse, and perform the play for a science or health class at your school.
3. Under the direction of your teacher, get information from different teachers concerning problems facing students at your school. Write an original play for shadow puppets or hand puppets demonstrating appropriate ways to solve the problems. Make the puppets for the show. Rehearse, produce, and perform the show for an audience. Think of classes on your campus that would enjoy and learn from your performance. You might invite other electives, ESL classes, Peer Assistant Leadership classes, or the student council.
4. Plan how to tell a children's story using masks and pantomime. Construct the masks and share the story.
5. Create a sound effects tape. Record ten different "live" sounds appropriate for puppet shows.
6. Compile a list of twenty different special effects that might be used in puppet shows. Invent a simple way to achieve each special effect.
7. Collect ten photographs for ideas for creating puppets. Look in magazines for pictures of real or stuffed animals, birds, or reptiles. Explain to your acting company or group why you chose each one and how you would turn each into a puppet.
8. Collect twenty magazine photographs illustrating facial features suitable for puppets. Include a variety of eyes, ears, noses, mouths, and hairstyles.

The Playbook

Monologues For Males

Winners
by Cynthia Mercati

Scene: Male monologue.
Character: **ZEKE CARTER,** a popular football player.
Setting: Central High School.
Time: The present.
Situation: This is a contemporary play concerned with the priorities of high school students—fitting in, making friends, and being oneself. For three years Zeke has been an all-conference football player at Central High School and the big man on campus. His football career comes to a sudden end when the principal suspends him and kicks him off the team after finding out about his stash of drugs.

■ ■ ■

ZEKE   A chip off the old block. That's what my Dad calls me. He was a big football star in high school—and he's still got every one of his trophies to prove it. Games 30 years old, he can remember every play! But he never made it big. He never got that scholarship. Good as he was—he wasn't good enough. But his son's gonna be. Oh, yeah, his son's gonna be the best. *(Grimly)* He better be.

. . .

"Big game tonight," my Dad always says. Every game is a big game to him. "Everyone's counting on you," he always says. "Your coach, the school. The whole town! And me. Especially me. Don't let me down, Zeke."

. . .

(Bitterly) Then after the game, the old man always says, "You could have done better. You *should* have done better."

. . .

"Play pro ball and you count for something in this world." That's what my Dad always says. "Football's your chance to make it big!" *(Angrily)* But it's not my chance—it's his! I gotta do what he never did—I gotta give him what he never got for himself! *(Fiercely)* Someday I'm gonna tell him, "You don't get a second chance in life! This is my life and my chance! And if I want to blow it—I will! *(Desperately)* But if I blow it, I'll be a nobody, going nowhere—counting for nothing. *(Bitterly)* Just ask my Dad.

. . .

"You put too much pressure on the boy!" That's what Mom always says. "He can take it," Dad says. "He's a man—he's a *jock!* He can handle it." And I guess I can.

. . .

"Don't let me down," that's what the old man always says. "I'm counting on you!" Well, you can't count on me anymore, Dad. And I did let you down. I found out I'm off the team permanently. And I'm outta school—for good. And I am going to court. "He can handle it," the old man always says. "He can take it!" But you know what, Dad—I can't. Oh, getting high'll help—*(Starkly, the veneer gone)* For awhile. See I found out something else today, Dad. Take away the uniform and there's nothing left. Take away the cheers—and I can't hear my name. I was always looking for me in other people's eyes—trying to find a reflection so I'd know I was real. But now—there's nothing there. Or maybe—there never was anything there. *(And he exits)*

Simply Heavenly
by Langston Hughes

Scene: Male monologue.
Character: **JESSE B. SIMPLE,** a likeable young man who is down on his luck.
Setting: A hospital room in Harlem.
Time: The present

Situation: While joy-riding with a few friends, Simple was injured in a car accident. When this scene opens, he is lying in a hospital bed with both of his legs in traction. When Joyce, the woman he loves, comes to visit, he feels guilty about the accident and reminisces an incident from his childhood.

■ ■ ■

SIMPLE Aunt Lucy is dead and gone to glory, Joyce. But it were Aunt Lucy taught me right from wrong. When I were a little young child, I didn't have much raising. I knocked around every-which-where, pillar to post. But when Aunt Lucy took me, she did her best to whip me and *raise* me, too—'cause Aunt Lucy really believed in her Bible. "Spare the rod and spoil the child." I were *not* spoiled. But that last whipping is what did it—made me the man I am today. . . . I could see that whipping coming, Joyce, when I sneaked out of the hen-house one of Aunt Lucy's best hens and give it to that girl to roast for her Sunday School picnic, because that old girl said she was aiming to picnic *me*—except that she didn't have nothing much to put in her basket. I was trying to jive that girl, you know. Anyhow, Aunt Lucy found out about it and woke me up the next morning with a switch in her hand. . . . But I got all mannish that morning, Joyce. I said, "Aunt Lucy, you ain't gonna whip me no more. I'se a man now—and you ain't gonna whip me." Aunt Lucy said, "You know you had no business snatching my best laying hen right off her nest." Aunt Lucy was angry. And big as I was, I was scared. . . . Yet I was meaning not to let her whip me, Joyce. But, just when I was aiming to snatch that switch out of her hand, I seed Aunt Lucy was crying. I said, "What you crying for?" She said, "I'm crying 'cause here you is a man and don't know how to act right *yet*, and I done did my best to raise you so you'll grow up to be a good man. I wore out so many switches on your back—still you tries my soul. But it *ain't* my soul I'm thinking of, son, it's you. Jess, I wants you to carry yourself right. You understand me? I'm getting too old to be using my strength up like this. Here!" Aunt Lucy hollered, "Bend over and lemme whip you one more time!" . . . Big as I was,

Joyce, you know I bended. When I seen her crying, I would have let Aunt Lucy kill me before I raised a hand. When she got through, I said, "Aunt Lucy, you ain't gonna have to whip me no more—I'm going to do my best to do right from now on, and not try your soul. And I am sorry about that hen. . . ." Joyce, from that day to this, I have tried to behave myself. Aunt Lucy is gone to Glory, now, but if she's looking down, she knows that's true. That was my last whipping. But it wasn't the whipping that taught me what I needed to know. It was because she cried and cried. When peoples care for you and cry for you—and *love* you—Joyce, they can straighten out your soul. (*Simple, lost in his story, had not been looking at Joyce. Instead, as he finishes, he is looking at the ceiling. Suddenly Joyce turns to bury her head on the back of her chair, sobbing aloud. Simple, forgetting that his legs are tied and that he cannot get out of bed, tries to rise.*) (*If he could, he would go to her and take her in his arms.*) Joyce, you're crying for me!

Harvey
by Mary Chase

Scene: Male monologue.
Character: **ELWOOD P. DOWD,** a 47-year-old man.
Setting: The library of the old Dowd family mansion.
Time: A spring afternoon. The 1940s.
Situation: Elwood P. Dowd, a lovable, slightly peculiar man is accompanied by an invisible six-foot-tall white rabbit named Harvey. His sister Veta and her daughter Myrtle, who live with him in the family home, are embarrassed and humiliated by Elwood's behavior. As the play opens, Elwood is playing pinochle at the Fourth Avenue Firehouse, and Veta and Myrtle are hosting an afternoon tea for the members of the Wednesday Forum in the family home. During the party, much to their disappointment, Elwood returns and visits on the phone with a magazine solicitor who has called the wrong number.

■ ■ ■

(Through door U.L. *enters Elwood P. Dowd. He is a man about 47 years old with a dignified bearing, and yet a dreamy expression in his eyes. His expression is benign, yet serious to the point of gravity. He wears an overcoat and a battered old hat. This hat, reminiscent of the Joe College era, sits on the top of his head. Over his arm he carries another hat and coat. As he enters, although he is alone, he seems to be ushering and bowing someone else in with him. He bows the invisible person over to a chair. His step is light, his movements quiet and his voice low-pitched.)*

ELWOOD   *(To invisible person.)* Excuse me a moment. I have to answer the phone. Make yourself comfortable, Harvey. *(Phone rings.)* Hello. Oh, you've got the wrong number. But how are you, anyway? This is Elwood P. Dowd speaking. I'll do? Well, thank you. And what is your name, my dear? Miss Elsie Greenawalt? *(To chair.)* Harvey, it's a Miss Elsie Greenawalt. How are you today, Miss Greenawalt? That's fine. Yes, my dear. I would be happy to join your club. I belong to several clubs now—the University Club, the Country Club and the Pinochle Club at the Fourth Avenue Firehouse. I spend a good deal of my time there, or at Charlie's Place, or over at Eddie's Bar. And what is your club, Miss Greenawalt? *(He listens—then turns to empty chair.)* Harvey, I get the Ladies Home Journal, Good Housekeeping and the Open Road for Boys for two years for six twenty-five. *(Back to phone.)* It sounds fine to me. I'll join it. *(To chair.)* How does it sound to you, Harvey? *(Back to phone.)* Harvey says it sounds fine to him also, Miss Greenawalt. He says he will join, too. Yes—two subscriptions. Mail everything to this address . . . . I hope I will have the pleasure of meeting you some time, my dear. Harvey, she says she would like to meet me. When? When would you like to meet me, Miss Greenawalt? Why not right now? My sister seems to be having a few friends in and we would consider it an honor if you would come and join us. My sister will be delighted. 343 Temple Drive—I hope to see you in a very few minutes. Goodbye, my dear. *(Hangs up.)* She's coming right over. *(Moves C. to Harvey.)* Harvey, don't you think we'd better freshen up? Yes, so do I. *(He takes up hats and coats and exits* L.)

Hamlet
by William Shakespeare
Act III, Scene i

Scene: Male monologue.
Character: **HAMLET,** Prince of Denmark.
Setting: A hall in the castle of Elsinore.
Time: The sixteenth century.
Situation: Hamlet is a troubled young man because his uncle, Claudius, has killed his father, married his mother, and taken over his father's kingdom. Hamlet pretends to be mad until the time is right to avenge his father's death. In this scene Hamlet gives acting advice to a troupe of players, friends of his, who are performing at the castle.

■ ■ ■

(Enter Hamlet and three of the players.)

HAMLET   Speak the speech, I pray you, as I pronounced it to you, trippingly on the tongue. But if you mouth it, as many of our players do, I had as lief the town crier spoke my lines. Nor do not saw the air too much with your hand, thus, but use all gently, for in the very torrent, tempest, and (as I may say) whirlwind of your passion, you must acquire and beget a temperance that may give it smoothness. O, it offends me to the soul to hear a robustious periwig-pated fellow tear a passion to tatters, to very rags, to split the ears of the groundlings, who for the most part are capable of nothing but inexplicable dumb show and noise. I would have such a fellow whipped for o'erdoing Termagant. It out-herods Herod. Pray you avoid it.

* * *

HAMLET   Be not too tame neither, but let your own discretion by your tutor. Suit the action to the word, the word to the action, with this special observance, that you o'step not the modesty of nature. For anything so overdone is from the purpose of playing, whose end, both at the first and now, was and is, to hold, as 'twere, the mirror up to nature, to show virtue her own feature, scorn her own image, and the very age and body of the time his form and pressure. Now this overdone, or come tardy off, though it make the unskillful laugh, cannot but make the judicious grieve, the censure of the which one must in your allowance o'erweigh a whole theatre of others. O, there be players that I have seen play, and heard others praise, and that highly (not to speak it profanely), that neither having th' accent of Christians, nor the gait of Christian, pagan, nor man, have so strutted and bellowed that I have thought some of Nature's journeymen had made men, and not made them well, they imitated humanity so abominably.

* * *

O, reform it altogether! And let those that play your clowns speak no more than is set down for them, for there be of them that will themselves laugh, to set on some quantity of barren spectators to laugh too, though in the mean time some necessary question of the play be then to be considered. That's villainous and shows a most pitiful ambition in the fool that uses it. Go make you ready.

Monologues For Females

The Star Spangled Girl
by Neil Simon

Scene: Female monologue.
Character: **SOPHIE RAUSCHMEYER,** an all-American girl with an Arkansas drawl.
Setting: A duplex studio apartment in San Francisco.
Time: A summer day in the present
Situation: When Sophie Rauschmeyer moves to San Francisco, she keeps her promise to her parents and introduces herself to her neighbors. The two young men, Norman Cornell and Andy Hobart, are poor young writers who publish a protest magazine. As soon as he sees her, Norman falls in love with Sophie and begins to pursue her in unconventional ways. In this scene Sophie rejects Norman's affection.

■ ■ ■

SOPHIE *(To Andy)* Excuse me. *(To Norman)* Mr. Cornell, Ah have tried to be neighborly, Ah have tried to be friendly and Ah have tried to be cordial . . . Ah don't know what it is that you're tryin' to be. That first night Ah was appreciative that you carried mah trunk up the stairs . . . The fact that it slipped and fell five flights and smashed to pieces was not your fault . . . Ah didn't even mind that personal message you painted on the stairs. Ah thought it was crazy, but sorta sweet. However, things have now gone too far . . . *(Goes down to the pole table)* Ah cannot accept gifts from a man Ah hardly know . . . *(Puts the basket on the pole table)* Especially canned goods. And Ah read your little note. Ah can guess the gist of it even though Ah don't speak Italian. *(Andy sits on the stool below the kitchen bar)* This has got to stop, Mr. Cornell. Ah can do very well without you leavin' little chocolate-almond Hershey bars in mah mailbox—they melted yesterday, and now Ah got three gooey letters from home with nuts in 'em—and Ah can do without you sneakin' into mah room after Ah go to work and paintin' mah balcony without tellin' me about it. Ah stepped out there yesterday and mah slippers are still glued to the floor. And Ah can do without you tying big bottles of eau de cologne to mah cat's tail. The poor thing kept swishin' it yesterday and nearly beat herself to death . . . And most of all, Ah can certainly do without you watchin' me get on the bus every day through that high-powered telescope. You got me so nervous the other day Ah got on the wrong bus. In short, Mr. Cornell, and An don't want to have to say this again, *leave me ay-lone!*
(She turns and starts to go)

. . .

SOPHIE *(To Norman)* Ah am going to repeat this to you once more and for the last time. Ah am ingaged to be married to First Lieutenant Burt Fenneman of the United States Marine Corps. *(To Andy)* And in six weeks Ah will be *Mrs.* First Lieutenant Burt Fenneman of the United States Marine Corps. *(To Norman)* And Ah intend to be happily married to him for the rest of mah natural life. *(She takes a step left)* Do you understand that?

Scene: Female monologue.
Character: **TARA LACEY,** an attractive, intelligent, and well dressed new student.
Setting: Central High School.
Time: The present.
Situation: After an attempted suicide, Tara's parents have moved to protect Tara's secret and give her a fresh start. At her new school, Tara's parents want her to wear the right clothes, fit in with the popular crowd, and maybe even try out for cheerleader. When Tara's secret is discovered, she chooses to tell her story herself in the last scene of the play.

■ ■ ■

TARA *(Firmly)* No, Jan—I'm going to tell them. *(The bell rings, the lights dim, a single spot coming up on Tara as she crosses DC)*

. . .

TARA *(Hesitantly, with apparent nervousness)* This is supposed to be a speech about a personal experience. My experience is really hard for me to talk about. But I *need* to talk about it. *(A breath, then, with difficulty)* I tried to commit suicide last year. I didn't do any of the stuff you see on TV. No last phone call. I didn't leave a note. I just swallowed a whole bottle of pills. It was pretty much on impulse—but I had been thinking about it. It was *all* I thought about. And I'd been talking about it. It's not true, that the people who talk about suicide don't try it. Just the opposite. You talk about it alot—to anyone who'll listen. Hoping, I guess, that someone will give you a reason not to. I talked to my Mom and Dad. In a general sort of way. *(With sadness)* They thought I was doing research for a paper or something. I talked to some of my friends, too. One girl said she thought suicide was romantic—like *Romeo and Juliet. (Angrily)* But that's only a story—and nobody really died! Suicide isn't romantic—it's a *waste!* But I was lucky—my Mom got me to the hospital in time.

I—can't tell you exactly *why* I did it. I know I didn't think too much of myself—so it didn't seem to matter if I was around or not. But I've learned alot in the last year—and I think it's time I started using what I learned. Like who I am! *(With growing surety)* I'm a girl who has a problem who's working on solving it. I'm not proud of what I did. But it happened. I can't pretend it didn't. It's a part of me. I'd like people to like me in spite of what I did—or at least accept me. *(Firmly)* But if they can't—if they call me nuts or psycho—I'm just going to have to like myself enough not to let it get me down. That's something else I'm working on. Liking me. The *real* me. Not the Tara I made up to please my parents or get popular. *(Bursting out with it)* I don't think any of us like ourselves enough! We're always worrying that our hair isn't right or our face is all wrong—or our body isn't like somebody's on TV! Or we want to be good at dancing when we're good at math—or we wish we were outgoing when we're shy! But those are the things that make us *special*—not weird! They set us apart—but they bring us together, too. Because everybody's different—and everybody's okay.

Scene: Female monologue.
Character: **LENA YOUNGER (MAMA),** a strong, full-bodied woman in her sixties.
Setting: The Younger family's worn living room in a Chicago apartment.
Time: The 1950s.
Situation: Three generations of the Younger family live together in a small apartment in Chicago's Southside ghetto. The anticipation of an insurance check for ten thousand dollars brings to light individual dreams and family conflicts. Mama wants to buy a house for the family; Walter, her son, dreams of investing the money in a business of his own; and Beneatha, her daughter, dreams of medical school. Walter feels his mother doesn't trust him to invest the insurance money. Mama sees Walter slipping away, and in this scene, she admits that she has been wrong.

MAMA   I've helped do it to you, haven't I, son? Walter, I been wrong.

...

MAMA   Listen to me, now. I say I been wrong, son. That I been doing to you what the rest of the world been doing to you. *(She stops and he looks up slowly at her and she meets his eyes pleadingly.)* Walter—what you ain't never understood is that I ain't got nothing, don't own nothing, ain't never really wanted nothing that wasn't for you. There ain't nothing as precious to me. . . . There ain't nothing worth holding on to, money, dreams, nothing else—if it means—if it means it's going to destroy my boy. *(She puts her papers in front of him and he watches her without speaking or moving.)* I paid the man thirty-five hundred dollars down on the house. That leaves sixty-five hundred dollars. Monday morning I want you to take this money and take three thousand dollars and put it in a savings account for Beneatha's medical schooling. The rest you put in a checking account—with your name on it. And from now on any penny that come out of it or that go in it is for you to look after. For you to decide. *(She drops her hands a little helplessly.)* It ain't much, but it's all I got in this world and I'm putting it in your hands. I'm telling you to be the head of this family from now on like you supposed to be.

...

MAMA   I ain't never stop trusting you. Like I ain't never stop loving you.

The Taming of the Shrew
by William Shakespeare

Scene: Female monologue.
Character: **KATHARINA,** the older daughter of Baptista.
Setting: Baptista's house in Padua, Italy.
Time: The sixteenth century.
Situation: An elderly gentleman, Baptista, has two daughters he would like to see married. However, the older daughter must marry before the younger one. Katharina, the hot tempered, older daughter, has discouraged many young men with her sharp tongue and fighting ways. Petruchio, a young suitor from Verona, comes to their home in Padua and after working out the financial arrangements with Baptista, tries to win Katharina's heart and take her for his wife. Petruchio proves to be a good match for the shrewish, spitfire Katharina, and succeeds in winning her. In this scene, we listen to the changed Katharina.

■■■

KATHARINA   Fie, fie! unknit that threat'ning unkind brow,
And dart not scornful glances from those eyes
To wound thy lord, thy king, thy governor!
It blots thy beauty as frosts do bite the meads,
Confounds thy fame as whirlwinds shake fair buds,
And in no sense is meet or amiable.
A woman mov'd is like a fountain troubled,
Muddy, ill-seeming, thick, bereft of beauty;
And while it is so, none so dry or thirsty
Will deign to sip or touch one drop of it.
Thy husband is thy lord, thy life, thy keeper.
Thy head, thy sovereign; one that cares for thee
And for thy maintenance; commits his body
To painful labor both by sea and land,
To watch the night in storms, the day in cold,
Whilst thou li'st warm at home, secure and safe;
And craves no other tribute at thy hands
But love, fair looks, and true obedience—
Too little payment for so great a debt.
Such duty as the subject owes the prince,
Even such a woman oweth to her husband;
And when she is froward, peevish, sullen, sour,
And not obedient to his honest will,
What is she but a foul contending rebel
And graceless traitor to her loving lord?
I am asham'd that women are so simple
To offer war where they should kneel for peace;
Or seek for rule, supremacy, and sway
When they are bound to serve, love, and obey.
Why are our bodies soft and weak and smooth,
Unapt to toil and trouble in the world,
But that our soft conditions and our hearts
Should well agree with our external parts?
Come, come, you froward and unable worms!

My mind hath been as big as one of yours,
My heart as great, my reason haply more,
To bandy word for word and frown for frown;
But now I see our lances are but straws,
Our strength as weak, our weakness past compare,
That seeming to be most which we indeed least are.
Then vail your stomachs, for it is no boot,
And place your hands below your husband's foot;
In token of which duty, if he please,
My hand is ready, may it do him ease.

Saint Joan
by Bernard Shaw

Scene: Female monologue.
Character: **JOAN OF ARC,** a simple, country girl, still in her teens.
Setting: The great stone hall at Rouen, France.
Time: The fifteenth century.
Situation: This is the story of Joan of Arc, the young woman who, after hearing "voices" from heaven, dressed like a man and led the French soldiers into battle against the English. In this scene, after being told she will be imprisoned for life, we hear her speak to her inquisitors.

■ ■ ■

JOAN   *[rising in consternation and terrible anger]* Perpetual imprisonment! Am I not then to be set free?

. . .

JOAN   Give me that writing. *[She rushes to the table; snatches up the paper; and tears it into fragments]* Light your fire: do you think I dread it as much as the life of a rat in a hole? My voices were right.

. . .

JOAN   Yes: they told me you were fools *[the word gives great offense]*, and that I was not to listen to your fine words nor trust to your charity. You promised me my life; but you lied *[indignant exclamations]*. You think that life is nothing but not being stone dead. It is not the bread and water I fear: I can live on bread:

when have I asked for more? It is no hardship to drink water if the water be clean. Bread has no sorrow for me, and water no affliction. But to shut me from the light of the sky and the sight of the fields and flowers; to chain my feet so that I can never again ride with the soldiers nor climb the hills; to make me breathe foul damp darkness, and keep from me everything that brings me back to the love of God when your wickedness and foolishness tempt me to hate Him: all this is worse than the furnace in the Bible that was heated seven times. I could do without my warhorse; I could drag about in a skirt; I could let the banners and the trumpets and the knights and soldiers pass me and leave me behind as they leave the other women, if only I could still hear the wind in the trees, the larks in the sunshine, the young lambs crying through the healthy frost, and the blessed blessed church bells that send my angel voices floating to me on the wind. But without these things I cannot live; and by your wanting to take them away from me, or from any human creature, I know that your counsel is of the devil, and that mine is of God.

. . .

JOAN   His ways are not your ways. He wills that I go through the fire to His bosom; for I am His child, and you are not fit that I should live among you. That is my last word to you.

Duet Scenes For Males

A Raisin in the Sun
by Lorraine Hansberry

Scene: Two males.
Characters: **TRAVIS YOUNGER**, a ten- or eleven-year-old male.
                 WALTER LEE YOUNGER, an intense young man in his early thirties.
Setting: The Younger family's worn living room in a Chicago apartment.
Time: The 1950s.
Situation: Walter and Ruth Younger and their son Travis share a small ghetto apartment with

Walter's mother and Beneatha, his sister. Problems arise as to what is to be done with the money Walter's mother receives from the insurance company after her husband's death. Walter wants to use the money to invest in a business of his own, but his mother purchases a home for the family with part of the money. When Walter's mother sees how she has hurt her son and how his dream has dried up, "like a raisin in the sun," she gives him more than just money. She reassures him of her trust and her love. In this scene Walter shares his happiness and his dreams for a better life with his young son. (For further background, read the introductions to other scenes from the play.)

■ ■ ■

WALTER   Son, I feel like talking to you tonight.
TRAVIS   About what?
WALTER   Oh, about a lot of things. About you and what kind of man you going to be when you grow up. . . . Son—son, what do you want to be when you grow up?
TRAVIS   A bus driver.
WALTER   (Laughing a little.) A what? Man, that ain't nothing to want to be!
TRAVIS   Why not?
WALTER   'Cause, man—it ain't big enough—you know what I mean.
TRAVIS   I don't know then. I can't make up my mind. Sometimes Mama asks me that too. And sometimes when I tell her I want to be like you—she says she don't want me to be like that and sometimes she says she does. . . .
WALTER   (Gathering him up in his arms.) You know what, Travis? In seven years you going to be seventeen years old. And things is going to be very different with us in seven years, Travis. . . . One day when you are seventeen I'll come home—home from my office downtown somewhere—
TRAVIS   You don't work in no office, Daddy.
WALTER   No—but after tonight. After what your daddy gonna do tonight, there's going to be offices—a whole lot of offices. . . .
TRAVIS   What you gonna do tonight, Daddy?
WALTER   You wouldn't understand yet, son, but your daddy's gonna make a transaction . . . a business transaction that's going to change our lives. . . . That's how come one day when

you 'bout seventeen years old I'll come home and I'll be pretty tired, you know what I mean, after a day of conferences and secretaries getting things wrong the way they do . . . 'cause an executive's life is hell, man—(The more he talks the farther away he gets.) And I'll pull the car up on the driveway . . . just a plain black Chrysler, I think, with white walls—no—black tires. More elegant. Rich people don't have to be flashy . . . though I'll have to get something a little sportier for Ruth—maybe a Cadillac convertible to do her shopping in. . . . And I'll come up the steps to the house and the gardener will be clipping away at the hedges and he'll say, "Good evening, Mr. Younger." And I'll say, "Hello, Jefferson, how are you this evening?" And I'll go inside and Ruth will come downstairs and meet me at the door and we'll kiss each other and she'll take my arm and we'll go up to your room to see you sitting on the floor with the catalogues of all the great schools in America around you. . . . All the great schools in the world! And—and I'll say, all right, son—it's your seventeenth birthday, what is it you've decided? . . . Just tell me where you want to go to school and you'll *go.* Just tell me, what it is you want to be—and you'll *be* it. . . . Whatever you want to be—Yessir! (He holds his arms open for Travis.) You just name it, son . . .
(Travis leaps into them.)
and I hand you the world! (Walter's voice has risen in pitch and hysterical promise and on the last line he lifts Travis high.)

Cyrano de Bergerac
by Edmond Rostand

Scene: Two males.
Characters: **CYRANO DE BERGERAC,** a noble, homely hero.
THE BORE, an onlooker.
Setting: A hall of the Hotel de Bourgogne.
Time: 1640
Situation: Cyrano de Bergerac is a clever, witty, bold seventeenth-century cavalier, who is known not only for his good deeds but also for his big nose. A patron of the theatre, Cyrano has ordered Montfleury, a pathetic actor, not

to perform onstage for a month. When Cyrano attends a performance of *La Clorise*, he finds Montfleury performing onstage. Cyrano becomes angry, ordering Montfleury to "Get off the stage." Montfleury, continuing to act, agitates Cyrano so much that Cyrano leaves his seat in the audience to sit upon the stage. Once Cyrano has succeeded in canceling the performance, the audience begins to exit. A young man from the crowd stops Cyrano to protest his actions and is caught staring at Cyrano's nose. In this scene Cyrano responds to him.

■ ■ ■

CYRANO Face about, I say . . . or else, tell me why you are looking at my nose.

THE BORE *[Bewildered.]* I . . .

CYRANO *[Advancing upon him.]* In what is it unusual?

THE BORE *[Backing.]* Your worship is mistaken.

CYRANO *[Same business as above.]* Is it flabby and pendulous, like a proboscis?

THE BORE I never said . . .

CYRANO Or hooked like a hawk's beak?

THE BORE I . . .

CYRANO Do you discern a mole upon the tip?

THE BORE But . . .

CYRANO Or is a fly disporting himself thereon? What is there wonderful about it?

THE BORE Oh . . .

CYRANO Is it a freak of nature?

THE BORE But I had refrained from casting so much as a glance at it!

CYRANO And why, I pray, should you not look at it?

THE BORE I had . . .

CYRANO So it disgusts you?

THE BORE Sir . . .

CYRANO Its color strikes you as unwholesome?

THE BORE Sir . . .

CYRANO Its shape, unfortunate?

THE BORE But far from it!

CYRANO Then wherefore that depreciating air? . . . Perhaps monsieur thinks it a shade too large?

THE BORE Indeed not. No, indeed. I think it small . . . small—I should have said, minute!

CYRANO What? How? Charge me with such a ridiculous defect? Small, my nose? Ho! . . .

THE BORE Heavens!

CYRANO Enormous, my nose! . . . Contemptible stutterer, snub-nosed and flatheaded, be it known to you that I am proud, proud of such an appendage! inasmuch as a great nose is properly the index of an affable, kindly, courteous man, witty, liberal, brave, such as I am! and such as you are for evermore precluded from supposing yourself, deplorable rogue! For the inglorious surface my hand encounters above your ruff, is no less devoid—*[Strikes him.]*

THE BORE Aï! aï! . . .

CYRANO Of pride, alacrity, and sweep, of perception and of gift, of heavenly spark, of sumptuousness, to sum up all, of NOSE, than that *[turns him around by the shoulders and suits the action to the word]* which stops my boot below your spine!

THE BORE *[Running off.]* Help! The watch! . . .

CYRANO Warning to the idle who might find entertainment in my organ of smell. . . . And if the facetious fellow be of birth, my custom is, before I let him go, to chasten him, in front, and higher up, with steel, and not with hide!

In Splendid Error
by William Branch

Scene: Two males.

Characters: **FREDERICK DOUGLASS,** an escaped slave and abolition orator. **JOHN BROWN,** an abolitionist.

Setting: The parlor of the Douglass home in Rochester, New York.

Time: A late spring afternoon in 1859, two years before the Civil War.

Situation: Frederick Douglass, an escaped slave, has become a leading advocate of the abolition of slavery through the publication of his newspapers and his public speeches. As one of the stations on the Underground Railroad, his home has been open to many runaway slaves. Frederick Douglass is surprised when Nelson Hawkins, an unexpected visitor, turns out to be John Brown. In this scene, he welcomes John Brown into his home.

■ ■ ■

DOUGLASS (*Slowly recognition—and joy—come into Douglass's face.*) Why . . . bless my soul, it's Captain Brown! (*He rushes to him.*) John! John! (*Brown laughs and they embrace warmly.*)

. . .

DOUGLASS But that beard!—You were always clean-shaven. And these clothes! Why, if it hadn't been for your voice I never would have—!

BROWN (*Laughs loudly.*) You're looking well, Frederick!

DOUGLASS Why, so are you, only—well, come and sit down, John. How did you ever manage to get through? Why, there's an alarm out for you in seven States!

BROWN (*Laughs.*) Oh, I have means, Frederick. I have means.

. . .

DOUGLASS And how's your family, John?

. . .

DOUGLASS (*Concerned.*) Sit down, John. Tell us about it.

BROWN (*Sitting.*) Thank you. I am a little tired.

. . .

DOUGLASS John, we've had no word of you for months. We didn't know if you were alive or dead.

BROWN (*Smiling.*) Oh, I'm still above ground, Douglass. It will take more than a few cowardly ruffians in the Territories to put John Brown in his grave. And a lot more to keep him there! (*Sobers.*) They did get one of my sons, though. My Frederick.

DOUGLASS Oh, no . . . !

BROWN Yes. They shot him down one night, not far from Ossawatomie. Owen, too—the big one. But Owen still lives. Back on the farm at North Elba, Mary's nursing him back to health. He's . . . paralyzed. The waist down.

DOUGLASS (*Softly.*) . . . And you, John, are you well?

BROWN Oh, yes. I've been a little tired, but I'm gathering strength to go on with the work.

DOUGLASS To go on? But John, Kansas is won! Surely now you can rest. You've done what no other man has been able to do: you've stopped the slave power dead in its tracks!

BROWN Not quite, Douglass, not quite. Try as we might, the Free Soil constitution adopted in Kansas says nothing about the emancipation of slaves. It offers sanctuary to not a

blessed black soul. I must get back to my true work: to free enslaved black folk, and not further waste my energies and resources on political partridges like Kansas. That is why I am here.

DOUGLASS Yes?

BROWN I shall want you to put me up for a time, Frederick. Several weeks, a month perhaps.

DOUGLASS You know, John, that my house is always yours.

BROWN Good. I knew I could count on you. I will pay for my accommodations. Oh no—no, I insist! I will not stay with you unless I can contribute my share to the household expenses. What shall it be?

DOUGLASS Now, now, John—

BROWN Come, come, Douglass! You must be practical.

DOUGLASS Well, all right. Shall we say—three dollars a week for room and board? No, not a penny more! You are my guest.

BROWN All right, settled then. (*He withdraws a purse and hands to Douglass three dollars in silver coin.*) For the first week.

DOUGLASS You are now a member of the Douglass household, in good financial standing.

BROWN Fine! And one other thing, Frederick. While I am here I wish to be known in public only as "Nelson Hawkins." I want John Brown to be thought still in the Territories. Though Kansas is won, still there's a price on my head some enterprising young scamp might be ambitious to collect.

DOUGLASS Ha! I shall turn you in at once! (*They laugh.*) As you wish, John. I shall inform the entire household at supper.

Teahouse of the August Moon
by John Patrick

Scene:	Two males.
Characters:	**CAPTAIN FISBY,** a young Army officer.
	SAKINI, the local interpreter.
Setting:	Outside Captain Fisby's quarters, Tobiki, Okinawa.
Time:	Following World War II.

Situation: During the American occupation of Okinawa after World War II, Captain Fisby is stationed in the remote Tobiki village. His assignment is to teach democracy to the villagers and help them become more independent. He doesn't like his new job and is not prepared for the ingenuity of Sakini, the local interpreter. In this scene, Sakini's cleverness forces Captain Fisby to go against army policy.

■ ■ ■

Scene: Outside Captain Fisby's quarters.
Time: A few minutes later.
At Rise: Captain Fisby and Sakini enter from left and cross before the panels, all of which are now down.

SAKINI Everything all ready, boss. We go to Tobiki now?

FISBY I guess so. Well, wish me luck, Sakini. I'm going out to spread the gospel of Plan B.

SAKINI You already lucky, boss. You got me.

FISBY *[Smiles.]* Thanks . . . do you know the road?

SAKINI No road, boss—just path for wagon cart and goat.

FISBY Will a jeep make it?

SAKINI We find out, boss.

FISBY Naturally. How long will it take us?

SAKINI Oh—not know until we arrive, boss.

FISBY Naturally. Well, we might as well get started. I'll drive and you give directions.

SAKINI Oh, very happy to go home.

FISBY Where is the jeep?

SAKINI Right here, boss.

[He turns and claps his hands. The panels go up. The laundry line has been removed and the jeep pulled down center. The jeep is piled with Fisby's belongings. Perched high on the top of this pyramid sits a very old and very wrinkled Native Woman. Sakini pays no attention to her as he goes around the jeep test-kicking the tires. And the Old Woman sits disinterested and aloof from what goes on below her.]

FISBY Hey, wait a minute! What's she doing up there? *[He points to her. The Old Woman sits with hands folded serenely, looking straight ahead.]*

SAKINI She nice old lady hear we go to Tobiki village. She think she go along to visit grandson.

FISBY Oh, she does. Well, you explain that I'm very sorry but she'll have to take a bus.

SAKINI No buses to Tobiki. People very poor—can only travel on generosity.

FISBY I'm sorry, but it's against regulations.

SAKINI She not fall off, boss. She tied on.

FISBY Well, untie her and get her down. She'll just have to find some other way to visit her grandson.

SAKINI Her grandson mayor of Tobiki village. You make him lose face if you kick old grandmother off jeep.

FISBY She's the mayor's grandmother?

SAKINI Oh yes, boss.

FISBY Well, since she's already tied on, I guess we can take her. *[He looks at the bundles.]* Are all those *mine?*

SAKINI Oh, no. Most of bundles belong to old lady. She think she visit three or four months so she bring own bed and cooking pots.

FISBY Well, tell her to yell out if she sees any low branches coming. *[He starts to get in.]* Let's get started.

SAKINI Oh, can't go yet, boss.

FISBY Why not?

SAKINI Old lady's daughter not here.

FISBY *[Glances at watch.]* We can't wait for a lot of good-byes, Sakini!

SAKINI *[Looking behind Fisby.]* Oh, she come now—right on dot you bet.

[Captain Fisby turns to witness a squat young Native Woman come on pushing a wheelbarrow loaded with bundles. She stops long enough to bow low to Fisby—then begins to tie bundles onto the jeep.]

FISBY Sakini, can't the old lady leave some of that stuff behind?

SAKINI Not her things, boss. Belong to daughter.

FISBY Wait a minute. Is the daughter planning on going with us, too?

SAKINI Old lady very old. Who take care of her on trip?

FISBY Well, I—*[The Daughter takes the wheelbarrow and hurries off.]* Hey—you come back. Sakini—tell her to come back. We can't carry any more bundles.

SAKINI *[Calmly.]* Oh, she not go to get bundles, boss. She go to get children.

FISBY Come here, Sakini. Now look—this sort of thing is always happening to me and I have to put a stop to it some place. This time I'm determined to succeed. It's not that I don't *want* to take them. But you can see for yourself, *there's no room left for kids!*

SAKINI But daughter not go without children and old lady not go without daughter. And if old lady not go, mayor of Tobiki be mad at you.

[Turns to see the Daughter hurry back with three children in tow. They all bow politely to Fisby. Their mother then piles them on the hood of the jeep.]

FISBY For Pete's sake, Sakini, how does she expect me to see how to drive!

SAKINI Old lady got very good eyesight. She sit on top and tell us when to turn.

[At this point one of the Children climbs off the hood and points offstage.]

. . .

[The child dashes offstage.]

FISBY . . . Where's *he* going?

SAKINI *[To Fisby.]* He go to get goat.

FISBY A goat!

SAKINI Can't go and leave poor goat behind.

. . .

FISBY Well, right here is where we start seeing who's going to lose face. No goat is going to travel on this jeep.

SAKINI You not like goats, boss?

FISBY It has nothing to do with whether I like goats or not. I'm positive the colonel wouldn't like it.

SAKINI But children not go without goat, mother not go without children, old lady not go without daughter—

FISBY *[Repeats with Sakini.]*—and if old lady not go, the mayor of Tobiki be mad at you! *[Fisby sees the goat being led on by the Small Boy.]* Oh, no!

SAKINI Everybody here, boss. Goat not got children. Goat unmarried lady goat.

FISBY All right, all right. Put it on the hood with the kids. *[The goat is placed on the hood and held by the Children.]* We've got to get started or we'll never get off the ground.

SAKINI All ready to go, boss. You get in now. Nobody else going.

The Odd Couple
Neil Simon

Scene: Two males.

Characters: **FELIX UNGER,** recently divorced man.
OSCAR MADISON, friend of Felix.
Setting: Oscar's apartment.
Time: 1960s
Situation: Felix, who is a stickler for neatness and cleanliness and fancies himself a gourmet cook, has recently separated from his wife and has temporarily moved into his friend Oscar's apartment. Felix is having a hard time getting over the separation and being away from his children and home. The night before the following scene takes place, Felix ruined a double date that Oscar had arranged by talking all night about his wife, his children, and his home. Oscar, who is eager for some female companionship, and who is comfortable in his disorganized, messy lifestyle, is furious with Felix for ruining the date.

(Felix comes out of the kitchen carrying a tray with steaming dish of spaghetti. As he crosses behind Oscar to the table, he smells it "deliciously" and passes it close to Oscar to make sure Oscar smells the fantastic dish he's missing. As Felix sits and begins to eat, Oscar takes can of aerosol spray from the bar, and circling the table sprays all about Felix, puts can down next to him and goes back to his newspaper.

FELIX *(Pushing spaghetti away.)* All right, how much longer is this gonna go on?

OSCAR *(Reading his paper.)* Are you talking to me?

FELIX That's right, I'm talking to you.

OSCAR What do you want to know?

FELIX I want to know if you're going to spend the rest of your life not talking to me. Because if you are, I'm going to buy a radio. *(No reply.)* Well? *(No reply.)* I see. You're not going to talk to me. *(No reply.)* All right. Two can play at this game. *(Pause)* If you're not going to talk to me, I'm not going to talk to you. *(No reply.)* I can act childish too, you know. *(No reply.)* I can go on without talking just as long as you can.

OSCAR Then why the hell don't you shut up?

FELIX Are you talking to me?

OSCAR You had your chance to talk last night. I begged you to come upstairs with me. From now on I never want to hear a word from that shampooed head as long as you live. That's a warning, Felix.

FELIX (*Stares at him.*) I stand warned. Over and out!

OSCAR (*Gets up taking key out of his pocket and slams it on the table.*) There's a key to the back door. If you stick to the hallway and your room, you won't get hurt. (*Sits back down on couch.*)

FELIX I don't think I gather the entire meaning of that remark.

OSCAR Then I'll explain it to you. Stay out of my way.

FELIX (*Picks up key and moves to couch.*) I think you're serious. I think you're really serious. . . . Are you serious?

OSCAR This is my apartment. Everything in my apartment is mine. The only thing here that's yours is you. Just stay in your room and speak softly.

FELIX Yeah, you're serious. . . . Well, let me remind you that I pay half the rent and I'll go into any room I want. (*He gets up angrily and starts towards hallway.*)

OSCAR Where are you going?

FELIX I'm going to walk around your bedroom.

OSCAR (*Slams down newspaper.*) You stay out of there.

FELIX (*Steaming.*) Don't tell me where to go. I pay a hundred and twenty dollars a month.

OSCAR That was off-season. Starting tomorrow the rates are twelve dollars a day.

FELIX All right. (*He takes some bills out of his pocket and slams them down on table.*) There you are. I'm paid up for today. Now I'm going to walk in your bedroom. (*He starts to storm off.*)

OSCAR Stay out of there! Stay out of my room! (*He chases after him. Felix dodges around the table as Oscar blocks the hallway.*)

FELIX (*Backing away, keeping table between them.*) Watch yourself! Just watch yourself, Oscar!

OSCAR (*With a pointing finger.*) I'm warning you. You want to live here, I don't want to see you. I don't want to hear you and I don't want to smell your cooking. Now get this spaghetti off my poker table.

FELIX Ha! Haha!

OSCAR What the hell's so funny?

FELIX It's not spaghetti. It's linguini! (*Oscar picks up the plate of linguini, crosses to the doorway, and hurls it into the kitchen.*)

OSCAR Now it's garbage! (*Paces above the couch.*)

FELIX (*Looks at Oscar unbelievingly.*) What an insane thing to do. You are crazy! . . . I'm a neurotic nut but *you are crazy!*

OSCAR *I'm* crazy, heh? That's really funny coming from a fruitcake like you.

FELIX (*Goes to kitchen door and looks in at the mess. Turns back to Oscar.*) I'm not cleaning that up.

OSCAR Is that a promise?

FELIX Did you hear what I said? I'm not cleaning it up. It's your mess. (*Looking into kitchen again.*) Look at it. Hanging all over the walls.

OSCAR (*Crosses up on landing and looks at kitchen door.*) I like it. (*Closes door and paces Right.*)

FELIX (*Fumes.*) You'd just let it lie there, wouldn't you? Until it turns hard and brown and . . . yich. . . . It's disgusting. . . . I'm cleaning it up. (*He goes into the kitchen. Oscar chases after him. There is the sound of a struggle and falling pots.*)

OSCAR (*Off.*) Leave it alone!. . . You touch one strand of that linguini—and I'm gonna punch you right in your sinuses.

FELIX (*Dashes out of kitchen with Oscar in pursuit. Stops and tries to calm Oscar down.*) Oscar. . . . I'd like you to take a couple of phenobarbital.

OSCAR (*Points.*) Go to your room! . . . Did you hear what I said? Go *to your room!*

Duet Scenes For Females

The Glass Menagerie
by Tennessee Williams

Scene: For two females.
Characters: AMANDA WINGFIELD
LAURA WINGFIELD, her daughter
Setting: The Wingfield apartment.
Time: An afternoon in the 1930s.
Situation: Amanda Wingfield has reared her children, Tom and Laura, alone after her hus-

band deserted her. Laura's shy and withdrawn personality has been shaped by her embarrassment at having a deformed foot. She escapes reality through her collection of glass animals. Mrs. Wingfield has been paying to send Laura to typing school so that she can find a job as a secretary. Laura hates the school and quits attending without telling her mother. In this scene Mrs. Wingfield has just discovered Laura's secret.

■ ■ ■

LAURA Hello, Mother, I was—
(*She makes a nervous gesture toward the chart on the wall. Amanda leans against the shut door and stares at Laura with martyred look.*)
AMANDA Deception? Deception?
(*She slowly removes her hat and gloves, continuing the sweet suffering stare. She lets the hat and gloves fall on the floor—a bit of acting.*)
LAURA (*Shakily*) How was the D.A.R. meeting?
(*Amanda slowly opens her purse and removes a dainty white handkerchief which she shakes out delicately and delicately touches to her lips and nostrils.*)
Didn't you go to the D.A.R. meeting, Mother?
AMANDA (*Faintly, almost inaudibly*)—No—No. (*Then more forcibly*) I did not have the strength—to go to the D.A.R. In fact, I did not have the courage! I wanted to find a hole in the ground and hide myself in it forever!
(*She crosses slowly to the wall and removes the diagram of the typewriter keyboard. She holds it in front of her for a second, staring at it sweetly and sorrowfully—then bites her lips and tears it in two pieces.*)
LAURA (*Faintly*) Why did you do that, Mother?
(*Amanda repeats the same procedure with the chart of the Gregg Alphabet.*) Why are you—
AMANDA Why? Why? How old are you, Laura?
LAURA Mother, you know my age.
AMANDA I thought that you were an adult; it seems that I was mistaken.
(*She crosses slowly to the sofa and sinks down and stares at Laura.*)
LAURA Please don't stare at me, Mother.
(*Amanda closes her eyes and lowers her head. Count ten.*)
AMANDA What are we going to do, what is going to become of us, what is the future?
(*Count ten.*)

LAURA Has something happened, Mother?
(*Amanda draws a long breath and takes out the handkerchief again. Dabbing process*) Mother, has—something happened?
AMANDA I'll be all right in a minute. I'm just bewildered—(*Count five.*)—by life . . . .
LAURA Mother, I wish that you would tell me what's happened.
AMANDA As you know, I was supposed to be inducted into my office at the D.A.R. this afternoon. But I stopped off at Rubicam's Business College to speak to your teachers about your having a cold and ask them what progress they thought you were making down there.
LAURA Oh . . .
AMANDA I went to the typing instructor and introduced myself as your mother. She didn't know who you were. Wingfield, she said. We don't have any such student enrolled at the school!

I assured her she did, that you have been going to classes since early in January.

"I wonder," she said, "if you could be talking about the terribly shy little girl who dropped out of school after only a few days' attendance?" "No," I said, "Laura, my daughter, has been going to school every day for the past six weeks!"

"Excuse me," she said. She took the attendance book out and there was your name, unmistakably printed, and all the dates you were absent until they decided that you had dropped out of school.

I still said, "No, there must have been some mistake! There must have been some mix-up in the records?"

And she said, "No—I remember her perfectly now. Her hands shook so that she couldn't hit the right keys! The first time we had a speedtest, she broke down completely—was sick at the stomach and almost had to be carried into the wash-room! After that morning she never showed up any more. We phoned the house but never got any answer"—while I was working at Famous and Barr, I suppose, demonstrating those—Oh!

I felt so weak I could barely keep on my feet!

I had to sit down while they got me a glass of water!

Fifty dollars' tuition, all of our plans—my hopes and ambitions for you—just gone up the spout, just gone up the spout like that. (*Laura draws a long breath and gets awkwardly to her feet. She crosses to the victrola and winds it up.*) What are you doing?

LAURA   Oh! (*She release the handle and returns to her seat.*)

AMANDA   Laura, where have you been going when you've gone out pretending that you were going to business college?

LAURA   I've just been going out walking.

AMANDA   That's not true.

LAURA   It is. I just went walking.

AMANDA   Walking? Walking? In winter? Deliberately courting pneumonia in that light coat? Where did you walk to, Laura?

LAURA   All sorts of places—mostly in the park.

AMANDA   Even after you'd started catching that cold?

LAURA   It was the lesser of two evils, Mother. I couldn't go back up. I—threw up—on the floor!

AMANDA   From half past seven till after five every day you mean to tell me you walked around in the park, because you wanted me to think that you were still going to Rubicam's Business College?

LAURA   It wasn't as bad as it sounds. I went inside places to get warmed up.

AMANDA   Inside where?

LAURA   I went in the art museum and the birdhouses at the Zoo. I visited the penguins every day! Sometimes I did without lunch and went to the movies. Lately I've been spending most of my afternoons in the Jewel-box, that big glass house where they raise the tropical flowers.

AMANDA   You did all this to deceive me, just for deception? (*Laura looks down.*) Why?

LAURA   Mother, when you're disappointed, you get that awful suffering look on your face, like the picture of Jesus' mother in the museum!

AMANDA   Hush!

LAURA   I couldn't face it!

(*Pause. A whisper of strings*)

AMANDA   (*Hopelessly fingering the huge pocketbook*) So what are we going to do the rest of our lives? Stay home and watch the parades go by? Amuse ourselves with the glass menagerie, darling? Eternally play those worn-out phonograph records your father left as a painful reminder of him.

We won't have a business career—we've given that up because it gave us nervous indigestion! (*Laughs wearily*) What is there left but dependency all our lives? I know so well what becomes of unmarried women who aren't prepared to occupy a position. I've seen such pitiful cases in the South—barely tolerated spinsters living upon the grudging patronage of sister's husband or brother's wife!—stuck away in some little mouse-trap of a room—encouraged by one in-law to visit another—little birdlike women without any nest—eating the crust of humility all their life!

Is that the future that we've mapped out for ourselves? I swear it's the only alternative I can think of! It isn't a very pleasant alternative, is it? Of course—some girls *do marry*. (*Laura twists her hands nervously.*)

Haven't you ever liked some boy?

LAURA   Yes. I liked one once. (*Rises*) I came across his picture a while ago.

AMANDA   (*With some interest*) He gave you his picture?

LAURA   No, it's in the year-book.

AMANDA   (*Disappointed*) Oh—a high-school boy.

LAURA   Yes. His name was Jim. (*Laura lifts the heavy annual from the claw-foot table.*) Here he is in *The Pirates of Penzance*.

AMANDA   (*Absently*) The what?

LAURA   The operetta the senior class put on. He had a wonderful voice and we sat across the aisle from each other Mondays, Wednesdays and Fridays in the Aud. Here he is with the silver cup for debating! See his grin?

AMANDA   (*Absently*) He must have had a jolly disposition.

LAURA   He used to call me—Blue Roses.

AMANDA   Why did he call you such a name as that?

LAURA   When I had that attack of pleurosis—he asked me what was the matter when I came back. I said pleurosis—he thought I said Blue Roses! So that's what he always called me after that. Whenever he saw me, he'd holler, "Hello, Blue Roses!" I didn't care for the girl that he went out with. Emily Meisenbach. Emily was the best-dressed girl at Soldan. She never struck me, though, as being sincere. . . . It says in the Personal Section—they're engaged. That's—six years ago! They must be married by now.

AMANDA Girls that aren't cut out for business careers usually wind up married to some nice man. (*Gets up with a spark of revival*) Sister, that's what you'll do!

(*Laura utters a startled, doubtful laugh. She reaches quickly for a piece of glass.*)

LAURA But, Mother—

AMANDA Yes? (*Crossing to photograph*)

LAURA (*In a tone of frightened apology*) I'm—crippled!

AMANDA Nonsense! Laura, I've told you never, never to use that word. Why, you're not crippled, you just have a little defect—hardly noticeable, even! When people have some slight disadvantage like that, they cultivate other things to make up for it—develop charm—and vivacity—and—*charm!* That's all you have to do! (*She turns again to the photograph.*) One thing your father had *plenty of*—was *charm!*

The Importance of Being Earnest
by Oscar Wilde

Scene: For two females.
Characters: **GWENDOLEN FAIRFAX,** a sophisticated young lady in her mid-twenties from London.
CECILY CARDEW, an English country girl in her late teens.
Setting: The garden of an English country manor house.
Time: An afternoon in the late 1890s.
Situation: Two young ladies, who have just met, believe they are both engaged to be married to the same man, Mr. Ernest Worthing. They begin insulting each other while at the same time participating in the very polite British social custom of taking tea.

■ ■ ■

(*Enter Gwendolen. Exit Merriman.*)

CECILY (*Advancing to meet her*) Pray let me introduce myself to you. My name is Cecily Cardew.

GWENDOLEN Cecily Cardew? (*Moving to her and shaking hands*) What a very sweet name! Something tells me that we are going to be great friends. I like you already more than I can say. My first impressions of people are never wrong.

CECILY How nice of you to like me so much after we have known each other such a comparatively short time. Pray sit down.

GWENDOLEN (*Still standing up*) I may call you Cecily, may I not?

CECILY With pleasure!

GWENDOLEN And you will always call me Gwendolen, won't you?

CECILY If you wish.

GWENDOLEN Then that is all quite settled, is it not?

CECILY I hope so.

(*A pause. They both sit down together.*)

GWENDOLEN Perhaps this might be a favorable opportunity for my mentioning who I am. My father is Lord Bracknell. You have never heard of papa, I suppose?

CECILY I don't think so.

GWENDOLEN Outside the family circle, papa, I am glad to say, is entirely unknown. I think that is quite as it should be. The home seems to me to be the proper sphere for the man. And certainly once a man begins to neglect his domestic duties he becomes painfully effeminate, does he not? And I don't like that. It makes men so very attractive. Cecily, mamma, whose views on education are remarkably strict, has brought me up to be extremely shortsighted; it is part of her system; so do you mind my looking at you through my glasses?

CECILY Oh, not at all, Gwendolen. I am very fond of being looked at.

GWENDOLEN (*After examining Cecily carefully through a lorgnette*) You are here on a short visit, I suppose.

CECILY Oh, no, I live here.

GWENDOLEN (*Severely*) Really? Your mother, no doubt, or some female relative of advanced years, resides here also?

CECILY Oh, no. I have no mother, nor, in fact, any relations.

GWENDOLEN Indeed?

CECILY My dear guardian, with the assistance of Miss Prism, has the arduous task of looking after me.

GWENDOLEN Your guardian?

CECILY Yes, I am Mr. Worthing's ward.

GWENDOLEN Oh! It is strange he never mentioned to me that he had a ward. How secretive of him! He grows more interesting hourly. I am not sure, however, that the news inspires me with feelings of unmixed delight. (*Rising and going to her*) I am very fond of you Cecily; I have liked you ever since I met you. But I am bound to state that now that I know that you are Mr. Worthing's ward, I cannot help expressing a wish you were well, just a little older than you seem to be and not quite so very alluring in appearance. In fact, if I may speak candidly—

CECILY Pray do! I think that whenever one has anything unpleasant to say, one should always be quite candid.

GWENDOLEN Well, to speak with perfect candor, Cecily, I wish that you were fully forty-two, and more than usually plain for your age. Ernest has a strong upright nature. He is the very soul of truth and honor. Disloyalty would be as impossible to him as deception. But even men of the noblest possible moral character are extremely susceptible to the influence of the physical charms of others. Modern, no less Ancient History, supplies us with many most painful examples of what I refer to. If it were not so, indeed, History would be quite unreadable.

CECILY I beg your pardon, Gwendolen, did you say Ernest?

GWENDOLEN Yes.

CECILY Oh, but it is not Mr. Ernest Worthing who is my guardian. It is his brother—his elder brother.

GWENDOLEN (*Sitting down again*) Ernest never mentioned to me that he had a brother.

CECILY I am sorry to say they have not been on good terms for a long time.

GWENDOLEN Ah! that accounts for it. And now that I think of it, I have never heard any man mention his brother. The subject seems distasteful to most men. Cecily, you have lifted a load from my mind. I was growing almost anxious. It would have been terrible if any cloud had come across a friendship like ours, would it not? Of course you are quite, quite sure that it is not Mr. Ernest Worthing who is your guardian?

CECILY Quite sure. (*A pause*) In fact, I am going to be his.

GWENDOLEN (*Inquiringly*) I beg your pardon?

CECILY (*Rather shy and confidingly*) Dearest Gwendolen, there is no reason why I should make a secret of it to you. Our little county newspaper is sure to chronicle the fact next week. Mr. Ernest Worthing and I are engaged to be married.

GWENDOLEN (*Quite politely rising*) My darling Cecily, I think there must be some slight error. Mr. Ernest Worthing is engaged to me. The announcement will appear in the *Morning Post* on Saturday at the latest.

CECILY (*Very politely rising*) I am afraid you must be under some misconception. Ernest proposed to me exactly ten minutes ago. (*Shows diary*)

GWENDOLEN (*Examines diary through her lorgnette carefully*) It is certainly very curious, for he asked me to be his wife yesterday afternoon at 5:30. If you would care to verify the incident, pray do so. (*Produces diary of her own*) I never travel without my diary. One should always have something sensational to read on the train. I am so sorry, dear Cecily, if it is any disappointment for you, but I am afraid *I* have the prior claim.

A Young Lady of Property
by Horton Foote

Scene: Two females.
Characters: **WILMA THOMPSON**, a fifteen-year-old female.
ARABELLA COOKENBOO, Wilma's friend and shadow, also fifteen.
Setting: A swing in the front yard of Wilma's vacant house in Harrison, Texas.
Time: 1925.
Situation: Wilma became a "young lady of property" when her mother died and willed her the family home so that her father

wouldn't gamble it away. Now, Wilma lives with her Aunt Gert and enjoys visiting the house when there are no tenants. Arabella, Wilma's best friend, does everything to please her, so it is no surprise that when Wilma wants to have a Hollywood screen test, Arabella pretends to want one too. In this scene, the girls discuss their futures.

■ ■ ■

(They both sit dejectedly at the table. The lights fade in the area D. L. *as they come up on the area* D. R. *Wilma comes in from* U. C. *of the* D. R. *area. It is the yard of her house. She sits in the swing rocking back and forth, singing "Birmingham Jail" in her hill billy style. Arabella comes running in* R. C. *of the yard area.)*

WILMA   Heh, Arabella. Come sit and swing.

ARABELLA   All right. Your letter came.

WILMA   Whoopee. Where is it?

ARABELLA   Here. *(She gives it to her. Wilma tears it open. She reads.)*

WILMA   *(Reading.)* Dear Miss Thompson. Mr. Delafonte will be glad to see you any time next week about your contemplated screen test. We suggest you call the office when you arrive in the city and we will set an exact time. Yours truly, Adele Murray. Well. . . . Did you get yours?

ARABELLA   Yes.

WILMA   What did it say?

ARABELLA   The same.

WILMA   Exactly the same?

ARABELLA   Yes.

WILMA   Well, let's pack our bags. Hollywood, here we come.

ARABELLA   Wilma . . .

WILMA   Yes?

ARABELLA   I have to tell you something. . . . Well . . . I . . .

WILMA   What is it?

ARABELLA   Well . . . promise me you won't hate me, or stop being my friend. I never had a friend, Wilma, until you began being nice to me, and I couldn't stand it if you weren't my friend any longer . . .

WILMA   Oh, my cow. Stop talking like that. I'll never stop being your friend. What do you want to tell me?

ARABELLA   Well . . . I don't want to go to see Mr. Delafonte, Wilma . . .

WILMA   You don't?

ARABELLA   No. I don't want to be a movie star. I don't want to leave Harrison or my mother or father . . . I just want to stay here the rest of my life and get married and settle down and have children.

WILMA   Arabella . . .

ARABELLA   I just pretended like I wanted to go to Hollywood because I knew you wanted me to, and I wanted you to like me . . .

WILMA   Oh, Arabella . . .

ARABELLA   Don't hate me, Wilma. You see, I'd be afraid . . . I'd die if I had to go to see Mr. Delafonte. Why, I even get faint when I have to recite before the class. I'm not like you. You're not scared of anything.

WILMA   Why do you say that?

ARABELLA   Because you're not. I know.

WILMA   Oh, yes, I am. I'm scared of lots of things.

ARABELLA   What?

WILMA   Getting lost in a city. Being bitten by dogs. Old lady Leighton taking my daddy away . . . *(A pause.)*

ARABELLA   Will you still be my friend?

WILMA   Sure. I'll always be your friend.

ARABELLA   I'm glad. Oh, I almost forgot. Your Aunt Gert said for you to come on home.

WILMA   I'll go in a little. I love to swing in my front yard. Aunt Gert has a swing in her front yard, but it's not the same. Mama and I used to come out here and swing together. Some nights when Daddy was out all night gambling, I used to wake up and hear her out here swinging away. Sometimes she'd let me come and sit beside her. We'd swing until three or four in the morning. *(A pause. She looks out into the yard.)* The pear tree looks sickly, doesn't it? The fig trees are doing nicely though. I was out in back and the weeds are near knee high, but fig trees just seem to thrive in the weeds. The freeze must have killed off the banana trees. . . . *(A pause. Wilma stops swinging—she walks around the yard.)* Maybe I won't leave either. Maybe I won't go to Hollywood after all.

ARABELLA   You won't?

WILMA   No. Maybe I shouldn't. That just comes to me now. You know sometimes my old house looks so lonesome it tears at my heart. I used to think it looks lonesome just whenever it had no tenants, but now it comes to me it has looked lonesome ever since Mama died and we moved away, and it will look lonesome until some of us move back here. Of course, Mama can't, and Daddy won't. So it's up to me.

ARABELLA   Are you gonna live here all by yourself?

WILMA   No. I talk big about living here by myself, but I'm too much of a coward to do that. But maybe I'll finish school and live with Aunt Gert and keep on renting the house until I meet some nice boy with good habits and steady ways, and marry him. Then we'll move here and have children and I bet this old house won't be lonely any more. I'll get Mama's old croquet set and put it out under the pecan trees and play croquet with my children, or sit in this yard and swing and wave to people as they pass by.

ARABELLA   Oh, I wish you would. Mama says that's a normal life for a girl, marrying and having children. She says being an actress is all right, but the other's better.

WILMA   Maybe I've come to agree with your mama. Maybe I was going to Hollywood out of pure lonesomeness. I felt so alone with Mrs. Leighton getting my daddy and my mamma having left the world. Daddy could have taken away my lonesomeness, but he didn't want to or couldn't. Aunt Gert says nobody is lonesome with a house full of children, so maybe that's what I just ought to stay here and have . . .

ARABELLA   Have you decided on a husband yet?

WILMA   No.

ARABELLA   Mama says that's the bad feature of being a girl, you have to wait for the boy to ask you and just pray that the one you want wants you. Tommy Murray is nice, isn't he?

WILMA   I think so.

ARABELLA   Jay Godfrey told me once he wanted to ask you for a date, but he didn't dare because he was afraid you'd turn him down.

WILMA   Why did he think that?

ARABELLA   He said the way you talked he didn't think you would go out with anything less than a movie star.

WILMA   Maybe you'd tell him different . . .

ARABELLA   All right. I think Jay Godfrey is very nice. Don't you?

WILMA   Yes. I think he's very nice and Tommy is nice . . .

ARABELLA   Maybe we could double-date sometimes.

WILMA   That might be fun.

ARABELLA   Oh, Wilma. Don't go to Hollywood. Stay here in Harrison and let's be friends forever. . . .

WILMA   All right. I will.

ARABELLA   You will?

WILMA   Sure, why not? I'll stay here. I'll stay and marry and live in my house.

ARABELLA   Oh, Wilma. I'm so glad. I'm so very glad. *(Wilma gets back in the swing. They swing vigorously back and forth)*

Picnic
by William Inge

Scene: Two females.

Characters: **MADGE OWENS**, a beautiful young woman.
MILLIE OWENS, Madge's tomboyish younger sister.

Setting: The Owens' front porch in a small Kansas town.

Time: A late Labor Day afternoon in the 1950s.

Situation: Mrs. Potts, the Owens' neighbor, has arranged for Hal Carter, a good-looking vagabond who works for her, to escort Millie to the annual Labor Day picnic. Millie, usually a tomboy, has dressed for the picnic and is feeling out-of-place wearing an attractive party dress. In this scene, she shares with her older sister Madge her worries that she won't know what to say or do on her date.

■ ■ ■

Act Two

Scene: *It is late afternoon, the same day. The sun is beginning to set and fills the atmosphere with radiant orange. When the curtain goes up, Millie is on the porch alone. She has permitted herself to "dress up" and wears a becoming, feminine dress in which* *she cannot help feeling a little strange. She is quite attractive. Piano music can be heard offstage, somewhere past Mrs. Potts' house, and Millie stands listening to it for a moment. Then she begins to sway to the music and in a moment is dancing a strange, impromptu dance over the porch and yard. The music stops suddenly and Millie's mood is broken. She rushes upstage and calls off, left.*

MADGE *(Crossing to center and sitting on chair)* I don't know why you couldn't have helped us in the kitchen.

MILLIE *(Lightly, giving her version of the sophisticated belle)* I had to dress for the ball.

MADGE I had to make the potato salad and stuff the eggs and make three dozen bread-and-butter sandwiches.

MILLIE *(In a very affected accent)* I had to *bathe*—and dust my limbs with powder—and slip into my frock . . .

MADGE Did you clean out the bathtub?

MILLIE Yes, I cleaned out the bathtub. *(She becomes very self-conscious)* Madge, how do I look? Now tell me the truth.

MADGE You look very pretty.

MILLIE I feel sorta funny.

MADGE You can have the dress if you want it.

MILLIE Thanks. *(A pause)* Madge, how do you talk to boys?

MADGE Why, you just talk, silly.

MILLIE How d'ya think of things to say?

MADGE I don't know. You just say whatever comes into your head.

MILLIE Supposing nothing ever comes into my head?

MADGE You talked with him all right this morning.

MILLIE But now I've got a *date* with him, and it's *different!*

MADGE You're crazy.

MILLIE I think he's a big show-off. You should have seen him this morning on the high diving board. He did real graceful swan dives, and a two and a half gainer, and a back flip—and kids stood around clapping. He just ate it up.

MADGE *(Her mind elsewhere)* I think I'll paint my toenails tonight and wear sandals.

MILLIE And he was braggin' all afternoon how he used to be a deep-sea diver off Catalina Island.

MADGE Honest?

MILLIE And he says he used to make hundreds of dollars doin' parachute jumps out of a balloon. Do you believe it?

MADGE I don't see why not.

MILLIE You never hear Alan bragging that way.

MADGE Alan never jumped out of a balloon.

MILLIE Madge, I think he's girl crazy.

MADGE You think every boy you see is something horrible.

MILLIE Alan took us into the Hi Ho for Cokes and there was a gang of girls in the back booth—Juanita Badger and her gang. *(Madge groans at hearing this name)* When they saw him, they started giggling and tee-heeing and saying all sorts of crazy things. Then Juanita Badger comes up to me and whispers, "He's the cutest thing I ever saw." Is he, Madge?

MADGE *(Not willing to go overboard)* I certainly wouldn't say he was "the cutest thing I ever *saw.*"

MILLIE Juanita Badger's an old floozy. She sits in the back row at the movie so the guys that come in will see her and sit with her. One time she and Rubberneck Krauss were asked by the management to leave—and they weren't just kissin', either!

MADGE *(Proudly)* I never even speak to Juanita Badger.

MILLIE Madge, do you think he'll like me?

MADGE Why ask me all these questions? You're supposed to be the smart one.

MILLIE I don't really care. I just wonder.

The Chalk Garden
by Enid Bagnold

Scene: Two females.

Characters: **MISS MADRIGAL,** the governess.
LAUREL, Mrs. St. Maugham's sixteen-year-old granddaughter.

Setting: A sitting room in a manor house, Sussex, England.

Time: Mid-morning, 1950s.

Situation: Mrs. St. Maugham, a wealthy English woman, spends most of her time tending to a garden that will not grow and advertising for a companion for her unmanageable granddaughter. Miss Madrigal applies for the job, and Mrs. St. Maugham hires her, even though Miss Madrigal is slightly mysterious and comes with no references. Laurel is fascinated by the strange older woman and is determined to uncover her mysterious past. While questioning Miss Madrigal during a painting lesson, Laurel discovers that she has been to a trial.

■ ■ ■

LAUREL   (*moving to* R *of table*) So you've been to a trial?

MADRIGAL   (*crossing to the couch*) I did not say I hadn't.

LAUREL   (*moving to* L *of Madrigal*) Why did you not say—when you know what store we both lay by it?

MADRIGAL   (*picking up the paintings from the floor*) It may be I think you lay too much store by it. (*She puts the paintings on the table below the couch*)

LAUREL   (*relaxing her tone and asking as though an ordinary light question*) How does one get in?

MADRIGAL   It's surprisingly easy. (*She sits on the couch and picks up the paintbox*)

LAUREL   Was it a trial for murder?

MADRIGAL   (*closing the box*) It would have to be to satisfy you.

LAUREL   *Was* it a trial for murder?

MADRIGAL   (*picking up Laurel's painting block*) Have you finished that flower?

LAUREL   (*yawning*) As much as I can. I get tired of it. (*Wandering to the window*) In my house—at home—there were so many things to do.

MADRIGAL   What was it like?

LAUREL   My home? (*She moves the small table by the couch and sets it* R *of the armchair*)

MADRIGAL   Yes.

LAUREL   (*as though caught unaware*) There was a stream. And a Chinese bridge. And yew trees cut like horses. And a bell on the weathervane, and a little wood called mine . . .

MADRIGAL   Who called it that?

LAUREL   (*unwillingly moved*) She did. My mother. And when it was raining we made an army of her cream pots and a battlefield of her dressing-table—I used to thread her rings on safety pins . . .

MADRIGAL   Tomorrow I will light that candle in the green glass candlestick and you can try to paint that.

LAUREL   What—paint the flame? (*She collects the loose paintings and the jar of water and puts them on the table up* C)

MADRIGAL   Yes.

LAUREL   (*putting the vase and rose on the desk*) I'm tired of fire, too, Boss.

MADRIGAL   (*putting the painting book on the downstage end of the couch*) Why do you sign your name a thousand times?

LAUREL   I am looking for which is me.

MADRIGAL   Shall we read?

LAUREL   (*sitting on the desk chair*) Oh, I don't want to read.

MADRIGAL   Let's have a game.

LAUREL   All right. (*With meaning*) A *guessing* game.

MADRIGAL   Very well. Do you know one?

LAUREL   (*rising and moving above the armchair*) Maitland and I play one called "The Sky's the Limit".

MADRIGAL   How do you begin?

(*Laurel takes the cushion from the armchair, puts it on the floor beside the couch and sits on it*)

LAUREL   We ask three questions each but if you don't answer one, I get a fourth.

MADRIGAL   What do we guess about?

LAUREL   Let's guess about each other. We are both mysterious . . .

MADRIGAL   (*sententious*) The human heart is mysterious.

LAUREL   We don't know the first thing about each other, so there are so many things to ask.

MADRIGAL   But we mustn't go too fast. Or there will be nothing left to discover. Has it got to be the truth?

LAUREL   One can lie. But I get better and better at spotting lies. It's so dull playing with Maitland. He's so innocent.

(*Madrigal folds her hands and waits*)

Now! First question. Are you a—*maiden* lady?

MADRIGAL   (*after a moment's reflection*) I can't answer that.

LAUREL   Why?

MADRIGAL   Because you throw the emphasis so oddly.

LAUREL   Right! You don't answer. so now I have an extra question. *(She pauses)* Are you living under an assumed name?

MADRIGAL   No.

LAUREL   Careful! I'm getting my lie-detector working. Do you take things here at their face value?

MADRIGAL   No.

LAUREL   Splendid! You're getting the idea.

MADRIGAL   *(warningly)* This is to be your fourth question.

LAUREL   *(rising, moving* C *and turning)* Yes. Yes, indeed. I must think—I must be careful. *(She shoots her question hard at Madrigal)* What is the full name of your married sister?

(Madrigal covers the paintbox with her hand and stares for a brief second at Laurel)

MADRIGAL   Clarissa Dalrymple Westerham.

LAUREL   Is Dalrymple Westerham a double name?

MADRIGAL   *(with ironical satisfaction)* You've *had* your questions.

LAUREL   *(gaily accepting defeat)* Yes, I have. Now yours. You've only three unless I pass one. *(She resumes her seat on the cushion)*

MADRIGAL   *(after a pause)* Was your famous affair in Hyde Park on the night of your mother's marriage?

LAUREL   *(wary)* About that time.

MADRIGAL   What was the charge by the police?

LAUREL   *(wary)* The police didn't come into it.

MADRIGAL   *(airily)* Did someone follow you? And try to kiss you?

LAUREL   *(off her guard)* Kiss me! It was a case of Criminal Assault.

MADRIGAL   *(following that up)* How do you know—if there wasn't a charge by the Police?

LAUREL   *(after a brief pause; triumphant)* That's one too many questions. *(She rises) Now* for the deduction. *(She picks up the cushion, replaces it on the armchair and sits)*

MADRIGAL   You didn't tell me there was a deduction.

LAUREL   I forgot. It's the whole point. Mine's ready.

MADRIGAL   What do you deduce?

LAUREL   *(taking a breath; then fast, as though she might be stopped)* That you've changed so much you must have been something quite different. When you came here you were like a rusty

hinge that wanted oiling. You spoke to yourself out loud without knowing it. You had been *alone.* You may have been a missionary in Central Africa. You may have escaped from a private asylum. But as a maiden lady you are an impostor. *(She changes her tone slightly; slower and more penetrating)* About your assumed name I am not so sure. *But you have no married sister.*

MADRIGAL   *(lightly)* You take my breath away.

LAUREL   *(leaning back in her chair; as lightly)* Good at it, aren't I?

MADRIGAL   *(gaily)* Yes, for a mind under a cloud.

LAUREL   Now for *your* deduction.

MADRIGAL   *(rising)* Mine must keep. *(She moves to the door down* R, *taking the paintbox with her)*

LAUREL   *(rising)* But it's the game! Where are you going?

MADRIGAL   *(pleasantly)* To my room. To be sure I have left no clues unlocked. *(She opens the door)*

LAUREL   To your past life?

MADRIGAL   Yes. You have given me so much warning.

(Madrigal exits down R. *Laurel, taken aback, stands for a moment looking after her, looks around the room, then moves to the table up* C, *picks up the handbell, rings it and stands waiting, looking* R.

Maitland rushes in from the pantry, putting on his jacket.)

Lemonade
by James Prideaux

Scene: Two females.

Characters: **MABEL LAMSTON,** an affluent matron lady in her mid- or late fifties.

EDITH NORTHRUP, similar to Mabel, but slightly younger.

Setting: A deserted highway at the edge of a Midwestern town.

Time: Memorial Day, the late 1960s.

Situation: Much in the same way that children set up lemonade stands, two lonely ladies meet unexpectedly on the highway to sell lemonade. Edith is more confident and vocal, while Mable is slightly timid, but neither seem to be very good salespeople. Since no cars stop and there are no sales, the ladies pass the time in friendly competition bragging about their personal accomplishments.

■ ■ ■

The curtain rises on a bare stage.

Mabel Lamston appears R. *She is a matronly lady in her mid or late fifties. There is about her a smug air of affluence and well being. She is dressed for a warm Spring day in a simple—but expensive—frock. A voluminous straw bag hangs from her shoulder. She carries a large pitcher of lemonade in one hand, and drags a wooden box behind her with the other. She places the wooden box on end at* R. *and carefully puts the pitcher on top of it.*

MABEL There! *(Satisfied, she exits* R. *for a moment, returning with a stool and a large poster. She puts the stool behind the box, and then leans the poster against the front of the box so that it faces the audience. It reads:* LEMONADE—2¢ A GLASS. *She sits on the stool and rummaging in her bag, produces paper cups, which she arranges next to the pitcher. Now she is ready for business, she and her stand facing the audience. Her head moves slowly from left to right. Calling in a timid, cultured voice.)* Lemonade. *(A little louder.)* Lemonade. Get your ice cold lemonade here. *(Edith Northrup appears* L. *She is cut of the same cloth as Mabel, but she is slighter, smaller, perhaps a little younger. A bag hangs from her shoulder, and she also carries a pitcher of lemonade and drags a box. She stops dead upon seeing Mabel.)*

EDITH Why, Mabel Lamston!

MABEL Edith!

EDITH Of all people! I never expected—

MABEL What a surprise! *(Mabel rises, Edith approaches, and they touch cheeks.)*

EDITH What are you doing here?

MABEL Now don't laugh. I'm selling lemonade. I've got this little stand and I'm selling lemonade. *(She looks at Edith's pitcher.)* You don't mean—! *(They shriek with laughter.)*

EDITH *(Politely.)* I'll go down the road.

MABEL You'll do nothing of the kind. There's plenty of business for both of us.

EDITH Sure you don't mind?

MABEL *(Helping her place the box beside hers, facing the audience.)* I'll be glad for the company. Where's your stool?

EDITH It's over by the telephone pole. I won't be a minute.

MABEL *(Sitting.)* I'll mind the store. *(Edith exits* L., *returning immediately with her stool and sign.)*

EDITH I can't get over meeting you like this.

MABEL I've always said it's a small world.

EDITH It certainly is *here*. *(Puts her sign up—it reads the same as Mabel's—and, sitting, pulls paper cups out of her bag.)*

MABEL All set? *(Edith puts the cups beside the pitcher.)*

EDITH I'm open for business. *(Suddenly they both half rise and, leaning forward, read each other's signs. They smile at one another and sit down. Her head moving left to right, taking off gloves.)* I've never seen so many cars.

MABEL It's the holiday weekend. Happy Decoration Day!

EDITH We always called it Memorial Day. Happy *Memorial* Day! *(They laugh socially.)*

MABEL Now what I do is, I shout lemonade every so often. Like this. *(Softly, meekly.)* Lemonade!

EDITH I don't know if I've got the nerve.

MABEL Well, you'll never make a sale if you don't, Edith. Try it.

EDITH *(Meekly.)* Lemonade.

MABEL That's very good.

EDITH *(Louder.)* Lemonade!

MABEL Wonderful!

EDITH *(Quite loud.)* Lemonade!

MABEL Talent will out!

EDITH I used to sing, you know.

MABEL Really?

EDITH Years ago. I was with a singing group. You probably heard of us. The Cincinnati Songbirds?

MABEL *(She hasn't.)* I'm trying to think.

EDITH We sang in hotel lobbies a lot. That's how I met Herbert. In the lobby of the Seqwaunie Hotel. He was sitting and I was singing and one thing led to another.

MABEL *(Conversationally.)* Oh, yes?

EDITH I miss my singing.

MABEL I've always been sorry *I* didn't have a career.

EDITH Well, Mabel, now you have.

MABEL This? This is just a diversion. I don't expect it to *lead* anywhere. Do you?

EDITH   (*Laughing.*) Gracious, no! It's just an excuse to get out of the house.

MABEL   I know how you feel.

EDITH   Now that the children are gone, things are just too quiet for me around there. I like things stirring. All these cars whizzing by!

MABEL   I was sorry to hear about the children, Edith.

EDITH   (*Pleasantly.*) Don't give it a thought. Have you sold any?

MABEL   I just got here myself.

EDITH   If I only sell one glass I'll feel I've done something. I had such a shock the other day.

MABEL   What in the world—?

EDITH   Elizabeth Arden's obituary. Did you read it?

MABEL   Let me think.

EDITH   When I saw what she'd accomplished, I just went limp in the knees. There she was, all her life, up to her earrings in liniments and lotions. Inventing things, discovering things. She made Madame Curie look like a *slouch!* And the money. Millions of dollars! She even kept race horses.

MABEL   I wouldn't care to keep race horses.

EDITH   When I think what *I've* done, I wonder why I was *put* on this earth. Do you ever feel like that?

MABEL   (*Sighing.*) It's all too clear to me, Edith.

EDITH   What is?

MABEL   We're *mothers*, that's what we're here for. And I for one am *exhausted*. Bringing them up, seeing them through college, making good marriages. And with my brood, it was especially difficult. Marilyn cross-eyed and Randolph a cripple. I had to do double-duty. Anyway, I did it and that's that.

EDITH   I don't mean to pry, but what are you doing out here on the highway selling lemonade?

MABEL   I don't know, I really don't. I just got up this morning and I looked at Raymond reading his newspaper over the breakfast coffee and I thought: wouldn't it be fun to go out to the highway and set up a lemonade stand! I don't mind admitting I feel pretty peculiar. The president of the League of Women Voters.

EDITH   Well, *I'm* Grand Matron of the Order of Eastern Star. (*They laugh.*) Lemonade!

MABEL   Lemonade! (*More laughter.*)

EDITH   (*Head turning.*) Where do you suppose all these people are going?

MABEL   Just out driving, I guess. I used to enjoy that—especially on Sundays—but I don't so much anymore. Too many cars on the road.

EDITH   I suppose I should be at the cemetery doing something to the children's graves.

MABEL   I feel so guilty. I ought to be putting peonies on Raymond's mother. We do that every year. Put peonies. On Raymond's mother.

EDITH   Herbert's people are all in Sandusky so I just send his sister a check every year and she decorates *them*. But she has such poor taste. She buys plastic wreaths! I certainly hope when my time comes nobody puts a plastic wreath on me.

MABEL   You see plastic everywhere these days, Edith.

EDITH   I just pray that Herbert's sister goes *first*.

MABEL   (*Excitedly, half rising.*) Did you see the way that car slowed down?

EDITH   I wasn't looking.

MABEL   I thought we had our first sale. (*Waves her hand in front of her face.*) I don't see how cars on a paved highway can stir up so much dust.

EDITH   It's terrible. (*Conspiratorially.*) I think we ought to sample the product.

MABEL   (*Coyly.*) Now, we mustn't drink up the profits.

EDITH   One little cup? I want you to try mine.

MABEL   I'd love to. And you must have some of *mine*. (*They each pour a cup.*) I'm afraid it's tepid.

EDITH   It's impossible to keep it cold. Mine was *icy* when I left the house, but now I'm sure it's—(*She accepts a cup and hands Mabel one.*) Thank you.

MABEL   Thank you, dear.

EDITH   (*She sips.*) Oh, *Mabel!*

MABEL   Is it all right?

EDITH   It's just *perfect*. That certainly hits the spot.

Antigone
by Jean Anouilh

Scene: Two females

Characters: **ANTIGONE,** a young Grecian girl, daughter of Oedipus, the late king of Thebes.

ISMENE, her older sister.

Setting: The steps of the castle of Thebes.

Time: Early morning.

Situation: Following the death of Oedipus, his sons, Eteocles and Polynices, kill each other in a civil war over control of his kingdom. Creon, Oedipus's brother-in-law, upon becoming the king decrees that Eteocles be given a noble burial. Believing that Polynices began the war, Creon also decrees that his body be left unburied and anyone covering it be executed. Antigone defies the decree and gives her brother a religious burial so that his soul will not wander forever. This scene takes place the morning after the burial.

■ ■ ■

ISMENE Aren't you well?

ANTIGONE Of course I am. Just a little tired. I got up too early. *(She relaxes, suddenly tired.)*

ISMENE I couldn't sleep, either.

ANTIGONE Ismene, you ought not to go without your beauty sleep.

ISMENE Don't make fun of me.

ANTIGONE I'm not, Ismene, truly. This particular morning, seeing how beautiful you are makes everything easier for me. Wasn't I a miserable little beast when we were small? I used to fling mud at you, and put worms down your neck. I remember tying you to a tree and cutting off your hair. Your beautiful hair! How easy it must be never to be unreasonable with all that smooth silken hair so beautifully set round your head.

ISMENE *(Abruptly)* Why do you insist upon talking about other things?

ANTIGONE *(Gently)* I'm not talking about other things.

ISMENE Antigone, I've thought about it a lot.

ANTIGONE Have you?

ISMENE I thought about it all night long. Antigone, you're mad.

ANTIGONE Am I?

ISMENE We cannot do it.

ANTIGONE Why not?

ISMENE Creon will have us put to death.

ANTIGONE Of course he will. That's what he's here for. He will do what he has to do, and we will do what we have to do. He is bound to put us to death. We are bound to go out and bury our brother. That's the way it is. What do you think we can do to change it?

ISMENE *(Releases Antigone's hand; draws back a step)* I don't want to die.

ANTIGONE I'd prefer not to die, myself.

ISMENE Listen to me, Antigone. I thought about it all night. I'm older than you are. I always think things over and you don't. You are impulsive. You get a notion in your head and you jump up and do the thing straight off. And if it's silly, well, so much the worse for you. Whereas, I think things out.

ANTIGONE Sometimes it is better not to think too much.

ISMENE I don't agree with you! Oh, I know it's horrible. And I pity Polynices just as much as you do. But all the same, I sort of see what Uncle Creon means.

ANTIGONE. I don't want to "sort of see" anything.

ISMENE Uncle Creon is the king. He has to set an example!

ANTIGONE But I am not the king; and I don't have to set people examples. Little Antigone gets a notion in her head—the nasty brat, the wilful, wicked girl; and they put her in a corner all day, or they lock her up in the cellar. And she deserves it. She shouldn't have disobeyed!

ISMENE There you go, frowning, glowering, wanting your own stubborn way in everything. Listen to me. I'm right oftener than you are.

ANTIGONE I don't want to be right!

ISMENE At least you can try to understand.

ANTIGONE Understand! The first word I ever heard out of any of you was that word "understand." Why didn't I "understand" that I must not play with water—cold, black, beautiful flowing water—because I'd spill it on the palace tiles. Or with earth, because earth dirties a little girl's frock. Why didn't I "understand" that nice children don't eat out of every dish at once; or give everything in their pockets to beggars; or run in the wind so fast that they fall down; or ask for a drink when they're perspiring; or want to go swimming when it's either too early or too late, merely because they happen to feel like swimming. Understand! I don't want to understand. There'll be time enough to understand when I'm old. . . . If I ever *am* old. But not now.

ISMENE   He is stronger than we are, Antigone. He is the king. And the whole city is with him. Thousands and thousands of them, swarming through all the streets of Thebes.

ANTIGONE   I am not listening to you.

ISMENE   His mob will come running, howling as it runs. A thousand arms will seize our arms. A thousand breaths will breathe into our faces. Like one single pair of eyes, a thousand eyes will stare at us. We'll be driven in a tumbrel through their hatred, through the smell of them and their cruel, roaring laughter. We'll be dragged to the scaffold for torture, surrounded by guards with their idiot faces all bloated, their animal hands clean-washed for the sacrifice, their beefy eyes squinting as they stare at us. And we'll know that no shrieking and no begging will make them understand that we want to live, for they are like slaves who do exactly as they've been told, without caring about right or wrong. And we shall suffer, we shall feel pain rising in us until it becomes so unbearable that we *know* it must stop. But it won't stop, it will go on rising and rising, like a screaming voice. Oh, I can't, I can't, Antigone! *(A pause)*

ANTIGONE   How well you have thought it all out.

ISMENE   I thought of it all night long. Didn't you?

ANTIGONE   Oh, yes.

ISMENE   I'm an awful coward, Antigone.

ANTIGONE   So am I. But what has that got to do with it?

ISMENE   But, Antigone! Don't you want to go on living?

ANTIGONE   Go on living! Who was it that was always the first out of bed because she loved the touch of the cold morning air on her bare skin? Who was always the last to bed because nothing less than infinite weariness could wean her from the lingering night? Who wept when she was little because there were too many grasses in the meadow, too many creatures in the field, for her to know and touch them all?

ISMENE *(Clasps Antigone's hands, in a sudden rush of tenderness)*   Darling little sister!

ANTIGONE *(Repulsing her)*   No! For heaven's sake! Don't paw me! And don't let us start sniveling! You say you've thought it all out. The howling mob—the torture—the fear of death . . . they've made up your mind for you. Is that it?

ISMENE   Yes.

ANTIGONE   All right. They're as good excuses as any.

ISMENE   Antigone, be sensible. It's all very well for men to believe in ideas and die for them. But you are a girl!

ANTIGONE.   Don't I know I'm a girl? Haven't I spent my life cursing the fact that I was a girl?

ISMENE *(With spirit)*   Antigone! You have everything in the world to make you happy. All you have to do is reach out for it. You are going to be married; you are young; you are beautiful—

ANTIGONE   I am not beautiful.

ISMENE   Yes, you are! Not the way other girls are. But it's always you that the little boys turn to look back at when they pass us in the street. And when you go by, the little girls stop talking. They stare and stare at you, until we've turned a corner.

ANTIGONE *(A faint smile)*   "Little boys—little girls."

ISMENE *(Challengingly)*   And what about Haemon?

ANTIGONE   I shall see Haemon this morning. I'll take care of Haemon. You always said I was mad; and it didn't matter how little I was or what I wanted to do. Go back to bed now, Ismene. The sun is coming up, and as you see, there is nothing I can do today. Our brother Polynices is as well guarded as if he had won the war and were sitting on his throne. Go along. You are pale with weariness.

ISMENE   What are you going to do?

. . .

ANTIGONE   I don't feel like going to bed. However, if you like, I'll promise not to leave the house till you wake up. Nurse is getting me breakfast. Go and get some sleep. The sun is just up. Look at you: You can't keep your eyes open. Go.

ISMENE   And you will listen to reason, won't you? You'll let me talk to you about this again? Promise?

ANTIGONE I promise. I'll let you talk. I'll let all of you talk. Go to bed, now. *(Ismene goes to arch and exits.)* Poor Ismene!

. . .

(Ismene enters again.)

ISMENE I can't sleep, I know. I'm terrified. I'm so afraid that even though it is daylight, you will still try to bury Polynices. Antigone, little sister, we all want to make you happy—Haemon, and Nurse, and I, and Puff whom you love. We love you, we are alive, we need you. And you remember what Polynices was like. He was our brother, of course. But he's dead; and he never loved you. He was a bad brother. He was like an enemy in the house. He never thought of you. Why should you think of him? What if his soul does have to wander through endless time without rest or peace? Don't try something that is beyond your strength. You are always defying the world, but you're only a girl, after all. Stay at home tonight. Don't try to do it, I beg you. It's Creon's doing, not ours.

ANTIGONE You are too late, Ismene. When you first saw me this morning, I had just come in from burying him.

(Antigone exits through arch.)

Duet Scenes For One Male and One Female

Step on a Crack
by Susan Zeder

Scene: One male and one female.
Characters: **ELLIE MURPHY,** a ten-year-old girl.
             MAX MURPHY, her father, about thirty-seven.
Setting: Their home.
Time: The present
Situation: Ellie was content until her widowed father remarried. In this scene, Ellie has spilled grease on the new carpet in her room. Lucille, Ellie's stepmother, is unhappy because she can't get the stain out. In retaliation, Ellie

tells Lucille that she will never be her real mother. Lucille exits, leaving the angry Ellie and the depressed and angry Max.

■ ■ ■

ELLIE It's not my fault.

MAX You hurt her feelings.

ELLIE I have feelings too you know. Just because you're a kid doesn't mean you're junk!

MAX Come off it Ellie.

ELLIE That spot is almost out.

MAX *[Really down]* Yeah!

ELLIE Maybe we could put something over it.

MAX Yeah.

ELLIE With a sign that says "Don't look here."

MAX *[With a slight laugh]* Sure.

ELLIE *[Trying to get him out of his mood.]* Knock, knock.

MAX Not now, Ellie.

ELLIE Let's wrestle.

MAX Uh uh! You're getting too big for me.

ELLIE Do you think I'm too fat?

MAX You? Naw you're fine.

ELLIE Hey Pop, do you remember the time we went camping and you drove all afternoon to get out to the woods? It was dark when we pitched the tent and we heard all those funny sounds and you said it was MONSTERS. Then in the morning we found out we were in somebody's front lawn.

MAX *[Responding a bit.]* I knew where we were all the time.

ELLIE Or when we went to the Super Bowl and I got cold, and you said yell something in your megaphone.

MAX Yeah, and you yelled "I'm cold and I want to go home." *[They both laugh.]*

ELLIE *[Tentatively.]* Hey Pop, tell me about my real mother.

MAX How come you want to hear about her all the time these days? *[Ellie sits at his feet and rests against his knees.]*

ELLIE I just do. Hey do you remember the time it was my birthday and you brought Mom home from the hospital, and I didn't know she was coming that time? I remember I was already in bed and you guys wanted to surprise me. She just came into my room, kissed me goodnight and tucked me in, just like it was any other night.

MAX [*Moved*] How could you remember that? You were just four years old.

ELLIE I just remember.

MAX Your mother was a wonderful person and I loved her very much.

ELLIE As much as you . . . like Lucille?

MAX Ellie.

ELLIE Was she pretty?

MAX She was beautiful.

ELLIE Do I look like her?

MAX Naw, you look more like me, you mug.

ELLIE [*Suddenly angry*] Why does everything have to change?

MAX Hey.

ELLIE How come Lucille is always so neat and everything? I bet she never even burps.

MAX She does.

ELLIE HUH!

MAX I heard her once.

ELLIE Do you think I'd look cute with make-up on?

MAX You? You're just a kid.

ELLIE But Lucille wears make-up. Lots of it.

MAX Well she's grown up.

ELLIE Hey do you know how old she is?

MAX Sure. Thirty-five.

ELLIE How come you married such an old one?

MAX That's not old.

ELLIE Huh!

MAX Why I am older than that myself.

ELLIE You are??

MAX Ellie, you know how you get to go to camp in the summer. You get to go away all by yourself.

ELLIE Yeah but I'm not going any more.

MAX: You're not?

ELLIE Nope, look what happened the last time I went. You and Lucille get to be good friends, then as soon as I get back you get married. Who knows if I go away again I might get back and find out you moved to Alaska.

MAX We wouldn't do that.

ELLIE: You might.

MAX Ellie, kids can't always go where parents go. Sometimes parents go away all by themselves.

ELLIE How come ever since you got married I am such a kid. You never used to say I was a kid. We did everything together. Now all I hear is, "Kids can't do this," "Kids can't do that,"

"Kids have to go to bed at eight-thirty." "Kids have to clean up their rooms." Why does everything have to change?

MAX Nothing's changed. I still love you the same. Now there's just two of us who love you.

ELLIE HUH!

POP I just wish you'd try a little harder to. . . .

ELLIE To like Lucille? Why should I? She doesn't like me. She likes cute little girls who play with dollies.

MAX Well she got herself a messy little mug that likes junk. [*Ellie pulls away.*]

MAX I'm just kidding. She likes you fine the way you are.

ELLIE Oh yeah, well I don't like her.

MAX Why not?

[*Lucille enters and overhears the following.*]

ELLIE Cause . . . Cause . . Cause she's a wicked stepmother . . . . [*Ellie giggles in spite of herself. Max is really angry.*]

MAX That's not funny!

ELLIE You shout at me all the time!

MAX [*Shouting.*] I'm not shouting!

Trouble in Mind
by Alice Childress

Scene: One male and one female

Characters: **WILETTA MAYER,** a middle-aged actress.

HENRY, the elderly, hard-of-hearing theatre doorman.

Setting: The stage of a Broadway theatre in New York City.

Time: Ten o'clock Monday morning, fall, 1957.

Situation: We hear banging sounds growing louder and louder from offstage. As the scene opens, we see the stage with props and leftovers from the last show. Wiletta Mayer enters, expressing her unhappiness at finding the stage door locked. She is greeted by Henry, the kind old doorman who remembers her from her younger days, when she was the star.

■ ■ ■

WILETTA   My Lord, I like to have wore my arm off bangin' on that door! What you got it locked for?

(LIGHTS up brighter.)

Had me standin' out there in the cold, catchin' my death of pneumonia!

(Henry, the elderly doorman, enters.)

HENRY   I didn't hear a thing . . . I didn't know . . .

WILETTA   *(Is suddenly moved by the sight of the theater. She holds up her hand for silence, looks out and up at the balcony. She loves the theater. She turns back to Henry.)* A theater always makes me feel that way . . . gotta get still for a second.

HENRY   *(Welcomes an old memory.)* You . . . you are Wiletta Mayer . . . more than twenty years ago, in the old Galy Theater. . . .

(Is pleased to be remembered.)

You was singin' a number, with the lights changin' color all around you. . . . What was the name of that show?

WILETTA   *Brownskin Melody.*

HENRY   That's it . . . and the lights . . .

WILETTA   Was a doggone rainbow.

HENRY   And you looked so pretty and sounded so fine, there's no denyin' it.

WILETTA   Thank you, but I . . . I . . . *(Hates to admit she doesn't remember him.)*

HENRY   I'm Henry.

WILETTA   Mmmmm, you don't say.

HENRY   I was the electrician. Rigged up all those lights and never missed a cue. I'm the doorman here now. I've been in show business over fifty years. I'm the doorman . . . Henry.

WILETTA   That's a nice name. I . . . I sure remember those lights.

HENRY   Bet you can't guess how old I am, I'll betcha.

WILETTA   *(Would rather not guess.)* Well . . . you're sure lookin' good.

HENRY   Go ahead, take a guess.

WILETTA   *(Being very kind.)* Ohhhhh, I'd say you're in your . . . late fifties.

HENRY   *(Laughs proudly.)* I fool 'em all! I'm seventy-eight years old! How's that?

WILETTA   Ohhhh, don't be tellin' it. *(She places her script and purse on the table, removes her coat.)*

(Henry takes coat and hangs it on a rack.)

HENRY   You singin' in this new show?

WILETTA   No, I'm actin'. I play the mother.

HENRY   *(Is hard of hearing.)* How's that?

WILETTA   I'm the mother!

HENRY   Could I run next door and get you some coffee? I'm goin' anyway, no bother.

WILETTA   No, thank you just the same.

HENRY   If you open here, don't let 'em give you dressin' room "C." It's small and it's got no "john" in it . . . excuse me, I mean . . . no commode . . . Miss Mayer.

WILETTA   *(Feeling like the star he's made her.)* Thank you, I'll watch out for that.

HENRY   *(Reaches for a small chair, changes his mind and draws the gilt armchair to the table.)* Make yourself comfortable. The old Galy. Yessir, I'm seventy-eight years old.

WILETTA   Well, I'm not gonna tell you my age. A woman that'll tell her age will tell anything.

HENRY   *(Laughs.)* Oh, that's a good one! I'll remember that! A woman that'll tell her age . . . what else?

WILETTA   Will tell anything.

HENRY   *Will tell.* Well, I'll see you a little later. *(He exits stage Left.)*

WILETTA   *(Saying goodbye to the kind of gentle treatment she seldom receives.)* So long. *(Rises and walks downstage, strikes a pose from the "old Galy" and sings a snatch of an old song.)*

Oh, honey babe
Oh, honey baby . . .

(She pushes the memory aside.) Yes indeed!

Look Homeward Angel
by Kettie Frings
Based on the novel by Thomas Wolfe

Scene: One male, one female

Characters: **LAURA JAMES,** an attractive boarder, twenty-three years old. **EUGENE GANT,** an awkward young man of seventeen.

Setting: The Dixieland Boarding House, Altamont, North Carolina

Time: A fall evening, 1916.

Situation: Mrs. Gant runs a boarding house, the Dixieland, in Altamont. Her husband is a failure, and she must provide for the family by renting rooms. Eugene, the youngest Gant, has a craving for knowledge. He would like to go away to college, but there isn't enough money. In this scene Laura, a new boarder from Richmond, Virginia, makes friends with Eugene.

■ ■ ■

LAURA   Good evening.

EUGENE   What!

LAURA   I said good evening.

EUGENE   *(Flustered.)* Goodyado. *(Rises, moves Down Left of her.)*

LAURA   I beg your pardon?

EUGENE   I mean—I meant to say good evening, how do you do?

LAURA   Goodyado! I like that much better. Goodyado! *(They shake hands, Laura reacting to Eugene's giant grip. Eugene sits Left on unit.)* Don't you think that's funny?

EUGENE   It's about as funny as most things I do.

LAURA   May I sit down?

EUGENE   *(Leaping up.)* Please.

LAURA   *(As she sits.)* I'm Laura James.

EUGENE   I know. My name's Eugene Gant.

LAURA   You know, I've seen you before.

EUGENE   Yes, earlier this afternoon.

LAURA   I mean before that. I saw you throw those advertising cards in the gutter.

EUGENE   You did?

LAURA   I was coming from the station. You know where the train crosses the street? You were just standing there staring at it. I walked right by you and smiled at you. I never got such a snub before in my whole life. My, you must be crazy about trains.

EUGENE   *(Sits Left of her.)* You stood right beside me? *(Ben plays a record on the PHONOGRAPH.)* Where are you from?

LAURA   Richmond, Virginia.

EUGENE   Richmond! That's a big city, isn't it?

LAURA   It's pretty big.

EUGENE   How many people?

LAURA   Oh, about a hundred and twenty thousand, I'd say.

EUGENE   Are there a lot of pretty parks and boulevards?

LAURA   Oh, yes—

EUGENE   And fine tall buildings, with elevators?

LAURA   Yes, it's quite a metropolis.

EUGENE   Theatres and things like that?

LAURA   A lot of good shows come to Richmond. Are you interested in shows?

EUGENE   You have a big library. Did you know it has over a hundred thousand books in it?

LAURA   No, I didn't know that.

EUGENE   Well, it does. I read that somewhere. It would take a long time to read a hundred thousand books, wouldn't it?

LAURA   Yes, it would.

EUGENE   I figure about twenty years. How many books do they let you take out at one time?

LAURA   I really don't know.

EUGENE   They only let you take out two here!

LAURA   That's too bad.

EUGENE   You have some great colleges in Virginia. Did you know that William and Mary is the second oldest college in the country?

LAURA   Is it? What's the oldest?

EUGENE   Harvard! I'd like to study there! First Chapel Hill. That's our state university. Then Harvard. I'd like to study all over the world, learn all its languages. I love words, don't you?

LAURA   Yes; yes I do.

EUGENE   Are you laughing at me?

LAURA   Of course not.

EUGENE   You are smiling a lot!

LAURA   I'm smiling because I'm enjoying myself. I like talking to you.

EUGENE   I like talking to you, too. I always talk better with older people.

LAURA   Oh!

EUGENE   They know so much more.

LAURA   Like me?

EUGENE   Yes. You're very interesting.

LAURA   Am I?

EUGENE   Oh yes! You're very interesting!

. . .

LAURA   You do like trains, don't you?

EUGENE   Mama took us on one to St. Louis to the Fair, when I was only five. Have you ever touched one?

LAURA   What?

EUGENE   A locomotive. Have you put your hand on one? You have to feel things to fully understand them.

LAURA   Aren't they rather hot?

EUGENE   Even a cold one, standing in a station yard. You know what you feel? You feel the shining steel rails under it—and the rails send a message right into your hand—a message of all the mountains that engine ever passed—all the flowing rivers, the forests, the towns, all the houses, the people, the washlines flapping in the fresh cool breeze—the beauty of the people in the way they live and the way they work—a farmer waving from his field, a kid from the school yard—the faraway places it roars through at night, places you don't even know, can hardly imagine. Do you believe it? You feel the rhythm of a whole life, a whole country clicking through your hand.

LAURA *(Impressed.)* I'm not sure we all would. I believe *you* do.

(There is a moment while Laura looks at Eugene. Ben moves up to the veranda and the phonograph plays another RECORD. Eugene and Laura speak simultaneously.)

EUGENE How long do } **LAURA** How you plan to stay here—? } old are you, Gene?

EUGENE I'm sorry—please. *(Draws a chair close to Laura, straddles it, facing her.)*

LAURA No, you.

EUGENE How long do you plan to stay here, Miss James?

LAURA My name is Laura. I wish you'd call me that.

EUGENE Laura. It's a lovely name. Do you know what it means?

LAURA No.

EUGENE I read a book once on the meaning of names. Laura is the laurel. The Greek symbol of victory.

LAURA Victory. Maybe some day I'll live up to that! *(After a second.)* What does Eugene mean?

EUGENE Oh, I forget.

LAURA *You*, forget?

EUGENE It means "well born."

LAURA How old are you?

EUGENE Why?

LAURA I'm always curious about people's ages.

EUGENE So am I. How old are you?

LAURA I'm twenty-one. You?

EUGENE Nineteen. Will you be staying here long?

LAURA I don't know exactly.

EUGENE You're only twenty-one?

LAURA How old did you think I was?

EUGENE Oh, about that. About twenty-one, I'd say. That's not old at all!

LAURA *(Laughs.)* I don't feel it is!

EUGENE I was afraid you might think I was too young for you to waste time with like this!

LAURA I don't think nineteen is young at all!

EUGENE It isn't, really, is it?

LAURA *(Rises.)* Gene, if we keep rushing together like this, we're going to have a collision.

The Miracle Worker
by William Gibson

Scene: One male, one female
Characters: ANAGNOS, a Greek man who is an administrator at the Perkins Institution for the Blind.
ANNIE SULLIVAN, a 20-year-old girl who is outspoken, impudent, and stubborn, but intelligent and likable.
Setting: Anagnos's office in the Perkins Institution for the Blind in Boston, Massachusetts.
Time: A day in the year 1887.
Situation: Annie Sullivan grew up in a bleak and horrifying poorhouse with her brother Jimmie prior to coming to the Perkins Institution for the Blind. She has been summoned into Anagnos's office for guidance and a good-bye before leaving the institution to be the governess and teacher of Helen Keller, a deaf, blind, and mute girl who does not know how to properly communicate.

■ ■ ■

ANAGNOS —who could do nothing for the girl, of course. It was Dr. Bell who thought she might somehow be taught. I have written the family only that a suitable governess, Miss Annie Sullivan, has been found here in Boston— *(The LIGHTS begin to come up, Down Left, on a long table and chair. The table contains equipment for teaching the blind by touch—a small replica of the human skeleton, stuffed animals, models of flowers and plants, piles of books. The chair contains a girl of 20, Annie Sullivan, with a face which in repose is grave and rather obstinate, and* *when active is impudent, combative, twinkling with all the life that is lacking in Helen's, and handsome; there is a crude vitality to her. Her suitcase is at her knee. Anagnos, a stocky bearded man, comes into the light only towards the end of his speech.)* — and will come. It will no doubt be difficult for you there, Annie. But it has been difficult for you at our school too, hm? Gratifying, yes, when you came to us and could not spell your name, to accomplish so much here in a few years, but always an Irish battle. For independence. *(He studies Annie, humorously; she does not open her eyes.)* This is my last time to counsel you, Annie, and you do lack some—by some I mean *all*—what, tact or talent to bend. To others. And what has saved you on more than one occasion here at Perkins is that there was nowhere to expel you to. Your eyes hurt?

ANNIE   My ears, Mr. Anagnos. *(And now she has opened her eyes; they are inflamed, vague, slightly crossed, clouded by the granular growth of trachoma, and she often keeps them closed to shut out the pain of light.)*

ANAGNOS   *(Severely.)* Nowhere but back to Tewksbury, where children learn to be saucy. Annie, I know how dreadful it was there, but that battle is dead and done with, why not let it stay buried?

ANNIE   *(Cheerily.)* I think God must owe me a resurrection.

ANAGNOS   *(A bit shocked.)* What?

ANNIE   *(Taps her brow.)* Well, He keeps digging up that battle!

ANAGNOS   That is not a proper thing to say, Annie. It is what I mean.

ANNIE   *(Meekly.)* Yes. But I know what I'm like, what's this child like?

ANAGNOS   Like?

ANNIE   Well— Bright or dull, to start off.

ANAGNOS   No one knows. And if she is dull, you have no patience with this?

ANNIE   Oh, in grownups you have to, Mr. Anagnos. I mean in children it just seems a little—precocious, can I use that word?

ANAGNOS   Only if you can spell it.

ANNIE   Premature. So I hope at least she's a bright one.

ANAGNOS   Deaf, blind, mute—who knows? She is like a little safe, locked, that no one can open. Perhaps there is a treasure inside.

ANNIE   Maybe it's empty, too?

ANAGNOS   Possible. I should warn you, she is much given to tantrums.

ANNIE   Means something is inside. Well, so am I, if I believe all I hear. Maybe you should warn *them.*

ANAGNOS   *(Frowns.)* Annie, I wrote them no word of your history. You will find yourself among strangers now, who know nothing of it.

ANNIE   Well, we'll keep them in a state of blessed ignorance.

ANAGNOS   Perhaps *you* should tell it?

ANNIE   *(Bristling.)* Why? I have enough trouble with people who don't know.

ANAGNOS   So they will understand. When you have trouble.

ANNIE   The only time I have trouble is when I'm right. *(But she is amused at herself, as is Anagnos.)* Is it my fault it's so often? I won't give them trouble, Mr. Anagnos, I'll be so ladylike they won't notice I've come.

ANAGNOS   Annie, be—humble. It is not as if you have so many offers to pick and choose. You will need their affection, working with this child.

ANNIE   *(Humorously.)* I hope I won't need their pity.

ANAGNOS   Oh, we can all use some pity. *(Crisply.)* So. You are no longer our pupil, we throw you into the world, a teacher. *If* the child can be taught. No one expects you to work miracles, even for twenty-five dollars a month. Now, in this envelope a loan, for the railroad, which you will repay me when you have a bank account. But in this box, a gift. With our love. *(Annie opens the small box he extends, and sees a garnet ring. She looks up, blinking, and down.)* I think other friends are ready to say goodbye. *(He moves as though to open doors.)*

ANNIE   Mr. Anagnos. *(Her voice is trembling.)* Dear Mr. Anagnos, I— *(But she swallows over getting the ring on her finger, and cannot continue until she finds a woebegone joke.)* Well, what should I say, I'm an ignorant opinionated girl, and everything I am I owe to you?

ANAGNOS   *(Smiles.)* That is only half true, Annie.

ANNIE   Which half? I crawled in here like a drowned rat, I thought I died when Jimmie died, that I'd never again—come alive. Well, you say with love so easy, and I haven't *loved* a soul since and I never will, I suppose, but this place gave me more than my eyes back. Or taught me how to spell, which I'll never learn anyway, but with all the fights and the trouble I've been here it taught me what help is, and how to live again, and I don't want to say good-bye. Don't open the door, I'm crying.

ANAGNOS *(Gently.)* They will not see.

The Rainmaker
by N. Richard Nash

Scene:	One male and one female.
Characters:	**LIZZIE CURRY,** a plain girl.
	BILL STARBUCK, the rainmaker.
Setting:	A tack room on the Curry ranch in a western state.
Time:	A summer night.
Situation:	During a long drought, dying cattle, lack of rain, and an unmarried daughter are problems Lizzie Curry's father must face. Her two brothers, afraid that Lizzie will become an old maid, try unsuccessfully to get her married. When a rainmaker arrives promising relief from the drought, not only does he bring rain, but he also helps Lizzie recognize her beauty and worth. In this scene Starbuck shares with Lizzie the power in believing in oneself.

■ ■ ■

STARBUCK *(This time he grabs her fully, holding her close.)* Lizzie—

LIZZIE Please—

STARBUCK I'm sorry, Lizzie! I'm sorry!

LIZZIE It's all right—let me go!

STARBUCK I hope your dreams come true, Lizzie—I hope they do!

LIZZIE They won't—they never will!

STARBUCK Believe in yourself and they will!

LIZZIE I've got nothing to believe in!

STARBUCK You're a woman! Believe in that!

LIZZIE How can I when nobody else will?

STARBUCK *You* gotta believe it first! *(Quickly)* Let me ask you, Lizzie—are you pretty?

LIZZIE *(With a wail)* No—I'm plain!

STARBUCK There! You see?—you don't know you're a woman!

LIZZIE I am a woman! A plain one!

STARBUCK There's no such thing as a plain woman! Every real woman is pretty! They're all pretty in a different way—but they're all pretty!

LIZZIE Not me! When I look in the looking glass—

STARBUCK Don't let Noah be your lookin' glass! It's gotta be inside you! And then one day the lookin' glass will be the man who loves you! It'll be his eyes maybe! And you'll look in that mirror and you'll be more than pretty!—you'll be beautiful!

LIZZIE *(Crying out)* It'll never happen!

STARBUCK Make it happen! Lizzie, why don't you think "pretty"? and take down your hair! *(He reaches for her hair.)*

LIZZIE *(In panic)* No!

STARBUCK Please, Lizzie! *(He is taking the pins out of her hair. Taking her in his arms)* Now close your eyes, Lizzie—close them! *(As she obeys)* Now—say: I'm pretty!

LIZZIE *(Trying)* I'm—I'm—I can't!

STARBUCK Say it! Say it, Lizzie!

LIZZIE I'm—pretty.

STARBUCK Say it again!

LIZZIE *(With a little cry)* Pretty!

STARBUCK Say it—mean it!

LIZZIE *(Exalted)* I'm pretty! I'm pretty! I'm pretty! *(He kisses her. A long kiss and she clings to him, passionately, the bonds of her spinsterhood breaking away. The kiss over, she collapses on the sacks, sobbing.)*

(Through the sobs) Why did you do that?!

STARBUCK *(Going beside her on the sacks)* Because when you said you were pretty, it was true!

(Her sobs are louder, more heartrending because for the first time, she is happy.)

Lizzie—look at me!

LIZZIE I can't!

STARBUCK *(Turning her to him)* Stop cryin' and look at me! Look at my eyes! What do you see?

LIZZIE *(Gazing through her tears)* I can't *believe* what I see!

STARBUCK Tell me what you see!

LIZZIE (*With a sob of happiness*) Oh, is it me?! Is it really me?! (*Now she goes to him with all her giving.*)

A Raisin in the Sun
by Lorraine Hansberry

Scene: One male, one female
Characters: **RUTH YOUNGER,** a woman in her thirties.
TRAVIS, their son, about ten.
Setting: The Younger family's worn living room in a Chicago apartment.
Time: The 1950s.
Situation: In the small apartment where three generations of the Younger family live, they must share a hall bath with other tenants. As the play opens, Ruth is trying to get her family up for the day. (*For further background, read the introductions to other scenes from this play.*)

■ ■ ■

TRAVIS (*Watching the bathroom.*) Daddy, come on!
(*Walter gets his bathroom utensils and flies out to the bathroom.*)
RUTH Sit down and have your breakfast, Travis.
TRAVIS Mama, this is Friday. (*Gleefully.*) Check coming tomorrow, huh?
RUTH You get your mind off money and eat your breakfast.
TRAVIS (*Eating.*) This is the morning we supposed to bring the fifty cents to school.
RUTH Well, I ain't got no fifty cents this morning.
TRAVIS Teacher say we have to.
RUTH I don't care what teacher say. I ain't got it. Eat your breakfast, Travis.
TRAVIS I *am* eating.
RUTH Hush up now and just eat!
(*The boy gives her an exasperated look for her lack of understanding, and eats grudgingly.*)
TRAVIS You think Grandmama would have it?

RUTH No! And I want you to stop asking your grandmother for money, you hear me?
TRAVIS (*Outraged.*) Gaaaleee! I don't ask her, she just gimme it sometimes!
RUTH Travis Willard Younger—I got too much on me this morning to be—
TRAVIS Maybe Daddy—
RUTH TRAVIS!
(*The boy hushes abruptly. They are both quiet and tense for several seconds.*)
TRAVIS (*Presently.*) Could I maybe go carry some groceries in front of the supermarket for a little while after school then?
RUTH Just hush, I said.
(*Travis jabs his spoon into his cereal bowl viciously, and rests his head in anger upon his fists.*)
If you through eating, you can get over there and make up your bed.
(*The boy obeys stiffly and crosses the room, almost mechanically, to the bed and more or less carefully folds the covering. He carries the bedding into his mother's room and returns with his books and cap.*)
TRAVIS (*Sulking and standing apart from her unnaturally.*) I'm gone.
RUTH (*Looking up from the stove to inspect him automatically.*) Come here. (*He crosses to her and she studies his head.*) If you don't take this comb and fix this here head, you better!
(*Travis puts down his books with a great sigh of oppression, and crosses to the mirror. His mother mutters under her breath about his "slubborness."*)
'Bout to march out of here with this head looking just like chickens slept in it! I just don't know where you get your slubborn ways. . . . And get your jacket, too. Looks chilly out this morning.
TRAVIS (*With conspicuously brushed hair and jacket.*) I'm gone.
RUTH Get carfare and milk money—(*Waving one finger.*)—and not a single penny for no caps, you hear me?
TRAVIS (*With sullen politeness.*) Yes'm. (*He turns in outrage to leave.*)
(*His mother watches after him as in his frustration he approaches the door almost comically. When she speaks to him, her voice has become a very gentle tease.*)
RUTH (*Mocking; as she thinks he would say it.*) Oh, Mamma makes me so mad sometimes, I don't know what to do! (*She waits and continues*

to his back as he stands stock still in front of the door.) I wouldn't kiss that woman goodbye for nothing in this world this morning!

(The boy finally turns around and rolls his eyes at her, knowing the mood has changed and he is vindicated; he does not, however, move toward her yet.)

Scenes For Groups

Julius Caesar
by William Shakespeare

Scene: Four males
Characters: **FLAVIUS** and **MARULLUS,** tribunes. Two **COMMONERS,** a carpenter and a cobbler.
Setting: A street in ancient Rome.
Time: 44 A.D.
Situation: Flavius and Marullus confront a group of workmen taking a holiday from work. The cobbler and the carpenter, unconcerned with political issues, are eager to share in Caesar's triumphs. Marullus accuses the workmen of dishonoring Pompey and commands they return home. This opening scene of the play introduces the political and social conflict of the times and at the same time shows the fickleness of the common people.

■ ■ ■

FLAVIUS Hence! Home, you idle creatures, get you home!
Is this a holiday? What, know you not,
Being mechanical, you ought not walk
Upon a laboring day without the sign
Of your profession? Speak, what trade art thou?

CARPENTER Why, sir, a carpenter.

MARULLUS Where is thy leather apron and thy rule?
What dost thou with thy best apparel on?
You, sir, what trade are you?

COBBLER Truly, sir, in respect of a fine workman, I am but, as you would say, a cobbler.

MARULLUS But what trade are thou? Answer me directly.

COBBLER A trade, sir, that, I hope, I may use with a safe conscience, which is indeed, sir, a mender of bad soles.

FLAVIUS What trade, thou knave? Though naughty knave, what trade?

CARPENTER Nay, I beseech you, sir, be not out with me: yet, if you be out, sir, I can mend you.

MARULLUS What mean'st thou by that? Mend me, thou saucy fellow?

COBBLER Why, sir, cobble you.

FLAVIUS Thou art a cobbler, art thou?

COBBLER Truly sir, all that I live by is with the awl: I meddle with no tradesman's matters, nor women's matters; but withal, I am indeed, sir, a surgeon to old shoes: when they are in great danger, I recover them. As proper men as ever trod upon neat's leather have gone upon my handiwork.

FLAVIUS But wherefore art not in thy shop today?
Why dost thou lead these men about the street?

COBBLER Truly, sir, to wear out their shoes, to get myself into more work. But indeed, sir, we make holiday to see Caesar and to rejoice in his triumph.

MARULLUS Wherefore rejoice? What conquest brings he home?
What tributaries follow him to Rome,
To grace in captive bonds his chariot wheels?
You blocks, you stones, you worse than senseless things!
O you hard hearts, you cruel men of Rome,
Knew you not Pompey? Many a time and oft
Have you climbed up to walls and battlements,
To tow'rs and windows, yea, to chimney tops.
Your infants in your arms, and there have sat
The livelong day, with patient expectation,
To see great Pompey pass the streets of Rome.
And when you saw his chariot but appear,
Have you not made an universal shout,
That Tiber trembled underneath her banks
To hear the replication of your sounds
Made in her concave shores?
And do you now put on your best attire?
And do you now cull out a holiday?
And do you now strew flowers in his way
That comes in triumph over Pompey's blood?

Be gone!
Run to your houses, fall upon your knees,
Pray to the gods to intermit the plague
That needs must light on this ingratitude.

FLAVIUS   Go, go, good countrymen, and, for this fault,
Assemble all the poor men of your sort;
Draw them to Tiber banks and weep your tears
Into the channel, till the lowest stream
Do kiss the most exalted shores of all.

(Exeunt all the Commoners.)

See, whe'r their basest mettle be not moved;
They vanish tongue-tied in their guiltiness.
Go you down that way towards the Capitol;
This way will I. Disrobe the images,
If you do find them decked with ceremonies.

MARULLUS   May we do so?
You know it is the feast of Lupercal.

FLAVIUS   It is no matter; let no images
Be hung with Caesar's trophies. I'll about
And drive away the vulgar from the streets;
So do you too, where you perceive them thick.
These growing feathers plucked from Caesar's wing
Will make him fly an ordinary pitch,
Who else would soar above the view of men
And keep us all in servile fearfulness.

(Exeunt.)

The Miracle Worker
by William Gibson

Scene:	One male, two females
Characters:	**CAPTAIN KELLER,** father of Helen Keller, who is blind, deaf, and mute.
	KATE KELLER, wife of Captain Keller, Helen's mother.
	MISS ANNIE SULLIVAN, a 20-year-old girl who has been hired by Captain and Mrs. Keller to teach Helen.
Setting:	The Kellers' garden house.
Time:	An hour after sundown in the year 1887.
Situation:	Captain and Mrs. Keller's child, Helen, became deaf and blind after having a very high fever when she was just 19 months old. Helen is now 7 years old, quite ill-tempered, lacking in civility, and unable to properly communicate. The Kellers hired Annie to be her governess and teacher. In this scene, Captain Keller has brought Kate to their garden house to privately ask her to fire Annie. He is furious that Helen seems to have become worse in behavior since Annie's arrival. He is also angered by Annie's impertinence. Their discussion is interrupted by Annie knocking on the garden house door.

■ ■ ■

KELLER   Katie, I will not *have* it! Now you did not see when that girl after supper tonight went to look for Helen in her room—

KATE   No.

KELLER   The child practically climbed out of her window to escape from her! What kind of teacher *is* she? I thought I had seen her at her worst this morning, shouting at me, but I come home to find the entire house disorganized by her—Helen won't stay one second in the same room, won't come to the table with her, won't let herself be bathed or undressed or put to bed by her, or even by Viney now, and the end result is that *you* have to do more for the child than before we hired this girl's services! From the moment she stepped off the train she's been nothing but a burden, incompetent, impertinent, ineffectual, immodest—

KATE   She folded her napkin, Captain.

KELLER   What?

KATE   Not ineffectual. Helen did fold her napkin.

KELLER   What is heaven's name is so extraordinary about folding a napkin?

KATE   *[with some humor]* Well. It's more than you did, Captain.

KELLER   Katie, I did not bring you all the way out here to the garden house to be frivolous. Now, how does Miss Sullivan propose to teach a deaf-blind pupil who won't let her even touch her?

KATE   *[a pause]* I don't know.

KELLER   The fact is, today she scuttled any chance she ever had of getting along with the child. If you can see any point or purpose to her staying on here longer, it's more than—

KATE What do you wish me to do?

KELLER I want you to give her notice.

KATE I can't.

KELLER Then if you won't, I must. I simply will not—

(He is interrupted by a knock at the back door. Keller after a glance at Kate moves to open the door; Annie in her smoked glasses is standing outside. Keller contemplates her, heavily.)

Miss Sullivan.

ANNIE Captain Keller.

(She is nervous, keyed up to seizing the bull by the horns again, and she assumes a cheeriness which is not unshaky.)

Viney said I'd find you both over here in the garden house. I thought we should—have a talk?

KELLER *[reluctantly]* Yes, I— Well, come in.

(Annie enters, and is interested in this room; she rounds on her heel, anxiously, studying it. Keller turns the matter over to Kate, sotto voce.)

Katie.

KATE *[turning it back, courteously]* Captain.

(Keller clears his throat, makes ready.)

KELLER I, ah—wanted first to make my position clear to Mrs. Keller, in private. I have decided I—am not satisfied—in fact, am deeply dissatisfied—with the manner in which—

ANNIE *[intent]* Excuse me, is this little house ever in use?

KELLER *[with patience]* In the hunting season. If you will give me your attention, Miss Sullivan.

(Annie turns her smoked glasses upon him; they hold his unwilling stare.)

I have tried to make allowances for you because you come from a part of the country where people are—women, I should say—come from who—well, for whom—

(It begins to elude him.)

—allowances must—be made. I have decided, nevertheless, to—that is, decided I—

(Vexedly)

Miss Sullivan, I find it difficult to talk through those glasses.

ANNIE *[eagerly, removing them]* Oh, of course.

KELLER *[dourly]* Why do you wear them, the sun has been down for an hour.

ANNIE *[pleasantly, at the lamp]* Any kind of light hurts my eyes.

(A silence; Keller ponders her, heavily.)

KELLER Put them on. Miss Sullivan. I have decided to—give you another chance.

ANNIE *[cheerfully]* To do *what*?

KELLER To—remain in our employ.

(Annie's eyes widen.)

But on two conditions. I am not accustomed to rudeness in servants or women, and that is the first. If you are to stay, there must be a radical change of manner.

ANNIE *[a pause]* Whose?

KELLER *[exploding]* Yours, young lady, isn't it obvious? And the second is that you persuade me there's the slightest hope of your teaching a child who flees from you now like the plague, to anyone else she can find in this house.

ANNIE *[a pause]* There isn't.

(Kate stops sewing, and fixes her eyes upon Annie.)

KATE What, Miss Annie?

ANNIE It's hopeless here. I can't teach a child who runs away.

KELLER *[nonplussed]* Then—do I understand you—propose—

ANNIE Well, if we agree it's hopeless, the next question is what—

KATE Miss Annie.

(She is leaning toward Annie in deadly earnest; it commands both Annie and Keller.)

I am not agreed. I think perhaps you—underestimate Helen.

ANNIE I think everybody else here does.

KATE She did fold her napkin. She learns, she learns, do you know she began talking when she was six months old? She could say "water." Not really—"wahwah." "Wahwah," but she meant water, she knew what it meant, and only six months old, I never saw a child so—bright, or outgoing—

(Her voice is unsteady, but she gets it level.)

It's still in her, somewhere, isn't it? You should have seen her before her illness, such a good-tempered child—

ANNIE *[agreeably]* She's changed.

(A pause, Kate not letting her eyes go; her appeal at last is unconditional, and very quiet.)

KATE   Miss Annie, put up with it. And with us.

KELLER   Us!

KATE   Please? Like the lost lamb in the parable, I love her all the more.

ANNIE   Mrs. Keller, I don't think Helen's worst handicap is deafness or blindness. I think it's your love. And pity.

KELLER   Now what does that mean?

ANNIE   All of you here are so sorry for her you've kept her—like a pet, why, even a dog you housebreak. No wonder she won't let me come near her. It's useless for me to try to teach her language or anything else here. I might as well—

KATE   *[cuts in]* Miss Annie, before you came we spoke of putting her in an asylum.

(Annie turns back to regard her. A pause.)

ANNIE   What kind of asylum?

KELLER   For mental defectives.

KATE   I visited there. I can't tell you what I saw, people like—animals, with—*rats*, in the halls, and—

(She shakes her head on her vision.)

What else are we to do, if you give up?

ANNIE   Give up?

KATE   You said it was hopeless.

ANNIE   Here. Give up, why I only today saw what has to be done, to begin!

(She glances from Kate to Keller, who stares, waiting; and she makes it as plain and simple as her nervousness permits.)

I—want complete charge of her.

KELLER   You already have that. It has resulted in—

ANNIE   No, I mean day and night. She has to be dependent on me.

KATE   For what?

ANNIE   Everything. The food she eats, the clothes she wears, fresh—

(She is amused at herself, though very serious.)

—air, yes, the air she breathes, whatever her body needs is a—primer, to teach her out of. It's the only way, the one who lets her have it should be her teacher.

(She considers them in turn; they digest it, Keller frowning, Kate perplexed.)

Not anyone who *loves* her, you have so many feelings they fall over each other like feet, you won't use your chances and you won't let me.

KATE   But if she runs from you—*to* us—

ANNIE   Yes, that's the point. I'll have to live with her somewhere else.

KELLER   What!

ANNIE   Till she learns to depend on and listen to me.

KATE   *[not without alarm]* For how long?

ANNIE   As long as it takes.

(A pause. She takes a breath.)

I packed half my things already.

KELLER   Miss—Sullivan!

(But when Annie attends upon him he is speechless, and she is merely earnest.)

ANNIE   Captain Keller, it meets both your conditions. It's the one way I can get back in touch with Helen, and I don't see how I can be rude to you again if you're not around to interfere with me.

KELLER   *[red-faced]* And what is your intention if I say no? Pack the other half, for home, and abandon your charge to—to—

ANNIE   The asylum?

(She waits, appraises Keller's glare and Kate's uncertainty, and decides to use her weapons.)

I grew up in such an asylum. The state almshouse.

(Kate's head comes up on this, and Keller stares hard; Annie's tone is cheerful enough, albeit level as gunfire.)

Rats—why, my brother Jimmie and I used to play with the rats because we didn't have toys. Maybe you'd like to know what Helen will find there, not on visiting days? One ward was full of the—old women, crippled, blind, most of them dying, but even if what they had was catching there was nowhere else to move them, and that's where they put us. There were younger ones across the hall, . . . with T.B., . . . and some insane. The youngest were in another ward to have babies they didn't want, they started at thirteen, fourteen. They'd leave afterwards, but the babies stayed and we played with them, too, though a lot of them had—sores all over from diseases you're not supposed to talk about, but not many of them lived. The first year we had eighty, seventy died. The room Jimmie and I played in was the deadhouse, where they kept the bodies till they could dig—

KATE   *[closes her eyes]* Oh, my dear—

ANNIE   —the graves.

(She is immune to Kate's compassion.)

No, it made me strong. But I don't think you need send Helen there. She's strong enough.

(She waits again; but when neither offers her a word, she simply concludes.)

No, I have no conditions, Captain Keller.

KATE *[not looking up]* Miss Annie.

ANNIE Yes.

KATE *[a pause]* Where would you—take Helen?

ANNIE Ohh—

(Brightly)

Italy?

KELLER *[wheeling]* What?

ANNIE Can't have everything, how would this garden house do? Furnish it, bring Helen here after a long ride so she won't recognize it, and you can see her every day. If she doesn't know. Well?

KATE *[a sigh of relief]* Is that all?

ANNIE That's all.

KATE Captain.

(Keller turns his head; and Kate's request is quiet but firm.)

With your permission?

KELLER *[teeth in cigar]* Why must she depend on you for the food she eats?

ANNIE *[a pause]* I want control of it.

KELLER Why?

ANNIE It's a way to reach her.

KELLER *[stares]* You intend to *starve* her into letting you touch her?

ANNIE She won't starve, she'll learn. All's fair in love and war, Captain Keller, you never cut supplies?

KELLER This is hardly a war!

ANNIE Well, it's not love. A siege is a siege.

KELLER *[heavily]* Miss Sullivan. Do you *like* the child?

ANNIE *[straight in his eyes]* Do you?

(A long pause.)

. . .

KELLER Very well, I consent to everything!

(He shakes the cigar at Annie.)

. . . I'll give you two weeks . . . and it will be a miracle if you get the child to tolerate you.

ANNIE Two weeks. For only one miracle?

(She nods at him, nervously.)

I'll get her to tolerate me.

(Keller marches out, and slams the door. Kate on her feet regards Annie, who is facing the door.)

KATE *[then]* You can't think as little of love as you said.

(Annie glances questioning.)

Or you wouldn't stay.

ANNIE *[a pause]* I didn't come here for love. I came for money!

(Kate shakes her head to this, with a smile; after a moment she extends her open hand. Annie looks at it, but when she puts hers out it is not to shake hands, it is to set her fist in Kate's palm.)

KATE *[puzzled]* Hm?

ANNIE A. It's the first of many. Twenty-six!

(Kate squeezes her fist, squeezes it hard, and hastens out after Keller. Annie stands as the door closes behind her, her manner so apprehensive that finally she slaps her brow, holds it, sighs, and with her eyes closed, crosses herself for luck.)

The Diary of Anne Frank
by Frances Goodrich and Albert Hackett
Scene II

Scene:	Four females and one male (optional)
Characters:	**ANNE FRANK,** a young Jewish girl.
	MARGOT FRANK, her older sister.
	MRS. FRANK, her mother.
	MRS. VAN DAAN, Peter's mother.
	MR. DUSSEL, a Jewish dentist who shares Anne's room in the hiding place.
Setting:	The top floor of a warehouse and office building in Amsterdam, Holland.
Time:	During World War II.
Situation:	To escape Nazi persecution, the Otto Frank family moved from Germany to Amsterdam. When the Nazis took over the Netherlands, the family went into hiding on the top floor of a building where Mr. Frank had his warehouse and office. The Van Daans, another Jewish family, and Jan Dussel, a dentist, hide with the Franks. After almost eighteen months, Peter Van Daan, a shy sixteen-year-old boy, finally becomes Anne's friend. In this scene Anne is in her room, dressing for a visit with Peter.

■ ■ ■

It is evening, after supper. From outside we hear the sound of children playing. The "grownups," with the exception of Mr. Van Daan, are all in the main room. Mrs. Frank is doing some mending, Mrs. Van Daan is reading a fashion magazine. Mr. Frank is going over business accounts. Dussel, in his dentist's jacket is pacing up and down, impatient to get into his bedroom. Mr. Van Daan is upstairs working on a piece of embroidery in an embroidery frame.

In his room Peter is sitting before the mirror, smoothing his hair. As the scene goes on, he puts on his tie, brushes his coat and puts it on, preparing himself meticulously for a visit from Anne. On his wall are now hung some of Anne's motion picture stars.

In her room Anne too is getting dressed. She stands before the mirror in her slip, trying various ways of dressing her hair. Margot is seated on the sofa, hemming a skirt for Anne to wear.

In the main room Dussel can stand it no longer. He comes over, rapping sharply on the door of his and Anne's bedroom.

ANNE *(Calling to him)*

No, no, Mr. Dussel! I am not dressed yet. *(Dussel walks away, furious, sitting down and burying his head in his hands. Anne turns to Margot)* How is that? How does that look?

MARGOT *(Glancing at her briefly)*

Fine.

ANNE   You didn't even look.

MARGOT   Of course I did. It's fine.

ANNE   Margot, tell me, am I terribly ugly?

MARGOT   Oh, stop fishing.

ANNE   No. No. Tell me.

MARGOT   Of course you're not. You've got nice eyes . . . and a lot of animation, and . . .

ANNE   A little vague, aren't you?

(She reaches over and takes a brassière out of Margot's sewing basket. She holds it up to herself, studying the effect in the mirror. Outside, Mrs. Frank, feeling sorry for Dussel, comes over, knocking at the girl's door.)

MRS. FRANK *(Outside)*

May I come in?

MARGOT   Come in, Mother.

MRS. FRANK *(Shutting the door behind her)*

Mr. Dussel's impatient to get in here.

ANNE *(Still with the brassière)*

Heavens, he takes the room for himself the entire day.

MRS. FRANK *(Gently)*

Anne, dear, you're not going in again tonight to see Peter?

ANNE *(Dignified)*

That is my intention.

MRS. FRANK   But you've already spent a great deal of time in there today.

ANNE   I was in there exactly twice. Once to get the dictionary, and then three-quarters of an hour before supper.

MRS. FRANK   Aren't you afraid you're disturbing him?

ANNE   Mother, I have some intuition.

MRS. FRANK   Then may I ask you this much, Anne. Please don't shut the door when you go in.

ANNE   You sound like Mrs. Van Daan!

(She throws the brassière back in Margot's sewing basket and picks up her blouse, putting it on.)

MRS. FRANK   No. No. I don't mean to suggest anything wrong. I only wish that you wouldn't expose yourself to criticism . . . that you wouldn't give Mrs. Van Daan the opportunity to be unpleasant.

ANNE   Mrs. Van Daan doesn't need an opportunity to be unpleasant!

MRS. FRANK   Everyone's on edge, worried about Mr. Kraler. This is one more thing . . .

ANNE   I'm sorry, Mother. I'm going to Peter's room. I'm not going to let Petronella Van Daan spoil our friendship.

(Mrs. Frank hesitates for a second, then goes out, closing the door after her. She gets a pack of playing cards and sits at the center table, playing solitaire. In Anne's room Margot hands the finished skirt to Anne. As Anne is putting it on, Margot takes off her high-heeled shoes and stuffs paper in the toes so that Anne can wear them.)

MARGOT *(To Anne)*

Why don't you two talk in the main room? It'd save a lot of trouble. It's hard on Mother, having to listen to those remarks from Mrs. Van Daan and not say a word.

ANNE   Why doesn't she say a word? I think it's ridiculous to take it and take it.

MARGOT   You don't understand Mother at all, do you? She can't talk back. She's not like you. It's just not in her nature to fight back.

ANNE   Anyway . . . the only one I worry about is you. I feel awfully guilty about you.

(She sits on the stool near Margot, putting on Margot's high-heeled shoes.)

MARGOT   What about?

ANNE   I mean, every time I go into Peter's room, I have a feeling I may be hurting you.

(Margot shakes her head) I know if it were me, I'd be wild. I'd be desperately jealous, if it were me.

MARGOT Well, I'm not.

ANNE You don't feel badly? Really? Truly? You're not jealous?

MARGOT Of course I'm jealous . . . jealous that you've got something to get up in the morning for . . . But jealous of you and Peter? No.

(Anne goes back to the mirror.)

ANNE Maybe there's nothing to be jealous of. Maybe he doesn't really like me. Maybe I'm just taking the place of his cat . . . *(She picks up a pair of short white gloves, putting them on)* Wouldn't you like to come in with us?

MARGOT I have a book.

(The sound of the children playing outside fades out. In the main room Dussel can stand it no longer. He jumps up, going to the bedroom door and knocking sharply.)

DUSSEL Will you please let me in my room!

ANNE Just a minute, dear, dear Mr. Dussel. *(She picks up her Mother's pink stole and adjusts it elegantly over her shoulders, then gives a last look in the mirror)* Well, here I go . . . to run the gauntlet.

(She starts out, followed by Margot.)

DUSSEL *(As she appears—sarcastic)* Thank you so much.

(Dussel goes into his room. Anne goes toward Peter's room, passing Mrs. Van Daan and her parents at the center table.)

MRS. VAN DAAN My God, look at her! *(Anne pays no attention. She knocks at Peter's door)* I don't know what good it is to have a son. I never see him. He wouldn't care if I killed myself. *(Peter opens the door and stands aside for Anne to come in)* Just a minute, Anne. *(She goes to them at the door)* I'd like to say a few words to my son. Do you mind? *(Peter and Anne stand waiting)* Peter, I don't want you staying up till all hours tonight. You've got to have your sleep. You're a growing boy. You hear?

MRS. FRANK Anne won't stay late. She's going to bed promptly at nine. Aren't you, Anne?

ANNE Yes, Mother . . . *(To Mrs. Van Daan)* May we go now?

MRS. VAN DAAN Are you asking me? I don't know I had anything to say about it.

MRS. FRANK Listen for the chimes, Anne dear.

(The two young people go off into Peter's room, shutting the door after them.)

MRS. VAN DAAN *(To Mrs. Frank)* In my day it was the boys who called on the girls. Not the girls on the boys.

MRS. FRANK You know how young people like to feel that they have secrets. Peter's room is the only place where they can talk.

Little Women*
dramatized by Kristen Laurence

Scene:	Five females.
Characters:	The March sisters:
	JO
	BETH
	AMY
	MEG
	HANNAH, the housekeeper
Setting:	The well-worn living room of the March home.
Time:	A Christmas season in the 1800s.
Situation:	Times are hard in the March family. The girls' father is away at war and their mother, Marmee, has told the girls that this year there will be no Christmas presents. The play opens with the girls discussing the situation. Jo is seated on the ottoman before the fire. Beth is curled up in the big armchair. Meg is slumped in a chair working at her embroidery. Amy sits on the sofa drawing a picture of Meg.

■ ■ ■

SCENE: *The living-room of the March home. It is a comfortable old room with plain, well-worn furniture. There are three entrances to the room. In the R wall, downstage, is the door to the kitchen. There is another door in the L wall at center, which leads to Marmee's bedroom, while U L C is an archway which leads to the front hall and the outside. There is a fire burning in the fireplace at L stage. In front of the fireplace is an ottoman, while a bit above it, facing downstage, is a large armchair with an end table right of it. There is a smaller armchair just below the fireplace, and facing slightly upstage. In the rear wall, U R C, are casement windows and a window seat, with several pots of flowers blooming along the sill. (An ordinary window will do in place of casement windows, in which case use an easy chair in front of the window to replace the window seat.) To the right of the window is a small table, with a doily and a few knickknacks. At L C, at an angle, is a sofa with several pillows. There is a small work table right of the sofa, and on it is a small bowl of apples. Below the sofa, D L C, is an easy chair. Above and below the door L, against the wall, are bookcases. On the wall D L is a mirror. When the piano and bench are brought in for the second scene in Act One, they are placed U C, against the back wall of the set, where they remain throughout the rest of the play.]*

AT RISE OF CURTAIN: *Hannah, the family servant, is standing on a kitchen chair, nailing a Christmas wreath above the archway U L C. Jo is seated on the ottoman before the fire, and Beth is curled up in the big armchair upstage of the fireplace, humming softly as she knits. Amy, who is drawing a sketch of Jo, sits on the sofa. Meg slumped comfortably in the chair below the sofa, works carefully at her embroidery.]*

HANNAH *[with a last thump of the hammer]* There! That ought to be holdin' it. *[She climbs down and stands back to look at it.]*

AMY It looks very artistic, Hannah.

[Hannah beams at the compliment. Gathering the chair and her things together, she goes out D R, leaving the girls looking critically at the wreath.]

JO *[grumbling]* Christmas won't be Christmas without any presents.

MEG It's so dreadful to be poor.

AMY I don't think it's fair for some girls to have plenty of pretty things and other girls nothing at all.

BETH We've got Father and Mother, and each other.

JO *[rebelliously]* We haven't got Father and won't have for a long time. Maybe never.

BETH Oh, Jo—

MEG *[quickly]* You know the reason Mother proposed not having any presents this Christmas. The war is making it such a hard winter for everyone—and she thinks we shouldn't

spend money on pleasure when our men in the army are suffering so.

AMY Yes—it must be very disagreeable to be shot at, and have to sleep in a tent and drink out of a *tin mug! [She says this as if the tin mug were the worst of war's horrors.]*

MEG We can't do much to help, but ought to do gladly what we can. *[She sighs.]* But I'm afraid sometimes I don't.

JO *[laughing a little]* We've each got a dollar. I don't think the army would be much helped by that. *[Hugging her knees, she begins to rock back and forth on the footstool.]* I agree not to expect anything from you or Marmee, but I do want to buy "Undine and Sintram" for myself. I haven't bought a book for ever so long. *[She rocks too far, and the ottoman goes over, sending her sprawling.]*

AMY *[putting her drawing board down]* Josephine, you are impossible!

BETH *[as she helps Jo brush off her shirt]* I planned to spend mine for new music. If only we had a nice piano. *[She resumes her seat, after helping Jo.]*

AMY *[decidedly]* I shall get a nice box of new drawing pencils. I really need them.

JO Mother didn't say anything about our money, and she won't want us to give up everything. Let's each buy what we want and have a little fun. I think we work hard enough to earn it.

MEG I know I do—teaching those tiresome children all day. At least you don't have to be a governess, Jo.

JO You don't have half as hard a time as I do, being shut up all day with a fussy old lady like Aunt March. Every time I find an interesting book to read she starts calling—*[She imitates an old lady's voice.]*—"Josyphine! Josyphine!"—and I have to go help her wind yarn or wash the poodle!

AMY *[not wishing to be outdone]* I don't believe any of you suffer as I do. You don't have to go to school with impertinent girls who laugh at your dresses and *label* your father if he isn't rich.

JO *[laughing]* If you mean *libel*, I'd say so, and not talk about *labels*, as if Papa was a pickle bottle!

[The other girls laugh at Amy.]

AMY I know what I mean, and you needn't be *statirical* about it. It's proper to use elegant words and improve your *vocabilary*. Jo uses such slang. *[She picks up her pencil and goes back to her sketching.]*

JO *[in great disgust]* Elegant words! I like good strong words that mean something! *[She begins to whistle.]*

AMY Don't whistle, Jo. It's boyish.

JO That's why I do it. *[She continues to whistle.]*

AMY I detest rude, unladylike girls. *[She swishes her skirt as she hitches about on the sofa.]*

JO *[imitating Amy's gesture]* And I hate affected, niminy-piminy little school children.

MEG *[in her "eldest sister" manner]* Now, don't peck at one another.

JO Oh, Amy is always trying to be so elegant! She has even started wearing a clothespin on her nose when she goes to bed.

AMY *[with a little toss of her head]* My nose wouldn't be so flat and un-aristocratic if you hadn't dropped me in the coal hod when I was little.

BETH *[laughing]* Remember, Jo and Amy— "birds in their little nests agree."

[They all laugh, and peace is restored.]

MEG Really, though, Josephine, you are old enough to leave off boyish tricks and behave better. When you were younger it didn't matter so much, but now that you are so tall and turn up your hair, you should remember you are a young lady.

JO *[hotly, rising, and crossing to C stage]* I'm not a young lady! And if turning up my hair makes me one, I'll wear it in two tails till I'm twenty! *[She pulls off her net and shakes her head, letting her hair fall about her shoulders.]* I hate to think I've got to grow up and wear long gowns and be prim. *[She flops down on the hearth at Beth's feet.]* It's bad enough to be a girl, anyway. I wish I were a boy and could go away to war with Papa and fight, instead of staying at home like a poky old woman.

MEG But, Jo, Father is the chaplain of his regiment, and chaplains don't fight.

JO They don't knit socks, either!

BETH *[stroking Jo's head]* Poor Jo! It's too bad, but it can't be helped; so you must try to be content with having a boyish name and playing brother to us girls.

MEG *[continuing her sisterly lecture]* As for you, Amy, you are getting altogether too particular and prim. I like your nice manners, but your absurd words are as bad as Jo's slang. If you don't take care, you'll grow into an affected little goose.

[Jo grins up at Amy, who pretends not to notice.]

BETH *[suddenly jumping up]* Oh, I forgot to bring in Marmee's slippers!

JO *[getting up quickly]* Never mind. I'll get 'em!

[Jo dashes out L, into Marmee's bedroom.]

BETH *[moving up to the window]* Oh, look! There's Laurie, out riding his new pony!

AMY *[running to look over Beth's shoulder]* That boy is a perfect Cyclops, isn't he?

[On Amy's line, Jo enters L with Marmee's slippers.]

JO *[moving U C]* How dare you say that when he's got both his eyes?

AMY *[turning]* I didn't say anything about his eyes. I don't see why you fire up so just because I admire his riding.

JO *[laughing]* You mean a Centaur—not a Cyclops! *[She turns away, crosses to the fireplace and puts the slippers down on the hearth.]*

AMY Anyway, he's outside with his new pony. *[She turns away, crosses down to the sofa, and sits again.]*

JO *[rushing to the window]* He is! Where? *[She throws open the window and leans out, shouting.]* Laurie! Laurie! May I have that ride now?

MEG Jo, you mustn't shout so.

JO *[over her shoulder, to Meg]* How else can I make him hear me? *[She yells out the window again to Laurie.]* All right. I'll be right there. Wait a minute! *[She gathers her skirts up and climbs quickly out the window, shouting as she disappears:]* Be right back, Meg!

AMY *[moving U R C and closing the window firmly]* Well! Jo is certainly precipitous!

BETH *[anxiously, peering through the window]* I hope she doesn't catch cold, going out without her shawl and bonnet.

MEG What would Marmee say?

BETH Don't scold her, Meg. You know how Jo has been looking forward to riding the pony. *[She sits in the chair by the fireplace again.]*

AMY *[sitting down on the sofa and smoothing her skirt]* Even people who ride horses usually leave the house by the *door*. I declare, it was a sad day for Josephine's manners when Laurie and his grandfather came to live next door.

[Beth giggles, and Meg laughs outright.]

MEG   You know you were as glad as any of us to see the Laurences move into that huge old house. Marmee thinks it's good for us to share our fun with a boy our own age, since we have no brothers. And old Mr. Laurence is such a good friend of Father's.

AMY   Well, I just meant—

BETH   It must be very lonely to live in such a big house with no father or mother—just a grandfather and a tutor.

AMY   I think it would be wonderful.

BETH   Why, Amy!

AMY   To have a tutor like Mr. Brooke, I mean, and not have to go to school any more.

BETH   But Mr. Brooke is *old*—he must be twenty-five, at least.

MEG   He's very dignified. And twenty-five isn't so awfully old.

BETH   But Laurie is only Jo's age—

AMY   I don't care! You needn't have jumped on me so—I didn't mean it was a *really* sad day when the Laurences and Mr. Brooke moved here, but—*[She pouts a little.]*—even neighbors needn't go flying out windows at each other!

[There is the sound of much stomping about offstage U L, and Jo calling "Good-bye, Laurie. Thanks very much" In a moment, she enters U L C, wearing a huge pair of russet-colored boots.]

JO   *[clumping about the room at C stage]* Look! Aren't they wonderful? Real actor's boots! Laurie gave them to me to wear in our Christmas play.

AMY   Where did Laurie get actor's boots?

JO   He has a friend who has a friend who once knew an actor. It was certainly a lucky day for this family when Laurie and his grandfather moved in next door!

[Amy, Meg, and Beth all look at each other for a moment, and then burst into laughter. Jo looks at them, puzzled.]

BETH   *[quickly]* I think the boots are—simply plummy!

[Jo sits down on the ottoman and starts to tug at the boots to get them off.]

AMY   *[rising, moving to her, to help take off the boots]* You should exert a more *Herculaneum* effort, Jo. *[She starts to help, but stops when Jo*

laughs.] Well, you needn't be rude about it. If I did make a mistake, it's only a *lapse of lingy* as Mr. Davis says at school. *[She sighs deeply, and goes to the window.]* I only wish I had some of the money Laurie spent buying that horse.

MEG   Why, what would you do with it?

AMY   I really need it. I'm dreadfully in debt, and—

MEG   *[sharply]* In debt! What do you mean?

AMY   *[turning from the window and coming to C stage]* I owe at least a dozen pickled limes—

MEG   *[relieved]* Is that all?

AMY   It's a debt of honor. I should pay them back next month when the new term begins, but I can't until I have some money, for Marmee forbade my charging anything at the store. It's quite dreadful.

MEG   Are pickled limes the fashion now?

AMY   Oh, yes! Everybody buys them. The girls eat them during school time and trade them off for pencils and bead rings at recess. If one girl likes another she gives her a lime; if she's mad at her she eats one right before her, and doesn't even offer her a bite. They treat by turns. I've had ever so many, and I haven't returned them.

MEG   *[smiling]* How much will pay them off and restore your credit? Would a quarter do?

AMY   *[delighted, racing down to her]* And leave some over for a treat for you! Do you really think you can spare it?

MEG   *[teasingly]* Yes—since it is a debt of honor.

AMY   *[hugging Meg]* Oh, thank you! Ever so much!

[Jo, meanwhile, has not succeeded in removing the boots, and resigns herself to wearing them for the moment.]

JO   *[shaking her head]* I wish it were as easy to get Marmee new slippers. These are quite worn out! *[She pokes her finger through the hole in the toe of one, and holds it up for the others to see.]*

BETH   I think I'll buy her some with my dollar.

AMY   *[still glowing with new-found wealth]* No! I shall. *[She perches on the upstage arm of Meg's chair.]*

MEG   I'm the oldest, so I ought—

JO   *[cutting in decidedly]* I'm the man of the family, now that Father is away, and I shall get the slippers, for he told me to take special care of Marmee while he was away.

BETH   I'll tell you what! Let's each get Marmee something for Christmas and not get anything for ourselves.

JO   Good for you, Bethy! *[She continues thoughtfully.]* What will we get?

MEG   *[after a moment of sober consideration]* I shall give her a nice pair of gloves.

JO   Army shoes, best to be had.

BETH   Some handkerchiefs, all hemmed.

AMY   I'll get a small bottle of cologne. It won't cost very much, so I'll have enough left to buy my drawing pencils.

MEG   *[severely]* Amy!

AMY   *[defensively]* She likes cologne!

JO   Let's let Marmee think we are getting things for ourselves, and then surprise her.

The Ransom of Red Chief*
by Anne Coulter Martens
Based on the short story by O. Henry

Scene: Three males
Characters: **SAM BLAKE,** a schemer.
   BILL DRISCOLL, Sam's partner.
   RED CHIEF
Setting: A cave area near a small town.
Time: Summertime.
Situation: Sam and Bill, two schemers hoping to make some quick money, make the mistake of kidnapping Johnny Dorset, a feisty brat called "Red Chief." Red proves to be more than the two can handle and Bill ends up sending him home, much to Sam's dismay. In this scene, Bill confesses what has happened to Sam.

■ ■ ■

SCENE: *The cave.*
AT RISE OF CURTAIN: *It is later that night. There is faint moonlight and a dimly burning fire on the rock. Bill, wrapped in a blanket, is sleeping near the fire. With his even breathing there is a steady snoring sound. Sam comes in R with a box in his hand. He goes to Bill and shakes him several times.*

SAM   Bill, wake up! Wake up, I say!

BILL   *(sleepily)* What? *(Quickly.)* I'm innocent!

SAM   Shut up. It's me. Where's Red Chief?

BILL   Took his blanket and said he'd sleep in the cave.

SAM   Good. *(Shows box.)* See?

BILL   You got the ransom.

SAM   Bet your sweet life. It was delivered just the way we told him to.

BILL   Was anybody around? *(Raises himself on one elbow.)*

SAM   Just the kid on a bike who brought the ransom money.

BILL   I sure got to hand it to you, Sam.

SAM   Slickest job we ever pulled off.

BILL   Except I got my ribs all taped up.

SAM   What's a couple of broken ribs?

BILL   Easy to say when they're not yours. Go ahead, open the box.

SAM   I will, I will. Sure the kid's in the cave?

BILL   Sound asleep. It's nearly one o'clock.

SAM   Maybe you should have tied him up. *(Indicates rope lying near the cave.)*

BILL   Not Red Chief. He likes us too much to run away. Kind of pitiful, ain't it?

SAM   Why?

BILL   A holy terror like him liking *us.*

SAM   He's got funny ways of showing it.

BILL   Maybe he don't know no other way. Take me, when I was a kid . . .

SAM   You interested in this money, or not? *(Breaks string on box.)*

BILL   In another hour we can have the kid at old Ebenezer's back door and be on our way.

SAM   *(tearing paper from box)* He sure wrapped it up well.

BILL   Open it. What are we waiting for?

SAM   My hands are shaking. Guess I half thought there'd be a catch in it somewhere.

BILL   We're splitting fifty-fifty, remember.

SAM   But it all goes into the real estate deal.

BILL   A horse race is faster.

SAM   Oh, no, you don't!

BILL   Okay. Just let me get a look at that green stuff.

SAM   *(hand on lid)* This is the best part. When you have all those dreams of how rich you're going to be, all the great things you're going to do.

BILL   *(surprised)* You got dreams, too?

SAM   Sometimes I get real soft inside.

BILL No kidding? Maybe your old lady was nicer than mine.

SAM What old lady? I didn't have one. Orphan home, is all.

BILL Gee, that's tough.

SAM That's why *I* had to be tough. Understand?

BILL I guess so.

SAM Nobody ever gave me anything. What I wanted I had to take.

BILL Me, too. But Sam . . .

SAM What?

BILL I been thinking. This real estate scheme of ours ain't honest, you know.

SAM Sure, I know.

BILL How about if we just split this loot and go legit?

SAM *(after a pause)* Funny thing, I had the same idea.

BILL I could settle down somewhere, marry, and have a raft of kids to play with. *(Quickly.)* *Nice* kids.

SAM And what would you do for a living? Kids like to eat.

BILL I'd think of something.

SAM Like . . . work, maybe?

BILL *Work? (Shivers.)*

SAM An ugly word.

BILL Just forget it!

SAM *(weighing box in his hand)* First time I ever held so much money in my hand.

BILL Heavy?

SAM No, it's light—very light. But then, money's only paper.

BILL *Only* paper, he says.

SAM Small bills. But they should weigh . . . *(Takes lid from box, gasps in dismay, then searches in box frantically).*

BILL What's the matter?

SAM *(dismayed)* There's no money in here at all! *(Gets up, turning box upside down.)*

BILL Oh, no!

SAM Just one little piece of note paper. *(Holds it up.)*

BILL Maybe he says he'll pay later?

SAM *(leaning toward fire to see better)* Why did he have to wrap *this* up in a box?

BILL What does it say?

SAM *(reading)* "Two Desperate Men. Gentlemen: I received your letter this afternoon in regard to the ransom you ask for the return of my nephew . . . "

BILL Then he *is* going to pay?

SAM *(reading)* "I think you are a little high in your demands, and I hereby make you a counter-proposition which I am inclined to believe you will accept . . . "

BILL Tell him we'll accept even *one* thousand.

SAM *(reading)* "This is it. Bring Johnny home and pay me two hundred dollars, and I'll take him off your hands."

BILL *(stunned)* He wants *us* to pay *him?*

SAM *(reading)* "Come early in the morning because I can't be responsible for what the neighbors would do to anybody they saw bringing him back." *(His voice fades.)* Signed, "Very respectfully, Ebenezer Dorset."

BILL I knew it. Why'd anyone pay good money for that demon?

SAM Of all the gall!

BILL He wants to get rid of him.

SAM Fat chance! I found out things in town. He's the boy's legal guardian, and the kid inherited part of the house he's living in. I'll lay odds the old coot is collecting plenty just for taking care of him.

BILL He earns it.

SAM He'll lose a steady income if he loses the kid.

BILL Red's such a pest he probably doesn't care.

SAM Every penny counts, with that old skinflint.

BILL I almost feel sorry for Red—even his own uncle not wanting him.

SAM He'll get that boy back whether he wants him or not.

BILL Maybe he's got the law out looking for us.

SAM I saw the law, and I'm not worried.

BILL They'll be asking questions around and looking for clues.

SAM I didn't leave any clues. I'm smart.

BILL Sure, Sam, but . . .

SAM *(stopping short)* Oh! Maybe I *did!*

BILL Did what?

SAM I left my old newspaper on the park bench!

BILL So?

SAM Right after I told a talkative woman I was interested in the *latest* events.

BILL   I don't follow you.

SAM   She might get suspicious of a stranger in town. *(Glumly.)* I sure wish I could kick myself.

BILL   Want me to get up and do it for you?

SAM   Aw, shut up!

BILL   Sure, Sam. I still think you're *pretty* smart.

SAM   If old Dorset reports Red kidnaped, even that dumb constable might catch on. We'd better get out of here.

BILL   What about Red Chief?

SAM   Why don't *you* think of something for a change?

BILL   We can't just tie him up and leave him here.

SAM   Why not?

BILL   Even my old lady wouldn't pull a stunt like that.

SAM   I'm not your old lady.

BILL   I couldn't treat the kid that way. He *likes* me.

SAM   Quiet, and let me think. *(After a pause.)* No, we can't tie him up and leave him here.

BILL   Gee, thanks, Sam.

SAM   The letter says . . . *(Looks at it again.)* "Come early in the morning."

BILL   But we'll give him breakfast first.

SAM   He can have breakfast with his dear uncle. We'll just shove the kid in by the back door and leave fast.

BILL   He can't *make* us pay, can he?

SAM   I'd like to see him try! Red Chief's his headache.

BILL   *(putting a hand to his head)* Mine, too. Golly, Sam, I'm wore out and so sleepy I can't hardly keep my eyes open.

SAM   Go to sleep, then. I'm pretty tired, too. *(Picks up a blanket, goes L, wraps himself in it and lies down, his back to Bill.)*

(There is silence for a few moments. Bill snores again. Then Red sneaks out of the cave, a knife in his hand. He leaps on Bill, knife held high over his head. Bill gives an unearthly scream. Sam jumps up as Red is getting a grip on Bill's hair.)

BILL   *(yelling)* He's scalping me! *(Red is still war whooping when Sam gets him by the back of his shirt and pulls him off Bill.)*

SAM   I'll tan your hide, you varmint! *(Takes the knife from Red. Red breaks away from him. Bill gets up shakily, taking his blanket.)*

BILL   Did I say he *liked* me? *(Explores his scalp.)*

RED   Aw, it was only the old bacon knife.

SAM   Back into that cave, and don't let me hear another word!

RED   But I *told* him I was going to scalp him!

SAM   *(pointing).* Inside! *(Red goes back into the cave.)*

BILL   Me, I'm finding another place to sleep. *(Goes L.)*

SAM   Where?

BILL   Far enough away so I'll hear him coming.

SAM   The kid was only fooling.

BILL   It's *my* scalp, and I want to stay attached to it.

SAM   It's an awful thing to hear a strong fat man scream desperately like that. *(Puts his blanket around his shoulders and sits in front of the old post.)*

BILL   How come *you're* not lying down?

SAM   I don't feel sleepy right now.

BILL   He said you'd be burned at daybreak. You afraid he'll try it?

SAM   Don't be funny.

BILL   See you in the morning—if you're still alive. *(Goes out L.)*

(Sam leans against the post. His eyes close and he opens them quickly, shaking his head to stay awake. They close again. Red peeks out and reaches for the coil of rope which is near the cave. When Sam's eyes close for the third time, Red tiptoes out, goes behind the post, and ties the rope to the top of it. Then, very quietly, he passes the rope around Sam, over his arms. He does this about three times before Sam awakes.)

SAM   *(yelling)* Hey, what's going on? *(Although he is not securely tied, his arms are pinned to his sides. Beginning to whoop, Red carries sticks of wood from near the fire and piles them by Sam.)*

SAM   Bill! Bill, wake up! Help! *(Red puts more wood around him and whoops.)* Bill! Help, help!

RED   Where do you keep the matches?

(Bill hurries in L and over to Sam.)

SAM   He wants to burn me at the stake! *(As Red comes near with wood in his arms, Sam kicks out, tripping him. Bill leaps on top of Red, finally getting hold of his arms.)* Hold him till I get loose from this rope. *(Manages to free himself and stand up.)*

BILL   This kid sure tries to keep his word!

SAM   This does it! We guard him till morning. And then we'll *make* the old coot pay! *(He and Bill wrap the struggling Red securely in a blanket* *and lay him down. Then they sit on either side of him, eyes wide open.)*

RED   Why does everybody have to spoil my fun?

Selections For Readers Theatre

The Fun They Had
Isaac Asimov

NARRATOR 1
NARRATOR 2
MARGIE
TOMMY
INSPECTOR
MECHANICAL TEACHER

■ ■ ■

NARRATOR 1   Margie even wrote about it that night in her diary. On the page headed May 17, 2157, she wrote . . .

MARGIE   Today Tommy found a real book!

NARRATOR 2   It was a very old book. Margie's grandfather once said that when he was a little boy *his* grandfather told him that there was a time when all stories were printed on paper.

NARRATOR 1   They turned the pages, which were yellow and crinkly, and it was awfully funny to read words that stood still instead of moving the way they were supposed to—on a screen, you know. And then, when they turned back to the page before, it had the same words on it that it had had when they read it the first time. Tommy said . . .

TOMMY   Gee, what a waste. When you're through with the book, you just throw it away, I guess. Our television screen must have had a million books on it and it's good for plenty more. I wouldn't throw *it* away.

MARGIE   Same with mine.

NARRATOR 2   Margie was eleven and hadn't seen as many telebooks as Tommy had. He was thirteen. She said . . .

MARGIE   Where did you find it?

TOMMY   In my house.

NARRATOR 1   Tommy pointed without looking, because he was busy reading . . .

TOMMY   In the attic.

MARGIE   What's it about?

TOMMY   School.

NARRATOR 2   Margie was scornful.

MARGIE   School? What's there to write about school? I hate school.

NARRATOR 1   Margie always hated school, but now she hated it more than ever. The mechanical teacher had been giving her test after test in geography and she had been doing worse and worse until her mother had shaken her head sorrowfully and sent for the County Inspector.

NARRATOR 2   He was a round little man with a red face and a whole box of tools with dials and wires. He smiled at Margie and gave her an apple, then took the teacher apart.

NARRATOR 1   Margie had hoped he wouldn't know how to put it together again . . .

NARRATOR 2   But he knew all right, and after an hour or so, there it was again, large and ugly, with a big screen on which all the lessons were shown and the questions were asked.

NARRATOR 1   That wasn't so bad. The part Margie hated most was the slot where she had to put homework and test papers. She always had to write them out in a punch code they made her learn when she was six years old, and the mechanical teacher calculated the mark in no time.

NARRATOR 2   The Inspector had smiled after he was finished, and patted Margie's head. He said to her mother . . .

INSPECTOR   It's not the little girl's fault, Mrs. Jones. I think the geography sector was geared a little too quick. Those things happen sometimes. I've slowed it up to an average ten-year level. Actually, the overall pattern of her progress is quite satisfactory.

NARRATOR 1   And he patted Margie's head again.

NARRATOR 2   Margie was disappointed. She had been hoping they would take the teacher away altogether. They had once taken Tommy's teacher away for nearly a month because the history sector had blanked out completely. So she said to Tommy . . .

MARGIE   Why would anyone write about school?

NARRATOR 1 Tommy looked at her with very superior eyes.

TOMMY Because it's not our kind of school, stupid. This is the old kind of school that they had hundreds and hundreds of years ago.

NARRATOR 2 He added loftily, pronouncing the word carefully . . .

TOMMY *Centuries* ago.

NARRATOR 1 Margie was hurt.

MARGIE Well, I don't know what kind of school they had all that time ago.

NARRATOR 2 She read the book over his shoulder for a while, then said . . .

MARGIE Anyway, they had a teacher.

TOMMY Sure they had a teacher, but it wasn't a *regular* teacher. It was a man.

MARGIE A man? How could a man be a teacher?

TOMMY Well, he just told the boys and girls things and gave them homework and asked them questions.

MARGIE A man isn't smart enough.

TOMMY Sure he is. My father knows as much as my teacher.

MARGIE He can't. A man can't know as much as a teacher.

TOMMY He knows almost as much, I betcha.

NARRATOR 1 Margie wasn't prepared to dispute that. She said . . .

MARGIE I wouldn't want a strange man in my house to teach me.

NARRATOR 2 Tommy screamed with laughter.

TOMMY You don't know much, Margie. The teachers didn't live in the house. They had a special building and all the kids went there.

MARGIE And all the kids learned the same thing?

TOMMY Sure, if they were the same age.

MARGIE But my mother says a teacher has to be adjusted to fit the mind of each boy and girl it teaches and that each kid has to be taught differently.

TOMMY Just the same they didn't do it that way then. If you don't like it, you don't have to read the book.

MARGIE I didn't say I didn't like it . . .

NARRATOR 1 Margie said quickly. She wanted to read about those funny schools.

NARRATOR 2 They weren't even half-finished when Margie's mother called.

MARGIE Can I read the book some more with you after school?

TOMMY Maybe . . .

NARRATOR 1 He said nonchalantly. He walked away whistling, the dusty old book tucked beneath his arm.

NARRATOR 2 Margie went into the schoolroom. It was right next to her bedroom, and the mechanical teacher was on and waiting for her. It was always on at the same time except Saturday and Sunday, because her mother said little girls learned better if they learned at regular hours. The screen was lit up, and it said . . .

MECHANICAL TEACHER Today's arithmetic lesson is on the addition of proper fractions. Please insert yesterday's homework in the proper slot.

NARRATOR 1 Margie did so with a sigh. She was thinking about the old schools they had when her grandfather's grandfather was a little boy.

NARRATOR 2 All the kids from the whole neighborhood came, laughing and shouting in the schoolyard, sitting together in the schoolroom, going home together at the end of the day. They learned the same things, so they could help one another on the homework and talk about it. And the teachers were people . . .

NARRATOR 1 The mechanical teacher was flashing on the screen . . .

MECHANICAL TEACHER When we add the fractions $\frac{1}{2}$ and $\frac{1}{4}$ —

NARRATOR 2 Margie was thinking about how the kids must have loved it in the old days. She was thinking about the fun they had.

A Fable
Mark Twain

NARRATOR
ARTIST
CAT
HATHI THE ELEPHANT
COW
DONKEY
BALOO THE BEAR

NARRATOR   Once upon a time an artist who had painted a small and very beautiful picture placed it so that he could see it in the mirror. He said . . .

ARTIST   This doubles the distance and softens it, and it is twice as lovely as it was before.

NARRATOR   The animals out in the woods heard of this through the cat, who was greatly admired by them because he was so learned, and so refined, and so polite, and could tell them so much which they didn't know before, and were not certain about afterward. They were much excited about this new piece of gossip. And they asked questions, so as to get at a full understanding of it. They asked what a picture was, and the cat explained . . .

CAT   It is a flat thing, wonderfully flat, marvelously flat, enchantingly flat and elegant. And, oh, so beautiful!

NARRATOR   That excited them almost to a frenzy. And they said they would give the world to see it. Then the bear asked . . .

BEAR   What is it that makes it so beautiful?

CAT   It is the looks of it.

NARRATOR   This filled them with admiration and uncertainty, and they were more excited than ever. Then the cow asked . . .

COW   What is a mirror?

CAT   It is a hole in the wall. You look in it. There you see the picture, and it is so dainty and charming and ethereal and inspiring in its unimaginable beauty that your head turns round and round, and you almost swoon.

DONKEY   I have not said anything as yet; I have strong doubts. There has never been anything as beautiful as this before, and probably isn't now. When it takes a whole basketful of sesquipedalian adjectives to whoop up a thing of beauty, it is time for suspicion.

NARRATOR   It was easy to see that these doubts were having an effect upon the animals, so the cat went off offended. The subject was dropped for a couple of days. But in the meantime curiosity was taking a fresh start, and there was a revival of interest. Then the animals assailed the donkey for spoiling what could have been a pleasure to them, on a mere suspicion that the picture was not beautiful, without any evidence that such was the case.

The donkey was not troubled. He was calm and said . . .

DONKEY   There is one way to find out who is in the right, myself or the cat. I will go and look in that hole, and come back and tell what I find there.

NARRATOR   The animals felt relieved and grateful, and asked him to go at once—

DONKEY   Which I did.

NARRATOR   But he did not know where he ought to stand. And, so, through error, he stood between the picture and the mirror. The result was that the picture had no chance, and didn't show up. He returned home and said . . .

DONKEY   The cat lied. There was nothing in that hole but a donkey. There wasn't a sign of a flat thing visible. It was a handsome donkey, and friendly, but just a donkey, and nothing more.

NARRATOR   The elephant asked . . .

ELEPHANT   Did you see it good and clear? Were you close to it?

DONKEY   I saw it good and clear, O Hathi, King of Beasts. I was so close that I touched noses with it.

ELEPHANT   This is very strange, the cat was always truthful before—as far as we could make out. Let another witness try. Go, Baloo, look in the hole, and come and report.

NARRATOR   So the bear went. When he came back, he said . . .

BEAR   Both the cat and the donkey have lied. There was nothing in that hole but a bear.

NARRATOR   Great was the surprise and puzzlement of the animals. Each was now anxious to make the test and get the straight truth. The elephant said . . .

ELEPHANT   I will send them one at a time.

NARRATOR   First the cow. She found nothing in the hole but a cow. The tiger found nothing in it but a tiger. The lion found nothing in it but a lion. The leopard found nothing in it but a leopard. The camel found a camel, and nothing more. The Hathi was wroth, and said he would have the truth, if he had to go and fetch it himself. When he returned, he abused his whole subjectry for liars. And he was in an unappeasable fury with the moral and mental blindness of the cat. He said . . .

ELEPHANT   Anybody but a near-sighted fool could see that there was nothing in the hole but an elephant.

NARRATOR   MORAL, BY THE CAT

CAT   You can find in a text whatever you bring, if you will stand between it and the mirror of your imagination. You may not see your ears, but they will be there.

Otherwise Known As Sheila the Great
Judy Blume

NARRATOR   SHEILA   MOM   MARTY

■ ■ ■

NARRATOR   This afternoon I am going to take my swimming test. I hope it rains. I hope it rains and pours until we leave here. But when I checked the sky, the sun was shining. And when I turned on the radio and listened to the weather report, there was no rain forecast.

So I hope I get sick and the doctor says I can't go in the water for ten days. But I feel fine. Except for my stomach, which keeps jumping all around.

So I hope that when I get to the pool this afternoon Marty won't be there. And no one will be able to find him. Then I will never have to take my swimming test!

But when we got to the pool, Marty was there, waiting for me. That's when I knew there was no getting out of it. I would have to take my Beginner's Test and if I drowned, I drowned! It was better not to think about it. Besides, chances were I wouldn't drown. Marty would probably save me. But if he had to jump in and save me in front of everyone, that would be as bad as drowning. Maybe even worse!

When I was in my suit, Mom said . . .

MOM   Good luck, Sheila. And please don't be nervous.

SHEILA   Me . . . nervous? Ha, ha. That's really funny.

NARRATOR   When Marty saw me he called . . .

MARTY   Hi, Sheila. All set?

NARRATOR   I didn't answer him.

MARTY   Okay, now here's all you have to do. First you'll jump in and swim across the deep end of the pool. Then you'll tread water for two minutes.

NARRATOR   I don't know who Marty thought he was fooling. If he expected me to jump in and swim across the deep end of the pool, he was even nuttier than I thought. He was more than nutty. He was even more than crazy! He was also stupid, dumb, and an idiot! Then Marty asked . . .

MARTY   Are you listening to me?

SHEILA   Oh, sure. I'm listening. But you know I can't swim across the whole pool!

MARTY   Yes, you can.

NARRATOR   I folded my arms and gave him one of my best stares.

MARTY   You've got to try, Sheila. That's all I ask. You just can't give up without trying.

SHEILA   Who's giving up? I can swim. You know that. You've seen me.

MARTY   Okay. So I know it. So now I want you to prove it to everyone by swimming across the pool.

SHEILA   Maybe I just don't feel like it.

MARTY   Look, Sheila, there's absolutely nothing to be afraid of. If you can't make it, I'll be right there to help you.

SHEILA   I am not afraid!

MARTY   Then prove that you're not! Jump in right now and start swimming. I know you can make it. I have a lot of confidence in you.

NARRATOR   I didn't answer him.

MARTY   Please, Sheila. Please try . . . for me.

NARRATOR   I liked the way Marty said that. But when I looked across the pool, the other side seemed ten miles away. I asked . . .

SHEILA   You promise nothing bad will happen?

MARTY   I promise. Word of honor. I'll even clear this section of the pool while you take your test.

SHEILA   Do I have to keep my face in the water the whole time?

MARTY   No, you can swim any way you want.

SHEILA   How far is it across? About a mile?

NARRATOR   Marty laughed.

MARTY   It's only forty feet.

SHEILA   It looks like ten miles to me.

MARTY   It's not. Tell you what . . . I'll count to three. Then you jump in and start swimming. I'll walk along the side of the pool and if you have any trouble, I'll pull you out.

SHEILA   You'll really be near me?

MARTY   Yes. I told you that. Now get ready.

NARRATOR I stood at the edge of the pool. Marty counted . . .

MARTY One . . . and two . . . and three . . . jump!

NARRATOR I didn't move. Marty asked . . .

MARTY What are you waiting for?

SHEILA I wasn't quite ready. Let's try it again.

MARTY Okay. Here we go. And one . . . and two . . . and three . . . jump!

NARRATOR I held my nose and jumped in. When I came up, I looked for Marty. He was right where he said he'd be. He called . . .

MARTY Swim . . . swim, . . .

NARRATOR I started. First I tried blowing bubbles, but I felt like I wasn't getting anywhere. So I kept my head out and swam like a dog. That way I could see what was going on. And I could keep an eye on Marty to make sure he followed me all the way across. Every time I looked up at him, he yelled . . .

MARTY Go, Sheila, go!

NARRATOR I swam past the low diving board. Then past the high one. And then I started to get tired. I couldn't get my arms all the way out of the water. And my legs didn't want to kick anymore. I looked up at Marty.

MARTY Go, Sheila, go! Don't stop now!

NARRATOR Marty was wrong. The pool wasn't forty feet across. It was really forty miles. I never should have tried it.

MARTY Go . . . go . . .

NARRATOR Why didn't he just shut up? When I raised my head and looked straight across the pool, who did I see waiting for me but Mom and the twins. Mom was yelling . . .

MOM Go . . . go!

NARRATOR Just like Marty. I wanted to tell her to stop. That I would never get to their side. This was very stupid. Soon I would be dead. Why didn't Marty pull me out? What was he waiting for? Couldn't he see I wasn't going to make it? I tried to say . . .

SHEILA I can't make it.

NARRATOR But it came out so soft he didn't hear me. He said . . .

MARTY That's it. Keep on going . . .

NARRATOR I can't . . . I can't . . . I thought. Then my hand touched the ladder. Mom and the twins were cheering and jumping up and down. Marty was yelling . . .

MARTY You made it! You made it! I knew you would!

NARRATOR It was true. I swam across the deep end of the pool, and I was still alive! I really and truly did it! I tried to climb up the ladder, but Marty bent down and said . . .

MARTY Now all you've got to do is tread water for two minutes.

SHEILA No . . . no . . . let me up!

MARTY Relax, Sheila. You can do it. Just tread for two minutes.

NARRATOR Treading water is pretty easy. It's just like riding a bicycle, except you aren't on one. But I was so tired. I wanted to go to sleep. Marty was holding a watch. He talked to me the whole time I was treading. He said . . .

MARTY That's it, Sheila. Only one more minute to go. And what's one little minute?

NARRATOR When we got down to the last couple of seconds, Marty counted out loud . . .

MARTY Ten, nine, eight, seven, six, five, four, three, two, one . . . Hurray! You did it! You did it!

NARRATOR I climbed up the ladder, and Marty put his arms around me. Then he gave me a big kiss right in front of everybody, but I didn't mind. My mother ran over and wrapped me up in a towel, and Mom and the twins dragged a lounge chair to me.

SHEILA I really did it?

NARRATOR I asked over and over. Marty said . . .

MARTY You sure did.

SHEILA How about that?

NARRATOR Never mind that the twins are already working on their Advanced cards. Never mind that Libby is practically a Junior Life Saver. Never mind that I will never dive like Betsy Ellis or stand on my hands under the water. *I can swim.* I proved it to everyone, including myself! I am Sunny Tubman, girl swimmer! I am Super Sheila the Swimming Wonder. I am . . . I am . . . I am . . . Then I heard my mother say . . .

MOM Sheila . . . are you all right?

NARRATOR I think I nodded. Then another voice laughed and said . . .

MARTY She's asleep. That's all.

NARRATOR I think it was Marty. But I couldn't even open my eyes to thank him.

Glossary

A

Accent The manner in which people speak and the way words are pronounced in different parts of the world.

Act Major division of a play.

Acting An actor's assumed behavior for the purpose of projecting a character to an audience.

Acting areas Nine to fifteen divisions of the stage floor, used by directors when moving actors or placing furniture or scenery.

Actor viewpoint The way the cast members react to the audience and the situation.

Actors Males or females playing character roles.

Adapting Changing or cutting a literary piece.

Aesthetic appreciation The ability to recognize, understand, and value that which is pleasing, beautiful, cultured, and tasteful in the arts (theatre, music, visual art, and dance).

Aesthetic perception Insight into our world of images, sound, color, patterns, forms, and movements.

Analyze To study carefully or examine critically.

Animation Bringing something to life through movement and action.

Antagonist The character opposing the protagonist.

Apron The part of the stage extending past the proscenium arch toward the audience.

Arena stage A stage constructed so that the audience can sit on all sides; also known as "theatre-in-the-round."

Articulation The shaping and molding of sounds into syllables.

Artistic discipline Maintaining a balance between group cooperation and individual integrity.

Assistant director The person who helps the director with such duties as warming up the cast before rehearsal, checking roll, posting rehearsal schedules, writing directorial notes during rehearsal, running errands, and filling in as an understudy when an actor is absent.

Audience commitment Audience responsibility.

Audience etiquette Appropriate audience behavior at a theatrical event.

Audience focus A type of focus in readers theatre in which the characters focus on the audience.

Audience viewpoint The way the audience sees and responds to the cast members.

Auditions Tryouts for a production.

Auguste clown A rodeo or circus clown; a clown whose makeup is reddish brown instead of white. Makeup and costume usually consist of exaggerated designs and items, such as a huge painted mouth, accented eyes, a huge bow tie, large shirt and pants, and large shoes.

Authentic evaluation An evaluation involving real-life situations and role-playing to test skills and abilities for the real world.

B

Basic makeup Cosmetics applied to the face or body using the actor's natural features.

Blackout Turning out all the stage lights at one time.

Blocking Planning and working out the movements and stage grouping for a play.

Blocking rehearsals Rehearsals for planning stage movement and groupings.

Body positions The angle of the actor's body onstage in relationship to the audience: full front, full back, one-quarter, profile, and three-quarter.

Breaking character Losing concentration or getting out of character. Using dialogue or behavior inconsistent with the part you are creating.

Breath control The amount of force you use in inhaling and exhaling.

Breathing The necessary process of inhaling and exhaling air to live.

Business Small movements and actions that do not require the actor to move from place to place.

C

Callbacks Additional opportunities for the actor to audition.

Camera shots Camera angles.

Casting Selecting actors to play specific roles in a production.

Character The personality an actor portrays in a scene or play that is different from his own personality.

Character clown A type of clown who uses makeup and clothes to represent a specific person or image; for example, a tramp, hobo, Keystone Kop, and so on.

Character makeup Makeup used to change an actor's natural features.

Character mask A mask representing a specific character.

Characterization Developing and portraying a personality through thought, action, dialogue, costuming, and makeup.

Characterized Divided into characters for readers theatre.

Choreography The art of planning and composing a dance.

Climax Turning point in the action of a play.

Clowning The art of entertaining others by providing laughter; requires the use of personal resources, an understanding of human nature, effective timing, and comedy techniques.

Comedy A play that presents its theme and characters in a humorous way. All characters come together at the end of the play.

Commedia dell'arte A form of improvisational theatre begun during the Renaissance, in the early sixteenth century.

Community theatre Not-for-profit theatre that uses local talent of all ages to produce plays. The theatre may hire a professional staff but use volunteer actors and backstage workers.

Concentration The ability to focus and pay close attention.

Conflict The problem or obstacles a literary character must overcome. Often a struggle between opposing forces.

Constructive criticism Helpful comments and opinions that are expressed in a positive way.

Cooperation The act of working together, getting along, and sharing responsibility.

Copyright The registration of ownership of a literary or musical work.

Costume An outfit, including accessories and undergarments, worn by an actor in a production.

Costume crew The committee in charge of costuming the show.

Costume designer The person who designs or plans the costumes to be worn in a play or stage production.

Costume parade Actors modeling costumes under the appropriate stage lights. This parade gives the director and costume designer the opportunity to evaluate the costumes and make any needed changes before the production opens.

Costume plot A chart listing all characters, the acts or scenes in which they appear, and all garments, undergarments, and accessories needed.

Creative drama An improvisational, process-centered form of theatre in which participants are guided by a leader to imagine, enact, and reflect on human experiences.

Crew Committee of technicians who work behind the scenes creating the scenery, costumes, props, and so on.

Criteria Evaluation guidelines to use in judging or grading an activity.

Critique Opinions and comments based on predetermined criteria; used in an evaluation of a person or performance.

Cue sheet A chart or list for lighting or sound showing all of the changes that will occur during a production.

Cues The dialogue, sounds, movement, or business signaling an actor or technician to respond as rehearsed.

"Curtain" A verbal command starting or ending a scene.

Curtain call Following a performance, the appearance of the actors onstage to acknowledge the appreciation of the audience and to take a bow.

Cutting Reducing or condensing material for oral interpretation.

Cyclorama A large curtain covering the back and sides of the stage.

D

Designer A person who creates or plans a specific part of the production, such as the costumes, lighting, set, makeup, or sound.

Developing rehearsals Rehearsals in which the actors work under the director's guidance to prepare the show for performance; also called working rehearsals.

Dialect A pronunciation of words from different languages blended together to form a distinct language for a group of people.

Dialogue The conversation between actors on the stage.

Diaphragm The muscle located between the abdomen and the rib cage.

Diction A person's pronunciation of words, choice of words, and manner in which the person expresses himself or herself.

Director Person in charge of the artistic production of a play.

Double-cast Assign an actor to play two roles.

Drama A story written to be played out on the stage.

Dramatic play Children's creation of scenes when they play "pretend."

Dramatic structure The special literary style in which plays are written.

Dress rehearsal A rehearsal conducted as if it were an actual performance.

E

Emotions Strong feelings, such as joy, fear, hate, and happiness.

Ensemble A group of people working together cooperatively.

Evaluation An assessment of strengths and weaknesses.

Exposition Detailed information revealing the facts of the plot.

Expressive movement The ability to express feelings through physical action.

External traits Traits relating to a character's outwardly visible qualities.

F

Feedback Constructive comments or opinions.

Filmed Preserved on film as a moving photograph.

First person Indicates the speaker's point of view as "I."

Flexibility The process of varying inflections of the voice.

Flexible staging Any stage not classified as proscenium, arena, or thrust.

Flipping the lid Improperly manipulating a movable-mouth hand puppet, causing flapping of the upper jaw or head.

Floor plan A drawing of the stage setting as seen from above (bird's-eye view).

Focus In readers theatre, the place or people that the actors look at when they speak their lines.

Folklore Tales, beliefs, customs, and traditions that were passed down orally from one generation to another.

Formal drama Theatre that focuses on a performance in front of an audience as the important final product.

"Freeze" A verbal command given by the director to stop the dialogue and movement in a scene.

Full-body puppet A puppet worn over the puppeteer's head and body like a costume.

G

Grand drape The draperies covering the proscenium opening (picture frame), separating the audience from the stage.

Grotesque whiteface A type of whiteface clown whose makeup has exaggerated features.

Group process Two or more people taking a step-by-step course of action that takes place over a period of time and is aimed at achieving goals.

H

Hand puppet A puppet that fits over the puppeteer's hand, much like a mitten, and is manipulated by the puppeteer's fingers inside the puppet's head and hands.

House The section of the theatre where the audience sits; also called "out front."

House crew The group responsible for printing tickets and programs and managing the box office, audience, and physical theatre during a production.

I

Illusion Something that looks real but is false.

Imagination The power to create ideas and pictures in our minds.

Improvisation A spontaneous style of theatre using unrehearsed and unscripted acting scenes.

Improvisational Nonscripted and spontaneous.

Improvise To ad-lib, or invent dialogue and actions without a script or rehearsal.

In unison At the same time.

Inflection The rising and falling of pitch. Inflection adds meaning, color, and rhythm to spoken words.

Intermission A short break in the action of the play for the audience.

Internal traits Inner, personal qualities, invisible to the human eye.

Interpersonal relationships The contacts a person has with many different people.

Interpret Act out a meaning of a selection and understand it in a unique way.

Introduction Information that an interpreter gives to the audience at the beginning of the presentation to help the audience understand the selection.

L

Leader (or teacher) playing in role A leader (or teacher) who actively participates in the creative drama process by playing one of the characters.

Level The actual head height of the actor as determined by his or her body position (sitting, lying, standing, or elevated by an artificial means such as a step unit or platform). Meaning is created in stage pictures by placing actors at different levels.

Light crew The technicians responsible for planning, preparing, and running the stage lights for a production.

Lighting designer The person who plans and puts into effect the lighting for a play or stage production.

Lighting plot A floor plan of the set showing the placement of basic lighting and any special lighting. This plot should also include a list of what lights are turned on and off and where the switches are located. These cues are marked in the light technician's promptbook for use in production.

Line check A test run of the show's dialogue to ensure that all lines have been memorized; also called a line rehearsal.

Lip sync Synchronizing movement of a puppet's mouth with the spoken words.

Literary merit That quality of a story that gives readers and actors a deeper understanding about the human condition and human spirit just through experiencing the story. Usually, the story's protagonist must face and triumph over internal and external obstacles.

M

Makeup crew The crew in charge of designing and applying makeup for each character.

Makeup designer The person who plans and designs the makeup to be worn in a play or stage production. Sometimes this person is also the makeup artist, the person who applies the makeup to the performers.

Makeup plot A chart listing the makeup needs for each character in a play.

Manipulation The way a puppeteer moves or works a puppet.

Mannerisms Unconscious habits or peculiarities.

Marionette A puppet manipulated by strings connecting a control rod or paddle to the moving body parts.

Mask A covering worn over all or part of the actor's face to neutralize or create a new character.

Masking Any materials such as curtains or scenery used to block an audience's view of the backstage area.

Mass media Communication that can reach large audiences.

Melodrama An exaggerated, fast-moving play in which action is more important than characterization. The "good guys" win and the "bad guys" are punished.

Mime The silent art of using body movements to create an illusion of reality.

Mimesis To imitate an activity.

Monologue A long speech spoken by one person, revealing personal thoughts and feelings.

Motivation An inner drive that causes a person to act a certain way.

Mounting the show Adding the finishing touches—such as scenery, props, and costumes—to a theatrical production.

Movable-mouth puppet A hand puppet with a movable mouth.

Movement The ability to transform ideas into action.

N

Narrative bridge Description of characters, actions, and settings provided by one or more narrators.

Narrative pantomime A creative drama activity in which a leader reads a piece of literature while the entire class plays the action in unison without words.

Narrator A storyteller.

Neat whiteface A type of whiteface clown whose makeup is in proportion and looks normal in size.

Neutral mask A white, featureless facial covering worn to neutralize the actor's own face.

O

Observation The power of seeing and taking notice.

Offstage focus A type of focus in readers theatre in which the characters look above the heads of the audience, into an imaginary mirror, focusing on the reflected image of the person to whom they are speaking.

Onstage focus A type of focus in readers theatre in which the characters focus on each other, as in traditional theatre.

Oral interpretation The skill of reading aloud to convey an author's message to an audience.

Oscilloscope An instrument that can be used to record voice vibrations and show voice patterns.

P

Pantomime The use of mime techniques, acting without words, to tell a story.

Pantomimus All gestures used in support of a theme.

Paraphrase Put a story into your own words.

Performance evaluation An evaluation of a performance given before an audience.

Performance space An area set aside for a performance.

Personal resources Techniques and skills that we use to express ourselves emotionally, intellectually, socially, and physically.

Phrasing Grouping words to create a specific meaning.

Pitch The musical tone of a voice.

Planes Imaginary divisions giving depth to the proscenium stage. An actor moves through the stage planes as he or she moves downstage toward the audience or upstage away from the audience.

Play Story in dialogue form to be acted out by actors before a live audience.

Player-audience relationship The special interactive and "live" relationship that exists between the performers and the audience, connecting and bonding them into a team.

Playwright One who writes plays.

Plot The arrangement of the incidents that take place in a play.

Poetry Literature written in verse form, often in rhythmic patterns and in rhyme.

Point of view A position from which we perceive (understand) an object, person, or place.

Poise The effective control of all voice elements and body movements.

Polishing rehearsals Rehearsals used to correct problems that occurred in the run-throughs. The rehearsals give the actors the opportunities to fine-tune character believability, vocal projection, and "picking up cues."

Posture How we sit and stand.

Producer The person responsible for the entire production, including obtaining financial backing, paying the bills, and hiring the director and creative staff.

Production techniques The methods used to stage a play and the methods used to produce television programs and films.

Program Printed sheet of paper or booklet that provides information about the production.

Projection The placement and delivery of voice elements used effectively in communicating to an audience.

Promptbook Usually a loose-leaf notebook containing the script marked with all stage movement, entrances and exits, technical cues, and special instructions for the production. The stage manager is usually in charge of the promptbook.

Pronunciation The way sounds or syllables that represent a word are said and stressed according to the proper notation found in the dictionary.

Prop crew The crew in charge of stage properties (props).

Property master The person in charge of the stage properties, or props, for a production.

Props a. Stage properties or items that might be part of the stage decorations. b. Items used by the actors for stage business and characterization.

Proscenium stage A four-sided stage built like a box with one side cut away, enabling the audience to view the play as if it were in a picture frame.

Prose A composition written without patterns of rhyme or rhythm.

Protagonist The major character in a story.

Publicity crew The committee responsible for organizing and implementing all advertising for a production. Often in charge of ticket sales, this crew is sometimes combined with the house crew.

Puppet Almost anything brought to life by a human in front of an audience.

Q

Quality The voice element that makes one person sound different from everyone else.

R

Radio theatre The performance of a play or story on radio by readers using a script that is not memorized. This type of theatre is either broadcast live or taped for later use.

Rate The speed at which someone speaks.

Readers theatre A style of theatre in which two or more interpreters appear to be reading from a script.

Reading rehearsals Rehearsals for the purpose of reading and analyzing the script as well as discussing and understanding characterization.

Rehearsals Production sessions in which the actors and technicians prepare by repetition.

Relaxation Freedom from all bodily tensions.

Replaying Acting out again.

Respect Consideration for and acceptance of ourselves and others, including other people's property, backgrounds, and opinions.

Rhythmic movement The ability to move to a beat or pattern of beats.

Risks Actions that are different from the norm.

Ritual Repeated action that becomes a custom or ceremony.

Rod puppet A puppet constructed without shoulders, arms, or legs and manipulated by one or more rods.

Role-playing Trying on the role of others, or assuming the part of another person in society.

Royalty A fee required to produce a play or musical.

Run-throughs Rehearsals conducted without any stops.

S

Scene (1) A short situation to be acted out, as in improvisation, with a beginning, middle, and end. (2) A subdivision of an act in a play.

Scenery Curtains, backdrops, or any structures constructed to transform an empty stage into a suitable background for a play.

Screenplay The script written for a movie or television show.

Screenwriter A writer who writes television or movie scripts.

Script A written copy of the dialogue that the actors will speak.

Self-confidence Belief in your worth and abilities as a person.

Self-image The way we see ourselves.

Self-talk Mental comments and opinions we repeat to ourselves constantly.

Sensory awareness The ability to use sight, sound, touch, smell, and taste to become conscious of the environment.

Set Usually large items used to stage a scene or play.

Set designer The person who designs the set for a production.

Set pieces Large portable pieces of the stage setting.

Shadow play Projecting shadow images on a screen.

Shadow puppet A flat, two-dimensional puppet designed to cast a shadow or form a silhouette on a white screen.

Side-coaching A method by which the leader talks you through an activity by making suggestions or giving you ideas.

Sight lines Imaginary lines defining the areas of the stage where the actors can clearly be seen by the audience.

Soliloquy A monologue usually delivered while the character is alone onstage, thinking aloud.

Sound Artificially produced sound effects or music as well as the amplification of voices so that they can be heard.

Sound crew The group responsible for planning and preparing all sound effects needed for a production.

Sound designer The person who plans and puts into effect the sound for a production.

Sound plot The plan of all the sound effects and music needed for a production.

Spectacle All visual elements of production, such as scenery, properties, lighting, costumes, makeup, stage movement, and dance.

Spectacle viewing A medium through which film is viewed with wonder and amazement.

Stage The area where the players perform; usually a raised platform.

Stage crew The group of technicians responsible for building the scenery. During a production, this crew is in charge of any scene changes.

Stage directions Information provided by the playwright to give the actors instructions on how to feel or what to do when certain lines are spoken. These directions, usually in italics, are set apart from the dialogue by parentheses.

Stage lighting Illumination of the actors and acting area; includes any special lighting effects.

Stage makeup Any cosmetic effect, including hair, that enhances or changes an actor's appearance.

Stage manager The person in charge of supervising backstage.

Stage picture An appealing and meaningful arrangement of performers on the stage; the picture that the audience sees onstage.

Stereotypical character A familiar character identified by an oversimplified pattern of behavior that typically labels the character as being part of a group of people.

Stock character An easily recognizable character. A flat, one-dimensional character with predictable actions.

Story The narration of an event or series of events brought to life for listeners by a storyteller.

Story dramatization A playing/acting process to interpret and share a story by using improvisation rather than scripts.

Storyteller A person who tells stories or tales.

Storytelling The art of sharing stories with an audience.

Strike Take apart the stage setting, remove it from the stage, and store all parts of the production for future use.

Subtext The underlying meaning or interpretation of a line, which is not indicated in the script but is supplied by the actor.

Suspend belief Pretend that what is happening onstage is real.

T

Technical rehearsals Rehearsals emphasizing the performance of the production's technical elements—prop changes, scenery shifts, light changes, sound effects, and so on.

Theatre The writing or performing of plays, as well as the formal study of the art form. Also, a building in which plays are performed.

Theatre arts The term used to cover all parts of training or instruction in the field of theatre.

Theatre conventions Established techniques, practices, or devices unique to theatrical productions.

Theatre safety Keeping the crews, cast, and audience free from harm, danger, risk, or injury.

Theatre teacher An educator who specializes in theatre arts or drama.

Theme The basic idea or purpose of the play. It ties together all the characters and events.

Thrust stage A stage that extends into the seating area. The audience sits on three sides of the stage.

Tragedy A play that deals with a serious situation in a serious way. The protagonist dies or is defeated at the end of the play.

Transition Description of what is happening while the actors pantomime the action of a story.

Trust The ability to risk expressing yourself in front of your classmates without fear of being ridiculed.

U

Understudy A person who learns a part in order to substitute in a performance should the original actor not be able to appear in the show.

V

Vista shots Faraway shots.

Visualizing The act of imagining and seeing pictures in the mind.

Vocal folds Muscular membranes in the larynx that produce sound.

Volume How softly or loudly a person speaks.

W

Whiteface clown A clown whose makeup is an all-white face with features of black and red added for detail.

Wings Offstage spaces to the sides of the acting area.

Index

formal, 67
Golden Age of, 88
masks and, 347
mime and, 270
Neoclassical Ideals of, 88, 126
oral interpretation and, 288
puppetry and, 347
shadow play and, 347
See also Melodrama
Drama festivals/contests, 331
Dramatic play, 9, 51
Dramatic poetry, 127
Dramatic structure, 7, 8, 173
Dress rehearsal, 178, 184, 205
 costume parade and, 183
 makeup crew and, 208, 211
 technical rehearsals and, 183
"Dress stage," 164
Drury Lane Theatre, 272
Dunlap, William, 262
Duse, Eleonora, 206

E

Eastern (Asian) theatre, 72–73
Educational theatre
 curtain calls in, 183
 makeup crew and, 208
 masks and, 347
 props for, 201
 puppetry and, 347
El Teatro Campesino, 319
Elizabethan theatre, 88, 126–127, 142
 Restoration theatre compared
  with, 180
Emotions, 62
 body positions and, 157
 movement and, 61–62
 movtivation and, 62
 voice and, 83, 90
Emphasis
 composition and, 165
 radio theatre and, 341
 readers theatre and, 334
Encouragement, 37, 38
English plays, 126
 Renaissance and, 88, 180. *See also*
  Elizabethan theatre
 pantomime in, 272
 cycle plays, 58
 in early (colonial) U.S. theatre, 262
English Restoration theatre, 180–181
Ensemble, 36–39
 in Moscow Art Theatre, 253
 movement and, 61
Enthusiasm, storytelling and, 317
Entrances, 151, 173
 blocking of, 161
 masks and, 372
 puppetry and, 353

readers theatre and, 335, 337
 See also Wings
Environmental theatre, 354
Etiquette, 177, 226
 audience, 230, 232–234
Euripides, 35
Evaluation, 45–48, 226, 238, 240–244
 oral interpretation and, 297–312
 puppetry and, 366
 radio theatre and, 342–343
 story dramatization and, 77
 See also Constructive criticism;
  Critique; Feedback; Theatre
  appreciation
Exits, 151, 173
 blocking of, 164
 masks and, 372
 puppetry and, 353
 readers theatre and, 335, 337
 See also Wings
Experimental/nontraditional theatre,
 313, 322, 354
Exposition, 138
Expressive movement, 61–62,
 63–64, 269
Expressiveness (of voice), 339, 341–342
External characteristics/traits, 74, 125,
 128
Eye contact, 294, 298, 318

F

Facades, 88
Facial expressions, 62, 157
 evaluation of, 47
 masks and, 371
 mime and, 269
 oral interpretation and, 294, 296, 298
 pantomime and, 269, 272
 storytelling and, 317, 325
Fairy tales, 271, 357
Farce, 58, 272
Federal Theatre Project, 340
Feedback, 233, 294, 298
Fields, W. C., 270
Film. *See* Movies/film
First person, 134
"Flashbacks," 237
Flats (painted), 88–89, 197, 198
 in English Restoration theatre, 181
Flexibility (of voice), 83, 92–93
 oral interpretation and, 296
 radio theatre and, 339, 341–342
Flexible staging, 152, 156
Flipping the lid, 353
Floor, "racked" (slanted), 180
Floor plan, 173, 179, 182
 designers and, 257
 stage crew and, 194
Focus, 274

clowning and, 282
readers theatre and, 335, 337
See also Concentration
Folklore, 271, 323, 357
Ford Foundation, 322, 340
Formal drama, 67
Fort, Paul, 281
"Freezing," 119, 335, 353
French classical mime, 269
French 16th century theatre, 270. *See
 also* Commedia dell'arte
French 17th century theatre,
 158–159, 180
Full-body puppet, 348, 349, 350
Furniture
 blocking rehearsal and, 179
 designers and, 256, 257
 English Elizabethan theatre and, 180
 stage crew and, 197
 thank-you letters for, 185
 See also Props (properties)
Furniture pieces, 173

G

Galen, 364
Gallery seating, 181
Genet, Jean, 295
Gershwin, George, 276
Gesturing, 157, 269
 in live theatre vs. television and
  film, 237
 masks and, 370, 371, 372
 puppetry and, 352, 353
 readers theatre and, 335
 storytelling and, 325
"Give stage," 160
Gleason, Jackie, 270, 280
Globe Theatre, 126, 142
Goals, 36, 37
Goethe, Johann von, 240
Golden Age of drama, 88
Gorki, Maxim, 239
Government-run theatre, 340
Grand drape, 151
Greek literature, puppetry and, 364
Greek theatre/plays, 15, 35, 44
 burlesque in, 279
 chanting in, 138, 331
 clowning and, 279
 Italian Renaissance and, 88
 masks and, 35, 370
 mime and, 270
 monologues in, 131
 music in, 138, 276. *See also* Chorus
Grimaldi, Joseph, 270, 280
Grotesque whiteface clown, 282
Grotowsky, Jerzy, 354
Group process, 34, 36
Groups, 5, 6–7, 34–42

Tone (of voice), 128, 129
Tragedy, 139
    clowning and, 279, 283
    in English Restoration, 180
    Greek, 35, 270
    heroic, 180
    in Italian Renaissance, 89
    in melodrama, 141
    Roman, 44
Transition, 77
Trissino, Giangiorgio, 89
Trust, 36
"Turn in/out," 160
Tyler, Royall, 262

U

Understudy, 177, 192
Unison, 71
Unity of time/place/action, 88, 126
Upstage, 154, 155, 156, 165
Upstaging, 165

V

Valdez, Luis, 319
Van Dyke, Dick, 270, 280
Vaudeville, 276, 365
Ventriloquist, 279
Verbal communication, 62. *See also*
    Voice
Verisimilitude, 88
Vestris (Madame), 207
Vista shots, 237
Visual elements (of play), 139
Visual imagery/art, 88, 89
Visualizing, 53
    pantomime and, 272, 274
    radio theatre and, 330
    readers theatre and, 330, 331

Vocal folds, 89, 91
Vocalization/vocal expression, 128–129
    puppetry and, 355–356
    radio theatre and, 341, 342
    readers theatre and, 333
    storytelling and, 317, 324, 325
    See also Voice
Voice, 82–106
    articulation and. *See* Articulation
    evaluation of, 47, 240, 298
    flexibility of. *See* Flexibility (of
        voice)
    oral interpretation and, 294, 296
    pitch of, 83, 91–92
    placement of, 99, 101
    projection of. *See* Projection (of
        voice)
    pronunciation and. *See*
        Pronunciation
    puppetry and, 355–356
    radio theatre and, 330, 339, 341
    and rate of speech, 83, 99–101, 296
    readers theatre and, 330
    tone of, 128, 129
    volume of. *See* Volume
    See also Accent; Dialect; Vocalization
Voice quality, 83, 90–91, 143
    characterization and, 128, 129
    oral interpretation and, 296, 298
    storytelling and, 317
Volume, 83, 98–99
    evaluation of, 47
    oral interpretation and, 296
    radio theatre and, 341

W

Wagner, Richard, 207
Wakefield cycle, 58
Ward, Douglas Turner, 340
Wardrobe, 204

Washington Square Players, 313
Weigel, Helene, 336
Welles, Orson, 348
Well-made plays, 206
Whiteface clown, 274, 282–283
Wignell, Thomas, 262
Wilson, August, 340
Wings, 89, 126, 151
    in English Restoration theatre, 181
    in French 17th century theatre, 158
Women, in English Restoration
        theatre, 180
Wooster Group, 313
Words
    radio theatre and, 341
    storytelling and, 317
    See also Dialogue; Language
Working rehearsals, 182
Writing
    for movies/films, 250
    for television, 250
    of original monologues, 131–134
    for puppet shows, 357–359
    See also Playwrights

X

Xenophon, 364

Y

Yarnell, Lorene, 270
Yeats, William Butler, 281

Z

Zeami, 72
Zola, Émile, 239

Credits

■ Chapter 12

225 ©Eric R. Berndt, Unicorn; **227** ©Wayne Eastep, Tony Stone Images; **229a** ©David Brownell; **229b** ©Ron Chapple, FPG; **231** ©The Billy Rose Theatre Collection, The New York Public Library for the Performing Arts. Archival photography by Kate Kunz. **233** ©Wayne Eastep, Tony Stone Images; **235** ©Karen Moskowitz, Tony Stone Images; **236** ©Joseph Lederer, The Kobal Collection; **237** ©The Kobal Collection; **239** ©The Billy Rose Theatre Collection, The New York Public Library for the Performing Arts. Archival photography by Kate Kunz; **240** ©Don Milici; **242** ©Eric R. Berndt, Unicorn.

■ Chapter 13

246 ©Dave Schaefer, The Picture Cube, Inc.; **248** ©David Brownell; **249** ©Wolfgang Spunbarg, PhotoEdit; **253a** © The Bettmann Archive; **253b** © Sovfoto: **254** ©Mark Richards, PhotoEdit; **255a** ©Archive Photos; **255b** ©Henry Gris, FPG; **256** ©Anna E. Zuckerman, PhotoEdit; **257** ©Frank Siteman, Stock-Boston; **258** ©Michael LePoer Trench, Sygma; **259** ©Archive Photos; **262** ©Lawrence S. Williams, Inc.; **263** ©Mary Kate Denny, PhotoEdit; **266/267** ©Ken Karp, Omni Photo Communications.

■ Chapter 14

268 ©John Lei, Omni Photo Communications; **269** ©Robert Copeland, West Light; **270a** ©Archive Photos/Express Newspapers; **270b** ©John Lei, Omni Photo Communications; **271** ©The Bettmann Archive; **272** ©Corbis-Bettmann; **274a** ©FPG; **274b** ©Archive Photos; **276** ©The Bettmann Archive; **278** ©John Lei, Omni Photo Communications; **280a** ©Steve Starr, Stock-Boston; **280b** ©FPG; **281** ©The Billy Rose Theatre Collection, The New York Public Library for the Performing Arts. Archival photography by Kate Kunz. **282a** ©Jeff Greenberg, PhotoEdit; **282b** ©David Burnett, Stock-Boston; **282c** ©Charles Feil.

■ Chapter 15

286 ©Laima Druskis, Stock-Boston; **287** ©Batt Johnson, Unicorn; **289** ©Elena Rooraid, PhotoEdit; **290** ©Kathy Sloane; **292** Copyright © 1940 James Thurber. Copyright © 1968 Rosemary A. Thurber. From *Fables For Our Time*, published by HarperCollins; **294** ©David R. Frazier, Tony Stone Images; **295** ©Stan Wayman, Photo Researchers. The Billy Rose Theatre Collection, The New York Public Library for the Performing Arts. **299/300** "The Dentist and the Crocodile": "The Dentist and the Crocodile", from *Rhyme Stew* by Roald Dahl & Quentin Blake, illustrations. Copyright ©1989 by Roald Dahl. Used by permission of Viking Penguin, a division of Penguin Books USA Inc. **301/303** "Priscilla and the Wimps": "Priscilla and the Wimps" by Richard Peck, Copyright ©1984 by Richard Peck from *Sixteen: Short Stories* by Donald R. Gallo, ed. Used by permission of Dell Books, a division of Bantam Doubleday Dell Publishing Group, Inc. **303/305** "Humpty Dumpty in the Food Store": Reprinted by permission of UIL–University Interscholastic League, Austin, Texas. **305/307** *The Imaginary Invalid:* From *The Imaginary Invalid*, by Moliere, adapted by Fran Tanner, *BASIC DRAMA PROJECTS*, Clark Publishing, Inc.; **307/309** *The Diary of Anne Frank:* From *The Diary of Anne Frank*, by Frances Goodrich and Albert Hackett. Copyright ©1954, 1956 as an unpublished work.

Copyright ©1956 by Albert Hackett, Frances Goodrich Hackett and Otto Frank. Reprinted by permission of Random House, Inc.; **309/312** *A Raisin in the Sun*: From *A Raisin in the Sun* by Lorraine Hansberry. Copyright ©1958 by Robert Nemiroff as an unpublished work. Copyright ©1959, 1966, 1984 by Robert Nemiroff. Reprinted by permission of Random House, Inc.; **307** ©The Kobal Collection; **313** ©Carol Rosegg.

■ Chapter 16

315 ©Myrleen Ferguson, PhotoEdit; **316** ©The Bettmann Archive; **317** ©Jeffrey Dunn, Stock-Boston; **319** Courtesy *El Teatro Campesino;* **320** ©Lawrence Migdale, Stock-Boston; **321** ©Steve Skjold, PhotoEdit; **324a** ©Mark Lewis, Tony Stone Images; **324b** ©Bob Daemmrich, Stock-Boston; **326** "Mario the Beggar", "The Lost Donkey", and "Three Rolls and a Chocolate Eclair": From *Read for the Fun of It*, Copyright ©1992 by Caroline Feller Bauer and reprinted here by permission of The H. W. Wilson Company.

■ Chapter 17

329 ©Don Milici; **332** ©Don Milici; **333** ©Richard Pasley, Stock-Boston; **334** ©Kathy Sloane; **336** Courtesy of California Lutheran University Drama Department; photo by Brian Stethem, 1985; **340** ©Jon McGinty/Madison Repertory Theatre; **341** ©Corbis/Bettmann.

■ Chapter 18

345 ©Lawrence Migdale, Stock Boston; **346** ©Archive Photos; **349a** ©Bonnie Kamin, PhotoEdit; **349b** ©Stock-Boston; **349c** ©David Young-Wolff, PhotoEdit; **349d** ©Jeff Greenberg, Omni Photo Communications; **349e** ©Reuters/Bettmann; **349f** ©John Lei, Stock-Boston; **351** ©David Young-Wolff, PhotoEdit; **352** ©Archive Photos; **354** ©Culver Pictures, Inc.; **355** ©Steve Benbow, Stock-Boston; **360** ©Norman Mosallem, Tony Stone Images; **361** ©Jeff Greenberg, Unicorn; **363** Courtesy Nancy Prince; **364** ©Bob Daemmrich, Stock-Boston; **365** ©Michael S. Yamashita, West Light; **367a** ©Ilene; **367b** ©Tony Freeman, PhotoEdit; **370** ©Martin R. Jones, Unicorn; **371a** ©Lawrence Migdale, Stock-Boston; **371b** ©Shelley Rotner, Omni Photo Communications.

The Playbook

■ Monologues For Males

Winners: Copyright 1989 by Cynthia Mercati, permission granted by the publisher, Baker's Plays, Boston, MA.
Simply Heavenly: Reprinted by permission of Harold Ober Associates Inc. Copyright ©1953 by Langston Hughes; renewed 1981 by George Houston Bass.
Harvey: ©Copyright 1943, by Mary Chase (under the title, THE WHITE RABBIT). ©Copyright 1944, by Mary Chase (under the title, HARVEY). ©Copyrights, Renewed, 1970, 1971, by Mary Chase. CAUTION: The reprinting of HARVEY included in this volume is reprinted by permission of the owners and Dramatists Play Service, Inc. The amateur performance rights in this play are controlled exclusively by Dramatists Play Service, Inc., 440 Park Avenue South, New York, N.Y. 10016. No amateur production of the play may be given without obtaining in advance, the written permission of the Dramatists Play Service, Inc. and paying the requisite